AF352659

Andrew H. Plaks and Michael Nylan, Series Editors

Exemplary Figures / Fayan
Yang Xiong, translated by Michael Nylan

Zuo Tradition / Zuozhuan
Commentary on the "Spring and Autumn Annals"
Translated by Stephen Durrant, Wai-yee Li, and David Schaberg

ZUO TRADITION

ZUOZHUAN

左傳

Commentary on the "Spring and Autumn Annals"

Volume Two

TRANSLATED AND INTRODUCED BY

Stephen Durrant

Wai-yee Li

David Schaberg

UNIVERSITY OF WASHINGTON PRESS
Seattle and London

Publication of this book was made possible in part by generous gifts from Joseph and Lauren Allen, Nancy Alvord, Michael Burnap and Irene Tanake, Ruth and Alvin Eller, Griffith Way, and other donors.

Printed and bound in the United States of America
Design by Thomas Eykemans
Composed in Minion, typeface designed by Robert Slimbach
19   5   4   3   2

UNIVERSITY OF WASHINGTON PRESS
www.washington.edu/uwpress

VOLUME 2: ISBN 978-0-295-99916-6

LIBRARY OF CONGRESS CATALOGING-IN-PUBLICATION DATA
Names: Durrant, Stephen W., 1944– translator. | Li, Wai-yee, translator. | Schaberg, David, 1964– translator.
Title: Zuo tradition = Zuozhuan : commentary on the "Spring and autumn annals" / translated and introduced by Stephen Durrant, Wai-yee Li, David Schaberg.
Other titles: Zuozhuan. English. | Commentary on the "Spring and autumn annals"
Description: 1st edition. | Seattle : University of Washington Press, [2016] | Series: Classics of Chinese thought | Includes bibliographical references and indexes. Contents: Chronology of dynasties — Volume One — Lord Yin — Lord Huan — Lord Zhuang — Lord Min — Lord Xi — Lord Wen — Lord Xuan — Volume Two — Lord Cheng — Lord Xiang — Volume Three — Lord Zhao — Lord Ding — Lord Ai — Place name index — Personal name index.
Identifiers: LCCN 2016014414 | ISBN 9780295999159 (hardcover : acid-free paper)
Subjects: LCSH: Confucius. Chun qiu. | China—History—Zhou dynasty, 1122–221 B.C.—Early works to 1800. | China—History—Zhou dynasty, 1122–221 B.C.—Historiography. | Shandong Sheng (China)—History—Early works to 1800. | Shandong Sheng (China)—Historiography.
Classification: LCC PL2470.Z6 Z8713 2016 | DDC 895.18/107—dc23
LC record available at https://lccn.loc.gov/2016014414

To the memory of Livia Plaks and Anthony C. Yu

Contents

Acknowledgments

Our work on this project has extended across more springs and autumns than we originally envisaged. Perhaps at the outset we underestimated the difficulty of this great text, or perhaps we overestimated our own abilities as translators—or, possibly, both. Still, if our time spent with *Zuozhuan* has brought frustrations, it has also brought joys. The most obvious joy has come from slowly working our way together through this rich literary masterpiece in a desperate but sincere effort to beat translation's odds, to find *les mots justes*, to capture in English the austere, unmistakable style that we all admired in *Zuozhuan* prose. For what is translation but exceedingly slow, careful, interpretative reading, undertaken with and for other readers, born from the urge to share with others the pleasure one takes in a difficult, remote work of art? Chief among our frustrations was the realization that our English translation, no matter how much effort we have put into it, does not and could never reproduce the genius of the original. We can perhaps draw comfort from the realization that the higher the quality of a text, the more it defies perfect translation.

Another joy of our work together and individually over the years has been the support and encouragement of so many colleagues, students, friends, and family. The three of us extend our heartfelt appreciation to those who have read our translation and have offered valuable suggestions. Michael Nylan, Andrew Plaks, and Yuri Pines all worked through the entire manuscript with great meticulousness and helped us improve our translation in numerous ways. Many others have helped us with particular problems in *Zuozhuan* or have read and responded to portions of our work. Among these scholars are Lothar von Falkenhausen, David Keightley, Göran Malmqvist, Christoph Harbsmeier, Reinhard Emmerich, Enno Giele, Li Long-shien, David Pankenier, and Chang Su-ching. Lorri Hagman , Jacqueline Volin, Pamela Bruton, and other members of the staff at the University of Washington Press encouraged us at every stage of this project and have been more patient with us than we have sometimes deserved. We are grateful for their help. Our project has benefited from the financial support of the National Endowment for the Humanities, the Fairbank Center and the Asia Center at Harvard University, and the Oregon Humanities Center and the Department of East Asian Languages and Literatures at the University of Oregon. Sabbatical leaves funded by Harvard University, the American Council of Learned Societies, the Radcliffe Institute of Advanced Study, the University of California at Los Angeles, and the American Academy at Berlin allowed us to devote time to the translation of *Zuozhuan*, even as other projects claimed our attention.

During the last decade, each of the three of us has taught graduate seminars dealing with *Zuozhuan*. Our interaction with students in these seminars has convinced us once again of how much research and publication can benefit from engagement with good students in the classroom. We are deeply grateful to our students for their willingness both to encourage and to challenge us. We also express our gratitude to Bill Nelson at "Bill's Imac" for his help with maps and to several students who provided valuable assistance with technical details: Sara Higgins, Shijia Nie, and Xingwei Fu at the University of Oregon, and Ted Mingtak Hui at Harvard University. The image for the cover is based on a rubbing from a stele (dated 241) with fragments of the text of the *Spring and Autumn Annals* carved in three script styles. We thank the Special Collections in Fine Arts Library, Harvard University, for permitting the use of this image.

Numerous friends and members of our families have helped us in one way or another with this lengthy project. We cannot name them all but would like to thank Omer Bartov, Françoise Calin Durrant, and Daphne Pi-Wei Lei for their support and encouragement over the years.

Finally, we take full responsibility for the mistakes and infelicities that remain in this book and can only hope that, despite such possible problems, our work will help *Zuozhuan* achieve its deserved place among the masterpieces that have come to us from the ancient world.

Abbreviations

BMFEA	*Bulletin of the Museum of Far Eastern Antiquities*
EC	*Early China*
Gongyang	*Chunqiu Gongyang zhuan zhushu* 春秋公羊傳注疏
Guliang	*Chunqiu Guliang zhuan zhushu* 春秋穀梁傳注疏
HJAS	*Harvard Journal of Asiatic Studies*
JAOS	*Journal of the American Oriental Society*
Karlgren	Bernhard Karlgren, "Glosses on the *Tso Chuan*," *BMFEA* 41 (1969): 1–158
Legge	James Legge, trans., *The Ch'un Ts'ew with the Tso Chuen*, vol. 5 of *The Chinese Classics* (1872; repr., Hong Kong: Hong Kong University Press, 1895)
SBBY	*Sibu beiyao* 四部備要
SKQS	*Yingyin Wenyuan ge Siku quanshu* 影印文淵閣四庫全書
SSJZS	*Chongkan Song ben Shisan jing zhushu fu jiaokan ji* 重刊宋本十三經注疏附校勘記
Takezoe	Takezoe Kōkō 竹添光鴻, ed. and annotator, *Saden Kaisen* 左傳會箋 (1912; repr., Taipei: Fenghuang, 1961)
XBZZJC	*Xinbian zhuzi jicheng* 新編諸子集成
Yang	Yang Bojun 楊伯峻, ed. and annotator, *Chunqiu Zuozhuan zhu* 春秋左傳注, rev. ed., 4 vols. (Beijing: Zhonghua, 1990)
ZZ	*Chunqiu Zuozhuan zhengyi* 春秋左傳正義

Chronology of Dynasties

Xia	ca. 21st–16th BCE
Shang	ca. 1600–1045 BCE
Zhou	1045–256
Western Zhou	1045–771
Eastern Zhou	770–256
Spring and Autumn	770–476
Warring States	475–221
Qin	221–206
Han	202 BCE–220 CE
Former Han (also called Western Han)	202 BCE–9 CE
Xin (Wang Mang reign)	9–23
Gengshi Emperor	23–25
Later Han (also called Eastern Han)	25–220
Six Dynasties	220–589
Three Kingdoms	220–280
Jin	265–420
Northern and Southern Dynasties	420–589
Sui	581–618
Tang	618–907
The Five Dynasties and Ten Kingdoms	902–979
Song	960–1279
Northern Song	960–1127
Southern Song	1127–1279
Yuan	1279–1368
Ming	1368–1644
Qing	1644–1912

Adapted from Endymion Wilkinson, *Chinese History: A Manual* (Cambridge, MA: Harvard University Asia Center, 2000), 10–13.

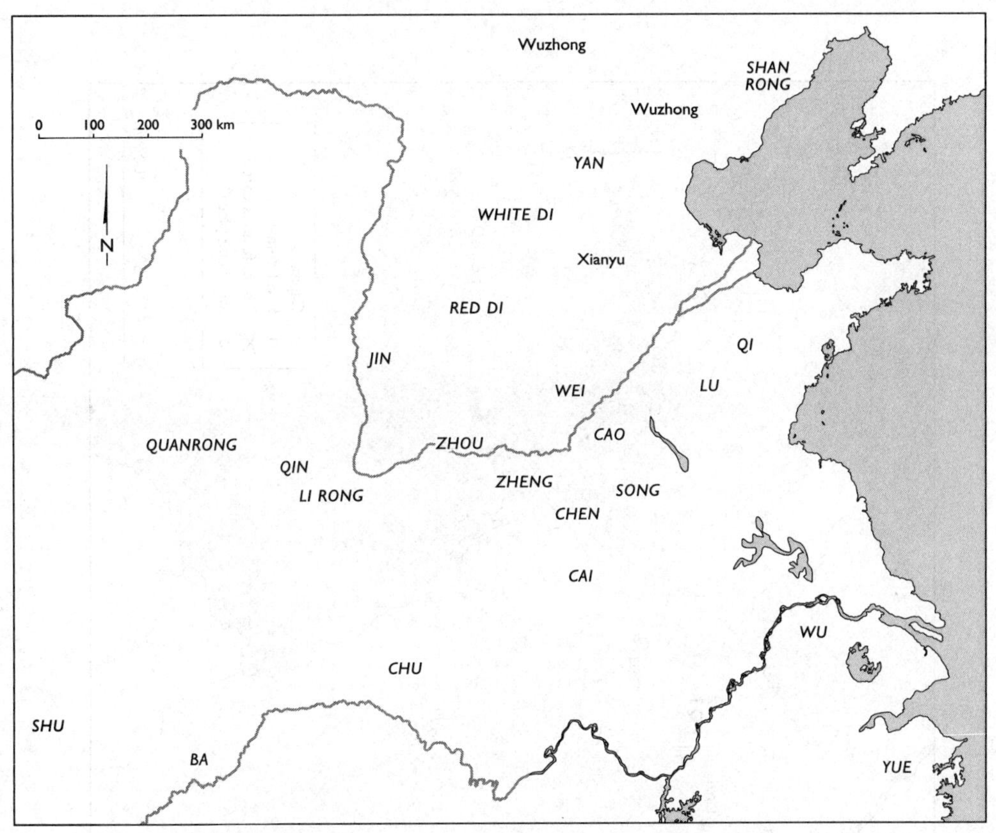

Map 1. Major domains and peoples during the Spring and Autumn Period

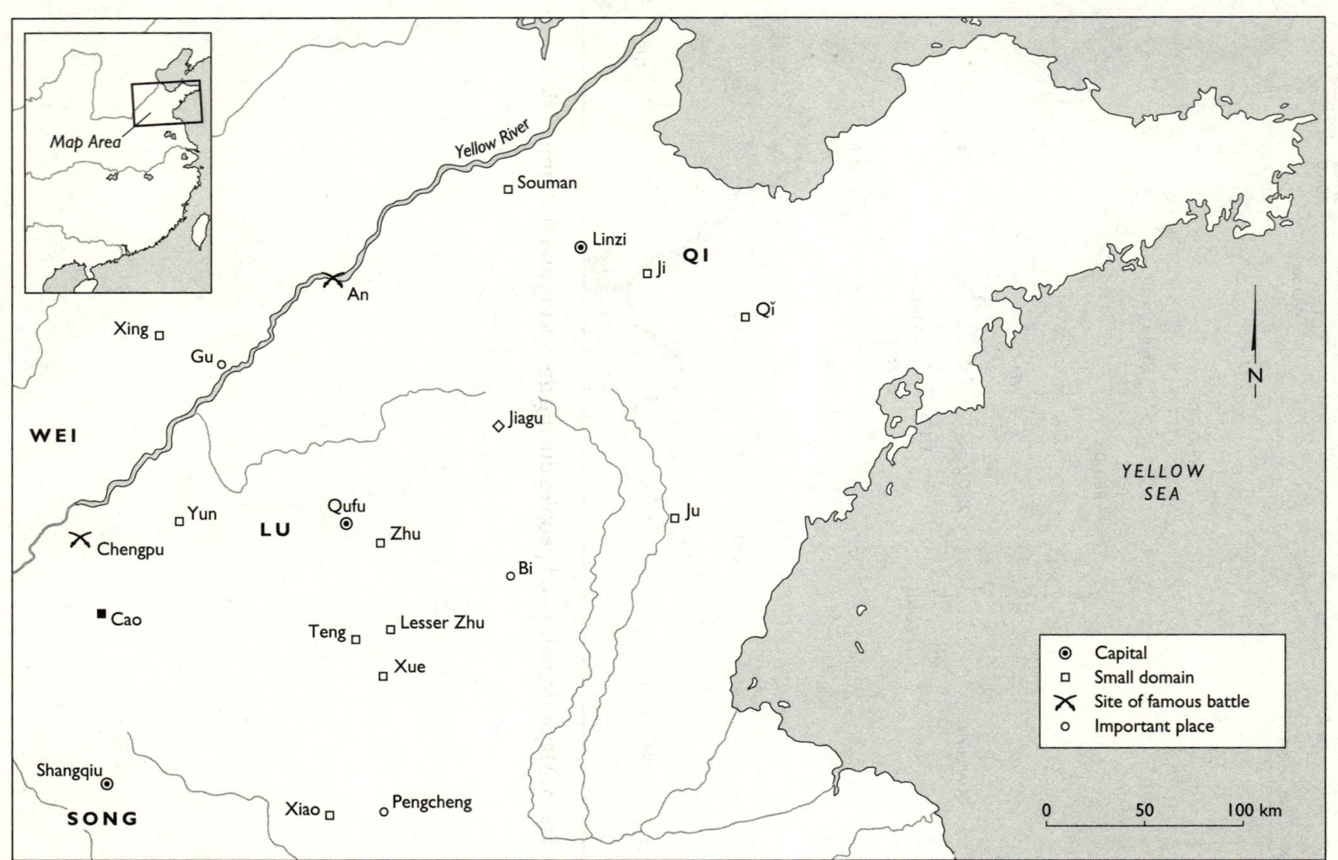

Map 2. Important places on the North China Plain

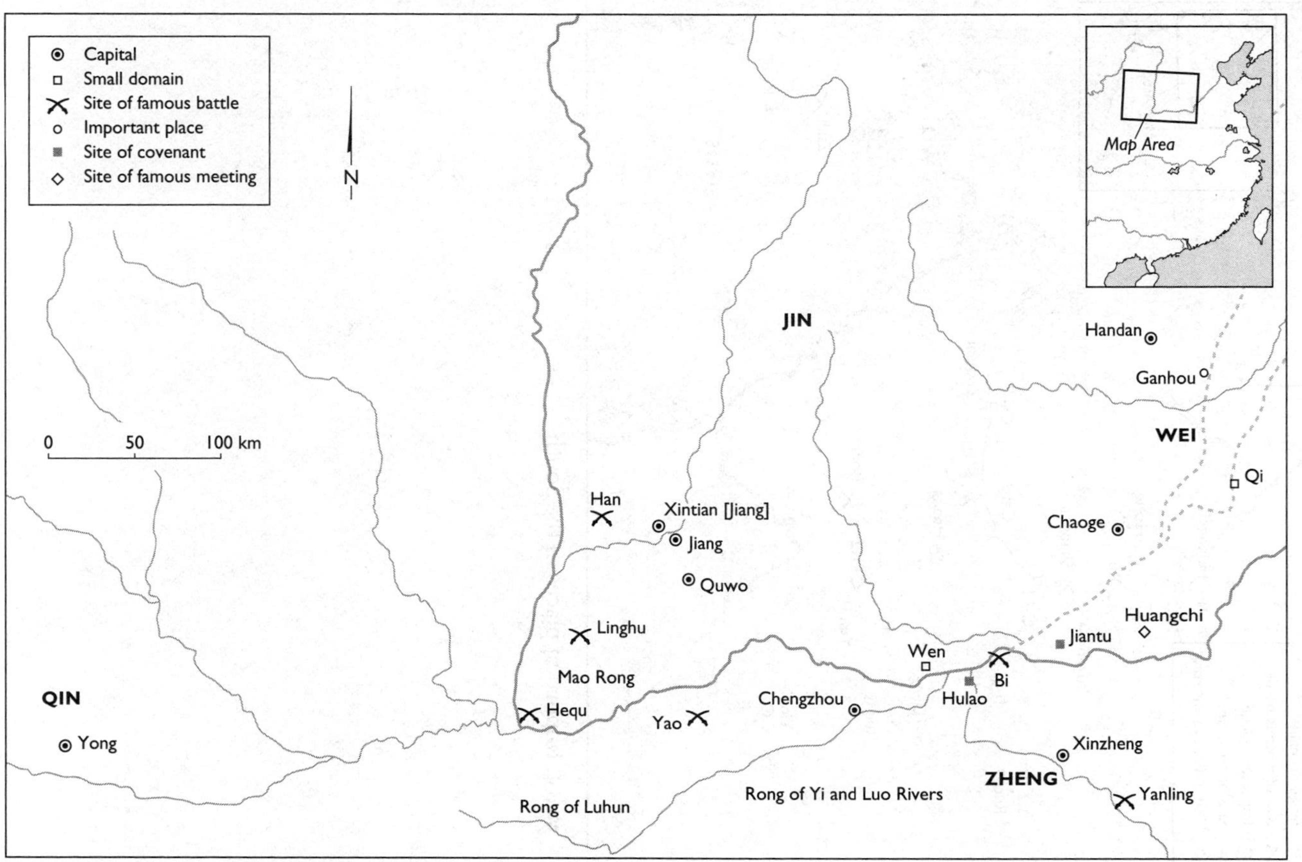

Map 3. Important places in the Upper Yellow River / Wei River Basin

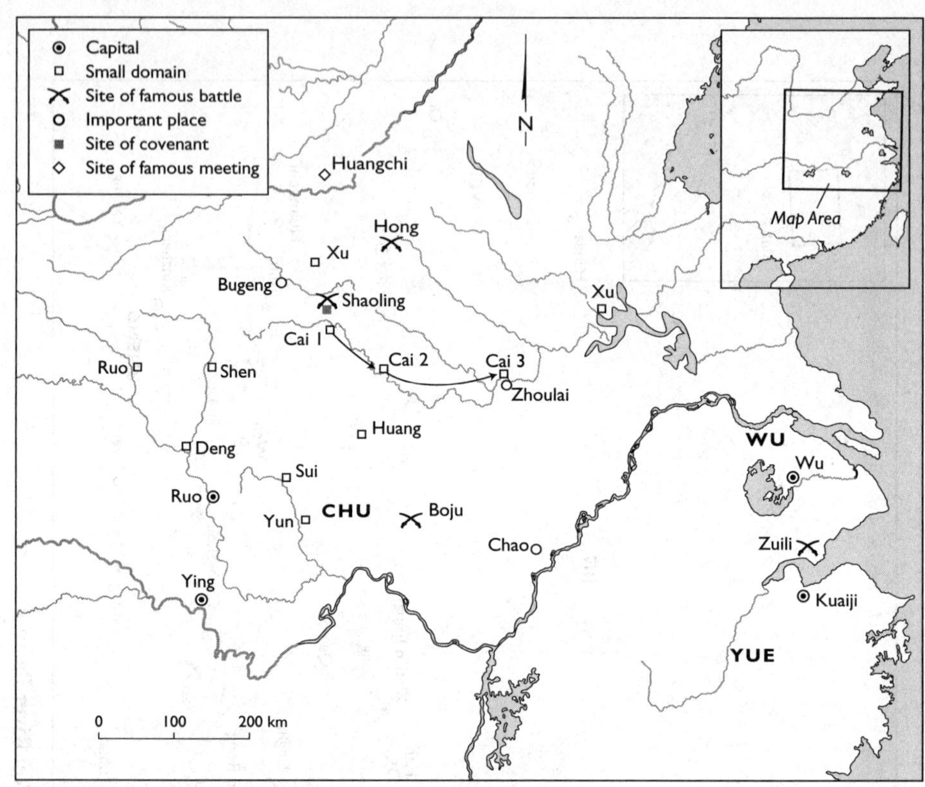

Map 4. Important places in the South

Zuo Tradition / *Zuozhuan*

成公

Lord Cheng
(590–573 BCE)

The period covered by Lord Cheng's reign is framed by two extended battle narratives—the battle of An (Cheng 2, 589 BCE) and the battle of Yanling (Cheng 16, 575 BCE). In both cases, victory is presented as inconclusive and even dangerous, unlike the alignment of moral rhetoric, superior tactics, and eventual victory in the campaigns at Chengpu (Xi 28, 632 BCE) and Bi (Xuan 12, 597 BCE). In the aftermath of Chu victory at Bi, smaller domains such as Zheng, Song, Chen, and Cai became dependents of Chu. The campaign at An may be seen as Jin's attempt to reassert its influence in the north, as it supports Lu and Wei, its allies from the Covenant of Duandao (Xuan 17, 592 BCE), against Qi. The Jin minister Xi Ke's desire for vengeance against the Qi ruler's mother, who laughed at his deformity during his official visit to Qi (Xuan 17.1), is presented as a key factor in the An campaign. Jin vindictiveness may explain why the most compelling rhetoric belongs to the defeated party—the speech of the Qi minister Guo Zuo (Bin Meiren) resisting Jin demands (Cheng 2.3). This is one of several famous pieces of diplomatic rhetoric in this section, which also includes Zhi Ying's dignified refusal to yield to the Chu king's demand for requittal (Cheng 3.4), Ji Wenzi's speech on the duties of an overlord (Cheng 8.1), and Lü Xiang's (Wei Xiang) speech or letter severing relations with Qin (Cheng 13.3).

The fruits of victory at An for Jin and its allies are hollow. Lu regains the lands north of the Wen River from Qi (Cheng 2.3), but Jin forces Lu to return the territories six years later after improving its ties with Qi (Cheng 8.1). Jin's position as covenant chief seems uncertain, despite its triumph at An and victory over Qin at Masui (Cheng 13.3). Chu confirms its ascendancy and gathers many domains, except Jin, for a covenant at Shu shortly after the An campaign (Cheng 2.8), and it continues its aggression against Wei (Cheng 2.8, 15.3), Zheng (Cheng 6.9, 7.4, 15.3), and Song (Cheng 18.2). Chu's image remains ambivalent, however. On the one

hand, we have the Lu minister Ji Wenzi's categorical rejection of Chu as not being "of the same kith and kin" as the central domains (Cheng 4.4). On the other hand, Zhong Yi, a Chu prisoner in Jin, impresses Jin leaders with his dignity and ritual propriety by strumming "southern tunes" and proudly proclaiming his hereditary vocation as a musician (Cheng 9.9), and he becomes an envoy seeking a Jin-Chu accord. Music serves an opposite function when the Chu minister Zifan (Gongzi Ce) uses it to intimidate the Jin minister Xi Zhi (Cheng 12.4), thus undermining the peace agreement between Jin and Chu (Cheng 12.2). That accord is brought about by the Song minister Hua Yuan (Cheng 11.8, 12.2), whose mediatory effort presages that of Xiang Xu, another Song minister seeking cessation of conflicts some thirty years later (Xiang 27.4, 546 BCE; Zhao 1.1, 541 BCE).

Jin-Chu conflict culminates in the battle of Yanling. As in analogous accounts earlier, we have a cluster of anecdotes about omens, predictions, and explanations that assess and justify the outcome. A heightened awareness of perspectives and spectacle adds to narrative interest. Unlike previous battles, ritualized respect toward rulers of the enemy camp here feeds allegations of conspiracy and treason (Cheng 17.10). The battle of Yanling produces no real victor. Whereas Chu defeat is moralized, notably in Shen Shushi's speech (Cheng 16.5), Jin victory is not presented as morally justified; instead, it is accompanied by the Jin minister Fan Hui's repeated predictions of imminent disaster, soon fulfilled in the annihilation of the Xi lineage (Cheng 17.10) and the Jin ruler's assassination (Cheng 18.1).

This bloody outcome in turn develops from the deepening rift between the Jin ruling house and its ministerial lineages, as well as from deadly rivalry among those lineages. Earlier we see the destruction of the Zhao lineage (Cheng 8.6), whose ancestor's fearsome ghost exacts vengeance against Lord Jing of Jin in a memorable dream visitation (Cheng 10.4). The sagacious Jin minister Bo Zong is slandered and killed by leaders of the Xi lineage (Cheng 15.5), in their turn maligned by Luan Shu (Cheng 17.10). Possibly as a response to such violence, we have passages celebrating the virtues of yielding, civility, and cohesion among Jin leaders (Cheng 2.3, 2.7, 4.4, 6.11, 8.2). There are other kinds of intriguing mixtures: Xi Ke is alternatively humble (Cheng 2.7) and arrogant (Cheng 3.9), the Zhou king's concern with the ritual propriety of Jin's act of presenting the spoils of its victory over Qi shades into a petulant complaint about the inferior rank of the Jin envoy (Cheng 2.9), Zhao Yingqi of Jin combines licentiousness with keen insight (Cheng 5.1), Zishu Shengbo of Lu is both unscrupulous (Cheng 11.3) and loyal (Cheng 16.8, 16.11), and his life ends with an enigmatic dream (Cheng 17.8).

We have accounts of internecine conflicts in many domains, although they are often less detailed than such narratives in Jin. In Song, complex negotiations between the Dai and Huan lines show how the sometimes-

春秋

1.1　元年，春，王正月，公即位。

1.2　二月辛酉，葬我君宣公。

1.3　無冰。

1.4(2)　三月，作丘甲。

1.5(3)　夏，臧孫許及晉侯盟于赤棘。

1　In his classification of female characters in *Zuozhuan*, Gu Donggao lists twelve in the highest rank of "integrity" (*jiexing* 節行), eleven in the middle rank of "sound judgment" (*mingzhe* 明哲), and thirty-four in the lowest rank of "unscrupulous excesses" (*zongzi budu* 縱恣不度). See Gu's "*Chunqiu* lienü biao" 春秋列女表, in *Chunqiu dashi biao*, 3:2628–30.

2　The ritual of collecting and storing ice in the second month of the Zhou calendar (for use in the summer) is mentioned in Zhao 4.2 and *Maoshi* 154, "Qiyue" 七月, 8A.276–88. Here "no ice" means that the ritual cannot be performed.

3　Commentators disagree on the size of the district (*qiu* 丘) and the number of armored soldiers (*jia* 甲). Suffice it to say that the two seem to have a proportional relationship. Fan Wenlan (cited in Yang, 2:784) suggests that this reform may be connected to

conflicting interests of individuals, lineages, and the domain are debated (Cheng 15.4, 15.5). Chu interference determines the balance of power between Song lineages (Cheng 18.5), just as Jin arbitrates disputes between the Wei ruler and the Sun lineage of Wei (Cheng 7.6, 14.1, 14.5). In Lu, the young Lord Cheng is threatened by his mother, Mu Jiang, who demonstrates her cultural competence (Cheng 9.5) but also plots with her lover Shusun Qiaoru to expel the Ji and Meng lineages by seeking Jin assistance (Cheng 16.5, 16.6, 16.8, 16.11). In Qi, adulterous relations between Lord Qing's mother, Sheng Meng Zi, and Qing Ke lead to violence against the Gao and Guo lineages (Cheng 17.6, 17.9, 18.2). In Chu, Qu Wuchen warns King Zhuang and Zifan against union with the femme fatale Xia Ji but acts against his own better judgment (Cheng 2.6). His marriage with Xia Ji and Zifan's consequent enmity, in addition to the grudges of another Chu minister, Zichong, lead to the annihilation of his line in Chu (Cheng 7.5). As Jin envoy in Wu, Qu Wuchen contributes to the rise of Wu and uses Wu attacks against Chu to wreak vengeance on Zifan and Zichong (Cheng 7.5). In all these cases, women are seductive and dangerous. There are, however, counterexamples, including Bo Zong's wife, who warns Bo Zong against excessive forthrightness (Cheng 15.5), and Ding Jiang of Wei, whose sagacity urges reconciliation and whose prescience predicts disaster (Cheng 14.1, 14.5).[1]

....

LORD CHENG 1 (590 BCE)
ANNALS

In the first year, in spring, in the royal first month, our lord acceded to his position. — 1.1

In the second month, on the *xinyou* day (27), we buried our ruler Lord Xuan. — 1.2

There was no ice.[2] — 1.3

In the third month, the system of having districts supply armored soldiers was instituted.[3] — 1.4(2)

In summer, Zangsun Xu (Zang Xuanshu) and the Prince of Jin swore a covenant at Chiji.[4] — 1.5(3)

---

the "tithe levied according to acreage" (*shuimu* 稅畝) mentioned in Xuan 15.8. The last *Zuozhuan* reference to Lu taxation is in Ai 12.1. Cf. the "levy according to district" 邱賦 in Zheng in Zhao 4.6. See Gu Donggao, *Chunqiu dashi biao*, 2:1423–33.

4   Chiji 赤棘 is of unknown location.

1.6(1)　秋，王師敗績于茅戎。

1.7　冬，十月。

左傳

1.1(6)　元年，春，晉侯使瑕嘉平戎于王，單襄公如晉拜成。劉康公徼戎，將遂伐之。叔服曰：「背盟而欺大國，此必敗。背盟，不祥；欺大國，不義；神、人弗助，將何以勝？」不聽，遂伐茅戎。三月癸未，敗績于徐吾氏。

1.2(4)　為齊難故，作丘甲。

1.3(5)　聞齊將出楚師，夏，盟于赤棘。

1.4　秋，王人來告敗。

1.5　冬，臧宣叔令脩賦、繕完、具守備，曰：「齊、楚結好，我新與晉盟，晉、楚爭盟，齊師必至。雖晉人伐齊，楚必救之，是齊、楚同我也。知難而有備，乃可以逞。」

5　The word *jiao* 徼 here is read as *jiao* (僥, 傲), as in *jiaoxing* 僥倖, "to trust one's luck." The Rong have let down their guard because of the peace negotiations.

6　Du Yu (ZZ 25.420) identifies Xuwushi as a subgroup of the Mao Rong (Rong tribe of the Mao), while Kong Yingda (ZZ-Kong 25.420) notes that Xuwushi was the place where the Mao Rong gathered their forces. We may surmise on the basis of Shufu's prediction that Zhou was defeated by Jin forces assisting the Mao Rong. The difference between the Zhou and Xia calendars, followed by the *Annals* and this *Zuozhuan* entry respectively, explains the temporal discrepancy. Whereas *Gongyang*, Cheng 1 (7.214), implies and *Guliang*, Cheng 1 (13.128), explicitly asserts that the lack of reference to Jin is "respectful concealment" of the royal house's plight, *Zuozhuan*, through Shufu, places the blame squarely on the Zhou house.

In autumn, the king's troops were completely defeated by the Rong tribe of Mao. 1.6(1)

Winter, the tenth month. 1.7

ZUO

Zhou defeated the Rong twenty years earlier (Wen 17.5) and hostilities persist. A Jin envoy brings about a peace agreement between Zhou and the Rong. Zhou attacks the Rong by surprise but is defeated, as Shufu (Wen 1.1), the prescient court scribe, predicts.

In the first year, in spring, the Prince of Jin sent Zhan Jia[a] to make peace with the Rong on behalf of the king. Shan Duke Xiang went to Jin to bow to affirm the alliance. Liu Duke Kang wanted to try his luck with the Rong[5] and thus planned to attack them. Shufu said, "To turn against a covenant and deceive a great domain like Jin will certainly end in defeat. To turn against a covenant is inauspicious; to deceive a great domain is undutiful; gods and men will not assist you; on what basis will you win?" Liu Duke Kang did not listen, and thereupon attacked the Rong tribe of Mao. In the third month, on the *guiwei* day (19), Zhou troops were completely defeated at Xuwushi.[6] 1.1(6)

New military preparations are undertaken as a consequence of Qi-Lu hostilities in the last two years (Xuan 17.1, 18.2).

On account of the troubles with Qi, the system of having districts supply armored soldiers was instituted. 1.2(4)

With the news of an impending Qi-Chu incursion, Lu affirms its alliance with Jin.

We heard that Qi was about to send forth Chu troops. In the summer, we swore a covenant at Chiji. 1.3(5)

In autumn, the king's men came to announce Zhou's defeat. 1.4

Zang Xuanshu of Lu prepares for war.

In winter, Zang Xuanshu ordered that military levies be exacted, city walls be repaired, and preparations for defense be made. He said, "Qi and Chu have cemented their ties. We have just sworn a covenant with Jin. With Jin and Chu fighting to become leader of the covenant, Qi troops will certainly descend on us. Although Jin will attack Qi, Chu will certainly go to its aid. That means Qi and Chu will together side against us. It is only when one is aware of dangers and makes preparations for them that one will prevail." 1.5

春秋

2.1(1)　二年，春，齊侯伐我北鄙。

2.2(2)　夏，四月丙戌，衛孫良夫帥師及齊師戰于新築，衛師敗績。

2.3(3)　六月癸酉，季孫行父、臧孫許、叔孫僑如、公孫嬰齊帥師會晉郤克、衛孫良夫、曹公子首及齊侯戰于鞌，齊師敗績。

2.4(3)　秋，七月，齊侯使國佐如師。己酉，及國佐盟于袁婁。

2.5(4)　八月壬午，宋公鮑卒。

2.6(5)　庚寅，衛侯速卒。

2.7(4)　取汶陽田。

2.8(8)　冬，楚師、鄭師侵衛。

2.9(8)　十有一月，公會楚公子嬰齊于蜀。

2.10(8)　丙申，公及楚人、秦人、宋人、陳人、衛人、鄭人、齊人、曹人、邾人、薛人、鄫人盟于蜀。

In the second year, in spring, the Prince of Qi attacked our northern marches.   2.1(1)

In summer, in the fourth month, on the *bingxu* day (29), Sun Liangfu of Wei led out troops and did battle with Qi troops at Xinzhu.[7] The Wei troops were completely defeated.   2.2(2)

In the sixth month, on the *guiyou* day (27), Jisun Hangfu (Ji Wenzi), Zangsun Xu (Zang Xuanshu), Shusun Qiaoru, and Gongsun Yingqi (Zishu Shengbo) led out troops, met with Xi Ke of Jin, Sun Liangfu of Wei, and Gongzi Shou of Cao, and did battle with the Prince of Qi at An. The Qi troops were completely defeated.   2.3(3)

In autumn, in the seventh month, the Prince of Qi sent Guo Zuo to the invading troops of the allies. On the *jiyou* day (23), they swore a covenant with Guo Zuo at Yuanlou.   2.4(3)

In the eighth month, on the *renwu* day (27), Bao, the Duke of Song, died.   2.5(4)

On the *gengyin* day (9), Su, the Prince of Wei, died.[8]   2.6(5)

We took lands to the north of the Wen River.[9]   2.7(4)

In winter, Chu troops and Zheng troops invaded Wei.   2.8(8)

In the eleventh month, our lord met with Gongzi Yingqi (Zichong) of Chu at Shu.   2.9(8)

On the *bingshen* day (12), our lord swore a covenant with a Chu leader, a Qin leader, a Song leader, a Chen leader, a Wei leader, a Zheng leader, a Qi leader, a Cao leader, a Zhu leader, a Xue leader, and a Zeng leader at Shu.   2.10(8)

---

7   Xinzhu 新築 was presumably in Wei or somewhere along the Qi-Wei border.
8   The *gengyin* day fell in the ninth month.
9   Jin made Qi return the fields to Lu.

2.1(1)　二年，春，齊侯伐我北鄙，圍龍。頃公之嬖人盧蒲就魁門焉。龍人囚之。齊侯曰：「勿殺，吾與而盟，無入而封。」弗聽，殺而膊諸城上。齊侯親鼓，士陵城。三日，取龍。遂南侵，及巢丘。

2.2(2)　衛侯使孫良夫、石稷、甯相、向禽將侵齊，與齊師遇。石子欲還。孫子曰：「不可。以師伐人，遇其師而還，將謂君何？若知不能，則如無出。今既遇矣，不如戰也。」

　　　夏，有……。

　　　石成子曰：「師敗矣，子不少須，眾懼盡。子喪師徒，何以復命？」皆不對。又曰：「子，國卿也。隕子，辱矣。子以眾退，我此乃止。」且告車來甚眾。齊師乃止，次于鞫居。新築人仲叔于奚救孫桓子，桓子是以免。

　　　既，衛人賞之以邑，辭，請曲縣、繁纓以朝。許之。

10　Lu borders Qi on the east. Qi attacks against Lu were usually from the west. Lu defenses on its western border were probably stronger than on its northern one, hence Qi's circuitous route of attack. The Prince of Qi is also referred to as Lord Qing in this entry.

11　During the battle of Chengpu in 632 BCE, the men of Cao also displayed Jin corpses on the city wall (Xi 28.3). Here the word *bo* 膊 indicates that Lupu Jiukui had been undressed before being exposed on the wall.

12　Long 龍 was located in the domain of Lu southeast of present-day Tai'an County 泰安縣, Shandong.

13　Chaoqiu 巢丘 would probably not have been far from Long.

14　This is also a recurrent theme in *Xunzi*; see *Xunzi* 9.165, 10.200, 19.419, 22.511.

15　Sima Qian (*Shiji* 37.1596) believes that Wei was trying to come to the aid of Lu. *Zuozhuan* does not specify where Qi and Wei troops met. According to the *Annals*, Qi and Wei fought at Xinzhu. It seems likely that Qi and Wei troops met at the border between Qi and Wei, and then the Qi army pursued Wei forces to Xinzhu in Wei, where the battle took place. Alternatively, Xinzhu could be at the border of Qi and Wei.

16　Here the text breaks off. The missing text presumably describes the Xinzhu campaign that took place in the fourth month.

17　Shi Chengzi and Sun Liangfu reverse their positions as the battle wears on.

18　The Zhou king used four-sided frames for suspending musical instruments such as bells and chime-stones; this was called "palace-style suspension" (*gongxuan* 宮縣、宮懸). The curved (three-sided) frames used by the princes were called *quxuan* 曲縣 or *xuanxuan* 軒縣. High officers were entitled to two-sided frames known as *panxuan* 判縣. The martingales of silken cords (*fanying* 繁纓) were a prerogative of the princes. In sum, Zhongshu Yuxi was requesting the ritual regalia and paraphernalia of the princes, which should be beyond his station as high officer.

Qi invades Lu, and tensions mount because the Qi ruler's male favorite is killed.

In the second year, in spring, the Prince of Qi attacked our northern marches and laid siege to Long.[10] Lord Qing's male favorite, Lupu Jiukui, stormed the city gate. The men of Long took him prisoner. The Prince of Qi said, "Do not put him to death. I will swear a covenant with you and will not enter your borders." The men of Long did not heed him, put Lupu Jiukui to death, and exposed his naked corpse on the city wall.[11] The Prince of Qi personally beat the war drum, and his officers scaled the city walls. In three days, the Qi army took Long.[12] It then made a southward incursion and advanced as far as Chaoqiu.[13]

2.1(1)

The forces of Wei and Qi meet. Wei is defeated at the battle of Xinzhu. Zhongshu Yuxi saves the Wei commander Sun Liangfu and is, against ritual propriety, rewarded with dignities beyond his station. On the importance of ritual distinctions and the dangers of their misuse, see also Zhuang 18.1 and Zhao 6.7.[14]

The prince of Wei sent Sun Liangfu, Shi Chengzi[a], Ning Xiang, and Xiang Qinjiang to invade Qi, and they encountered Qi troops on the way.[15] Shi Chengzi[b] wanted to return to Wei. Sun Liangfu[b] said, "This will not do. If we mobilize troops to attack another domain, and then turn back upon encountering its troops, what will we say to the ruler? Had we known that we could not fight, we would have done better not to have set forth at all. Now, since we have encountered them, it will be better to fight."

2.2(2)

In summer, there was . . .[16]

Shi Chengzi said, "Our troops are losing. If you, sir, do not hold out and wait a while for reinforcements, I fear that our entire force will be destroyed. If you lose all your men, how are you going to report on the discharge of your mission?"[17] None of the other commanders responded. Shi Chengzi continued, addressing Sun Liangfu, "You, sir, are a minister of the domain. If we lose you, it will be shameful indeed. You should retreat with the majority of the troops, while we remain here." Meanwhile, he also announced to Wei troops that many chariots were coming as reinforcement. Qi troops then stopped and set up camp at Juju. Zhongshu Yuxi, a man of Xinzhu, had come to the aid of Sun Liangfu[a], who thereby escaped harm.

Not long thereafter, the leaders of Wei rewarded Zhongshu Yuxi with settlements. He declined and requested instead curved frames for suspending musical instruments and the use of martingales of silken cords when he visited court.[18] His requests were granted.

仲尼聞之曰：「惜也，不如多與之邑。唯器與名，不可以假人，君之所司也。名以出信，信以守器，器以藏禮，禮以行義，義以生利，利以平民，政之大節也。若以假人，與人政也。政亡，則國家從之，弗可止也已。」

2.3a　孫桓子還於新築，不入，遂如晉乞師。臧宣叔亦如晉乞師。皆主郤獻子。晉侯許之七百乘。郤子曰：「此城濮之賦也。有先君之明與先大夫之肅，故捷。克於先大夫，無能為役，請八百乘。」許之。郤克將中軍，士燮佐上軍，欒書將下軍，韓厥為司馬，以救魯、衛。臧宣叔逆晉師，且道之。季文子帥師會之。

　　　及衛地，韓獻子將斬人，郤獻子馳，將救之。至，則既斬之矣。郤子使速以徇，告其僕曰：「吾以分謗也。」

19　The argument about the inviolability of "ritual objects" and "names" is repeated in Zhao 32.4 when Scribe Mo discusses the exile of Lord Zhao of Lu. This may be linked to the idea of "rectification of names" (*zhengming* 正名) (*Analects* 13.3), as Sima Guang asserts in *Zizhi tongjian* 1.4, when he refers to this passage as Confucius' programmatic affirmation of the political hierarchy of ruler and subject.

20　For other examples of such sequencing in the so-called thimble style (*dingzhen* 頂針) or anadiplosis in Western rhetoric, see Xi 15.4g, Zhao 9.5.

21　Xi Ke's vow of vengeance against Lord Qing of Qi (Xuan 17.1) must have become public knowledge.

22　See Xi 28.3.

23　Ma Zonglian believed that *xian dafu* refers to Xi Ke's ancestor Xi Hu, but the term probably includes all the Jin commanders responsible for victory at Chengpu (Yang, 2:789). The word *su* 肅 is usually associated with solemnity, caution, and discipline. Here we follow Wang Yinzhi (*Jingyi shuwen*, 696), who cites his father Wang Niansun's gloss of *su* 肅 as *minjie* 敏捷, "quickness." Wang also refers to the gloss of *su* as *su* 速 or *ji* 疾 ("quick," "swift") in *Erya*.

24　In other words, the troops under the assistant commander of the central army, the commander of the upper army, and the assistant commander of the lower army did not join the battle. That a partially mobilized Jin army should involve eight hundred chariots, compared with the seven hundred chariots that constituted the entire Jin army in the battle of Chengpu, demonstrates how the scale of warfare and the size of the Jin army had escalated.

Confucius[c] heard of this and said, "What a pity! It would have been better to give him many settlements. It is precisely ritual objects and names that cannot be granted to others, for these are the things by which a ruler governs.[19] The right names are for bringing forth trust; trust is for guarding ritual objects; ritual objects are for embodying ritual propriety; ritual propriety is for carrying out justice; justice is for bringing benefit; benefit is for governing the people.[20] These are the great principles of government. If these things are granted to others, it amounts to handing over government to others. Once the government is gone, then domain and patrimony follow, and the process cannot be stopped."

The commanders of Wei and Lu appeal to Xi Ke, chief commander of Jin, for assistance. Xi Ke, motivated by a personal grudge against Qi (see Xuan 17.1), requests a large force from the Jin ruler. He takes pains to foster unity among Jin commanders.

Sun Liangfu[a] returned to Xinzhu. Without entering the capital, he then went to Jin to plead for troops. Zang Xuanshu also went to Jin to plead for troops. Both looked to Xi Ke[a] as one who could decide the situation.[21] The Prince of Jin granted Xi Ke the use of seven hundred war chariots. Xi Ke[b] said, "This was the size of our force at the Chengpu campaign.[22] We then had the wisdom of our former ruler and the quick, judicious calculations of our former high officers[23]—hence our victory. I am not even fit to be a lackey of our former high officers. I request eight hundred chariots." His request was granted. Xi Ke was commander of the central army, Fan Xie[b] was assistant commander of the upper army, Luan Shu was commander of the lower army.[24] Han Jue was supervisor of the military. Thus did they go to the aid of Lu and Wei. Zang Xuanshu met the Jin troops and also guided them on their way. Ji Wenzi led out Lu troops and joined forces with them.

When they reached Wei territories, Han Jue[a] was about to execute someone. Xi Ke[a] raced there with the intention of saving him. By the time he arrived, that person had been executed. Xi Ke immediately had his corpse circulated among the troops as a warning, saying to his attendant, "Thus have I shared the blame."[25]

2.3a

---

25 In *Guoyu*, "Jin yu 5," 11.402, the attendant questions Xi Ke's about-face. The guilt or innocence of the executed person is not the issue. At first Xi Ke wants to have him spared, for fear that harsh military discipline would undermine morale. When he finds out that the person had been executed, he hastens to "share the blame" to preserve the unity among the commanders, perhaps in tacit recognition that division among the leaders had led to Jin defeat in the battle of Bi (Xuan 12.2). Xi Ke's act is castigated as a perversion of justice that "heightens blame" 益謗 in *Han Feizi* 36.811–12. See also *Zhuzi yulei*, 83.2167. Han Jue's and Xun Linfu's pursuit of Chu in the name of unity of command might have led to Jin's defeat in the battle of Bi (Xuan 12.2c), although Fan Hui's decision to "share the blame" of retreat is also praised (Xuan 2.12h).

2.3b　師從齊師于莘。六月壬申，師至于靡笄之下。齊侯使請戰，曰：「子以君師辱於敝邑，不腆敝賦，詰朝請見。」

　　對曰：「晉與魯、衛，兄弟也，來告曰：『大國朝夕釋憾於敝邑之地。』寡君不忍，使群臣請於大國，無令輿師淹於君地。能進不能退，君無所辱命。」

　　齊侯曰：「大夫之許，寡人之願也；若其不許，亦將見也。」齊高固入晉師，桀石以投人，禽之而乘其車，繫桑本焉，以徇齊壘，曰：「欲勇者賈余餘勇！」

2.3c(3)　癸酉，師陳于鞌。邴夏御齊侯，逢丑父為右。晉解張御郤克，鄭丘緩為右。齊侯曰：「余姑翦滅此而朝食。」不介馬而馳之。

26　Mount Miji 靡笄 is identified with what is now called Qianfo Mountain 千佛山, near Jinan City 濟南市, Shandong. Note that the battle of An is referred to as the battle of Miji 靡笄之役 in *Guoyu*, "Jin yu 5."

27　The Jin commanders are referring to the Qi ruler's request to commence battle on the morrow.

The allied troops caught up with Qi troops at Shen. In the sixth month, on the *renshen* day (16), the allied troops reached the foot of Mount Miji.[26] The Prince of Qi sent someone to request engagement in battle, saying, "You deigned to bring your lord's troops to our humble settlement. Insufficient as our modest forces are, we request to meet you tomorrow morning."

The Jin commanders responded, "Lu and Wei are the brothers of Jin. They came to notify us: 'That great domain had been day and night relieving its rancor in the territories of our humble settlements.' Our unworthy ruler could not bear their distress and sent a group of his subjects to plead with your great domain, charging that we should not let our chariots and troops remain long in your territory. We can only advance; we cannot retreat. The command from you, my lord, shall have no cause to be dishonored."[27]

The Prince of Qi said, "What you, high officers, granted is my own wish. Even had you not given us permission, we would still meet you in battle." Gao Gu of Qi entered the ranks of the Jin army, raised a stone and hurled it against a Jin man, took him captive, and then rode in his chariot, tying to it a mulberry trunk with its roots.[28] He paraded around the Qi fortifications, saying, "Those who want valor can buy my surplus!"

At the battle of An, Jin commanders and officers bear with injuries and persevere.

On the *guiyou* day, the troops formed their lines at An.[29] Bing Xia was the Qi Prince's chariot driver. Feng Choufu was the spearman on the right. On the Jin side, Xie Zhang was Xi Ke's chariot driver, and Zhengqiu Huan was the spearman on the right. The Prince of Qi said, "I might as well smite them and root them out before my morning meal!"[30] Without putting armor on his horse, he charged toward the enemy.

2.3b

2.3c(3)

---

28 Mulberry trees are hard to uproot. Gao Gu thereby demonstrates another feat of strength. The mulberry trunk also makes the captured chariot distinctly recognizable.

29 An 鞌 was located in the domain of Qi and is probably to be identified with Lixia 歷下, west of Jinan City 濟南市, Shandong.

30 Du Yu (ZZ 25.423) reads *jian* 翦 as *jin* 盡 (completely), but elsewhere in *Zuozhuan* the word means "to cut off" or "to destroy."

　　郤克傷於矢，流血及屨，未絕鼓音，曰：「余病矣！」張侯曰：「自始合，而矢貫余手及肘，余折以御。左輪朱殷，豈敢言病？吾子忍之！」緩曰：「自始合，苟有險，余必下推車，子豈識之？然子病矣！」張侯曰：「師之耳目，在吾旗鼓，進退從之。此車一人殿之，可以集事。若之何其以病敗君之大事也？擐甲執兵，固即死也，病未及死，吾子勉之！」左并轡，右援枹而鼓。馬逸不能止，師從之。齊師敗績。逐之，三周華不注。

2.3d　韓厥夢子輿謂己曰：「旦辟左右！」故中御而從齊侯。邴夏曰：「射其御者，君子也。」公曰：「謂之君子而射之，非禮也。」射其左，越于車下。射其右，斃于車中。

　　綦毋張喪車，從韓厥曰：「請寓乘！」從左右，皆肘之，使立於後。

31　In *Shiji* 32.1497, Xi Ke is said to want to "return to Jin ranks."

32　Alternatively, "an arrow went through my hand and reached my elbow."

33　He did not have time to take them out properly, so he just broke them off, leaving the tips of the arrows in his flesh.

34　Zhengqiu Huan assumes rightly that Xi Ke did not notice because he had been seriously wounded and also because he was devoting whatever remained of his energy and concentration to beating the war drums.

35　By acknowledging Xi Ke's wound, Zhengqiu Huan could have implied that a return to the Jin ranks might be admissible. This in turn provoked Xie Zhang's rebuttal.

36　The analogy of the army with the human body means that banners and drums define direction, unity, and purpose for the army—banners are what the soldiers see and drumbeats are what they hear. Cf. *Guoyu*, "Jin yu 5," 11.402: "The heart of the three armies is with this chariot. Their eyes and ears are with our banners and drums. If the chariot shows no retreating sign and the drum makes no retreating sound, our military endeavor will succeed." Cf. *Sunzi* 7.141.

37　Du Yu (*ZZ* 25.423) reads *dian* 殿 as *zhen* 鎮 ("control" or "guard"). Du derived his gloss from *Maoshi* 15A.502 (Hong Liangji, *Chunqiu Zuozhuan gu*, 439). Qian Zhongshu (*Guanzhui bian*, 1.204–5) suggests the phonological and semantic connections between *dian* 殿, *tian* 填 ("fill"), and *zhen* 鎮.

38　Xie Zhang was holding the reins in only one hand and thus could not control the horses properly.

39　The mountain called Huabuzhu 華不注 was located northeast of present-day Jinan.

40　For similar reasoning, see Xi 22.8, where Lord Xiang of Song refuses to attack Chu at the battle of Hong until the Chu army had crossed the river and arranged its troops; see also Zhao 26.4c, where Ran Shu does not lead troops against Chen Ziqiang of Qi because Ran calls Chen a "noble man." For the opposite argument, which maintains that warfare calls for a different kind of ritual propriety, see Xi 22.8 and Xuan 2.1a. In Zhao 21.6b, Hua Bao, having shot at and missed an enemy on the battlefield, agrees to give the latter his turn to shoot and is killed.

Xi Ke was wounded by an arrow. The blood flowed all the way to his shoes, but he never faltered in his drumbeat. He said, "I have been wounded!"[31] Xie Zhang[a] said, "From the moment the troops clashed, arrows pierced my arm and elbow.[32] I broke them off so as to drive the chariot.[33] The left wheel has turned dark red with blood. Did I dare to speak of my wounds? You, sir, should just bear it!" Zhengqiu Huan[a] said, "From the moment the troops clashed, whenever there is difficult terrain, I have without fail dismounted to push the chariot. How would you even know about it?[34] But you, sir, have indeed been wounded!"[35] Xie Zhang[a] said, "The eyes and ears of the army are with our banners and drums, and we advance and retreat in step with them.[36] We can complete our mission so long as there is one of us to control the chariot.[37] How can you let your injury ruin our ruler's great enterprise? To don armor and take up weapons is to be ready to meet death. You are wounded but not dying yet. You, sir, have to brace yourself!" Xie Zhang grasped all the reins together with his left hand while with his right he wielded the drumstick and beat the war drums. The horses raced forward and could not be stopped,[38] and the army followed his chariot. The Qi troops were completely defeated. Jin forces pursued the Qi army, whose remnants thrice circled Mount Huabuzhu.[39]

A dream saves the Jin commander Han Jue; a snakebite might have caused Qi's defeat. In the midst of such apparently random causality the etiquette of battle persists: the Qi ruler refuses to shoot Han Jue because he seems to be "a noble man"; Xi Ke pardons the Qi officer Feng Choufu because of his loyalty toward his ruler.

Han Jue had dreamed of his father, Ziyu, telling him: "Tomorrow morning, avoid the right and the left!" That was why he stood in the center driving the chariot as he pursued the prince of Qi. Bing Xia said, "Shoot the chariot driver, to all appearances a noble man." The Qi lord said, "To call him a noble man and yet shoot him would not be in accordance with ritual propriety."[40] He shot the archer on Han's left, who fell from the chariot, and he also shot the spearman man on his right, who died in it.

Qiwu Zhang lost his chariot and ran after Han Jue, saying, "Please let me ride in your chariot!" He followed Han Jue to his left and then his right; in both cases Han Jue elbowed him and made him stand behind

韓厥俛，定其右。逢丑父與公易位。將及華泉，驂絓於木而止。丑父寢
於轏中，蛇出於其下，以肱擊之，傷而匿之，故不能推車而及。

　　韓厥執縶馬前，再拜稽首，奉觴加璧以進，曰：「寡君使群臣為
魯、衛請，曰：『無令輿師陷入君地。』下臣不幸，屬當戎行，無所逃隱。
且懼奔辟，而忝兩君。臣辱戎士，敢告不敏，攝官承乏。」丑父使公下，如
華泉取飲。

　　鄭周父御佐車，宛茷為右，載齊侯以免。韓厥獻丑父，郤獻子將
戮之，呼曰：「自今無有代其君任患者，有一於此，將為戮乎？」郤子曰：
「人不難以死免其君，我戮之，不祥，赦之，以勸事君者。」乃免之。

2.3e　　齊侯免，求丑父三入，三出。每出，齊師以帥退。入于狄卒，狄卒皆抽戈
楯冒之。以入于衛師，衛師免之。遂自徐關入。

41　In the beginning, Lord Qing of Qi was in the center and Feng Choufu was his spearman on the right. Now Feng Choufu moves to the center and Lord Qing stands on his right. The ruler and the commander must have been wearing similar military garb; hence, changing places sufficed to confuse the enemy.

42　These were springs at the foot of Mount Huabuzhu.

43　The *zhan* 轏 ("army wagon") has been glossed as "carriage for sleeping" (*woche* 臥車) and as "military carriage" (*yiche* 役車) (Hong Liangji, *Chunqiu Zuozhuan gu*, 439).

44　Presumably he concealed the wound so as to retain his position as the Qi ruler's spearman on the right.

45　According to the received text, this line should be translated differently: "Han Jue held the bridle in front of the horses." But the word *ma* 馬 is probably included by mistake (Karlgren, gl. 362, following Duan Yucai). Du Yu (ZZ 25.424) claims that the horse trappings symbolize willingness to serve as attendant.

46　The horse trappings, the bowing, and the wine cup were all part of the standard etiquette for a commander addressing the ruler of the vanquished army. These details are repeated in Xiang 25.5, when Gongsun Shezhi of Zheng meets the defeated Chen ruler.

47　"The ranks of the army" (*ronghang* 戎行) may also be rendered as "military action" or "the battlefield."

48　Despite the elaborately polite rhetoric, Han Jue is announcing his intention to make a prisoner of the man he believes to be Lord Qing of Qi.

49　To give Lord Qing a chance to escape, Feng Choufu orders him to fetch water.

50　In *Gongyang*, Cheng 2 (17.215), Xi Ke executed Feng Choufu.

51　Following Liu Wenqi, *Chunqiu Zuoshi zhuan jiuzhu shuzheng*, 780. He enters to lead the Qi army in withdrawal but comes out again to look for Feng Choufu. Du Yu (ZZ 25.424) opines that Lord Qing enters and comes out of the Jin ranks three times trying to save Feng Choufu. Yang (2:795) asserts that Lord Qing deals with Jin in his first attempt and with the Di and Wei troops in his second and third attempts.

52　Di soldiers are found in the Jin army probably because Di men were awarded to Jin ministers as slaves or conscripts after Jin's victory over the Red Di (Xuan 15.3).

53　Karlgren (gl. 366), following Shen Qinhan, reads *mao* 冒 as "charge." Du Yu (ZZ 25.425) explains *mao* as "cover." According to the latter reading, the Di soldiers pull out dagger-axes to allay Jin suspicions, but they actually try to protect the Qi ruler by covering him with shields.

54　Both Di and Wei are Jin allies, but Wei (or both Di and Wei, if we read *mao* as "cover") is reluctant to harm Lord Qing, perhaps for fear of future Qi vengeance.

himself. As Han Jue bent to adjust the corpse of his attendant on the right, Feng Choufu and the Qi lord changed places.[41] When they were about to reach the Springs of Hua,[42] the flanking horses got caught in the trees and stopped. Feng Choufu had been sleeping in an army wagon[43] when a snake emerged from under it. He had hit it with his forearm, was bitten, and concealed his wound.[44] That was why he could not push the chariot free and his pursuers caught up with it.

Han Jue held the bridle and came forward,[45] bowed twice with his forehead touching the ground, and respectfully presented a wine cup, adding a jade disk as offering.[46] He said, "Our unworthy ruler sent a group of his subjects to plead with Qi on behalf of Lu and Wei, charging us not to let our troops penetrate deeply into your territory. Your humble servant unfortunately happens to be in the ranks of the army,[47] with no place to turn for escape or hiding. Moreover, he fears that fleeing or avoiding battle will bring shame to both rulers. Unworthy to be a warrior, I venture to tell of my lack of abilities, as I provisionally take up duties to attend you and offer inadequate service."[48] Choufu had the lord dismount and fetch a drink from the Springs of Hua.[49]

Meanwhile, Zheng Zhoufu was driving one of the auxiliary chariots, with Yuan Pei as his spearman on the right. They took in the Prince of Qi, who thus escaped capture. Han Jue presented Choufu to Xi Ke. Xi Ke[a] was about to put him to death, when Choufu cried out: "Henceforth there will be none who will take his ruler's place to bear his woe! There is one right here. Is he to be put to death?" Xi Ke[b] said, "It is inauspicious for us to put to death a man who does not balk at death if it will let his ruler escape. I will pardon him to encourage those who serve their lords." He thus spared him.[50]

The Qi ruler tries to retrieve Feng Choufu, causing further confusion in the Qi army. A Qi woman is rewarded for upholding the primacy of the ruler and the father. For another example of a Qi woman who upholds public duty as paramount, see Xiang 23.7.

Having evaded capture, the Prince of Qi searched for Choufu. Thrice he entered his army's ranks and thrice he came out of them.[51] Each time he came out, Qi troops withdrew with their commanders without following him. He entered the ranks of Di soldiers.[52] The Di soldiers all pulled out dagger-axes and shields as they charged at him.[53] He entered the ranks of Wei troops, which let him escape from harm.[54] He then entered Qi from Xuguan.[55]

2.3e

---

55   Xuguan 徐關, which could be translated as the "Pass of Xu," was a pass located just southwest of present-day Zibo City 淄博市, Shandong.

齊侯見保者，曰：「勉之！齊師敗矣！」辟女子。女子曰：「君免乎？」曰：「免矣。」曰：「銳司徒免乎？」曰：「免矣。」曰：「苟君與吾父免矣，可若何？」乃奔。齊侯以為有禮。既而問之，辟司徒之妻也。予之石窌。

晉師從齊師，入自丘輿。擊馬陘。

2.3f 齊侯使賓媚人賂以紀甗、玉磬與地。「不可，則聽客之所為。」

賓媚人致賂。晉人不可，曰：「必以蕭同叔子為質，而使齊之封內盡東其畝。」

對曰：

蕭同叔子非他，寡君之母也。若以匹敵，則亦晉君之母也。
吾子布大命於諸侯，而曰必質其母以為信，其若王命何？且
是以不孝令也。《詩》曰：

孝子不匱，
永錫爾類。

---

56   *Rui* 銳 is a spearlike weapon. The *rui situ* 銳司徒 is the leader of those who wield such weapons, who probably form the front line of the army. Alternatively, *ruishi* 銳士 can mean "crack troops"; see Karlgren, gl. 367.

57   He thought this because she asked first about the ruler and only then about her father, and she did not ask about her husband, which may be considered a more private concern.

58   Takezoe (12.18–19) notes that this is the first instance of a woman being granted a settlement.

59   Maxing 馬陘 was located southwest of Yidu County 益都縣, Shandong.

60   This might have been acquired when Lord Xiang of Qi annexed Ji in 690 BCE (Zhuang 4.2). The *yan* 甗, a kind of ancient double boiler, was made of pottery or bronze. Kong Yingda (ZZ-Kong 25.425) speculates that this *yan* is made of jade, which might have been a more appropriate gift. Karlgren (gl. 368) suggests that *yan* may simply be a mistake for *xian* 獻, a bronze vessel presented as an offering.

61   The Ji vessel and jade chiming stones are to be given to Xi Ke (or, according to the *Bamboo Annals*, cited by Du Yu, to the Jin ruler), while land is to be returned to Wei and Lu (ZZ 1063; Yang, 2:797).

62   That is, if Jin refuses, Qi would fight again.

63   Xiao Tongshu Zi was the mother of Lord Qing of Qi and a secondary consort of Lord Hui of Qi (*Soushen ji* 14.103). Her scornful laughter at Xi Ke's deformity in 592 BCE (Xuan 17.1) in part explains Xi Ke's readiness to attack Qi on behalf of Lu and Wei. She is called Xiao Tongzhi Zi 蕭同姪子 in *Gongyang*, Cheng 2 (17.216), and *Guliang*, Cheng 1–2 (13.129). Tong 同 is written as Tong 桐 in *Shiji* 32.1494, 39.1678. Du Yu (ZZ 25.425) glosses her name as "the daughter of Tongshu of Xiao." Her name has also been interpreted as Xiaotong Shu Zi, "middle daughter of [the ruler of] Xiaotong," Xiaotong here being understood as the name of a domain or as a combination of the names of two domains. Other commentators read "Zi" as the clan name of Song, to which Xiao was subsidiary, as indicated by the word *shu* (Liu Wenqi, *Chunqiu Zuoshi zhuan jiuzhu shuzheng*, 783).

When the Prince of Qi saw the guards for the city walls and gates, he said, "Brace yourselves! The Qi army was defeated!" The vanguard urged a woman to get out of the way. The woman said, "Has the ruler escaped harm?" They replied, "He has." "Has the leader of the spearmen escaped harm?"[56] "He has." She said, "If the ruler and my father have escaped harm, what more can I ask?" She then ran away. The Prince of Qi thought she acted in accordance with ritual propriety.[57] Inquiring about her subsequently, he found out that she was the wife of the leader of fortifications, and he gave her the settlement of Shiliu.[58]

The Jin army pursued the Qi army, entered Qi by way of Qiuyu, and attacked Maxing.[59]

Jin leaders demand total subjugation from Qi: its field divisions are to run east and west, thus linking Qi to Jin, and the Qi ruler's mother is to come to Jin as hostage, because Xi Ke wants revenge for her scornful laughter at his deformity three years ago (Xuan 17.1). The Qi envoy Guo Zuo rebuffs Jin demands by appealing, through citation of the Odes, *to the early Zhou moral and political order. He also emphasizes Qi's determination to resist Jin's encroachments.*

The Prince of Qi sent Guo Zuo[a] to offer the bronze *yan* vessel from Ji,[60]   2.3f
jade chiming stones, and land as gifts to the victors,[61] with this instruction: "If they refuse, let them do what they would."[62]

Guo Zuo[a] offered the gifts. The leaders of Jin refused: "Qi must give Xiao Tongshu Zi as hostage in Jin[63] and make the divisions between fields within its borders all run east and west."[64]

Guo Zuo replied,

> Xiao Tongshu Zi is none other than our unworthy ruler's mother.
> If we were to name someone as her counterpart, then it would
> in fact be the mother of the Jin ruler. If, as you lay your great
> command upon the princes, sir, you must make hostages of their
> mothers to secure a pledge, how can you answer to the Zhou king's
> charge? Moreover, this will amount to issuing commands that are
> unfilial. As it says in the *Odes,*
>
> > The filial son is unstinting,
> > And forever blesses your kind.[65]

---

64   Divisions between fields were made according to topography and patterns of irrigation. Jin was west of Qi, east–west divisions in Qi would mean irrigation canals and roads running in the same direction, which would facilitate Jin incursions into Qi. *Shangjun shu* 17.136, *Lüshi chunqiu* 8.441, and *Han Feizi* 34.250 all mention that after Lord Wen of Jin defeated Wei, Jin demanded that Wei make the divisions between fields run east to west.

65   *Maoshi* 247, "Jizui" 既醉, 17B.606. These lines are also quoted in Yin 1.4.

若以不孝令於諸侯，其無乃非德類也乎？先王疆理天下，物
土之宜，而布其利。故《詩》曰：

> 我疆我理，
> 南東其畝。

今吾子疆理諸侯，而曰「盡東其畝」而已，唯吾子戎車是利，
無顧土宜，其無乃非先王之命也乎？反先王則不義，何以為
盟主？其晉實有闕。四王之王也，樹德而濟同欲焉；五伯之
霸也，勤而撫之，以役王命。今吾子求合諸侯，以逞無疆之
欲，《詩》曰：

> 布政優優，
> 百祿是遒。

子實不優，而棄百祿，諸侯何害焉？不然，寡君之命使臣，
則有辭矣。曰：「子以君師辱於敝邑，不腆敝賦，以犒從者。
畏君之震，師徒橈敗。吾子惠徼齊國之福，不泯其社稷，使
繼舊好，唯是先君之敝器、土地不敢愛。子又不許，請收合
餘燼，背城借一。敝邑之幸，亦云從也；況其不幸，敢不唯
命是聽？」

---

66   *Maoshi* 210, "Xin Nanshan" 信南山, 13B.460.

67   Yang (2:798) identifies them as Shun, Yu, Tang, and Wu (or Wen). Shun was succes-
      sor to the sage-king Yao; the remaining three founded the Xia, Shang, and Zhou
      dynasties, respectively. The four eras are named together in Zhuang 32.3 and Cheng
      13.3. Du Yu (*ZZ* 25.426) identifies the four kings as Yu of Xia, Tang of Shang, and
      Kings Wen and Wu of Zhou.

68   Du Yu (*ZZ* 25.426) names Kunwu of Xia, Dapeng and Shiwei of Shang, Lord Huan
      of Qi, and Lord Wen of Jin as the "five overlords." The list coincides with those of Fu
      Qian (as cited in *Maoshi*-Kong, "Preface," 6), Ban Gu (*Baihu tong shuzheng* 1), and
      Ying Shao (*Fengsu tongyi* 1.2b–3b). "The five overlords of the Three Dynasties" are
      distinct from "the five overlords of the Spring and Autumn period," of which there
      are various versions (Gu Yanwu, *Rizhi lu jishi*, 4.95–96). Lord Huan of Qi and Lord
      Wen of Jin figure in all versions. *Xunzi* 11.232–33 and *Lüshi chunqiu* 2.95–96 add King
      Zhuang of Chu, King Helu of Wu, and King Goujian of Yue, while Lu Deming's *Jing-
      dian shiwen* includes Lord Xiang of Song, Lord Mu of Qin, and King Zhuang of Chu,
      as does Zhao Qi in his annotations to *Mencius* (*Mengzi*-Zhao 12B.218); Yan Shigu in
      his annotations to *Hanshu* (*Hanshu*-Yan 13.364) lists Lord Mu of Qin, Lord Xiang of
      Song, and King Fucha of Wu. It is likely that Guo Zuo is referring to "the five overlords
      of the Three Dynasties." It would be anachronistic, but not impossible, for Guo Zuo
      to refer to "the five overlords of the Spring and Autumn period." (In other words, the
      mid–Warring States author of this passage could have been guilty of anachronism.) In
      Zuozhuan itself, the only figures consistently referred to as overlords are Lord Huan
      of Qi and Lord Wen of Jin. The term is used more sporadically in relation to Lord Mu
      of Qin's expanding power over the Western Rong, Lord Xiang of Jin's continuation of
      his father's enterprise, and the resurgence of Jin power under Lord Dao. Often the term
      is used in policy debates or diplomatic negotiations to invoke varying visions of domi-
      nance or judicious authority. Cf. Li, *Readability*, 296–98.

69   *Maoshi* 304, "Changfa" 長發, 20D.802.

                                                        Zuo Tradition

If you should command the princes to be unfilial, is that not a contravention of moral example? When the former kings drew up boundaries for the land under heaven and divided it into geographical regions, they assessed what the land was suitable for and laid it out in accordance with the benefits to be gotten from it. That is why it says in the *Odes*,

> We draw up boundaries, we divide,
> Making fields run south, run east.[66]

Now you, sir, are setting up boundaries and divisions for the princes but demand that "divisions between fields should all run east and west." You are only considering the advantage for your war chariots, with no regard for what is suitable for the land. Is that not a violation of the former kings' commands? To go against the former kings is undutiful. How then can you be the covenant chief? It is Jin that is at fault. The four kings[67] became kings by establishing virtue and fulfilling desires shared by all. The five overlords[68] became overlords by being diligent and attending to the needs of other princes, and in this way put themselves in the service of the king's commands. Now you seek to gather the princes and unite them, only to give free rein to desires that go beyond all boundaries. As it says in the *Odes*,

> Gently and carefully he lays out his decrees.
> A hundred blessings he gathers around him.[69]

It is you, sir, who are not gentle and careful in this matter, and thus abandon the hundred blessings—how can that harm the other princes?[70] In the event that our offer is refused, our unworthy ruler has already charged his envoy with the following message: "You, sir, deigned to bring your lord's army to our humble settlement. Insufficient as our modest forces were, we strove to honor the exertions of your followers.[71] Awed by your ruler's mighty authority, our troops scattered and suffered defeat. If you will be kind enough to seek blessings for this domain of Qi, and not let the altars of its domain be obliterated, and if you instead allow our former good relations to be continued, then we do not dare begrudge the humble vessels and land of our former rulers. If you do not grant this, then we ask to collect the last remnants[72] of our army and fight one more time with our backs to our city walls. Even if our humble settlement is lucky in battle, we shall still obey you. How much more so if we are not lucky? Would we dare to abide by anything but your commands?"

---

70   That is, Jin alone will suffer.

71   Literally, "to offer provisions to your followers." It is customary diplomatic rhetoric to refer to battle as "the offering of provisions" (e.g., Xi 26.2). Karlgren (gl. 372) suggests that Guo Zuo may be referring specifically to how the provisions left behind by the Qi army in its hasty retreat were taken over by the Jin army.

72   What we translate as "last remnants" is literally "remnant embers" (*yujin* 餘燼), what remains after a devastating fire.

2.3g 魯、衛諫曰：「齊疾我矣。其死亡者，皆親暱也。子若不許，讎我必甚。唯子，則又何求？子得其國寶，我亦得地，而紓於難，其榮多矣。齊、晉亦唯天所授，豈必晉？」

晉人許之，對曰：「群臣帥賦輿，以為魯、衛請。若苟有以藉口，而復於寡君，君之惠也。敢不唯命是聽？」

2.3h(4, 7) 禽鄭自師逆公。

秋，七月，晉師及齊國佐盟于爰婁。使齊人歸我汶陽之田。公會晉師於上鄍。賜三帥先路三命之服。司馬、司空、輿帥、候正、亞旅皆受一命之服。

2.4(5) 八月，宋文公卒，始厚葬，用蜃、炭，益車、馬，始用殉，重器備。槨有四阿，棺有翰、檜。

君子謂華元、樂舉「於是乎不臣。臣，治煩去惑者也，是以伏死而爭。今二子者，君生則縱其惑，死又益其侈，是棄君於惡也，何臣之為？」

---

73 Lord Cheng of Lu was coming from Lu to meet the Jin army. Qin Zheng is a Lu high officer accompanying the Jin army.

74 The location of Yuanlou 爰婁 is unknown.

75 Shangming 上鄍 was located in present-day Yanggu County 陽穀縣, Shandong.

76 The three commanders are Xi Ke, Fan Xie, and Luan Shu. According to *Shangshu* 18.278 and *Liji* 25.480, ceremonial carriages have three gradations: great carriage, superior carriage, and inferior carriage. *Zhouli* 27.413 names five kinds of ceremonial carriages, made of jade, gold, ivory, leather, and wood, respectively. It is not clear how the two lists may be compared. The higher the number of commands, the more opulent the carriages and robes would be.

77 Du Yu (*ZZ* 25.427) glosses *yushuai* 輿帥 as "leader of war chariots." Karlgren (gl. 376) suggests that, since all military units have chariots, the title should refer to more specific duties, such as overseeing the repair and management of chariots and other military supplies.

78 Both lime (obtained by burning clamshells) and charcoal function to absorb humidity. Use of charcoal seems to have been common practice among the rich (*Lüshi chunqiu* 10.525). However, according to *Zhouli*-Zheng 16.251, only Zhou kings were entitled to use the ashes of burnt clamshells.

79 Since the Song ruling line was descended from Shang, for which human sacrifices and interment of humans to "accompany the dead" were common, it is not clear why the text says here that interment of humans began only with Lord Wen. It is possible that the practice had been discontinued for some generations and only restarted with Lord Wen. See also Xi 19.3.

80 Both the style of the outer coffin and the ornamentations on the coffin were prerogatives of the Zhou king. Also, Lord Wen was buried in the second month of the next year, seven months after his death. According to burial rites of the time, a Zhou king should be buried after seven months, and a prince after five months. Karlgren (gl. 379) argues that the association of *hankuai* 翰檜 with decorations is tenuous, and he proposes that the term may simply mean "on the side was a supporting cypress trunk" (reading *han* as *gan* 榦). Archaeological evidence suggests the "upgrading" of sumptuary norms for the tombs of lords and nobles (von Falkenhausen, *Chinese Society in the Age of Confucius*, 139–49).

Lu and Wei remonstrated with the Jin leaders: "Qi already resents us! The ones who died were all their ruler's kin and favorites. If you do not agree to these terms, Qi's enmity toward us will certainly be extreme! Even in your case, sirs, what more can you ask for? You will gain their treasures of the domain; we too will gain land and will have been relieved of our difficulties. The glory is great indeed! Qi and Jin are both endowed by Heaven. Why must it be Jin that prevails?"

2.3g

The Jin leaders granted the Qi request with this reply: "We, our lord's subjects, led war chariots to plead on behalf of Lu and Wei. If we have the wherewithal for an answer to report back to our unworthy ruler, it is due to your ruler's beneficence. Would we dare to abide by anything but your commands?"

Lu gains lands, and Jin commanders gain honor.

Qin Zheng came from the army to meet our lord.[73]

2.3h(4, 7)

In autumn, in the seventh month, Jin troops and Guo Zuo of Qi swore a covenant at Yuanlou.[74] Qi leaders were made to return to us the lands to the north of the Wen River. Our lord met with Jin troops at Shangming[75] and bestowed on the three Jin commanders superior ceremonial carriages as well as regalia appropriate to dignitaries of three commands.[76] The supervisor of the military, the overseer of works, the commander of military administration,[77] the leader of scouts, and officers second in command all received the regalia appropriate to dignitaries of one command.

Song ministers are blamed for the Song ruler's extravagant funeral. This, along with the next entry, explains the origins of certain funeral practices.

In the eighth month, Lord Wen of Song died. It was then that the extravagant burials began. The ashes of burnt clamshells and charcoal were used.[78] The number of carriages and horses accompanying the dead were increased. For the first time humans were sacrificed to follow the deceased in death.[79] The number of vessels and implements was multiplied. Four pillars supported the outer coffin, which had a roof in the palace style. The coffin was ornamented on three sides and on the top.[80]

2.4(5)

The noble man said of Hua Yuan and Yue Ju that "in this they did not behave as subjects should. A subject is one who brings order to chaos and removes confusion. That is why he braves death to fight for the right path. Now as for these two men, when the ruler was alive they abetted his desires, and when he died, they added to his extravagance. This amounted to abandoning the ruler to iniquities. How was this the proper behavior for a subject?"

2.5(6)　九月，衛穆公卒，晉三子自役弔焉，哭於大門之外。衛人逆之，婦人哭於門內。送亦如之。遂常以葬。

2.6a　楚之討陳夏氏也，莊王欲納夏姬。申公巫臣曰：「不可。君召諸侯，以討罪也；今納夏姬，貪其色也。貪色為淫，淫為大罰。周書曰：『明德慎罰』，文王所以造周也。明德，務崇之之謂也；慎罰，務去之之謂也。若興諸侯，以取大罰，非慎之也。君其圖之！」王乃止。

　　子反欲取之，巫臣曰：「是不祥人也。是夭子蠻，殺御叔，弒靈侯，戮夏南，出孔、儀，喪陳國，何不祥如是？人生實難，其有不獲死乎？天下多美婦人，何必是？」子反乃止。

81　According to *Liji* 41.727, officials on a mission to offer condolences for deaths in another domain should enter the hall. Here the three Jin commanders wailed outside the gate, perhaps because they were not official representatives sent by the Jin ruler.

82　According to *Liji* 44.765, women should wail in the hall. Here they are mourning "inside the gate," but the guests offering condolences are "wailing outside the main gate." Ministers and, in some cases, rulers attending the funerals of Jin lords and Chu kings during the Xiang and Zhao reigns are often asked to do more than this.

83　That is, officials from other domains offered condolences and were received outside the main gate.

84　In the parallel but briefer account in the bamboo document *Xinian*, Zifan and Qu Wuchen openly fight for Xia Ji (Pines, "Zhou History and Historiography"). Xia Ji had a grown son in the accounts from more than ten years earlier. At this point she must be in her forties or fifties. That she should remain seductive well into middle age becomes part of the lore about Xia Ji, who is said to rejuvenate herself through mastery of the art of sexual intercourse (*Lienü zhuan* 7.155–56). In the late Ming erotic novel *Unofficial History from the Forest* (Zhulin yeshi 株林野史), Xia Ji learns such secrets from her first lover, the immortal who visits her in a dream; and the first mortal with whom she has sexual relations is Ziman, her paternal uncle's son (who, according to the Chinese patrilineal system, counts as a brother).

In the ninth month, Lord Mu of Wei died. The three commanders of Jin,   2.5(6)
on their way back from the campaign, went to offer condolences. They
wailed outside the main gate of the capital.[81] The men of Wei went out to
meet them. The womenfolk wailed inside the gate.[82] There was the same
arrangement as they were sent off. This thus became the customary procedure for burial.[83]

*The femme fatale Xia Ji, who caused havoc in Chen (Xuan 9.6, 10.4, 11.5),
now sows discord in Chu. A Chu minister, Qu Wuchen, offers advice that
he himself cannot follow.[84]*

Having chastised the Xia lineage of Chen, King Zhuang wished to take   2.6a
Xia Ji into his harem. Qu Wuchen[a], Lord of Shen, said, "This will not do.
You, my lord, summoned the princes to chastise the guilty, but now you
are taking her into your harem because you covet her beauty. To covet
beauty is licentiousness, and licentiousness is a great transgression. The
Zhou Documents says, 'Illuminate virtue, be wary of transgression.' On
this basis King Wen created Zhou.[85] To illuminate virtue is to strive to
exalt it; to be wary of transgression is to strive to remove it. If you rouse
the princes only to become guilty of great transgression, you are not
being wary. My lord should consider this well!" The king thus desisted.

Zifan wanted to take her for himself. Wuchen said, "This is an inauspicious person. This is the one who brought about Ziman's early death,
killed Yushu, murdered Lord Ling, executed Xia Zhengshu[a], exiled Kong
and Yi, and destroyed Chen.[86] How can anyone be so inauspicious? Life
is difficult enough as it is. Would you want to suffer an unnatural death?[87]
There are many beautiful women under heaven. Why must you have that
one?" Zifan thus desisted.

---

85   Qu Wuchen is paraphrasing lines from "Kanggao" 康誥 in the *Documents* (*Shangshu*
     14.201).
86   Du Yu identifies Ziman as Xia Ji's older brother. According to Zhao 28.2, Xia Ji's older
     brother is Zimo, or Lord Ling of Zheng, who was murdered in the first year of his reign
     because of the turtle stew incident (Xuan 4.2). Ziman, identified as Xia Ji's cousin in
     the late Ming novel mentioned in n. 84, may be another name for Lord Ling of Zheng;
     or he may be another older brother or Xia Ji's first husband. Since she is said to have
     "killed three husbands" (Zhao 28.2), there should be another husband before Xia
     Zhengshu's father and Xiang the Elder. Yushu is identified as Xia Ji's second husband
     and Xia Zhengshu's father. "Kong and Yi" are the Chen ministers Gongsun Ning and
     Yi Hangfu.
87   Literally, "For any man, staying alive is difficult. Will you fail to find a natural death?"
     The implication is that life is hard to guard—the alternative reading is that life is pre-
     cious, hard to come by—and Zifan's proposed marriage will lead to his premature or
     violent death.

王以予連尹襄老。襄老死於邲，不獲其尸。其子黑要烝焉。巫臣使
道焉，曰：「歸，吾聘女。」又使自鄭召之，曰：「尸可得也，必來逆之。」
姬以告王。王問諸屈巫。對曰：「其信。知罃之父，成公之嬖也，而中行伯
之季弟也，新佐中軍，而善鄭皇戌，甚愛此子。其必因鄭而歸王子與襄
老之尸以求之。鄭人懼於邲之役，而欲求媚於晉，其必許之。」

2.6b　王遣夏姬歸。將行，謂送者曰：「不得尸，吾不反矣。」

巫臣聘諸鄭，鄭伯許之。及共王即位，將為陽橋之役，使屈巫聘于
齊，且告師期。巫臣盡室以行。申叔跪從其父，將適郢，遇之，曰：「異
哉！夫子有三軍之懼，而又有桑中之喜，宜將竊妻以逃者也。」及鄭，使
介反幣，而以夏姬行。將奔齊。齊師新敗，曰：「吾不處不勝之國。」遂
奔晉，而因郤至，以臣於晉。晉人使為邢大夫。

子反請以重幣錮之。王曰：「止！其自為謀也則過矣，其為吾先君
謀也則忠。忠，社稷之固也，所蓋多矣。且彼若能利國家，雖重幣，晉將
可乎？若無益於晉，晉將棄之，何勞錮焉？」

<hr>

88　Xiang the Elder was shot by the Jin commander Xun Shou during the battle of Bi (Xuan 12.2h).

89　Wuchen claims that Zhi Ying's father, Xun Shou, is a favorite of Lord Cheng of Jin, father of the reigning Lord Jing. Xun Linfu's recent victories over the Red Di (Xuan 15.6) confirm his position in Jin government. Such important connections mean that Xun Shou would be heeded. "The prince" refers to Gongzi Guchen, who was taken prisoner during the battle of Bi (Xuan 12.2h). Recall that the Xun line branched out as the Zhi and Zhonghang lineages, headed first by Xun Linfu (Zhonghang Huanzi) and Xun Shou (Zhi Zhuangzi).

90　The prince refers to Gongzi Guchen, whom Xun Shou captured at Bi (Xuan 12.2).

91　She, of course, has no intention of bringing back Xiang the Elder's body; she knows that she is not returning to Chu.

92　For the Yangqiao campaign, see Cheng 2.8 below. Yangqiao 陽橋 was located north-west of present-day Tai'an County 泰安縣, Shandong.

93　Wuchen should be anxious because of his diplomatic mission involving military affairs. "The delight of a mulberry patch tryst" refers to illicit union. See *Maoshi* 48, "Sang zhong" 桑中, 3A.113: *sang zhong* (in the mulberry patch) is where lovers have their rendezvous.

94　By this time Wuchen has completed his mission in Qi and is supposed to be on his way back to Chu. He sends his assistant to bring back the gifts and also to report to the Chu king the discharge of his mission.

95　Literally, "The way he planned for himself was indeed excessive, but the way he planned for our former rulers was loyal."

96　Since King Gong was only ten or eleven at this point, it is unlikely that he could have made such an elaborate statement. The balance between loyalty and self-interest (or self-preservation) is a persistent concern in *Zuozhuan*.

The king gave her to the court deputy Xiang the Elder.[88] Xiang the Elder died at Bi, and his corpse was not retrieved. His son Heiyao then consorted with Xia Ji. Wuchen sent word to her, saying, "Return to Zheng, and I will formalize engagement with you." He also had someone from Zheng summon her with this message: "The body of Xiang the Elder, the court deputy, can be obtained, but you must come and take it back." Xia Ji told the king about this, and the king consulted Qu Wuchen[b]. The latter replied, "This may well be credible. Zhi Ying's father was Lord Cheng's favorite and the youngest brother of Xun Linfu[c].[89] Recently made assistant commander of the central army, he is on good terms with Huang Xu of Zheng and loves this son very much. He must be trying to return the prince and the body of Xiang the Elder through Zheng in order to seek the release of his son.[90] The men of Zheng, fearful because of the Bi campaign, wish to court Jin's favor. They will certainly grant this arrangement."

Qu Wuchen pursues his scheme, marries Xia Ji, and becomes a high officer in Jin. King Gong of Chu rejects vengeance.

The king sent Xia Ji to return to Zheng. Upon leaving, she said to those seeing her off: "If I do not obtain the body, I will not return."[91]

Qu Wuchen[a] formalized his engagement with Xia Ji in Zheng, and the Liege of Zheng granted his assent. When King Gong acceded to his position, he intended to undertake a campaign at Yangqiao.[92] He sent Qu Wuchen[b] on an official visit to Qi and also to notify Qi of the date when his troops would move. Wuchen took all his valuables with him as he set out. Shen Shugui, who was accompanying his father, Shen Shushi, was about to go to Ying. He encountered him and said, "Strange indeed! That fine man should be full of vigilant anxiety for three armies, yet he shows all the delight of a mulberry patch tryst.[93] He must be someone on his way to an elopement!" Arriving in Zheng,[94] he sent his aide to carry the Qi gifts back to Chu, and then he set out with Xia Ji. They were going to flee to Qi, but the Qi army had recently been defeated, and he said, "I will not reside in any domain that is not victorious." He then fled to Jin, and, with the intercession of Xi Zhi, became a Jin subject. The leaders of Jin appointed him the high officer for Xing.

Zifan requested that generous bribes be given Jin to have Qu Wuchen forever barred from office. The king said, "Stop! The way he acted in his own interest may have been excessive, but he was loyal in the way he acted in the interest of our former rulers.[95] Loyalty is the firm foundation of the altars of the domain. It can cover up much indeed! Moreover, if he can benefit their domain and patrimony, even if we were to offer generous bribes, would Jin give approval? If he does not bring any gains to Jin, then Jin will abandon him. Why bother to have him barred from office?"[96]

2.7　晉師歸，范文子後入。武子曰：「無為吾望爾也乎？」對曰：「師有功，國人喜以逆之，先入，必屬耳目焉，是代帥受名也，故不敢。」武子曰：「吾知免矣。」

　　郤伯見，公曰：「子之力也夫！」對曰：「君之訓也，二三子之力也，臣何力之有焉？」范叔見，勞之如郤伯。對曰：「庚所命也，克之制也，燮何力之有焉？」欒伯見，公亦如之。對曰：「燮之詔也，士用命也，書何力之有焉？」

2.8a(8–10)　宣公使求好于楚，莊王卒，宣公薨，不克作好。公即位，受盟于晉，會晉伐齊。衛人不行使于楚，而亦受盟于晉，從於伐齊。故楚今尹子重為陽橋之役以救齊。將起師，子重曰：「君弱，群臣不如先大夫，師眾而後可。」

《詩》曰：

濟濟多士，
文王以寧。

97　Zhonghang Xuanzi (Xun Geng, Xun Linfu's son) was at the time commander of the central army and did not take part in the campaign. However, Fan Xie, as assistant commander, received orders from him.

98　See Xuan 18.2.

99　King Zhuang of Chu and Lord Xuan of Lu died in the same year (591 BCE).

100　See Cheng 1.3.

101　When King Gong is on his deathbed, he talks about his inexperience when he became king at age ten (Xiang 13.4).

Jin commanders and officers, upon their victorious return, show exemplary modesty and disinterestedness. The moral rhetoric stands in stark contrast to the violent power struggles among Jin ministerial lineages (Cheng 8.6, 17.10, Xiang 21.5).

When the Jin army returned, Fan Xie[f] was the last to enter the capital. Fan Hui[f] said, "Don't you know that I have been anxiously waiting for your return?" He replied, "The army has achieved victory. The inhabitants of the capital met it with joy. To enter first is by necessity to attract their attention and to usurp the commander in chief's good name. That was why I did not dare enter earlier." Fan Hui[f] said, "Now I know we will escape disaster!"

Xi Ke[d] presented himself for an audience with Lord Jing of Jin. The lord said, "This was due to your efforts!" He replied, "This was due to my lord's instructions and the efforts of all the leaders. How could my effort be credited for anything?" Fan Xie[d] presented himself for an audience, and the lord honored his exertions in the same manner as he did with Xi Ke[d]. He replied, "This was due to the leadership of Zhonghang Xuanzi[c][97] and the discipline of Xi Ke[e]. How could my effort be credited for anything?" Luan Shu[b] presented himself for an audience, and the lord said the same thing. He replied, "This was due to Fan Xie[d]'s direction and the fact that officers followed their orders. How could my effort be credited for anything?"

Lu and Wei side with Jin when Jin attacks Qi. Chu comes to Qi's aid, preparing for war by raising a large army and instituting reforms designed to boost morale.

Lord Xuan had sent someone to seek good relations with Chu.[98] But then King Zhuang died and Lord Xuan expired, so Lu and Chu did not manage to become allies.[99] Our lord acceded to his position and accepted a covenant with Jin just when Jin was attacking Qi.[100] The leaders of Wei did not send envoys to Chu and instead accepted a covenant with Jin and followed Jin in attacking Qi. That was why the Chu chief minister, Zichong, undertook the Yangqiao campaign to go to the aid of Qi. When the army was about to set forth, Zichong said, "The ruler is young,[101] and we are no match for our former high officers. Our troops must be numerous if we are to succeed.[102] As it says in the *Odes,*

> Mighty and splendid were the many officers,
> And relying on them King Wen enjoyed peace.[103]

---

102 Recall Xi Ke's similar argument when he requested eight hundred chariots before the An campaign (Cheng 2.3a).

103 *Maoshi* 235, "Wen wang" 文王, 16A.535.

夫文王猶用眾，況吾儕乎？且先君莊王屬之曰：『無德以及遠方，莫如惠恤其民，而善用之。』」乃大戶，已責，逮鰥，救乏，赦罪。悉師，王卒盡行。彭名御戎，蔡景公為左，許靈公為右。二君弱，皆強冠之。

2.8b

冬，楚師侵衛，遂侵我師于蜀。使臧孫往。辭曰：「楚遠而久，固將退矣。無功而受名，臣不敢。」楚侵及陽橋，孟孫請往賂之以執斲、執鍼、織紝，皆百人，公衡為質，以請盟。楚人許平。

十一月，公及楚公子嬰齊、蔡侯、許男、秦右大夫說、宋華元、陳公孫寧、衛孫良夫、鄭公子去疾及齊國之大夫盟于蜀。卿不書，匱盟也。於是乎畏晉而竊與楚盟，故曰「匱盟」。蔡侯、許男不書，乘楚車也，謂之失位。

君子曰：「位其不可不慎也乎！蔡、許之君，一失其位，不得列於諸侯，況其下乎！《詩》曰：

> 不解于位，
> 民之攸墍。

其是之謂矣。」

---

104 The census might have involved tracking down the tax status of each household; hence, "forgiving debts (owed the government)" followed from the census.

105 King Gong was too young to take part in the campaign, but his war chariot must have been used. Had he ridden in the chariot, he would have been in the middle, with the chariot driver on the left and the spearman on the right. Here the chariot driver sat in the middle because of the king's absence.

106 Assistants on the right and left of the chariot were supposed to have reached the age for the capping ceremony.

107 Du Yu (*ZZ* 25.429) identifies Gongheng as Lord Cheng's son, but Lord Cheng did not marry until twelve years later (Cheng 14.2). Gongheng might have been Lord Xuan's son (Shen Qinhan, *Chunqiu Zuozhuan buzhu*, cited in Yang, 2:809).

108 The *Annals* does not record the presence of the rulers of Cai and Xǔ because they act beneath their station when they ride in a Chu chariot as assistants on the right and the left.

109 *Maoshi* 249, "Jia le" 假樂, 17C.615–16. *Maoshi* has *jia* 假, while *Zhongyong* (*Liji* 52.885) and *Zuozhuan* have *jia* 嘉 when referring to this ode. This ode praising a ruler is also mentioned or cited in Wen 3.7, Xiang 26.7b, Zhao 21.2, and Ai 5.4.

If even King Wen used numerous troops, then how much more should the likes of us rely on them? Moreover, our former ruler King Zhuang enjoined us thus: 'Lacking the virtue to reach faraway places, it is better to show kindness and compassion to our own people and to use them well.'" Zichong therefore instituted a grand census, forgave debts,[104] let beneficence reach the old and the widowed, relieved the impoverished, and pardoned the guilty. He mobilized all the troops; even the king's guards all marched on. Peng Ming drove the war chariot, Lord Jing of Cai was on his left, and Lord Ling of Xǔ was on his right.[105] Those two rulers were young; both of them, though not of age, were made to undergo the capping ceremony.[106]

The Chu incursion reaches Yangqiao. Lu offers gifts and hostages to sue for peace. Bad faith on all sides mars the ensuing covenant. Lu, Song, and Wei join Jin in attacking Chu's ally Zheng, which will become their covenant partner the following year.

In winter, Chu troops invaded Wei and then also descended on our troops at Shu. The Lu ruler wanted to send Zang Xuanshu[a] there. He declined: "Chu came from afar and has been in the field a long time. Their army would, in any case, leave soon. I do not dare to accept the credit while lacking the merit." When the Chu incursion reached Yangqiao, Meng Xianzi[a] begged leave to go. With gifts of a hundred each of carpenters, needlewomen, and weavers, and with Gongheng[107] as hostage, he requested a covenant. The leaders of Chu agreed to make peace.

2.8b

In the eleventh month, our lord and Zichong[a] of Chu, the Prince of Cai, the Head of Xǔ, Yue (who was the high officer of the right of Qin), Hua Yuan of Song, Gongsun Ning of Chen, Sun Liangfu of Wei, Gongzi Quji of Zheng, and Qi high officers swore a covenant at Shu. The ministers were not recorded because this was a flawed covenant. At this time Lu feared Jin and secretly swore a covenant with Chu: that is why this was called a "flawed covenant." The Prince of Cai and the Head of Xǔ were not recorded because they were riding in a Chu chariot. This is called "losing one's rightful position."[108]

The noble man said, "Position is something for which one must not fail to be vigilant! The rulers of Cai and Xǔ, once they lost their rightful position, could not be listed among the princes. How much more so then with those of lesser rank! As it says in the *Odes*,

> He never slackens in what is due his position;
> He is the one in whom the people find repose.[109]

This is what is meant!"

2.8c 楚師及宋，公衡逃歸。臧宣叔曰：「衡父不忍數年之不宴，以棄魯國，國
將若之何？誰居？後之人必任是夫！國棄矣。」

是行也，晉辟楚，畏其眾也。君子曰：「眾之不可以已也。大夫為
政，猶以眾克，況明君而善用其眾乎？〈大誓〉所謂『商兆民離，周十人
同』者，眾也。」

2.9 晉侯使鞏朔獻齊捷于周。王弗見，使單襄公辭焉，曰：「蠻夷戎狄，不式
王命，淫湎毀常，王命伐之，則有獻捷。王親受而勞之，所以懲不敬、勸
有功也。兄弟甥舅，侵敗王略，王命伐之，告事而已，不獻其功，所以敬
親暱、禁淫慝也。今叔父克遂，有功于齊，而不使命卿鎮撫王室，所使
來撫余一人，而鞏伯實來，未有職司於王室，又奸先王之禮。余雖欲於

---

110   In the line *shui ju* 誰居, the word *ju* 居 has no substantive meaning but simply
       indicates an interrogative mood. "Who then?" may mean "who will bear the conse-
       quences?" or "whom can we send as hostage?" The compound also appears in Xiang
       23.5 ("Who could it be then?").

111   These lines seem to summarize the quotation from the "Great Oath" (Tai shi 泰誓)
       cited in Zhao 24.1 (*Shangshu* 11.155). The "Great Oath" is one of the Ancient Script
       chapters of the *Documents*. While Zichong's victory testifies to the importance of
       sheer number (as Zichong argued earlier in 2.8a), the noble man's comment rede-
       fines "multitude" (*zhong* 眾) as persons united by virtue and moral purpose. See also
       Cheng 6.11.

112   Shi Zhuangbo was a high officer in the upper army during the battle of Bi (Xuan
       12.2). It was not until the following year (Cheng 3.8) that he became a minister (*qing*),
       an appointment supposedly approved by the Zhou king. During this visit to the
       Zhou court he is thus not yet a "royally commissioned minister."

By the time the Chu army reached Song, Gongheng had escaped and returned to Lu. Zang Xuanshu said, "Gongheng[a] cannot bear a few years of discomfort and thus abandons Lu to its fate. What will happen to the domain? Who then?[110] Those who come after will certainly suffer the consequences. The domain is abandoned to its fate!" 2.8c

In this military action, Jin avoided Chu, fearing its multitudes. The noble man said, "Multitudes cannot be dispensed with. Even high officers in charge of government would prevail on the basis of multitudes. How much more then should an enlightened ruler who excelled in using his multitudes? Where the 'Great Oath' says 'the millions of Shang are divided, the ten persons of Zhou are united,' it is referring to the true meaning of multitudes."[111]

The Zhou king chides the Jin ruler for the impropriety of offering spoils from the victory over Qi and of sending an envoy of insufficiently high rank. On the appropriate ritual of "presenting spoils," see also Zhuang 31.1. Privately, however, the king treats the Jin envoy with courtesy, adding the provision that the royal feast and gifts, representing a ritual breach, should not be recorded in the annals.

The Prince of Jin sent Shi Zhuangbo[a] to present Qi captives and the spoils of victory at the Zhou court. The king did not receive him and sent the Shan Duke Xiang to decline the offering, saying, "When the Man, Yi, Rong, and Di tribes do not carry out royal commands, indulge in sensual excesses and wine, and flout the constants of order, and the king gives the command to attack them, then there is the presentation of captives and spoils of victory. The king will personally receive the offerings and honor the exertions of those who undertake the expedition, this being the means whereby he punishes the irreverent and encourages the meritorious. As for domains ruled by the brothers, nephews, and uncles of Zhou, when they encroach upon and undermine the king's rules and regulations, the king gives the command to attack them. In such cases, there is only report of mission accomplished but no presentation of the fruits of victory. This is the means whereby he shows respect for kin and allies and proscribes excesses and iniquities. Now you, Uncle, are able to succeed and achieve merit in Qi but have not sent a royally commissioned minister to bring stability and solace to the royal house. The man you have sent to comfort me, the lone one, is none other than Shi Zhuangbo[b], who has no office in the royal house.[112] Moreover, this visit 2.9

鞏伯，其敢廢舊典以忝叔父？夫齊，甥舅之國也，而大師之後也，寧不
亦淫從其欲以怒叔父，抑豈不可諫誨？」士莊伯不能對。

　　王使委於三吏，禮之如侯伯克敵使大夫告慶之禮，降於卿禮一
等。王以鞏伯宴，而私賄之。使相告之曰：「非禮也，勿籍！」

春秋

3.1(1)　三年，春，王正月，公會晉侯、宋公、衛侯、曹伯伐鄭。

3.2　辛亥，葬衛穆公。

3.3　二月，公至自伐鄭。

3.4　甲子，新宮災。三日哭。

3.5　乙亥，葬宋文公。

3.6(2)　夏，公如晉。

3.7(3)　鄭公子去疾帥師伐許。

3.8　公至自晉。

3.9(5)　秋，叔孫僑如帥師圍棘。

3.10　大雩。

3.11(6)　晉郤克、衛孫良夫伐廧咎如。

3.12(7)　冬，十有一月，晉侯使荀庚來聘。

3.13(7)　衛侯使孫良夫來聘。

violates the ritual propriety of the former kings. Even if I wish to be partial to Shi Zhuangbo[b], how dare I abandon old statutes and bring shame to my uncle? Now Qi is a domain ruled by our maternal nephews and maternal uncles, who are the descendants of the Grand Lord.[113] Did it not indulge in excessive desires and thereby anger my uncle? Was it indeed beyond remonstrance and instruction?" Shi Zhuangbo could not answer.

The king had the task of reception entrusted to the three officials and treated Shi Zhuangbo with the ritual appropriate for the occasion when a prince, having vanquished his enemy, sent a high officer to report the felicitous news. This was one rank lower than the ritual for ministers. The king feasted Shi Zhuangbo[b] and privately gave him gifts. He had his assistant tell him, "This is not in accordance with ritual propriety. Do not record it in the historical annals!"

LORD CHENG 3 (588 BCE)
ANNALS

In the third year, in spring, in the royal first month, our lord met with the Prince of Jin, the Duke of Song, the Prince of Wei, and the Liege of Cao and attacked Zheng.   3.1(1)

On the *xinhai* day (28), Lord Mu of Wei was buried.   3.2

In the second month, our lord arrived from the attack on Zheng.   3.3

On the *jiazi* day (12), there was a disastrous fire at the New Palace. For three days we wailed.   3.4

On the *yihai* day (23), Lord Wen of Song was buried.   3.5

In summer, our lord went to Jin.   3.6(2)

Gongzi Quji of Zheng led out troops and attacked Xǔ.   3.7(3)

Our lord arrived from Jin.   3.8

In autumn, Shusun Qiaoru led out troops and laid siege to Ji.   3.9(5)

There was a great rain sacrifice.   3.10

Xi Ke of Jin and Sun Liangfu of Wei attacked Qianggaoru.   3.11(6)

In winter, in the eleventh month, the Prince of Jin sent Xun Geng (Zhonghang Xuanzi) to us on an official visit.   3.12(7)

The Prince of Wei sent Sun Liangfu to us on an official visit.   3.13(7)

---

113   The ruling house of Qi was related to the Zhou house by marriage. King Ding's queen was a daughter of Qi (Xuan 6.2, 6.4). The Grand Lord (or "Grand Preceptor") was Lü Shang or Jiang Shang (Jiang Grand Lord 姜太公), ancestor of Qi. Recall how Cang Ge resists Jin aggression by appealing to his domain's (Yangfen) marital ties with the Zhou house (Xi 25.2).

3.14(7)　丙午，及荀庚盟。

3.15(7)　丁未，及孫良夫盟。

3.16　鄭伐許。

左傳

3.1(1)　三年，春，諸侯伐鄭，次于伯牛，討邲之役也，遂東侵鄭。鄭公子偃帥師禦之，使東鄙覆諸鄛，敗諸丘輿。皇戌如楚獻捷。

3.2(6)　夏，公如晉，拜汶陽之田。

3.3(7)　許恃楚而不事鄭，鄭子良伐許。

3.4　晉人歸楚公子穀臣與連尹襄老之尸于楚，以求知罃。於是荀首佐中軍矣，故楚人許之。王送知罃，曰：「子其怨我乎？」
　　　對曰：「二國治戎，臣不才，不勝其任，以為俘馘。執事不以釁鼓，使歸即戮，君之惠也。臣實不才，又誰敢怨？」

114　Zheng is punished for having vacillated between Jin and Chu.

115　Man 鄛 is of unknown location. Qiuyu 丘輿 was located in present-day Yidu County 益都縣, Shandong.

116　After Qi's defeat at the battle of An, Jin and Qi swear the Covenant of Yuanlou, by which Qi returns to Lu the lands north of the Wen River. See *Annals*, Cheng 2.4.

117　The word *guo* 馘, sometimes written with the "ear" 耳 radical, is glossed as ears cut off from the corpses of defeated soldiers (*Shuowen jiezi* 12A.4a) or, according to the Mao commentary, left ears cut off from recalcitrant prisoners of war (Mao 241, "Huang yi" 皇矣, 16D.574). Karlgren (gl. 179, 387) argues that *guo* refers to cut-off heads.

On the *bingwu* day (28), we swore a covenant with Xun Geng (Zhong-hang Xuanzi).

3.14(7)

On the *dingwei* day (29), we swore a covenant with Sun Liangfu.

3.15(7)

Zheng attacked Xǔ.

3.16

ZUO

Jin and its allies attack Zheng but are rebuffed.

In the third year, in spring, the princes attacked Zheng and set up camp at Boniu to chastise Zheng for its role in the Bi campaign.[114] They then made an eastward incursion into Zheng. Gongzi Yan of Zheng led troops to fight back. He had the troops of the eastern marches lay an ambush at Man and defeated the invaders at Qiuyu.[115] Huang Xu went to Chu to present the spoils of victory.

3.1(1)

In summer, our lord went to Jin to bow in thanks for the lands to the north of the Wen River.[116]

3.2(6)

Xǔ, relying on Chu, did not serve Zheng. Gongzi Quji[a] of Zheng attacked Xǔ.

3.3(7)

Zhi Ying, a Jin commander taken captive at the battle of Bi (Xuan 12.2), is about to be repatriated to Jin (see also Cheng 2.6). His exchange with King Gong is reminiscent of that between Chong'er and King Cheng of Chu a few years before the battle of Chengpu (Xi 23.6): both respond with pride, deference, and subtle aggression to the question of repaying Chu for its generosity. Zhi Ying later plays an important role in the resurgence of Jin under Lord Dao.

The leaders of Jin returned Gongzi Guchen and the body of the court deputy, Xiang the Elder, to Chu in order to seek the release of Zhi Ying. At that time Zhi Ying's father, Xun Shou, was assistant commander of the central army; that was why the leaders of Chu granted the exchange. When he was sending Zhi Ying off, the king asked, "Do you harbor any resentment toward me?"

3.4

He replied, "Our two domains were at war, and I, lacking talent and unequal to the duties of my position, became a captive awaiting decapitation.[117] That your men in charge have not used my blood to smear the war drum, and will instead send me back to meet my execution, is a result of your kindness, my lord. It is I who lack talent; whom do I dare blame?"

王曰：「然則德我乎？」對曰：「二國圖其社稷，而求紓其民，各懲其
忿，以相宥也。兩釋纍囚，以成其好。二國有好，臣不與及，其誰敢德？」

王曰：「子歸，何以報我？」對曰：「臣不任受怨，君亦不任受德，
無怨無德，不知所報。」王曰：「雖然，必告不穀。」

對曰：「以君之靈，纍臣得歸骨於晉，寡君之以為戮，死且不朽。
若從君之惠而免之，以賜君之外臣首；首其請於寡君，而以戮於宗，亦
死且不朽。若不獲命，而使嗣宗職，次及於事，而帥偏師，以修封疆。雖
遇執事，其弗敢違，其竭力致死，無有二心，以盡臣禮，所以報也。」王
曰：「晉未可與爭。」重為之禮而歸之。

3.5(9)　秋，叔孫僑如圍棘，取汶陽之田。棘不服，故圍之。

3.6(11)　晉郤克、衛孫良夫伐廧咎如，討赤狄之餘焉。廧咎如潰，上失民也。

118　Alternatively, "to whom would I dare to feel grateful?" Zhi Ying is saying that he
should not matter in the dealings between Jin and Chu. Chu is not releasing him
as a personal favor; thus, Zhi Ying for his part cannot presume to be grateful, especially when gratitude may involve the fortunes of his domain.

119　If the Jin ruler puts Zhi Ying to death for failing his duty and thereby being captured, it will be a fitting punishment and a just death. He would die but his spirit
would live on.

120　The subject from another domain is designated as "external subject." Zhi Ying refers
to his father, Xun Shou, by name because he is addressing a king; for other examples,
see Xuan 15.2, Cheng 16.5f, and Xiang 21.5. On the occasions when the taboo for calling one's father, ancestor, or ruler by name can be legitimately disregarded, see Gu
Yanwu, *Rizhi lu jishi*, 23.546. Zhi Ying is claiming that if his father puts him to death
at the Ancestral Temple for failing his duty, he will consider that too a just and rightful death.

The king said, "In that case, are you grateful to me?" He replied, "The leaders of our two domains are planning on behalf of the altars of their respective domains and seeking to bring succor to their people. Each side for its part, to bring about mutual forgiveness, cautions against anger. Both release captives to foster good relations. Our two domains will have good relations for which I play no role; to whom would I dare to feel beholden?"[118]

The king said, "After you return, how will you repay me?" He replied, "I will not be in a position to feel resentment, and you, my lord, will not be in a position to accept gratitude. Without resentment and gratitude, I do not know what there is to repay." The king said, "Even so, you have to tell me, the deficient one."

He replied, "If by my lord's blessing this captive subject's bones are returned to Jin, and if our unworthy ruler then put me to death, I will not perish even in death.[119] If, as a consequence of my lord's kindness, I am pardoned and bestowed upon my lord's external subject, Xun Shou[d], and if Xun Shou[d] then asks permission from our unworthy ruler to have me put to death at the lineage shrine, in that case too I will not perish even in death.[120] If he does not receive the command to put me to death and instead has me succeed him in his duties as lineage head, and if my turn comes to apply myself to affairs of the domain, and to lead a subsidiary army to oversee the domain's borders, then even if I were to meet your men in charge, I will not dare to avoid them. I will do my utmost, to the point of death, with an undivided heart, so as to fulfill the ritual propriety of a subject. That is how I will repay you."[121] The king said, "It is not yet time to contend with Jin." He enhanced the ritual entertainment for Zhi Ying and sent him back to Jin.

In autumn, Shusun Qiaoru laid siege to Ji,[122] taking the lands to the north of the Wen River. Ji did not submit, and that is why Lu laid siege to it.[123]   3.5(9)

Jin avenges the earlier incursions of the Red Di tribes (Xuan 13.3).

Xi Ke of Jin and Sun Liangfu of Wei attacked Qianggaoru to chastise the   3.6(11)
remnants of the Red Di tribes.[124] Qianggaoru collapsed and dispersed, because its leaders lost the support of the people.

---

121   Zhi Ying claims that while repayment does not really apply because there is no reason for resentment or gratitude, by loyally fulfilling his duty he will be justifying the Chu king's kindness in releasing him.

122   Ji 棘 was located in present-day Shandong. *Shuijing zhu* locates it north of the Wen River (Yang, 2:814).

123   This is the first of seven instances of a rebellious Lu city being besieged and subjugated recorded in *Zuozhuan* (Yang, 2:814).

124   For the Qianggaoru tribe, see Xi 23.6a, n. 288.

3.7(12–15)　冬，十一月，晉侯使荀庚來聘，且尋盟。衛侯使孫良夫來聘，且尋盟。公問諸臧宣叔曰：「中行伯之於晉也，其位在三；孫子之於衛也，位為上卿，將誰先？」對曰：「次國之上卿，當大國之中，中當其下，下當其上大夫。小國之上卿，當大國之下卿，中當其上大夫，下當其下大夫。上下如是，古之制也。衛在晉，不得為次國。晉為盟主，其將先之。」丙午，盟晉；丁未，盟衛，禮也。

3.8　十二月甲戌，晉作六軍。韓厥、趙括、鞏朔、韓穿、荀騅、趙旃皆為卿，賞鞌之功也。

3.9　齊侯朝于晉，將授玉。郤克趨進曰：「此行也，君為婦人之笑辱也，寡君未之敢任。」

125　At this time Xi Ke, as commander of the central army, ranks first; Xun Shou, as assistant commander of the central army, ranks second; while Zhonghang Xuanzi, as commander of the upper army, ranks third.

126　Yang (2:815) suggests that Wei can only be considered a small domain, which means that its high minister, Sun Liangfu, should be treated in the same way as Zhonghang Xuanzi, a low-rank minister in Jin. However, Jin's role as covenant chief gives Zhonghang Xuanzi priority.

127　Jin originally had three armies, whose commanders and assistant commanders (Xi Ke, Fan Xie, Luan Shu, Xun Shou, Zhonghang Xuanzi, Zhao Tong) were the six ministers. The additional three armies made for six more ministers. Han Jue was commander, and Zhao Kuo assistant commander, of the new central army; Shi Zhuangbo was commander, and Han Chuan assistant commander, of the new upper army; Xun Zhui was the commander, and Zhao Tong assistant commander, of the new lower army. The military expansion here presaged developments during the Warring States era. There is also the possibility that Warring States realities are being projected back into the Spring and Autumn period. Note that the entire military force of Western Zhou in Shaanxi consisted of six armies, in addition to eight armies in Luoyang in the east.

128　When princes met in court visits, there was the ceremony of delivering and receiving the ritual jade. The prince's bearing in this ceremony is often interpreted as a sign of his destiny; see Cheng 6.1 and Ding 15.1.

129　Xi Ke, as aide of ceremony, is in the central court, while the two rulers are in the hall above. In order to say something during the ceremony of delivering jade, Xi Ke must traverse the distance quickly. "Hastened forward" also indicates respect (Yang, 2:815–16, citing Tao Hongqing). Xi Ke is still harking back to the incivility of the Qi ruler's mother (Xuan 17.1) as the cause of the conflict. In the parallel account in *Guoyu*, "Jin yu 5," 11.404, Xi Ke humiliates the Qi ruler with "the ritual for rulers who escaped captivity." Fen Huang of Miao comments on how he is courting disaster by being "valorous but ignorant of ritual propriety."

A discussion of rules of precedence: the values of rank depend on the size and power of the domain. Compare this with the argument over seniority between the Prince of Teng and the Prince of Xue in 712 BCE (Yin 11.1) or Invocator Tuo's defense of Wei precedence over Cai in 506 BCE (Ding 4.1c), which both hinge on the interpretation of historical precedents. Forty years hence a Zheng nobleman will argue that rank does not depend on the size and power of the domain (Xiang 24.8). Cf. Liji 11.251.

In winter, in the eleventh month, the Prince of Jin sent Zhonghang Xuanzi[a] to us on an official visit and also to renew our covenant. The Prince of Wei sent Sun Liangfu to us on an official visit and also to renew our covenant. Our lord asked Zang Xuanshu about the matter: "Zhonghang Xuanzi[b] in Jin ranks third;[125] Sun Liangfu[b] in Wei has the rank of high minister. Who should have precedence?" He replied, "A high minister in a second-tier domain corresponds to a middle-rank minister in a great domain; a middle-rank minister corresponds to its low-rank minister; a low-rank minister corresponds to a senior high officer. A high minister in a small domain corresponds to a low-rank minister in a great domain; a middle-rank minister corresponds to its senior high officer; a low-rank minister corresponds to its low-rank high officer. Positions above and below should be like this; such were the regulations of old. Wei, compared to Jin, cannot be considered a second-tier domain.[126] However, Jin is acting as covenant chief, and we will therefore give Jin precedence." On the *bingwu* day, we swore a covenant with Jin; on the *dingwei* day, we swore a covenant with Wei. This was in accordance with ritual propriety.

3.7(12–15)

The Jin army expands, and its commanders in the battle of An become ministers. Note that Zhao Kuo, one of the prime culprits responsible for Jin's defeat at the battle of Bi (Xuan 12.2e, 12.2g), is here elevated, while Xian Hu, another commander blamed for defeat at Bi, was eliminated (Xuan 13.4).

In the twelfth month, on the *jiaxu* day (26), Jin created the six armies. Han Jue, Zhao Kuo, Shi Zhuangbo[a], Han Chuan, Xun Zhui, and Zhao Zhan all became ministers as reward for their merit in the victory at An.[127]

3.8

Xi Ke is still resentful, but Han Jue, with skillful rhetoric, rebuilds ties between Jin and Qi.

The Prince of Qi visited the court of Jin. As he was about to deliver the ritual jade,[128] Xi Ke hastened forward and said, "This visit is taking place because you, my lord, were shamed as a result of womenfolk's laughter. Our unworthy ruler may not presume to deserve this."[129]

3.9

晉侯享齊侯。齊侯視韓厥。韓厥曰：「君知厥也乎？」齊侯曰：「服改矣。」韓厥登，舉爵曰：「臣之不敢愛死，為兩君之在此堂也。」

3.10 荀罃之在楚也，鄭賈人有將寘諸褚中以出。既謀之，未行，而楚人歸之。賈人如晉，荀罃善視之，如實出己。賈人曰：「吾無其功，敢有其實乎？吾小人，不可以厚誣君子。」遂適齊。

春秋

4.1(1) 四年，春，宋公使華元來聘。

4.2 三月壬申，鄭伯堅卒。

4.3(2) 杞伯來朝。

4.4 夏，四月甲寅，臧孫許卒。

4.5(3) 公如晉。

4.6 葬鄭襄公。

4.7(4) 秋，公至自晉。

4.8 冬，城鄆。

4.9(5) 鄭伯伐許。

The Prince of Jin offered ceremonial toasts for the Prince of Qi. The Prince of Qi looked steadily at Han Jue. Han Jue said, "Do you, my lord, recognize Jue?" The Prince of Qi said, "Your costume is changed." Han Jue ascended the steps and raised his wine cup, saying, "The reason I dared not begrudge death was just so that the two rulers might be in this hall."[130]

This is one among other stories about merchants from Zheng (see also Xi 33.1 and Zhao 16.3) and is another example of a humble man with exemplary integrity. The proposed ruse is similar to what Chen Qi uses to smuggle Gongzi Yangsheng to the Qi court in Gongyang, Ai 6 (27.350–51).

When Zhi Ying[b] was in Chu, a Zheng merchant planned to take him out of Chu in a large sack used for carrying clothes. The plan had already been made, but before the trip could take place, the leaders of Chu repatriated him. When the merchant went to Jin, Zhi Ying[b] treated him as well as if it was he who had personally smuggled him out. The merchant said, "When I do not have the merit, do I dare enjoy the fruits of success? I am but a petty man; I cannot so grievously deceive a noble man." He thus went to Qi.

3.10

LORD CHENG 4 (587 BCE)
ANNALS

In the fourth year, in spring, the Duke of Song sent Hua Yuan to us on an official visit.

4.1(1)

In the third month, on the *renshen* day,[131] Jian, the Liege of Zheng, died.

4.2

The Liege of Qǐ came to visit our court.

4.3(2)

In summer, in the fourth month, on the *jiayin* day (8), Zangsun Xu (Zang Xuanshu) died.

4.4

Our lord went to Jin.

4.5(3)

Lord Xiang of Zheng was buried.

4.6

In autumn, our lord arrived from Jin.

4.7(4)

In winter, we fortified Yun.

4.8

The Liege of Zheng attacked Xǔ.

4.9(5)

---

130 Han Jue is trying to make up for Xi Ke's vindictive outburst. He claims that he fought bravely so that the Qi and Jin rulers can reach harmonious agreement at a feast. The Qi ruler recognizes Han Jue: recall how he refused to shoot Han Jue during the battle of An because Han appeared to be a "noble man" and how he narrowly escaped being arrested by Han by changing places with Feng Choufu (Cheng 2.3d).

131 There is no *renshen* day in the third month; *renshen* is the twenty-fifth day of the second month (Yang, 2:817).

左傳

4.1(1) 　四年，春，宋華元來聘，通嗣君也。

4.2(3) 　杞伯來朝，歸叔姬故也。

4.3(5) 　夏，公如晉。晉侯見公，不敬。季文子曰：「晉侯必不免。《詩》曰：

> 敬之敬之！
> 天惟顯思，
> 命不易哉！

夫晉侯之命在諸侯矣，可不敬乎！」

4.4(7) 　秋，公至自晉，欲求成于楚而叛晉。季文子曰：「不可。晉雖無道，未可叛也。國大、臣睦，而邇於我，諸侯聽焉，未可以貳。《史佚之志》有之曰：

> 非我族類，
> 其心必異。

楚雖大，非吾族也，其肯字我乎？」公乃止。

132　It was customary for a ruler who had newly acceded to his position, as with Lord Gong of Song here, to dispatch envoys to other domains on formal visits. This is the first of four formal visits from Song to the Lu court.

133　*Maoshi* 288, "Jing zhi" 敬之, 19C.740; also cited in Xi 22.7.

134　Note the dual meanings of *ming* 命 as "command" and "destiny." See also Wen 13.3.

135　Lord Cheng of Lu wants to turn against Jin because Lord Jing of Jin did not receive him with courtesy.

In the fourth year, in spring, Hua Yuan of Song came to us on an official visit: this was to establish relations between Lu and his new ruler.[132]

4.1(1)

Shu Ji was a daughter of a Lu Lord, though of which one is unclear. She was not the daughter of Lord Cheng, who was too young at this time, and probably not of Lord Xuan, whose oldest daughter married Duke Gong of Song four years later (see Cheng 9.5). Shu Ji will return to Lu in the following year (Annals, Cheng 5.1) and will die three years later (Cheng 8.9).

The Liege of Qi came to visit our court: this was because of the plan to send Shu Ji back.

4.2(3)

A Lu minister, Ji Wenzi, predicts doom for Lord Jing of Jin because of the latter's lack of respect toward the Lu ruler. Lord Jing will die six years later.

In summer, our lord went to Jin. The Prince of Jin granted our lord an audience and was disrespectful. Ji Wenzi said, "The Prince of Jin will certainly not be able to escape disaster. As it says in the *Odes*,

4.3(5)

> Be reverent, be reverent.
> Heaven is clear to see.
> Its command is not easy to guard![133]

Since the destiny of the Prince of Jin lies with the princes, how can he be disrespectful?"[134]

Jin Wenzi counsels against alliance with Chu because it is "not of the same kith and kin" as the central domains.

In autumn, our lord arrived from Jin. He wished to seek an accord with Chu and to turn against Jin.[135] Ji Wenzi said, "This will not do. Although Jin goes against the proper way, we cannot yet turn against it. That domain is great, and its ministers are harmonious. It is close to us and the other princes defer to it. We cannot yet switch allegiance. As it says in *Scribe Yi's Records*,

4.4(7)

> Those not of the same kith and kin,
> Their hearts and minds must be different.

Although Chu is great, its people are not our kin.[136] Will it be willing to care for us?" Our lord thus desisted.

---

136 Whereas Chu is more consistently presented as "barbarian" and opposed to the central domains in the *Gongyang* tradition (although praise for King Zhuang also abounds), Chu's image is marked by the balance or tension between approbation and critique, sameness and difference, in *Zuozhuan*.

4.5(9)　冬，十一月，鄭公孫申帥師疆許田。許人敗諸展陂。鄭伯伐許，取鉏任、泠敦之田。

晉欒書將中軍，荀首佐之，士燮佐上軍，以救許伐鄭，取氾、祭。

楚子反救鄭，鄭伯與許男訟焉，皇戌攝鄭伯之辭。子反不能決也，曰：「君若辱在寡君，寡君與其二三臣共聽兩君之所欲，成其可知也。不然，側不足以知二國之成。」

4.6　晉趙嬰通于趙莊姫。

春秋

5.1　五年，春王正月，杞叔姫來歸。

5.2(2)　仲孫蔑如宋。

5.3(3)　夏，叔孫僑如會晉荀首于穀。

5.4(4)　梁山崩。

5.5　秋，大水。

5.6(8)　冬，十有一月己酉，天王崩。

137　Zheng invaded Xǔ the year before (Cheng 3.3). Here Zheng tries to demarcate the boundaries taken from Xǔ during that incursion but is defeated by Xǔ. Ten years later, Zheng invades Xǔ again, and Xǔ finally gives up these territories. There is a long history of Zheng aggression against Xǔ dating back to Lord Zhuang of Zheng's invasion of Xǔ in 712 BCE (Yin 11.3).

138　Zhao Yingqi was the son of Zhao Cui, the brother of Zhao Tong and Zhao Kuo, and the half brother of Zhao Dun (Xi 24.1). He is also called Lou Ying because he was given the settlement of Lou (Xi 24.1). He fought in the battle of Bi as an officer of the central army (Xuan 12.2). Zhao Zhuang Ji was the wife of Zhao Shuo (Zhao Dun's son and Zhao Yingqi's nephew), whose posthumous honorific was "Zhuang."

In winter, in the eleventh month, Gongsun Shen of Zheng led out troops 4.5(9)
to demarcate the boundaries of lands taken from Xŭ.[137] The men of Xŭ
defeated them at Zhan Slope. The Liege of Zheng attacked Xŭ and took
the lands of Churen and Lingdun.

    Luan Shu of Jin was commander of the central army, and Xun Shou
was his assistant commander. Fan Xie[b] was assistant commander of the
upper army. In order to go to the aid of Xŭ, they attacked Zheng and took
Fan and Zhai.

    When Zifan of Chu went to the aid of Zheng, the Liege of Zheng and
the Head of Xŭ disputed their claims before him. Huang Xu spoke on
behalf of the Liege of Zheng. Zifan could not arbitrate the case and said,
"If you, my lords, deign to come to our unworthy ruler, he and his various subjects will listen to what you desire, and the resolution of your case
will be known. If we don't do it that way, I am not equal to the task of
resolving the claims of your two domains."

Zhao Yingqi[b] of Jin had a liaison with Zhao Zhuang Ji.[138] 4.6

LORD CHENG 5 (586 BCE)
ANNALS

In the fifth year, in spring, in the royal first month, Shu Ji of Qǐ came 5.1
home.

Zhongsun Mie (Meng Xianzi) went to Song. 5.2(2)

In summer, Shusun Qiaoru met with Xun Shou of Jin at Gu. 5.3(3)

Mount Liang collapsed.[139] 5.4(4)

In autumn, there was a great flood. 5.5

In winter, in the eleventh month, on the *jiyou* day (12), the Heaven- 5.6(8)
appointed king succumbed.

---

139 Mount Liang 梁山 was located along the Yellow River in present-day Hancheng
    County 韓城縣, Shaanxi.

5.7(7) 十有二月己丑，公會晉侯、齊侯、宋公、衛侯、鄭伯、曹伯、邾子、杞伯同盟于蟲牢。

左傳

5.1 五年，春，原、屏放諸齊。嬰曰：「我在，故欒氏不作。我亡，吾二昆其憂哉。且人各有能、有不能，舍我，何害？」弗聽。
　　嬰夢天使謂己：「祭余，余福女。」使問諸士貞伯。貞伯曰：「不識也。」既而告其人曰：「神福仁而禍淫。淫而無罰，福也。祭，其得亡乎？」祭之，之明日而亡。

5.2(2) 孟獻子如宋，報華元也。

5.3(3) 夏，晉荀首如齊逆女，故宣伯餫諸穀。

140　Chonglao 蟲牢 was located north of present-day Fengqiu County 封丘縣, Henan.

141　Lord Jing of Jin will eliminate almost the entire Zhao lineage three years later (Cheng 8.6).

142　At this time Luan Shu, as commander of the central army, is in charge of policies. Zhao Yingqi is arguing that if he is exiled, Luan Shu and his kinsmen will rise up against the Zhao lineage. While he cannot adhere to the rules of proper sexual conduct, he is capable of stopping the Luan lineage from destroying the Zhao lineage.

143　Shi Wozhuo disclaims any knowledge or judgment in the public exchange but gives his opinion in private communication. The same pattern obtains in the exchange between the Ousted Lord of Wei's messenger and Zigong (Ai 26.3).

In the twelfth month, on the *jichou* day (23), our lord met with the Prince   5.7(7)
of Jin, the Prince of Qi, the Duke of Song, the Prince of Wei, the Liege of
Zheng, the Liege of Cao, the Master of Zhu, and the Liege of Qǐ, and they
swore a covenant together at Chonglao.[140]

ZUO

The narrative is obviously continuous with the event described in Cheng
4.6. Zhao Yingqi's adulterous affair leads to his exile and doom for his
lineage, despite the false promise of succor from a messenger of Heaven in
Zhao Yingqi's dream. The equivocation of the numinous message reminds
us of the fickle spirit in Zhuang 32.3. For other dreams open to different
interpretations or offering misleading clues, see Zuozhuan, Xi 28.3f, Cheng
17.8, and Zhao 4.8, 7.3.

In the fifth year, in spring, Zhao Tong[a] and Zhao Kuo[b] banished Zhao   5.1
Yingqi to Qi. Zhao Yingqi[a] said, "It is because I am here that the Luan
lineage does not stir up any trouble. If I am exiled, my two older brothers
will have cause for concern![141] Moreover, each person has what he can
and cannot do. What harm would it do to let me off?"[142] They did not
heed him.

Zhao Yingqi[a] dreamed that a messenger from Heaven said to him,
"Offer sacrifice to me, and I will confer blessings on you." He sent someone to Shi Wozhuo[c] to inquire about it. Shi Wozhuo[d] said, "I do not
know." Afterward, however, Shi Wozhuo told the man,[143] "The gods confer blessings on the noble in spirit and inflict calamities on the licentious.
To be licentious and escape punishment is already a blessing. If you offer
sacrifices, how can you not be banished?"[144] He offered sacrifices, and the
following day he was banished.

Meng Xianzi went to Song: this was to reciprocate Hua Yuan's visit.[145]   5.2(2)

In summer, Xun Shou of Jin went to Qi to meet and escort the bride home.   5.3(3)
This is why Shusun Qiaoru[a] supplied him with provisions at Gu.

---

144 Yang (2:821–22) reads *wang* 亡 as *wu* 無: "how can there be no [calamitous conse-
     quences]?" Our translation, based on Yang's reading, implies that the offering of
     sacrifices is preposterous and will only provoke calamities and banishment. Du Yu
     (ZZ 26.439), on the other hand, interprets banishment as a blessing: "If he offers
     sacrifice, how can he not obtain banishment [as the lesser punishment that is
     already a blessing]?"
145 For Hua Yuan's visit to the Lu court in the previous year, see Cheng 4.1.

5.4(4)　梁山崩，晉侯以傳召伯宗。伯宗辟重，曰：「辟傳！」重人曰：「待我，不如捷之速也。」問其所。曰：「絳人也。」問絳事焉。曰：「梁山崩，將召伯宗謀之。」問將若之何。曰：「山有朽壤而崩，可若何？國主山川，故山崩川竭，君為之不舉、降服、乘縵、徹樂、出次，祝幣，史辭以禮焉。其如此而已。雖伯宗，若之何？」伯宗請見之。不可。遂以告，而從之。

5.5　許靈公愬鄭伯于楚。六月，鄭悼公如楚訟，不勝，楚人執皇戌及子國。故鄭伯歸，使公子偃請成于晉。秋，八月，鄭伯及晉趙同盟于垂棘。

5.6　宋公子圍龜為質于楚而歸，華元享之。請鼓譟以出，鼓譟以復入，曰：「習攻華氏。」宋公殺之。

5.7(7)　冬，同盟于蟲牢，鄭服也。

<hr>

146 *Guoyu*, "Jin yu 5," 11.406, gives an almost identical account. *Gongyang*, Cheng 4 (17.218), *Guliang*, Cheng 5 (13.131), and *Hanshi waizhuan* 8.341 all link the collapse of Mount Liang to the blockage of the Yellow River. The largely overlapping *Guliang* and *Hanshi waizhuan* accounts turn this into a story of how a humble man is initially abused (Bo Zong wants to whip the driver for not giving way) and then exploited (he is not given credit for his sound advice). Instead of being an exemplary figure, Bo Zong (or Bo Zun 伯尊 in *Guliang*) is criticized for not bringing a good adviser to the ruler's attention.

147 The Xǔ ruler thus follows Zifan's suggestion in Cheng 4.5.

148 Ziguo is the cognomen of Gongzi Fa, father of the famous Zheng minister Zichan.

149 Lord Gong of Song thus kills his brother or half brother to mollify a powerful minister.

Another commoner shows exemplary sagacity when he discourses on a ruler's appropriate response to natural calamities. For other examples of wise commoners, see Xi 31.1, Xiang 4.4, 15.4, 30.3a.

Mount Liang collapsed. The Prince of Jin used a courier-carriage to summon Bo Zong. Bo Zong sent a heavy wagon to one side, saying, "Make way for the courier-carriage!" The driver of the wagon said, "To wait for me will not be as fast as taking a shortcut." Bo Zong asked where he came from, and he replied, "I am a man of Jiang." He then asked about affairs in Jiang. He said, "Mount Liang collapsed. The ruler intends to summon Bo Zong to confer with him about it." Bo Zong asked what was to be done. He replied, "If a mountain has decayed soil and then collapses, what is there to be done? Mountains and rivers are the mainstay of the domain. Thus, when mountains collapse and rivers run dry, the ruler abstains from meat and elaborate food, reduces the splendor of his apparel, rides carriages without decoration, banishes music, and leaves his usual abode. The diviner displays objects to be sacrificed to the spirits; the scribe reads ritually appropriate words to honor them. And that is all. Even with Bo Zong, what can he do?" Bo Zong asked to present him at court, but he refused. He thus told the ruler the driver's words, which the ruler then followed.[146]

5.4(4)

Chu arbitrates the Zheng-Xǔ conflict in Xǔ's favor, and Zheng turns to Jin.

Lord Ling of Xǔ lodged a complaint against the Liege of Zheng at the Chu court.[147] In the sixth month, Lord Dao of Zheng went to Chu to dispute the charge. He did not win the case, and the men of Chu seized Huang Xu and Ziguo.[148] That is why when the Liege of Zheng returned, he sent Gongzi Yan to seek an accord with Jin. In autumn, in the eighth month, the Liege of Zheng and Zhao Tong of Jin swore a covenant at Chuiji.

5.5

Hua Yuan went to Chu as hostage in 594 BCE (Xuan 15.2) but had returned by 589, when he was criticized for mismanaging the burial of Lord Wen of Song (Cheng 2.4). It is possible that he was allowed to return from Chu only because Gongzi Weigui replaced him there as hostage; this would account for the latter's animus against Hua Yuan.

When Gongzi Weigui of Song returned from being a hostage in Chu, Hua Yuan offered him ceremonial toasts. He requested to leave Hua's residence with drumbeats and shouts and to enter again with drumbeats and shouts, saying, "I am practicing my attack on the Hua lineage." The lord of Song put him to death.[149]

5.6

In winter, the princes swore a covenant together at Chonglao: this was on account of Zheng's submission to Jin.

5.7(7)

諸侯謀復會，宋公使向為人辭以子靈之難。

5.8(6)　十一月己酉，定王崩。

春秋

6.1　六年，春王正月，公至自會。

6.2(2)　二月辛巳，立武宮。

6.3(3)　取鄟。

6.4(4)　衛孫良夫帥師侵宋。

6.5　夏，六月，邾子來朝。

6.6(7)　公孫嬰齊如晉。

6.7　壬申，鄭伯費卒。

6.8(8)　秋，仲孫蔑、叔孫僑如帥師侵宋。

6.9(9)　楚公子嬰齊帥師伐鄭。

6.10(10)　冬，季孫行父如晉。

6.11(11)　晉欒書帥師救鄭。

左傳

6.1　六年，春，鄭伯如晉拜成，子游相，授玉于東楹之東。士貞伯曰：「鄭伯其死乎！自棄也已。視流而行速，不安其位，宜不能久。」

150　There are various ideas about the status and location of Zhuan 鄟 (see Yang, 2:827). It was probably located somewhere near present-day Yanzhou 兖州, Shandong.

151　Jin and Zheng swore a covenant at Chuiji the previous year (Cheng 5.5).

152　As equals, rulers of domains should conduct the ceremony of "presenting and receiving jade" (*shou shou yu* 授受玉) between the eastern and western pillars, in the middle of the hall (*zhongtang* 中堂). If the guest has a lower status than the host, as might have been argued on the basis of Jin's status as covenant chief, he should move eastward, somewhere between the middle of the hall and the eastern pillar. In moving too quickly and going farther east, beyond even the eastern pillar, the Zheng ruler is demoting himself to the status of an official. In general, the more august a person's position is, the more slowly he moves, see Ding 5.4. In Xi 11.2, Lord Hui of Jin also invites dire predictions because of the negligent way he received a ritual jade.

When the princes planned to meet again, the Duke of Song sent Xiang Weiren to decline participation on his behalf because of the troubles provoked by Gongzi Weigui[a].

In the eleventh month, on the *jiyou* day, King Ding succumbed.   5.8(6)

LORD CHENG 6 (585 BCE)
ANNALS

In the sixth year, in spring, in the royal first month, our lord arrived from the meeting.   6.1

In the second month, on the *xinsi* day (16), the Martial Palace was established.   6.2(2)

We took Zhuan.[150]   6.3(3)

Sun Liangfu of Wei led out troops and invaded Song.   6.4(4)

In summer, in the sixth month, the Master of Zhu came to visit our court.   6.5

Gongsun Yingqi (Zishu Shengbo) went to Jin.   6.6(7)

On the *renshen* day (9), Fei, the Liege of Zheng, died.   6.7

In autumn, Zhongsun Mie (Meng Xianzi) and Shusun Qiaoru led out troops and invaded Song.   6.8(8)

Gongzi Yingqi (Zichong) of Chu led out troops and attacked Zheng.   6.9(9)

In winter, Jisun Hangfu (Ji Wenzi) went to Jin.   6.10(10)

Luan Shu of Jin led out troops and went to the aid of Zheng.   6.11(11)

ZUO

A Jin minister interprets the Zheng ruler's excessive self-abnegation as the sign of his imminent demise. Lord Dao of Zheng dies a few months later. For a similar case of wrong positioning and ritual failure, see Zhao 21.2.

In the sixth year, in spring, the Liege of Zheng went to Jin to bow to affirm the alliance.[151] Gongzi Yan[a] was his assistant. He received the ceremonial jade eastward of the eastern pillar. Shi Wozhuo[c] said, "The Zheng ruler will surely die! He has abandoned what he owes himself. His eyes have a roving expression and his movements are hasty. He is not secure in his position. It is fitting that he should not last long."[152]   6.1

6.2(2)　二月，季文子以鄃之功立武宮，非禮也。聽於人以救其難，不可以立武。立武由己，非由人也。

6.3(3)　取鄟，言易也。

6.4(4)　三月，晉伯宗、夏陽說、衛孫良夫、甯相、鄭人、伊雒之戎、陸渾、蠻氏侵宋，以其辭會也。師于鍼。衛人不保。說欲襲衛，曰：「雖不可入，多俘而歸，有罪不及死。」伯宗曰：「不可。衛唯信晉，故師在其郊而不設備。若襲之，是棄信也。雖多衛俘，而晉無信，何以求諸侯？」乃止。師還，衛人登陴。

Ji Wenzi's commemoration of Lu's victory in the An campaign (Cheng 2.3) is deemed improper self-aggrandizement, since Lu had to rely on Jin's assistance to defeat Qi. His vanity compares unfavorably with the restraint of King Zhuang of Chu in the aftermath of his victory at Bi (Xuan 12.2i).

In the second month, Ji Wenzi established the Martial Palace because of his meritorious achievement at the battle of An.[153] This was not in accordance with ritual propriety. If one has to rely on others in order to be saved from disaster, one cannot establish a martial palace. A martial palace is to be established because of one's own achievement, not because of what is achieved through the assistance of others.

We took Zhuan: this indicates that it was easily done.

The allies punish Song for not participating in the covenant at Chonglao (Cheng 5.7). A Jin commander is tempted to make a surprise attack on Jin's supposed ally Wei because of an earlier grudge (Xuan 13.5). Bo Zong refuses and maintains the importance of good faith in leadership.

In the third month, Bo Zong and Xiayang Yue of Jin,[154] Sun Liangfu and Ning Xiang of Wei, a Zheng leader, the Rong tribes of the Yi and Luo Rivers and of Luhun, together with the Man lineage, invaded Song because Song had declined to attend the meeting last year. The troops were stationed at Qian.[155] The men of Wei were not on guard. Xiayang Yue wanted to make a surprise attack on Wei: "Although we cannot enter the capital, so long as we come back with many captives, our offense will not be punishable by death." Bo Zong said, "This will not do. Precisely because Wei trusts Jin, it has not prepared for attacks, even though our troops are in its outskirts. For us to attack it is to abandon good faith. Although we may get many Wei captives, if Jin is faithless, how can we seek allegiance from the princes?" Xiayang Yue thus desisted. When Jin troops turned back, the men of Wei climbed the parapets.[156]

6.2(2)

6.3(3)

6.4(4)

---

153   Presumably, the Martial Palace (Wugong 武宮) was built to commemorate military achievement. It is obviously different from the Wugong mentioned in *Annals*, Zhao 15.2. The latter was the Ancestral Temple honoring Lord Wu of Lu.

154   The settlement called Xiayang 下陽 in Xi 2.3 (n. 15) is probably the same as this Xiayang 夏陽. It was in the domain of Guo that was annexed by Jin. Xiayang became the name of the lineage of officers put in power there.

155   For the Rong of Yi and Luo and Luhun, see Xi 11.3, Xi 22.4; the Rong of Man is mentioned in Zhao 16.2. Qian 鋮 was a Wei city not far from Wei's capital, Diqiu, and was located near present-day Puyang County 濮陽縣, Henan.

156   In other words, Wei was actually more vigilant than Xiayang Yue thought.

6.5　晉人謀去故絳，諸大夫皆曰：「必居郇、瑕氏之地，沃饒而近鹽，國利君樂，不可失也。」韓獻子將新中軍，且為僕大夫。公揖而入。獻子從。公立於寢庭，謂獻子曰：「何如？」對曰：「不可。郇、瑕氏土薄水淺，其惡易覯。易覯則民愁，民愁則墊隘，於是乎有沈溺重腿之疾。不如新田，土厚水深，居之不疾，有汾、澮以流其惡，且民從教，十世之利也。夫山、澤、林、鹽，國之寶也。國饒，則民驕佚。近寶，公室乃貧。不可謂樂。」公說，從之。夏，四月丁丑，晉遷于新田。

6.6(7)　六月，鄭悼公卒。

6.7(6)　子叔聲伯如晉，命伐宋。

6.8(8)　秋，孟獻子、叔孫宣伯侵宋，晉命也。

6.9(9)　楚子重伐鄭，鄭從晉故也。

6.10(10)　冬，季文子如晉，賀遷也。

157　The result of this discussion was that Jin moved its capital to Xintian (present-day Houma), which was renamed Jiang. The former capital was thus called "Old Jiang." See Yang, 1:44.

158　For Xun and Xia, see Xi 24 (n. 309) and Xi 30.3. Gu 蠱, which means "salt," is also called Yanchi 鹽池, or Salt Marsh (present-day Jiechi 解池). Xun lies to the northwest, and Xia to the south, of Jiechi. The argument here refers to a site in the general area of Xun and Xia, which is quite large.

159　The palaces of lords had three gates, leading to the outer court, the court of government, and the inner court. The discussion here took place either in the outer court or the court of government.

160　As the high officer of palace affairs, Han Jue should attend to the lord as he entered the inner court.

161　Gongfu Wenbo's mother offers the same argument in *Guoyu*, "Lu yu 2," 5.205. Han Jue is refuting the argument that Xun-Xia is "profitable for the domain and enjoyable for the ruler." He asserts that real profit lies in the people's obedience.

The leaders of Jin conferred about leaving Old Jiang.[157] The various high officers all said, "We must stay in the land of the Xun and Xia lineages. It is fertile and close to Gu:[158] it is profitable for the domain and enjoyable for the ruler. Such a site is not to be lost." Han Jue[a] was commander of the new central army and also served as high officer of palace affairs. The lord bowed to the various ministers and entered the inner gate.[159] Han Jue[b] followed.[160] The lord stood in the inner court and said to Han Jue[b], "What do you think?" He replied, "This will not do. At Xun and Xia the soil is thin and the water is shallow, and foul substances can easily accumulate. If such accumulation is easy, the people will be miserable; if they are miserable, they will be enfeebled; and they will thus be sick with rheumatism and swollen limbs. That area does not compare to Xintian. There the soil is thick and the water is deep; living there does not cause sicknesses; and the Fen and Hui Rivers allow foul substances to flow away. Moreover, the people there heed instruction. This will mean profit for ten generations. For mountains, marshes, forests, and salt are treasures of the domain. If the domain is rich in resources, the people will become arrogant and indolent.[161] Being close to treasures, the lord's house will be impoverished.[162] This cannot be called 'enjoyable' for the ruler." The lord was pleased and followed his advice. In summer, in the fourth month, on the *dingchou* day (13), Jin moved its capital to Xintian.

Shi Wozhuo's prophecy (Cheng 6.1) is fulfilled.

In the sixth month, Lord Dao of Zheng died.

Zishu Shengbo went to Jin: this was because Jin leaders ordered Lu to attack Song.

In autumn, Meng Xianzi and Shusun Qiaoru[b] invaded Song: this was Jin's command.

Zichong of Chu attacked Zheng: this was because Zheng followed Jin.

In winter, Ji Wenzi went to Jin: this was to congratulate Jin on the relocation of its capital.

---

162 It is not clear why proximity to "treasures" (in this case salt from Salt Marsh) should impoverish the ruling house. Kong Yingda (ZZ-Kong 26.442) suggests that "treasures," which represent alternative means of livelihood, will lure the people from agriculture to commerce. The poor will become poorer and less able to pay the levy, and the rich will gain in power and become more defiant toward the ruling house.

晉欒書救鄭，與楚師遇於繞角。楚師還。晉師遂侵蔡。楚公子申、公子成以申、息之師救蔡，禦諸桑隧。趙同、趙括欲戰，請於武子，武子將許之。知莊子、范文子、韓獻子諫曰：「不可。吾來救鄭，楚師去我，吾遂至於此，是遷戮也。戮而不已，又怒楚師，戰必不克。雖克，不令。成師以出，而敗楚之二縣，何榮之有焉？若不能敗，為辱已甚，不如還也。」乃遂還。

於是軍帥之欲戰者眾。或謂欒武子曰：「聖人與眾同欲，是以濟事，子盍從眾？子為大政，將酌於民者也。子之佐十一人，其不欲戰者，三人而已。欲戰者可謂眾矣。《商書》曰：『三人占，從二人』，眾故也。」武子曰：「善鈞從眾。夫善，眾之主也。三卿為主，可謂眾矣。從之，不亦可乎？」

---

163   According to Jiang Yong, Raojiao 繞角 was in Cai territory and located southeast of present-day Lushan County 魯山縣, Henan.

164   Sangsui 桑隧 was located east of present-day Queshan County 確山縣, Henan.

165   The same phrase (*chengshi yi chu* 成師以出) appears in the account of the battle of Bi; see Xuan 12.2 (Yang, 2:726).

166   That is, Shen and Xi.

167   "Hong fan" 洪範, *Shangshu* 12.174: "When three persons use divination, follow the opinions shared by two." For an instance of several diviners being simultaneously consulted, see Ai 9.6. Cf. Gu Yanwu, *Rizhi lu jishi*, 4.7–98 ("Yishi liangzhan" 一事兩占). "Hong fan" is also cited in Wen 5.5 and Xiang 3.4. In all three cases the quotations are identified as *Shang Documents*, although in the received text "Hong fan" belongs to the section "Zhou Documents."

Zheng is now siding with Jin at this point in the Jin-Chu conflict (last mentioned in Cheng 4.5, 5.5, 5.7). Three Jin ministers convince their commander, Luan Shu, to avoid military confrontation with Chu.

Luan Shu of Jin went to the aid of Zheng, and encountered Chu troops at Raojiao.[163] Chu troops turned back. Jin troops thereupon invaded Cai. Gongzi Shen and Gongzi Cheng of Chu led the troops of Shen and Xi to go to the aid of Cai, putting up a defense at Sangsui.[164] Zhao Tong and Zhao Kuo wanted to fight and requested permission from Luan Shu[c]. Luan Shu[c] was about to agree when Xun Shou[a], Fan Xie[c], and Han Jue[a] remonstrated with him: "This will not do. We came to aid Zheng. The Chu army moved away from us, and we thus reached this place. This is to move the site of killing. To kill and fail to stop and in addition to anger Chu troops—if we fight, we will surely not win. Even if we do win, it will not be good. To have organized troops and set forth[165] to defeat two dependencies of Chu[166]—what glory will there be in this? If we cannot defeat them, the humiliation will be extreme. It is better to turn back." The Jin army thus turned back.

Luan Shu defends his decision by redefining what constitutes a majority opinion. This echoes the noble man's ruminations on the meaning of "multitude" in Cheng 2.8c. To fulfill desires shared by the multitude (or the majority) is the definition of kingship (Cheng 2.3f) and effective government (Xi 20.5, Zhao 4.1c).

At that point many of the military leaders wished to fight. Someone said to Luan Shu[a]: "Wise men fulfill desires shared by the majority and thus achieve success. Why would you not follow the majority? You are the chief minister in charge of policies and should weigh the wishes of the people. Of your assistants there are eleven, and those who do not wish to fight amount to three only. Those who wish to fight can be called the majority. The *Shang Documents* said, 'When three persons use divination, follow the results obtained by two.'[167] It is because they are the majority." Luan Shu[c] said, "When the merits of different positions are equal, the majority can be followed. For merit is the master of the majority. Three ministers championing a position can be called the majority. Is it not acceptable to follow them?"[168]

---

168   The majority should be followed if the good points of different positions are equal. However, if they are not, then the merit of the position outweighs the number of supporters. Cf. Karlgren's different reading, gl. 395: "If the good ministers holding different views are equal in number, then follow the views supported by the multitude."

春秋

7.1　七年，春，王正月，鼷鼠食郊牛角，改卜牛。鼷鼠又食其角，乃免牛。

7.2(1)　吳伐郯。

7.3(3)　夏，五月，曹伯來朝。

7.4　不郊，猶三望。

7.5(4)　秋，楚公子嬰齊帥師伐鄭。

7.6(4)　公會晉侯、齊侯、宋公、衛侯、曹伯、莒子、邾子、杞伯救鄭。八月戊辰，同盟于馬陵。

7.7　公至自會。

7.8　吳入州來。

7.9　冬，大雩。

7.10(6)　衛孫林父出奔晉。

左傳

7.1(2)　七年，春，吳伐郯，郯成。
　　　　季文子曰：「中國不振旅，蠻夷入伐，而莫之或恤。無弔者也夫！《詩》曰：

169　For a similar record of how bulls were chosen or rejected for sacrifices, see *Annals*, Xi 31.3, Xuan 3.1, Ding 15.7, Ai 1.3.

170　See Xi 31.3, n. 470, Zhao 6.4, n. 116.

171　Maling 馬陵 was located southeast of present-day Daming County 大名縣, Hebei.

172　Wu is first mentioned here in the *Annals*, and in Xuan 8.3 in *Zuozhuan*. Zhoulai 州來, which will be mentioned frequently in the Lord Zhao years, was located near present-day Fengtai County 鳳台縣, Anhui (see map 4).

173　This demonstrable military order (*zhenlü* 振旅) is also associated with ceremonial functions; see Yin 5.1, Xi 28.6.

ANNALS

In the seventh year, in spring, in the royal first month, field mice had   7.1
gnawed at the horns of the bull designated for the sacrifice in the outskirts. We divined about using another bull. The field mice again gnawed
at its horns, so we spared the bull.[169]

Wu attacked Tan.   7.2(1)

In summer, in the fifth month, the Liege of Cao came to visit our court.   7.3(3)

We did not perform the sacrifice in the outskirts. Still we performed the   7.4
sacrifices to the Three Prospects.[170]

In autumn, Gongzi Yingqi (Zichong) of Chu led out troops and attacked   7.5(4)
Zheng.

Our lord met with the Prince of Jin, the Prince of Qi, the Duke of Song,   7.6(4)
the Prince of Wei, the Liege of Cao, the Master of Ju, the Master of Zhu,
and the Liege of Qǐ and went to the aid of Zheng. In the eighth month,
on the *wuchen* day (11), they swore a covenant together at Maling.[171]

Our lord arrived from the meeting.   7.7

Wu entered Zhoulai.[172]   7.8

In winter, there was a great rain sacrifice.   7.9

Sun Linfu of Wei departed and fled to Jin.   7.10(6)

ZUO

*Lamenting how none came to Tan's defense during the Wu incursion into
Tan, Ji Wenzi invokes the polarity of central domains and barbarians.
However, the concept of barbarian is fluid and relational. As a victim of
Wu, sometimes decried for its barbarian mores, Tan is considered one of
the central domains. However, when the Tan ruler comes to the Lu court
and shows unexpected mastery of esoteric knowledge (Zhao 17.3), Confucius declares that learning is lost at the center but found among "tribes of
the four quarters" (siyi 四夷). Compared with Lu, Tan's non-Zhou status
becomes obvious.*

In the seventh year, in spring, Wu attacked Tan. Tan reached an accord   7.1(2)
with Wu.

   Ji Wenzi said, "The central domains are not putting their forces in
order.[173] The Man and Yi tribes enter and attack, and none has any concern for the domain in its plight. Is this not because there is no good
leader? As it says in the *Odes*,

不弔昊天，
亂靡有定。

其此之謂乎！有上不弔，其誰不受亂？吾亡無日矣。」君子曰：「知懼如
是，斯不亡矣。」

7.2 鄭子良相成公以如晉，見，且拜師。

7.3(3) 夏，曹宣公來朝。

7.4(5, 6) 秋，楚子重伐鄭，師于氾。諸侯救鄭。鄭共仲、侯羽軍楚師，囚鄖公鍾
儀，獻諸晉。
八月，同盟于馬陵，尋蟲牢之盟，且莒服故也。
晉人以鍾儀歸，囚諸軍府。

7.5a(8) 楚圍宋之役，師還，子重請取於申、呂以為賞田。王許之。申公巫臣曰：
「不可。此申、呂所以邑也，是以為賦，以御北方。若取之，是無申、呂
也，晉、鄭必至于漢。」王乃止。子重是以怨巫臣。

---

174 *Maoshi* 191, "Jie nanshan" 節南山, 12A.396.

175 Ju was under Qi's sway. Qi's recognition of Jin's hegemonic status thus entailed Ju's
submission.

176 The small domain of Shen has been frequently mentioned above (for location see
map 4). Lü 呂 was a small domain located west of Nanyang City 南陽市, Henan.

  Zuo Tradition

High Heaven has no compassion,
And there is no end to disorder.[174]

This is what is meant! If there is no good leader above, who will be spared disorder? The day of my death will not be far off." The noble man said, "He who knows fearful vigilance to this extent will surely not perish."

Gongzi Quji[a] of Zheng acted as Lord Cheng's assistant when the latter went to Jin. They had an audience with the Jin ruler and also bowed to thank Jin for its military assistance.

In summer, Lord Xuan of Cao came to visit our court.

Zheng commanders take a Chu officer, Zhong Yi, prisoner and present him to Jin leaders. Zhong Yi will impress Jin leaders two years hence (Cheng 9.9).

In autumn, Zichong of Chu attacked Zheng, stationing the troops at Fan. The princes went to the aid of Zheng. Gong Zhong and Hou Yu of Zheng encircled Chu troops, took Zhong Yi, Lord of Yun, prisoner, and offered him to Jin.

In the eighth month, they swore a covenant together at Maling. This was to renew the covenant of Chonglao and also to recognize Ju's submission to Jin.[175]

The leaders of Jin returned with Zhong Yi and imprisoned him at the arsenal.

Internecine conflict in Chu erupts: Zichong and Zifan, who resent Qu Wuchen because of the aftermath of the Chu-Song conflict (Xuan 14.3, 15.2) and intrigues surrounding Xia Ji (Cheng 2.6), decimate Qu Wuchen's lineage in Chu. Heiyao, who had adulterous relations with Xia Ji (Cheng 2.6), is also killed. In Lienü zhuan 7.155–56, the destruction of Wuchen's lineage supplies the moral for a story about the baleful consequences of desire. But in Zuozhuan, Qu Wuchen is able to exact revenge.

When the troops returned after the campaign in which Chu had laid siege to Song, Zichong requested certain lands from Shen and Lü as reward.[176] The king assented. Qu Wuchen[a], Lord of Shen, said, "This will not do. It is with these lands that Shen and Lü could become full-fledged settlements. From thence have come the levies and soldiers with which we defend ourselves against the north. If he takes those lands, there will be no more Shen and Lü. Jin and Zheng will certainly reach the Han River." The king then desisted. As a result Zichong resented Wuchen.

子反欲取夏姬，巫臣止之，遂取以行，子反亦怨之。及共王即位，子重、子反殺巫臣之族子閻、子蕩及清尹弗忌及襄老之子黑要，而分其室。子重取子閻之室，使沈尹與王子罷分子蕩之室，子反取黑要與清尹之室。

巫臣自晉遺二子書，曰：「爾以讒慝貪惏事君，而多殺不辜，余必使爾罷於奔命以死。」

7.5b 巫臣請使於吳，晉侯許之。吳子壽夢說之。乃通吳於晉，以兩之一卒適吳，舍偏兩之一焉。與其射御，教吳乘車，教之戰陳，教之叛楚。寘其子狐庸焉，使為行人於吳。吳始伐楚、伐巢、伐徐，子重奔命。馬陵之會，吳入州來，子重自鄭奔命。子重、子反於是乎一歲七奔命。蠻夷屬於楚者，吳盡取之，是以始大，通吳於上國。

7.6(10) 衛定公惡孫林父。冬，孫林父出奔晉。衛侯如晉，晉反戚焉。

Zifan had wished to marry Xia Ji. Qu Wuchen[a] stopped him, then married her himself and left Chu. Thus, Zifan also resented Wuchen. After King Gong acceded to his position, Zichong and Zifan put to death Ziyan, Zidang, and Fuji, deputy of Qing, all of them from Wuchen's lineage, as well as Heiyao, the son of Xiang the Elder, and divided their property. Zichong took Ziyan's property and had the Shen deputy and Wangzi Pi divide Zidang's property, and Zifan took the property of Heiyao and of the Qing deputy.

From Jin, Wuchen sent Zichong and Zifan a letter, saying, "You serve your ruler with slander, malice, and avarice, and you have killed many innocent persons. I will certainly make you die from exhaustion as you rush about trying to fulfill commands."

Qu Wuchen teaches Wu chariot warfare and battle formation and facilitates relations between Wu and the central domains. Wu becomes a real threat to Chu. In this sense the femme fatale Xia Ji, through her influence on Qu Wuchen's decisions, plays a role in redefining the balance of power in the sixth century BCE.

Qu Wuchen[a] asked to be sent on a mission to Wu, and the Prince of Jin assented. Shoumeng, the Master of Wu, was pleased with him. Wuchen thereupon established relations between Wu and Jin. He took thirty Chu chariots to Wu, left half of them there,[177] along with archers and chariot drivers. He taught the men of Wu how to ride chariots, he taught them battle formations, and he taught them to rebel against Chu. He left his son Qu Huyong[a] there and made him an envoy in Wu. Wu began to attack Chu, Chao, and Xu. Zichong rushed about to fulfill commands. At the meeting at Maling, Wu entered Zhoulai, and Zichong rushed from Zheng to fulfill commands. As a result, Zichong and Zifan in one year rushed about seven times to fulfill commands to stave off Wu incursions. Man and Yi tribes that had submitted to Chu were all taken over by Wu. That was how Wu began to expand; and relations opened between Wu and the domains above it.[178]

7.5b

Lord Ding of Wei hated Sun Linfu. In winter, Sun Linfu departed and fled to Jin. The Prince of Wei went to Jin, and Jin returned Qī.[179]

7.6(10)

---

177   The same expression, *pianliang* 偏兩, is used for tallying chariots in Xuan 12 (Yang, 2:731).

178   Du Yu (*ZZ* 26.444) glosses *shangguo* ("domains above it") as *zhuxia* (central domains). *Shang* ("above") may have the spatial sense of "to the north" or the historical sense of "culturally superior."

179   Qī might have been the territories that Sun Linfu offered to Jin when he fled there.

8.1(1)　八年，春，晉侯使韓穿來言汶陽之田，歸之于齊。

8.2(2)　晉欒書帥師侵蔡。

8.3(3)　公孫嬰齊如莒。

8.4(4)　宋公使華元來聘。

8.5(5)　夏，宋公使公孫壽來納幣。

8.6(6)　晉殺其大夫趙同、趙括。

8.7(7)　秋，七月，天子使召來賜公命。

8.8(9)　冬，十月癸卯，杞叔姬卒。

8.9(10)　晉侯使士燮來聘。

8.10(10)　叔孫僑如會晉士燮、齊人、邾人伐郯。

8.11(11)　衛人來媵。

8.1(1)　八年，春，晉侯使韓穿來言汶陽之田，歸之于齊。季文子餞之，私焉，曰：「大國制義，以為盟主，是以諸侯懷德畏討，無有貳心。謂汶陽之田，敝邑之舊也，而用師於齊，使歸諸敝邑。今有二命，曰『歸諸齊』。信以行義，義以成命，小國所望而懷也。信不可知，義無所立，四方諸侯，其誰不解體？《詩》曰：

180　This is the only time that the Zhou king is referred to as "the Son of Heaven" (*tianzi*) in the *Annals*. The term "Heaven-appointed king" (*tian wang*) is more commonly applied. By contrast, the term "Son of Heaven" appears much more frequently than "Heaven-appointed king" in *Zuozhuan*.

181　For Shu Ji of Qǐ, see *Annals*, Cheng 4.2.

182　These were women who were to accompany Bo Ji in her marriage to the Song ruler.

183　The private communication between ministers sometimes differs markedly from official pronouncements; see also Cheng 2.9, 5.1, Zhao 3.3. Cf. Wen 4.7, n. 71.

ANNALS

In the eighth year, in spring, the Prince of Jin sent Han Chuan to us to speak about returning the lands to the north of the Wen River to Qi.

8.1(1)

Luan Shu of Jin led out troops and invaded Cai.

8.2(2)

Gongsun Yingqi (Zishu Shengbo) went to Ju.

8.3(3)

The Duke of Song sent Hua Yuan to us on an official visit.

8.4(4)

In summer, the Duke of Song sent Gongsun Shou to us to present betrothal gifts.

8.5(5)

Jin put to death its high officers Zhao Tong and Zhao Kuo.

8.6(6)

In autumn, in the seventh month, the Son of Heaven sent the Shao Liege to us to bestow an appointment on our lord.[180]

8.7(7)

In winter, in the tenth month, on the *guimao* day (23), Shu Ji of Qǐ died.[181]

8.8(9)

The Prince of Jin sent Shi Xie (Fan Xie) to us on an official visit.

8.9(10)

Shusun Qiaoru met with Shi Xie (Fan Xie) of Jin, a Qi leader, and a Zhu leader and attacked Tan.

8.10(10)

A Wei leader brought secondary consorts.[182]

8.11(11)

ZUO

Lu gained the lands to the north of the Wen River in the aftermath of the battle of An (Cheng 2.3). Jin, having cemented ties with Qi through marriage (Cheng 5.3), pressures Lu to return the territories to Qi. Ji Wenzi privately protests to Han Chuan by appealing to an overlord's supposed good faith.

In the eighth year, in spring, the Prince of Jin sent Han Chuan to us to speak about returning the lands to the north of the Wen River to Qi. Ji Wenzi provided a feast to send him off and said to him privately,[183] "A great domain sets up just measures whereby it rules as covenant chief. As a result the princes cherish its virtues and fear being chastised and will not have divided allegiance. You had said that the lands to the north of the Wen River formerly belonged to our humble settlement and thus used your troops against Qi to facilitate their return to us. Now there is a second command, saying 'Return them to Qi.' Good faith is for realizing dutifulness, dutifulness is for fulfilling commands—this is what a small domain hopes for and cherishes. If good faith cannot be ascertained and dutifulness has no basis to be established, who among the princes from the four directions would not break away from you? As it says in the *Odes*,

8.1(1)

女也不爽，
士貳其行。
士也罔極，
二三其德。

七年之中，一與一奪，二三孰甚焉？士之二三，猶喪妃耦，而況霸主？霸主將德是以，而二三之，其何以長有諸侯乎？《詩》曰：

猶之未遠，
是用大簡。

行父懼晉之不遠猶而失諸侯也，是以敢私言之。」

8.2(2)　晉欒書侵蔡，遂侵楚，獲申驪。
　　楚師之還也，晉侵沈，獲沈子揖初，從知、范、韓也。君子曰：「從善如流，宜哉！《詩》曰：

愷悌君子，
遐不作人？

求善也夫！作人，斯有功績矣。」
　　是行也，鄭伯將會晉師，門于許東門，大獲焉。

8.3(3)　聲伯如莒，逆也。

8.4(4)　宋華元來聘，聘共姬也。

8.5(5)　夏，宋公使公孫壽來納幣，禮也。

184　*Maoshi* 58, "Mang" 氓, 3C.135. The word translated here as "gentleman" is *shi* 士, which has a wide semantic range and here probably refers to an officer or official. The last line cited is, literally, "making two and three things of his virtues," with the numbers "two" and "three" functioning as transitive verbs. This is one of many examples in which the relationship between men and women is used as an analogy for interdomain relations. See also Xiang 8.9, 27.5, Zhao 1.4.

185　*Maoshi* 254, "Ban" 板, 17D.632.

186　Note that Cai's proximity to Chu was the ostensible reason for the northern domains' incursions into Chu; see also Xi 4.1. Shen Li was a Chu official.

187　*Maoshi* 239, "Hanlu" 旱麓, 16C.560, following Du Yu's reading (*ZZ* 26.446). Yang (2:836) proposes a different reading: "Joyous and pleased is the noble man. / Why would he not raise true talents?"

188　Gong Ji was Mu Jiang's daughter and Lord Cheng's sister (Cheng 9.5). "Gong" is the posthumous honorific for her husband, Lord Gong of Song.

> She does not fail him,
> But the gentleman is duplicitous in his ways.
> He keeps not to rules and standards,
> And is inconstant in his virtue.[184]

Within seven years, we have had one round of giving and another round of seizing. What inconstancy could be more extreme than that? Since even a gentleman's inconstancy can cost him a worthy mate, how much greater the loss then for an overlord? If an overlord, who should abide by his virtue, is constantly making changes, how can he maintain the princes' allegiance for long? As it says in the *Odes*,

> Plans that will not go far
> Call for great remonstrance.[185]

I fear that Jin will lose the princes' support because its plans will not go far, and that is why I presume to speak about this privately."

By not fighting Chu at Raojiao (Cheng 6.11), Jin achieves victory in Shen. The sound advice of various Jin ministers is credited with Jin victory.

Luan Shu of Jin invaded Cai and then invaded Chu, capturing Shen Li.[186]   8.2(2)

With the Chu troops turning back, Jin invaded Shĕn and captured Jichu, the Master of Shĕn. This was a consequence of following the advice of Xun Shou[c], Fan Xie[e], and Han Jue[c]. The noble man said, "It is proper indeed to follow good as naturally as water flowing! As it says in the *Odes*,

> Joyous and pleased is the noble man.
> From afar he raises true talents.[187]

Surely this is about seeking good! To raise true talents is to achieve merit."

On that journey, the Liege of Zheng planned to join forces with Jin troops and to storm the Eastern Gate of Xŭ. They took many captives.

Zishu Shengbo[a] went to Ju to meet and escort home a bride.   8.3(3)

Hua Yuan of Song came to us on an official visit: this was to formalize   8.4(4)
the Song ruler's engagement with Gong Ji.[188]

In summer, the Duke of Song sent Gongsun Shou to us to present   8.5(5)
betrothal gifts. This was in accordance with ritual propriety.

8.6(6)　晉趙莊姬為趙嬰之亡故，譖之于晉侯，曰：「原、屏將為亂。」欒、郤為
徵。六月，晉討趙同、趙括。武從姬氏畜于公宮。以其田與祁奚。韓厥言
於晉侯曰：「成季之勳，宣孟之忠，而無後，為善者其懼矣。三代之今王
皆數百年保天之祿。夫豈無辟王？賴前哲以免也。《周書》曰：『不敢侮
鰥寡』，所以明德也。」乃立武，而反其田焉。

8.7(7)　秋，召桓公來賜公命。

8.8　晉侯使申公巫臣如吳，假道于莒。與渠丘公立於池上，曰：「城已惡。」
莒子曰：「辟陋在夷，其孰以我為虞？」對曰：「夫狡焉思啟封疆以利社
稷者，何國蔑有？唯然，故多大國矣。唯或思或縱也。勇夫重閉，況國
乎？」

8.9(8)　冬，杞叔姬卒。來歸自杞，故書。

189　The word translated as "put to death" here is *tao* 討 (literally, "chastise" or
　　　"punish").

190　Zhao Wu was the son of Zhao Shuo (Zhao Dun's son) and Zhao Zhuang Ji. Zhuang
　　　Ji was the daughter of Lord Jing of Jin (r. 599–581), but it is not clear why Zhao Wu
　　　should be raised in Lord Jing's palace. Various commentators suggest that Zhao
　　　Wu hid in the palace with his mother to escape being put to death like the rest of the
　　　Zhao lineage (Yang, 2:839). The word *xu* 畜 ("raised") suggests a more long-term
　　　arrangement, yet it is not clear whether it was common to have widowed daughters
　　　of lords keep their children in the lord's palace. A very different account of the Zhao
　　　lineage's near extinction and miraculous continuation, told in *Shiji* 43.1783–85, is the
　　　basis of the Yuan play *The Orphan of Zhao* (Zhao shi gu'er 趙氏孤兒) by Ji Junxiang
　　　紀君祥 (thirteenth cent.). For translations of the Yuan and Ming editions of this
　　　play, see Hsia, Li and Kao, *The Columbia Anthology of Yuan Drama*, 17–73.

191　Zhao Cui assisted Chong'er during his years of exile and was rewarded with lands
　　　and titles when Chong'er became Lord Wen (Xi 23.6, 24.1). Zhao Dun was Zhao Cui's
　　　son by the Di wife he married in exile (Xi 23.6, 24.1). Despite Zhao Dun's role in the
　　　murder of Lord Ling of Jin (Xuan 2.3), he is cited here as the exemplary loyal
　　　official.

Zhao Zhuang Ji, on account of the exile of her lover, Zhao Yingqi (Cheng 4.6, 5.1), plots the downfall of the Zhao lineage. Her son, Zhao Wu, eventually continues the Zhao lineage due to the intercession of the Jin minister Han Jue, who was raised by Zhao Dun (Cheng 17.10).

Zhao Zhuang Ji of Jin, because of Zhao Yingqi[b]'s banishment, slandered his brothers to the Prince of Jin, saying, "Zhao Tong[a] and Zhao Kuo[b] are about to rebel." The Luan and Xi lineage heads confirmed the charge. In the sixth month, Jin put to death Zhao Tong and Zhao Kuo.[189] Zhao Wu[d], following his mother Zhao Zhuang Ji[a], was raised in the lord's palace.[190] The Jin ruler gave the lands of the Zhao lineage to Qi Xi. Han Jue said to the Jin prince, "If for all the achievements of Zhao Cui[c] and the loyalty of Zhao Dun[e],[191] the Zhao lineage will nevertheless be without progeny, those who do good will surely be fearful! The sage-kings of the Three Dynasties all preserved their Heaven-endowed position for several hundred years. Now, how could there have been no benighted kings? They relied on the former sage-kings to keep them from disasters. As it says in the *Zhou Documents*, 'Do not dare to humiliate widows and widowers': this is to illuminate virtue."[192] The Jin ruler thus established Zhao Wu[d] as head of the Zhao lineage and returned the lands to him.

8.6(6)

In autumn, Shao Duke Huan came to us to bestow an appointment on our lord.

8.7(7)

Ju, last mentioned as the victim of Qi aggression (Xuan 13.2), will fall prey to Chu the following year (Cheng 9.10). Qu Wuchen cautions the Ju ruler against carelessness.

The Jin ruler sent Qu Wuchen[a], Lord of Shen, to Wu. Passing through Ju, he stood with the Master of Ju[a] by the moat and said, "The city walls are too dilapidated." The Master of Ju said, "Who will care to prey on us, a remote domain among the barbarians?" Wuchen replied, "Scheming ones who plan to expand territories beyond their borders and profit the altars of their domains are everywhere. What domain can be free from their threat? It is for that reason that there are many big domains. Everything hinges on caution or the lack of vigilance. Since even a brave man keeps his gates shut, how much more should a domain do so!"

8.8

In winter, Shu Ji of Qǐ died. She had come home from Qǐ; hence, her death was recorded.

8.9(8)

---

192 The quote, which appears in "Kang gao" and "Wu yi" 無逸 (*Shangshu* 14.201, 16.241), is meant to encourage Lord Jing to follow King Wen's example of mercy. As Takezoe (12.62) points out, Han Jue appeals to Lord Jing's compassion, instead of debating the injustice of the charge and the persecution, probably because this better serves the purpose of reinstating the Zhao lineage.

8.10(9, 10)　晉士燮來聘，言伐郯也，以其事吳故。公賂之，請緩師。文子不可，曰：「君命無貳，失信不立。禮無加貨，事無二成。君後諸侯，是寡君不得事君也。燮將復之。」季孫懼，使宣伯帥師會伐郯。

8.11(11)　衛人來媵共姬，禮也。凡諸侯嫁女，同姓媵之，異姓則否。

春秋

9.1(1)　九年，春，王正月，杞伯來逆叔姬之喪以歸。

9.2(2)　公會晉侯、齊侯、宋公、衛侯、鄭伯、曹伯、莒子、杞伯，同盟于蒲。

9.3　公至自會。

9.4(3)　二月，伯姬歸于宋。

9.5(5)　夏，季孫行父如宋致女。

9.6(6)　晉人來媵。

9.7　秋，七月丙子，齊侯無野卒。

193　See Cheng 7.1.

194　Fan Xie will be going back on his word if he fails to fulfill his mission. He justifies his mission of aggression with the language of duty and good faith.

195　In other words, bribes are not allowed, and he can undertake the military offensive only as planned.

196　Fan Xie is threatening that Jin will sever relations with Lu.

Wu's subjugation of Tan was lamented as a consequence of Jin weakness (Cheng 7.1), and Tan is now under attack from Jin and its allies for having submitted to Wu. Lu tries to ameliorate Tan's plight, to no avail, and joins Jin in punishing Tan.

Fan Xie[b] of Jin came to us on an official visit: this was to speak about attacking Tan because it was serving Wu.[193] Our lord sent him gifts and requested that they delay military action. Fan Xie[a] refused, saying, "A ruler's command cannot bear divided allegiance. Losing good faith, I cannot establish myself.[194] Ritual propriety admits of no extra gifts; an appointed task cannot be fulfilled in two ways.[195] If you, my lord, fall behind other princes in joining the attack, it means our unworthy ruler will not be able to serve you.[196] I plan to thus report on my mission." Ji Wenzi[b] was fearful, and sent Shusun Qiaoru[a] to lead out troops to join the forces attacking Tan. — 8.10(9, 10)

A Wei leader brought secondary consorts for Gong Ji. This was in accordance with ritual propriety. In all cases when the daughters of princes married, ruling houses with the same clan name sent secondary consorts, while ruling houses with different clan names did not do so. — 8.11(11)

LORD CHENG 9 (582 BCE)
ANNALS

In the ninth year, in spring, in the royal first month, the Liege of Qǐ came to meet Shu Ji's funeral cortege and took it home with him. — 9.1(1)

Our lord met with the Prince of Jin, the Prince of Qi, the Duke of Song, the Prince of Wei, the Liege of Zheng, the Liege of Cao, the Master of Ju, and the Liege of Qǐ, and they swore a covenant together at Pu. — 9.2(2)

Our lord arrived from the meeting. — 9.3

In the second month, Bo Ji went to marry in Song. — 9.4(3)

In summer, Jisun Hangfu (Ji Wenzi) went to Song to convey a message to the bride.[197] — 9.5(5)

A Jin leader brought secondary consorts.[198] — 9.6(6)

In autumn, in the seventh month, on the *bingzi* day,[199] Wuye, the Prince of Qi, died. — 9.7

---

197   When a lord and a lady of ruling houses were wed, the bride's family sent a missive to the bride on the occasion of her presentation at the Ancestral Temple three months after the union. For this ritual, see also *Zuozhuan*, Huan 3.7 (Yang, 1:99; Legge, 371).

198   They were going to accompany Gong Ji in her marriage to the Song ruler.

199   According to the Lu calendar as we know it, there was no *bingzi* day in the seventh month.

9.8(7)　　晉人執鄭伯。

9.9(8)　　晉欒書帥師伐鄭。

9.10　　　冬，十有一月，葬齊頃公。

9.11(10)　楚公子嬰齊帥師伐莒。庚申，莒潰。楚人入鄆。

9.12(11)　秦人、白狄伐晉。

9.13(12)　鄭人圍許。

9.14(13)　城中城。

左傳

9.1(1)　　九年，春，杞桓公來逆叔姬之喪，請之也。杞叔姬卒，為杞故也。逆叔姬，為我也。

9.2(2)　　為歸汶陽之田故，諸侯貳於晉。晉人懼，會於蒲，以尋馬陵之盟。季文子謂范文子曰：「德則不競，尋盟何為？」范文子曰：「勤以撫之，寬以待之，堅彊以御之，明神以要之，柔服而伐貳，德之次也。」
　　　　　是行也，將始會吳，吳人不至。

9.3(3)　　二月，伯姬歸于宋。

9.4　　　楚人以重賂求鄭，鄭伯會楚公子成于鄧。

200　Lu and Ju fought over control of the city of Yun throughout most of the Spring and Autumn era; see *Annals*, Wen 12.8 (Yang, 2:586).

201　She died because she had been abandoned by Lord Huan of Qi.

202　Fan Xie's defense of Jin virtue contains a barely veiled threat to use force against Lu.

Jin leaders arrested the Liege of Zheng. 9.8(7)

Luan Shu of Jin led out troops and attacked Zheng. 9.9(8)

In winter, in the eleventh month, Lord Qing of Qi was buried. 9.10

Gongzi Yingqi of Chu led out troops and attacked Ju. On the *gengshen* day (17), Ju collapsed. The men of Chu entered Yun.[200] 9.11(10)

Qin leaders and the White Di tribe attacked Jin. 9.12(11)

Zheng leaders laid siege to Xǔ. 9.13(12)

We fortified the inner city. 9.14(13)

ZUO

Continuing the account of Shu Ji of Qǐ, who is also mentioned in Cheng 4.2, 8.9, and Annals, Cheng 5.1.

In the ninth year, in spring, Lord Huan of Qǐ came to meet Shu Ji's funeral cortege: this was because we requested it. Shu Ji of Qǐ died on account of Qǐ.[201] The Qǐ ruler came to meet Shu Ji's funeral cortege because of our request. 9.1(1)

Disaffection spreads among Jin's allies because Lu is asked to return the lands to the north of the Wen River. Fan Xie defends Jin policies with the rhetoric of virtue that conceals a threat.

On account of the return of the lands to the north of the Wen River to Qi, the princes shifted their allegiance from Jin. Fearful, the leaders of Jin met with other leaders in Pu to renew the covenant of Maling. Ji Wenzi said to Fan Xie[c], "What use is it to renew the covenant if one's virtue is insufficient?" Fan Xie[c] said, "To care for other domains assiduously, to treat them leniently, to control them firmly, to invoke bright spirits to deter them, to deal gently with the submissive, and to attack those with divided allegiance—these are the next best things after virtue."[202] 9.2(2)

On this occasion, Jin had planned to have a first meeting with Wu, but the leaders of Wu did not come.

In the second month, Bo Ji went to marry in Song. 9.3(3)

The leaders of Chu used valuable gifts to seek Zheng's support. The Liege of Zheng met with Gongzi Cheng of Chu at Deng.[203] 9.4

---

203 There were two places by the name of Deng 鄧. One was a domain that was assimilated into Chu in 688 BCE (see Zhuang 6.3). The other, probably meant here, was a Cai settlement.

9.5(4)　夏，季文子如宋致女，復命，公享之。賦〈韓奕〉之五章。穆姜出于房，再拜，曰：「大夫勤辱，不忘先君，以及嗣君，施及未亡人，先君猶有望也。敢拜大夫之重勤。」又賦〈綠衣〉之卒章而入。

9.6(6)　晉人來媵，禮也。

9.7(7)　秋，鄭伯如晉，晉人討其貳於楚也，執諸銅鞮。

9.8(9)　欒書伐鄭，鄭人使伯蠲行成，晉人殺之，非禮也。兵交，使在其間可也。楚子重侵陳以救鄭。

Mu Jiang, widow of Lord Xuan and mother of Lord Cheng and Gong Ji, demonstrates her mastery of polite, refined communication by chanting lines from the Odes *(fushi). This is the only example of a woman reciting from the* Odes *in a public setting in Zuozhuan. (Lady Mu of Xǔ is said to have composed an ode in Min 2.5a.) Her story continues in Cheng 11.3, 16.5, and Xiang 2.3, 9.3. She will later show herself to be equally knowledgeable about the Zhou Changes. Her later schemes against her son and the Ji lineage put her in the chapter on "Pernicious Favorites" (Niebi* 孽嬖*) in* Lienü zhuan *7.155–56.*

In summer, Ji Wenzi went to Song to convey a message to the bride. He reported the completion of his mission, and our lord offered him ceremonial toasts. He chanted the fifth stanza of "The Lofty Han."[204] Mu Jiang came out of her chamber to the inner court, bowed twice, and said, "You, sir, deigned to be assiduous. You do not forget the former lord, and your regard reaches to his heir and even extends to his soon-to-perish widow.[205] The former ruler indeed expected this from you. I presume to bow in gratitude for your repeated, assiduous service." She also chanted the final stanza of "Green Coat"[206] before entering her chamber.

9.5(4)

A Jin leader brought secondary consorts. This was in accordance with ritual propriety.

9.6(6)

In autumn, the Liege of Zheng went to Jin. Jin leaders, chastising him for switching allegiance to Chu, arrested him at Tongti.[207]

9.7(7)

Luan Shu attacked Zheng. The leaders of Zheng sent Bojuan to negotiate for peace. The men of Jin killed him. This was not in accordance with ritual propriety. When armies are engaged in conflict, envoys should be allowed to move between them.

Zichong of Chu invaded Chen in order to go to the aid of Zheng.

9.8(9)

---

204 *Maoshi* 261, "Hanyi" 韓奕, 18D.682–83. The fifth stanza describes how Han Ji, daughter of Quefu, finds honor and happiness in her marriage with the Prince of Han.

205 The term for "widow" here is the conventional expression *wei wang ren* 未亡人, literally, "the one who is not yet dead" or "the one who can only await death." The term also appears in Zhuang 28.3 and Cheng 14.5.

206 *Maoshi* 27, "Lüyi" 綠衣, 2A.77. Her emphasis is presumably on the last two lines: "I long for the ancients. / Indeed, they had what my heart seeks" 我思古人，實獲我心. She is comparing Ji Wenzi to the virtuous ancients. Mu Jiang's high regard for Ji Wenzi turns into enmity seven years later, when Ji Wenzi's rival Shusun Qiaoru becomes her lover (Cheng 16.5).

207 Tongti 銅鞮 was located in the domain of Jin and was south of present-day Qin County 沁縣, Shanxi.

晉侯觀于軍府，見鍾儀。問之曰：「南冠而縶者，誰也？」有司對曰：「鄭人所獻楚囚也。」使稅之。召而弔之。再拜稽首。問其族。對曰：「泠人也。」公曰：「能樂乎？」對曰：「先父之職官也，敢有二事？」使與之琴，操南音。

公曰：「君王何如？」對曰：「非小人之所得知也。」固問之。對曰：「其為大子也，師、保奉之，以朝于嬰齊而夕于側也。不知其他。」公語范文子。文子曰：「楚囚，君子也。言稱先職，不背本也；樂操土風，不忘舊也；稱大子，抑無私也；名其二卿，尊君也。不背本，仁也；不忘舊，信也；無私，忠也；尊君，敏也。仁以接事，信以守之，忠以成之，敏以行之。事雖大，必濟。君盍歸之，使合晉、楚之成？」公從之，重為之禮，使歸求成。

Zhong Yi of Chu, taken prisoner two years earlier (Cheng 7.4), here describes himself as a musician and responds to his Jin captors with dignity and ritual propriety. Music is linked to peaceful accord, which becomes Zhong Yi's mission upon his repatriation to Chu.

The Prince of Jin surveyed the arsenal and saw Zhong Yi. He asked about him, "That bound person with a southern cap, who is he?"[208] The officer in charge said, "This is the Chu prisoner presented by the men of Zheng." The lord had his bonds released, summoned him, and spoke sympathetically to him. Zhong Yi bowed twice, with his forehead touching the ground. The lord asked about his lineage. He replied, "We are musicians." The lord asked, "Can you play music?" He replied, "This is the hereditary office of our ancestors. Dare I have another vocation?" The lord had a level lute given to him, and he strummed southern tunes. The lord said, "What is your lord and king like?" He replied, "That is not what a humble person like me can know." The lord persisted with the question. He replied, "When he was the prince and heir apparent, his teacher and guardian served him. Every morning he was with Yingqi and every evening with Ce.[209] I do not know the rest."

The lord told Fan Xie[c] about him. Fan Xie[a] said, "The Chu prisoner is a noble man. In speaking, he named his forebears' vocation—thus, he did not turn against his origins. In playing music, he strummed his native tunes—thus, he did not forget his old ties. He spoke of what his ruler was like as heir apparent—thus, he had no partiality.[210] He called the two Chu ministers by name—this showed respect for you, my lord. Not turning against one's origins is nobility of spirit; not forgetting old ties is good faith; not being partial is loyalty; respecting the ruler with such attention to etiquette is adroit intelligence. Nobility of spirit is for taking up important affairs, good faith for guarding them, loyalty for completing them, adroit intelligence for executing them. No matter how momentous the affair, there will be certain success. Why don't you, my lord, send him back, and have him bring about peace between Jin and Chu?" The lord followed his advice, treated Zhong Yi with redoubled courtesy and ceremony, and sent him back to seek an accord between Jin and Chu.

---

208   This is another indication that the style of Chu headdress (and probably costumes) was different from that of the central domains.

209   That is, day and night he sought instruction from Gongzi Yingqi (Zichong), the chief minister, and from Gongzi Ce (Zifan), the supervisor of the military. It is ritually proper to use the given name of one's superior or father when addressing someone honored as superior to the person one is referring to. See n. 120.

210   The implication is that Zhong Yi is sincere: he is not motivated by partiality to aggrandize his ruler. He speaks about what the Chu king was like when he was heir apparent, because that is what he knows.

9.10a(11) 　冬，十一月，楚子重自陳伐莒，圍渠丘。渠丘城惡，眾潰，奔莒。戊申，楚入渠丘。莒人囚楚公子平。楚人曰：「勿殺，吾歸而俘。」莒人殺之。楚師圍莒。莒城亦惡，庚申，莒潰。楚遂入鄆，莒無備故也。

9.10b 　君子曰：「恃陋而不備，罪之大者也，備豫不虞，善之大者也。莒恃其陋，而不修城郭，浹辰之間，而楚克其三都，無備也夫！《詩》曰：

> 雖有絲、麻，
> 無棄菅、蒯；
> 雖有姬、姜，
> 無棄蕉萃；
> 凡百君子，
> 莫不代匱。

言備之不可以已也。」

9.11(12) 　秦人、白狄伐晉，諸侯貳故也。

9.12(13) 　鄭人圍許，示晉不急君也。是則公孫申謀之，曰：「我出師以圍許，偽將改立君者，而紓晉使，晉必歸君。」

9.13(14) 　城中城，書，時也。

211　Ququ 渠丘 was probably located southeast of present-day Ju County 莒縣, Shandong.

212　The word *chen* 辰 refers to two-hour units for measuring the twelve blocks of time in a day. From *moushen* to *gengshen*, one cycle of twelve earthly stems is completed.

213　This is not in the received text of *Maoshi*.

Ju falls: the Ju ruler erred in thinking that his domain was too insignificant to merit proper defensive measures. No potential conquest is too meager, and Chu destroys Ju because it has not made preparations, as Qu Wuchen predicted (Cheng 8.8).

In winter, in the eleventh month, Zichong of Chu attacked Ju from Chen and laid siege to Quqiu.[211] The city walls of Quqiu were dilapidated, and the people dispersed, fleeing to Ju. On the *wushen* day (5), Chu entered Quqiu. The men of Ju took Gongzi Ping of Chu prisoner. The men of Chu said, "Do not kill him; we will return your captives." But the men of Ju killed Gongzi Ping, and Chu troops laid siege to Ju. The city walls of Ju were also dilapidated, and on the *gengshen* day, Ju collapsed. Chu thereupon entered Yun. This came about because Ju had not made any preparations.

9.10a(11)

The noble man said, "To count on one's insignificance and make no defensive preparations is the greatest of offenses; to be prepared even for the unexpected is the greatest good. Ju counted on its insignificance and did not repair its city walls, so that in the course of twelve days[212] Chu vanquished its three major cities. Is this not because of the lack of defensive preparation? As it says in the *Odes*,

9.10b

> Even if you have silk and hemp,
> Do not abandon the grasses with coarse fibers.
> Even if you have the ladies of Ji and Jiang,
> Do not abandon the homely and weathered ones.
> All types of noble men
> Without exception suffer want of this or that.[213]

This is to say how defensive preparation cannot be neglected."

Qin leaders and the White Di tribe attacked Jin: this was because the princes shifted their allegiance.

9.11(12)

Lord Cheng of Zheng went to Jin and was detained (Cheng 9.7). Zheng leaders plot to appear indifferent. By laying siege to Xǔ, Zheng shows itself capable of military action despite the detainment of Lord Cheng.

Zheng leaders laid siege to Xǔ: this was to show Jin that it was not anxious about its ruler. This was the plot of Gongsun Shen, who said, "We will send out troops to lay siege to Xǔ, pretend that we are planning to establish another ruler, and temporarily dispense with sending envoys to Jin. Jin will surely return our ruler."

9.12(13)

We fortified the inner city: this was recorded because it was timely.

9.13(14)

9.14　十二月，楚子使公子辰如晉，報鍾儀之使，請修好、結成。

春秋

10.1(2)　十年，春，衛侯之弟黑背帥師侵鄭。

10.2　夏，四月，五卜郊，不從，乃不郊。

10.3(3)　五月，公會晉侯、齊侯、宋公、衛侯、曹伯，伐鄭。

10.4　齊人來滕。

10.5(4)　丙午，晉侯獳卒。

10.6(6)　秋，七月，公如晉。

10.7　冬，十月。

左傳

10.1　十年，春，晉侯使糴茷如楚，報大宰子商之使也。

10.2(1)　衛子叔黑背侵鄭，晉命也。

10.3(3)　鄭公子班聞叔申之謀。三月，子如立公子繻。夏，四月，鄭人殺繻，立髡頑，子如奔許。欒武子曰：「鄭人立君，我執一人焉，何益？不如伐鄭而歸其君，以求成焉。」

214　According to earlier entries in *Zuozhuan* (Cheng 8.11, 9.6), only domains that share the same clan name should send secondary consorts. The houses of Qi and Lu, however, did not have the same clan name.

215　According to *Shiji* 42.1770, Gongzi Xu was Lord Xiang's son and Lord Cheng's half brother, and he was made ruler when Luan Shu laid siege to Zheng, not, as *Zuozhuan* records, because Gongzi Ban sought to carry out Gongsun Shen's plot.

216　Kunwan was Lord Cheng's son and heir apparent, later Lord Xi (*Annals*, Xiang 7.9). Sima Qian (*Shiji* 42.1770) does not mention Kunwan and also records that Xu was killed after Lord Cheng returned to Zheng.

Jīnthe twelfth month, the Chu ruler sent the grand steward Zishang[a] to   9.14
in response to Zhong Yi's mission, requesting that the two domains
cultivate good relations and reach an accord.

LORD CHENG 10 (581 BCE)
ANNALS

In the tenth year, in spring, Heibei, the younger brother of the Prince of   10.1(2)
Wei, led out troops and invaded Zheng.

In summer, in the fourth month, we divined five times about per-   10.2
forming the sacrifice in the outskirts. The results were not favorable, so
we did not perform the sacrifice in the outskirts.

In the fifth month, our lord met with the Prince of Jin, the Prince of Qi,   10.3(3)
the Duke of Song, the Prince of Wei, and the Liege of Cao and attacked
Zheng.

A Qi leader brought secondary consorts.[214]   10.4

On the *bingwu* day, Nou, the Prince of Jin, died.   10.5(4)

In autumn, in the seventh month, our lord went to Jin.   10.6(6)

Winter, the tenth month.   10.7

ZUO

In the tenth year, in spring, the Prince of Jin sent Di Pei to Chu. This was   10.1
in response to the diplomatic mission of Zishang, the grand steward.

Zishu Heibei of Wei invaded Zheng: this was because Jin had com-   10.2(1)
manded it to do so.

*The plan of the Zheng minister Gongsun Shen (Cheng 9.12) is carried out,
and Jin lets Lord Cheng return to Zheng.*

Gongzi Ban of Zheng learned of Gongsun Shen[a]'s plan. In the third   10.3(3)
month, Gongzi Ban[a] established Gongzi Xu as ruler.[215] In summer, in the
fourth month, the Zheng leaders put Gongzi Xu[a] to death and established Kunwan as ruler.[216] Gongzi Ban[a] fled to Xŭ. Luan Shu[a] said, "The
Zheng leaders have established a ruler. Of what benefit will it be for us to
hold this one man? It would be better to attack Zheng and repatriate its
ruler to seek an accord with them."

晉侯有疾，五月，晉立大子州蒲以為君，而會諸侯伐鄭。鄭子罕賂以襄鐘，子然盟于脩澤，子駟為質。辛巳，鄭伯歸。

10.4(5)　晉侯夢大厲，被髮及地，搏膺而踊，曰：「殺余孫，不義。余得請於帝矣！」壞大門及寢門而入。公懼，入于室。又壞戶。公覺，召桑田巫。巫言如夢。公曰：「何如？」曰：「不食新矣。」

公疾病，求醫于秦。秦伯使醫緩為之。未至，公夢疾為二豎子，曰：「彼，良醫也，懼傷我，焉逃之？」其一曰：「居肓之上、膏之下，若我何？」醫至，曰：「疾不可為也，在肓之上、膏之下，攻之不可，達之不及，藥不至焉，不可為也。」公曰：「良醫也。」厚為之禮而歸之。

六月丙午，晉侯欲麥，使甸人獻麥，饋人為之。召桑田巫，示而殺之。將食，張，如廁，陷而卒。小臣有晨夢負公以登天，及日中，負晉侯出諸廁，遂以為殉。

<hr>

217　The received text has Zhoupu 州蒲, but Kong Yingda (ZZ-Kong 26.449) argued, based on references in Ying Shao's *Jiujun huiyi*, that the name should be Zhouman 州滿. *Shiji* (39.1679) records a phonetically similar name, Shouman 壽曼. He becomes Lord Li of Jin. Note that Lord Jing was still alive when Zhouman was instated as ruler. Gu Yanwu (*Rizhi lu jishi*, 14.338–39) cites this as the first instance of "internal abdication" (*neishan* 內禪).

218　Xiu Marsh 脩澤 was located in the domain of Zheng southwest of present-day Yuanyang County 原陽縣, Henan.

219　For *li* 厲 ("vengeful spirit"), see also Xiang 17.2, Zhao 7.7, and Zhao 7.9. A person who dies without surviving progeny and therefore is denied sacrificial offering will likely become a *li*.

220　In Xi 10.3, the ghost of the Jin prince Shensheng also mentions permission from the high god to punish his half brother, Lord Hui of Jin.

221　Sangtian 桑田 was in Guo, which was annexed by Jin (Xi 5.8).

222　Literally, "the space between the heart and the diaphragm, and below the fat at the tip of the heart." This becomes the idiom *bing ru gaohuang* 病入膏肓: an incurable malady is one that "has entered the space between the diaphragm and the heart." The dream of the boys concretizes the tension between agency and the loss of control (Wai-yee Li, "Dreams of Interpretation").

223　See Zhao 1.12e for another example of a Qin doctor diagnosing the illness of a Jin ruler.

The Prince of Jin had been ill. In the fifth month, Jin established the heir apparent Zhouman[217] as ruler, met with the princes, and attacked Zheng. Zihan of Zheng sent the Xiang Temple bells as a gift, and Ziran swore a covenant with the allies at Xiu Marsh.[218] Zisi became a hostage in Jin. On the *xinsi* day (11), the Liege of Zheng returned.

A vengeful ghost and a strange dream set the stage for Lord Jing of Jin's dramatic death. The vengeful ghost, presumably an ancestor of the Zhao lineage, demands retribution because Lord Jing wiped out almost the entire Zhao lineage on account of the false accusation of Zhao Zhuang Ji (Cheng 8.6). Victims of political turmoil and violent deaths often appear in dreams to demand vengeance; see also Xiang 18.3, Zhao 7.9, and Ai 17.5. The ghosts of unjustly killed ministers haunt rulers in Mozi ("Minggui").

The Prince of Jin dreamed of a huge vengeful ghost[219] with disheveled hair hanging to the ground. It beat its chest, leapt up and down, and said, "For you to murder my descendants was unjust. I have the high god's approval of my request for revenge!"[220] It smashed the main gate and the door to his private quarters and made its entry. Terrified, the lord entered the inner chamber, and the ghost smashed that door also. The lord woke up and summoned the shaman of Sangtian (Mulberry Fields).[221] What the shaman described corresponded exactly to the dream. The lord said, "What then?" He replied, "You will not eat the grain of the new harvest!"

The lord fell seriously ill and sought a physician from Qin. The Liege of Qin sent a physician named Huan to treat him. Before he arrived, the lord dreamed that his illness assumed the form of two boys, who said, "He is a skilled physician. I fear he will harm us. Where can we escape?" One of them said, "If we lodge above the diaphragm and below the heart,[222] then what can he do to us?" The physician arrived and said, "There is nothing to be done about the illness. It is above the diaphragm and below the heart, where it can neither be overcome with heat treatment nor reached through acupuncture. Medicine will not get to it. There is nothing to be done." The lord said, "He is a good physician."[223] He gave him handsome gifts and sent him back.

In the sixth month, on the *bingwu* day (6), the Prince of Jin wanted to taste the new grain. He had the official in charge of sacrificial grains present it and the cook prepare it. He summoned the shaman of Sangtian, showed him the new grain, and had him killed. When he was about to eat, he became bloated, went to the privy, fell in, and died. A eunuch had dreamed in the morning of ascending to heaven with the lord on his back. By midday, he was carrying the Prince of Jin out of the privy. And then he was killed to attend his lord after death.

10.5　鄭伯討立君者，戊申，殺叔申、叔禽。君子曰：「忠為令德，非其人猶不可，況不令乎？」

10.6(6)　秋，公如晉。晉人止公，使送葬。於是糴茷未反。

10.7　冬，葬晉景公。公送葬，諸侯莫在。魯人辱之，故不書，諱之也。

春秋

11.1(1)　十有一年，春，王三月，公至自晉。

11.2(2)　晉侯使郤犨來聘，己丑，及郤犨盟。

11.3(4)　夏，季孫行父如晉。

11.4(6)　秋，叔孫僑如如齊。

11.5　冬，十月。

Lord Cheng of Zheng returns from captivity in Jin (Cheng 9.7) and wreaks vengeance on those whose ploy might have secured his return (Cheng 9.12, 10.3).

The Liege of Zheng chastised those who had established another ruler. On the *wushen* day (8), he put Gongsun Shen[a] and Shuqin[224] to death. The noble man said, "Loyalty is an admirable virtue. Even so, it cannot be realized when its object is not the right person—how much less so when the loyalty itself may not be worthy!"[225]

10.5

In autumn, our lord went to Jin. The men of Jin detained him and made him attend the funeral. At this point Di Pei had still not returned to Jin.[226]

10.6(6)

In winter, Lord Jing of Jin was buried. Our lord attended the funeral, but no other princes were present. Lu leaders considered this a disgrace; that was why the burial was not recorded. This was to conceal it.

10.7

LORD CHENG 11 (580 BCE)
ANNALS

In the eleventh year, in spring, in the royal third month, our lord arrived from Jin.

11.1(1)

The Prince of Jin sent Xi Chou to us on an official visit. On the *jichou* day (24), we swore a covenant with Xi Chou.

11.2(2)

In summer, Jisun Hangfu (Ji Wenzi) went to Jin.

11.3(4)

In autumn, Shusun Qiaoru went to Qi.

11.4(6)

Winter, the tenth month.

11.5

---

224 Shuqin is the younger brother of Gongsun Shen.

225 "Not the right person" has been taken to mean either Lord Cheng (following Du Yu, ZZ 26.450) or Gongsun Shen (Lu Can, cited by Gu Yanwu in *Zuozhuan Du jie buzheng*; Yang, 2:850). According to the latter reading, the sentence should be rendered: "it cannot be realized when it is not practiced by the right person." Alternatively, "not the right person" refers to Lord Cheng (i.e., he is not worthy of loyalty), and the virtue that "may not be worthy" refers to Gongsun Shen's dubious motives. Kong Yingda (ZZ-Kong 22.380) quotes these lines to discuss another case of what he judged to be misapplied loyalty: Xie Ye's ill-fated attempt to remonstrate with Lord Ling of Chen in Xuan 9.6.

226 The fact that Di Pei had not returned meant that peace between Jin and Chu had yet to be cemented. Lord Cheng of Lu was detained because Jin suspected Lu of leaning toward Chu; this would not have been an issue if Jin and Chu had made peace.

左傳

11.1(1) 十一年，春，王三月，公至自晉。晉人以公為貳於楚，故止公。公請受盟，而後使歸。

11.2(2) 郤犨來聘，且涖盟。

11.3 聲伯之母不聘，穆姜曰：「吾不以妾為姒。」生聲伯而出之，嫁於齊管于奚，生二子而寡，以歸聲伯。聲伯以其外弟為大夫，而嫁其外妹於施孝叔。郤犨來聘，求婦於聲伯。聲伯奪施氏婦以與之。婦人曰：「鳥獸猶不失儷，子將若何？」曰：「吾不能死亡。」婦人遂行。生二子於郤氏。郤氏亡，晉人歸之施氏。施氏逆諸河，沈其二子。婦人怒曰：「己不能庇其伉儷而亡之，又不能字人之孤而殺之，將何以終？」遂誓施氏。

11.4(3) 夏，季文子如晉報聘，且涖盟也。

---

227 Note that Lord Cheng's detainment is not mentioned in the *Annals*.

228 The new Jin ruler did not come, probably because he was in mourning.

229 Recall that Mu Jiang is Lord Xuan's wife and Lord Cheng's mother. Zishu Shengbo is the son of Shu Xi, Lord Xuan's brother.

230 The terms used here are *waidi* 外弟 and *waimei* 外妹, literally, "external younger brother" and "external younger sister."

Jin leaders detain Lord Cheng, suspecting him of leaning toward Chu (Cheng 4.7, 10.6; Annals, Cheng 4.4).

In the eleventh year, in spring, the royal third month, our lord arrived from Jin. The leaders of Jin thought that our lord was shifting allegiance to Chu and thus detained him.[227] Our lord asked to be granted a covenant; after that, he was sent back.

11.1(1)

Xi Chou came to us for an official visit and also to oversee the covenant.[228]

11.2(2)

A mother and a daughter are passed back and forth between lineages as pawns and appendages. Both Zishu Shengbo's mother and his half sister are sent away by their first husbands. The latter, used by her half brother Zishu Shengbo to curry favor with Xi Chou, suffers an even more pitiable fate, as her first husband drowns her children from her second marriage. The story also illustrates the reach of Xi Chou's power.

Zishu Shengbo[a]'s mother had not formalized her engagement before marriage. Mu Jiang said, "I will not have a concubine for a sister-in-law."[229] After giving birth to Shengbo, she was sent away by her husband Shu Xi and married Guan Yuxi of Qi. Having borne two children, she was widowed and was sent back to Zishu Shengbo[a]. Shengbo made his younger half brother a high officer and married his younger half sister to Shi Xiaoshu.[230] When Xi Chou came for an official visit, he sought a wife by turning to Zishu Shengbo[a].[231] Zishu Shengbo[a] procured by force his half sister, who had become Shi Xiaoshu[a]'s wife, and gave her to him. The woman said to Shi Xiaoshu, "Even birds and animals do not lose their mates. What are you going to do?" He said, "I am not willing to die or be banished for this." The woman thus went. She bore two children as Xi Chou's wife. When the Xi lineage was destroyed,[232] the men of Jin returned her to Shi Xiaoshu[a], who met her at the Yellow River and drowned her two children. Enraged, the woman said, "You could not protect your own wife and allowed her to be sent away, and you also could not cherish another man's orphans and killed them. How do you expect to die?" She then, with a vow, cursed Shi Xiaoshu[a].[233]

11.3

In summer, Ji Wenzi went to Jin: this was in response to Jin's official visit and also to oversee the covenant.

11.4(3)

---

231 We may surmise that Xi Chou had heard about the beauty of Shengbo's younger half sister.

232 See Cheng 17.10.

233 Following Karlgren, gl. 405. Du Yu (ZZ 27.456) glossed this slightly differently: she vowed to sever relations with Shi Xiaoshu.

11.5　周公楚惡惠、襄之偪也，且與伯與爭政，不勝，怒而出。及陽樊，王使劉子復之，盟于鄭而入。三日復出，奔晉。

11.6　秋，宣伯聘于齊，以修前好。

11.7　晉郤至與周爭鄇田，王命劉康公、單襄公訟諸晉。郤至曰：「溫，吾故也，故不敢失。」劉子、單子曰：「昔周克商，使諸侯撫封，蘇忿生以溫為司寇，與檀伯達封于河。蘇氏即狄，又不能於狄而奔衛。襄王勞文公而賜之溫，狐氏、陽氏先處之，而後及子。若治其故，則王官之邑也，子安得之？」晉侯使郤至勿敢爭。

11.8　宋華元善於令尹子重，又善於欒武子，聞楚人既許晉糴茷成，而使歸復命矣。冬，華元如楚，遂如晉，合晉、楚之成。

234　The Zhou Duke Chu might have been from the same lineage as the Zhou Duke Yue (Xi 30.4). The lineages of Hui and Xiang were descendants of King Hui and King Xiang of Zhou.

235　The precise location of Juan 鄭 is unknown but was probably in the royal domain of Zhou.

236　The fields of Hou 鄇 were part of Wen 溫, and Wen was granted to Xi's lineage. Hou was located to the northwest of present-day Wushe County 武涉縣, Henan.

237　Tan was a Zhou town and not a polity. Zhou control over Su Fensheng and Wen was tenuous; see Yin 11.5.

238　This foreshadows the mediatory efforts by another Song minister, Xiang Xu, some thirty years later (Xiang 27.4, Zhao 1.1c, 1.1d).

Zhou Duke Chu resented the oppression from the lineages of Hui and **11.5**
Xiang,[234] and he was also contending with Bo Yu for control of the government. Failing to win, he left Zhou in anger. When he reached Yang-fan, the king sent Liu Duke Kang[a] to bring him back. Having sworn a covenant with the latter at Juan,[235] he entered the Zhou capital. Three days later he departed again and fled to Jin.

Lu uses diplomacy to try to ease tensions between Qi and Lu, antagonists in the earlier battle of An (Cheng 2).

In autumn, Shusun Qiaoru[a] went on an official visit to Qi: this was to **11.6**
restore the former good relations between Qi and Lu.

A territorial dispute occurs between a Jin high officer and the Zhou court. Both sides appeal to precedents, but Zhou nobles prevail (Cf. Zhao 9.3a). The story of Su Fensheng, who at one point possessed Wen, appears in Xi 10.1.

Xi Zhi of Jin contended with Zhou for the lands of Hou. The king **11.7**
ordered Liu Duke Kang and Shan Duke Xiang to dispute the issue with Xi Zhi at Jin. Xi Zhi said, "Wen has been ours from former times; that is why I do not dare lose it."[236] Liu Duke Kang[a] and Shan Duke Xiang[a] said, "In the old days Zhou vanquished Shang and sent the princes to take care of the lands they had been granted. Su Fensheng, using Wen as a base, served as supervisor of corrections and, together with Tan Liege Da, was placed in power next to the Yellow River.[237] A subsequent Su clan leader went over to the Di; he was not able to get along with the Di, and he fled to Wei. King Xiang, to honor Lord Wen's exertions, bestowed Wen on him. The lineages of Hu and Yang first stayed there, and then it came to you. If we were to examine its past, then it was a settlement held by the king's official. How can you, sir, lay claim to it?" The Prince of Jin brought it about that Xi Zhi did not dare to contend for it.

The Song minister Hua Yuan tries to negotiate for peace between Chu and Jin.

Hua Yuan of Song was on good terms with Zichong, the chief minister **11.8**
of Chu, and he was also on good terms with Luan Shu[a]. He heard that the leaders of Chu had already agreed to the accord proposed by Di Pei of Jin, and that they had sent the latter to report the completion of his mission. In winter, Hua Yuan went to Chu, and then also to Jin, to cement the accord between Jin and Chu.[238]

11.9　秦、晉為成，將會于令狐。晉侯先至焉。秦伯不肯涉河，次于王城，使史顆盟晉侯于河東。晉郤犫盟秦伯于河西。范文子曰：「是盟也何益？齊盟，所以質信也。會所，信之始也。始之不從，其可質乎？」秦伯歸而背晉成。

春秋

12.1(1)　十有二年，春，周公出奔晉。

12.2(2)　夏，公會晉侯、衛侯于瑣澤。

12.3(3)　秋，晉人敗狄于交剛。

12.4　冬，十月。

左傳

12.1(1)　十二年，春，王使以周公之難來告。書曰「周公出奔晉」，凡自周無出，周公自出故也。

239　See Xi 15.8, n. 219. Note that this Wangcheng is in Qin.
240　Suo Marsh 瑣澤 was located in present-day Daming County 大名縣, Hebei.
241　The Di here are probably the White Di, because the remnants of the Red Di were destroyed in 588 BCE (Cheng 3.6). Jiaogang 交剛 was located near present-day Xi County 隰縣, Shanxi.

Mutual suspicion and failure to agree on the place of meeting mar the peace agreement between Qin and Jin.

Qin and Jin reached an accord, and planned to have a meeting at Linghu. The Prince of Jin arrived first. The Liege of Qin refused to cross the Yellow River, set up camp at Wangcheng,[239] and sent the scribe Ke to swear a covenant with the Prince of Jin east of the Yellow River. Xi Chou of Jin swore a covenant with the Liege of Qin west of the Yellow River. Fan Xie[c] said, "What good would this covenant do? A covenant preceded by fasting and purification is for ensuring good faith. To agree on the place of meeting is the beginning of good faith. If the beginning does not go smoothly, how can it ensure anything?" The Liege of Qin returned and turned against his accord with Jin.

11.9

LORD CHENG 12 (579 BCE)
ANNALS

In the twelfth year, in spring, the Zhou Duke departed and fled to Jin.

12.1(1)

In summer, our lord met with the Prince of Jin and the Prince of Wei at Suo Marsh.[240]

12.2(2)

In autumn, Jin leaders defeated the Di at Jiaogang.[241]

12.3(3)

Winter, the tenth month.

12.4

ZUO

The Zhou Duke again left Zhou and fled to Jin despite his earlier rehabilitation (Cheng 11.5).

In the twelfth year, in spring, the king sent someone to notify us about the troubles connected with Zhou Duke Chu[a]. The text says, "The Zhou Duke departed and fled to Jin." In all cases concerning Zhou, there is no "departing." The word *chu*—meaning "depart"—is used because the Zhou Duke Chu[a] cast himself out.[242]

12.1(1)

---

242 Or perhaps less dramatically: "he departed of his own volition." This exegetical comment is based on the idea that since Zhou laid claim to all lands under heaven (e.g., *Maoshi* 205, "Beishan" 北山), there could be no "departing from Zhou." King Xiang is said to "leave the capital and reside in Zheng" because of a rebellion (Xi 24.5), presumably to emphasize the crisis. The word *chu* is not used when Wangzi Xia and Wangzi Zhao fled Zhou (see *Annals*, Xiang 30.5, Zhao 26.7). The commentator surmises that the use of the word *chu* here draws attention to the Zhou Duke Chu's willful act of casting himself out (*zichu* 自出) despite his earlier rehabilitation by the king.

12.2(2) 宋華元克合晉、楚之成，夏，五月，晉士燮會楚公子罷、許偃。癸亥，盟于宋西門之外，曰：「凡晉、楚無相加戎，好惡同之，同恤菑危，備救凶患。若有害楚，則晉伐之；在晉，楚亦如之。交贄往來，道路無壅；謀其不協，而討不庭。有渝此盟，明神殛之，俾隊其師，無克胙國。」鄭伯如晉聽成，會于瑣澤，成故也。

12.3(3) 狄人間宋之盟以侵晉，而不設備。秋，晉人敗狄于交剛。

12.4 晉郤至如楚聘，且涖盟。楚子享之，子反相，為地室而縣焉。郤至將登，金奏作於下，驚而走出。

　　　子反曰：「日云莫矣，寡君須矣，吾子其入也！」

　　　賓曰：「君不忘先君之好，施及下臣，貺之以大禮，重之以備樂。如天之福，兩君相見，何以代此？下臣不敢。」

---

243 This last sentence—four lines in the original—also appears in the covenant that Wangzi Hu made with the lords in 632 BCE (Xi 28.3). The term *buting* 不庭, which means literally "do not come to court" (Yin 10.3), and which we translate here as "turn against us," also appears in Xiang 16.1.

244 Literally, "the sun is setting," because 莫 and 暮 are variant graphs with the same meaning of "evening." But various ritual texts use the word 暯, which means the middle of the day. Here it may refer to the middle of the day or simply indicates that time is passing.

245 King Cheng of Chu feasted Chong'er (later Lord Wen of Jin) during the latter's exile (Xi 23.6).

The Song minister Hua Yuan finalizes the peace agreement between Jin and Chu. The text of the covenant proclaims ideals soon to be betrayed.

Hua Yuan of Song finalized the accord between Jin and Chu. In summer, in the fifth month, Fan Xie[b] of Jin met with Gongzi Pi and Xu Yan of Chu. On the *guihai* day (4), they swore a covenant outside the west gate of Song to this effect: "In all cases, Jin and Chu are not to take up weapons against each other. They shall have the same friends and enemies. Together they shall cherish those suffering calamities and perils and come to the assistance of the famished and the afflicted. If another domain harms Chu, Jin shall attack it; with Jin, Chu shall act likewise. For envoys going back and forth with diplomatic offerings, the roads shall not be blocked. We shall confer about domains that disagree with us and chastise those who turn against us. Whoever betrays this covenant, may the glorious spirits destroy him, bring about his army's defeat, and bestow no blessings on his domain."[243] The Liege of Zheng went to Jin to accept the terms of the accord. They met at Suo Marsh: this was because of the accord.

The Di took advantage of the covenant at Song to invade Jin, but they did not make defensive preparations. In autumn, Jin leaders defeated the Di at Jiaogang.

When the Chu nobleman Zifan ceremoniously entertains the Jin envoy Xi Zhi, supposedly to finalize the peace agreement, the misuse of music shows a lack of good faith and sets the stage for war. By offering an envoy the kind of musical performance appropriate for the meeting of rulers, Zifan signifies the readiness to renew conflict. On the improper use of music, see also Zhuang 20.1, Zhao 1.12. The Lu minister Shusun Bao will similarly decline to be entertained by excessively grand music ten years hence (Xiang 4.3).

Xi Zhi of Jin went to Chu on an official visit and also to oversee the covenant. The Master of Chu offered him ceremonial toasts. Zifan was the Chu king's assistant. He had had an underground chamber made in which bells and drums were suspended. Xi Zhi was about to ascend to the hall when the music of bells, chimes, and drums sounded from down below. He was so startled that he ran out.

Zifan said, "Time is passing;[244] our unworthy ruler is waiting. You, sir, should enter!"

His guest said, "Your ruler has not forgotten the good relations between our former rulers[245] and extends his favor to this humble servant, bestowing on him great ceremony, adding to that grandly prepared music. If, by the blessing of Heaven, our two rulers should meet, what can replace this? Your humble servant does not dare receive this honor."

子反曰：「如天之福，兩君相見，無亦唯是一矢以相加遺，焉用樂？寡君須矣，吾子其入也！」

賓曰：「若讓之以一矢，禍之大者，其何福之為？世之治也，諸侯間於天子之事，則相朝也，於是乎有享、宴之禮。享以訓共儉，宴以示慈惠。共儉以行禮，而慈惠以布政。政以禮成，民是以息。百官承事，朝而不夕，此公侯之所以扞城其民也。故《詩》曰：

> 赳赳武夫，
> 公侯干城。

及其亂也，諸侯貪冒，侵欲不忌，爭尋常以盡其民，略其武夫，以為己腹心、股肱、爪牙。故《詩》曰：

> 赳赳武夫，
> 公侯腹心。

天下有道，則公侯能為民干城，而制其腹心。亂則反之。今吾子之言，亂之道也，不可以為法。然吾子，主也，至敢不從？」遂入，卒事。

歸以語范文子。文子曰：「無禮，必食言，吾死無日矣夫！」

冬，楚公子罷如晉聘，且蒞盟。十二月，晉侯及楚公子罷盟于赤棘。

---

246 Yu Qiang (cited in Yang, 2:897) glossed the word *rang* 讓 (yield) as *rang* 饢 (also pronounced *shang* or *xiang*, "to offer food and wine," here translated as "receive"). Xi Zhi persists with the metaphor of feasting.

247 The food and wine in ceremonial toasts (*xiang* 享) are not consumed by the participants of sacrifices—they are left for the spirits—hence, they constitute a lesson in reverence and restraint.

248 Literally, "this is how the lords act as shields and walls for their people." By the logic of the quotation from the *Odes*, Xi Zhi is referring to how the lords can use warriors as "shields and walls" for their people.

249 Xi Zhi presents this quotation and the next one, both from *Maoshi* 7, "Tu ju" 兔罝, 1C.40, as having opposite meanings. But in the *Odes* these lines are obviously analogous: both celebrate the importance of the warrior for his lord. Xi Zhi's fashioning of lines from the *Odes* to fit his own intent and the context is common practice in *Zuozhuan*. Cf. Xiang, nn. 342 and 932.

Zifan said, "If, by the blessing of Heaven, our two rulers should meet, they will have nothing but an arrow to exchange with each other. What use will there be for music? Our unworthy ruler is waiting. You, sir, should enter!"

His guest said, "If they receive[246] each other with an arrow, that is the greatest of disasters. What blessing is there? In an era of good government, when there are intervals of leisure from the affairs of the Son of Heaven, princes visit one another's courts. Then there will be rituals of ceremonial toasts and feastings—ceremonial toasts to offer instruction in reverence and restraint;[247] feasts to show kindness and beneficence. With reverence and restraint one practices proper ritual; with kindness and beneficence one lays out government policies. Government is realized through ritual propriety, and the people therewith find rest. The myriad officials receive orders, seeking morning audiences but not evening ones. This is how the lords and princes protect their people like shields and walls.[248] Thus, it says in the *Odes*,

> Bold and stalwart warriors,
> Shields and walls of their lord and prince.[249]

But when there is disorder, the princes in their greed have no compunctions about invading other domains or pursuing their desires. Fighting over a mere stretch of land, they drive their people to the limit, conscripting the fighting men among them to be their own bellies and hearts, legs and rumps, claws and teeth. Thus, it says in the *Odes*,

> Bold and stalwart warriors,
> Belly and heart of their lord and prince.

When the proper way prevails under heaven, the lords can be shields and walls for their people, disciplining their own hearts and minds. With disorder, the situation is reversed. Now your words embody the way of disorder; they cannot be held up as a model. But you, sir, are the host. Dare I not follow?" He thus entered, and completed the business.

Upon his return he told Fan Xie[c] about this. Fan Xie[a] said, "Without ritual propriety, they are sure to eat their own words. Our death cannot be many days away!"

Jin and Chu swear a covenant that will prove to be short-lived.

In winter, Gongzi Pi of Chu went to Jin on an official visit and also to oversee the covenant. In the twelfth month, the Prince of Jin and Gongzi Pi of Chu swore a covenant at Chiji.

春秋

13.1(1)　十有三年，春，晉侯使郤錡來乞師。

13.2(2)　三月，公如京師。

13.3(3)　夏，五月，公自京師，遂會晉侯、齊侯、宋公、衛侯、鄭伯、曹伯、邾人、滕
人伐秦。

13.4　曹伯盧卒于師。

13.5　秋，七月，公至自伐秦。

13.6(5)　冬，葬曹宣公。

左傳

13.1(1)　十三年，春，晉侯使郤錡來乞師，將事不敬。孟獻子曰：「郤氏其亡乎！
禮，身之幹也；敬，身之基也。郤子無基。且先君之嗣卿也，受命以求
師，將社稷是衛，而惰，棄君命也，不亡，何為？」

13.2(2)　三月，公如京師。宣伯欲賜，請先使。王以行人之禮禮焉。孟獻子從。王
以為介而重賄之。

250　In other words, Shusun Qiaoru received no gifts.

ANNALS

In the thirteenth year, in spring, the Prince of Jin sent Xi Yi to us to plead for troops.

13.1(1)

In the third month, our lord went to the Zhou capital.

13.2(2)

In summer, in the fifth month, our lord was coming from the Zhou capital. He then met with the Prince of Jin, the Prince of Qi, the Duke of Song, the Prince of Wei, the Liege of Zheng, the Liege of Cao, a Zhu leader, and a Teng leader and attacked Qin.

13.3(3)

Lu, the Liege of Cao, died among the troops.

13.4

In autumn, in the seventh month, our lord arrived from the attack on Qin.

13.5

In winter, Lord Xuan of Cao was buried.

13.6(5)

ZUO

A Lu minister, Meng Xianzi, predicts doom for the Jin minister Xi Yi (Xi Ke's son and head of the Xi lineage) because of the latter's irreverence in conducting his mission of asking for troops. The prophecy is fulfilled four years later (Cheng 17.10). Lack of reverence (bujing 不敬) often leads to predictions of a person's doom in Zuozhuan.

In the thirteenth year, in spring, the Prince of Jin sent Xi Yi to us to plead for troops. The way he conducted his mission was not reverential. Meng Xianzi said, "The Xi lineage will likely perish! Ritual propriety is a person's trunk; reverence, a person's foundation. Xi Yi[b] does not have that foundation. Moreover, as a hereditary minister of the former ruler, he had received the charge to request troops. This was for the sake of defending the altars of the domain, and yet he was slack. This amounts to abandoning the ruler's charge. How can he not perish?"

13.1(1)

One Zhou noble, Liu Duke Kang, predicts doom for another, Cheng Duke Su, because of his irreverent attitude in receiving sacrificial meat. The prophecy, fulfilled two months later (Cheng 13.3), is premised on the multiple meanings of the word ming 命 (translated here as "charge"), which can also mean "command," "life," and "destiny" (see also Wen 13.3, Cheng 4.3).

In the third month, our lord went to the Zhou capital. Shusun Qiaoru[a] hoped to have gifts bestowed upon him and asked to be sent on beforehand. The king treated him with the ritual proper to intermediaries.[250] Meng Xianzi followed; the king, treating him as our lord's assistant, rewarded him amply.

13.2(2)

公及諸侯朝王，遂從劉康公、成肅公會晉侯伐秦。成子受脤于社，不敬。劉子曰：「吾聞之：民受天地之中以生，所謂命也。是以有動作禮義威儀之則，以定命也。能者養以之福，不能者敗以取禍。

是故君子勤禮，小人盡力。勤禮莫如致敬，盡力莫如敦篤。敬在養神，篤在守業。

國之大事，在祀與戎。祀有執膰，戎有受脤，神之大節也。今成子惰，棄其命矣，其不反乎！」

13.3a(3)　夏，四月戊午，晉侯使呂相絕秦，曰：

昔逮我獻公及穆公相好，戮力同心，申之以盟誓，重之以昏姻。天禍晉國，文公如齊，惠公如秦。無祿，獻公即世。穆公不忘舊德，俾我惠公用能奉祀于晉。又不能成大勳，而為韓之師。亦悔于厥心，用集我文公，是穆之成也。

---

251 Lord Cheng of Lu and the other lords all passed through Zhou on the way to Jin, presumably to legitimize Jin's aggression against Qin.

252 We follow Kong Yingda (ZZ-Kong 27.460–61), who reads *zhong* as "the energy (or spirit) of central harmony" 天地中和之氣, and Hui Dong, who reads *zhong* as "centrality" (Liu Wenqi, *Chunqiu Zuoshi zhuan jiuzhu shuzheng*, 883–84). Cf. Karlgren, gl. 412: "humans are granted the central realm between heaven and earth to sustain life."

253 Cf. Karlgren's (gl. 413) different reading, following Lin Yaosou: "reverence lies in nurturing one's spirit."

254 For references to sacrifice or warfare as "a great affair," see Yin 5.1, Xi 15.4b, 32.4, Wen 2.5.

255 That is, Lord Xian of Jin and Lord Mu of Qin.

256 Lord Mu of Qin married one of Lord Xian's daughters; she is called Mu Ji in the text. She interceded on behalf of her half brother, Lord Hui of Jin, after the defeat of Jin in the battle of Han (Xi 15.4). Wen Ying and Huai Ying, both daughters of Lord Mu of Qin, married Lord Wen of Jin. Lord Xiang was Bi Jí's son (Wen 6.6), but Wen Ying as principal wife was his official mother. Wen Ying urged Lord Xiang of Jin to release three captured Qin commanders (Xi 33.3b).

257 Chong'er (later Lord Wen) was in exile from 656 to 637 BCE, and Yiwu (later Lord Hui) was in exile from 656 to 651 BCE. Chong'er sojourned in many domains (including Qi), and Yiwu resided in Liang before he came to Qin.

258 *Wulu* 無祿 is a special term used in notification about a lord's death in communications between domains (Karlgren, gl. 415).

259 Lord Mu of Qin supported Yiwu's return to Jin as ruler (Xi 9.6). On the conditions of Lord Mu's assistance, as well as the background to and the course of the battle of Han, see Xi 15.4.

Our lord and the other princes visited the court of the king, and then, led by Liu Duke Kang and Cheng Duke Su, they joined forces with the Prince of Jin to attack Qin.[251] When Cheng Duke Su[a] received the sacrificial meat at the altar of earth, he was not reverent. Liu Duke Kang[a] said, "I have heard that humans are born of the spirit of central harmony between heaven and earth and this is what is called their charge.[252] That is why there are models for action and movement, ritual propriety and duty, majesty and bearing for securing this charge. The able ones nurture this charge and find their way to good fortune; the feckless ones ruin this charge and bring on disaster.

That is why noble men are assiduous in fulfilling ritual propriety, while common men exert themselves to the utmost in physical labor. In being assiduous in fulfilling ritual propriety, there is nothing equal to offering reverence. In exerting oneself to the utmost in physical labor, there is nothing equal to steady dedication. Reverence lies in nurturing the spirits;[253] dedication lies in keeping to one's vocation.

The great affairs of the domain lie with sacrifice and warfare.[254] With sacrifices, there is the ritual of distributing roasted sacrificial meat; with warfare, there is the ritual of receiving sacrificial meat. These are the critical junctures in serving the spirits. In the present case, Cheng Duke Su[a] was slack; he has cast aside his charge. Surely he will not return!"

The Jin envoy Lü Xiang (Wei Xiang) threatens to sever relations with Qin by giving a purportedly historical retrospective of Qin-Jin relations over the last eighty years. This famous piece of rhetoric, delivered in an elevated style and laced with compelling examples, presents Jin as invariably righteous and victimized and Qin as ungrateful and aggressive. It skillfully distorts events chronicled elsewhere in Zuozhuan.

In summer, in the fourth month, on the *wuwu* day (5), the Prince of Jin sent Lü Xiang to sever relations with Qin with these words:

> In former times our Lord Xian and Lord Mu[255] shared good rela-
> tions. They joined their efforts and were of the same heart and
> mind, extending their good relations with oaths and covenants
> and strengthening their relationship with marriage ties.[256] When
> Heaven inflicted calamities on Jin, Lord Wen went to Qi, and
> Lord Hui went to Qin.[257] Misfortune befell us,[258] and Lord Xian
> passed away. Lord Mu did not forget the old ties of beneficence
> and allowed our Lord Hui to uphold ancestral sacrifices in the
> domain of Jin. Yet he was not able to complete his great meritori-
> ous service to Jin and deployed his army at Han.[259] He did, how-
> ever, have regret in his heart and brought about the success of our
> Lord Wen. All these were due to the mediation of Lord Mu.

13.3a(3)

文公躬擐甲冑，跋履山川，踰越險阻，征東之諸侯，
虞、夏、商、周之胤 而朝諸秦，則亦既報舊德矣。鄭人怒君
之疆場，我文公帥諸侯及秦圍鄭。秦大夫不詢于我寡君，
擅及鄭盟。諸侯疾之，將致命于秦。文公恐懼，綏靜諸侯，
秦師克還無害，則是我有大造于西也。

　　無祿，文公即世，穆為不弔，蔑死我君，寡我襄公，迭
我殽地，奸絕我好，伐我保城，殄滅我費滑，散離我兄弟，
撓亂我同盟，傾覆我國家。我襄公未忘君之舊勳，而懼社稷
之隕，是以有殽之師。猶願赦罪于穆公。穆公弗聽，而即楚
謀我。天誘其衷，成王隕命，穆公是以不克逞志于我。

　　穆、襄即世，康、靈即位。康公，我之自出，又欲闕翦
我公室，傾覆我社稷，帥我蝥賊，以來蕩搖我邊疆，我是以
有令狐之役。康猶不悛，入我河曲，伐我涑川，俘我王官，翦
我羈馬，我是以有河曲之戰。東道之不通，則是康公絕我
好也。

260　There is no record of this in *Zuozhuan* or other early texts.

261　Qin and Jin were about to join forces to attack Zheng in 630 BCE when Zhu Zhiwu
of Zheng, in a masterful rhetorical performance, persuaded Lord Mu of Qin that
Zheng's capitulation could only benefit Jin, to the detriment of Qin (Xi 30.3). Jin's
military ambition vis-à-vis Zheng, fueled by old grudges and eventually deflected
by Qin, is here presented as an attempt to defend Qin.

262　It was Hu Yan who wanted to attack Qin, but Lord Wen, recalling Qin's earlier
assistance, refused (Xi 30.3). Jin "restraint" in this instance, probably based on strategic calculations, is here described as a great favor toward Qin.

263　Yang (2:832, 862) reads *diao* 弔 as *shu* 叔、淑 ("good," "kind," "scrupulous"), following evidence from oracle bones and bronze inscriptions; see also the similar views
of Wang Yinzhi and Yu Yue (cited in Karlgren, gl. 416). Takezoe (13.13), Legge (382),
and Watson (*Tso Chuan*, 123) all read *budiao* more literally as "offered no condolences" or "showed no compassion."

264　Lu Deming cites this line as "defied our deceased lord" (*mie wo sijun* 蔑我死君) in
Jingdian shiwen, and Hui Dong cites other examples of the compound *sijun* (Hong
Liangji, *Chunqiu Zuozhuan gu*, 467). A literal translation of the received text is
"defied our lord as if he were deceased" (*mie si wojun* 蔑死我君). "Defied our
deceased lord" makes for a better parallelism with the line that follows.

265　Since the ruling houses of Zheng and Hua both had the clan name Ji, they are
referred to as "brother domains." The original has Bihua: Bi was the capital of Hua.

266　For the battle of Yao, which ended with Qin defeat, see Xi 33.3.

267　This phrase *tian you qi zhong* 天誘其衷 recurs in *Zuozhuan*. See Xi 28.4, Xiang 25.10,
Ding 4.3, and Ai 16.2 (Yang, 1:469, 3:1105, 4:1547, 4:1698).

268　According to the account given in Wen 14.10, the alliance between Qin and Chu did
not come to fruition because of the intrigues of two Chu ministers, not because of
King Cheng's death.

269　Both Lord Mu of Qin and Lord Xiang of Jin died in 621 BCE. They were succeeded
by Lord Kang of Qin (r. 620–609) and Lord Ling of Jin (r. 620–607). Lord Kang was
born of the union between Lord Mu and Mu Ji, the daughter of Lord Xian of Jin.

270　Lü Xiang is accusing Lord Kang of Qin of trying to destabilize Jin by supporting
Gongzi Yong, a rival claimant to the throne. In fact, it was Zhao Dun, chief minister
of Jin, who advocated the establishment of Gongzi Yong as Jin ruler (Wen 6.5)

Lord Wen personally donned armor and headpiece, traversed mountains and rivers, overcame perils and obstacles, and vanquished the princes of the east, making the descendants of Yu, Xia, Shang, and Zhou visit the court of Qin.[260] Thus did he already requite the old ties of beneficence. When the men of Zheng unleashed their fury at the borders of your domain, our Lord Wen led the princes and Qin in laying siege to Zheng.[261] The high officers of Qin, without consulting our unworthy ruler, unilaterally swore a covenant with Zheng. The princes were outraged by such conduct and wanted to brave death to attack Qin. Lord Wen, fearing for Qin, pacified the princes; and the Qin army succeeded in returning without suffering any harm. With this we thus performed a great service for the domain in the west.[262]

Misfortune befell us, and Lord Wen passed away. Lord Mu was ruthless.[263] He defied our deceased lord,[264] belittled our Lord Xiang as young and weak, encroached upon our land of Yao, cut us off from our allies and friends, attacked our city walls and fortresses, eliminated our domain of Hua, scattered and drove away our brothers,[265] brought about strife and chaos among our covenant partners, and threatened to topple our domain and patrimony. Our Lord Xiang had still not forgotten your earlier meritorious service, yet he feared the destruction of the altars of the domain, and that was why the armies were deployed at Yao.[266] Even then he was willing to resolve with Lord Mu the causes for recrimination. Yet Lord Mu refused to listen and turned to Chu to plot against us. Heaven's sentiments were swayed,[267] King Cheng of Chu perished, and because of that Lord Mu did not succeed in exerting his will at our expense.[268]

When Lords Mu and Xiang passed away, Lords Kang and Ling acceded to their positions.[269] Lord Kang was of our Jin extraction, yet he wished to disrupt and ruin our lord's house and to overturn the altars of our domain. He led noxious vermin from our line to destabilize our borders; that is why we had the Linghu campaign.[270] Even then Lord Kang did not repent. He entered our territory at Hequ, attacked our Su River area, took captives from among our people at Wangguan, and plundered our Jima. That was why we had the battle of Hequ.[271] That the way eastward was blocked for you was because Lord Kang terminated good relations with us.[272]

---

before he backed down and switched allegiance to Lord Ling. The battle of Linghu was fought in 620 BCE (Wen 7.4).

271   The battle of Hequ was fought in 615 BCE. According to *Zuozhuan*, Qin attacked Jin and occupied Jima in retaliation for the battle of Linghu (Wen 12.5).

272   "The way eastward" means "the road from Qin to Jin" and also refers to contact with other states farther to the east. Recall that Qin was referred to earlier as "the domain in the west."

及君之嗣也，我君景公引領西望曰：「庶撫我乎！」君亦不惠稱盟，利 吾有狄難，入我河縣，焚我箕、郜，芟夷我農功，虔劉我邊陲，我是以有輔氏之聚。君亦悔禍之延，而欲徼福于先君獻、穆，使伯車來命我景公曰：「吾與女同好棄惡，復修舊德，以追念前勳。」言誓未就，景公即世，我寡君是以有令狐之會。

君又不祥，背棄盟誓。白狄及君同州，君之仇讎，而我昏姻也。君來賜命曰：「吾與女伐狄。」寡君不敢顧昏姻，畏君之威，而受命于吏。君有二心於狄，曰：「晉將伐女。」狄應且憎，是用告我。

楚人惡君之二三其德也，亦來告我曰：「秦背令狐之盟，而來求盟于我：『昭告昊天上帝、秦三公、楚三王曰：余雖與晉出入，余唯利是視。』不穀惡其無成德，是用宣之，以懲不壹。」諸侯備聞此言，斯是用痛心疾首，暱就寡人，寡人帥以聽命，唯好是求。君若惠顧諸侯，矜哀寡人，而賜之盟，則寡人之願也，其承寧諸侯以退，豈敢徼亂？君若不施大惠，寡人不佞，其不能以諸侯退矣。

---

273   In 594 BCE, Jin attacked the Red Di (Xuan 15.3).

274   We follow Du Yu's (ZZ 27.462) reading of *qianliu* 虔劉 as "killing." Kong Yingda, in his subcommentary to "Lüxing" 呂刑 in the *Documents* (*Shangshu*-Kong 19.296), cites Zheng Xuan's reading of the term as "unsettle" or "cause disorder."

275   See Xuan 15.5.

276   Both sides came to the meeting with suspicions and ill will; see Cheng 11.9.

277   This is one of several references in the text to intermarriage between the central domains and the "barbarians"; see also Xi 23.6, Xi 24.2, and Xuan 15.3.

278   We follow Wang Yinzhi's (*Jingyi shuwen*, 698) reading of *ying* 應 as *shou* 受 ("receive"). Wang cites Wei Zhao's gloss of the phrase *ying qie zeng* 應且憎 in *Guoyu*, "Jin yu 8," 14.455: "Outside they receive and accept us; inside they abhor our error."

279   The phrase "being inconstant in your virtue" (literally, "making two and three things of your virtue") also appears in Cheng 8.1.

280   "The three lords of Qin" are Lord Mu, Lord Kang, and Lord Gong; the "three kings of Chu" are King Cheng, King Mu, and King Zhuang.

281   Recall that Jin and Chu made a peace agreement brokered by Hua Yuan of Song (Cheng 12.2).

282   Here Lord Li seems to be speaking in his own voice instead of through the voice of his envoy. Yang (2:864) notes the inconsistencies in the uses of the terms "our ruler" (*wojun* 我君), "our unworthy ruler" (*guajun* 寡君), and "I, the unworthy one" (*guaren* 寡人), in Lü Xiang's speech or letter.

When the time came for you, my lord, to succeed your father, our 13.3b
ruler Lord Jing craned his neck and gazed westward, saying, "Perhaps he will cherish us with compassion!" But you, my lord, did not grace us with participation in a covenant. Taking advantage of our troubles with the Di,[273] you entered our dependency by the Yellow River, burned our settlements of Ji and Gao, cut down the fruits of our agricultural labor, and committed slaughter at our borders:[274] that was why we gathered troops at Fushi.[275] You, my lord, also regretted the spreading of calamities and, wishing to elicit the blessings of our former rulers, Lords Xian and Mu, sent Qian[b] to command our Lord Jing thus: "You and I will share good relations and will abandon hostilities. We will return to the cultivation of former cordiality, so as to honor the memory of earlier meritorious services." Before the oaths were completed, Lord Jing passed away; that is why our unworthy ruler held the meeting at Linghu.[276]

You, my lord, were again merciless and turned against the covenant oaths. The White Di and you, my lord, shared the same region; they are your enemies and our partners in marriage.[277] You bestowed this command on us: "You and I shall attack the Di." Our unworthy ruler did not dare consider marriage ties; fearing your authority, he gave the command of war to the officers. Yet you, my lord, had divided allegiance regarding the Di and said to them, "Jin is planning to attack you." The Di received your notification,[278] even as they abhorred it; that is why they notified us about your perfidy.

The men of Chu hated your way of being inconstant in your virtue[279] and also came to notify us: "Qin turned against the Covenant of Linghu and came to us seeking a covenant with these words, 'We clearly declare to the god on high of the boundless heavens, to the three lords of Qin, and to the three kings of Chu:[280] Although we have maintained relations with Jin, our gaze is on nothing but gain.' I, the deficient one, detest Qin's lack of steadfast virtue. I thereby reveal these things, so that it can be punished for its inconstancy!"[281] Having heard all these words, the princes, aggrieved in heart and pained in mind, drew close to me.[282] I, the unworthy one, led them to await your commands, seeking nothing but amity. If you, my lord, deign to look with beneficence upon the princes, feel compassion for me, and bestow upon us a covenant, that will indeed be my wish. We shall then pacify the princes and retreat, for how would we dare to provoke disorder? If you do not bestow on us any great beneficence, then I, for all my ineptness, will not be able to lead the princes to retreat.

敢盡布之執事，俾執事實圖利之。

13.3c 秦桓公既與晉厲公為令狐之盟，而又召狄與楚，欲道以伐晉，諸侯是以
睦於晉。

晉欒書將中軍，荀庚佐之；士燮將上軍，郤錡佐之；韓厥將下軍，
荀罃佐之；趙旃將新軍，郤至佐之。郤毅御戎，欒鍼為右。孟獻子曰：
「晉帥乘和，師必有大功。」五月丁亥，晉師以諸侯之師及秦師戰于麻
隧。秦師敗績，獲秦成差及不更女父。曹宣公卒于師。師遂濟涇，及侯
麗而還。迓晉侯于新楚。

成肅公卒于瑕。

13.4 六月丁卯夜，鄭公子班自訾求入于大宮，不能，殺子印、子羽，反軍于
市。己巳，子駟帥國人盟于大宮，遂從而盡焚之，殺子如、子駹、孫叔、
孫知。

---

283 They support Jin as the more trustworthy ally.

284 Xi Yì (Xi Zhi's younger brother) is not to be confused with his more powerful kinsman Xi Yi, the lineage head of his generation. The two names are written with different characters.

285 Karlgren (gl. 421), following Shen Qinhan, reads *cheng* 乘 as a verb ("to use," "to take advantage of"). Du Yu (ZZ 27.463) reads *sheng* 乘 as a noun, "chariots (with their armored soldiers)": "The Jin commanders and the armored soldiers on the chariots are in harmonious cohesion."

286 Masui 麻隧 was located in present-day Jingyang County 涇陽縣, Shaanxi.

287 "Captain" is our translation of the unusual term *bugeng*. According to *Hanshu* 19A.739, *bugeng* 不更 and *shuzhang* 庶長 (mentioned in Xiang 11.6) were Qin ranks instituted by Shang Yang during the reign of Lord Xiao of Qin (r. 361–338) (ZZ-Kong 27.463). The Song scholar Zheng Qiao (*Liujing aolun*, j. 4) uses this as one of the "facts" to date *Zuozhuan* after the reign of Lord Hui of Qin (r. 399–387). We do not know much about the Qin administrative system prior to Shang Yang's reforms, however, and Shang might have redefined ranks that already existed during the Spring and Autumn period. Liu Wenqi (*Chunqiu Zuoshi zhuan jiuzhu shuzheng*, 896) cites Liu Shao, who glosses *bugeng* as the highest rank for an officer (*shi* 士) and "the spearman on the right in a chariot" in a Han text. But since he was singled out for mention, Rufu might have been of an even higher rank.

I have presumed to fully set forth the matter before those in
charge, so that they will indeed consider the most advantageous
course of action.

Lü Xiang's dire presentation of Qin-Jin relations turns out to be a declaration of war. Jin and its allies fight Qin at Masui. The Zhou noble Cheng Duke Su dies as predicted (Cheng 13.2).

Lord Huan of Qin had already sworn the Covenant of Linghu with Lord   13.3c
Li of Jin, yet he summoned the Di and Chu, hoping to lead them to attack
Jin. That was why the princes had cordial relations with Jin.[283]

Luan Shu of Jin commanded the central army, with Zhonghang
Xuanzi[a] assisting him. Fan Xie[b] commanded the upper army, with Xi Yi
assisting him. Han Jue commanded the lower army, with Zhi Ying[b]
assisting him. Zhao Zhan commanded the new army, with Xi Zhi assisting him. Xi Yì was the chariot driver,[284] with Luan Qian as his spearman
on the right. Meng Xianzi said, "The Jin commanders are taking advantage of the troops' harmonious cohesion.[285] Jin troops will certainly
accomplish great things." In the fifth month, on the *dinghai* day (4), Jin
troops led the troops of the princes and did battle with Qin troops at
Masui.[286] Qin troops were completely defeated, and Cheng Cha of Qin as
well as Captain Rufu[287] were taken captives. Lord Xuan of Cao died
among the troops. The allied troops then crossed the Jing River, advancing as far as Houli before turning back.[288] They met the Jin ruler at
Xinchu.

Cheng Duke Su died at Xia.

The disaffected Gongzi Ban, whose plan to install a proxy Zheng ruler was thwarted (Cheng 10.3), foments unrest in Zheng.

In the sixth month, on the night of *dingmao* (15), Gongzi Ban of Zheng,   13.4
coming from Zi,[289] sought to enter the Zheng Ancestral Temple. Failing
to do so, he killed Ziyin and Ziyu and returned to station his troops at
the marketplace. On the *jisi* day (17), Zisi led the inhabitants of the capital and swore a covenant at the Ancestral Temple. He then pursued the
rebels and burned them all, killing Gongzi Ban[a], Ban's younger brother
Zimang, Ban's son Sunshu, and Zimang's son Sunzhi.

---

288   Jing River 涇水 and Houli 侯麗, both of unknown location, were presumably deep
       in Qin territory.
289   Zi 訾 was located in the domain of Zheng between present-day Xinzheng County
       新鄭縣 and Xuchang City 許昌市, Henan.

13.5　曹人使公子負芻守，使公子欣時逆曹伯之喪。秋，負芻殺其大子而自立也。諸侯乃請討之。晉人以其役之勞，請俟他年。冬，葬曹宣公。既葬，子臧將亡，國人皆將從之。成公乃懼，告罪，且請焉。乃反，而致其邑。

春秋

14.1　十有四年，春，王正月，莒子朱卒。

14.2(1)　夏，衛孫林父自晉歸于衛。

14.3(2)　秋，叔孫僑如如齊逆女。

14.4(3)　鄭公子喜帥師伐許。

14.5(4)　九月，僑如以夫人婦姜氏至自齊。

14.6(5)　冬，十月庚寅，衛侯臧卒。

14.7　秦伯卒。

Jin leaders protect Gongzi Fuchu, a usurper who made himself the ruler of Cao, because of his assistance in the campaign against Qin. Fuchu's brother Gongzi Xinshi protests by trying to leave Cao.

The men of Cao had Gongzi Fuchu guard the domain and sent Gongzi Xinshi to meet the Liege of Cao's funeral cortege. In autumn, Fuchu killed the heir apparent and established himself as ruler. The princes therefore petitioned Jin to chastise him. The leaders of Jin, because of his service in the campaign against Qin, asked to wait till another year. In winter, Lord Xuan of Cao was buried. After he had been buried, Gongzi Xinshi[a] planned to go into exile. The inhabitants of the capital all intended to follow him. Lord Cheng [the usurper Fuchu] thus became fearful, acknowledged his guilt, and moreover implored Gongzi Xinshi to stay. Gongzi Xinshi thus returned and offered his settlement to the lord [to mend their rift].

13.5

LORD CHENG 14 (577 BCE)
ANNALS

In the fourteenth year, in spring, in the royal first month, Zhu, the Master of Ju, died.

14.1

In summer, Sun Linfu of Wei went home from Jin to Wei.

14.2(1)

In autumn, Shusun Qiaoru went to Qi to meet and escort home a bride.[290]

14.3(2)

Gongzi Xi (Zihan) of Zheng led out troops and attacked Xǔ.

14.4(3)

In the ninth month, Qiaoru, bringing our lord's wife, Lady Jiang, arrived from Qi.

14.5(4)

In winter, in the tenth month, on the *gengyin* day (16), Zang, the Prince of Wei, died.

14.6(5)

The Liege of Qin died.

14.7

---

290 The text is referring to a bride for Lord Cheng.

14.1(2)　十四年，春，衛侯如晉，晉侯強見孫林父焉。定公不可。夏，衛侯既歸，晉侯使郤犨送孫林父而見之。衛侯欲辭。定姜曰：「不可。是先君宗卿之嗣也，大國又以為請。不許，將亡。雖惡之，不猶愈於亡乎？君其忍之！安民而宥宗卿，不亦可乎？」衛侯見而復之。

衛侯饗苦成叔，甯惠子相。苦成叔傲。甯子曰：「苦成家其亡乎！古之為享食也，以觀威儀、省禍福也，故《詩》曰：

> 兕觥其觩，
> 旨酒思柔。
> 彼交匪傲，
> 萬福來求。

今夫子傲，取禍之道也。」

14.2(3)　秋，宣伯如齊逆女。稱族，尊君命也。

14.3(4)　八月，鄭子罕伐許，敗焉。戊戌，鄭伯復伐許。庚子，入其郛。許人平以叔申之封。

291　Sun Linfu's father, Sun Liangfu, was a minister during the reign of Lord Mu of Wei, father of Lord Ding. According to *Shiben*, the Sun lineage was descended from Lord Wu of Wei (ZZ-Kong 27.464).

292　Sun Linfu regained his position and the settlement that had supplied his revenue.

293　Xi Chou is called Kucheng Shu 苦成叔 here in the Chinese original. He is also called Kucheng shujia 苦成叔家 in the Kanazawa Bunko version. According to Wang Fu (*Qianfu lun*), Ku 苦 is the same as Xi 郤, the area that supplied revenue for the Xi lineage, and Cheng 成 is the honorific for Xi Chou. Shu is the order of seniority. Another theory is that Kucheng 苦成 was a place in Jin, presumably associated with Xi Chou (Yang, 2:869). There is a brief account of the Xi lineage's downfall among the Shanghai Museum Manuscripts, where Xi Chou is called Gucheng Jiafu 姑成家父 or Kucheng Jiafu 苦成家父 (*Shanghai Bowu guan cang Zhanguo Chu zhushu*, 5:69–78, 239–49) and has a much more positive image than in *Zuozhuan* or *Guoyu*. See Li Long-shien, "Xian Qin chuanben/jianben xushi juyu"; Zhou Fengwu, "Shangbo wu 'Gucheng jiafu' chongbian xinshi."

294　*Maoshi* 215, "Sanghu" 桑扈, 14B.481.

295　The fact that Lord Cheng marries only in the fourteenth year of his reign indicates that he was a small child when he became ruler.

The Wei minister Sun Linfu, who fled to Jin seven years earlier (Cheng 7.6), returns through Jin's intercession and because the Wei ruler's wife, Ding Jiang, urges the Wei ruler to accept the reconciliation. Xi Chou, the Jin minister who accompanies Sun Linfu, behaves arrogantly, and this is taken as another omen of the ruin of the Xi lineage. On Xi Chou's abuse of power, see also Cheng 11.3, 16.6, and 16.11.

In the fourteenth year, in spring, the Prince of Wei went to Jin. The Prince of Jin insisted on having Sun Linfu brought to the Wei ruler for an audience. The Prince of Wei, Lord Ding, refused. In summer, after the Prince of Wei had returned, the Prince of Jin had Xi Chou take Sun Linfu to Wei to seek an audience. The Prince of Wei wanted to decline. His wife, Ding Jiang, said, "This will not do. He is the successor to a hereditary minister of the former lord.[291] Moreover, a great domain is interceding on his behalf. If you refuse, the domain will perish. Even though you hate him, is it not better to bear his presence than to perish? My lord should endure this! To bring peace to the people and to pardon a hereditary minister, is that not the right thing to do?" The Prince of Wei granted him an audience and restored his position.[292]

    The Prince of Wei offered ceremonious toasts for Xi Chou[a],[293] and Ning Zhi[a] acted as the prince's assistant. Xi Chou[a] was arrogant. Ning Zhi[b] said, "Xi Chou[a] and his patrimony will probably perish! The ancients set forth feasts and ceremonious toasts in order to observe the participants' majesty and bearing and to discern disaster or blessings. That is why it says in the *Odes*,

> The rhinoceros drinking horns curve up;
> The fine wine is soothing.
> Neither haughty nor arrogant—
> Myriad blessings come and gather.[294]

Now that fine man is arrogant. This is the way to bring on disaster!"

14.1(2)

In autumn, Shusun Qiaoru[a] went to Qi to meet and escort home a bride.[295] The designation of his lineage honors the ruler's command.

14.2(3)

Zheng victory over Xŭ determines the outcome of a territorial dispute that sparked a conflict ten years earlier (Cheng 4.5).

In the eighth month, Zihan of Zheng attacked Xŭ and was defeated. On the *wuxu* day (23), the Liege of Zheng again attacked Xŭ. On the *gengzi* day (25), Zheng troops breached the outer city walls. The leaders of Xŭ sued for peace by offering the lands that Gongsun Shen[a] had demarcated as Zheng territories.

14.3(4)

14.4(5) 九月，僑如以夫人婦姜氏至自齊。舍族，尊夫人也。故君子曰：「《春秋》之稱，微而顯，志而晦，婉而成章，盡而不汙，懲惡而勸善，非聖人，誰能脩之？」

14.5(6) 衛侯有疾，使孔成子、甯惠子立敬姒之子衎以為大子。冬十月，衛定公卒。夫人姜氏既哭而息，見大子之不哀也，不內酌飲，歎曰：「是夫也，將不唯衛國之敗，其必始於未亡人。烏呼！天禍衛國也夫！吾不獲鱄也使主社稷。」大夫聞之，無不聳懼。孫文子自是不敢舍其重器於衛，盡寘諸戚，而甚善晉大夫。

---

296 In our translation of the word *cheng* 稱 we follow Karlgren (gl. 422), who in turn follows Lin Yaosou. *Cheng* can mean "to name" and may refer to the way Qiaoru is designated by his given name (rather than by his courtesy name "Xuanbo") here. However, in this passage the word seems to have broader implications and extends to the ways whereby the *Annals* articulates judgment by naming people and events in specific ways.

297 We read *wu* 汙 as *kua* 夸 or 誇; see Qian Zhongshu, *Guanzhui bian*, 1:161–66.

The following passage is an oft-quoted panegyric to the Annals, *which is described in terms that might well apply to* Zuozhuan *itself (see also Zhao 31.5). "The sage," commonly understood as Confucius, is said to have shaped it, although elsewhere in Zuozhuan Confucius is never referred to as "the sage."*

In the ninth month, Qiaoru, bringing our lord's wife, Lady Jiang, arrived from Qi. The lineage name of Qiaoru is left out to honor the lord's wife. That is why the noble man said, "Such is the way that the *Annals* articulates judgment:[296] subtle yet pointed, clear yet indirect, restrained yet richly patterned, exhaustive yet not excessive,[297] chastising evil and encouraging goodness.[298] Who but the sage could have shaped it?"

14.4(5)

Ding Jiang, who advised reconciliation with Sun Linfu earlier, again shows her prescience.[299] She predicts doom because the newly bereaved Wei ruler shows no grief. He will be driven into exile by Sun Linfu and Ning Zhi eighteen years later (Xiang 14.4).

The Prince of Wei became very ill. He had Kong Chengzi and Ning Zhi[a] establish Jing Si's[300] son, Kan, as heir apparent. In winter, in the tenth month, Lord Ding of Wei died. His wife, Lady Jiang, was resting after she had wailed, and when she saw that the heir apparent was not grieving, she would not drink so much as a ladle of water but sighed and said, "As for this man—not only will he destroy the domain of Wei, but also he will begin his iniquities with this soon-to-perish widow. Alas! Heaven is bringing disaster upon Wei! What a pity that we could not have Zhuan[301] preside over the altars of the domain!" When the high officers heard this, they were without exception filled with fear and dread. From that time on, Sun Linfu[a] did not dare leave his precious vessels in Wei and placed them all in his lands at Qī.[302] He also maintained very good relations with the high officers of Jin.

14.5(6)

---

298 There are verbal echoes here of *Xunzi* 8.138: "The noble man effaces himself yet manifests his intent, he is subtle yet clear; his words are yielding, yet they prevail" 君子隱而顯, 微而明, 辭讓而勝. The characterization of the *Annals* as "subtle" (*wei* 微) and as "restrained and not quickly grasped" (*yue er busu* 約而不速) in *Xunzi* 1.10 and 1.15 also resonates with this passage.

299 Ding Jiang is included in the chapter "Exemplary Mothers" (Muyi 母儀) in *Lienü zhuan* (1.9–11).

300 Jing Si was Lord Ding's concubine.

301 Zhuan was Kan's younger brother by the same mother.

302 Qī was the land supplying revenue for Sun Linfu. When Sun fled to Jin, Jin had returned Qī to Wei. Lord Ding of Wei restored the land to Sun Linfu upon his reinstatement in Wei.

春秋

15.1 十有五年，春，王二月，葬衛定公。

15.2 三月乙巳，仲嬰齊卒。

15.3(1) 癸丑，公會晉侯、衛侯、鄭伯、曹伯、宋世子成、齊國佐、邾人，同盟于戚。晉侯執曹伯歸于京師。

15.4 公至自會。

15.5(2) 夏，六月，宋公固卒。

15.6(3) 楚子伐鄭。

15.7(4) 秋，八月庚辰，葬宋共公。

15.8(4) 宋華元出奔晉。

15.9(4) 宋華元自晉歸于宋。

15.10(4) 宋殺其大夫山。

15.11(4) 宋魚石出奔楚。

15.12(6) 冬，十有一月，叔孫僑如會晉士燮、齊高無咎、宋華元、衛孫林父、鄭公子鰍、邾人會吳于鍾離。

15.13 許遷于葉。

In the fifteenth year, in spring, in the royal second month, Lord Ding of Wei was buried.

15.1

In the third month, on the *yisi* day (3), Zhong Yingqi died.[303]

15.2

On the *guichou* day (11), our lord met with the Prince of Jin, the Prince of Wei, the Liege of Zheng, the Liege of Cao, the Song heir apparent Cheng, Guo Zuo of Qi, and a Zhu leader, and they swore a covenant together at Qī. The Prince of Jin arrested the Liege of Cao and presented him at the Zhou capital.

15.3(1)

Our lord arrived from the meeting.

15.4

In summer, in the sixth month, Gu, the Duke of Song, died.

15.5(2)

The Master of Chu attacked Zheng.

15.6(3)

In autumn, in the eighth month, on the *gengchen* day (10), Lord Gong of Song was buried.

15.7(4)

Hua Yuan of Song departed and fled to Jin.

15.8(4)

Hua Yuan of Song went home from Jin to Song.

15.9(4)

Song put to death its high officer Shan.

15.10(4)

Yu Shi of Song departed and fled to Chu.

15.11(4)

In winter, in the eleventh month, Shusun Qiaoru met with Shi Xie (Fan Xie) of Jin, Gao Wujiu of Qi, Hua Yuan of Song, Sun Linfu of Wei, Gongzi Qiu of Zheng, and a Zhu leader and then met with Wu at Zhongli.[304]

15.12(6)

Xǔ relocated to She.

15.13

---

303   Zhong Yingqi is the son of Dongmen Xiangzhong and the younger brother of Gong-sun Guifu.

304   The *Gongyang* commentary emphasizes that Wu is mentioned separately to desig-nate Wu as being "external" to the central domains (*wai wu ye* 外吳也) and therefore disparaged as "barbarians" (*yidi* 夷狄).

15.1(3) 十五年，春，會于戚，討曹成公也。執而歸諸京師。書曰「晉侯執曹伯」，不及其民也。凡君不道於其民，諸侯討而執之，則曰：「某人執某侯」，不然則否。

諸侯將見子臧於王而立之。子臧辭曰：「前志有之曰：『聖達節，次守節，下失節。』為君非吾節也。雖不能聖，敢失守乎？」遂逃，奔宋。

15.2(5) 夏，六月，宋共公卒。

15.3(6) 楚將北師，子囊曰：「新與晉盟而背之，無乃不可乎？」子反曰：「敵利則進，何盟之有？」申叔時老矣，在申，聞之，曰：「子反必不免。信以守禮，禮以庇身，信、禮之亡，欲免，得乎？」

楚子侵鄭，及暴隧。遂侵衛，及首止。鄭子罕侵楚，取新石。

欒武子欲報楚。韓獻子曰：「無庸，使重其罪，民將叛之。無民，孰戰？」

305　There are plenty of exceptions to this rule (i.e., a ruler can be "arrested" irrespective of whether he "violated the proper way"), but one other instance of similar usage and presumed logic is found in Xi 28.8.

306　Kong Yingda (ZZ-Kong 27.466) cites sages who, as subjects, accept rulership (e.g., Shun, Yu) and those who started new dynasties (e.g., the founders of Shang and Zhou) as instances of "reaching optimal positions with their principles." But the idea of going beyond fixed rules certainly has broader applications. Whereas "to keep one's principles" (*shoujie*) and "to lose one's principles" (*shijie*) become common idioms, "to reach optimal positions with one's principles" (*dajie*) is not often used. *Da* implies efficacy, flexibility, and expediency and is in many cases associated with the word *quan* 權, which conveys the idea of "weighing options" and which Huang Kan glosses as "going against constancy and yet abiding by the Way" 反常而合於道 (Huang Kan's gloss to *Analects* 9.30). See Qian Zhongshu, *Guanzhui bian*, 1:206–10. Cf. Xuan 4.2, n. 80. Gongzi Xinshi as an example of one "keeping his principles" is mentioned in Xiang 14.2.

307　Baosui 暴隧 is probably the same place as Bao 暴 in *Annals*, Wen.8.5.

308　Xinshi 新石 in Chu was located in Ye County 葉縣, Henan.

309　Chu will have redoubled its guilt by turning against a covenant and driving its people into wars of invasion. This logic of biding one's time and letting an enemy "heighten its errors [or crimes]" appears often in *Zuozhuan* (e.g., Yin 1.4, Xuan 15.2, Zhao 4.1, 11.2).

Gongzi Xinshi, who earlier showed distress at his brother Lord Cheng's usurpation (Cheng 13.5), refuses to be installed as ruler after the princes arrest Lord Cheng and take him to the Zhou capital. The explanation of the wording in the Annals *implies that a ruler who failed his people should be arrested by leaders of other domains.*

In the fifteenth year, in spring, the princes met at Qī: this was to confer about chastising Lord Cheng of Cao. They arrested him and presented him at the Zhou capital. The text says, "The Prince of Jin arrested the Liege of Cao": it was because the punishment did not extend to his people. In all cases when a ruler violated the proper way with his people, and the princes chastised and arrested him, the text would say, "A leader of such and such a domain seized the prince of such and such a domain." If it were not so, no such formulation is used.[305]   15.1(3)

The princes were about to present Gongzi Xinshi[a] to the king and establish him as ruler. Gongzi Xinshi[a] declined, saying, "An ancient record has this to say: 'Sages reach optimal positions with their principles;[306] second to them are those who keep their principles; the lowest are those who lose their principles.' To become the ruler is not my idea of principles. Although I cannot be a sage, dare I fail to keep my principles?" He then escaped and fled to Song.

In summer, in the sixth month, Duke Gong of Song died.   15.2(5)

Chu turns against its covenant with Jin (Cheng 12.4) and invades Zheng and Wei. The Jin minister Han Jue counsels against an immediate military response. Shen Shushi's dire prediction about the Chu commander Zifan is fulfilled the following year (Cheng 16.5).

Chu planned a northward military expedition. Zinang said, "To have newly sworn a covenant with Jin and yet to turn against it, is that not unacceptable?" Zifan said, "We advance when we can press our advantages against the enemy. What difference does a covenant make?" Shen Shushi, already old by then, was living in Shen. He heard of this and said, "Zifan will certainly not escape disaster. Good faith serves to guard ritual propriety; ritual propriety serves to protect one's person. With the loss of good faith and ritual propriety, even if one wants to escape disaster, how will one succeed?"   15.3(6)

The Master of Chu invaded Zheng, advancing as far as Baosui.[307] He thereupon invaded Wei, advancing as far as Shouzhi. Zihan of Zheng invaded Chu and took Xinshi.[308]

Luan Shu[a] wanted retaliation against Chu. Han Jue[a] said, "No need. Let Chu redouble its crimes,[309] and its own people will rebel against it. Without the people, who will do battle for it?"

15.4a(7–11)　秋，八月，葬宋共公。於是華元為右師，魚石為左師，蕩澤為司馬，華喜為司徒，公孫師為司城，向為人為大司寇，鱗朱為少司寇，向帶為大宰，魚府為少宰。蕩澤弱公室，殺公子肥。華元曰：「我為右師，君臣之訓，師所司也。今公室卑，而不能正，吾罪大矣。不能治官，敢賴寵乎？」乃出奔晉。

15.4b　二華，戴族也；司城，莊族也；六官者皆桓族也。魚石將止華元。魚府曰：「右師反，必討，是無桓氏也。」魚石曰：「右師苟獲反，雖許之討，必不敢。且多大功，國人與之，不反，懼桓氏之無祀於宋也。右師討，猶有戌在。桓氏雖亡，必偏。」魚石自止華元于河上。請討，許之，乃反。使華喜、公孫師帥國人攻蕩氏，殺子山。書曰「宋殺其大夫山」，言背其族也。

310　Hua Yuan and Hua Xi were descended from Lord Dai of Song (r. 799–766), Gongsun Shi was descended from Lord Zhuang (r. 710–692), and the other six nobles (Yu Shi, Dang Ze, Xiang Weiren, Lin Zhu, Xiang Dai, and Yu Fu) were descendants of Lord Huan (r. 681–651).

311　Xiang Xu was also of the Huan lineage. Yu Shi surmised that Xiang Xu would not be implicated, perhaps because he was a close associate of Hua Yuan.

Internecine conflicts in Song: Dang Ze of the Huan lineage instigates unrest, and Hua Yuan flees to Jin because of his failure to resolve the conflicts between the ruling house and aristocratic lineages in Song.

In autumn, in the eighth month, Lord Gong of Song was buried. At that time Hua Yuan was minister of the right, Yu Shi was minister of the left, Dang Ze was supervisor of the military, Hua Xi was supervisor of conscripts, Gongsun Shi was supervisor of fortifications, Xiang Weiren was the senior supervisor of corrections, Lin Zhu was the junior supervisor of corrections, Xiang Dai was the senior steward, and Yu Fu was the junior steward. Dang Ze wanted to weaken the lord's house and killed Gongzi Fei. Hua Yuan said, "I am minister of the right. The instruction on proper relations between ruler and subjects is what the minister oversees. Now the lord's house is brought low, and I cannot correct it. My offense is great indeed. When I am unable to fulfill the function of my office, do I dare rely on the lord's favor?" He thus departed and fled to Jin.

15.4a(7–11)

Complex negotiations take place among the Dai, Zhuang, and Huan lineages in Song: leaders of the Huan lineage decide to sacrifice one of their own (Dang Ze) so that stability in Song may be maintained. Hua Yuan of the Dai lineage, who defended Song at critical junctures (Xuan 15.2) and was important in interdomain negotiations (Cheng 11.8, 12.2), returns to Song and puts Dang Ze to death.

The two Huas were of the Dai house, the supervisor of fortifications was of the Zhuang house, and the other six officers were all of the Huan house.[310] Yu Shi planned to stop Hua Yuan from fleeing. Yu Fu said, "Should the minister of the right return, he will certainly chastise Dang Ze and those related to him, and that means there will be no more Huan lineage." Yu Shi said, "Should the minister of the right manage to return, then even if he is given permission to chastise the offenders, he will certainly not dare to do so. Moreover, he has many great accomplishments, and the inhabitants of the capital support him. If he does not come back, I fear the Huan lineage will not maintain its sacrifices in Song. The minister of the right may chastise the offenders, but still Xiang Xu[c] will remain.[311] Even if the Huan lineage is to be destroyed, surely only one branch will suffer." Yu Shi personally stopped Hua Yuan by the banks of the Yellow River. Hua Yuan requested to chastise Dang Ze, Yu Shi allowed it, and he thus returned. He sent Hua Xi and Gongsun Shi to lead the inhabitants of the capital to attack the Dang lineage, and they killed Dang Ze[a]. The text says, "Song put to death its high officer Shan (Dang Ze)": this is to indicate that he had turned against his house.

15.4b

15.4c　魚石、向為人、鱗朱、向帶、魚府出舍於睢上，華元使止之，不可。冬十月，華元自止之，不可，乃反。魚府曰：「今不從，不得入矣。右師視速而言疾，有異志焉。若不我納，今將馳矣。」登丘而望之，則馳。騁而從之。則決睢澨、閉門登陴矣。左師、二司寇、二宰遂出奔楚。華元使向戌為左師、老佐為司馬，樂裔為司寇，以靖國人。

15.5　晉三郤害伯宗，譖而殺之，及欒弗忌。伯州犁奔楚。韓獻子曰：「郤氏其不免乎！善人，天地之紀也，而驟絕之，不亡，何待？」

　　　　　　初，伯宗每朝，其妻必戒之曰：「『盜憎主人，民惡其上。』子好直言，必及於難。」

15.6(12)　十一月，會吳于鍾離，始通吳也。

15.7(13)　許靈公畏偪于鄭，請遷于楚。辛丑，楚公子申遷許于葉。

312　Hua Yuan breaks the dam and uses the water to stop the nobles of the Huan lineage from returning.

313　Versions of this saying are found in *Guoyu*, "Zhou yu 2," 2.82; and *Shuoyuan* 10.338. According to Yang (2:876), this means that Bo Zong, lacking the power and position, should not offer criticism in a forthright manner, just as thieves cannot afford to loathe owners (of wealth) and as commoners must not hate their betters. It is also possible that Bo Zong's wife is comparing him to "owners" or "commoners' betters," whose resources and superior position would incur jealousy and calumny. Cf. the parallel accounts in *Guoyu*, "Jin yu 5," 11.407, and *Lienü zhuan* 3.56–57, in which Bo Zong's wife also suggests that Bo Zong should seek an ally to whom he can entrust his heir. Those accounts end with Bo Zong's heir, Bo Zhouli, being spared because he had been sent to Chu with the help of Bi Yang, another Jin high officer.

314　Zhongli 鍾離 was a small city situated between Chu and Wu. It could still be a sovereign domain, or it might have been annexed by Wu or partitioned by Chu and Wu at this point. Zhongli is identified as a place to the east of present-day Fengyang County 鳳陽縣, Anhui.

315　She 葉 was located in present-day Ye County 葉縣, Henan. Zheng took over the original Xǔ capital and called it "Old Xǔ." From this point, Xǔ becomes Chu's subservient ally.

Hua Yuan half-heartedly invites members of the Huan lineage to return to Song. They end up leaving and fleeing to Chu. Xiang Xu remains as the representative of the Huan lineage in Song government.

Yu Shi, Xiang Weiren, Lin Zhu, Xiang Dai, and Yu Fu left the capital and stayed by the banks of the Sui River. Hua Yuan sent someone to stop them from leaving, but they refused. In winter, in the tenth month, Hua Yuan personally tried to stop them, but they refused. He thus turned back. Yu Fu said, "Now that we have not gone along with him, we will not be able to gain entry! The minister of the right had flitting eyes and hasty words; he had other intentions. If he did not really want to take us in, he will certainly drive off swiftly." They climbed a hill and saw that Hua Yuan was already driving off swiftly. They let their horses gallop to follow Hua Yuan, who was already breaking the dam of the Sui River,[312] closing the city gates, and ascending the parapets. The minister of the left, the two supervisors of corrections, and the two stewards thereupon departed and fled to Chu. Hua Yuan appointed Xiang Xu as minister of the left, Lao Zuo as supervisor of the military, and Yue Yi as supervisor of corrections to calm the inhabitants of the capital.

The Jin minister Bo Zong, known for his sagacity (Xuan 15.2, Cheng 5.2, 6.4), falls victim to the machinations of the Xi lineage (Xi Yi, Xi Chou, Xi Zhi). The foresight of Bo Zong's wife earns her a place in the chapter on "Benevolent Sagacity" (Renzhi 仁智) in Lienü zhuan 3.56–57.

The three Xis of Jin destroyed Bo Zong: they slandered and killed him, implicating Luan Fuji. Bo Zong's son, Bo Zhouli, fled to Chu. Han Jue[a] said, "The Xi lineage will not escape disaster! Good men are the ordering principles of heaven and earth, yet the Xi lineage leaders cut them down again and again. If they do not go into exile, then what else will await them?"

Earlier, whenever Bo Zong had attended court, his wife would always caution him: "'Thieves loathe owners; commoners hate their betters.' Since you, sir, love to speak the truth in a forthright manner, you will certainly be overtaken by disaster."[313]

Wu, first mentioned as a covenant partner for Chu (Xuan 8.3), now extends its ties to the central domains.

In the eleventh month, the lords met with Wu at Zhongli.[314] This was the beginning of relations with Wu.

Xǔ continues to fear Zheng.

Lord Ling of Xǔ, fearing Zheng's oppression, asked Chu's permission to relocate. On the *xinchou* day (3), Gongzi Shen of Chu relocated Xǔ to She.[315]

春秋

16.1　　　十有六年，春，王正月，雨，木冰。

16.2(2)　　夏，四月辛未，滕子卒。

16.3(3)　　鄭公子喜帥師侵宋。

16.4　　　六月丙寅朔，日有食之。

16.5(5)　　晉侯使欒黶來乞師。

16.6(5)　　甲午晦，晉侯及楚子、鄭伯戰于鄢陵。楚子、鄭師敗績。

16.7(5)　　楚殺其大夫公子側。

16.8(6)　　秋，公會晉侯、齊侯、衛侯、宋華元、邾人于沙隨，不見公。

16.9　　　公至自會。

16.10(8)　 公會尹子、晉侯、齊國佐、邾人伐鄭。

16.11(10)　曹伯歸自京師。

16.12(11)　九月，晉人執季孫行父，舍之于苕丘。

16.13(11)　冬，十月乙亥，叔孫僑如出奔齊。

16.14(11)　十有二月，乙丑，季孫行父及晉郤犨盟于扈。

16.15　　　公至自會。

16.16(11)　乙酉，刺公子偃。

In the sixteenth year, in spring, in the royal first month, it rained, and the trees were encrusted with ice.   16.1

In summer, in the fourth month, on the *xinwei* day (5), the Master of Teng died.   16.2(2)

Gongzi Xi (Zihan) of Zheng led out troops and invaded Song.   16.3(3)

In the sixth month, on the *bingyin* day, the first day of the month, there was an eclipse of the sun.[316]   16.4

The Prince of Jin sent Luan Yan to us to plead for troops.   16.5(5)

On the *jiawu* day, the last day of the month, the Prince of Jin did battle with the Master of Chu and the Liege of Zheng at Yanling. The Master of Chu and the Zheng troops were completely defeated.   16.6(5)

Chu put to death its high officer Gongzi Ce (Zifan).   16.7(5)

In autumn, our lord met with the Prince of Jin, the Prince of Qi, the Prince of Wei, Hua Yuan of Song, and a Zhu leader at Shasui, but the Prince of Jin would not have an audience with him.   16.8(6)

Our lord arrived from the meeting.   16.9

Our lord met with the Yin Master, the Prince of Jin, Guo Zuo of Qi, and a Zhu leader and attacked Zheng.   16.10(8)

The Liege of Cao went home from the Zhou capital.   16.11(10)

In the ninth month, Jin leaders arrested Jisun Hangfu (Ji Wenzi) and kept him at Tiaoqiu.   16.12(11)

In winter, in the tenth month, on the *yihai* day (12), Shusun Qiaoru departed and fled to Qi.   16.13(11)

In the twelfth month, on the *yichou* day (3), Jisun Hangfu (Ji Wenzi) and Xi Chou of Jin swore a covenant at Hu.   16.14(11)

Our lord arrived from the meeting.   16.15

On the *yiyou* day (23), Gongzi Yan was cut down.   16.16(11)

---

316   The solar eclipse took place on 9 May 575 BCE.

左傳

16.1 十六年，春，楚子自武城使公子成以汝陰之田求成于鄭。鄭叛晉，子駟從楚子盟于武城。

16.2(2) 夏，四月，滕文公卒。

16.3(3) 鄭子罕伐宋，宋將鉏、樂懼敗諸汋陂。退，舍於夫渠，不儆。鄭人覆之，敗諸汋陵，獲將鉏、樂懼。宋恃勝也。

16.4 衛侯伐鄭，至于鳴雁，為晉故也。

16.5a(5–7) 晉侯將伐鄭。范文子曰：「若逞吾願，諸侯皆叛，晉可以逞。若唯鄭叛，晉國之憂，可立俟也。」欒武子曰：「不可以當吾世而失諸侯，必伐鄭。」乃興師。欒書將中軍，士燮佐之；郤錡將上軍，荀偃佐之；韓厥將下軍，郤至佐新軍。荀罃居守。郤犨如衛，遂如齊，皆乞師焉。欒黶來乞師。孟獻子曰：「晉有勝矣。」戊寅，晉師起。

---

317 Wucheng was located in Nanyang in Henan (see Xi 6.4). Ruyin 汝陰 (meaning "south of the Ru River") was located between Jia 郟 and Ye Counties 葉縣 in Henan.

318 Zhuo Hill 汋陵 was located south of present-day Ningling County 寧陵縣, Henan.

319 Mingyan 鳴雁 was in the domain of Zheng north of present-day Qi County 杞縣, Henan.

320 Whereas Luan Shu fears losing Zheng's allegiance, Fan Xie hopes for their disaffection, for without that outside threat Jin leaders will persist in their errors. The word *cheng* 逞 ("fulfill," "satisfy," "exert"), used twice, thus has very different implications. Yang Shuda argues that the second *cheng* is a loanword for *ting* 綎, meaning "slow" or "relieved" (Yang, 2:880). An alternative is to read *wu* 吾 as "my"—that is, Fan Xie is stating his wish that the lords rebel against Jin: "If my wish is fulfilled, and the princes rebel against Jin, then Jin's hopes for reprieve can be fulfilled." Fan Xie gives a more elaborate account of his reasoning in the analogous passage in *Guoyu*, "Jin yu 6," 12.418–19. That passage presents the annihilation of the Xi lineage and Lord Li's assassination as the direct consequence of Jin victory.

Zheng turns against Jin and sides with Chu when the latter offers territories.

In the sixteenth year, in spring, the Master of Chu, from Wucheng, sent Gongzi Cheng to use the lands of Ruyin to seek an accord with Zheng.[317] Zheng turned against Jin; Zisi of Zheng went to join the Master of Chu and swore a covenant with him at Wucheng.

16.1

In summer, in the fourth month, Lord Wen of Teng died.

16.2(2)

Zheng is emboldened by its alliance with Chu to attack Song, and Song suffers defeat because its commanders are overconfident.

Zihan of Zheng attacked Song. Jiang Chu and Yue Ju of Song defeated Zheng at Zhuo Slope. The Song forces retreated, bivouacked at Fuqu, and posted no guard. The men of Zheng ambushed them, defeated them at Zhuo Hill,[318] and captured Jiang Chu and Yue Ju. This came about because Song counted on its earlier victory.

16.3(3)

Wei, as Jin's ally, attacks Zheng for its alliance with Chu.

The Prince of Wei attacked Zheng and advanced as far as Mingyan.[319] This was for Jin's sake.

16.4

Jin prepares for battle with Chu. Luan Shu, who praised Chu and urged caution during the Bi campaign twenty-two years earlier (Xuan 12.2e), is now eager to fight. Fan Xie is filled with foreboding, and his prediction of internal troubles in Jin will soon be fulfilled after Jin's victory at Yanling. Meng Xianzi's prediction parallels Shen Shushi's below.

The Prince of Jin planned to attack Zheng. Fan Xie[c] said, "If we fulfill our wishes, and the lords all rebel against us, then Jin's hopes for reprieve can be fulfilled.[320] If it is only Zheng that rebels against us, then we will not have to wait long for misfortunes and grief to come to Jin!" Luan Shu[a] said, "We cannot in our generation lose the allegiance of the princes. We must attack Zheng." Jin thus mobilized its troops. Luan Shu was commander of the central army, and Fan Xie[b] assisted him. Xi Yi was commander of the upper army, and Zhonghang Yan[a] assisted him. Han Jue was commander of the lower army, and Xi Zhi was the assistant commander in the new army. Zhi Ying[b] remained to guard the domain. Xi Chou went to Wei and then to Qi, all in order to plead for troops. Luan Yan came to us to plead for troops. Meng Xianzi said, "Jin will have its victory!" On the *wuyin* day (12), Jin troops set out.

16.5a(5–7)

16.5b 鄭人聞有晉師，使告于楚，姚句耳與往。楚子救鄭。司馬將中軍，令尹將左，右尹子辛將右。過申，子反入見申叔時，曰：「師其何如？」

對曰：「德、刑、詳、義、禮、信，戰之器也。德以施惠，刑以正邪，詳以事神，義以建利，禮以順時，信以守物。民生厚而德正，用利而事節，時順而物成，上下和睦，周旋不逆，求無不具，各知其極。故《詩》曰：

立我烝民，
莫匪爾極。

是以神降之福，時無災害，民生敦厖，和同以聽，莫不盡力以從上命，致死以補其闕，此戰之所由克也。今楚內棄其民，而外絕其好；瀆齊盟，而食話言，奸時以動，而疲民以逞。民不知信，進退罪也。人恤所底，其誰致死？子其勉之！吾不復見子矣。」

---

321 *Maoshi* 275, "Si wen" 思文, 19B.721. The "you" in the sacrificial hymn refers to Lord Millet, the Zhou ancestor, who is praised for providing livelihood and moral guidance to the people.

322 This is based on Du Yu's interpretation (*ZZ* 28.473). Lu Can believes that "gap" (*que* 闕) means "the gap in military supplies" (cited in Liu Wenqi, *Chunqiu Zuoshi zhuan jiuzhu shuzheng*, 918).

323 Chu was mobilizing its forces in spring, the time for agricultural labors.

When the leaders of Zheng heard that Jin had mobilized its troops, they sent someone to notify Chu, with Yao Gou'er coming along. The Master of Chu went to the aid of Zheng. The supervisor of the military, Zifan, was commander of the central army; the chief minister, Zichong, was commander of the left army; and the minister of the right, Zixin, was commander of the right army. As they passed through Shen, Zifan entered the city to see Shen Shushi and said, "What do you make of our military expedition?"

He replied, "Virtue, punishment, circumspection, duty, ritual propriety, good faith: these are the instruments of battle. Virtue is for extending beneficence; punishment, for correcting deviance; circumspection, for serving the spirits; duty, for establishing advantage; ritual propriety, for according with the times; good faith, for guarding all things. If the people's livelihood is abundant, then their virtues will be in proper order. If actions bring advantages, then affairs will be regulated. If the right timing is followed, then all things will come to fruition. When those in positions above and below are in harmony, they maneuver in all situations without going against the proper course. Whatever is sought for will already have been prepared, and each will know the apposite standards. That is why it says in the *Odes*,

> You have established our multitudinous people.
> None fails to observe your apposite standards.[321]

In this way, the spirits will bestow blessings upon them, the seasons will pass with no calamity or injury, the people's livelihood will be prosperous and abundant, and in harmonious unity they will heed orders. Without exception, the people will exert themselves to the utmost to follow their superiors' commands, braving death to fill the gap left by the fallen soldiers.[322] This is the course by which victory is achieved in battle. But now Chu has abandoned its people at home and has cut off good relations abroad; it desecrates the covenant made after fasting and purification and eats its own words; it violates the right timing in moving its troops[323] and exhausts the people to fulfill selfish desires. The people do not know what is good faith, and they will be held guilty whether they advance or retreat. When people worry where they will end up, who will brave death to fight? You, sir, should try your best! I will not see you again!"

16.5b

　　　姚句耳先歸，子駟問焉。對曰：「其行速，過險而不整。速則失志，不整，喪列。志失、列喪，將何以戰？楚懼不可用也。」

16.5c　五月，晉師濟河。聞楚師將至，范文子欲反，曰：「我偽逃楚，可以紓憂。夫合諸侯，非吾所能也，以遺能者。我若群臣輯睦以事君，多矣。」武子曰：「不可。」

　　　六月，晉、楚遇於鄢陵。范文子不欲戰。郤至曰：「韓之戰，惠公不振旅；箕之役，先軫不反命；邲之師，荀伯不復從，皆晉之恥也。子亦見先君之事矣。今我辟楚，又益恥也。」

　　　文子曰：「吾先君之亟戰也，有故。秦、狄、齊、楚皆彊，不盡力，子孫將弱。今三彊服矣，敵楚而已。惟聖人能外內無患。自非聖人，外寧必有內憂，盍釋楚以為外懼乎？」

324　According to Yu Yue (cited in Liu Wenqi, *Chunqiu Zuoshi zhuan jiuzhu shuzheng*, 920; Yang, 2:882; Karlgren, gl. 428), the word *wei* 偽 should be read as *wei* 為, meaning "if"—"if we flee the Chu army." If we read *wei* in its usual sense of "pretend," then Jin would appear to be fleeing from Chu when in fact it only wanted to avoid war. The appearance of weakness will presumably stave off unrest in Jin.

Yao Gou'er came back first, and Zisi asked him about Chu. He replied, "They move quickly, and when they pass through dangerous terrain, their ranks are irregular. To move quickly is to lose the will to deliberate; to be irregular is to forgo the order of the ranks. With the will lost and the order forgone, on what grounds are they going to fight? I am afraid Chu will not be of use to us."

Even when Jin and Chu forces meet at Yanling, Fan Xie remains opposed to battle. He emphasizes again that only an external threat can stave off internecine struggles in Jin. However, other Jin commanders, such as Xi Zhi and Luan Shu, are eager to fight.

In the fifth month, Jin troops crossed the Yellow River. When they heard that Chu troops were about to arrive, Fan Xie^c wanted to turn back. He said, "If we flee the Chu army,[324] we can perhaps relieve the cause for grief in our domain. Now, uniting the princes under our leadership is not something we can achieve. We should leave that to abler men. If we ministers can act in concert and harmony when serving our lord, that will be no mean feat." Luan Shu^c said, "That will not do!"

In the sixth month, the Jin and the Chu forces met at Yanling.[325] Fan Xie^c did not want to engage in battle. Xi Zhi said, "At the battle of Han, Lord Hui did not rouse his troops; in the Ji campaign, Xian Zhen did not return to report on his mission; with the troops at Bi, Xun Linfu^c did not persist in confronting the enemy.[326] All of these were to the disgrace of Jin. You too, sir, have seen the achievements of our former rulers. Now if we avoid Chu, it will add to our shame."

Fan Xie^a said, "Our former rulers engaged in battle again and again for a reason. Qin, the Di, Qi, and Chu were all powerful. Had our former rulers not exerted themselves to the utmost, their descendants would have been reduced to weakness. Now three of those powerful enemies have submitted, and Chu remained our sole enemy. Only sages are capable of handling the situation of being without troubles both at home and abroad. And of course we are not sages: with pacification abroad there will certainly be causes for grief at home. Why do we not let Chu go so that it may inspire fear from abroad?"

16.5c

---

325 Yanling 鄢陵 was located in the state of Zheng. It was just north of present-day Yanling in Henan (see map 3).

326 For Lord Hui's defeat at the battle of Han in 645 BCE, see Xi 15.4. Xian Zhen was killed during Jin's Ji campaign against the Di in 627 BCE (Xi 33.6). During the battle of Bi (597 BCE), Xun Linfu could have used the Jin upper army, which remained intact, to continue fighting, but he did not (Xuan 12.2).

甲午晦，楚晨壓晉軍而陳。軍吏患之。范匄趨進，曰：「塞井夷竈，陳於軍中，而疏行首。晉、楚唯天所授，何患焉？」文子執戈逐之，曰：「國之存亡，天也，童子何知焉！」

　　欒書曰：「楚師輕窕，固壘而待之，三日必退。退而擊之，必獲勝焉。」

　　郤至曰：「楚有六間，不可失也。其二卿相惡，王卒以舊，鄭陳而不整，蠻軍而不陳，陳不違晦，在陳而囂，合而加囂。各顧其後，莫有鬭心；舊不必良，以犯天忌，我必克之。」

327　The Chu forces pressed close so quickly that the Jin ranks were not yet formed. Fan Gai is thus urging that battle formations be established within the encampment, and that this could be better accomplished once the encampment ground is leveled, with the wells filled up and the stoves destroyed. The phrase *hangshou* 行首, glossed by Du Yu (*ZZ* 28.475) and Shen Qinhan as "vanguard troops" (Yang, 2:883), is here understood as *xingdao* 行道, following Wang Yinzhi, *Jingyi shuwen*, 699. Wang suggests the same reading of *shou* as *dao* for the term *mengshou* 盟首 (which he reads as *mengdao* 盟道) in Xiang 23.5e.

328　The word *jian* 間 means, literally, "cracks," "interstices," or "space."

329　Zichong will drive Zifan to commit suicide after Chu's defeat at Yanling.

330　The translation here follows Karlgren's gloss (gl. 431) of 以 as 已. Takezoe (13.39) glosses 以 as 用: "the king's personal troops have been drawn from old families." This latter reading is plausible, but the logic of Karlgren's interpretation seems more compelling.

Chu's apparent readiness for battle inspires different responses among Jin commanders. Fan Gai suggests setting up battle formations within the encampment but is silenced by his father, Fan Xie. Luan Shu wants to strengthen fortifications, but Xi Zhi urges a speedy engagement. The different strategic recommendations of Luan Shu and Xi Zhi in part explain the rift between the two (Cheng 17.10; Guoyu, "Jin yu 6").

On the *jiawu* day, the last day of the month, at dawn Chu pressed close   16.5d
to Jin forces and deployed battle formations. The Jin military officers
were alarmed at this. Fan Gai hastened forward with small steps and
said, "Fill in the wells and level the stoves, deploy battle formations here
in the encampment, and open passages for the troops.[327] Whether victory
is handed to Jin or to Chu is for Heaven to decide. What good does it do
to be alarmed at this?" Fan Xie[a] seized a dagger-axe and chased him
away, saying, "The preservation or destruction of the domain is up to
Heaven. What can you, a mere child, know about it!"

Luan Shu said, "The Chu troops are insecure and changeable. Let us
strengthen our fortifications and wait it out; they will certainly retreat
in three days. If we attack as they retreat, we shall certainly achieve
victory."

Xi Zhi said, "Chu leaves for us six openings[328] that we cannot afford
to miss: its two ministers commanding the army, Zifan and Zichong,
hate each other;[329] the king's personal troops have been on the battlefield
for a long time;[330] Zheng's formations are deployed but in a disorderly
fashion; the forces of the Man tribes have joined the army but they do
not keep the battle formations;[331] battle formations are made without
regard for avoiding the last day of the month;[332] its soldiers are raucous
in their battle formations, and even more so as they press forward for
engagement. Each man looks behind him,[333] and none has the will to
fight. Troops that have been on the field for a long time will fail to obey
orders for sure. They have, moreover, flouted Heaven's taboos. We are
certain to overcome them."

---

331   The Man tribes lived in the area south of Chu and served here as supplementary
    troops.
332   There was a taboo at the time against beginning military action on the last day of
    the month.
333   That is, the troops would all look behind for assistance (Karlgren, gl. 432). In *Guoyu*,
    "Jin yu 6," 12.414, we have Xi Zhi predicting that the forces of Zheng, Chu, and Yi
    (the Man tribes) will all hope to escape the brunt of the fighting: "Zheng will look
    to Chu; Chu will look to the Yi."

16.5e　楚子登巢車，以望晉軍。子重使大宰伯州犂侍于王後。

王曰：「騁而左右，何也？」

曰：「召軍吏也。」

「皆聚於中軍矣。」

曰：「合謀也。」

「張幕矣。」

曰：「虔卜於先君也。」

「徹幕矣。」

曰：「將發命也。」

「甚囂，且塵上矣。」

曰：「將塞井夷竈而為行也。」

「皆乘矣，左右執兵而下矣。」

曰：「聽誓也。」

「戰乎？」

曰：「未可知也。」

「乘而左右皆下矣。」

曰：「戰禱也。」

伯州犂以公卒告王。

苗賁皇在晉侯之側，亦以王卒告。

皆曰：「國士在，且厚，不可當也。」

苗賁皇言於晉侯曰：「楚之良，在其中軍王族而已。請分良以擊其左右，而三軍萃於王卒，必大敗之。」

公筮之。史曰：「吉。其卦遇復䷗，曰：『南國蹙，射其元王，中厥目。』國蹙、王傷，不敗何待？」公從之。

334　The towered chariot or *chaoche* 巢車 (literally, "nest chariot") was probably similar to the *louche* 樓車 mentioned in Xuan 15.2.

335　The implication is that Bo Zhouli's vision is blocked (at least partially) by the king, but he has the knowledge to explain what the king sees.

336　This means that the Jin commanders actually act upon Fan Gai's suggestion.

337　"The best man of the domain" refers to Bo Zhouli. Alternatively, we could translate as "men," referring to the many talented persons in Chu.

338　At the time Jin had four armies. Wang Yinzhi (*Jinyi shuwen*, 699–700) believes that *san* is a mistake for 三. Cf. Xiang 26.10c, where Shengzi quotes Fen Huang's speech and also refers to "four armies."

There is a distinct sense of symmetry, shifting perspectives, and cinematic spectacle, first as Bo Zhouli (son of Bo Zong), exiled from Jin, interprets for King Gong of Chu, from a high perch, the meaning of various movements of Jin troops, and then as Fen Huang (son of Dou Jiao), exiled from Chu, strategizes for Lord Li of Jin.

The Master of Chu ascended a towered chariot[334] in order to survey the Jin troops. Zichong sent Bo Zhouli to stand behind the king in attendance.[335]

The Chu king said, "Chariots are racing right and left. Why is that?"

"So as to summon the military officers."

"They are all gathered around the central army!"

"So as to plot their strategy together."

"They are setting up tents!"

"So as to piously divine before the spirit tablets of the former rulers."

"They are taking down the tents!"

"They are about to issue orders."

"It is very noisy; and the dust is also rising."

"They are about to fill in the wells and level the stoves so as to make passages and form their lines."[336]

"Will they fight now?"

"It is impossible to know yet."

"They mounted their chariots, but are all now dismounting right and left."

"They are listening to the oaths of battle."

Bo Zhouli reported to the king about the lord's personal troops.

Fen Huang[a] was at the side of the Prince of Jin and also told the lord about the king's personal troops.

All on the Jin side said, "The best man of the domain is there![337] Further, their force is formidable. We are no match for them."

Fen Huang[a] said to the Prince of Jin, "The finest fighters of Chu are only with the royal soldiers in the central army. I submit that you should separate out your finer fighters and attack from the left and right sides and then concentrate the best of your four armies against the king's personal troops.[338] You are sure to inflict a great defeat on them."

The lord divined about this with milfoil. The scribe said, "Auspicious. The hexagram encountered is 'Return' ☷. It says, 'The domain in the south is in dire straits. Shoot its prime king. Hit his eye.' A domain in dire straits, a king injured: what could they expect but defeat?" The lord acted accordingly.

16.5f　有淖於前，乃皆左右相違於淖。步毅御晉厲公，欒鍼為右。彭名御楚共王，潘黨為右。石首御鄭成公，唐苟為右。

　　　欒、范以其族夾公行。陷於淖。欒書將載晉侯。鍼曰：「書退！國有大任，焉得專之？且侵官，冒也；失官，慢也；離局，姦也。有三罪焉，不可犯也。」乃掀公以出於淖。

16.5g　癸巳，潘尪之黨與養由基蹲甲而射之，徹七札焉。以示王，曰：「君有二臣如此，何憂於戰？」王怒曰：「大辱國！詰朝爾射，死藝。」

　　　呂錡夢射月，中之，退入於泥。占之，曰：「姬姓，日也；異姓，月也，必楚王也。射而中之，退入於泥，亦必死矣。」及戰，射共王中目。王召養由基，與之兩矢，使射呂錡，中項，伏弢。以一矢復命。

339　Here the narrative flashes back to the day before *jiawu* (29).

340　Pan Dang is specified as Pan Wang's son (literally, "Pan Wang's Dang"), perhaps because there was another Pan Dang. There are several references in Warring States and early Han texts to suits of armor made of seven layers of leather. Despite the Chu king's misgivings, Yang Youji's skill in archery will prove useful (Cheng 16.5g, 16.5j).

341　The Jin house has the same clan name as the Zhou royal house, Ji. The diviner claims that the sun symbolizes the ruling houses with the name Ji; while the moon symbolizes ruling houses with other clan names (such as Mi, clan name of the Chu kings).

Lord Li's chariot is mired in a bog, and Luan Qian reprimands his father, Luan Shu, for leaving his post to try to haul the Jin ruler out. His peremptory tone and manner of calling his father by name indicate the primacy of political hierarchy over family hierarchy and also mark the distinction between duty owed the ruler and duty owed the domain.

There was a bog in front of the encampment, and everybody was trying   16.5f
to avoid it by going around to the right or left of it. Xi Yì[a] was driving the
chariot for Lord Li of Jin, and Luan Qian was the spearman on the right.
Peng Ming was driving the chariot for King Gong of Chu, and Pan Dang
was the spearman on the right. Shi Shou was driving the chariot for Lord
Cheng of Zheng, and Tang Gou was the spearman on the right.

Luan Shu and Fan Xie led their lineage troops, flanking the lord on
either side as they proceeded. Lord Li's chariot became mired in a bog.
Luan Shu was about to take the Prince of Jin into his own chariot when
Luan Qian said, "Shu, retreat! The domain has given you a great responsibility as commander, how can you take it all upon yourself? Moreover,
to encroach upon another's office is presumption; to abandon one's own
office is negligence; and to leave one's post is dereliction. In what you are
doing there are these three offenses. You must not be guilty of them!" He
then hauled the lord's chariot out of the bog.

The Chu king regards his warriors' ostentatious display of skill in archery as ill-considered and shameful. Wei Yi, who, despite his valor and courtesy, contributed to Jin's defeat in the battle of Bi (Xuan 12.2g), here fulfills the meaning of an ominous dream.

On the *guisi* day (28),[339] Pan Wang's son, Pan Dang, and Yang Youji   16.5g
heaped up leather for armor and shot at them, penetrating seven layers.[340] They showed the results to the king, saying, "When you have two
subjects like us, my lord, what is there to worry about in battle?" The
king burst out in anger, "You are a great disgrace to our domain! When
you shoot tomorrow morning, your skill in archery will be the death of
you!"

Wei Yi[c] dreamed of shooting at the moon. The arrow hit it, while he
withdrew and sank into mud. He sought divination about this, and the
result said: "The Ji clan is the sun; a different clan, the moon.[341] The moon
must mean the king of Chu. If you shot at him and hit him and then
withdrew and sank into the mud, then you too will certainly die." When
the day of the battle came, Wei Yi shot at King Gong and hit him in the
eye. The king summoned Yang Youji and gave him two arrows and had
him shoot at Wei Yi[c]. He hit Wei Yi in the neck, and the latter slumped
over his quiver. Handing one arrow back to the king, Yang Youji reported
on the discharge of his mission.

16.5h 郤至三遇楚子之卒，見楚子，必下，免冑而趨風。楚子使工尹襄問之以弓，曰：「方事之殷也，有韎韋之跗注，君子也。識見不穀而趨，無乃傷乎？」

　　郤至見客，免冑承命，曰：「君之外臣至從寡君之戎事，以君之靈，間蒙甲冑，不敢拜命。敢告不寧，君命之辱。為事之故，敢肅使者。」三肅使者而退。

16.5i 晉韓厥從鄭伯，其御杜溷羅曰：「速從之！其御屢顧，不在馬，可及也。」韓厥曰：「不可以再辱國君。」乃止。

　　郤至從鄭伯，其右茀翰胡曰：「諜輅之，余從之乘，而俘以下。」郤至曰：「傷國君有刑。」亦止。

342　We understand the expression *qufeng* 趨風 here as *qu jiu xiafeng* 趨就下風. To hasten with small steps (*qu* 趨) is a sign of respect, as in Fan Gai's case earlier (Cheng 16.5d). In *Zhuangzi* 12.243 and *Lüshi chunqiu* 20.1336, the sage-king Yu "hastened with small steps to the subordinate position" (*qu jiu xiafeng*) when he seeks the counsel of a wise man; cf. *Zhuangzi* 11.381, 31.1026. Male and female are said to belong to the "superior position" (*shangfeng* 上風) and "subordinate position" (*xiafeng* 下風) in *Zhuangzi* 14.32 and *Huainanzi* 20.668. In *Sunzi* 12.225, *xiafeng* seems to refer to the less important part of the army.

343　The Chu king is expressing his concern that Xi Zhi might have injured himself by rushing past or that he might have rushed because he had been injured.

344　We read *ning* 寧 as *yin* 懲, meaning "wounded" (*shang* 傷) (Liu Wenqi, *Chunqiu Zuoshi zhuan jiuzhu shuzheng*, 931). Takezoe (13.44) reads *buning* 不寧 as 丕寧 or simply 寧.

345　A deep bow (*bai* 拜) or kneeling and knocking one's head on the ground (*dunshou* 頓首) require bending at the waist. Xi Zhi had armor on, and armored soldiers were supposed to execute short bows (*subai* 肅拜), in which they bent forward slightly and brought their hands together in salutation.

346　Han Jue may be referring to the battle of An, when he caught up with Lord Qing of Qi (Cheng 2.3). Alternatively, he may be referring to the injury that King Gong had already suffered.

Xi Zhi, who visited the Chu court four years earlier (Cheng 12.4), behaves toward King Gong of Chu with exemplary decorum, and this is later used against him (Cheng 17.10a).

Three times Xi Zhi encountered the Master of Chu's personal troops. Whenever he saw the Master of Chu, he invariably dismounted, doffed his helmet, and hastened with small steps to the subordinate position.[342] The Master of Chu sent the deputy for artisans Xiang to salute him with a bow as gift, saying, "Just now when we were in the thick of battle, there was one with brownish-red leather gaiters: he was a noble man. A moment ago he saw me, the deficient one, and made hasty steps. Could he have been injured?"[343]

Xi Zhi received the visitor, doffed his helmet, and accepted the message with these words: "I, Zhi, as your external subject, have followed my own unworthy ruler into battle. With your blessing, my lord, I have participated in the ranks of those donning armor and helmets. I do not dare bow to your command but presume to report that I am not wounded.[344] For the condescension of your command, I will presume to salute your envoy with short bows in view of the business we have at hand."[345] He withdrew after three short bows to the envoy.

Lord Cheng of Zheng is also spared because the Jin commanders Xi Zhi and Han Jue respect the dignity of an enemy ruler. Such generosity, however, can also be faulted as a breach of military discipline (Guoyu, "Zhou yu 2," 2.84). Despite Zheng's defeat, its warriors show valor and resourcefulness.

Han Jue of Jin was pursuing the Liege of Zheng when the driver of his chariot, Du Hunluo, said, "Let us pursue him with all speed! His driver is constantly looking back instead of paying attention to his horses. We can catch up with them." Han Jue said, "I must not for a second time bring shame on the ruler of a domain."[346] They thus gave up the chase.

Xi Zhi was pursuing the Liege of Zheng when his spearman on the right, Fu Hanhu, said, "Let us intercept them with a light chariot.[347] I will catch up with the chariot and board it, then take the Zheng ruler captive and bring him down." Xi Zhi said, "Injuring the ruler of a domain will incur punishment." They also gave up the chase.

---

347 Du Yu (*ZZ* 28.477) glosses *die* 諜 as "light chariot," although the usual meaning of *die* in *Zuozhuan* is "spy." Kong Yingda tries to reconcile the two meanings by claiming that both rely on stealth and speed (ZZ-Kong 28.477). Jiao Xun, citing *Guangya* 廣雅, notes the connection between *die* and *yi* 驛 (posthaste carriage); see Liu Wenqi, *Chunqiu Zuoshi zhuan jiuzhu shuzheng*, 932. Liu Wenqi (932) also points out that the old reading of *lu* 輅 as *ya* 迓 informs Du's gloss of *lu* as "to meet," "to advance," and, by implication, "to intercept."

石首曰：「衛懿公唯不去其旗，是以敗於熒。」乃內旌於弢中。
唐苟謂石首曰：「子在君側，敗者壹大。我不如子，子以君免，我請止。」
乃死。

16.5j 楚師薄於險，叔山冉謂養由基曰：「雖君有命，為國故，子必射。」乃射，
再發，盡殪。叔山冉搏人以投，中車，折軾。晉師乃止。囚楚公子茷。
　　　樂鍼見子重之旌，請曰：「楚人謂夫旌，子重之麾也，彼其子重
也。日臣之使於楚也，子重問晉國之勇，臣對曰：『好以眾整。』曰：『又
何如？』臣對曰：『好以暇。』今兩國治戎，行人不使，不可謂整；臨事而
食言，不可謂暇。請攝飲焉。」公許之。使行人執榼承飲，造于子重，曰：
「寡君乏使，使鍼御持矛，是以不得犒從者，使某攝飲。」子重曰：「夫
子嘗與吾言於楚，必是故也。不亦識乎！」受而飲之，免使者而復鼓。旦
而戰，見星未已。

348　See Min 2.5. Xing is the same as Xing Marsh (239).

349　The "one thing of primary importance" is the safety of the ruler (Gu Yanwu, *Rizhi lu jishi*, 27.623). Tang Gou is saying that Shi Shou is in a better position to protect the Zheng ruler.

350　This is the type of parallelism that prose masters like Fang Bao praise as "mutual illumination" (*xiangying* 相映); see his *Guwen yifa juyao* 1.54.

351　The Chu king must have forbidden Yang Youji to shoot. Recall the king's earlier disapproval when Yang Youji boasted about his skill in archery, although Yang Youji has already shot once at the king's behest.

The Zheng ruler's chariot driver, Shi Shou, said, "It was only because Lord Yi of Wei did not take down his banner that he was defeated at Xing."[348] He thus put the pennant inside his quiver. Tang Gou said to Shi Shou, "You stay by the ruler's side. For those suffering defeat, one thing is of primary importance. I do not compare to you—you take the ruler with you and escape; I beg permission to stay."[349] He then died in battle.

Chu warriors continue with spectacular feats of martial prowess. Luan Qian, Xi Zhi's spearman on the right, displays great courtesy toward the Chu commander Zichong, in part to fulfill his own earlier description of orderliness and leisurely ease in the Jin army. The polite exchange here echoes that between Xi Zhi and the Chu king earlier (16.5h).[350]

16.5j

The Chu army was driven into dangerous terrain. Shushan Ran said to Yang Youji, "Despite the ruler's command,[351] you must shoot for the sake of the domain." He thus shot one and then another arrow, each time killing his man. Shushan Ran seized a captured Jin man and hurled him; the body struck a Jin chariot and broke its crossbar. The Jin army thus halted its advance, having taken Gongzi Pei of Chu captive.

Luan Qian, seeing Zichong's pennant, made this request: "The men of Chu said of this pennant that it is Zichong's flag of command. That man must be Zichong. Formerly, when I was an envoy in Chu, Zichong asked how the valor of Jin men is shown. I submitted, 'We love the orderly arrangement of the troops.' He asked, 'And how is that shown?' I replied, 'We love to calmly take our time.' Now the two domains are engaged in warfare, yet we are not sending an envoy; that cannot be called orderly arrangement. Facing battle, we eat our words; that cannot be called calmly taking our time.[352] I beg permission to send someone in my stead to offer a drink." The lord assented. Luan Qian sent an envoy, holding the wine vessel and offering a drink, to go to Zichong with these words: "Our unworthy ruler, lacking proper envoys, has made Qian bear the spear in attendance. He therefore cannot honor the exertions of your followers in person and has sent me, a nonentity, to offer you a drink in his stead." Zichong said, "That fine man once spoke to me about this in Chu. This must be the reason. Did he then remember?"[353] He received the wine and drank it, and he resumed beating the war drums only after dismissing the envoy. The battle began at dawn and had not ended by the time stars appeared.

---

352   That is, they failed to sustain their claim of love of "orderly arrangement."

353   The translation follows the interpretation of Yang (2:889) and Takezoe (13.37). According to Legge (397) and Watson (136), Zichong is the subject of the "remembering": thus, "Do I not remember?" or "How well I recall it!"

子反命軍吏察夷傷，補卒乘，繕甲兵，展車馬，雞鳴而食，唯命是聽。晉人患之。苗賁皇徇曰：「蒐乘、補卒，秣馬、利兵，修陳、固列，蓐食、申禱，明日復戰！」乃逸楚囚。王聞之，召子反謀。穀陽豎獻飲於子反，子反醉而不能見。王曰：「天敗楚也夫！余不可以待。」乃宵遁。

晉入楚軍，三日穀。范文子立於戎馬之前，曰：「君幼，諸臣不佞，何以及此？君其戒之！《周書》曰：『惟命不于常』，有德之謂。」

楚師還，及瑕，王使謂子反曰：「先大夫之覆師徒者，君不在。子無以為過，不穀之罪也。」子反再拜稽首曰：「君賜臣死，死且不朽。臣之卒實奔，臣之罪也。」

---

354   That is, the lost men are replaced by soldiers from the reserves.

355   We follow Karlgren (gl. 445) and read *zhan* 展 as "inspect" (*Zhouli*-Zheng 19.296). Du Yu (ZZ 28.478) reads *zhan* as *chen* 陳, "array." Jia Kui reads *zhan* as *zheng* 整, "put in order" (Liu Wenqi, *Chunqiu Zuoshi zhuan jiuzhu shuzheng*, 935).

356   For different interpretations of the phrase *rushi* 蓐食, see Wen 7.4 (Yang, 1:560; Takezoe, 8.50), n. 114.

357   Takezoe (13.47) notes that Fen Huang's orders are substantially the same as Zichong's, but his more abrupt syntax conveys a greater sense of urgency. The Chu prisoners were released so that they could spread the word about Jin's preparations for battle.

358   The story of how Zifan's fondness for wine leads to his downfall and how Guyang's loyalty and affection toward Zifan lead to disastrous consequences is told in *Guoyu*, "Chu yu 1," 17.557; *Han Feizi* 10.165, 19.308–9; *Lüshi chunqiu* 15.865; *Huainanzi* 18.593; *Shuoyuan* 10.334; *Shiji* 39.1680, 40.1703. Most of these texts use the story to exemplify how "petty loyalty" (*xiaozhong* 小忠) undermines "great loyalty" (*dazhong* 大忠).

359   Recall that the same thing happened during the Chengpu campaign (Xi 28.3), a fact mentioned in the aftermath of the Bi campaign (Xuan 12.5).

360   *Shangshu*, "Kang gao" 康誥, 14.206. That is, the Mandate to rule depends on the ruler's virtue. This line is also cited in Xiang 23.2; see also Xiang n. 653.

361   Xia was in the small domain of Sui and is mentioned during Chu's invasion of Sui (Huan 6.2). Sui seems to have been annexed by Chu or was under Chu control.

362   The former great officer refers to Cheng Dechen, the Chu commander at the battle of Chengpu in 632 BCE (Xi 28). King Cheng of Chu was not present at that battle, and Cheng Dechen was held responsible for Chu's defeat.

Both Jin and Chu prepare for battle in an expeditious and circumspect fashion. Zifan's inebriation at a critical juncture leads to Chu's defeat. Fan Xie, however, considers Jin's victory ill deserved and a cause for anxiety rather than celebration.

Zifan gave orders to the military officers to attend to the wounded, to replenish the ranks of the infantry and soldiers in chariots,[354] to repair the armor and the weapons, and to inspect[355] the chariots and horses. They were to eat at cockcrow and to abide by none but his commands. The men of Jin were troubled by this. Fen Huang[a] circulated the following order: "Inspect the chariots, replenish the ranks, feed the horses, sharpen the weapons, put in order the battle formations, strengthen your ranks, have a good meal,[356] and repeat the prayer before battle. Tomorrow we fight again!" He thereupon released the Chu prisoners.[357] The Chu king heard about these preparations and summoned Zifan for consultation. Guyang, the young servant to Zifan, had been offering him wine, and Zifan was so drunk that he could not present himself for an audience.[358] The king said, "Heaven is defeating Chu! I cannot afford to wait." He thus escaped with his troops during the night.

Jin entered Chu's encampment and for three days fed on the store of grains there.[359] Fan Xie[c] stood in front of Lord Li's chariot and horses and said, "The ruler is young, and the various subjects are inept—how did we come to this? The ruler should be vigilant! The *Zhou Documents* says, 'It is the Mandate that does not remain constant';[360] this means that only those with virtue can secure it."

In the aftermath of Chu's defeat, the Chu commander Zifan, goaded by the other commander, Zichong, kills himself, fulfilling Qu Wuchen's curse nine years earlier. Then we are presented with a flashback on the role of Jin's allies in this conflict: Lord Cheng of Lu is somewhat tardy in joining Jin forces because he was threatened by his mother, Mu Jiang, and had to make defensive preparations. Mu Jiang might have gained sway in Lu politics because Lord Cheng was so young when he acceded to his position. (Lord Cheng married only two years earlier.)

Chu troops turned back. When they reached Xia,[361] the king sent someone to speak to Zifan, "When a former great officer brought about the army's defeat, the ruler was not present.[362] You, sir, have nothing to blame yourself for. The guilt is mine, the deficient one." Zifan bowed twice, knocking his head to the ground, and said, "If the ruler should grant me the gift of death, I will not perish even in death. It was my troops who fled. The guilt is mine."

子重使謂子反曰：「初隕師徒者，而亦聞之矣。盍圖之！」對曰：
「雖微先大夫有之，大夫命側，側敢不義？側亡君師，敢忘其死？」王使
止之，弗及而卒。

戰之日，齊國佐、高無咎至于師，衛侯出于衛，公出于壞隤。宣伯
通於穆姜，欲去季、孟而取其室。將行，穆姜送公，而使逐二子。公以晉
難告，曰：「請反而聽命。」姜怒，公子偃、公子鉏趨過，指之曰：「女不
可，是皆君也。」公待於壞隤，申宮、儆備、設守，而後行，是以後。使孟
獻子守于公宮。

16.6(8)　秋，會于沙隨，謀伐鄭也。宣伯使告郤犨曰：「魯侯待于壞隤，以待勝者。」
郤犨將新軍，且為公族大夫，以主東諸侯。取貨于宣伯，而訴公于晉
侯。晉侯不見公。

363　Zichong is referring again to Cheng Dechen, who committed suicide after Chu's
defeat at the battle of Chengpu. By thus driving Zifan to do the same, Zichong confirms Xi Zhi's earlier judgments that the two commanders "hate each other."

364　Some other Warring States and Han accounts claim that Zifan was executed (*Han
Feizi* 19.309; *Lüshi chunqiu* 15.865; *Huainanzi* 18.593). In *Shiji* 40.1703 Zifan is shot by
the king; while *Shiji* 39.1680 follows the story in *Zuozhuan*.

365　The Kanazawa Bunko version has 戰之明日, "on the day after the battle"; the
received text in other versions has 戰之日, "on the day of battle."

366　Jin had acted on its own, so it was only on the day of the battle that the Qi army
arrived and that the rulers of Wei and Lu started their march toward Yanling. Huaitui 壞隤 belonged to Lu and was located in present-day Qufu County 曲阜縣,
Shandong.

367　Lord Cheng, obviously disagreeing with his mother, is trying to postpone consideration of the matter.

Zichong sent someone to Zifan with these words, "As for the man who earlier brought defeat to the troops, you too must have heard what happened to him.[363] Why don't you make your own plans?" Zifan replied, "Even had I not had the example of the former high officer, with you, sir, thus commanding me, how dare I act against duty? I have brought about the loss of the ruler's troops—would I dare to forget that I should die?" The king sent an envoy to stop him, but before he reached him, Zifan had died.[364]

On the day of battle,[365] Guo Zuo and Gao Wujiu of Qi reached the Jin troops, the Prince of Wei set out from the Wei capital, and our lord set out from Huaitui.[366] Shusun Qiaoru[a], who had been having a liaison with Mu Jiang, wished to do away with the Ji and Meng lineages and to appropriate their property. When our lord was about to leave, Mu Jiang saw him off and urged that he drive out the heads of the Ji and Meng lineages. Our lord told her about troubles in Jin, saying, "I beg to abide by your command upon my return."[367] Mu Jiang was furious. At that moment Gongzi Yan and Gongzi Chu hastened past with small steps, and she pointed to them, saying, "If you refuse, either of these could be ruler."[368] Our lord waited at Huaitui and left only after having extended the palace's defenses, prepared the fortifications, and appointed sentries. That was why he was late in joining the Jin forces. He had Meng Xianzi keep watch at the lord's palace.[369]

Shusun Qiaoru, the lover of Lord Cheng's mother, Mu Jiang, slanders the Lu ruler to the Jin minister Xi Chou, who convinces the Jin ruler not to grant an audience to the Lu ruler.

In autumn, the lords met at Shasui:[370] this was to plan the attack against Zheng. Shusun Qiaoru[a] sent someone to notify Xi Chou: "The Prince of Lu was waiting at Huaitui to see which side would win." Xi Chou was commander of the new army, and he was also hosting the princes from the east in his capacity as a high officer of ruling lineages. Having taken a bribe from Shusun Qiaoru[a], he accused our lord to the Prince of Jin, who consequently would not have an audience with him.   16.6(8)

---

368   Mu Jiang is threatening to have Lord Cheng deposed and one of his younger brothers (Gongzi Yan or Gongzi Chu) instated in his place if he refuses to drive out Ji Wenzi and Meng Xianzi.

369   Ji Wenzi accompanied Lord Cheng in the expedition to join Jin in attacking Zheng, while Meng Xianzi stayed behind to guard the lord's palace. Lord Cheng's reliance on these two ministers showed that he had no intention of obeying his mother.

370   Shasui 沙隨 was located in the domain of Song north of present-day Ningling County 寧陵縣, Henan.

16.7　曹人請于晉曰：「自我先君宣公即世，國人曰：『若之何？憂猶未弭。』而又討我寡君，以亡曹國社稷之鎮公子，是大泯曹也，先君無乃有罪乎？若有罪，則君列諸會矣。君唯不遺德、刑，以伯諸侯，豈獨遺諸敝邑？敢私布之。」

16.8(10)　七月，公會尹武公及諸侯伐鄭。將行，姜又命公如初。公又申守而行。諸侯之師次于鄭西，我師次于督揚，不敢過鄭。子叔聲伯使叔孫豹請逆于晉師，為食於鄭郊。師逆以至。聲伯四日不食以待之，食使者而後食。

16.9　諸侯遷于制田，知武子佐下軍，以諸侯之師侵陳，至于鳴鹿。遂侵蔡。未反，諸侯遷于潁上。戊午，鄭子罕宵軍之，宋、齊、衛皆失軍。

371　See Cheng 13.5.

372　For Gongzi Xinshi's exile to Song, see Cheng 15.1.

373　According to Du Yu (ZZ 28.479), this refers to the inclusion of Lord Cheng in the meeting at Qī, where he was seized (Cheng 15.1). Takezoe (13.50–51) rightly points out that it would be more logical if the sentence referred to Lord Xuan of Cao's inclusion in the Covenant of Duandao (*Annals*, Xuan 17.6).

374　The precise location of Duyang 督揚 is unknown.

The leaders of Cao petitioned Jin: "Ever since our former ruler Lord Xuan passed away,[371] the inhabitants of the capital have been saying, 'What is to be done? The troubles have not eased.' And you also chastised our unworthy ruler, causing the noble son who would stabilize the altars of the domain in Cao to go into exile.[372] This amounts to putting an end to Cao forever. Could it be that our former ruler was guilty? But if he was guilty, how did it happen that you, my lord, included him in the meeting of princes?[373] It is precisely because you, my lord, do not neglect the principles of virtuous conduct and just punishment that you have become the overlord of the princes. How can it be that it is only with our humble settlement that you neglect these principles? We presume to privately set forth our case."

16.7

Lu ministers try to regain Jin's favor as Lu joins Jin and its allies to attack Zheng.

In the seventh month, our lord met with Yin Duke Wu and the princes and attacked Zheng. When he was about to leave, Mu Jiang[a] gave him the same commands as before. Again our lord set out only after he had made arrangements for extending the defenses of the palace and appointing sentries. The troops of the princes set up camp in the west of Zheng. Not daring to pass through Zheng, our troops set up camp at Duyang.[374] Zishu Shengbo sent Shusun Bao to seek permission from Qi to represent Lu, so that he could petition Jin troops to meet the Lu forces.[375] Shengbo prepared food for Jin troops in the outskirts of the Zheng capital. Jin troops came to meet our troops. Waiting for the Jin troops, Zishu Shengbo[a] had not eaten for four days. It was only after he had fed the Jin envoy that he himself ate.

16.8(10)

The Zheng commander Zihan's surprise attack inflicts losses on the allies.

The princes moved to Zhitian. Zhi Ying[a], acting as assistant commander of the lower army, led the troops of the princes to invade Chen, advancing as far as Minglu. He then invaded Cai.[376] Before he turned back, the princes had moved to the banks of the Ying River. On the *wuwu* day (24), Zihan of Zheng attacked them under the cover of night, and Song, Qi, and Wei all lost troops.[377]

16.9

---

375 Shushu Bao, Shusun Qiaoru's younger brother, was at this point in Qi and might have been accompanying Guo Zuo in the Qi army.

376 Chen and Cai were then subordinate to Chu.

377 Yu Yue (cited in Yang, 2:892) reads *shi qi jun* 失其軍 as "lost their encampment ground," which is also plausible.

16.10(11)　曹人復請于晉。晉侯謂子臧：「反，吾歸而君。」子臧反，曹伯歸。子臧盡致其邑與卿而不出。

16.11a　宣伯使告郤犨曰：「魯之有季、孟，猶晉之有欒、范也，政令於是乎成。
(12–14,16)　今其謀曰：『晉政多門，不可從也。寧事齊、楚，有亡而已，蔑從晉矣。』若欲得志於魯，請止行父而殺之，我斃蔑也，而事晉，蔑有貳矣。魯不貳，小國必睦。不然，歸必叛矣。」九月，晉人執季文子于苕丘。

公還，待于鄆，使子叔聲伯請季孫于晉。郤犨曰：「苟去仲孫蔑，而止季孫行父，吾與子國，親於公室。」

對曰：「僑如之情，子必聞之矣。若去蔑與行父，是大棄魯國，而罪寡君也。若猶不棄，而惠徼周公之福，使寡君得事晉君，則夫二人者，魯國社稷之臣也。若朝亡之，魯必夕亡。以魯之密邇仇讎，亡而為讎，治之何及？」

378　Shusun Qiaoru is here both pointing out a widely shared perception that the powerful lineages in Jin create disunity and instability there and also appealing to Xi Chou's probable jealousy of the dominant Luan and Fan lineages.

379　Tiaoqiu 苕丘 is a place of unknown location.

380　Recall that Zishu Shengbo married his younger half sister to Xi Chou (Cheng 11.3). Xi Chou adopts a conspiratorial tone with his brother-in-law and tries to convince Zishu Shengbo to improve his lot by betraying the Ji and Meng lineages.

381　Shengbo is referring to Shusun Qiaoru's adulterous relations with Mu Jiang and his intrigues against the Ji and Meng lineages.

382　Cf. *Analects* 18.10: a noble man "does not abandon an old associate, unless there is a momentous reason."

383　Shengbo is arguing that if Lu perishes, it will only be absorbed by Qi and Chu, domains that are hostile to Jin.

The Cao noble son Gongzi Xinshi, in self-imposed exile in Song, demonstrates his integrity and disinterestedness once again (see also Cheng 13.5, 15.1) and insists on supporting his brother, Lord Cheng, despite the latter's usurpation. Lord Cheng returns to Cao from Zhou. Gongzi Xinshi is praised as a paragon of integrity in Xinxu 7.216–17 (where he is called Gongzi Xishi).

The leaders of Cao again petitioned Jin. The Prince of Jin said to Gongzi Xinshi[a], "Go back, I will return your ruler." Gongzi Xinshi[a] returned, and the Liege of Cao went home. Gongzi Xinshi[a] surrendered all his settlements and his position as minister to the Cao ruler and did not come out to serve in the government.

16.10(11)

Shusun Qiaoru continues his intrigues against the Ji and Meng lineages by trying to turn Xi Chou against them; in the process he arouses suspicions against the Luan and Fan lineages in Xi Chou. Lord Cheng of Lu sends Zishu Shengbo to counter the charges and suspicions fomented by Shusun Qiaoru. Zishu Shengbo turns down an offer to profit by the fall of the Ji and Meng lineages from Xi Chou (his brother-in-law). The Jin leaders relent.

Shusun Qiaoru[a] sent someone to report to Xi Chou: "Lu has the Ji and Meng lineages, just as Jin has Luan and Fan. It is by them that the orders of government are determined. Now they are plotting thus: 'Jin policies are decided by many noble lineages; Jin is not to be followed. We would rather serve Qi and Chu. Even if we were to perish, so be it: we would not follow Jin.'[378] If you wish to achieve your aims in Lu, permit me to request that you detain Ji Wenzi[c] and put him to death. I will eradicate Meng Xianzi[c], and then we will serve Jin, and Lu will not waver in its allegiance to Jin. If Lu does not waver in its allegiance, other small domains will peacefully submit to Jin for sure. Otherwise, Lu will certainly rebel upon Ji Wenzi's return." In the ninth month, Jin leaders arrested Ji Wenzi at Tiaoqiu.[379]

16.11a
(12–14,16)

Our lord returned and waited at Yun. He sent Zishu Shengbo to petition Jin about Ji Wenzi[b]. Xi Chou said, "If Meng Xianzi[b] is removed and Ji Wenzi[a] is detained, I will let you control the government in Lu and will treat you with greater regard than I treat the Lu Lord's house."[380]

Zishu Shengbo replied, "You must have heard the story about Shusun Qiaoru[c].[381] To remove Meng Xianzi[c] and Ji Wenzi[c] would amount to abandoning Lu completely and laying the blame on our unworthy ruler.[382] If, nevertheless, you do not abandon Lu and, looking to the blessings of the Zhou Duke, allow our unworthy ruler to serve the Jin ruler, then those two men can become the ministers who uphold the altars of the domain in Lu. If they perish in the morning, Lu will certainly perish in the evening. With Lu being in such proximity to domains that are your enemies, its destruction will turn it into enemy territory.[383] How could Jin then save the situation?"

　　　　郤犨曰：「吾為子請邑。」對曰：「嬰齊，魯之常隸也，敢介大國以求厚焉？承寡君之命以請，若得所請，吾子之賜多矣，又何求？」

　　　　范文子謂欒武子曰：「季孫於魯，相二君矣。妾不衣帛，馬不食粟，可不謂忠乎？信讒慝而棄忠良，若諸侯何？子叔嬰齊奉君命無私，謀國家不貳，圖其身不忘其君。若虛其請，是棄善人也。子其圖之！」乃許魯平，赦季孫。

16.11 b(13–15)　冬，十月，出叔孫僑如而盟之。僑如奔齊。十二月，季孫及郤犨盟于扈。歸，刺公子偃。召叔孫豹于齊而立之。

16.11c　齊聲孟子通僑如，使立於高、國之間。僑如曰：「不可以再罪。」奔衛，亦間於卿。

16.12　晉侯使郤至獻楚捷于周，與單襄公語，驟稱其伐。單子語諸大夫曰：「溫季其亡乎！位於七人之下，而求掩其上。怨之所聚，亂之本也。多怨而階亂，何以在位？《夏書》曰：

384　The rulers were Lords Xuan and Cheng. Fan Xie's judgment below is similar to the praise of Ji Wenzi in Xiang 5.10.

385　For Gongzi Yan, a potential rival to Lord Cheng as Lu ruler, see the end of Cheng 16.5.

386　Sheng Meng Zi was a daughter of Song and the mother of Lord Ling. Shusun Qiaoru later married his own daughter to Lord Ling of Qi (Xiang 25.2).

387　Literally, "he was established in the midst of Gao and Guo." The Gao and Guo lineages, both related to the Qi ruling house, took up the positions of hereditary high ministers in Qi.

Xi Chou said, "I can request a settlement for you in Lu." He replied, "I am only a lowly servant in the domain of Lu. Would I dare rely on a great domain to seek rich emolument? I made this petition on the command of our unworthy ruler. If what is requested is granted, then you, sir, will have rewarded me richly. What more can I ask?"

Fan Xie[c] said to Luan Shu[a], "Ji Wenzi[b] has been chief minister for two rulers in Lu.[384] His concubines do not wear silk, and his horses do not eat grain. Can he not be called loyal? If we believe the devious and slanderous and abandon the loyal and good, how are we to deal with the princes? Zishu Shengbo[c] upheld the ruler's command with no wish for private gain and made plans for his domain and patrimony with unwavering allegiance toward Jin. Fending for himself, he did not forget his ruler. If we send him away empty-handed, it will amount to abandoning good men. You should consider this!" Jin thus agreed to peace with Lu and pardoned Ji Wenzi[b].

Shusun Bao becomes the head of the Shusun lineage after the exile of his older brother Shusun Qiaoru. The content of the covenant stating the latter's guilt and the justification of his exile is given later (Xiang 23.5).

In winter, in the tenth month, the leaders of Lu expelled Shusun Qiaoru and swore a covenant against him. Shusun Qiaoru[c] fled to Qi. In the twelfth month, Ji Wenzi[b] and Xi Chou swore a covenant at Hu. On his return, Ji Wenzi cut down Gongzi Yan and summoned Shusun Bao from Qi to establish him as the leader of the Shusun line.[385]

16.11b(13–15)

Shusun Qiaoru retains the rank of minister in Qi and Wei despite his misdemeanors.

Sheng Meng Zi of Qi had a liaison with Shusun Qiaoru[c386] and secured him a position on a par with Gao and Guo.[387] Shusun Qiaoru[c] said, "I cannot offend a second time." He fled to Wei, where he was also included in the ranks of ministers.

16.11c

A Zhou noble predicts doom for Xi Zhi on account of his arrogance and the ill-will he arouses. In the much longer analogous passage in Guoyu, *"Zhou yu 2," 2.80–81, Xi Zhi credits himself with Jin victory at Yanling, and Shan Duke Xiang faults him for "stealing Heaven's accomplishment and making it his own."*

The Prince of Jin sent Xi Zhi to present the spoils of victory over Chu at the Zhou court. As he spoke to Shan Duke Xiang, he repeatedly boasted about his military achievements. Shan Duke Xiang[a] said to the various high officers, "Xi Zhi[a] will surely perish! He was positioned below seven persons, yet he sought to supersede those above him. Where rancor gathers, there lie the origins of disorder. When he arouses so much rancor and opens up a path to disorder, how can he stay in his position? The *Xia Documents* says,

16.12

怨豈在明？
不見是圖。

將慎其細也。今而明之，其可乎？」

春秋

17.1(1)　十有七年，春，衛北宮括帥師侵鄭。

17.2(2)　夏，公會尹子、單子、晉侯、齊侯、宋公、衛侯、曹伯、邾人伐鄭。

17.3(4)　六月乙酉，同盟于柯陵。

17.4　秋，公至自會。

17.5(6)　齊高無咎出奔莒。

17.6　九月辛丑，用郊。

17.7　晉侯使荀罃來乞師。

17.8(7)　冬，公會單子、晉侯、宋公、衛侯、曹伯、齊人、邾人伐鄭。

17.9　十有一月，公至自伐鄭。

17.10(8)　壬申，公孫嬰齊卒于貍脤。

17.11　十有二月丁巳朔，日有食之。

17.12　邾子貜且卒。

17.13(10)　晉殺其大夫郤錡、郤犨、郤至。

17.14(11)　楚人滅舒庸。

When is rancor only out in the open?
What lies invisible is the thing to consider.[388]

This is to caution us about details betraying rancor. Now that he has brought this resentment into the open, is it at all acceptable?"

LORD CHENG 17 (574 BCE)
ANNALS

In the seventeenth year, in spring, Beigong Kuo of Wei led out troops and invaded Zheng.   17.1(1)

In summer, our lord met with the Yin Master, the Shan Master, the Prince of Jin, the Prince of Qi, the Duke of Song, the Prince of Wei, the Liege of Cao, and a Zhu leader and attacked Zheng.   17.2(2)

In the sixth month, on the *yiyou* day (26), they swore a covenant together at Keling.   17.3(4)

In autumn, our lord arrived from the meeting.   17.4

Gao Wujiu of Qi departed and fled to Ju.   17.5(6)

In the ninth month, on the *xinchou* day (13), there was a sacrifice in the outskirts.   17.6

The Prince of Jin sent Xun Ying to us to plead for troops.   17.7

In winter, our lord met with the Shan Master, the Prince of Jin, the Duke of Song, the Prince of Wei, the Liege of Cao, a Qi leader, and a Zhu leader and attacked Zheng.   17.8(7)

In the eleventh month, our lord arrived from the attack on Zheng.   17.9

On the *renshen* day,[389] Gongsun Yingqi (Zishu Shengbo) died at Lishen.   17.10(8)

In the twelfth month, on the *dingsi* day, the first day of the month, there was an eclipse of the sun.[390]   17.11

Jueju, the Master of Zhu, died.   17.12

Jin put to death its high officers Xi Yi, Xi Chou, and Xi Zhi.   17.13(10)

A Chu leader extinguished Shuyong.   17.14(11)

---

388   These lines are incorporated into "Wuzi zhi ge" 五子之歌 (*Shangshu* 7.99–100) in the Ancient Script version of the *Documents*.

389   According to the Lu calendar as we know it, there was no *renshen* day in the eleventh month.

390   This complete solar eclipse took place on 22 October 574 BCE, according to the Gregorian calendar.

左傳

17.1(1) 十七年，春，王正月，鄭子駟侵晉虛、滑。衛北宮括救晉，侵鄭，至于高氏。夏，五月，鄭大子髡頑、侯獳為質於楚，楚公子成、公子寅戍鄭。

17.2(2) 公會尹武公、單襄公及諸侯伐鄭，自戲童至于曲洧。

17.3 晉范文子反自鄢陵，使其祝宗祈死，曰：「君驕侈而克敵，是天益其疾也，難將作矣。愛我者唯祝我，使我速死，無及於難，范氏之福也。」六月戊辰，士燮卒。

17.4(3) 乙酉，同盟于柯陵，尋戚之盟也。

17.5 楚子重救鄭，師于首止。諸侯還。

17.6(5) 齊慶克通于聲孟子，與婦人蒙衣乘輦而入于閎。鮑牽見之，以告國武子。武子召慶克而謂之。慶克久不出，而告夫人曰：「國子謫我。」夫人怒。

　　國子相靈公以會，高、鮑處守。

---

391 Gaoshi 高氏 was located in the southwest of present-day Yu County 禹縣 in Henan.

392 Xitong 戲童, also known simply as Xi 戲, is a mountain in the northeast of present-day Songshan County 嵩山縣, Henan.

393 Keling 柯陵 was in the domain of Zheng and was located north of present-day Linying County 臨潁縣, Henan.

394 Being shrouded in outer clothing (*mengyi* 蒙衣) seems to have been standard practice for women going out. Female disguise is also employed in Xiang 23.3c and Ai 15.5.

　　　　　　　　　　　　　　　　　　　　　　　　　　　Zuo Tradition

Zheng continues to side with Chu against Jin and its allies (Cheng 16.6, 16.8, 16.9).

In the seventeenth year, in spring, in the royal first month, Zisi of Zheng invaded Xu and Hua in Jin. Beigong Kuo of Wei came to the aid of Jin and invaded Zheng, advancing as far as Gaoshi.[391] In summer, in the fifth month, the Zheng heir apparent Kunwan and the Zheng high officer Hou Nou became hostages in Chu. Gongzi Cheng and Gongzi Yin of Chu garrisoned Zheng.

17.1(1)

Our lord met with Yin Duke Wu, Shan Duke Xiang, and the princes and attacked Zheng. Moving from Xitong,[392] they advanced as far as the bend of the Wei River.

17.2(2)

Fan Xie's forebodings about disorder in Jin deepen. His death is presented as self-willed. For a similar act of praying for death, see also Zhao 25.6h.

When Fan Xie[c] returned from Yanling, he had the invocator and ancestral attendant of his lineage pray for his death. He said, "The ruler is arrogant and extravagant, and yet he overcame the enemy: Heaven is adding to his sickness. Disaster is brewing. Let any man who loves me curse me, nothing more, and make me die soon, so that I will not be overtaken by disaster. That will be a blessing for the Fan lineage." In the sixth month, on the *wuchen* day (9), Fan Xie[b] died.

17.3

On the *yiyou* day (26), we swore a covenant together at Keling:[393] this was to renew the covenant at Qī.

17.4(3)

Zichong of Chu went to the aid of Zheng, stationing the army at Shouzhi. The princes turned back.

17.5

The Qi ruler's mother, Sheng Meng Zi, who earlier had a liaison with the exiled Lu minister Shusun Qiaoru (Cheng 16.11), now wreaks havoc in Qi because her new lover, Qing Ke, is reproved by a Qi minister.

Qing Ke of Qi had a liaison with Sheng Meng Zi. Shrouded in a woman's outer clothing[394] and accompanied by women, he rode in a carriage drawn by eunuchs and entered the palace compound by way of an alleyway gate. Bao Qian saw him and told Guo Zuo[b]. Guo Zuo[c] summoned Qing Ke and spoke to him. For a long while Qing Ke did not leave his abode, telling the former lord's wife, Sheng Meng Zi: "Guo Zuo[d] reproved me." She was furious.

17.6(5)

Guo Zuo[d] acted as Lord Ling's assistant at the meeting, while Gao Wujiu[a] and Bao Qian[a] stayed behind on guard.

及還，將至，閉門而索客。孟子訴之曰：「高、鮑將不納君，而立公子角，國子知之。」

秋，七月壬寅，刖鮑牽而逐高無咎。無咎奔莒。高弱以盧叛。齊人來召鮑國而立之。

初，鮑國去鮑氏而來為施孝叔臣。施氏卜宰，匡句須吉。施氏之宰有百室之邑。與匡句須邑，使為宰，以讓鮑國而致邑焉。施孝叔曰：「子實吉。」對曰：「能與忠良，吉孰大焉？」鮑國相施氏忠，故齊人取以為鮑氏後。

仲尼曰：「鮑莊子之知不如葵，葵猶能衛其足。」

17.7(8) 冬，諸侯伐鄭。十月庚午，圍鄭。楚公子申救鄭，師于汝上。十一月，諸侯還。

17.8(10) 初，聲伯夢涉洹，或與己瓊瑰食之，泣而為瓊瑰盈其懷，從而歌之曰：

---

395 Lú was a settlement that belonged to the Gao lineage.

396 Both Takezoe (13.60–61) and Yang (2:899) note that this *kui* is not the sunflower (translated as *kui* in modern Chinese) but an edible vegetable mentioned often in ancient texts. *Kui* leaves were picked carefully so that the roots remained behind to produce more leaves—hence these lines from an ancient poem: "Pick the *kui* without injuring its roots. / Injure its roots and the *kui* will not live" 採葵不傷根, 傷根葵不生. "Not suffering injury in the roots" is here compared to "being able to protect one's feet." For another story on someone who cannot "protect his feet," see Zhuang 16.3.

397 The Huan 洹 River is the present-day Anyang River 安陽河, Henan.

By the time the lord's party had returned and was about to reach the city, the gates were closed and the travelers were being searched. Sheng Meng Zi[a] made accusations to the lord, saying, "Gao Wujiu[a] and Bao Qian[a] meant not to take you in and to establish Gongzi Jiao as ruler instead. Guo Zuo[d] was party to this."

In autumn, in the seventh month, on the *renyin* day (13), Bao Qian's feet were chopped off as punishment and Gao Wujiu was expelled. Gao Wujiu[b] fled to Ju. His son Gao Ruo used Lú as a base for revolt.[395] The leaders of Qi came to Lu to summon Bao Qian's brother Bao Guo and establish him as the head of the Bao lineage.

Bao Guo is chosen to continue the Bao lineage because of his loyal service as Shi Xiaoshu's retainer in Lu. Confucius criticizes Bao Qian for failing to protect himself, using a logic reminiscent of his earler disparagement of Xie Ye's forthright remonstrance (Xuan 9.6).

Earlier, Bao Guo had left the Bao lineage estate to come and serve as Shi Xiaoshu's retainer in Lu. Shi Xiaoshu[a] divined about the choice of steward, and the result was auspicious for the appointment of Kuang Quxu. The steward of the Shi lineage was entitled to a settlement of a hundred households. Kuang Quxu was given the settlement and appointed steward, but he yielded in favor of Bao Guo and also offered him the settlement. Shi Xiaoshu said, "It was you who was the auspicious choice." He replied, "What could be more auspicious than being able to give to the loyal and good?" Bao Guo served loyally as the steward of the Shi lineage; that was why the leaders of Qi chose him as successor of the Bao lineage.

Confucius[c] said, "Bao Qian[b]'s wisdom was not equal to that of a *kui* plant; even a *kui* plant can protect its feet."[396]

In winter, the princes attacked Zheng. In the tenth month, on the *gengwu* day (12), they laid siege to Zheng. Gongzi Shen of Chu came to Zheng's aid, stationing the army by the banks of the Ru River. In the eleventh month, the princes turned back.

17.7(8)

The Lu minister Zishu Shengbo, who bows to expediency (Cheng 11.3) but also upholds the interests of the domain (Cheng 16.8, 16.11), dies while trying to determine the meaning of an ominous dream. For other dreams open to different interpretations or offering misleading clues, see Zuozhuan, Xi 28.3f, Cheng 5.1, Zhao 4.8, 7.3.

Earlier, Zishu Shengbo[a] had dreamed of wading across the Huan River.[397] Someone gave him agate pieces to eat. He wept, and his tears became agate pieces that filled his arms. Following these events he sang this song:

17.8(10)

濟洹之水，
贈我以瓊瑰。
歸乎歸乎，
瓊瑰盈吾懷乎！

懼不敢占也。還自鄭，壬申，至于貍脤而占之，曰：「余恐死，故不敢占也。今眾繁而從余三年矣，無傷也。」言之，之莫而卒。

17.9　齊侯使崔杼為大夫，使慶克佐之，帥師圍盧。國佐從諸侯圍鄭，以難請而歸。遂如盧師，殺慶克，以穀叛。齊侯與之盟于徐關而復之。十二月，盧降。使國勝告難于晉，待命于清。

17.10a(13)　晉厲公侈，多外嬖。反自鄢陵，欲盡去群大夫，而立其左右。胥童以胥克之廢也，怨郤氏，而嬖於厲公。郤錡奪夷陽五田，五亦嬖於厲公。郤犫與長魚矯爭田，執而梏之，與其父母妻子同一轅。既，矯亦嬖於厲公。

<hr>

398　Zishu Shengbo fears that his dream portends death because agate pieces are put in the mouths of the dead. After three years during which the number of his followers grew, he decides that the dream is already fulfilled in the increased number of his supporters (i.e., the agate pieces symbolize his followers). In pursuing this logic, he is trying to control the meaning of his dream. The moment he is confident of mastery, however, destiny mocks him. Once Zishu Shengbo seeks divination, the meaning of his dream as foretelling his death is concretized in words, and it becomes public and inescapable. Cf. Wai-yee Li, "Dreams of Interpretation."

399　There are several places by the name of Qing 清 in *Zuozhuan*. This one probably was in Qi and located in the west of present-day Liaocheng County 聊城縣, Shandong.

I crossed the Huan River,
And someone gave me agate pieces.
Return! Return!
Agate pieces filled my arms!

He was fearful and did not dare to prognosticate about the dream's meaning. Returning from Zheng, he reached Lishen on the *renshen* day and sought prognostication about the dream, saying: "It was because I feared death that I dared not seek prognostication. Now that a growing multitude of people have been following me for three years, there is no harm in prognostication." He spoke about his dream and died by the evening.[398]

Allegations of Guo Zuo's revolt become reality when he joins the disaffected Gao Ruo in Lú and kills Qing Ke. He returns to Qi after swearing a covenant with Lord Ling of Qi.

The Prince of Qi sent Cui Zhu as the high officer in command, with Qing Ke assisting him, to lead troops to lay siege to Lú. Guo Zuo had accompanied the princes in laying siege to Zheng; citing troubles in Qi, he requested to return. He thereupon went to the troops at Lú, killed Qing Ke, and used Gu as a base for revolt. The Prince of Qi swore a covenant with him at Xuguan and reinstated him. In the twelfth month, Lú surrendered. The Qi ruler sent Guo Sheng, Guo Zuo's son, to notify Jin of Qi's troubles and to await Jin's command at Qing.[399]

17.9

Enmity festers between the Xi lineage and the favorites of Lord Li of Jin at court. Calumny from the rival Luan lineage gains ground, and the Jin ruler suspects Xi Zhi of treason.

Lord Li of Jin was extravagant, and he also had many favorites at court.[400] Upon his return from Yanling, he wanted to remove the entire cohort of high officers and to establish the men close to him in the high officers' positions. Xu Tong, who resented the Xi lineage on account of the dismissal of his father, Xu Ke,[401] was favored by Lord Li. Xi Yi forcibly appropriated fields from Yiyang Wu, who was also favored by Lord Li. Xi Chou and Changyu Jiao had a dispute over some fields. Xi Chou arrested and fettered him, binding him and his parents, wife, and children to the shaft of a single carriage. Not long after, Changyu Jiao[a] also gained Lord Li's favor.

17.10a(13)

---

400 Du Yu's (*ZZ* 28.483) gloss of *waibi* 外嬖 as "high officers favored by him" (*aixing dafu* 愛幸大夫) suggests that these might be his male lovers.

401 See Xuan 8.4.

欒書怨郤至，以其不從己而敗楚師也，欲廢之。使楚公子茷告
公曰：「此戰也，郤至實召寡君，以東師之未至也，與軍帥之不具也，曰：
『此必敗，吾因奉孫周以事君。』」公告欒書，書曰：「其有焉。不然，豈
其死之不恤，而受敵使乎？君盍嘗使諸周而察之？」郤至聘于周，欒書
使孫周見之。公使覘之，信。遂怨郤至。

厲公田，與婦人先殺而飲酒，後使大夫殺。郤至奉豕，寺人孟張奪
之，郤至射而殺之。公曰：「季子欺余！」

17.10b 厲公將作難，胥童曰：「必先三郤。族大，多怨。去大族，不逼；敵多怨，
有庸。」

公曰：「然。」郤氏聞之，郤錡欲攻公，曰：「雖死，君必危。」

---

402 Xi Zhi's courtesy toward the Chu king during the battle of Yanling is used against him.

403 Zhouzi (Sun Zhou), later Lord Dao of Jin, was at this point serving Shan Duke Xiang at the court of Zhou. Ever since Lord Xian's time, Jin had made it a policy not to keep the noble sons within the domain; see Xuan 2.4.

404 Takezoe (13.64) and Yang (2:901) gloss 欺 as "defy": "Xi Zhi defied me!" Mengzhang was Lord Li's personal attendant, so for Xi Zhi to kill him without first making a case to Lord Li about it was a sign of defiance. Karlgren (gl. 451) argues that in

Luan Shu, who resented Xi Zhi because the latter did not follow his proposal and yet still defeated the Chu army, wanted to destroy him. He sent Gongzi Pei of Chu to tell the lord: "In that battle, it was Xi Zhi who summoned our unworthy ruler. On the grounds that the armies from the east had not yet arrived and that the ranks of military commanders were not fully staffed, Xi Zhi claimed, 'We are sure to be defeated on this occasion. I will use the opportunity to support Zhouzi[a] as Jin ruler in order to serve you, my lord.'" The lord told Luan Shu about this. Luan Shu[e] said, "There is something to that. Otherwise, why would he have disregarded the danger of death and received the enemy's envoy?[402] Why don't you, my lord, send him as envoy to Zhou and thereby observe his conduct?"[403] Xi Zhi went on an official visit to Zhou, and Luan Shu had Zhouzi[a] give him an audience. The lord sent an agent to spy on him and came to believe the accusations against him. He thereupon resented Xi Zhi.

Lord Li went hunting. Accompanied by his women, he killed the animals first and drank wine, and only then did he allow the high officers to kill the animals. Xi Zhi was holding a boar he had shot when the eunuch Mengzhang snatched it away. Xi Zhi shot and killed him. The lord said, "Xi Zhi[b] deceived me!"[404]

The demise of the Xi lineage, repeatedly predicted in the last few years (Cheng 13.1, 14.1, 15.5, 16.12), is nevertheless presented not as just punishment but rather as private vengeance wrought by the Jin ruler's personal favorites and by rival ministers like Luan Shu. Xi Zhi's dignified refusal to rebel makes the violence against him and his kinsmen seem all the more heinous. In the Shanghai Museum Manuscript, it is Xi Chou who upholds integrity and avows the imperative of martyrdom.

Lord Li was about to instigate a purge of the high officers. Xu Tong said, "You must begin with the three Xis.[405] Their house is large, and they have incurred much rancor. Remove a big house, and the lord's house will not be oppressed; with their enemies harboring so much rancor, it will be easy for us to achieve success."

The lord said, "That is so." The Xi lineage head heard about this. Xi Yi wanted to attack the lord, saying, "Even though we will die, the ruler too will be in peril."

17.10b

---

pre-Han texts the word is used only to mean "deceive." Lord Li is saying that Xi Zhi was the one who snatched Mengzhang's boar (ZZ 28.483), or that Xi Zhi's disrespect shows that he was deceiving Lord Li in his earlier dealings with Chu during the battle of Yanling.

405 Xu Tong is claiming that Lord Li will have to first get rid of Xi Yi, Xi Chou, and Xi Zhi. In the Shanghai Museum Manuscript, it is Luan Shu who "wanted to instigate a purge and to destroy the three Xis."

郤至曰：「人所以立，信、知、勇也。信不叛君，知不害民，勇不作
亂。失茲三者，其誰與我？死而多怨，將安用之？君實有臣而殺之，其謂
君何？我之有罪，吾死後矣。若殺不辜，將失其民，欲安，得乎？待命而
已。受君之祿，是以聚黨。有黨而爭命，罪孰大焉？」

　　壬午，胥童、夷羊五帥甲八百將攻郤氏，長魚矯請無用眾，公使清
沸魋助之。抽戈結衽，而偽訟者。三郤將謀於榭，矯以戈殺駒伯、苦成
叔於其位。溫季曰：「逃威也。」遂趨。矯及諸其車，以戈殺之。皆尸諸
朝。

17.10c　胥童以甲劫欒書、中行偃於朝。矯曰：「不殺二子，憂必及君。」

　　公曰：「一朝而尸三卿，余不忍益也。」

　　對曰：「人將忍君。臣聞：亂在外為姦，在內為軌。御姦以德，御軌
以刑。不施而殺，不可謂德；臣偪而不討，不可謂刑。德、刑不立，姦、
軌並至，臣請行。」遂出奔狄。

406　Xi Zhi is saying that if they are indeed guilty, then the death they deserve is late in
coming. If they are innocent, then Lord Li will imperil his position, even without
the Xi lineage starting an insurrection against him. On the justification of the ruler's
absolute authority, see also Xuan 4.3b, Zhao 4.3e.

407　We follow *Liji*-Zheng 6.120, cited by Shen Qinhan: the word *wei* 威, used interchangeably with wei 畏, refers to death by persecution for those unable to defend
themselves (Liu Wenqi, *Chunqiu Zuoshi zhuan jiuzhu shuzheng*, 961). Xi Zhi had
earlier proclaimed his willingness to accept the command of death, but the assassination and unannounced slaughter did not even have the legitimacy of a formal
command.

408　The place where the corpses of offenders are exposed was determined by rank: the
court for high officers and above, the marketplace for officers and below (see
Shangshu-Zheng 3.44–45; *Zhouli*-Zheng 35.529; *Liji*-Zheng 3.56; *Lunyu*-Zheng
14.129). Ministers and high officers who had their corpses exposed at the marketplace (Xiang 28.11, Zhao 14.7) or the main road (Zhao 2.4) were implicitly demoted
because of their crimes.

　　　　　　　　　　　　　　　　　　　　　　　　　　Zuo Tradition

Xi Zhi said, "A person is established through good faith, wisdom, and valor. Good faith means not revolting against the ruler; wisdom means not harming the people; valor means not stirring up disorder. If we lose these three things, who will be on our side? If we die and incur so much rancor, then what use will it be? It is the ruler who has the authority over his subjects to put them to death; what can be done to the ruler? If we are guilty, then our death is late in coming. If the ruler is killing the innocent, then he will lose the people's support.[406] Even if he wants stability, how can he obtain it? We can only await our command. With the emoluments from the ruler we have gathered followers. What offense could be greater if we keep these followers and then dispute his commands?"

On the *renwu* day (26), Xu Tong and Yiyang Wu[a] were at the head of eight hundred armored soldiers on their way to attack the Xi lineage. Changyu Jiao asked to dispense with the multitude, and the lord sent Qing Feitui to assist him. They drew out dagger-axes and tied their lapels, pretending to be disputers requiring the Xis' mediation. The three Xis were preparing to discuss their case in the chamber on the platform when Changyu Jiao[a] used his dagger-axe to kill Xi Yi[a] and Xi Chou[a] where they were sitting. Xi Zhi[a] said, "I will flee this slaughter of the innocent,"[407] and then ran. Changyu Jiao[a] caught up with his carriage and killed him with the dagger-axe. All their corpses were exposed in the court.[408]

Lord Li's favorite, Changyu Jiao, uses elevated rhetoric to urge Lord Li to ruthlessly eliminate other ministerial lineages. Lord Li recoils from the excessive violence, then falls victim to the ministers he tries to spare. The ministers who do not want to be party to his murder also refuse to intervene. The ruler is compared to an "old ox," a metaphor used earlier in reference to the murder of Lord Ling of Zheng (Xuan 4.2).

Xu Tong led armored men to seize Luan Shu and Zhonghang Yan at court. Changyu Jiao[a] said, "If we do not kill these two, troubles will surely overtake you, my lord." 17.10c

The lord said, "In a single morning the corpses of three ministers have been exposed. I cannot bear to add to that."

Changyu Jiao replied, "Others can bear to act against your lordship. I have heard that disorder outside the court is dereliction, while disorder inside the court is treason. Use virtue to deal with dereliction; use punishment to deal with treason. To kill without bestowing instruction and leniency cannot be called virtue; and to fail to chastise when oppressed by one's subjects cannot be called just punishment. If virtue and just punishment are not established, dereliction and treason will arrive hand in hand. I beg leave to go." He then departed and fled to the Di.

公使辭於二子曰：「寡人有討於郤氏，郤氏既伏其辜矣，大夫無辱，其復職位！」

皆再拜稽首曰：「君討有罪，而免臣於死，君之惠也。二臣雖死，敢忘君德？」乃皆歸。公使胥童為卿。

公遊于匠麗氏，欒書、中行偃遂執公焉。召士匄，士匄辭，召韓厥，韓厥辭，曰：「昔吾畜於趙氏，孟姬之讒，吾能違兵。古人有言曰：『殺老牛莫之敢尸』，而況君乎？二三子不能事君，焉用厥也？」

17.11(14)　舒庸人以楚師之敗也，道吳人圍巢，伐駕，圍釐、虺，遂恃吳而不設備。楚公子橐師襲舒庸，滅之。

17.12(18.1)　閏月乙卯晦，欒書、中行偃殺胥童。民不與郤氏，胥童道君為亂，故皆書曰「晉殺其大夫。」

409　When Zhao Zhuang Ji slandered Zhao Tong and Zhao Kuo, the Luan and Xi lineages joined forces with Lord Jing of Jin to destroy the Zhao lineage. Han Jue, however, refused to participate and also convinced the Jin ruler to allow Zhao Wu to continue the Zhao lineage (Cheng 8.6).

410　People would not dare to preside over the slaying of an old ox because of its service in tilling the land. Gongzi Guisheng cited a similar saying when he protested against the plan to murder Lord Ling of Zheng: "Even with an aging domestic animal, one is reluctant to kill it. How much more so then with the ruler?" (Xuan 4.2).

The lord sent word of apology to the two ministers Luan Shu and Zhonghang Yan: "I, the unworthy one, chastised the Xi lineage, and the Xi lineage had already submitted to their punishment. You, the high officers, should not feel disgraced by your arrest. Resume your positions!"

They both bowed twice with their foreheads touching the ground, "You, my lord, chastised the guilty and absolved us from the punishment of death. This was your beneficence, my lord. Even if we two are to die, how can we forget your virtue?" Both of them then returned home. The lord appointed Xu Tong as a minister.

The lord was rambling on the grounds of the Jiang Li lineage, when Luan Shu and Zhonghang Yan seized him there. They summoned Fan Gai[a] to join them, but Fan Gai[a] declined. They summoned Han Jue, but Han Jue declined with these words, "Formerly I was brought up in the Zhao household. During the troubles brought on by Zhao Zhuang Ji[b]'s slander, I managed to not take up arms.[409] The ancients had this saying, 'No one dares to preside at the slaying of an old ox'—how much less so with a ruler![410] You are the ones who cannot serve the ruler—what use would you have for me?"

The leaders of Shuyong, because of the defeat of Chu troops, led the men of Wu to lay siege to Chao, attack Jia, and lay siege to Li and Hui.[411] They thereupon counted on Wu and did not make any defensive preparations. Gongzi Tuoshi of Chu made a surprise attack on Shuyong and extinguished it.

Internecine conflict in Jin continues.

In the intercalary month, on the *yimao* day (29), the last day of the lunar month, Luan Shu and Zhonghang Yan killed Xu Tong. The people did not support the Xi lineage, and Xu Tong had led the ruler to foment unrest. That was why in both cases the text says, "Jin put to death its high officer."[412]

17.11(14)

17.12(18.1)

---

411 On Chao 巢, see Wen 12.3. Jia 駕 and Li 釐 were probably in present-day Wuwei County 無為縣, Anhui, while Hui 虺 was in nearby present-day Lujiang County 廬江縣, Anhui.

412 This refers to *Annals*, Cheng 17.13, 18.1. The Lu annal uses the Zhou calendar, while the Jin records adhere to the Xia calendar—hence the discrepancy in dating the death of Xu Tong. Du Yu (ZZ 27.485) believes that the *Annals* entry follows the official notification (*cong fu, cong gao*) while the *Zuozhuan* entry pertains to the actual date of the event. For similar examples, see Xi 9.4 and *Annals*, Xi 10.3, 10.4, 11.1, 23.4, and 24.5.

春秋

18.1(17.12)　十有八年，春，王正月，晉殺其大夫胥童。

18.2(1)　庚申，晉弒其君州蒲。

18.3(2)　齊殺其大夫國佐。

18.4(4)　公如晉。

18.5(5)　夏，楚子、鄭伯伐宋。宋魚石復入于彭城。

18.6(6)　公至自晉。

18.7(6)　晉侯使士匄來聘。

18.8(7)　秋，杞伯來朝。

18.9(9)　八月，邾子來朝。

18.10(10)　築鹿囿。

18.11(11)　己丑，公薨于路寢。

18.12(12)　冬，楚人、鄭人侵宋。

18.13(13)　晉侯使士魴來乞師。

18.14(14)　十有二月，仲孫蔑會晉侯、宋公、衛侯、邾子、齊崔杼，同盟于虛杅。

18.15(15)　丁未，葬我君成公。

ANNALS

In the eighteenth year, in spring, in the royal first month, Jin put to death its high officer Xu Tong. — 18.1(17.12)

On the *gengshen* day (5), Jin assassinated its ruler, Zhouman.[413] — 18.2(1)

Qi put to death its high officer Guo Zuo. — 18.3(2)

Our lord went to Jin. — 18.4(4)

In summer, the Master of Chu and the Liege of Zheng attacked Song. Yu Shi of Song again entered Pengcheng. — 18.5(5)

Our lord arrived from Jin. — 18.6(6)

The Prince of Jin sent Shi Gai (Fan Gai) to us on an official visit. — 18.7(6)

In autumn, the Liege of Qǐ came to visit our court. — 18.8(7)

In the eighth month, the Master of Zhu came to visit our court. — 18.9(9)

The Deer Park was built. — 18.10(10)

On the *jichou* day (7), our lord expired in the Grand Chamber. — 18.11(11)

In winter, a Chu leader and a Zheng leader invaded Song. — 18.12(12)

The Prince of Jin sent Shi Fang to us to plead for troops. — 18.13(13)

In the twelfth month, Zhongsun Mie (Meng Xianzi) met with the Prince of Jin, the Duke of Song, the Prince of Wei, the Master of Zhu, and Cui Zhu of Qi, and they swore a covenant together at Xucheng. — 18.14(14)

On the *dingwei* day (26), we buried our ruler, Lord Cheng. — 18.15(15)

---

413 On the variants of Lord Li's name, see n. 217. Du Yu believes that to have "Jin" instead of "Jin ministers" as the subject implies condemnation of the ruler (*ZZ* 28.485). In *Guoyu*, "Lu yu 1," 4.181, the Lu minister Li Ge blames Lord Li for his own assassination.

18.1(2) 十八年，春，王正月庚申，晉欒書、中行偃使程滑弒厲公，葬之于翼東門之外，以車一乘。使荀罃、士魴逆周子于京師而立之，生十四年矣。大夫逆于清原。

周子曰：「孤始願不及此，雖及此，豈非天乎！抑人之求君，使出命也。立而不從，將安用君？二三子用我今日，否亦今日。共而從君，神之所福也。」

對曰：「群臣之願也，敢不唯命是聽？」

庚午，盟而入，館于伯子同氏。辛巳，朝于武宮。逐不臣者七人。周子有兄而無慧，不能辨菽麥，故不可立。

18.2(3) 齊為慶氏之難故，甲申晦，齊侯使士華免以戈殺國佐于內宮之朝。師逃于夫人之宮。

---

414   Lord Li was seized in the twelfth month of the previous year, an intercalary month passed, and he was murdered in the first month of this year. He was thus in captivity for three months, a point that finds collaboration in accounts in *Lüshi chunqiu* 20.1404 and *Huainanzi* 18.591.

415   Yi was the former capital of Jin; see Yin 5.2 (Yang, 1:44). Jin's former rulers were all buried in Jiang. Lord Li's inglorious murder might have meant that he was not to be buried with his ancestors. The use of one carriage to accompany him in burial was also a vastly diminished version of burial rites for princes (ZZ 28.485). "Li" 厲, his posthumous honorific, means "violent" and "murderous."

416   Shi Fang is Fan Hui's son. The trunk lineage of the Shi line has Fan as a power base; hence, it is also called the Fan lineage. Shi Fang belongs to a branch lineage that is put in power in Zhi 彘, and Shi Fang is posthumously honored as Zhi Gongzi.

417   By invoking Heaven, Zhouzi (the future Lord Dao) is saying that he owes his new position not only to the support of those who murdered Lord Li but also to Heaven. In *Guoyu*, "Jin yu 7," 13.429, Lord Dao gives a longer speech and asserts his authority more forcefully.

418   Lord Dao is implicitly announcing his hope of creating greater unity and stability in Jin by transferring power from the great lineages to the lord's house.

419   This could refer to either the men who led Lord Li down the path of disorder, such as Yiyang Wu, or those who were opposed to the new ruler.

420   "The crowd" refers to those present at the scene of the assassination. The event was so unexpected that the crowd dispersed and ran to the palace of the lord's wife, which would have been adjacent to the inner court.

The Jin ministers Luan Shu and Zhonghang Yan send an assassin to murder Lord Li of Jin. A Jin noble son in the Zhou court, Zhouzi, is brought back as the new Jin ruler. Posthumously honored as Lord Dao, the young man shows remarkable skills in negotiating with the ministers implicated in the assassination of his uncle and predecessor. Keenly aware of the weakened state of the ruling house, Lord Dao does not seek to punish the murderers.

In the eighteenth year, in spring, in the royal first month, on the *gengshen* day (5), Luan Shu and Zhonghang Yan of Jin sent Cheng Hua to assassinate Lord Li.[414] They buried him outside the eastern gate of the city of Yi, furnishing his grave with one single carriage.[415] They sent Zhi Ying[b] and Shi Fang[416] to meet Zhouzi at the Zhou capital, escorted him back to Jin, and established him as ruler. He was fourteen years old at this time. The high officers came out to meet him at Qingyuan.

Zhouzi said, "I, the orphaned one, did not at first wish to come to this position. And even if I have now come to this, is it not by the workings of Heaven?[417] Yet men seek a ruler to have him issue commands. If they establish him as a ruler and then do not follow him, what use would they have for a ruler? Today is the day when you, sirs, can use me; it is also the day when you can fail to use me. Those who are respectful and follow the ruler are the ones who receive blessings from the spirits."[418]

They replied, "Such is the wish of your many subjects. How dare we abide by any but your commands!"

On the *gengwu* day (15), Zhouzi entered the capital after swearing a covenant, then lodged at the residence of Bo Zitong. On the *xinsi* day (26), he paid his respects at Lord Wu's temple. He drove away seven who did not conduct themselves like worthy subjects.[419] Zhouzi did have an elder brother, but he was so devoid of intelligence that he could not distinguish beans from wheat. That was why he could not be established as ruler.

18.1(2)

The Qi ruler's reconciliation with Guo Zuo (Cheng 17.9) turns out to be a mere ploy to lure him back to Qi, where Guo Zuo is assassinated. Guo Zuo, despite his accomplishments as a Qi minister and diplomat (Cheng 2.3), is judged negatively in this passage. Qing Feng, from the resurgent Qing lineage, will wreak much havoc in Qi (Xiang 25.2, 27.7, 28.9).

In Qi, because of the troubles with the Qing lineage, the Prince of Qi, on the *jiashen* day, the last day of the month, sent the officer Hua Mian to kill Guo Zuo with a dagger-axe during a court audience in the inner palace. The crowd escaped into the palace of the lord's wife.[420]

18.2(3)

　　書曰「齊殺其大夫國佐」，棄命、專殺、以穀叛故也。使清人殺國勝。國弱來奔。王湫奔萊。慶封為大夫，慶佐為司寇。既，齊侯反國弱，使嗣國氏，禮也。

18.3 二月乙酉朔，晉悼公即位于朝。始命百官，施舍、已責，逮鰥寡，振廢滯，匡乏困，救災患，禁淫慝，薄賦斂，宥罪戾，節器用，時用民，欲無犯時。使魏相、士魴、魏頡、趙武為卿；荀家、荀會、欒魘、韓無忌為公族大夫，使訓卿之子弟共儉孝弟。使士渥濁為大傅，使修范武子之法；右行辛為司空，使修士蒍之法。弁糾御戎，校正屬焉，使訓諸御知義。荀賓為右，司士屬焉，使訓勇力之士時使。卿無共御，立軍尉以攝之。祁奚為中軍尉，羊舌職佐之；魏絳為司馬，張老為候奄。鐸遏寇為上軍尉，籍偃為之司馬，使訓卒乘，親以聽命。程鄭為乘馬御，六騶屬焉，使

421　See Cheng 17.9.

422　Lord Ling of Qi had asked Guo Sheng, Guo Zuo's son, to "await orders at Qing" (Cheng 17.9). Guo Ruo was Guo Sheng's younger brother. Wang Jiao was presumably one of Guo Zuo's associates.

423　Qing Feng was made a high officer (*dafu*), which in Qi seems to have been the equivalent of *qing* (minister) in other domains. Qing Zuo became a supervisor of corrections (*sikou* 司寇), which in other domains held ministerial rank but in Qi indicated a rank below *dafu*; Qing Zuo was promoted to the rank of *dafu* in 552 BCE (Xiang 21.3). Both Qing Feng and Qing Zuo were Qing Ke's sons.

424　According to the *Guoyu* passage cited in Kong Yingda's subcommentary (*ZZ-Kong* 28.486), Lord Dao's accession took place "in the first month, on the *yiyou* day." (The received text [*Guoyu*, "Jin yu 7," 13.432] has "the second month.") It is possible that the first month in the Zhou calendar (used in Lu) corresponded to the second month in the Xia calendar (used in Jin). (There should be a two-month difference between the two calendrical systems, but the intercalary month in the Lu records last year might have fallen in this year in the Xia-Jin calendar.)

425　The same policies are attributed to Lord Wen after he quelled disorder in Jin; see *Lüshi chunqiu* 23.1577.

426　Lü Xiang was the person who delivered the proclamation severing relations with Qin (Cheng 13.3); Shi Fang was Fan Hui's son; Wei Jie was Wei Ke's (Xuan 15.6) son; Zhao Wu was the survivor who continued the Zhao lineage after the persecution of his lineage (Cheng 8.6). Zhao Wu became minister after the death of Lü Xiang. The account here is thus a summary of Lord Dao's entire reign rather than policies and appointments instituted at the beginning of his reign.

427　Han Wuji was Han Jue's eldest son.

428　See Xuan 16.1.

429　Shi Wei, the grandfather of Fan Hui, was Lord Xian's supervisor of works; see Zhuang 26.1.

The text says, "Qi put to death its high officer Guo Zuo": this is because Guo Zuo abandoned the ruler's charge, took it upon himself to kill Qing Ke, and used Gu as a base for revolt.[421] The Qi ruler sent the men of Qing to put to death Guo Sheng. Guo Ruo came to us in flight. Wang Jiao fled to Lai.[422] Qing Feng served as high officer, and Qing Zuo as supervisor of corrections.[423] Later, the Prince of Qi allowed Guo Ruo to return and made him succeed as head of the Guo lineage. This was in accordance with ritual propriety.

The following passage is a stylized, formulaic account enumerating the various judicious deeds and appointments that allow Lord Dao to become overlord and lead Jin to resurgence. The analogous passage in Guoyu *("Jin yu 7," 13.432–35) is much longer: it includes Lord Dao's explanation of how the ministers' merits and virtues justify his appointments.*

In the second month, on the *yiyou* day,[424] the first day of the month, Lord Dao of Jin acceded to his position in court. He began to issue charges to the various officials. He bestowed favors, forgave debts, extended dispensations to widows and widowers, redressed the cause of the worthy ones who had been dismissed or kept back, relieved the needy and deprived, came to the aid of those suffering calamities and troubles, prohibited excesses and wickedness, lightened the burden of service and taxation, showed leniency toward offenders, moderated the use of extravagant vessels, and employed the people at the proper time, endeavoring not to interfere with the seasons.[425] He appointed Lü Xiang[a], Shi Fang, Wei Jie, and Zhao Wu as ministers.[426] He made Xun Jia, Xun Hui, Luan Yan, and Han Wuji[427] high officers of ruling lineages: he had them instruct the sons of ministers in the virtues of respect, frugality, filial piety, and fraternity. He appointed Shi Wozhuo the grand guardian to revive and revise the laws of Fan Hui[i];[428] Jia Xin[a] the supervisor of works to revive and revise the laws of Shi Wei;[429] Luan Jiu[a] the principal chariot driver, with overseers of horses under him, to instruct all the chariot drivers in principles of duty; Xun Bin the attendant on the right, with the supervisors of officers under him, to instruct officers in valor and strength, so that they could be available at the right time. Ministers who served as commanders in battle would no longer have specific chariot drivers; army commandants were established to assume their duties. Qi Xi was made commandant of the central army; Yangshe Zhi assisted him. Wei Jiang became supervisor of the military; Zhang Lao became the leader of scouts. Duo Ekou was made commandant of the upper army, with Ji Yan as his supervisor of the military, to instruct soldiers in the infantry and around chariots to synchronize their march and obey commands. Cheng Zheng was made principal horseman, with the grooms of six stables under him, to instruct all the grooms in ritual propriety. All the

18.3

訓群騶知禮。凡六官之長，皆民譽也。舉不失職，官不易方，爵不踰德，師不陵正，旅不偪師，民無謗言，所以復霸也。

18.4(4)　公如晉，朝嗣君也。

18.5(5)　夏，六月，鄭伯侵宋，及曹門外。遂會楚子伐宋，取朝郟。楚子辛、鄭皇辰侵城郜，取幽丘。同伐彭城，納宋魚石、向為人、鱗朱、向帶、魚府焉，以三百乘戍之而還。

　　　　書曰「復入」。凡去其國，國逆而立之，曰「入」；復其位，曰「復歸」；諸侯納之，曰「歸」；以惡曰「復入」。

　　　　宋人患之。西鉏吾曰：「何也？若楚人與吾同惡，以德於我，吾固事之也，不敢貳矣。大國無厭，鄙我猶憾。不然，而收吾憎，使贊其政，以間吾釁，亦吾患也。今將崇諸侯之姦而披其地，以塞夷庚。逞姦而攜服，毒諸侯而懼吳、晉，吾庸多矣，非吾憂也。且事晉何為？晉必恤之。」

430　Chaojia 朝郟 was located near present-day Luyi County 鹿邑縣, Henan.

431　Both Chenggao 城郜 and Youqiu 幽丘 were probably located in present-day Xiao County 蕭縣, Anhui.

432　This refers to two branches of the army: one headed by Lord Cheng of Zheng and King Gong of Chu, the other headed by Zixin and Huang Chen.

433　These Song noblemen fled to Chu in 576 BCE (Cheng 15.4).

434　There are many exceptions to these enumerated "rules" in the *Annals*.

435　Chu installed the exiled Song nobles in Pengcheng (see map 2), which was on the main routes of communication between various domains.

　　　　　　　　　　　　　　　　　　　　　Zuo Tradition

leaders of the six departments were men praised by the people. Those raised to various positions were not remiss in fulfilling their duties; officials did not alter the normative rules and received statutes; the ranks received did not exceed the recipients' virtues. High officials did not challenge the authority of the highest chief officials; officials did not infringe upon the authority of high officials. Among the people there were no words of dissatisfaction or slander. That was how Jin regained the position of overlord.

Our lord went to Jin: this was to visit the court of the ruler who had just succeeded to his position.   18.4(4)

Zheng and Chu invade Song and end up installing Song noblemen of the Huan lineage who were exiled because of intrigues against the Dai lineage (Cheng 15.4). Song looks to Jin for support.

In summer, in the sixth month, the Liege of Zheng invaded Song, advancing as far the area outside the Cao Gate. He then joined the Master of Chu in attacking Song, taking Chaojia.[430] Zixin of Chu and Huang Chen of Zheng invaded Chenggao and took Youqiu.[431] Together they[432] attacked Pengcheng and installed Yu Shi, Xiang Weiren, Lin Zhu, Xiang Dai, and Yu Fu in Song.[433] They returned only after using three hundred chariots to garrison their gains.   18.5(5)

The text says, "again entered." In all cases concerning persons who left their domains, if the leaders of their domains escorted them in and established them, the text says, "entered." If their positions were restored, the text says, "again returned." If the princes installed them, the text says, "returned." If the princes did so by force and violence, the text says, "again entered."[434]

The men of Song were troubled by this. Xichu Wu said, "What now? Had the men of Chu shared our worries and showed us virtuous consideration, we would of course have served them, and we would not have dared to shift our allegiance. But that great domain is insatiable; even if it were to turn our domain into its borderland, it would still not be satisfied. Even had Chu not done all that, had it taken in those whom we abhor and let them assist in its government, so as to spy out opportunities to attack us, it would mean affliction for us. But now Chu intends to raise up the miscreants from the princes' realms, whose land is partitioned for these malefactors, thereby blocking the level roads for carriages and horses.[435] Chu has given satisfaction to those miscreants and alienated those who had submitted to them; it has poisoned the realms of princes and instilled fear in Wu and Jin. All these will benefit us greatly and should not trouble us. Besides, to what end have we served Jin? Jin will surely show sympathetic concern for us."

18.6(6, 7)　公至自晉。晉范宣子來聘，且拜朝也。君子謂晉於是乎有禮。

18.7(8)　秋，杞桓公來朝，勞公，且問晉故。公以晉君語之。杞伯於是驟朝于晉而請為昏。

18.8　七月，宋老佐、華喜圍彭城，老佐卒焉。

18.9(9)　八月，邾宣公來朝，即位而來見也。

18.10(10)　築鹿囿，書不時也。

18.11(11)　己丑，公薨于路寢，言道也。

18.12(12)　冬，十一月，楚子重救彭城，伐宋。宋華元如晉告急。韓獻子為政，曰：「欲求得人，必先勤之。成霸、安彊，自宋始矣。」晉侯師于台谷以救宋。遇楚師于靡角之谷，楚師還。

18.13(13)　晉士魴來乞師。季文子問師數於臧武仲，對曰：「伐鄭之役，知伯實來，下軍之佐也。今彘季亦佐下軍，如伐鄭可也。事大國，無失班爵而加敬焉，禮也。」從之。

436　That is, Lord Cheng died where he should have died; see also *Annals*, Zhuang 32.4.

437　The location of Taigu 台谷 and the Valley of Mijiao 靡角之谷 are unknown. The latter, however, should be in the vicinity of Pengcheng (Yang, 2:913).

438　In a long speech explaining how "Chu talents have been employed by Jin," Shengzi claims that the Chu army was defeated at Valley of Mijiao because Jin followed the plan offered by Yongzi, a Chu nobleman who had fled to Jin (Xiang 26.10).

439　See *Annals*, Cheng 17.7.

Our lord arrived from Jin. Fan Gai[c] of Jin came on an official visit and also to thank Lu for visiting its court. The noble man said that Jin in this situation showed ritual propriety.

In autumn, Lord Huan of Qí came to visit our court: this was to honor our lord's exertions and also to inquire about Jin. Our lord told him about the Jin ruler. For this reason, the Liege of Qí rushed to visit the Jin court and requested a marriage alliance with Jin.

In the seventh month, Lao Zuo and Hua Xi of Song laid siege to Pengcheng. Lao Zuo died there.

In the eighth month, Lord Xuan of Zhu came to visit our court. He came for an audience upon acceding to his position.

The Deer Park was built: this was recorded because it was not the proper season.

On the *jichou* day (7), our lord expired in the Grand Chamber: this is to say that it was proper.[436]

Jin reasserts itself and fights Chu on behalf of Song.

In winter, in the eleventh month, Zichong of Chu went to the aid of Pengcheng and attacked Song. Hua Yuan of Song went to Jin to announce the urgent situation. Han Jue[a], who was in charge of policies, said, "If we want to obtain the support of others, we must first exert ourselves on their behalf. Establishing ourselves as overlord and reining in a powerful rival will begin with Song." The Prince of Jin stationed troops at Taigu to go to the aid of Song. They encountered Chu troops at the Valley of Mijiao.[437] Chu troops turned back.[438]

The Lu minister Zang Wuzhong explains that the rank and title of an envoy seeking military assistance determine how his mission will be fulfilled. On how ranks have to be considered in tandem with the size of a domain in considering ritual protocol, see also Cheng 3.7.

Shi Fang of Jin came to us to plead for troops. Ji Wenzi asked Zang Wuzhong about the size of the troops to be sent to assist Jin. He replied, "For the campaign to attack Zheng, it was Zhi Ying[c] who came, and he was the assistant commander of the lower army. Now Shi Fang[a] is also assistant commander of the lower army.[439] We can send the same number of troops as in the attack against Zheng. In serving a great domain, we should not go against the rank and title of the envoy and, therefore, have to redouble our respect. This is in accordance with ritual propriety." Ji Wenzi followed his advice.

 十二月，孟獻子會于虛杅，謀救宋也。宋人辭諸侯而請師以圍彭城。孟獻子請于諸侯而先歸會葬。

 丁未，葬我君成公，書，順也。

In the twelfth month, Meng Xianzi met with the other leaders at Xu-   18.14(14)
ding[440] and conferred about going to the aid of Song. The leaders of Song
declined their offer and requested troops for laying siege to Pengcheng.
Meng Xianzi obtained permission from the princes to return first for
Lord Cheng's funeral.

On the *dingwei* day (26), we buried our ruler, Lord Cheng: this was   18.15(15)
recorded to show that it was properly done.

---

440   The location of Xuding 虛打 is unknown.

襄公

Lord Xiang
(572–542 BCE)

The previous section ends with the assassination of Lord Li of Jin and a laudatory account of how the judicious appointments made by the new Jin ruler, the fourteen-year-old Lord Dao (r. 573–558), allow him to regain the status of overlord. The first half of the period covered here can be read as an account of Jin resurgence. Unlike earlier Jin overlords who sought legitimation through Zhou blessings (Lord Wen in Xi 28.3h, 28.9; Lord Xiang in Wen 1.5), Lord Dao focuses on achieving peace with the Rong tribes, which according to his adviser Wei Jiang will result in the princes being "awed into submission" (Xiang 4.7). In a reversal of a covenant chief's supposed duty to defend the Zhou house and fend off the barbarians, Jin arrests a Zhou envoy seeking Jin help against Rong incursions (Xiang 5.2). The exchange between Lord Dao and Wei Jiang on the symbolic power of music implies that the most visible token of Jin's achievement as covenant chief is the gift of chariots, musicians, and sets of bells and chime-stones that Zheng offers to Jin (Xiang 11.5). In fact, Zheng's submission during these years is at best intermittent, and Zheng remains torn between Chu and Jin in various policy debates (Xiang 2.5, 8.7, 9.8, 11.2). Zheng and Jin publicly argue over the terms of Zheng allegiance during the swearing of a covenant oath (Xiang 9.5), and at one point Jin gives up the siege of Zheng as the Jin minister Zhi Ying acknowledges that Jin has no right to punish Zheng, since it "can neither stop Chu nor protect Zheng" (Xiang 10.11).

Lu and Song remain loyal Jin allies, although Jin needs to confirm Song allegiance through the gift of the settlement of Biyang (Xiang 10.2). Qi reluctantly complies with Jin pressure (Xiang 3.3), while Wu defies Jin outright (Xiang 3.5). Even temporary sway over Chen, a Chu ally, arouses anxiety among Jin ministers (Xiang 4.1, 5.9). A Qin-Chu coalition invades Jin and meets with little resistance (Xiang 9.4). In retaliation for its defeat by Qin at Li (Xiang 11.6), Jin leads its allies in a disastrous

"Campaign of Changes and Procrastinations" (Xiang 14.3). Jin military operations during these years are characterized by indecisiveness and contention among its leaders and merely half-hearted support from its allies (Xiang 9.5, 10.2, 10.11, 14.3). Juxtaposed with these signs of weakness and division are categorical descriptions of good government in Jin and of its leaders' virtues (Xiang 9.4, 9.9, 13.3). The idea of Jin resurgence seems to be an attempt on the part of the *Zuozhuan* compiler (or one of its compilers) to wrest moments of triumph from a mixed record.

Toward the end of Lord Dao's reign, Jin faces a new challenge with Qi disaffection (Xiang 14.10). Lord Ling of Qi (r. 581–554), though mocked for cowardice (Xiang 18.3), extinguishes the small domain of Lai to its east (Xiang 6.7) and also pursues an aggressive policy against Jin's ally Lu (Xiang 15.5, 16.4, 17.3, 18.3). Jin's campaign against Qi attains high drama when its commander Zhonghang Yan dreams of disputing a court case with, and being decapitated by, Lord Li of Jin (Xiang 18.3), whom he had murdered eighteen years earlier (Cheng 18.1). The meanings of the dream are fulfilled in the Jin victory at Pingyin (Xiang 18.3) and Zhonghang Yan's own death (Xiang 19.1). Qi-Jin conflicts continue despite peace agreements (Xiang 19.12, 20.2), and Qi offers refuge to Luan Ying and his followers, who are persecuted by the Fan lineage in Jin (Xiang 21.8, 22.3). Relations deteriorate further after Qi attacks Wei and Jin (Xiang 23.4) and moves toward an alliance with Chu (Xiang 24.5, 24.8). It is only with the assassination of Lord Zhuang of Qi, who was largely responsible for Qi's aggression against Jin, that Qi and Jin achieve a more lasting peace (Xiang 25.3).

By this time there is also a more comprehensive effort to halt military conflict between Jin and Chu and their respective allies. First mentioned by the Jin minister Zhao Wu (Xiang 25.7) and noted by the Zheng minister Zichan (Xiang 26.11) as a possible development, these peace negotiations are initiated by the Song minister Xiang Xu (Xiang 27.4), who seems to be repeating the efforts at mediation of another Song minister, Hua Yuan, more than thirty years earlier (Cheng 11.8, 12.2). Throughout the period covered here, Jin's main rival remains Chu, which continues intermittent campaigns against Song (Xiang 1.3, 10.3, 12.4), Zheng (Xiang 2.1, 2.5, 8.7, 9.8, 11.4, 18.4, 24.8, 26.11), Chen (Xiang 3.8, 4.2, 7.8), and Lu (Xiang 10.6) in its bid to expand its power and influence. Jin cultivates an alliance with Wu (Cheng 15.6; Xiang 5.5, 5.8, 10.1), because Wu poses a new threat to Chu (Xiang 3.1, 13.5, 14.7, 24.4). Chu commanders collapse in exhaustion as they "rush about trying to fulfill commands," as Qu Wuchen predicted in his vow of vengeance (Cheng 7.5).

By the time Xiang Xu mediates the accord between Jin and Chu, both sides see gains in the cessation of conflict. From the beginning, the peace process is marred, however, by Xiang Xu's self-interest (Xiang 27.4a, 27.6) and by the mutual suspicions of Jin and Chu. The Chu minister Qu Jian's readiness to outmaneuver Jin by deception and his insistence on Chu

precedence in swearing the Covenant of Song mean that the laudable goal of halting conflict merely provides some cover for Jin decline (Xiang 27.4c). Jin is praised for its good faith (Xiang 27.4d), almost as apology for yielding to Chu the position of de facto covenant chief, a status that will become evident in the gatherings of princes in the beginning of the next section (Zhao 1.1, 1.2, 1.3, 4.1). Confucius is said to consider the Covenant of Song an occasion "replete with finely patterned arguments" (Xiang 27.4b), a statement that seems to convey implicit criticism. Indeed, the covenant does not lead to lasting peace and brings no tangible benefits. It only heightens the burden of court visits and offerings for the smaller domains, which are now required also to attend the courts of their respective leaders' rivals (Xiang 28.2, 28.8, 28.12, 29.1, 29.3). Song, the domain that hosts the covenant, obtains no relief in the wake of its disastrous fire despite the pledges made to it by other domains (Xiang 30.12). Jin decline finds a palpable symbol in its chief minister, Zhao Wu: for all his cultural competence, his words are "torpid" (Xiang 31.1). Lord Ping of Jin (r. 557–532), who succeeds Lord Dao, also provokes widespread disaffection by forcing his allies to fortify and to return land to Qi (Xiang 29.8, 29.11), the natal domain of Lord Ping's mother.

In domestic affairs in many domains, the pattern of weak rulers and powerful ministers continues. Lord Xiang of Lu was only four years old when he acceded to his position, and during his reign Lu government was effectively in the hands of the Jisun (Ji) lineage and, to a lesser extent, the Zhongsun (Meng) and Shusun lineages. Ji Wenzi, head of the Jisun lineage, is vindictive toward Lord Xiang's grandmother Mu Jiang (Xiang 2.3)[1] and dismissive toward his birth mother, Ding Si (Xiang 4.4)—for all that he is fervently praised for his integrity and loyalty when he dies (Xiang 5.10). Under his son Ji Wuzi, the shift of power from the Lu ruling house to the Jisun, Zhongsun, and Shusun lineages is formalized in the reorganization of the Lu armies (Xiang 11.1). Ji Wuzi continues to aggrandize his lineage (Xiang 7.3, 29.4), so much so that Lord Xiang, returning from a diplomatic mission, wonders whether he should reenter Lu at all (Xiang 29.4), and he lacks even the archers to provide entertainment at an official feast (Xiang 29.10). Attending court in Jin (Xiang 3.2, 4.5, 8.1, 12.6, 21.2) and Chu (Xiang 29.1), Lord Xiang is often no more than a pawn forced to negotiate the terms of Lu's subservience to more powerful domains.

The decline of the Lu ruling house is representative of general trends in various domains. While earlier in *Zuozhuan* such rulers as Lord Huan of Qi, Lord Wen of Jin, and King Zhuang of Chu took center stage as agents for positive political action, in these pages rulers are often in the

---

1   Mu Jiang plotted with her lover Shusun Qiaoru to bring about the downfall of the Jisun and Zhongsun lineages (Cheng 16.5).

shadows or portrayed negatively, with the possible exception of Lord Dao of Jin. A ruler's moment of glory comes only when he acknowledges error or affirms the rights of his minister (Xiang 3.7, 13.4). Rulers who fall victim to assassination are often said to deserve their fate because of ritual impropriety toward their ministers (Lord Xi of Zheng, 7.9), debauchery (Lord Zhuang of Qi, 25.2), adultery (Lord Jing of Cai, 30.5), inconstancy and tyranny (Lord Libi of Ju, 31.8). When Lord Xian of Wei is driven into exile by his ministers Sun Linfu and Ning Zhi, various prescient characters, including his father's wife Ding Jiang and the Lu minister Zang Wuzhong, denounce his crimes (Xiang 14.4). The music master Kuang justifies Lord Xian's expulsion and articulates a political vision wherein a ruler can validate his position only by good government, and the exercise of power on all levels is tempered by advice, remonstrance, and correction (Xiang 14.6).

Given the dominance of ministers and noble lineages, it is perhaps not surprising that power struggles among rival lineages as well as between rulers and ministers are often the focus of narrative attention. In Jin, the Fan lineage secures alliances with other lineages and ruthlessly eliminates Luan Ying and his followers (Xiang 21.5). The fanatical loyalty of Luan Ying's followers, who brave death to support him, already in some ways foreshadows Warring States stories about the bonds between lords and retainers based on the motif of recognition (Xiang 23.3, 23.6). (Alternatively, this example may reflect Warring States concerns retrospectively projected onto narration of events from the Spring and Autumn era.) In Qi, Cui Zhu murders Lord Zhuang, whom he himself installed (Xiang 19.5), when Lord Zhuang cuckolds him (Xiang 25.2). Cui Zhu and his lineage in turn fall victim to his co-conspirator Qing Feng (Xiang 27.7), who is eventually driven into exile by self-styled defenders of the Qi ruling house (Xiang 28.9). The most frequently cited scene in this tangled story of betrayals and deception is that of the Qi scribes who defy death to preserve truthful historical records (Xiang 25.2d). They become symbols of the historian's integrity in the tradition.[2]

In Wei, Lord Xian's insults to his ministers culminate in an irreparable breach, and he is driven into exile by Sun Linfu and Ning Zhi (Xiang 14.4). Ning Zhi's son Ning Xi restores Lord Xian (Xiang 26.2), only to be put to death by the Wei ruler, who is unwilling to share power (Xiang 27.3). Qi intervention in Luan Ying's rebellion in Jin and Jin involvement in the conflict between Sun Linfu and the Wei ruler show how domestic conflicts can widen in scope and involve other domains. At one point Jin leaders arrest Lord Xian of Wei and release him only

---

2   As noted in the Introduction (LXXIV), Wen Tianxiang's "Zhengqi ge" names them, together with the Jin scribe Dong Hu (Xuan 2.3), as representatives of the "righteous breath" between heaven and earth.

after Qi and Zheng ministers intercede by reciting selections from the *Odes* (Xiang 26.7). In Zheng, the struggle for control of the government overlaps with the tension between pro-Jin and pro-Chu factions (Xiang 10.9, 15.4, 18.4, 19.9), and even Zichan's rise to power (Xiang 19.9) does not put a stop to the violent power struggles. In Chu alone is there little evidence of overreaching lineages or power struggles between rival lineages. Instead, Chu kings execute ministers when subordinate domains defect (Xiang 2.8, 5.7) or when ministers seem corrupt or simply too rich and powerful (Xiang 22.6). Thus, Wei Ziping feigns illness to avoid an appointment (Xiang 21.4) and, after becoming minister, narrowly escapes disaster by exercising restraint in time (Xiang 22.6). His son Wei Yan is not so fortunate: Gongzi Wei, soon to usurp the Chu throne (Zhao 1.13), puts him to death and appropriates his possessions (Xiang 30.11).

These pages yield memorable images of several wise and capable ministers. These are clusters of anecdotes that develop around a single historical character, although in the present form they are sometimes scattered over different years. Shusun Bao of Lu shows his ritual knowledge, perspicacity, and rhetorical prowess on numerous occasions, often citing apposite lines from the *Odes* to make his point (Xiang 4.3, 7.7, 14.3, 16.5, 19.12, 22.1, 24.1, 24.4, 27.2, 27.4, 28.9, 28.11, 28.12, 29.1, 30.1, 31.1, 31.3, 31.4), although errors of judgment will bring about his downfall (Zhao 4.8, 5.1). Yue Xi of Song combines incorruptible integrity (Xiang 15.8), political acumen (Xiang 6.2, 27.6), and practical aplomb in responding to crisis (Xiang 9.1, 29.7), but he refuses to recognize the right of the lower orders to appraise those in power, even when those judgments involve only praise for himself (Xiang 17.6). Zang Wuzhong shows good judgment (Xiang 4.2, 11.5, 13.6, 14.4, 22.2), especially when he remonstrates with Ji Wuzi on the dangers of flaunting martial might (Xiang 19.4) and on the consequences of a leader's example (Xiang 21.2). He falls short of his grandfather Zang Wenzhong, however, when the Lu army under his command is defeated by Zhu (Xiang 4.8). He also uses his cleverness for a more dubious goal when he manipulates the succession in the Jisun lineage (Xiang 23.5), an apparently gratuitous exploit that leads to his exile.

Such mixtures are not uncommon. Xiang Xu combines moral judgments (Xiang 15.1) and strivings for peace (Xiang 27.4) with political machinations (Xiang 26.8). The perspicacious Shuxiang of Jin (Xiang 18.3, 21.5, 21.7, 27.4, 27.5) is not above partisan wrangling (Xiang 26.1). Yan Ying of Qi adheres to ritual propriety (Xiang 17.7) but is also capable of calculating political assessments (Xiang 22.3, 22.5, 23.4). He mourns Lord Zhuang of Qi in a ritually proper fashion but refuses to die or go into exile for him and manages to avoid complicity in the new government headed by Cui Zhu and Qing Feng (Xiang 25.2). His philosophy of self-preservation is evident in his refusal to get involved in power struggles in Qi (Xiang 28.9, Zhao 10.2) and his decision to keep wealth "within

春秋

1.1 元年，春，王正月，公即位。

1.2(1) 仲孫蔑會晉欒黶、宋華元、衛甯殖、曹人、莒人、邾人、滕人、薛人，圍宋彭城。

1.3(2) 夏，晉韓厥帥師伐鄭，仲孫蔑會齊崔杼、曹人、邾人、杞人，次于鄫。

1.4(3) 秋，楚公子壬夫帥師侵宋。

---

3   To some imperial commentators, Qu Boyu's withdrawal looks suspiciously like a cowardly refusal to confront evil. Gu Dongguo, for example, describes him as "Feng Dao (882–954) of the Spring and Autumn Period." (Feng Dao of the Five Dynasties was notorious for switching allegiance between different rulers.) See Gu, *Chunqiu dashi biao*, 3:2623–24.

proper measure" (Xiang 28.11). Like Yan Ying, Zichan exemplifies a noble man's choices and dilemmas in an age of violence and disorder. He urges compromises and tolerates hypocrisy (Xiang 10.9, 30.13, Zhao 1.7, 1.9), even as he tries to maintain his neutrality and impartiality in internecine conflicts in Zheng (Xiang 29.17, 30.2, 30.10, Zhao 2.4, 7.9, 7.10. 19.8). A master of diplomatic language, Zichan seems to be making up for Zheng weakness by grand rhetoric in many speeches (and one letter) that defend Zheng's rights vis-à-vis Jin (Xiang 22.2, 24.2, 25.10, 28.8, 31.6, Zhao 13.3, 16.3). The principles of government that he defines (Xiang 25.14, 30.12) seem to be tied to a program of reform embraced only after initial hostility (Xiang 30.13, Zhao 4.6). Unlike Yue Xi, he welcomes criticism expressed by those outside government (Xiang 30.11). The value he places on worthy opinions is part of a larger concern with appraising worth and employing the right men (Xiang 30.10), a recurrent issue in these pages (Xiang 3.4, 7.5, 15.3, 15.4, 21.8, 26.10, 30.3).

Of a different order are characters who choose to withdraw from the political struggles of their times. Qu Boyu leaves via a nearby pass when disorder threatens to engulf Wei (Xiang 14.4, 26.2).[3] Jizha accurately appraises the histories and fortunes of various domains by observing the performance of music and odes associated with them (Xiang 29.13). In his case, "knowing music" (*zhiyin* 知音) is also "knowing people" (*zhiren* 知人), for he offers unerring advice to contemporary statesmen on how to negotiate the dangers of public life. To guard his integrity, however, Jizha would not accept kingship (Xiang 14.2, 31.9). Jizha is thus an idealized figure who combines a kind of historical knowledge with the promise of escape from history.

....

LORD XIANG 1 (572 BCE)
ANNALS

In the first year, in spring, in the royal first month, our lord acceded to his position.   1.1

Zhongsun Mie (Meng Xianzi) met with Luan Yan of Jin, Hua Yuan of Song, Ning Zhi of Wei, a Cao leader, a Ju leader, a Zhu leader, a Teng leader, and a Xue leader and laid siege to Pengcheng in Song.   1.2(1)

In summer, Han Jue of Jin led out troops and attacked Zheng. Zhongsun Mie (Meng Xianzi) met with Cui Zhu of Qi, a Cao leader, a Zhu leader, and a Qǐ leader and set up camp at Zeng.   1.3(2)

In autumn, Gongzi Renfu of Chu led out troops and invaded Song.   1.4(3)

1.5 九月辛酉，天王崩。

1.6(4) 邾子來朝。

1.7(5) 冬，衛侯使公孫剽來聘。晉侯使荀罃來聘。

左傳

1.1(2) 元年，春，己亥，圍宋彭城。非宋地，追書也。於是為宋討魚石，故稱宋，且不登叛人也，謂之宋志。
　　　彭城降晉，晉人以宋五大夫在彭城者歸，寘諸瓠丘。
　　　齊人不會彭城，晉人以為討。二月，齊大子光為質於晉。

1.2(3) 夏，五月，晉韓厥、荀偃帥諸侯之師伐鄭，入其郛，敗其徒兵於洧上。於是東諸侯之師次于鄫，以待晉師。晉師自鄭以鄫之師侵楚焦、夷及陳。晉侯、衛侯次于戚，以為之援。

1.3(4) 秋，楚子辛救鄭，侵宋呂、留。鄭子然侵宋，取犬丘。

4　There was no *jihai* 己亥 day in the first month of this year, and *jihai* might be a
mistake for *yihai* 乙亥 day (25).

5　If Pengcheng is not designated as a Song city, then it would seem that the rebels'
sovereignty over Pengcheng is recognized.

6　Yang (3:917) suggests that *zhi* 志 indicates secret intention; cf. Yin 1.4b, n. 22. In Yin
1.4b, it was Lord Zhuang's hidden intention to get rid of his younger brother by
drawing the latter into conflict. Here, however, the intention of Song leaders (especially the Hua lineage) to retake Pengcheng seems manifest. On how *zhi* can be an
explicitly avowed aim (e.g., Xiang 1.1, Zhao 16.3) or a secret, often illicit goal (e.g., Yin
1.4, Zhuang 7.1), see Qian Zhongshu, *Guanzhui bian*, 1:172–73.

7　Huqiu 瓠丘 (Gourd Mound), also called Huqiu 壺丘 (Flask Mound), was in present-
day Shanxi, southeast of Yuanqu County 垣曲縣. This should not confused with
Huqiu in Wen 9.7.

8　Jiao and Yi were originally Chen towns that had been seized earlier by Chu (see Xi
23.3).

9　Lü 呂 was southeast of present-day Xuzhou City 徐州市, Jiangsu, and Liu 留 was to
the north of Xuzhou City.

10　Ziran is the son of Lord Mu of Zheng, last mentioned in Cheng 10.3. His death is
mentioned in Xiang 19.9, and his son Ran Dan will become an important minister
in the court of King Ling of Chu.

11　Quanqiu 犬丘 (Dog Mound) was northwest of present-day Yongcheng County 永
城縣, Henan.

In the ninth month, on the *xinyou* day (15), the Heaven-appointed king succumbed.   1.5

The Master of Zhu came to visit our court.   1.6(4)

In winter, the Prince of Wei sent Gongsun Piao to come on an official visit. The Prince of Jin sent Xun Ying (Zhi Ying) to come on an official visit.   1.7(5)

ZUO

The narrative of the Huan lineage's rebellion in Song (Cheng 15.4, 18.5) continues: Chu and Jin side with opposing factions in Song, as a Jin-Lu-Song coalition punishes the rebels who were supported by Chu and Zheng forces the year before (Cheng 18.5, 18.12). The ability to stabilize Song has always been a key component of the claim to overlordship (Zhuang 13.1, Xi 28.3).

In the first year, in spring, on the *jihai* day,[4] we laid siege to Pengcheng in Song. Pengcheng was no longer Song territory: it was designated as such retrospectively. At that time the princes were chastising Yu Shi on behalf of Song; that is why the text makes reference to Song. Furthermore, the text does not countenance rebels.[5] It says that this was "Song's intention."[6]   1.1(2)

Pengcheng surrendered to Jin. The leaders of Jin took the five Song high officers at Pengcheng and returned with them, placing them at Huqiu.[7]

The leaders of Qi did not join in the siege of Pengcheng, and because of this the leaders of Jin chastised them. In the second month, the heir apparent Guang of Qi became a hostage in Jin.

The resurgence of Jin is demonstrated by military victories over Zheng, Chu, and Chen.

In summer, in the fifth month, Han Jue and Zhonghang Yan[a] of Jin led out the troops of the princes and attacked Zheng. They entered its outer city walls and defeated its infantry on the bank of the River Wei. At that time the troops of the princes of the eastern domains set up camp at Zeng to await the Jin forces. Jin troops, coming from Zheng, led the troops at Zeng to invade Jiao and Yi of Chu, advancing as far as Chen.[8] The Prince of Jin and the Prince of Wei set up camp at Qī in order to provide support for them.   1.2(3)

In autumn, Zixin of Chu went to the aid of Zheng and invaded Lü and Liu of Song.[9] Ziran[10] of Zheng invaded Song and took Quanqiu.[11]   1.3(4)

1.4(6)　九月，邾子來朝，禮也。

1.5(7)　冬，衛子叔、晉知武子來聘，禮也。凡諸侯即位，小國朝之，大國聘焉，以繼好、結信、謀事、補闕，禮之大者也。

春秋

2.1　二年，春，王正月，葬簡王。

2.2(1)　鄭師伐宋。

2.3(3)　夏，五月庚寅，夫人姜氏薨。

2.4(5)　六月庚辰，鄭伯睔卒。

2.5(5)　晉師、宋師、衛甯殖侵鄭。

2.6(5)　秋，七月，仲孫蔑會晉荀罃、宋華元、衛孫林父、曹人、邾人于戚。

2.7　己丑，葬我小君齊姜。

2.8(6)　叔孫豹如宋。

2.9(7)　冬，仲孫蔑會晉荀罃、齊崔杼、宋華元、衛孫林父、曹人、邾人、滕人、薛人、小邾人于戚，遂城虎牢。

2.10(8)　楚殺其大夫公子申。

12　Du Yu (*ZZ* 29.497) glosses que 闕 as "errors." By this reading, *buque* 補闕 ("repair breaches in alliances") would be "mend errors." For the distinction between types of court visit, see *Annals*, Yin 7.4, n. 110.

13　King Jian was buried four months after his death, instead of the ritually proper seven months, as mentioned in *Zuozhuan*, Yin 1.6.

14　Lady Jiang was the wife of Lord Cheng of Lu.

15　The *Zuozhuan* entry has "the seventh month." The *gengchen* and *gengyin* were fifty days apart. Du Yu (*ZZ* 29.497) identifies *gengchen* as the ninth day of the seventh month.

Long-standing hostilities between Lu and Zhu temporarily abate.

In the ninth month, the Master of Zhu came to visit our court. This was in accordance with ritual propriety. — 1.4(6)

In winter, Gongsun Piao[a] of Wei and Zhi Ying[a] of Jin came to us on an official visit. This was in accordance with ritual propriety. In all cases when princes accede to their positions, the small domains attend their courts, and the great domains undertake an official visit to them, so as to continue amity, cement good faith, confer on affairs, and repair breaches in alliances.[12] These are important aspects of ritual propriety. — 1.5(7)

LORD XIANG 2 (571 BCE)
ANNALS

In the second year, in spring, in the royal first month, King Jian of Zhou was buried.[13] — 2.1

Zheng troops attacked Song. — 2.2(1)

In summer, in the fifth month, on the *gengyin* day (18), our lord's wife, Lady Jiang,[14] expired. — 2.3(3)

In the sixth month, on the *gengchen* day,[15] Gun, the Liege of Zheng, died. — 2.4(5)

Jin troops and Song troops, together with Ning Zhi of Wei, invaded Zheng. — 2.5(5)

In autumn, in the seventh month, Zhongsun Mie (Meng Xianzi) met with Xun Ying (Zhi Ying) of Jin, Hua Yuan of Song, Sun Linfu of Wei, a Cao leader, and a Zhu leader at Qī. — 2.6(5)

On the *jichou* day (18), we buried our former lord's wife, Qi Jiang.[16] — 2.7

Shusun Bao went to Song.[17] — 2.8(6)

In winter, Zhongsun Mie (Meng Xianzi) met with Xun Ying (Zhi Ying) of Jin, Cui Zhu of Qi, Hua Yuan of Song, Sun Linfu of Wei, a Cao leader, a Zhu leader, a Teng leader, a Xue leader, and a Lesser Zhu leader at Qī. They then fortified Hulao. — 2.9(7)

Chu put to death its high officer Gongzi Shen. — 2.10(8)

---

16 "Qi" was the posthumous honorific for Lady Jiang (Du Yu, *ZZ* 29.498), the wife of Lord Cheng of Lu. Both Qi Jiang and her mother-in-law Mu Jiang are sometimes called "Lady Jiang" in the text.

17 For Shusun Bao, see Cheng 16.8. From about this point on, Shusun Bao becomes active in Lu policy decisions.

左傳

2.1(2)　　二年，春，鄭師侵宋，楚令也。

2.2　　　齊侯伐萊，萊人使正輿子賂夙沙衛以索馬牛，皆百匹，齊師乃還。君子
是以知齊靈公之為「靈」也。

2.3(3)　　夏，齊姜薨。初，穆姜使擇美檟，以自為櫬與頌琴，季文子取以葬。
　　　　君子曰：「非禮也。禮無所逆。婦，養姑者也。虧姑以成婦，逆莫大
焉。《詩》曰：

> 其惟哲人，
> 告之話言，
> 順德之行。

季孫於是為不哲矣。且姜氏，君之妣也。《詩》曰：

> 為酒為醴，
> 烝畀祖妣，
> 以洽百禮，
> 降福孔偕。」

18　The *Annals* has the word "attacked" (*fa* 伐), while *Zuozhuan* uses the word "invaded" (*qin* 侵).

19　For "Ling" 靈 as a negative posthumous honorific, see our introductory remarks to Lord Xuan and also Xiang 13.4 (Yang, 3:1001). For the disorder in Qi preceding and following Lord Ling's death, see Xiang 19.5.

20　*Jia* 檟 is a hard and fine-grained wood considered superior for making coffins. Often equated with *qiu* 楸 (catalpa), it is also mentioned as a valuable wood in *Mencius* 6A.14. See also Xiang 4.4 and Ai 11.4. The more august a person's station, the more layers there were to his or her coffin. Here the "inner coffin" refers to the one in contact with the body. The *song* ("lauds") lute (*song qin* 頌琴) was intended as one of the items to be buried with Mu Jiang.

21　This echoes the negative judgment of the reversal of generational sequence in sacrificial order (*nisi* 逆祀) in Wen 2.5.

22　*Maoshi* 256, "Yi" 抑, 18A.658.

23　*Maoshi* 279, "Fengnian" 豐年, 19C.731.

In the second year, in spring, Zheng troops invaded Song.[18] This was upon Chu's order.   2.1(2)

The Qi ruler is said to have earned a negative posthumous honorific by allowing his favorite, the eunuch Susha Wei, to intervene in Qi policies.

The Prince of Qi attacked Lai. The men of Lai sent Zheng Yuzi to bribe Susha Wei with a hundred choice horses and as many choice oxen. The Qi troops thereupon turned back. Thus did the noble man know why Lord Ling of Qi was given the posthumous honorific of "Ling" (Disordered).[19]   2.2

Four years earlier, Mu Jiang, Lord Cheng's mother and Lord Xiang's grandmother, plotted unsuccessfully to remove the Ji and Meng lineages (Cheng 16.5), and she is at this point under virtual house arrest in the Eastern Palace (Xiang 9.3). Ji Wenzi's vengeful appropriation of Mu Jiang's inner coffin and lute for the burial of Lord Cheng's wife Qi Jiang is deemed a violation of ritual propriety.

In summer, Qi Jiang expired. Earlier, Mu Jiang had arranged to have fine *jia* wood chosen for her own inner coffin and a *song* lute. Ji Wenzi took these things and buried Qi Jiang with them.[20]   2.3(3)

The noble man said, "This was not in accordance with ritual propriety. Ritual propriety does not allow contravention.[21] A daughter-in-law is one who nurtures her mother-in-law. There is no greater contravention than to diminish a mother-in-law in order to supply the needs of a daughter-in-law. As it says in the *Odes*,

> It is thus only with wise men—
> Admonish them with good words,
> And they follow the path of virtue.[22]

In this matter, Ji Wenzi[b] was unwise. Moreover, Mu Jiang was the ruler's grandmother. As it says in the *Odes*,

> Make wine; make sweet liquor—
> Offer them to grandfather and grandmother
> So as to fulfill a hundred rites,
> And bring down blessings shared far and wide."[23]

2.4 齊侯使諸姜、宗婦來送葬，召萊子。萊子不會，故晏弱城東陽以偪之。

2.5(4–6) 鄭成公疾，子駟請息肩於晉。公曰：「楚君以鄭故，親集矢於其目，非異人任，寡人也。若背之，是棄力與言，其誰暱我？免寡人，唯二三子。」
　　秋，七月庚辰，鄭伯睔卒。於是子罕當國，子駟為政，子國為司馬。晉師侵鄭。諸大夫欲從晉。子駟曰：「官命未改。」
　　會于戚，謀鄭故也。孟獻子曰：「請城虎牢以偪鄭。」知武子曰：「善。鄶之會，吾子聞崔子之言，今不來矣。滕、薛、小邾之不至，皆齊故也。寡君之憂不唯鄭。縈將復於寡君而請於齊。得請而告，吾子之功也。若不得請，事將在齊。吾子之請，諸侯之福也，豈唯寡君賴之！」

2.6(8) 穆叔聘于宋，通嗣君也。

24　Women were not supposed to leave the domain to attend funerals or to offer condolences (*ZZ* 29.499; *Liji* 9.164).

25　Dongyang 東陽 was a Qi settlement located east of Linqu County 臨朐縣, Shandong.

26　Literally, "to rest its shoulders by Jin" (*xi jian yu Jin* 息肩於晉). Zisi, who was a hostage in Jin (Cheng 10.3), is arguing that by switching allegiance from Chu to Jin, Zheng can be freed of the many burdens that Chu imposes on it.

27　See Karlgren, gl. 464.

28　*Guanming* ("the ruler's command") is literally "the command whose authority is based on the ruler's office." Although Lord Cheng of Zheng had died, his charge remained effective until his burial or until his successor's official accession in the following year. In the absence of a newly elevated ruler, no one has the authority to put aside the Chu alliance and submit to Jin. Alternatively, "the command to this officeholder has not yet changed."

29　The leaders of Jin, Lu, Wei, and Song were conferring on how to induce Zheng to submit to Jin.

30　It appears that Jin had occupied Hulao (see map 3) by this point.

31　For the meeting at Zeng, see Xiang 1.2.

32　Zhi Ying is saying that Jin also worries about Qi and Chu. If Qi, Chu, and Zheng form an alliance against Jin, Jin will not be able to maintain its status as covenant chief.

33　That is, Jin will attack Qi. The "affair" 事 refers to one of the two "great affairs of the domain" (*guo zhi dashi* 國之大事) (Cheng 13.2): warfare.

Zuo Tradition

During Qi Jiang's funeral, Lord Ling of Qi flouts ritual propriety by sending Qi ladies to escort the funeral cortege of Qi Jiang, further evidence of his bad judgment (Xiang 2.2). Qi meets with insubordination from Lai. Qi had attacked Lai earlier (Xuan 7.2, Xiang 2.2).

The Prince of Qi sent various ladies of the Jiang line married to Qi high officers, as well as the wives of Qi high officers who shared the name of the lord's house, to escort the funeral cortege.[24] He sent for the Master of Lai. The Master of Lai did not meet with him, and so Yan Ruo fortified the walls of Dongyang to exert pressure on him.[25]

2.4

Zheng leaders follow Lord Cheng's deathbed wish to side with Chu. Jin, wary not only of Zheng insubordination but also of Qi designs, seeks to enlist Qi help with the fortification of Hulao.

When Lord Cheng of Zheng was ill, Zisi requested that Zheng ease its burden by turning to Jin.[26] The lord said, "The Chu ruler, on account of Zheng, took an arrow in his very own eye. None but I, the unworthy one, should bear the responsibility.[27] If we turn against Chu, it will amount to casting away the Chu ruler's efforts and our own words. Who would draw close to us then? Only you, sirs, can save me from that offense."

2.5(4–6)

In autumn, in the seventh month, on the *gengchen* day, Gun, the Liege of Zheng, died. At that time Zihan was managing the domain, Zisi was in charge of policies, and Ziguo was the supervisor of the military. Jin troops invaded Zheng. The various high officers in Zheng wanted to submit to Jin. Zisi said, "The ruler's command has not yet changed."[28]

The leaders met at Qī: this was to confer about Zheng.[29] Meng Xianzi said, "I request that Hulao[30] be fortified to exert pressure on Zheng." Zhi Ying[a] said, "Excellent. At the meeting at Zeng, you, sirs, heard the words of Cui Zhu[e].[31] He will not come this time. That Teng, Xue, and Lesser Zhu did not come was on account of Qi in every case. Our unworthy ruler's worries pertain not only to Zheng.[32] I will report on my mission to our unworthy ruler and make our request to Qi to join the coalition. If our request is granted, and Qi reports their intention to assist at Hulao, the merit will be yours. If our request is not granted, then our affair will be to tackle Qi.[33] This request of yours regarding Hulao will confer blessings on the princes. How can it be our unworthy ruler alone who will rely on it?"

Shusun Bao[a] went on an official visit to Song: this was to establish relations between Song and our new ruler.

2.6(8)

2.7(9)　冬，復會于戚，齊崔武子及滕、薛、小邾之大夫皆會，知武子之言故也。遂城虎牢。鄭人乃成。

2.8(10)　楚公子申為右司馬，多受小國之賂，以偪子重、子辛。楚人殺之，故書曰「楚殺其大夫公子申。」

春秋

3.1(1)　三年，春，楚公子嬰齊帥師伐吳。

3.2(2)　公如晉。

3.3(2)　夏，四月壬戌，公及晉侯盟于長樗。

3.4　公至自晉。

3.5(5)　六月，公會單子、晉侯、宋公、衛侯、鄭伯、莒子、邾子、齊世子光。己未，同盟于雞澤。

3.6(6)　陳侯使袁僑如會。

3.7(6)　戊寅，叔孫豹及諸侯之大夫及陳袁僑盟。

3.8　秋，公至自會。

3.9(9)　冬，晉荀罃帥師伐許。

The Jin minister Zhi Ying's plans to confirm Qi's allegiance and to bring Zheng to submission are realized. This means Zisi and his allies relent.

In winter, the leaders met again at Qī. That Cui Zhu[a] of Qi, as well as high officers from Teng, Xue, and Lesser Zhu, all came to the meeting was on account of Zhi Ying[a]'s words. They then fortified Hulao. The leaders of Zheng thus reached an accord with Jin.   2.7(9)

Zichong again emerges victorious in internecine conflicts in Chu. The fall of Gongzi Shen may be explained by Zheng's shift of allegiance to Jin after the fortification of Hulao.

Gongzi Shen of Chu was the supervisor of the military on the right. Having received many gifts from small domains, he used them to exert pressure on Zichong and Zixin. The leaders of Chu put him to death. That is why the text says, "Chu put to death its high officer Gongzi Shen."   2.8(10)

LORD XIANG 3 (570 BCE)
ANNALS

In the third year, in spring, Gongzi Yingqi (Zichong) of Chu led out troops and attacked Wu.   3.1(1)

Our lord went to Jin.   3.2(2)

In summer, in the fourth month, on the *renxu* day (25), our lord and the Prince of Jin swore a covenant at Changchu.   3.3(2)

Our lord arrived from Jin.   3.4

In the sixth month, our lord met with the Shan Master, the Prince of Jin, the Duke of Song, the Prince of Wei, the Liege of Zheng, the Master of Ju, the Master of Zhu, and the Qi heir apparent Guang. On the *jiwei* day (23), they swore a covenant together at Ji Marsh.[34]   3.5(5)

The Prince of Chen sent Yuan Qiao to the meeting.   3.6(6)

On the *wuyin* day (13),[35] Shusun Bao and the high officers of the princes swore a covenant with Yuan Qiao of Chen.   3.7(6)

In autumn, our lord arrived from the meeting.   3.8

In winter, Xun Ying (Zhi Ying) of Jin led out troops and attacked Xǔ.   3.9(9)

---

34   Ji Marsh 雞澤 was located northeast of the city of Hangdan 邯鄲 in Hebei.

35   The *wuyin* day fell on the thirteenth day of the seventh month. Assuming that the meeting did not last that long, *wuyin* may be a mistake. Alternatively, the lords might have been waiting for the Chen envoy.

左傳

3.1(1)　三年，春，楚子重伐吳，為簡之師。克鳩茲，至于衡山。使鄧廖帥組甲三
百、被練三千，以侵吳。吳人要而擊之，獲鄧廖。其能免者，組甲八十、被
練三百而已。
　　　　子重歸，既飲至三日，吳人伐楚，取駕。駕，良邑也；鄧廖，亦楚之
良也。君子謂子重於是役也，所獲不如所亡。楚人以是咎子重。子重病
之，遂遇心疾而卒。

3.2(2, 3)　公如晉，始朝也。夏，盟于長樗。孟獻子相。公稽首。知武子曰：「天子
在，而君辱稽首，寡君懼矣。」孟獻子曰：「以敝邑介在東表，密邇仇讎，
寡君將君是望，敢不稽首？」

36　Hengshan 衡山, or Heng Mountain, was located in Wu. Known by the same name
　　today, it is in present-day Dangtu County 當涂縣, Anhui.

37　Commentators give different explanations of *zujia* 組甲 and *pilian* 被練. *Zujia* is
　　variously glossed as "string pattern lacquered on leather" (Du Yu), "armor padded
　　with woven silk (for those of higher ranks)" (Ma Rong), and "armor sewn with cords
　　(for soldiers on chariots)" (Jia Kui). *Pilian* is glossed as "silk coat" (Du Yu), "armor
　　sewn with plain silk (for infantry soldiers)" (Jia Kui), and "armor padded with plain
　　silk (for those of lower ranks)" (Ma Rong). See Liu Wenqi, *Chunqiu Zuoshi zhuan
　　jiuzhu shuzheng*, 991. Here we choose to read *zujia* as a more elaborate type of sewn
　　armor and *pilian* as a coarser type of defensive clothing.

38　For the ritual toasts to celebrate the army's return (*yinzhi* 飲至), see Yin 5.1.

Conflicts between Wu and Chu (Cheng 7.5) continue. After initial victories, Chu suffers grave reversals, which lead to the Chu commander Zichong's death, fulfilling Qu Wuchen's vow of vengeance fourteen years ago (Cheng 7.5).

In the third year, in spring, Zichong of Chu attacked Wu, having organized his forces based on rigorous selection and training. After overcoming Jiuzi and advancing as far as Hengshan,[36] he sent Deng Liao to lead three hundred soldiers in sewn armor and three thousand soldiers in armored coats to invade Wu.[37] The men of Wu struck them in the center of their lines, seizing Deng Liao. Those who managed to escape amounted to only eighty in sewn armor and three hundred in armored coats.

3.1(1)

Zichong returned. Three days after the ritual toasts to celebrate their arrival,[38] the men of Wu attacked Chu and took Jia.[39] Jia was a fine settlement, and Deng Liao had also been a fine man of Chu. The noble man said that with this battle, what Zichong gained did not amount to what he lost. For this reason the men of Chu blamed Zichong. Zichong was so distressed by this that he came to be afflicted with a sickness of the heart and died.[40]

The six-year-old Lord Xiang of Lu bows low to the seventeen-year-old Lord Dao of Jin with rituals appropriate for the Zhou king. The Lu minister Meng Xianzi deems such self-abnegation necessary to secure Jin support to stave off threats posed by Qi, Chu, and Wu.

Our lord went to Jin: that was the first time he visited the court of Jin. In summer, they swore a covenant at Changchu.[41] Meng Xianzi assisted our lord. Our lord bowed with his forehead touching the ground. Zhi Ying[a] said, "The Son of Heaven is still there. Yet you, my lord, deigned to bow with your forehead touching the ground. Our unworthy ruler is fearful." Meng Xianzi said, "Because our humble settlement is on the eastern rim and in close proximity to our enemies, it is to you, my lord, that our unworthy ruler must look. How should he dare not bow with his forehead touching the ground?"

3.2(2, 3)

---

39   The "fine settlement" of Jia 駕 has already appeared in Cheng 17.11.

40   Since the heart was supposed to be the organ of thought and emotions, "sickness of the heart" 心疾 (see also Zhao 1.12, 21.1) refers to mental disorder or emotional imbalance (Yang, 3:926). Another reference to "sickness of the heart" seems to refer to a more physiological malfunction (Zhao 22.3).

41   Changchu 長樗 was located in the outskirts of the Jin capital.

3.3 晉為鄭服故，且欲修吳好，將合諸侯。使士匄告于齊曰：「寡君使匄，以歲之不易，不虞之不戒，寡君願與一二兄弟相見，以謀不協。請君臨之，使匄乞盟。」齊侯欲勿許，而難為不協，乃盟於邴外。

3.4 祁奚請老，晉侯問嗣焉。稱解狐，其讎也，將立之而卒。又問焉。對曰：「午也可。」於是羊舌職死矣，晉侯曰：「孰可以代之？」對曰：「赤也可。」於是使祁午為中軍尉，羊舌赤佐之。

　　君子謂祁奚「於是能舉善矣。稱其讎，不為諂；立其子，不為比；舉其偏，不為黨。《商書》曰：

42　"The difficulties over the years" refers to conflicts among the princes; with such conflicts it would be hard to "guard against the unexpected." "Those in discord with us" include Qi.

43　The northwestern outskirts of the Qi capital, Linzi 臨淄, were close to the Er River.

44　On the different versions of this story, see Petersen, "The *Zuozhuan* Story about Qi Xi and His Recommendations and Its Sources."

45　Qi Xi was made senior officer of the central army in 573 BCE (Cheng 18.3).

46　Yangshe Zhi was Qi Xi's aide or adjutant (Cheng 18.2). Yangshe Chi was Yangshe Zhi's son. Qi Xi thus ends up recommending his own son and his adjutant's son, but the noble man argues that Qi Xi is not being partial (*bi* 比) or factional (*dang* 黨). On how the noble man should not be partial or factional, see the *Analects* 2.14, 7.31.

Jin demands and receives a demonstration of allegiance from Qi, despite Qi's reluctance.

Jin, on account of Zheng's submission and also because it wished to cultivate good relations with Wu, planned to assemble the princes. Jin sent Fan Gai[a] to notify Qi: "Our unworthy ruler has sent me here. Because of the difficulties over the years and the failure to guard against the unexpected, our unworthy ruler wishes to meet with his brothers to confer about those in discord with us.[42] He requests that you, my lord, attend the meeting and has sent me to beg for a covenant." The Prince of Qi wished to decline, but finding it hard to be the one "in discord," he thus swore the covenant by the Er River.[43]

3.3

The Jin army commandant Qi Xi is praised for his unbiased recommendations of men for office; the same judiciousness will lead him to defend his adversary Shuxiang (Yangshe Xi) in Xiang 21.5b. Qi Xi demonstrates his impartiality by recommending his enemy Xie Hu, who conveniently dies. Qi's eventual recommendation of his son Qi Wu and his ally Yangshe Chi, which results in a pattern of sons succeeding to their fathers' positions, is proleptically defended as impartiality and virtuous affinity. For another example of recommending an enemy, see Ai 5.1. For similarly elevated rhetoric justifying a politically convenient fait accompli, see Zhao 28.3b, where Wei Shu parcels out rewards after the destruction of the Qi and Yangshe lineages. Versions of this anecdote also appear in Lüshi chunqiu *1.55,* Xinxu *1.11–12,* Shiji *39.1682, and* Han Feizi *33.705 (this last version has different actors but analogous elements). Whereas all these parallel accounts emphasize impartiality (gong 公) and feature the actual elevation of an enemy, the Zuozhuan account is unique in using the rhetoric of impartiality to justify hereditary succession. In* Guoyu, *"Jin yu 7," 13.439–40, Xie Yang is not mentioned. Qi Xi recommends his son right away and gives a long panegyric of his virtues.[44]*

Qi Xi requested to retire on account of old age.[45] The Prince of Jin asked about his successor. Qi Xi named Xie Hu, who was his enemy. The Jin ruler was about to establish Xie Hu in the position when the latter died. He asked again. Qi Xi replied, "Qi Wu[a] would be acceptable." At that time Yangshe Zhi had just died, and the Prince of Jin asked, "Who can take his place?" He replied, "Yangshe Chi[b] would be acceptable." Thus, Qi Wu was made commandant of the central army, with Yangshe Chi assisting him.[46]

3.4

The noble man said that Qi Xi "in this case showed himself capable of recommending good men. He named his enemy, but that was not ingratiation. He established his son in office, but that was not favoritism. He recommended his adjutant, but that was not about forming factions. As it says in the *Shang Documents*,

無偏無黨，
王道蕩蕩。

其祁奚之謂矣。解狐得舉，祁午得位，伯華得官，建一官而三物成，能舉善也。夫唯善，故能舉其類。《詩》云：

惟其有之，
是以似之。

祁奚有焉。」

3.5(5) 六月，公會單頃公及諸侯。己未，同盟于雞澤。
晉侯使荀會逆吳子于淮上，吳子不至。

3.6(6, 7) 楚子辛為令尹，侵欲於小國，陳成公使袁僑如會求成。晉侯使和組父告于諸侯。秋，叔孫豹及諸侯之大夫及陳袁僑盟，陳請服也。

3.7 晉侯之弟揚干亂行於曲梁，魏絳戮其僕。晉侯怒，謂羊舌赤曰：「合諸侯，以為榮也。揚干為戮，何辱如之？必殺魏絳，無失也！」
　　對曰：「絳無貳志，事君不辟難，有罪不逃刑，其將來辭，何辱命焉？」

---

47   *Shangshu*, "Hong fan" 洪範, 12.173. The word for both "adjutant" and "partial" is *pian* 偏.

48   The commandant and his adjutant attend to the same affair, hence "one office." The three things refer to the recommendation, the position, and the office.

49   *Maoshi* 214, "Chang chang zhe hua" 裳裳者華, 14B.280. The word *si* 似 in the poem seems to refer to the correspondence of internal and external qualities. Here the "resemblance" refers to Qi Xi and those he recommends, or to him and his progeny. Yang (3:928) suggests that *si* 似 ("resemble") may be a loan for *si* 嗣 ("heir").

50   It is Wei Jiang's duty as supervisor of the military to enforce military discipline. Unable to execute Yanggan (because of his rank), he kills Yanggan's driver as a substitute.

51   Covenants involved gatherings of chariots (*bingche zhi hui* 兵車之會) or of carriages (*chengche zhi hui* 乘車之會). In either case there were accompanying soldiers in ranks. Quliang 曲梁 was close to Ji Marsh and northeast of Handan City.

> Not being partial, not forming factions,
> The kingly way is great and boundless.[47]

This could refer to Qi Xi! Xie Hu received his recommendation, Qi Wu his position, and Yangshe Chi[a] his office. When he established one office, these three things were accomplished.[48] This was because he was capable of recommending worthy men. It was quite simply because he was worthy that he was capable of recommending those of his kind. As it says in the *Odes,*

> It is precisely because he has the virtues
> That they resemble him.[49]

And so it was with Qi Xi."

Wu defies Jin.

In the sixth month, our lord met with the Shan Duke Qing and the princes. On the *jiwei* day (23), they swore a covenant together at Ji Marsh.

    The Prince of Jin sent Xun Hui to meet the Master of Wu on the banks of the Huai River, but the Master of Wu did not arrive.

Chen shifts its allegiance from Chu to Jin.

Zixin of Chu became chief minister and rapaciously invaded the small domains. Lord Cheng of Chen sent Yuan Qiao to the meeting to seek an accord. The Prince of Jin sent He Zufu to notify the princes. In autumn, Shusun Bao, the high officers of the princes, and Yuan Qiao of Chen swore a covenant: this was because Chen had requested to submit to Jin.

The Jin supervisor of the military Wei Jiang punishes the Jin ruler's younger brother Yanggan by proxy in order to enforce military discipline.[50] Lord Dao of Jin, initially enraged, comes to acknowledge his own error. Wei Jiang is rewarded with the rank of minister (assistant commander of the new army) for "knowing how to use punishment."

The Prince of Jin's younger brother, Yanggan, caused disorder in the ranks at Quliang.[51] Wei Jiang executed Yanggan's driver. Furious, the Prince of Jin said to Yangshe Chi, "Assembling the princes is something we do for the sake of glory. What shame can possibly compare to having Yanggan disgraced and punished? We must put Wei Jiang to death without fail!"

    Yangshe Chi replied, "Wei Jiang has never had disloyal intent. In serving his ruler he does not avoid difficulties, and having offended he does not flee punishment. Surely he will come to explain his case. Why deign to issue a command?"

言終，魏絳至，授僕人書，將伏劍。士魴、張老止之。公讀其書，
曰：「日君乏使，使臣斯司馬。臣聞：『師眾以順為武，軍事有死無犯為
敬。』君合諸侯，臣敢不敬？君師不武，執事不敬，罪莫大焉。臣懼其
死，以及揚干，無所逃罪。不能致訓，至於用鉞，臣之罪重，敢有不從以
怒君心？請歸死於司寇。」

公跣而出，曰：「寡人之言，親愛也；吾子之討，軍禮也。寡人有
弟，弗能教訓，使干大命，寡人之過也。子無重寡人之過，敢以為請。」

晉侯以魏絳為能以刑佐民矣，反役，與之禮食，使佐新軍。張老為
中軍司馬，士富為候奄。

3.8　楚司馬公子何忌侵陳，陳叛故也。

3.9(9)　許靈公事楚，不會于雞澤。冬，晉知武子帥師伐許。

52　The implication is that he extends his own fear to Yanggan and empathizes with his
anticipated plight. An alternative reading is "I fear death, and thus extended punishment to Yanggan."

53　This may be a subtle reminder that the Jin ruler has himself "neglected instruction"
(*shijiao* 失教); cf. Yin 1.4b. Yanggan would have been younger than sixteen.

As he finished speaking, Wei Jiang arrived, handed a letter to one of the lord's attendants, and prepared to fall on his sword. Shi Fang and Zhang Lao stopped him. The lord read out his letter: "Formerly, you, my lord, lacked better men to serve you and appointed me to this office as supervisor of the military. I have heard, 'For troops, to obey orders constitutes martial virtue; in military affairs, to die rather than commit transgressions constitutes reverence.' When you, my lord, have assembled the princes, should we dare to be irreverent? If the ruler's army lacks martial virtue and those in charge lack reverence, no offense can be greater. I feared that I would be put to death for it and that Yanggan would then be implicated in a crime.[52] We would have no way to escape the consequences of our guilt. I failed to offer instruction to him[53] and came to use the axe. My offense is grave. Could I presume not to submit, and so infuriate you? I beg leave to put my death in the hands of the supervisor of corrections."

The lord ran out barefoot[54] and said, "The words I, the unworthy one, spoke were for love of kin; the chastising that you, sir, meted out was for the sake of military protocol. I have a younger brother but was unable to instruct him, causing him to violate the great command. This was my offense. You are not to compound my offense.[55] That is what I presume to request of you."

The Prince of Jin considered Wei Jiang a man who knew how to use punishment to aid in governing the people. After they had returned from their mission, the Jin ruler bestowed upon him a ceremonious meal and made him assistant commander in the new army. Zhang Lao became supervisor of the military in the central army; Shi Fu became leader of scouts.

Chu punishes Chen for shifting its allegiance to Jin, as evinced by its participation in the Ji Marsh covenant.

The Chu supervisor of the military Gongzi Heji invaded Chen because   3.8
Chen had revolted.

Jin attacks Xǔ because the latter sides with Chu and does not join the Ji Marsh covenant.

Lord Ling of Xǔ served Chu and did not come to the meeting at Ji Marsh.   3.9(9)
In winter, Zhi Ying[a] of Jin led out troops and attacked Xǔ.

---

54   For another example of a ruler forgetting his shoes in his eagerness to act, see Xuan 14.3.

55   Had the Jin ruler allowed Wei Jiang to commit suicide, he would have committed an even graver offense.

春秋

4.1(2)　四年，春，王三月。己酉，陳侯午卒。

4.2(3)　夏，叔孫豹如晉。

4.3(4)　秋，七月戊子，夫人姒氏薨。

4.4　　葬陳成公。

4.5　　八月辛亥，葬我小君定姒。

4.6(5)　冬，公如晉。

4.7(6)　陳人圍頓。

左傳

4.1　　四年，春，楚師為陳叛故，猶在繁陽。韓獻子患之，言於朝曰：「文王帥
殷之叛國以事紂，唯知時也。今我易之，難哉！」

4.2(1)　三月，陳成公卒。楚人將伐陳，聞喪乃止。陳人不聽命。臧武仲聞之，曰：
「陳不服於楚，必亡。大國行禮焉，而不服，在大猶有咎，而況小乎？」
夏，楚彭名侵陳，陳無禮故也。

56　Fanyang 繁揚 (繁陽) was located north of present-day Xincai County 新蔡縣, Henan.

57　See *Yi Zhou shu* 2.12.176; *Analects* 8.20. For an interesting newly discovered version of King Wen's loyalty to Shang, see the "Rong Cheng shi" 容成氏 manuscript, in *Shanghai bowuguan cang Zhanguo Chu zhushu*, vol. 2.

58　In Xiang 19.6, the Jin army on the way to attack Qi turns back upon receiving news of the Qi ruler's death.

ANNALS

In the fourth year, in spring, in the royal third month, on the *jiyou* day, Wu, the Prince of Chen, died. 4.1(2)

In summer, Shusun Bao went to Jin. 4.2(3)

In autumn, in the seventh month, on the *wuzi* day (28), our lord's wife, Lady Si, expired. 4.3(4)

Lord Cheng of Chen was buried. 4.4

In the eighth month, on the *xinhai* day (22), we buried our former lord's consort, Ding Si. 4.5

In winter, our lord went to Jin. 4.6(5)

Chen leaders laid siege to Dun. 4.7(6)

ZUO

The Jin minister Han Jue argues that it is not timely for Jin to accept Chen's submission, because Jin is not yet in a position to challenge Chu.

In the fourth year, in spring, Chu troops were still in Fanyang because Chen had revolted.[56] Han Jue[a] was worried about this and spoke at court: "King Wen led the rebellious domains of Yin (Shang) to serve its last ruler Zhòu.[57] This was precisely because he knew the proper time to act. Now because we have acted differently, it will surely be difficult for us!" 4.1

The Lu minister Zang Wuzhong criticizes Chen for failing to submit to Chu despite the latter's restraint and ritual propriety. This view of Chu stands in sharp contrast to that of another Lu minister, Ji Wenzi, who sees Chu as untrustworthy, "not of the same kith and kin" (Cheng 4.4).

In the third month, Lord Cheng of Chen died. The leaders of Chu had been planning to attack Chen but stopped when they heard of the funeral.[58] The men of Chen did not heed Chu's commands. Zang Wuzhong heard about this and said, "Since Chen does not submit to Chu, it will surely perish. When a great domain acts according to ritual propriety, failure to submit to it will incur blame even for a large domain. How much more so for a small one?" 4.2(1)

   In summer, Peng Ming of Chu invaded Chen because Chen lacked ritual propriety.

4.3(2)　穆叔如晉，報知武子之聘也。晉侯享之，金奏〈肆夏〉之三，不拜。工歌〈文王〉之三，又不拜。歌〈鹿鳴〉之三，三拜。

　　　韓獻子使行人子員問之曰：「子以君命辱於敝邑，先君之禮，藉之以樂，以辱吾子。吾子舍其大，而重拜其細。敢問何禮也？」

　　　對曰：「三夏，天子所以享元侯也，使臣弗敢與聞。〈文王〉，兩君相見之樂也，使臣不敢及。〈鹿鳴〉，君所以嘉寡君也，敢不拜嘉？〈四牡〉，君所以勞使臣也，敢不重拜？〈皇皇者華〉，君教使臣曰：『必諮於周。』臣聞之：訪問於善為咨，咨親為詢，咨禮為度，咨事為諏，咨難為謀。臣獲五善，敢不重拜？」

59　Xiang 1.5.

60　This is the only instance in *Zuozhuan* where musical performance is mentioned in connection with the ritual of ceremonial toasts (*xiang* 享).

61　In the parallel passage in *Guoyu*, "Lu yu 2," 5.185–86, "the three forms of Xia" are identified as Fan 樊, E 遏, and Qu 渠, which Wei Zhao further equates with Si Xia 肆夏, Shao Xia 韶夏, and Na Xia 納夏.

62　The received text can be understood as "three stanzas of 'King Wen'" and "three stanzas of 'Deer Cry.'" However, in *Guoyu*, "Lu yu 2," 5.185–86, Shusun Bao explains *sanzhang* 三章 as "three songs in the sequence of"—thus including two songs that follow the one named (according to the arrangement of the songs in the received text): "King Wen" ("Wen wang" 文王), "Great Brightness" ("Da ming" 大明), "Spreading" ("Mian" 緜) (*Maoshi* 235–37), and "Deer Cry" ("Lu ming" 鹿鳴), "Four Stallions" ("Si mu" 四牡), and "Resplendent Are the Flowers" ("Huanghuang zhe hua" 皇皇者華) (*Maoshi* 161–63). The reference to "Four Stallions" and "Resplendent Are the Flowers" in Shusun Bao's reply confirms this reading.

63　"Deer Cry" (*Maoshi* 161, "Lu ming," 9B.315–17) is a feast poem that praises the "fine guest" (*jiabin* 嘉賓) who has the "voice of virtue" (*deyin* 德音) and whose exemplary conduct demonstrates "the great way" (or the way of Zhou, *zhouxing* 周行). Shusun Bao is accepting such compliments on behalf of the Lu ruler.

Shusun Bao[a] went to Jin: this was in answer to Zhi Ying[a]'s official visit to Lu.[59] The Prince of Jin offered him ceremonial toasts.[60] The bells played out three forms of "The Great Xia," and he did not bow.[61] The musicians sang three songs in the sequence of "King Wen," and again he did not bow. When they sang three songs in the sequence of "Deer Cry," he bowed thrice.[62]

4.3(2)

Han Jue[a] sent the envoy Ziyun to ask about it: "You, sir, by your ruler's command have deigned to come to our humble settlement. We have used the former rulers' rituals, performed through music, to receive you in a fashion requiring your condescension. Now you, sir, have not acknowledged the great ones but have repeatedly bowed to the minor ones. Dare we ask what ritual this is?"

He replied, "The three 'Xias' are what the Son of Heaven uses as he offers ceremonial toasts to the leader of princes. I, as a subject on a mission, did not dare to hear of it. 'King Wen' is the music for the meeting of two rulers. I did not dare to have anything to do with it. 'Deer Cry' was what your ruler used to praise our unworthy ruler.[63] How would I dare not bow to such praise? 'Four Stallions' was what your ruler used to honor my exertions.[64] How would I dare not bow again? With 'Resplendent Are the Flowers,' your ruler was instructing me: 'You must seek counsel from all.' According to what I have heard, to look for and solicit excellent men is to seek counsel; to seek counsel about kith and kin is inquiry; to seek counsel about ritual is deliberation; to seek counsel about affairs of the domain is consultation; and to seek counsel about difficulties is proper planning.[65] Since I have now received five good instructions, how would I dare not bow repeatedly?"

---

64   In "Four Stallions" (*Maoshi* 162, "Simu," 9B.317–18), the officer or emissary endures the hardships of journeys and suppresses longing for home because "the king's affairs admit of no rest" (*wangshi mi gu* 王事靡鹽).

65   Shusun Bao here paraphrases, summarizes, and explains lines from "Resplendent Are the Flowers" (*Maoshi* 163, "Huanghuang zhe hua," 9B.318–20), which contains four lines that repeat the words *zhou* 周 ("all" or "everywhere"), *yuan* 爰 ("from"), and *zi* 諮 or 咨 ("seek counsel") and vary only in the last word: *zou* 諏 ("consultation"), *mou* 謀 ("planning"), *du* 度 ("deliberation"), and *xun* 詢 ("inquiry"). He "translates" *yuan* as *yu* 於 and then elaborates the meanings of *zi, zou, mou, du,* and *xun*.

4.4(3)　秋，定姒薨。不殯于廟，無櫬，不虞。匠慶謂季文子曰：「子為正卿，而小君之喪不成，不終君也。君長，誰受其咎？」
　　初，季孫為己樹六檟於蒲圃東門之外，匠慶請木，季孫曰：「略。」匠慶用蒲圃之檟，季孫不御。
　　君子曰：「志所謂『多行無禮，必自及也』，其是之謂乎！」

4.5(6)　冬，公如晉聽政。晉侯享公，公請屬鄆。晉侯不許。孟獻子曰：「以寡君之密邇於仇讎，而願固事君，無失官命。鄆無賦於司馬，為執事朝夕之命敝邑，敝邑褊小，闕而為罪，寡君是以願借助焉。」晉侯許之。

4.6(7)　楚人使頓間陳而侵伐之，故陳人圍頓。

66　For such *yu* 虞 rituals, see *Yili* 14.493. For the ritual of "lying in state," see Xi 8.3, n. 111. The omissions in Ding Si's funeral contrasts with the pomp and circumstance of the funeral for Qi Jiang, Lord Cheng's principal wife, in Xiang 2.3.

67　We follow Ma Zonglian's reading, cited in Liu Wenqi, *Chunqiu Zuoshi zhuan jiuzhu shuzheng*, 1008. To keep the funeral rituals simple, Ding Si's coffin would not have to be made from fine wood. Yet Ji Wenzi's reply is also deliberately noncommittal, and he does not stop Qing from cutting down the trees. Du Yu (*ZZ* 29.506) glosses *lue* 略 (which we render as "simple") as "to obtain in an improper way" 不以道取, possibly averring that Ji Wenzi's own wood would have been improperly appropriated if it was used to make Ding Si's coffin, or (less likely) Ji may be suggesting that the wood for the coffin can be obtained by some other improper means. On the use of *jia* timber for coffin, see also Xiang 2.3, Ai 11.4.

68　For Dun, a small domain close to Chen, see Xi 23.3, n. 281.

Zuo Tradition

The funeral for Lord Xiang's birth mother and Lord Cheng's concubine, Ding Si, raises ritual questions. The Lu minister Ji Wenzi is criticized for his deliberate or inadvertent negligence. Again, a humble character voices authoritative arguments. (Cf. the builders in Xuan 2.1b, the wagon driver in Cheng 5.4, the musicians in Xiang 15.4, and the old man of Jiang in Xiang 30.3a.).

In autumn, Ding Si expired. Her coffin did not lie in state, there was no inner coffin, and they did not offer sacrifices to appease her spirit after burial.[66] The carpenter Qing said to Ji Wenzi, "You are the chief minister. That the funeral rituals of our former lord's wife should be so incomplete means that you are not allowing the ruler to fulfill his filial duty to the utmost. When the ruler grows up, who will bear the blame for this?"

    Earlier, Ji Wenzi[b] had planted for himself six *jia* trees outside the eastern gate of Pu Gardens. When the carpenter Qing asked about the wood for Ding Si's coffin, Ji Wenzi[b] said, "Make it simple."[67] But when the carpenter Qing used the *jia* wood from Pu Gardens, Ji Wenzi[b] did not stop him.

    The noble man said, "When the *Records* says, 'Having acted against ritual propriety many times, he will certainly be overtaken by disaster,' surely this is what is meant!"

Reiterating Lu's perilous situation (Xiang 3.2), the Lu minister Meng Xianzi seeks and obtains Jin's sanction for Lu's control of Zeng. Meng argues that Lu can meet the demands that Jin imposes upon it only by claiming Zeng as a subsidiary domain.

In winter, our lord went to Jin to attend to its commands. The Prince of Jin offered our lord ceremonial toasts, and our lord requested that Zeng be made subordinate to Lu. The Prince of Jin did not permit it. Meng Xianzi said, "For all our unworthy ruler's close proximity to our enemies, he is nevertheless willing to serve you, my lord, with unwavering resolve, and he does not fail to fulfill the commands of your offices. Zeng contributes no levies to your supervisors of the military. Your functionaries day and night make demands upon our humble settlement. Our humble settlement is remote and small, and if we are remiss, we will incur offense. That is why our unworthy ruler is hoping to get help from Zeng." The Prince of Jin granted permission.

The men of Chu had Dun[68] watch for any lapse in Chen's vigilance and then invade and attack it. That was why Chen leaders laid siege to Dun.

4.4(3)

4.5(6)

4.6(7)

無終子嘉父使孟樂如晉，因魏莊子納虎豹之皮，以請和諸戎。晉侯曰：
「戎狄無親而貪，不如伐之。」

魏絳曰：「諸侯新服，陳新來和，將觀於我。我德，則睦，否，則攜
貳。勞師於戎，而楚伐陳，必弗能救，是棄陳也。諸華必叛。戎，禽獸也。
獲戎失華，無乃不可乎？《夏訓》有之曰：『有窮后羿——』」

公曰：「后羿何如？」

---

69   Commentators believe this means that Archer Yi shoots nine suns out of ten to save
the world from being burnt up during the reign of Yao (*Huainanzi* 8.254–55).
According to *Huainanzi* 6.217, Yi also gets the elixir of immortality from the Queen
Mother of the West.

70   Wuzhong is a domain of the Shanrong tribe, at this time in Shanxi.

71   The Rong are characterized in the same terms in Yin 9.6.

72   Compare Guan Zhong's assertion in Min 1.2: "The Rong and the Di are jackals and
wolves and cannot be satisfied. The old Xia domains are close intimates and cannot
be abandoned." Note that while Guan Zhong uses the bestial metaphor to justify
military confrontation, Wei Jiang employs similar imagery to explain the need to
make peace. In *Shiji*, the "birds and beasts" analogy is used to justify both wars and
marriage diplomacy with the Xiongnu. See Wai-yee Li, "Hua Yi zhi bian yu yizu
tonghun"; "Historical Understanding in 'The Account of the Xiongnu' in *Shiji*."

Wei Jiang of Jin advocates peace with the Rong tribes. His remonstrance with Lord Dao on the subject includes an excursus on the dangers of indulging in hunting. The rhetorical connection between wars with the Rong and hunting may be found in the comparison of the Rong to "birds and beasts." Both represent an inappropriate or excessive use of martial power. Archer Yi appears in many early texts (e.g., Analects, Mencius, Xunzi, Zhuangzi, Han Feizi*) as a master archer. "Encountering Sorrow"* (Lisao) *mentions his sensual excesses and indulgence in hunting and also refers to Han Zhuo and Ao (Chuci buzhu 1.21–22). "Questions to Heaven"* (Tianwen) *asks, "How did Archer Yi shoot the suns?" (Chuci buzhu 3.96); the story of how Archer Yi "shoots ten suns" to save a parched world is also found in* Huainanzi 8.255.[69] *The focus of this passage in Zuozhuan, however, is on the warning posed by Archer Yi's errors of judgment. Archer Yi is mentioned in Zhao 28.2 as the destroyer of the evil Bofeng, and the legend of Ao is also told in Wu Zixu's remonstrance in Ai 1.2.*

The Master of Wuzhong,[70] Jiafu, sent Meng Yue to Jin. Through Wei Jiang[a] he presented furs of tigers and leopards, requesting with these gifts that Jin should reach a peace agreement with the various Rong tribes. The Prince of Jin said, "The Rong and Di, knowing nothing of kith and kin, are avaricious.[71] It would be better to attack them."

Wei Jiang said, "The princes have only recently submitted, and Chen has only recently come to seek peace. They are going to observe our every act. If we are virtuous, they will be in concord with us; if not, they will fall away and turn against us. If we are wearing our troops out in a conflict with the Rong and Chu attacks Chen, we will certainly not be able to go to the aid of the latter, and that will amount to abandoning Chen. The various central domains will certainly then rebel. The Rong tribes are birds and beasts.[72] Would it not be unacceptable to win control over the Rong and to lose the allegiance of the central domains? As the *Xia Instructions* has it, 'Archer Yi of the Youqiong lineage—'"[73]

The lord said, "What about Archer Yi?"

4.7a

---

73   This is incorporated into "Wuzi zhi ge" 五子之歌 (*Shangshu* 7.100) in the Ancient Script version of the *Documents*. Youqiong 有窮 lay to the west of present-day Luoyang 洛陽 in Henan. Lord Dao of Jin interrupts Wei Jiang. For another example of one character interrupting another, see Xiang 25.2. For examples of a character interrupting himself, see Zhao 6.3, 8.5. Qian Zhongshu (*Guanzhui bian*, 1:211–12) enumerates other examples from later historiography and fiction. Jin Shengtan applauds this mode of representing speech as suggestive of verisimilitude; see his comment in chapter 5 in *Shuihu zhuan huiping ben*, 146.

對曰：「昔有夏之方衰也，后羿自鉏遷于窮石，因夏民以代夏政。
恃其射也，不修民事，而淫于原獸，棄武羅、伯因、熊髡、尨圉，而用寒
浞。寒浞，伯明氏之讒子弟也，伯明后寒棄之，夷羿收之，信而使之，以
為己相。浞行媚于內，而施賂于外，愚弄其民，而虞羿于田。樹之詐慝，
以取其國家，外內咸服。羿猶不悛，將歸自田，家眾殺而亨之，以食其
子，其子不忍食諸，死于窮門。靡奔有鬲氏。浞因羿室，生澆及豷，恃其
讒慝詐偽，而不德于民，使澆用師，滅斟灌及斟尋氏。處澆于過，處豷
于戈。靡自有鬲氏，收二國之燼，以滅浞而立少康。少康滅澆于過，后杼
滅豷于戈，有窮由是遂亡，失人故也。昔周辛甲之為大史也，命百官，官
箴王闕。於〈虞人之箴〉曰：

---

74   Both Chu 鉏 and Qiongshi 窮石 are identified as places in Henan; Qiongshi lies to
the south of Luoyang. Archer Yi is called "Lord Yi" (Hou Yi 后羿) and "Yi from Yí"
or "Yi among the Yi tribe" (Yí Yi 夷羿, reading Yí as the name of a line [*ZZ* 29.507]
or a place) in the text.

75   We read *yu* 虞 as *wu* 誤, "mislead" or "deceive," following Wang Niansun (Karlgren,
gl. 470). Du Yu (*ZZ* 29.507) glosses *yu* 虞 as *le* 樂: "he amused Yi with hunting" or
"he induced Yi to be engrossed with hunting." Li Shan describes *yu* 虞 and *yu* 娛
("to amuse") as interchangeable (Liu Wenqi, *Chunqiu Zuoshi zhuan jiuzhu shuzheng*, 1013).

76   Alternatively, we could translate this line as "Having established for Archer Yi a bad
name for deceit and iniquities" (Karlgren, gl. 471) or "Having set up his deceptions
and evil deeds."

77   Yang (3:937) cites *Xiao erya* 小爾雅, which glosses *quan* 悛 as "aware" 覺, which is
also plausible: "even then Archer Yi was unaware" or "even then Archer Yi was
oblivious."

78   Lei Xueqi identifies this as the aforementioned Qiongshi (Yang, 3:927), while Du Yu
(*ZZ* 29.507) glosses it as "gate of the capital city." On the legends of Archer Yi's igno-
minious death, see "Encountering Sorrow" and "Questions to Heaven" (*Chuci buzhu*
1.21–22, 3.100). In *Mencius* 4B.24, Archer Yi is murdered by a jealous disciple.

79   Mi was a Xia minister who also served Archer Yi. Youge 有鬲 is identified as a place
in Shandong, southeast of Dezhou City 德州市.

80   Zhenguan and Zhenxun, both related to the Xia ruling house (ZZ-Kong 29.506), are
identified as places in present-day Shandong (Yang, 3:937).

81   Guo 過 is identified as a place in Shandong and is sometimes linked to an ancient
domain of the same name (Yang, 3:938). According to Du Yu (*ZZ* 29.507), Ge 戈 lay
between Song and Zheng.

He replied, "Formerly, just as Xia was in decline, Archer Yi moved from Chu to Qiongshi[74] and, with the support of the Xia people, took over Xia rule. Relying on his archery, he did not attend to the affairs of the people but indulged in hunting beasts of the plain. He cast off Wuluo, Boyin, Xiong Kun, and Mangyu and instead employed Han Zhuo. Han Zhuo was the deviant, slanderous son of the Boming lineage. Boming Lord Han had cast him off, and Archer Yi took him in, trusted him, and gave him assignments, making him his own assistant. Han Zhuo[a] flattered and seduced those inside the palace, offered bounties to those outside it, fooled and cajoled the people, and misled Archer Yi, making him engrossed with hunting.[75] Having planted in him deceit and iniquities,[76] he took Archer Yi's domain and patrimony from him, and those inside and outside all submitted to him. Even then Archer Yi did not repent.[77] When he was about to return to the court from the fields, his own men killed him, boiled him, and fed his flesh to his sons. His sons could not bear to eat it and died at the Gate of Qiong.[78] Mi fled to the Youge lineage.[79] Han Zhuo[a] took over Archer Yi's wives and concubines and fathered Ao and Yi. Relying on his slanderous wickedness and deceitful treachery, he showed no virtue toward the people and sent Ao to employ troops to eliminate the Zhenguan and Zhenxun lineages.[80] He placed Ao in Guo and Yi in Ge.[81] Mi, coming from the Youge lineage, collected the last embers—the remnant forces of Zhenguan and Zhenxun—to extinguish Han Zhuo[a] and establish Shaokang as ruler.[82] Shaokang killed Ao at Guo, and his son Lord Zhu killed Yi at Ge. That the Youqiong lineage thus perished was because it had failed in the proper use of men.[83] Formerly, when Xin Jia of Zhou was the grand scribe, he commanded the hundred officials, in keeping with their official duties, to remonstrate with the king on his shortcomings.[84] It is said in the 'Remonstrance of the Overseer of Hunts,'

---

82 Wu Zixu cites the story of Shaokang's resurgence as a cautionary tale to warn the Wu ruler Fucha against leniency toward the defeated Yue ruler Goujian (Ai 1.2).

83 Archer Yi's Youqiong lineage perished because he trusted Han Zhuo. Han Zhuo then usurped the name of the Youqiong lineage. Shaokang is remembered as a capable Xia king.

84 In *Shiji* 4.116, Xin Jia was a Shang minister who, after being repeatedly ignored by the last king of Shang, changed sides and became a Zhou minister. *Hanshu* 30.1729 lists "*Xin Jia*, twenty-nine chapters," which is no longer extant, but whose fragments were collected by Ma Guohan in *Yuhan shanfang jiyi shu*. The "Remonstrance of the Overseer of Hunts" 虞人之箴 might have been taken from *Xin Jia*. In *Wenxin diaolong* 11.409, Liu Xie names Xin Jia's "Remonstrances of the Hundred Officials" (Baiguan zhen 百官箴) as the most ancient example in the genre of remonstrances. He includes Wei Jiang's speech as another example (*Wenxin diaolong* 11.413). The Zhou minister Xin You (Xi 22.4) may be from the same line as Xin Jia.

芒芒禹跡，
畫為九州，
經啟九道。
民有寢、廟，
獸有茂草；
各有攸處，
德用不擾。
在帝夷羿，
冒于原獸，
忘其國恤，
而思其麀牡。
武不可重，
用不恢于夏家。
獸臣司原，
敢告僕夫。

〈虞箴〉如是，可不懲乎？」於是晉侯好田，故魏絳及之。

4.7b　公曰：「然則莫如和戎乎？」

　　對曰：「和戎有五利焉：戎狄荐居，貴貨易土，土可賈焉，一也。邊鄙不聳，民狎其野，稼人成功，二也。戎狄事晉，四鄰振動，諸侯威懷，三也。以德綏戎，師徒不勤，甲兵不頓，四也。鑒于后羿，而用德度，遠至邇安，五也。君其圖之！」

　　公說，使魏絳盟諸戎。修民事，田以時。

85　That is, the people have their places of repose in life and death.

86　In other words, there is no conflict between the nature of humans and animals (what they are) and their functions (what they do). Hunting would be optimal, just enough to provide the needs of humans.

87　In the phrase *youmu* 麀牡, *you* means "female deer" and *mu* means "male beasts."

88　For the connection between martial drills and hunting, see Yin 5.1. The word *sou* 蒐, which we have translated as "muster" (see Xi 31.4, Wen 6.1, 6.8, 8.7, 17.4, Xuan 14.2, Xiang 13.3, Zhao 4.3, 8.4, 11.5, 15.7, 29.5), also refers to "spring hunt." In reading *zhong* 重 as "grand" or "large scale," we have followed Fu Qian (Hong Liangji, *Chunqiu Zuozhuan gu*, 501). In Du Yu's (*ZZ* 29.508) reading, *chong* 重 means "repeated" or "frequent." It is because Archer Yi loved hunting that Xia was diminished under his rule.

89　Takezoe (14.25) suggests that Archer Yi's loss of the people's support may be linked to the threat of Jin losing the allegiance of the central domains, and Han Zhuo's expeditions against Zhenguan and Zhenxun may serve as a warning against the careless use of military resources.

Far-flung were the tracks of Yu—
Charting out nine regions,
He laid out and opened up nine routes.
The people had their bedchambers and temple chambers,[85]
The beasts had their luxuriant grass.
All had their place of abode,
And their qualities and functions were not confused.[86]
Archer Yi, in his position as king,
Coveted the hunt for beasts of the plains.
He forgot the concerns of state,
And thought only of does and stags.[87]
Martial drills must not become too grand,
For with them the Xia patrimony abjured greatness.[88]
The manager of beasts, in charge of the plains,
Presumes to notify my lord's servant.

Thus went the 'Remonstrance of the Overseer of Hunts.' Would it not be right to heed the warning?" At that time the Prince of Jin loved hunting; that was why Wei Jiang broached this topic.[89]

The lord said, "In that case, would it be better to seek peace with the Rong?" 4.7b

He replied, "Peace with the Rong has five advantages. First: the Rong and Di live off grasslands, they value goods and disdain land, and so lands can be purchased from them. Second: if those at the frontiers and borderlands are not fearful, the people will feel close to their fields,[90] and the harvesters will achieve success.[91] Third: if the Rong and Di serve Jin, our neighbors on four sides will be shaken, and the princes will be awed into submission. Fourth: if we use our virtue to pacify the Rong, the soldiers and officers will not toil, and armor and weapons will not be ruined. Fifth: if we regard Archer Yi as our cautionary mirror[92] and employ the standards of virtue, those from afar will come to us and those close by will be at ease. You, my lord, should consider this!"

The lord was pleased and sent Wei Jiang to swear a covenant with the various Rong tribes. He attended to the affairs of the people and hunted only at the proper seasons.

---

90   Karlgren, gl. 474. Du Yu (ZZ 29.508) glosses *xia* 狎 as *xi* 習, "to become familiar with."

91   "Harvesters" (*seren* 穡人) may refer to the people who reap the harvest or to the overseers who manage the farmers.

92   On the idea of history as a mirror, see also Xi 2.5, n. 24, Zhao 23.9, 26.10.

4.8　冬，十月，邾人、莒人伐鄶，臧紇救鄶，侵邾，敗於狐駘。國人逆喪者皆
髽，魯於是乎始髽。國人誦之曰：

> 臧之狐裘，
> 敗我于狐駘。
> 我君小子，
> 朱儒是使。
> 朱儒朱儒，
> 使我敗於邾。

春秋

5.1(1)　五年，春，公至自晉。

5.2(3)　夏，鄭伯使公子發來聘。

5.3(4)　叔孫豹、鄶世子巫如晉。

5.4(5)　仲孫蔑、衛孫林父會吳于善道。

93　Hutai 狐駘 was located in the domain of Zhu south of Teng County 滕縣, Shandong.

94　According to Kong Yingda's annotations to *Liji* 32.589, *zhua* 髽 was the mourning headdress for women. There are different types of *zhua*, whereby the hair was tied with hempen cloth and tied or braided with hemp strings. Here we probably have the simplest form of *zhua*—hair tied with hemp strings—taken up by both men and women. That this simplest form of mourning headdress was adopted for all implies that a great number of Lu soldiers died and there was no time for more elaborate preparation.

95　This is one of the *Zuozhuan* entries that explain the beginning of a custom (see also Xi 33.3, Xuan 8.5, and n. 134 in Xuan).

96　The battle took place in the tenth month according to the Lu calendar or in the eighth month according to the Xia calendar. This was not the season for wearing fox furs, which is mentioned only to indicate Zang Wuzhong's status as a dignitary of the domain. "Fox" may also come up by affective association (*xing* 興) with Hutai, a place name that contains the word for "fox" (*hu* 狐).

In winter, in the tenth month, the men of Zhu and Ju attacked Zeng. Zang Wuzhong[a] went to the aid of Zeng, invaded Zhu, and was defeated at Hutai.[93] The inhabitants of the capital who met the dead being brought back all had their hair tied in hemp strings.[94] It was then that hemp strings were first used to tie the hair of mourners in funeral rites.[95] The inhabitants of the capital chanted about this:

4.8

> Zang, in robes of fox fur,
> Brought us to defeat at Hutai.[96]
> Our ruler, the little one,
> Sends a midget, that's what he sends.[97]
> Midget, midget—
> You have brought about our defeat by Zhu.[98]

LORD XIANG 5 (568 BCE)
ANNALS

In the fifth year, in spring, our lord arrived from Jin.

5.1(1)

In summer, the Liege of Zheng sent Gongzi Fa (Ziguo) to come on an official visit.[99]

5.2(3)

Shusun Bao, the Zeng heir apparent Wu, went to Jin.[100]

5.3(4)

Zhongsun Mie (Meng Xianzi) and Sun Linfu of Wei met with Wu at Shandao.[101]

5.4(5)

---

97 Lord Xiang was only seven at this point; but the fact that his mother just died also renders the use of the term "little one" (*xiaozi* 小子) appropriate. Midgets belonged to a debased class of entertainers. Zang Wuzhong, as an aristocrat, could not have belonged to that class, and the derogatory term is used only to describe his small stature.

98 Lu was defeated by a much smaller domain, Zhu, which made it even more humiliating.

99 Ziguo, a son of Lord Mu of Zheng, was father of the famous Zichan. His lineage came to be known as the Guo lineage.

100 Since the point of the exegetical comment in Xiang 5.4 is the omission of the word "and" (*ji* 及), we have omitted the conjunction although English grammar requires it.

101 Shandao 善道 was in the domain of Wu and located north of present-day Xuyi County 盱眙縣, Anhui.

5.5(6)　秋，大雩。

5.6(7)　楚殺其大夫公子王夫。

5.7(8)　公會晉侯、宋公、陳侯、衛侯、鄭伯、曹伯、莒子、邾子、滕子、薛伯、齊
世子光、吳人、鄫人于戚。

5.8　公至自會。

5.9(9)　冬，戍陳。

5.10(9)　楚公子貞帥師伐陳。

5.11(9)　公會晉侯、宋公、衛侯、鄭伯、曹伯、莒子、邾子、滕子、薛伯、齊世子光
救陳。

5.12　十有二月，公至自救陳。

5.13(10)　辛未，季孫行父卒。

左傳

5.1(1)　五年，春，公至自晉。

5.2　王使王叔陳生愬戎于晉，晉人執之。士魴如京師，言王叔之貳於戎也。

5.3(2)　夏，鄭子國來聘，通嗣君也。

5.4(3)　穆叔覿鄫大子于晉，以成屬鄫。書曰「叔孫豹、鄫大子巫如晉」，言比諸
魯大夫也。

102　Alternatively, "Wangshu Chengsheng had shifted his allegiance to the Rong." Yu
Chang (cited in Yang, 3:942) speculates that Jin, having made peace with the Rong,
might be falsely accusing Chensheng in order to ignore the Zhou king's request for
help.

103　Lord Xi of Zheng acceded to his position two years earlier, in 570 BCE (Xiang 3).
Zheng's visits to Lu and other northern domains had become more irregular with
its submission to Chu.

104　This is to explain why the conjunction "and" (*ji* 及) is omitted in the *Annals* entry.
According to Kong Yingda (ZZ-Kong 30.514), when two Lu high officers are mentioned together, the conjunction *ji* is often omitted.

In autumn, there was a great rain sacrifice. 5.5(6)

Chu put to death its high officer Gongzi Renfu (Zixin). 5.6(7)

Our lord met with the Prince of Jin, the Duke of Song, the Prince of Chen, the Prince of Wei, the Liege of Zheng, the Liege of Cao, the Master of Ju, the Master of Zhu, the Master of Teng, the Liege of Xue, the Qi heir apparent Guang, a Wu leader, and a Zeng leader at Qī. 5.7(8)

Our lord arrived from the meeting. 5.8

In winter, we garrisoned Chen. 5.9(9)

Gongzi Zhen (Zinang) of Chu led out troops and attacked Chen. 5.10(9)

Our lord met with the Prince of Jin, the Duke of Song, the Prince of Wei, the Liege of Zheng, the Liege of Cao, the Master of Ju, the Master of Zhu, the Master of Teng, the Liege of Xue, and the Qi heir apparent Guang and went to the aid of Chen. 5.11(9)

In the twelfth month, our lord arrived from the expedition that went to the aid of Chen. 5.12

On the *xinwei* day (20), Jisun Hangfu (Ji Wenzi) died. 5.13(10)

ZUO

In the fifth year, in spring, our lord arrived from Jin. 5.1(1)

A Zhou noble coming to Jin to seek help against Rong incursions into Zhou territory is arrested by Jin leaders on charges of being in league with the Rong. This represents an inversion of the political goal of defending the Zhou court against barbarians often avowed by covenant chiefs.

The Zhou king sent Wangshu Chensheng to make an accusation against the Rong at the Jin court. The leaders of Jin arrested him. Shi Fang went to the Zhou capital and claimed that Wangshu Chensheng[a] was a double agent for the Rong.[102] 5.2

In summer, Ziguo (Gongzi Fa) of Zheng came to us on an official visit: this was to establish relations with the new ruler.[103] 5.3(2)

Jin recognizes Lu's subjugation of Zeng.

Shusun Bao[a] presented the heir apparent of Zeng at the court of Jin in order to formalize the submission of Zeng to Lu. The text says, "Shusun Bao, the Zeng heir apparent Wu, went to Jin": this is to treat the latter as the equal of a Lu high officer.[104] 5.4(3)

5.5(4) 吳子使壽越如晉，辭不會于雞澤之故，且請聽諸侯之好。
晉人將為之合諸侯，使魯、衛先會吳，且告會期。故孟獻子、孫文子會吳于善道。

5.6(5) 秋，大雩，旱也。

5.7(6) 楚人討陳叛故，曰：「由令尹子辛實侵欲焉。」乃殺之。書曰「楚殺其大夫公子王夫」，貪也。
君子謂「楚共王於是不刑。《詩》曰：

周道挺挺，
我心扃扃。
講見不令，
集人來定。

己則無信，而殺人以逞，不亦難乎！《夏書》曰：『成允成功。』」

5.8(7) 九月丙午，盟于戚，會吳，且命戍陳也。
穆叔以屬鄫為不利，使鄫大夫聽命于會。

---

105 This ode is an "uncollected ode" not found in the received text of *Maoshi*.

106 The line comes to be included in "Da Yu mo" 大禹謨 (*Shangshu* 4.55) in the Ancient Script version of the *Documents*. Cf. Zhuang n. 31, Xi n. 344, Wen n. 126, Xiang nn. 583, 832, Ai. n. 434.

107 Shusun Bao wants Zeng to attend the meeting and to receive commands from the covenant chief, Jin, as an independent sovereign domain. His position on Zeng thus

Jin is eager to accept Wu overtures and makes its allies meet with Wu.

The Master of Wu sent Shou Yue to Jin to explain why Wu had not come to the meeting at Ji Marsh and further to request that Wu be allowed to enjoy amity with the princes.　　5.5(4)

　　For his sake, the leaders of Jin planned to assemble the princes. They sent Lu and Wei to meet first with Wu and moreover to notify them of the meeting date. That was why Meng Xianzi and Sun Linfu[a] met with Wu at Shandao.

In autumn, there was a great rain sacrifice, this was because of the drought.　　5.6(5)

The Chu minister Zixin (Gongzi Renfu) is put to death because of Chu's troubles with Chen. Chen leaders blame their defection on Zixin's rapacity (Xiang 3.6). An exegetical comment accepts this reasoning, but a noble man criticizes King Gong for his miscarriage of justice.

The leaders of Chu demanded an explanation for Chen's revolt. The men of Chen said, "It was all on account of the chief minister, Zixin, who rapaciously invaded us." Chu therefore put him to death. The text says, "Chu put to death its high officer Gongzi Renfu (Zixin)": this was because of his rapacity.　　5.7(6)

　　The noble man said, "King Gong of Chu in this case used punishment improperly. As it says in the Odes,

> The great road is level and straight;
> My mind is keen and discerning.
> If the affairs planned are going awry,
> Gather wise men to decide on them.[105]

He himself lacked good faith, and he put others to death to satisfy his own wishes. Is this not difficult? As it says in the *Xia Documents*, 'Fulfill good faith, and achievements will be fulfilled.'"[106]

Jin and its allies plan to defend Chen against Chu.

In the ninth month, on the *bingwu* day (23), the princes swore a covenant at Qī. This was to meet with Wu leaders and further to issue the command to garrison Chen.　　5.8(7)

　　Shusun Bao[a] considered it disadvantageous to have Zeng as a subordinate and had the high officers of Zeng await commands at the meeting.[107]

---

differs from Meng Xianzi's (Xiang 4.5), possibly as a result of Lu's luckless intervention on behalf of Zeng (Xiang 4.8).

5.9(9–11)　楚子囊為令尹。范宣子曰：「我喪陳矣。楚人討貳而立子囊，必改行，而疾討陳。陳近于楚，民朝夕急，能無往乎？有陳，非吾事也；無之而後可。」

　　　　　　冬，諸侯戍陳。子囊伐陳。十一月甲午，會于城棣以救之。

5.10(13)　季文子卒。大夫入斂，公在位。宰庀家器為葬備，無衣帛之妾，無食粟之馬，無藏金玉，無重器備，君子是以知季文子之忠於公室也：「相三君矣，而無私積，可不謂忠乎？」

春秋

6.1(1)　六年，春，王三月，壬午，杞伯姑容卒。

6.2(2)　夏，宋華弱來奔。

6.3　秋，葬杞桓公。

6.4(3)　滕子來朝。

6.5(4)　莒人滅鄫。

6.6(5)　冬，叔孫豹如邾。

6.7(6)　季孫宿如晉。

6.8(7)　十有二月，齊侯滅萊。

108　Zinang, replacing Zixin, is King Gong's younger brother.

109　Chengdi 城棣 was in the domain of Zheng and located north of present-day Yuan-yang County 原陽縣, Henan.

Wise ministers distrust the apparent affirmation of power. Just like Shusun Bao of Lu (Xiang 5.8), the Jin minister Fan Gai regards a smaller domain's submission as a liability, echoing Han Jue's earlier judgment (Xiang 4.1).

Zinang of Chu became chief minister.[108] Fan Gai[c] said, "We have lost Chen. The men of Chu chastised the disloyal and established Zinang in office, and they will certainly change their ways and swiftly chastise Chen. Chen is close to Chu, so its people are anxious day and night. Can they do otherwise than turn to Chu? It is not our business to keep Chen. Only when we cede control over Chen will things turn out all right." 5.9(9–11)

In winter, the princes garrisoned Chen. Zinang attacked Chen. In the eleventh month, on the *jiawu* day (12), the princes met at Chengdi to go to Chen's aid.[109]

The Lu chief minister, Ji Wenzi, who is said to have shown his integrity and loyalty by refusing to aggrandize his lineage, dies.

Ji Wenzi died. Since it was a high officer who was being laid in his coffin, our lord took his rightful place to observe the procedure. Ji Wenzi's steward set forth patrimonial vessels as preparation for the burial. There were no concubines who wore silk, no horses that were fed grains, no stored-up gold and jade, no doubled set of utensils. Thus did the noble man know that Ji Wenzi was loyal to our lord's house:[110] "He assisted three rulers, and yet he had no private accumulation of wealth. Can this not be called loyalty?" 5.10(13)

LORD XIANG 6 (567 BCE)
ANNALS

In the sixth year, in spring, in the royal third month, on the *renwu* day (2), Gurong, the Liege of Qi, died. 6.1(1)

In summer, Hua Ruo of Song came to us in flight. 6.2(2)

In autumn, Lord Huan of Qi was buried. 6.3

The Master of Teng came to visit our court. 6.4(3)

Ju leaders extinguished Zeng. 6.5(4)

In winter, Shusun Bao went to Zhu. 6.6(5)

Jisun Su (Ji Wuzi) went to Jin. 6.7(6)

In the twelfth month, the Prince of Qi extinguished Lai. 6.8(7)

---

110 Fan Xie appraised Ji Wenzi in similar terms in Cheng 16.11. Active in Lu politics since Wen 6 (621 BCE), Ji Wenzi was chief minister for thirty-three years (601–568).

左傳

6.1(1)　六年，春，杞桓公卒。始赴以名，同盟故也。

6.2(2)　宋華弱與樂轡少相狎，長相優，又相謗也。子蕩怒，以弓梏華弱于朝。平
公見之，曰：「司武而梏於朝，難以勝矣。」遂逐之。夏，宋華弱來奔。
　　　司城子罕曰：「同罪異罰，非刑也。專戮於朝，罪孰大焉？」亦逐子
蕩。子蕩射子罕之門，曰：「幾日而不我從！」子罕善之如初。

6.3(4)　秋，滕成公來朝，始朝公也。

6.4(5)　莒人滅鄫，鄫恃賂也。

6.5(6)　冬，穆叔如邾，聘，且修平。

---

111 The minister of the right (*youshi* 右師) held the highest rank in Song. Yue Xi, as supervisor of fortifications (*sicheng* 司城), ranked fifth among the six ministers of Song.

112 Both were descended from Duke Dai of Song. This Yue Pei is to be distinguished from the supervisor of fortifications Yue Pei (Ai 26.1, 26.2).

113 According to Du Yu and Kong Yingda (ZZ 30.516), Yue Pei puts the bow around Hua Ruo's neck, "binding him as manacles bind hands." Here we imagine Yue Pei putting his bow over Hua Ruo and using the bowstrings to bind his hands (Takezoe, 14.35; Karlgren, gl. 477).

114 Kong Yingda (ZZ-Kong 30.516) suggests that this is part of Yue Xi's speech: "We should also drive Yue Pei away."

115 Being defied, Yue Xi is shown to be unequal to his office, just like Hua Ruo.

116 It is not clear which domain received the bribes. Zeng is no longer Lu's protectorate at this point.

A Qǐ ruler, earlier designated as "Master of Qǐ" (Xi 24.3), dies: he is said to have his name recorded in the Annals *now because Qǐ and Lu had become covenant partners (Annals, Cheng 5.7, 7.6, 9.2).*

In the sixth year, in spring, Lord Huan of Qǐ died. For the first time Qǐ sent the notice of its ruler's death by name. This was because Lu and Qǐ were covenant partners.   6.1(1)

Yue Xi, dominant in Song government for twenty-four years (Xiang 6–29, 576–544),[111] shows his impartiality by castigating a kinsman. That he relents can be seen as either weakness (Fu Qian) or necessary compromise (Kong Yingda). In similar scenarios, the Song minister Xiang Xu does not punish Hua Chen (Xiang 17.5), and Zichan of Zheng refrains from driving out Gongsun Hei (Zhao 1.7).

Hua Ruo and Yue Pei,[112] both of Song, were on overly familiar terms when they were young. They taunted each other when grown and also slandered each other. Yue Pei[a] in a rage used his bow to manacle Hua Ruo in court.[113] Lord Ping saw this and said, "If he allows himself to be manacled in court, even though he is a supervisor of the military, it will be hard for him to live up to his office!" He thus drove him away. In summer, Hua Ruo of Song came to us in flight.   6.2(2)

The supervisor of fortifications, Yue Xi[b], said, "To mete out different sentences to those guilty of the same offense is not proper punishment. He acted on his own authority to humiliate another at court. What offense can be greater than that?" He also drove Yue Pei[a] away.[114] Yue Pei[a] shot an arrow at Yue Xi[a]'s gate, saying, "In a few days, will you not be following me?"[115] Yue Xi[a] treated him well as before.

After a lapse of forty-eight years, a Teng ruler comes to the Lu court, probably in the hope of seeking Jin protection through the Jin-Lu accord.

In autumn, Lord Cheng of Teng came to visit our court. This was the first time he had visited the court of our lord.   6.3(4)

Ju leaders extinguished Zeng: this was because Zeng was relying on bribery for protection.[116]   6.4(5)

Lu and Zhu went to war over Zeng in Xiang 4.8. Control over Zeng is by now a dead issue, and Lu and Zhu can reach a peace agreement. This is the only recorded friendly visit of Lu to Zhu in the Annals.

In winter, Shusun Bao[a] went to Zhu on an official visit and also to cultivate peaceful relations.   6.5(6)

6.6(7)　晉人以鄫故來討，曰：「何故亡鄫？」季武子如晉見，且聽命。

6.7(8)　十一月，齊侯滅萊，萊恃謀也。

於鄭子國之來聘也，四月，晏弱城東陽，而遂圍萊。甲寅，堙之環城，傅於堞。及杞桓公卒之月，乙未，王湫帥師及正輿子、棠人軍齊師，齊師大敗之。丁未，入萊。萊共公浮柔奔棠，正輿子、王湫奔莒，莒人殺之。四月，陳無宇獻萊宗器于襄宮。晏弱圍棠，十一月丙辰而滅之。遷萊于郳。高厚、崔杼定其田。

117　It should be "the twelfth month," as in the *Annals*.

118　See *Annals*, Xiang 5.2.

119　The piling of earthen mounds around city walls to allow better surveillance of the enemy is called *juyin* 距闉 in *Sunzi* 3.93 (Wu Jing'an, *Chunqiu Zuoshi zhuan jiuzhu shuzheng xu*, 8). There is no *jiayin* day in the fourth month.

120　That is, the third month of this year; see *Annals* 6.1.

121　Zheng Yuzi bribed Susha Wei of Qi four years earlier (Xiang 2.2). Tang 棠 was a settlement in Lai and was located north of present-day Yutai County 魚臺縣, Shandong.

Lu sought Jin sanction for its control over Zeng (Xiang 4.5, 5.4) but lacked the power to control or defend Zeng (Xiang 4.8, 5.8, 6.4). Ji Wuzi (Ji Wenzi's son) goes to Jin to explain Lu's position and to seek recognition of his position as the new de facto chief minister of Lu.

The men of Jin, on account of Zeng, came to demand an explanation, saying, "Why did you allow Zeng to be destroyed?" Ji Wuzi went to Jin to seek an audience and also to await its commands.   6.6(7)

The small domain of Lai, whose rulers had the same clan name as Qi (Jiang), harbors the disaffected Qi officer Wang Jiao (Cheng 18.2) and relies on bribes (Xiang 2.2) to defy Qi (Xiang 2.4). Qi first attacked Lai thirty-five years earlier (Xuan 7.2). Here it extinguishes Lai, chiefly through the strategies of Yan Ruo (Xiang 2.4), father of the famous Qi minister Yan Ying.

In the eleventh month,[117] the Prince of Qi extinguished Lai because Lai was relying on its schemes.   6.7(8)

In the fourth month of the year when Ziguo of Zheng came to us on an official visit,[118] Yan Ruo fortified Dongyang and then laid siege to Lai. On the *jiayin* day, he piled up mounds of earth to encircle the city wall, pressing close to the parapets.[119] When it came to the month in which Lord Huan of Qǐ died,[120] on the *yiwei* day (15) Wang Jiao led an army and, together with Zheng Yuzi and an army of the men of Tang, confronted the Qi army.[121] The Qi army roundly defeated them. On the *dingwei* day (27), the Qi army entered Lai. Lord Gong of Lai, Furou, fled to Tang. Zheng Yuzi and Wang Jiao fled to Ju, and the men of Ju put them to death. In the fourth month, Chen Wuyu presented Lai ancestral vessels at the temple of Lord Xiang.[122] Yan Ruo laid siege to Tang, and in the eleventh month, on the *bingchen* day (10), extinguished it.[123] The people of Lai were relocated to Ni.[124] Gao Hou and Cui Zhu demarcated the boundaries of the fields of Lai.[125]

---

122   Chen Wuyu was the great-great-grandson of Jingzhong of Chen, who fled to Qi in 672 BCE (Zhuang 22.1). Takezoe (14.36) suggests that Lord Xiang is a mistake for Lord Hui (Xiang 6.36–37), who had attacked Lai in 602 and 600 BCE (Xuan 7.2; *Annals*, Xuan 9.4).

123   Tang might have been singled out for mention because the ruler of Lai, Furou, died in this siege.

124   The precise location of Ni 郳 is unknown.

125   Gao Hou and Cui Zhu survey the lands to be divided among Qi nobles.

春秋

7.1(1)　　七年，春，郳子來朝。

7.2(2)　　夏，四月，三卜郊，不從，乃免牲。

7.3(4)　　小邾子來朝。

7.4(3)　　城費。

7.5(5)　　秋，季孫宿如衛。

7.6　　　八月，螽。

7.7(7)　　冬，十月，衛侯使孫林父來聘。壬戌，及孫林父盟。

7.8(8)　　楚公子貞帥師圍陳。

7.9(9)　　十有二月，公會晉侯、宋公、陳侯、衛侯、曹伯、莒子、邾子于鄬。鄭伯髠頑如會，未見諸侯，丙戌，卒于鄵。

7.10(10)　陳侯逃歸。

左傳

7.1(1)　　七年，春，郳子來朝，始朝公也。

7.2(2)　　夏，四月，三卜郊，不從，乃免牲。
　　　　　孟獻子曰：「吾乃今而後知有卜、筮。夫郊祀后稷，以祈農事也。是故啟蟄而郊，郊而後耕。今既耕而卜郊，宜其不從也。」

126　See also Xi 31.3, Cheng 7.1.

127　This is the first instance of high officers being named in sieges.

128　According to *Zuozhuan*, Xiang 7.9, the Zheng ruler was murdered. The record of his death here may indicate that Zheng notified Lu that he died from illness. Cf. similar discrepancies in *Annals*, Zhao 1.10 and Ai 10.3.

129　Divination by milfoil is here mentioned by association. In the *Annals*, divination is always done with turtle shell, whereas both types of divination are common in *Zuozhuan*.

130　*Qizhi* 啟蟄 or *jingzhi* 驚蟄, the awakening of insects from winter dormancy, later becomes one of the twenty-four terms for seasonal changes in the Chinese calendar. Meng Xianzi decries the divination as untimely, but the very propriety of conducting divination for regular sacrifices is questioned (Xi 31.3).

ANNALS

In the seventh year, in spring, the Master of Tan came to visit our court. 7.1(1)

In summer, in the fourth month, we divined three times about performing the sacrifice in the outskirts. The results were not favorable, so we spared the sacrificial animals.[126] 7.2(2)

The Master of Lesser Zhu came to visit our court. 7.3(4)

We fortified Bi. 7.4(3)

In autumn, Jisun Su (Ji Wuzi) went to Wei. 7.5(5)

In the eighth month, there were locusts. 7.6

In winter, in the tenth month, the Prince of Wei sent Sun Linfu to come on an official visit. On the *renxu* day (21), we swore a covenant with Sun Linfu. 7.7(7)

Gongzi Zhen (Zinang) of Chu led out troops and laid siege to Chen.[127] 7.8(8)

In the twelfth month, our lord met with the Prince of Jin, the Duke of Song, the Prince of Chen, the Prince of Wei, the Liege of Cao, the Master of Ju, and the Master of Zhu at Wei. Kunwan, the Liege of Zheng, was going to the meeting, but before he had an audience with the princes, on the *bingxu* day (16), he died at Cao.[128] 7.9(9)

The Prince of Chen fled homeward to Chen. 7.10(10)

ZUO

In the seventh year, in spring, the Master of Tan came to visit our court. This was the first time he had visited the court of our lord. 7.1(1)

According to the Lu minister Meng Xianzi, untimely and irrelevant divination yields unfavorable results.

In summer, in the fourth month, we divined three times about performing the sacrifice in the outskirts. The results were not favorable, so we spared the sacrificial animals. 7.2(2)

Meng Xianzi said, "Only now do I know that there really is such a thing as divination by turtle shell and by milfoil![129] Now sacrifice in the outskirts is offered to Lord Millet as we pray for blessings in agricultural matters. That is why sacrifice in the outskirts is performed after the insects have stirred from their winter dormancy; and plowing begins only after performing sacrifice in the outskirts. Since on this occasion we had plowed and only then divined about sacrifice in the outskirts, it is fitting that the divination was unfavorable."[130]

7.3(4)　南遺為費宰。叔仲昭伯為隧正，欲善季氏，而求媚於南遺。謂遺：「請城費，吾多與而役。」故季氏城費。

7.4(3)　小邾穆公來朝，亦始朝公也。

7.5(5)　秋，季武子如衛，報子叔之聘，且辭緩報，非貳也。

7.6　冬，十月，晉韓獻子告老，公族穆子有廢疾，將立之。辭曰：「《詩》曰：

> 豈不夙夜？
> 謂行多露。

又曰：

> 弗躬弗親，
> 庶民弗信。

無忌不才，讓，其可乎？請立起也。與田蘇游，而曰『好仁』。《詩》曰：

131　Takezoe (14.39) observes that while Shuzhong Zhaobo's grandfather, Shuzhong Huibo, died defending the rights of the legitimate heir of Lord Wen (Wen 18.5), Shuzhong Zhaobo was eager to flatter the usurping Ji lineage; and whereas Ji Wenzi was lauded for his loyalty (Xiang 5.10), Ji Wuzi was interested in buttressing his own power.

132　Han Jue was supervisor of the military at the battle of An in 589 BCE (Cheng 2.3) and commander of the lower army at the battle of Yanling in 575 (Cheng 16.5). He assumed charge of government as commander of the central army in 573 (Cheng 18.12).

133　Han Wuji was appointed as high officer of ruling lineages in 573 BCE (Cheng 18.3); for the explanation of that position, see Xuan 2.4. *Feiji* 廢疾 has also been glossed as "incurable illness" or "long-lasting illness" (Yang, 3:951, citing *Shuowen jiezi*).

134　*Maoshi* 17, "Xinglu" 行露, 1D.55. Han Wuji uses the hesitation of the speaker who is torn between desire and fear of impropriety as analogy for his own conflicting wish to serve and reservation on account of his sickness. The same lines are cited in Xi 20.4 to aver the importance of "weighing one's strength."

135　*Maoshi* 191, "Jie nan shan" 節南山, 12A.395. Han Wuji is saying that his sickness means he cannot personally attend to his duties, and this will arouse discontent among the people.

136　Han Qi was Han Wuji's younger brother.

　Zuo Tradition

Bi, a settlement granted to Gongzi You (Ji You) almost a century earlier (Xi 1.6), is here fortified, a sign of the Ji lineage's rising power. The stewards of Bi, increasingly entrenched, will in turn challenge Ji leaders; see the rebellions of Nan Kuai (Zhao 12.10) and Gongshan Buniu (Ding 5.4, 8.10).

Nan Yi was the steward of Bi. Shuzhong Dai[a] was the director of conscripts. Wishing to please the Ji lineage head, Ji Wuzi, he sought to ingratiate himself with Nan Yi. He said to Nan Yi[a], "Request to fortify Bi. I will give you more conscripts for the work." That was why the Ji lineage head fortified Bi.[131]

7.3(4)

Lord Mu of Lesser Zhu came to visit our court: this was also the first time he had visited the court of our lord.

7.4(3)

Lu returns Wei's official visit (Xiang 1.5) only after an interval of six years, possibly because of the setbacks Lu suffered in Zeng. The relative weakness of Wei also accounts for this neglect. Lu has sent five missions to Jin over the same period.

In autumn, Ji Wuzi went to Wei to reciprocate the official visit of Gongsun Piao[a] and also to explain that the delay in the return visit was not on account of double-dealing.

7.5(5)

Han Jue retires, and his eldest son, Han Wuji, who is supposed to succeed to the position of chief minister of Jin, yields the position to his younger brother Han Qi. He justifies his decision with apposite quotations from the Odes. Anecdotes explaining why an appointment is just despite suspicions of impropriety or partiality are common in Jin-related materials.

In winter, in the tenth month, Han Jue[a] of Jin announced his retirement on account of old age.[132] Han Wuji[a] had a debilitating illness,[133] but there was a plan to establish him as successor. He declined, saying, "It says in the *Odes*,

7.6

> How could I not want to go morning and night?
> Yet what is to be done—for walking there is too much dew.[134]

It also says,

> He does not attend to things personally; he does not take charge himself;
> That is why the common people have no faith in him.[135]

I lack talent. Is it not acceptable that I should yield? I request to have Han Qi[d] established as successor.[136] He associates with Tian Su, who says he 'loves nobility of spirit.' As it says in the *Odes*,

靖共爾位，
好是正直。
神之聽之，
介爾景福。

恤民為德，正直為正，正曲為直，參和為仁。如是則神聽之，介福降之。
立之，不亦可乎？」
　　庚戌，使宣子朝，遂老。晉侯謂韓無忌仁，使掌公族大夫。

7.7(7)　衛孫文子來聘，且拜武子之言，而尋孫桓子之盟。公登亦登。叔孫穆子
相，趨進，曰：「諸侯之會，寡君未嘗後衛君。今吾子不後寡君，寡君未
知所過。吾子其少安！」孫子無辭，亦無悛容。
　　穆叔曰：「孫子必亡。為臣而君，過而不悛，亡之本也。《詩》曰：

退食自公，
委蛇委蛇。

謂從者也。衡而委蛇，必折。」

7.8(8)　楚子囊圍陳，會于鄬以救之。

137　*Maoshi* 207, "Xiaoming" 小明, 13A.447.

138　What is "straight" (*zhi* 直) does not need to be "aligned" or "rectified" (*zheng* 正):
the verb may indicate "furthering" or "full realization," or it may imply that even
those who are basically just may still have minor flaws. The "three" are virtue (*de*),
rectification (*zheng*), and straightening (*zhi*).

139　See Xiang 7.5.

140　Sun Liangfu, father of Sun Linfu, swore a covenant with Lu in 588 BCE (*Annals*,
Cheng 3.11).

141　According to *Yili* 22.262, the envoy should thrice yield precedence to the hosting
ruler, and he should be two steps behind the ruler as they ascend the seven steps
linking the central court to the palace hall (*Yili* 20.242). Backed by Jin, Sun Linfu
may be dismissive of the Lu ruler because the latter is only nine or ten years old.

142　Sun Linfu is said to have behaved arrogantly toward the Lu ruler because he defies
his own ruler in Wei.

143　*Maoshi* 18, "Gaoyang" 羔羊, 1D.57.

144　The ode "Gaoyang" praises the free and easy gait of the official who presumably has
fulfilled his duties. Sun Linfu's disregard for Lord Xiang's rightful precedence and
his lack of remorse might have been described as a kind of "free and easy" demeanor,
which, however, is here the mark of transgression.

Be loyal and vigilant with the duties of your position;
Be eager to be the one who rectifies and straightens.
The spirits will listen to you
And will help you, bestowing great blessings.[137]

To have compassion for the people is virtue; to align the straight is perfect rectification; to rectify the crooked is perfect straightening. And to be in harmony with these three[138] is nobility of spirit. In this way, the spirits will listen to you and will confer great blessings on you. Is it not acceptable to establish him as successor?"

On the *gengxu* day (9), Han Jue had Han Qi[b] attend court and retired forthwith. The Prince of Jin considered Han Wuji noble in spirit and put him in charge of the high officers of ruling lineages.

The Lu minister Shusun Bao predicts exile for the visiting Wei dignitary Sun Linfu because of the latter's incivility toward the Lu ruler. Sun's conflict with Wei rulers (Cheng 7.6, 14.1) culminates in exile for Lord Xian of Wei (Xiang 14.4), whose restoration, in turn, results in Sun Linfu's exile (Xiang 26.2). This anecdote is debated in Han Feizi *39.870–71, unfolding as arguments on whether the Wei ruler's failure or Sun Linfu's presumption deserves greater censure and on whether and when a subject may claim a ruler's prerogative.*

Sun Linfu of Wei came to us on an official visit and also to bow in respect for Ji Wuzi[c]'s words of apology.[139] Further, he was renewing the covenant sworn by Sun Liangfu[a].[140] When our lord ascended the steps, Sun Linfu also ascended.[141] Shusun Bao[b], acting as our lord's assistant, hastened forward and said, "At meetings of the princes, our unworthy ruler has never come after the Wei ruler. Now you, sir, did not stay behind our unworthy ruler. Our unworthy ruler does not yet know where he was at fault. You, sir, should proceed at greater leisure!" Sun Linfu[b] did not offer any explanation, nor did he appear remorseful.

    7.7(7)

Shusun Bao[a] said, "Sun Linfu[b] will certainly go into exile. Being a subject, he behaves like a ruler, and having erred, he does not repent: these are the root causes of exile.[142] As it says in the *Odes*,

> Retreating from court for supper,
> With steps free and easy.[143]

This refers only to those who follow the right course of action. But when the recalcitrant ones are free and easy, they are sure to be broken."[144]

Zinang of Chu laid siege to Chen. The princes joined forces at Wei to come to Chen's aid.

    7.8(8)

7.9(9) 鄭僖公之為大子也，於成之十六年與子罕適晉，不禮焉。又與子豐適楚，亦不禮焉。及其元年朝于晉，子豐欲愬諸晉而廢之，子罕止之。及將會于鄬，子駟相，又不禮焉。侍者諫，不聽；又諫，殺之。及鄬，子駟使賊夜弒僖公，而以瘧疾赴于諸侯。簡公生五年，奉而立之。

7.10(10) 陳人患楚。慶虎、慶寅謂楚人曰：「吾使公子黃往，而執之。」楚人從之。二慶使告陳侯于會，曰：「楚人執公子黃矣。君若不來，群臣不忍社稷宗廟，懼有二圖。」陳侯逃歸。

---

145   *Gongyang*, Xiang 7 (19.244), claims that this turn of events was "concealed on behalf of the central domains" (*wei zhongguo hui* 為中國諱) in the *Annals*.

146   Cf. Gao Shiqi, *Zuozhuan jishi benmo*, 612.

147   The first year of Lord Xi's reign corresponded to the third year of Lord Xiang's (570 BCE).

148   The received text has *nüeji* 瘧疾, the modern Chinese term for malaria. *Nüe* 瘧 is the same as *nüe* 虐 ("severe"). *Shiji* 42.1771 records that Lord Xi was poisoned and the funeral notification claimed that he had died of "sudden, serious illness" 暴病, which would have been derived from *nüeji* 瘧疾. See also Yu Yue, quoted in Karlgren, gl. 482.

When Lord Xi of Zheng was heir apparent and went with Zihan to Jin in the sixteenth year of Lord Cheng of Lu, he did not treat Zihan with ritual propriety. He went with Zifeng to Chu as well and again did not treat him with ritual propriety. By the first year of his reign,[147] when they visited the court of Jin, Zifeng wanted to accuse him before the Jin leaders and depose him, but Zihan stopped him. When he was about to attend the meeting at Wei, Zisi was his assistant, and again he did not treat him with ritual propriety. His attendant remonstrated with him, and he did not heed him; when he remonstrated again, the lord put him to death. When they reached Cao, Zisi sent brigands to assassinate Lord Xi at night and sent to the princes a notice of his death, claiming that it was the result of a sudden, serious illness.[148] They supported Lord Jian, who was five years old, and established him as ruler.

Chen is torn between Jin and Chu (Xiang 3.6, 3.8, 5.7, 5.8, 5.9, 7.8). Chen high officers, fearful of offending Chu, maneuver to force Lord Ai of Chen to leave the meeting of the princes led by Jin at Wei.

The men of Chen were troubled about Chu. Qing Hu and Qing Yin told the men of Chu, "We will send Gongzi Huang to you, and you will arrest him."[149] The men of Chu acted accordingly. The two Qings sent someone to tell the Prince of Chen at the meeting, "The men of Chu have arrested Gongzi Huang! If you, my lord, do not come back, your subjects will find it hard to bear what will happen to the altars of our domain as well as our Ancestral Temples. We fear there will be another plan."[150] The Prince of Chen fled homeward to Chen.

7.9(9)

7.10(10)

---

149   Qing Hu and Qing Yin are ministers in charge of government in Chen. Gongzi Huang is the younger brother of Lord Ai, who is attending the meeting at Wei.

150   Qing Hu and Qing Yin are implicitly threatening to establish another Chen ruler who will be more conciliatory toward Chu.

春秋

8.1(1) 八年，春，王正月，公如晉。

8.2 夏，葬鄭僖公。

8.3(3) 鄭人侵蔡，獲蔡公子燮。

8.4(4) 季孫宿會晉侯、鄭伯、齊人、宋人、衛人、邾人于邢丘。

8.5 公至自晉。

8.6(5) 莒人伐我東鄙。

8.7(6) 秋，九月，大雩。

8.8(7) 冬，楚公子貞帥師伐鄭。

8.9(8) 晉侯使士匄來聘。

左傳

8.1(1) 八年，春，公如晉，朝，且聽朝聘之數。

8.2 鄭群公子以僖公之死也，謀子駟。子駟先之。夏，四月庚辰，辟殺子狐、子熙、子侯、子丁。孫擊、孫惡出奔衛。

ANNALS

In the eighth year, in spring, in the royal first month, our lord went to Jin.   8.1(1)

In summer, Lord Xi of Zheng was buried.   8.2

Zheng leaders invaded Cai and captured Gongzi Xie of Cai.   8.3(3)

Jisun Su (Ji Wuzi) met with the Prince of Jin, the Liege of Zheng, a Qi   8.4(4)
leader, a Song leader, a Wei leader, and a Zhu leader at Xingqiu.[151]

Our lord arrived from Jin.   8.5

Ju leaders invaded our eastern marches.   8.6(5)

In autumn, in the ninth month, there was a great rain sacrifice.   8.7(6)

In winter, Gongzi Zhen (Zinang) of Chu led out troops and attacked   8.8(7)
Zheng.

The Prince of Jin sent Shi Gai (Fan Gai) to us on an official visit.   8.9(8)

ZUO

In the eighth year, in spring, our lord went to Jin to visit its court and also   8.1(1)
to await commands on the appropriate frequency for visiting its court
and for official visits.[152]

The noble sons of Zheng, on account of Lord Xi's death, plotted against   8.2
Zisi. Zisi acted first. In summer, in the fourth month, on the *gengchen*
day (12), he trumped up some charge and put to death Zihu, Zixi, Zihou,
and Ziding. Sunji and Sun'e left the domain and fled to Wei.[153]

---

151   Xingqiu was last mentioned in Xuan 6.3.

152   Du Yu (ZZ 30.520) glosses *chaopin zhi shu* 朝聘之數 as specifications on the amount
       of gifts and money to be offered and considers this a sign of Jin resurgence under
       Lord Dao; Kong Yingda (ZZ-Kong 30.520), citing You Ji's comment on how princes
       came on official visits (*pin*) to Jin every three years and attended its court (*chao*)
       every five years during the reigns of Lords Wen and Xiang (Zhao 3.1), argues that
       chaopin zhi shu refers to the frequency of visits. That this was already Lord Xiang's
       third visit to attend court in Jin in eight years suggests that the demands Jin made
       on the smaller domains had increased significantly since the times of Lords Wen
       and Xiang.

153   Du Yu (ZZ 30.520) identifies the two as sons of Zihu.

8.3(3)　庚寅，鄭子國、子耳侵蔡，獲蔡司馬公子燮。鄭人皆喜，唯子產不順，曰：「小國無文德而有武功，禍莫大焉。楚人來討，能勿從乎？從之，晉師必至。晉、楚伐鄭，自今鄭國不四、五年弗得寧矣。」子國怒之曰：「爾何知！國有大命，而有正卿，童子言焉，將為戮矣！」

8.4(4)　五月甲辰，會于邢丘，以命朝聘之數，使諸侯之大夫聽命。季孫宿、齊高厚、宋向戌、衛甯殖、邾大夫會之。鄭伯獻捷于會，故親聽命。大夫不書，尊晉侯也。

8.5(6)　莒人伐我東鄙，以疆鄫田。

8.6(7)　秋，九月，大雩，旱也。

8.7a(8)　冬，楚子囊伐鄭，討其侵蔡也。

154　The chief minister at this point is Zisi, who plotted Lord Xi's assassination and served as regent for the new young Zheng ruler. "Great command" refers here to decisions to mobilize an army. On the limits "great command" imposes on remonstrance, see *Xunzi* 13.294.

155　Zichan died forty-four years later (Zhao 20.9) and must have been quite young at this point.

156　According to Du Yu (*ZZ* 30.520), the logic seems to be that Lord Dao of Jin deserved respect and narrative attention because he was reasserting Jin's status as overlord by emphasizing ritual propriety in interdomain relations.

157　Zeng must have been situated between Lu and Ju. Ju had annexed Zeng two years earlier (Xiang 6.4). Lu might have made incursions eastward into former Zeng territories, which would have in turn provoked Ju to invade Lu's eastern border and to define the boundary between Zeng and Lu.

Even as a child Zichan shows great foresight. While Zheng celebrates its victory over Cai, Zichan worries about retaliation from Cai's ally, Chu, and about Jin reprisals if Zheng capitulates to Chu demands. A child who speaks out precociously to the dismay of his elders is a common trope in early Chinese literature. For another example of a father rebuking a son despite the son's good judgment, see Cheng 16.5a. A variant of the Zichan story, with further emphasis on the danger of speaking forthrightly, appears in Han Feizi 33.709.

On the *gengyin* day (22), Ziguo and Zi'er of Zheng invaded Cai and captured the Cai supervisor of the military, Gongzi Xie. The leaders of Zheng were all pleased. Only Zichan did not go along but said, "For a small domain, there is no greater calamity than to lack civil virtue and to have instead martial achievement. When the men of Chu come to chastise us, can we not submit to them? But if we submit to them, Jin troops will certainly come. And if both Jin and Chu attack Zheng, Zheng will have no peace for at least the next four or five years." Infuriated, his father, Ziguo, said, "What can you know! The domain has its great command, for which it has its chief minister.[154] This is a child speaking—for this you may be executed!"[155] 8.3(3)

With the meeting at Xingqiu, Lord Dao of Jin seems to reassert Jin's status as overlord.

In the fifth month, on the *jiachen* day (7), the princes met at Xingqiu for Jin to issue commands on the appropriate frequency for court visits and official visits, and for the high officers of the princes to await commands. Ji Wuzi[b], Gao Hou of Qi, Xiang Xu of Song, Ning Zhi of Wei, and the high officers of Zhu attended the meeting. The Liege of Zheng presented the spoils of victory at the meeting; that was why he personally attended to the Jin ruler's commands. That the names of the high officers were not recorded was to show respect for the Prince of Jin.[156] 8.4(4)

Ju leaders attacked our eastern marches in order to mark the boundaries of the fields of Zeng.[157] 8.5(6)

In autumn, in the ninth month, there was a great rain sacrifice: this was because of the drought. 8.6(7)

Facing Chu aggression, Zheng leaders debate the pros and cons of allegiance to Jin and to Chu. The pro-Jin faction is presented as having more compelling moral reasoning.

In winter, Zinang of Chu attacked Zheng: this was to chasten it for invading Cai. 8.7a(8)

子駟、子國、子耳欲從楚，子孔、子蟜、子展欲待晉。子駟曰：「《周詩》有之曰：

> 俟河之清，
> 人壽幾何？
> 兆云詢多，
> 職競作羅。

謀之多族，民之多違，事滋無成。民急矣，姑從楚，以紓吾民。晉師至，吾又從之。敬共幣帛，以待來者，小國之道也。犧牲玉帛，待於二竟，以待彊者而庇民焉。寇不為害，民不罷病，不亦可乎？」

子展曰：「小所以事大，信也。小國無信，兵亂日至，亡無日矣。五會之信，今將背之，雖楚救我，將安用之？親我無成，鄙我是欲，不可從也。不如待晉。晉君方明，四軍無闕，八卿和睦，必不棄鄭。楚師遼遠，糧食將盡，必將速歸，何患焉？舍之聞之：杖莫如信。完守以老楚，杖信以待晉，不亦可乎？」

8.7b　子駟曰：「《詩》云：

> 謀夫孔多，
> 是用不集。
> 發言盈庭，
> 誰敢執其咎？

158　One can wait for the Yellow River to clear up, but it will never happen in one's lifetime. Analogously, one may hope for Jin's assistance (or, more generally, consensus, order, and peace), but it will not happen easily.

159　Alternatively: "They are no more than a net of disputations" (Takezoe, 14.45). Yang (3:957), citing *Erya*, reads *xun* 詢 as *xin* 信 ("indeed"): "The signs of divination are indeed too many." This is an uncollected ode not found in the received text of *Maoshi*.

160　Karlgren (gl. 484) reads *zu* 族 as "category": "to deliberate on too many categories is to have people turn against each other."

161　The same line appears in Xiang 22.3 and Ai 7.4a.

162　Meetings took place at Ji Marsh (Xiang 3.5), Qī and Chengdi (Xiang 5.8, 5.9), Wei (Xiang 7.8), and Xingqiu (Xiang 8.4).

163　Reading *cheng* 成 as *zhong* 終 ("last"), following Wang Niansun (Karlgren, gl. 485). For *bi* 鄙 as a verb ("to regard as borders or margins"), see also Xuan 14.3; Wang Yinzhi, *Jingyi shuwen*, 702–3.

164　Jin's four armies referred to the middle, upper, lower, and new armies. There were no deficiencies in the ranks of soldiers or in military supplies.

165　The eight ministers (the commanders and assistant commanders of the four armies) are Zhi Ying, Fan Gai, Zhonghang Yan, Han Qi, Luan Yan, Shi Fang, Zhao Wu, and Wei Jiang.

Zisi, Ziguo, and Zi'er wanted to follow Chu. Zikong, Zijiao, and Gongsun Shezhi[a] wanted to wait for Jin to come to the aid of Zheng. Zisi said, "As the *Zhou Odes* has it:

> Wait for the clearing up of the Yellow River—
> Yet how long is the span of human life?[158]
> Deliberations over omens, so many, are
> No more than the weaving of a net to ensnare ourselves.[159]

The more lineages[160] are in on the deliberations, the more the people are divided, and the more likely the affair is to come to nothing. The people are so desperate—let us follow Chu for now to bring relief to our people. Then when the Jin army arrives, we can also follow it. Respectfully offering bolts of silk and waiting for others to come is the way of small domains. Let us wait with sacrificial animals, jade, and silk at the two borders, so as to wait for the stronger one and put our people under its protection. The enemies will do no harm, and the people will not be ill-used and exhausted. Is that not acceptable?"

Gongsun Shezhi[a] said, "The thing whereby the small domain serves the great domain is good faith.[161] If a small domain is faithless, war and disorder will come upon it day after day, and its doom will not be far off. Good faith has been built up over five meetings,[162] and now we plan to turn against it. Even if Chu were to come to our aid, of what use would it be? Chu's kindred feeling for us will come to nothing; its desire is to turn us into its borderland.[163] We cannot follow them. It is better to wait for Jin. Right now the Jin ruler is enlightened, its four armies have no deficiencies,[164] and its eight ministers are in harmony:[165] it will certainly not cast off Zheng. The Chu army is far from home, its provisions are nearly exhausted, and it will certainly depart soon. Why be troubled about it? I have heard: nothing offers support like good faith. Would it not be acceptable to complete our defensive fortifications in order to wear out the Chu army and to support ourselves on good faith as we wait for Jin?"

Zisi explains Zheng's defection with masterful rhetoric, but Jin, unappeased, threatens to punish Zheng. Zichan's dire prediction comes true.

Zisi said, "As it says in the *Odes*,   8.7b

> The counselors are very many;
> That is why nothing will be accomplished.
> The words spoken fill the court.
> Who will dare to bear the blame?

如匪行邁謀，
是用不得于道。

請從楚，騑也受其咎。」

　　乃及楚平，使王子伯駢告于晉曰：「君命敝邑：『修而車賦，儆而師徒，以討亂略。』蔡人不從，敝邑之人不敢寧處，悉索敝賦，以討于蔡，獲司馬燮，獻于邢丘。今楚來討曰：『女何故稱兵于蔡？』焚我郊保，馮陵我城郭。敝邑之眾，夫婦男女，不遑啟處，以相救也。翦焉傾覆，無所控告。民死亡者，非其父兄，即其子弟。夫人愁痛，不知所庇。民知窮困，而受盟于楚。孤也與其二三臣不能禁止，不敢不告。」

　　知武子使行人子員對之曰：「君有楚命，亦不使一个行李告于寡君，而即安于楚。君之所欲也，誰敢違君？寡君將帥諸侯以見于城下。唯君圖之！」

8.8(9)　晉范宣子來聘，且拜公之辱，告將用師于鄭。

166　Reading *fei* 匪 as *bi* 彼 (ZZ 30.521): those seeking counsel while walking will get so many different kinds of advice that they will become lost. Zheng Xuan reads *fei* 匪 as *fei* 非 (*Maoshi*-Zheng 12B.413): "They are like those seeking counsel while not walking, / And because of that cannot get on their way."

167　*Maoshi* 195, "Xiaomin" 小旻, 12B.412–13.

168　Zisi was initially pro-Jin (Xiang 2.5). Zichan later implies (Xiang 22.2) that it was Jin incivility toward Zisi during the meeting at Xingqiu this year that alienated him and induced him to become pro-Chu.

They are like those who seek counsel even while walking,[166]
And because of that cannot gain the right way.[167]

I submit that we follow Chu, and I will take the blame."[168]

They therefore made peace with Chu, sending Wangzi Bopian[169] to notify Jin: "You, my lord, issued this command to our humble settlement: 'Repair your contingent of chariots and put your soldiers on guard so as to chastise the disorderly and deviant.'[170] The men of Cai did not submit. The men of our humble settlement did not dare to stand by quietly and therefore mustered our whole meager contingent to chastise Cai. We seized Xie, its supervisor of the military, and presented the spoils of victory at Xingqiu. Now Chu has come to chastise us, saying: 'For what reason did you raise an army against Cai?' It has burned the forts in our outskirts and has breached our city walls. The multitudes of our humble settlement, husbands and wives, men and women, have not had time to tarry or dwell[171] as they tried to give each other succor. With the domain cut to pieces and thrown topsy-turvy, there is no place to turn to for appeal. Those among the people who perished were either fathers and older brothers or sons and younger brothers. Everyone is in sorrow and pain, not knowing where to find protection. The people realize that they are in dire straits and have therefore accepted the covenant from Chu. I, the lone one, along with my various subjects, cannot put a stop to this, and we would not presume to fail to notify you."

Zhi Ying[a] sent the envoy Ziyun to reply with these words: "You, my lord, received Chu's command, and without sending a single envoy to notify our unworthy ruler, you have quickly settled into concord with Chu. If this is your wish, who would dare to oppose you, my lord? Our unworthy ruler plans to lead the princes to have an audience with you beneath the city walls. You, my lord, should consider this."

A Jin minister enlists Lu's assistance in attacking Zheng. The prospective military alliance is couched in quotations on amity from the Odes.

Fan Gai[c] of Jin came to us on an official visit and also to bow for our lord's condescension in visiting Jin. He notified us that Jin planned to use its forces against Zheng. 8.8(9)

---

166   Although the term "Wangzi" ("the king's son") usually indicates royal lineage, Wangzi Bopian, like Wangzi Boliao (Xuan 6.6), is a Zheng noble.

170   Yang (3:958) glosses *lue* 略 as "not following the proper way." Takezoe (14.46) reads *lue* 略 as "border" and *luanlue* 亂略 as "those who wrought havoc at the borders." Karlgren (gl. 487), following Lin Yaosou, reads *lue* 略 as a loan for *lue* 掠, "to rob." The translation here follows Yang's reading. Wangzi Bopian is claiming that Zheng was carrying out Jin's command when it attacked Cai.

171   These words echo a line in *Maoshi* 162, "Simu," referred to in Xiang 4.3 and also cited in Xiang 29.4.

公享之。宣子賦〈摽有梅〉。季武子曰：「誰敢哉？今譬於草木，寡
君在君，君之臭味也。歡以承命，何時之有？」武子賦〈角弓〉。賓將出，
武子賦〈彤弓〉。宣子曰：「城濮之役，我先君文公獻功于衡雍，受彤弓
于襄王，以為子孫藏。匄也，先君守官之嗣也，敢不承命？」君子以為
知禮。

春秋

9.1(1) 九年，春，宋災。

9.2(2) 夏，季孫宿如晉。

9.3(3) 五月辛酉，夫人姜氏薨。

9.4 秋，八月癸未，葬我小君穆姜。

9.5(5) 冬，公會晉侯、宋公、衛侯、曹伯、莒子、邾子、滕子、薛伯、杞伯、小邾
子、齊世子光伐鄭。十有二月己亥，同盟于戲。

9.6(8) 楚子伐鄭。

---

172 *Maoshi* 20, "Piao you mei" 摽有梅, 1E.62–63. This is a song celebrating timely courtship. Fan Gai, using the analogy between courtship and interdomain relations, is
expressing his hope that Lu will supply military assistance to Jin in a timely fashion.
On this analogy, see also Cheng 8.1, Zhao 1.4.

173 Ji Wuzi was acting as aide to Lord Xiang, who was eleven at the time.

174 Our translation is based on Du Yu's (ZZ 30.522) comment that the comparison
implies that "both are of the same kind"—that is, the Lu and Jin rulers are related
as "attribute" and "substance" and are inseparable. Cf. Karlgren (gl. 490): "our
unworthy ruler is drawn to your ruler by his fragrance (like the fragrance of flowers
and fruit)." Zichan employs the same metaphor in Xiang 22.2.

175 Ji Wuzi is responding to Fan Gai's plea for "timely assistance" by confirming Lu's
unconditional support, for which "the season," or timeliness, is not even an issue.

176 *Maoshi* 223, "Jiao gong" 角弓, 15A.503–5. The ode celebrates the mutual assistance
of brothers and is here used to confirm the ties between Jin and Lu as "brother
domains."

Our lord offered him ceremonial toasts. Fan Gai[b] recited "Plop Fall the Plums."[172] Ji Wuzi[173] said, "Who would dare to miss the right time? Now if we take our analogies from plants, our unworthy ruler is to your ruler what fragrance is to flowers and fruits.[174] Gladly we take your decree as our own. What does the season have to do with it?"[175] Ji Wuzi[c] recited "Horn Bow."[176] When the guests were about to leave, Ji Wuzi[c] recited "Red Bow."[177] Fan Gai[b] said, "After the Chengpu campaign, our former ruler Lord Wen offered the spoils of victory at Hengyong and received from King Xiang the red bow, which is to be kept by his descendants. I am the successor of one who guarded his office under our former ruler. How dare I not take your decree as my own?" The noble man considered this a sound understanding of ritual propriety.

LORD XIANG 9 (564 BCE)
ANNALS

In the ninth year, in spring, there was a disastrous fire in Song.   9.1(1)

In summer, Jisun Su (Ji Wuzi) went to Jin.   9.2(2)

In the fifth month, on the *xinyou* day (29), our lord's wife, Lady Jiang, expired.   9.3(3)

In winter, in the eighth month, on the *guiwei* day (23), we buried our former lord's wife, Mu Jiang.   9.4

In winter, our lord met with the Prince of Jin, the Duke of Song, the Prince of Wei, the Liege of Cao, the Master of Ju, the Master of Zhu, the Master of Teng, the Liege of Xue, the Liege of Qĭ, the Master of Lesser Zhu, and the Qi heir apparent Guang and attacked Zheng. In the twelfth month, on the *jihai* day,[178] they swore a covenant together at Xi.   9.5(5)

The Master of Chu attacked Zheng.   9.6(8)

---

177 *Maoshi* 175, "Tong gong" 彤弓, 10A.351–53. The ode celebrates the joys of convivial feasting as the host welcome the guests. The unstrung red bow in the first line of the ode is a "beginning affective image" (*qixing* 起興) that does not have a direct logical connection with the rest of the poem. The red bow was one of the gifts bestowed by King Xiang of Zhou on Lord Wen of Jin. Fan Gai thus interprets "Red Bow" as a reminder of how Jin should guard (or regain) its status as overlord. Du Yu (ZZ 30.522) opines that Ji Wuzi also intends that association, although the recitation would also have made sense as a celebration of his guests. Note that Ning Wuzi of Wei declines to accept "Red Bow" in Wen 4.7 because it is too grandiose.

178 There was no *jihai* day in the twelfth month; it fell on the tenth day of the eleventh month.

左傳

9.1a(1)　九年，春，宋災，樂喜為司城以為政，使伯氏司里。火所未至，徹小屋，塗大屋，陳畚、挶；具綆、缶，備水器；量輕重，蓄水潦，積土塗；巡丈城，繕守備，表火道。使華臣具正徒，令隧正納郊保，奔火所。使華閱討右官，官庀其司。向戌討左，亦如之。使樂遄庀刑器，亦如之。使皇鄖命校正出馬，工正出車，備甲兵，庀武守。使西鉏吾庀府守，令司宮、巷伯儆宮。二師令四鄉正敬享，祝宗用馬于四墉，祀盤庚于西門之外。

9.1b　晉侯問於士弱曰：「吾聞之：宋災於是乎知有天道，何故？」

179　Cf. Xuan 16.2: a fire sent by Heaven is called "disastrous fire" (*zai* 災).

180　The supervisor of fortifications ranked fifth among the six ministers of Song (Wen 7.3, Cheng 15.3). Yue Xi was in charge of policies presumably because of his superior talents.

181　We follow Karlgren, gl. 490, and read *zhang* 丈 as a loanword for *chang* 長. Du Yu (ZZ 30.523) reads *zhang* as "measure," but that violates the syntactic pattern of the three-character lines in this passage (first character a verb, followed by a noun consisting of the second and third characters).

182　Du Yu (ZZ 30.523) identifies Yue Chuan as "supervisor of punishment" and reads *xingqi* 刑器 ("instruments of punishment") as *xingshu* 刑書 ("writings on punishment"). Karlgren (gl. 493) reminds us that such writings were often inscribed on bronze vessels (*qi* 器) (Zhao 6.3, 29.5), and *xingqi* would thus mean "vessels with penal codes."

183　The Song capital was divided into four districts (*xiang* 鄉). What we translate as "the elder of the lord's household" (*xiangbo* 巷伯) may be a eunuch; see *Maoshi* 200, "Xiangbo" 巷伯, 12C.428–30. The "two ministers" referred to here are the minister of the right (*youshi* 右師) and the minister of the left (*zuoshi* 左師), who ranked highest among the six ministers in charge of government in Song.

184　Pangeng, the tenth Shang king, is here honored as the ancestor of Song. According to Yang (3:963), Pangeng moved the Shang capital to Yinxu (Ruins of Yin), by the Anyang River in Anyang, Henan; and Yinxu was situated to the northwest of the Song capital (present-day Shangqiu). Hence, the sacrifices are performed at the western gate.

185　We follow Yu Yue's reading, cited in Takezoe (Xiang 14.53) and Karlgren, gl. 496: the question implies that Song understood the Way of Heaven because of the fire, not that Song could predict the fire because it understood the Way of Heaven (ZZ 30.524). Song seemed to have continued the Shang tradition of linking disastrous fires to planetary movements and turmoil in the realm (ZZ-Kong 30.526). As in Zhao 9.4, 11.2 and 11.5, where the Year-Planet's cycle is linked to retributory laws deciding the fate of Chen, Chu and Cai, "the Way of Heaven" is here linked to the movements of stars.

With Yue Xi delegating responsibilities and making necessary preparations, Song leaders manage to control a disastrous fire. For a comparable account, see Zichan's measures for dealing with a fire in Zhao 18.3.

In the ninth year, in spring, there was a disastrous fire in Song.[179] Yue Xi, as supervisor of fortifications, was in charge of policies.[180] He sent the Bo lineage head to oversee the streets and alleys. He removed the small houses where the fire had not yet reached, covered the big ones with mud, set out baskets and containers for carrying earth, had ropes and urns ready for drawing water, prepared vessels for holding water, assessed the lightness and heaviness of tasks, stored up water, accumulated earth, made inspection tours of the long city walls,[181] repaired the equipment for keeping guard, and indicated the path the fire would follow. He sent Hua Chen to bring together the regular conscripts. Hua Chen ordered the director of distant outlying districts to send their conscripts into the capital and hasten to the site of the fire. Yue Xi sent Hua Yue to sternly admonish officials commanding the right, so that each official would make sure that his subordinates were ready. Xiang Xu sternly admonished officials commanding the left in like fashion. Yue Xi also sent Yue Chuan to have implements of punishment ready in like fashion.[182] He sent Huang Yun to charge the manager of horses to bring out horses and the manager of carriages to bring out carriages, prepare armor and weapons, and to be ready for guarding the arsenal. He sent Xichu Wu to be ready for guarding the storehouses and archives. He ordered the supervisor of the palace and the elder of the lord's household to watch over the palace. The two ministers charged the four district directors to reverently offer sacrifices.[183] The invocator and the ancestral attendant sacrificed horses at the four city walls and made offerings to Pangeng outside the western gate.[184]

9.1a(1)

The Jin minister Shi Ruo explains how disastrous fires, planetary movements, and the Way of government are connected. However, he ends up confirming the primacy of "the Way of government" over the knowledge of such connections (see also Zhao 7.14). The implicit praise for Yue Xi's efficacious measures for combating the fire also shifts attention to the human realm.

The Prince of Jin asked Shi Ruo, "I have heard that as a result of the disastrous fire Song knows there is such a thing as the Way of Heaven. Why is that so?"[185]

9.1b

對曰：「古之火正，或食於心，或食於咮，以出內火。是故咮為鶉火，心為大火。陶唐氏之火正閼伯居商丘，祀大火，而火紀時焉。相土因之，故商主大火。商人閱其禍敗之釁，必始於火，是以日知其有天道也。」

公曰：「可必乎？」

對曰：「在道。國亂無象，不可知也。」

9.2(2)　夏，季武子如晉，報宣子之聘也。

9.3(3)　穆姜薨於東宮。始往而筮之，遇艮䷳之八。史曰：「是謂艮之隨䷐。隨，其出也。君必速出！」

186　See also Zhao 29.4, where the Jin scribe Cai Mo describes how the five phases have their corresponding "offices."

187　The Heart Asterism is the equivalent of Scorpio.

188　Explanations vary, but most commentators agree that the use of fire (in pottery and metal works) depends on the positions of these two constellations during different seasons of the year. The expression *chu nei huo* 出內火 has been glossed as "to set fire and to prohibit the setting of fire" (ZZ 30.524) or "to take fire outside and to bring it indoors" (*Zhouli-Zheng* 30.458). Hong Liangji (*Chunqiu Zuozhuan gu*, 510), citing Hui Dong, notes that *nei* 內 is interchangeable with *ru* 入, not *na* 納, in early texts.

189　That is, the sacrifices that Ebo (identified as Gaoxin's son) established were inherited by Shang (Zhao 1.12).

190　That is why Great Fire is also called Chen 辰 (Zhao 1.12). The seasons are marked by the rising of specific constellations at specific times in the year.

191　Great Fire came to be known as the "Shang Stars" (Zhao 1.12).

192　Mu Jiang was banished to the Eastern Palace after threatening to depose her son, Lord Cheng, when the latter hesitated to bring down the Ji and Meng lineages, whose property was coveted by Mu Jiang's lover Shusun Qiaoru (Cheng 16.5).

193　For explanations of the enigmatic "eight of 'Restraint,'" see Yang, 3:964; Takezoe, 14.57–58. The "eight" of a hexagram is also mentioned in *Guoyu*, "Jin yu 4," 10.365–66. These cases involve one unchanging line in the juxtaposition of two hexagrams, in contradistinction to the focus on the changing line in two juxtaposed hexagrams in all other instances of divination by the *Zhou Changes*. Fu Qian claims that the unchanging line is the focus of divination in the Lianshan 連山 and Guicang 歸藏

He replied, "The director for fire[186] in ancient times offered matching sacrifices sometimes to the Heart Asterism[187] and sometimes to the Beak Asterism, so as to regulate the bringing out or taking in of fire.[188] That is why the Beak is Quail Fire, and the Heart is Great Fire. Ebo, the director for fire of the Taotang lineage, stayed in Shangqiu.[189] He offered sacrifices to Great Fire and used it to regulate the seasons.[190] Xiangtu, the ancestor of Shang, followed this, and that is why Shang made Great Fire the basis of its sacrifices.[191] The men of Shang observed how the omens of its calamities and defeat invariably started with fire. That was how in the past they knew there was such a thing as the Way of Heaven."

The lord asked, "Can this be regarded as certain?"

He replied, "It depends on the Way of government. A domain in disorder has no interpretable signs, and the Way of Heaven cannot be known."

In summer, Ji Wuzi went to Jin: this was in answer to Fan Gai[b]'s official visit. 9.2(2)

Mu Jiang, wife of Lord Xuan of Lu, dies. The narrative harks back to the moment eleven years earlier when she was banished to the Eastern Palace in the aftermath of a failed conspiracy against the Ji and Meng lineages (Cheng 16). She maintains that divination results depend on character (on this issue, see also Zhao 12.10). Her understanding of the Changes *echoes her knowledge of the* Odes *(Cheng 9.5). Mu Jiang's self-indictment might have stemmed from the perceived need to control the subversive forces she embodies.*

Mu Jiang expired in the Eastern Palace.[192] When she first went there, she 9.3(3)
divined by milfoil and encountered the "eight" of "Restraint" ䷳. The scribe said, "This is called 'Restraint' going to 'Following'" ䷐.[193] 'Following' is about leaving.[194] You are sure to leave soon!"

---

traditions (cited in *Zhouli-Jia* 24.370). Thus, here "Restraint" ䷳ (Gen 艮, hexagram 52) and "Following" ䷐ (Sui 隨, hexagram 17) have the same second line with all five other lines being different. The line statement of the second line in "Following" emphasizes dependence: "Tied to the child, losing the grown man" 係小子，失丈夫 (*Zhouyi* 3.56). The corresponding line in "Restraint" has this statement: "Restrain the calves, and one cannot raise up what follows (the toes). The heart feels discontent" 艮其腓，不拯其隨。其心不快 (*Zhouyi* 5.116). One may argue that the images of dependence and constraint pointedly refer to Mu Jiang's condition. However, the ensuing speech deals with the judgment of the hexagram "Following" rather than the second line of "Restraint" or of "Following."

194　The scribe may be taking his cue from the reference to "leave the gate" (*chumen* 出門) in the line statement of the first unbroken line of "Following" (*Zhouyi* 3.56). According to Hui Dong, "Yin follows yang, just as the mother follows the son. That is why 'Following' is about 'leaving'" 陰隨陽，猶母隨子，故隨其出也。 (Hong Liangji, *Chunqiu Zuozhuan gu*, 511).

姜曰：「亡！是於《周易》曰：『隨，元、亨、利、貞，無咎。』元，體
之長也；亨，嘉之會也；利，義之和也；貞，事之幹也。體仁足以長人，嘉
德足以合禮，利物足以和義，貞固足以幹事。然，故不可誣也，是以雖
隨無咎。今我婦人，而與於亂。固在下位，而有不仁，不可謂元。不靖國
家，不可謂亨。作而害身，不可謂利。棄位而姣，不可謂貞。有四德者，
隨而無咎。我皆無之，豈隨也哉？我則取惡，能無咎乎？必死於此，弗
得出矣。」

9.4　秦景公使士雃乞師于楚，將以伐晉，楚子許之。子囊曰：「不可，當今吾
不能與晉爭。晉君類能而使之，舉不失選，官不易方；其卿讓於善，其
大夫不失守，其士競於教，其庶人力於農穡，商、工、皁、隸不知遷業。
韓厥老矣，知罃稟焉以為政。范匄少於中行偃而上之，使佐中軍。韓起
少於欒黶，而欒黶、士魴上之，使佐上軍。魏絳多功，以趙武為賢，而為
之佐。君明臣忠，上讓下競。當是時也，晉不可敵，事之而後可。君其
圖之！」

195　Elsewhere in *Zuozhuan* (Xi 33.6), the head is referred to as *yuan* 元, the word trans-
　　lated here as "prime."

196　The above eight lines also appear (with two variant characters) in the "Wenyan" com-
　　mentary (*Zhouyi* 1.12) on hexagram 1, "Pure Yang" ䷀ (Qian 乾) of the *Changes*.

197　Precisely because the words explained above have such meanings, failure to fulfill
　　those meanings amounts to deception or distorted application of the hexagram.

198　Although Mu Jiang was a noblewoman, just by virtue of being a woman she was in a
　　"lowly position." She was "inhumane" because she threatened her son and the Ji and
　　Meng lineages.

199　*Jiao* 姣 means "beauty" or "to adorn oneself." As a widow, Mu Jiang was not supposed
　　to adorn herself. Yet she abandoned her position as the lord's mother and engaged in
　　adulterous relations with Shusun Qiaoru (Yang 3:966). Du Yu glosses *jiao* as "licen-
　　tiousness." Yu Yue links it to *xiao* 佼, "to give rein to desires" (Wu Jing'an, *Chunqiu
　　Zuoshi zhuan jiuzhu shuzheng xu*, 57–58).

200　Cf. *Lienü zhuan* 7.6a–6b. The noble man comments at the end of that account: "What
　　a pity! Although Mu Jiang had qualities of intelligence and keen understanding, they
　　could not finally cover up her offense of wreaking disorder through licentiousness."

201　The translation follows Yang's (3:966) reading of *fang* 方 as "methods and policies,"
　　as in Zhao 29.4. Du Yu (ZZ 30.527) glosses *fang* as "what was appropriate"; Takezoe
　　(14.60) reads it as "what was constant."

Mu Jiang said, "Not so! About this, the *Zhou Changes* says, "'Following: prime, offering, benefit, constancy, no blame.' Prime is the most important part of the body;[195] offerings are made when blessings gather; benefit is the harmony of dutifulness; constancy is the mainstay of endeavors. Embodying humaneness suffices to improve a person, bringing blessings to virtue suffices to meld ritual propriety, benefiting others suffices to harmonize dutifulness, and never wavering in one's constancy suffices to build the mainstay of endeavors.[196] Since this is so, there cannot be any deception.[197] That is how even with 'Following,' there is 'no blame.' Now I, as a woman, was yet party to fomenting disorder; and undeniably in a lowly position, I was yet inhumane;[198] this cannot be called 'prime.' I did not bring peace and stability to the domain and patrimony; there cannot be 'offerings.' My action harmed my person; this cannot be called 'benefit.' I abandoned my position to indulge in licentiousness; this cannot be called 'constancy.'[199] With these four virtues, 'Following' is yet 'no blame.' But since I have none of them, how can this be deemed 'Following'? Since I have taken up evil, how can there be 'no blame'? I am sure to die here. I will not be able to leave!"[200]

Zinang of Chu lauds the virtues of yielding and disinterestedness among Jin leaders, although other Zuozhuan *accounts tell of their bitter strife. Despite Zinang's positive assessment of Jin power, Jin cannot fight back when a Qin-Chu coalition invades Jin, and Jin is defeated by Qin in the Li campaign (Xiang 11.6).*

Lord Jing of Qin sent Shi Qian to Chu to plead for troops. He planned to use these to attack Jin. The Master of Chu granted his request. Zinang said, "This will not do. At the present time we cannot contend with Jin. The Jin ruler sorts out different talents and employs them accordingly. So in making appointments, there are no mistakes with his choices, and in filling offices, there are no changes of methods and policies.[201] His ministers yield to men of greater excellence. His high officers do not fail to fulfill their duties. His officers assiduously apply themselves to instruction. His people exert themselves in agricultural labor. Merchants, artisans, servants, and slaves know nothing of changing their inherited employments. Han Jue has grown old, and Zhi Ying defers to him in taking charge of government. Fan Gai is younger than Zhonghang Yan, but the latter honors him as his superior and he has been made assistant commander of the central army. Han Qi is younger than Luan Yan, but Luan Yan and Shi Fang honor him as their superior, and he has been made assistant commander of the upper army. Wei Jiang has many meritorious achievements, but he considers Zhao Wu worthy and acts as his assistant. The ruler is enlightened, the subjects are loyal, those above are yielding, and those below apply themselves assiduously. At this moment, Jin cannot be opposed. The only acceptable course is to serve them. You, my lord, should consider this!"

9.4

王曰：「吾既許之矣，雖不及晉，必將出師。」

秋，楚子師于武城，以為秦援。

秦人侵晉。晉饑，弗能報也。

9.5a(5) 　冬十月，諸侯伐鄭。庚午，季武子、齊崔杼、宋皇鄖從荀罃、士匄門于鄟門，衛北宮括、曹人、邾人從荀偃、韓起門于師之梁，滕人、薛人從欒黶、士魴門于北門，杞人、郳人從趙武、魏絳斬行栗。甲戌，師于氾。令於諸侯曰：「修器備，盛餱糧，歸老幼，居疾于虎牢，肆眚，圍鄭。」

　　鄭人恐，乃行成。中行獻子曰：「遂圍之，以待楚人之救也，而與之戰，不然，無成。」

　　知武子曰：「許之盟而還師，以敝楚人。吾三分四軍，與諸侯之銳，以逆來者，於我未病，楚不能矣。猶愈於戰。暴骨以逞，不可以爭。大勞未艾。君子勞心，小人勞力，先王之制也。」

　　諸侯皆不欲戰，乃許鄭成。十一月己亥，同盟于戲，鄭服也。

202　Wucheng in Chu was first mentioned in Xi 6.4.

203　Gao Shiqi identifies the Zhuan Gate and Shizhiliang Gate as the eastern and western gates of the Zheng capital (Yang, 3:967).

204　The purpose is probably to open up roads, to get a supply of wood, or to destroy livelihood.

205　A Jin-Zheng peace agreement would provoke Chu to attack Zheng, and Chu would be worn out by the war effort. Note that differences between Zhonghang Yan and Zhi Ying belie the Chu commander Zinang's portrayal of harmony among Jin leaders.

206　Yang (3:968) explains that the three crack contingents will take turns harrying the advancing Chu force.

207　What we have translated as "resorting to slaughter" is literally "exposing bones." The biggest struggle is yet to come, so they should not persist in battle now.

The king said, "I have already given my word to Qin. Even though we are no match for Jin, we must dispatch our army."

In autumn, the Master of Chu stationed his troops at Wucheng[202] in order to assist Qin.

The men of Qin invaded Jin. Jin, suffering from a famine, could not retaliate.

Jin and its allies lay siege to Zheng. Despite initial dissension, Jin leaders grant Zheng's request for a peace accord.

In winter, in the tenth month, the princes attacked Zheng. On the *gengwu* day (11), Ji Wuzi, Cui Zhu of Qi, and Huang Yun of Song followed the lead of Zhi Ying[b] and Fan Gai[a] to storm the Zhuan Gate. Beigong Kuo of Wei and the men of Cao and Zhu followed the lead of Zhonghang Yan[a] and Han Qi to storm the gate at Shizhiliang.[203] The men of Teng and Xue followed the lead of Luan Yan and Shi Fang to storm the northern gate. The men of Qi and Ni followed the lead of Zhao Wu and Wei Jiang to cut down chestnut trees along the road.[204] On the *jiaxu* day (15), the troops were stationed at the Fan River. Jin leaders commanded the princes in these words: "Repair your instruments of war, prepare dried food, send home the old and the young, let the sick stay at Hulao, treat leniently those who are guilty, and lay siege to Zheng."

The men of Zheng were fearful and thus sued for peace. Zhonghang Yan[b] said, "Let us go ahead with the siege so as to wait for the men of Chu to come to its aid, and then we will engage in battle with them. Otherwise, nothing will be accomplished."

Zhi Ying[a] said, "Grant them a covenant and then let the troops turn back, so as to tire out the men of Chu.[205] We will divide our four armies into three. Together with the crack troops of the princes, we will confront the advancing Chu forces.[206] For us this will not be too draining, but Chu will not be able to endure it. This is still better than persisting in battle. Resorting to slaughter to satisfy our desire is not the way to contend for victory, for our great toil is not yet at an end.[207] Noble men should toil with their minds while common men toil with their strength:[208] that is the rule of former kings."

None of the princes wanted to fight. They thus granted Zheng an accord. In the eleventh month, on the *jihai* day (10), they swore a covenant together at Xi:[209] Zheng had submitted.

9.5a(5)

---

208   The same lines appear in *Guoyu*, "Lu yu 2," 5.208, when Gongfu Wenbo's mother uses her own weaving to talk about the importance of labor and assiduous application. Cf. *Mencius* 3A.4: "Those who toil with their minds govern others; those who toil with their strength are governed by others"; Cheng 13.2: "noble men are assiduous in fulfilling ritual propriety, while common men exert themselves to the utmost in physical labor."

209   Xi 戲 was located in Zheng and probably refers to Xitong Mountain 戲童山, northeast of present-day Songshan County 嵩山縣, Henan.

9.5b　將盟，鄭六卿，公子騑、公子發、公子嘉、公孫輒、公孫蠆、公孫舍之及其大夫、門子，皆從鄭伯。晉士莊子為載書，曰：「自今日既盟之後，鄭國而不唯晉命是聽，而或有異志者，有如此盟！」

公子騑趨進曰：「天禍鄭國，使介居二大國之間，大國不加德音，而亂以要之，使其鬼神不獲歆其禋祀，其民人不獲享其土利，夫婦辛苦墊隘，無所厎告。自今日既盟之後，鄭國而不唯有禮與彊可以庇民者是從，而敢有異志者，亦如之！」

荀偃曰：「改載書！」

公孫舍之曰：「昭大神要言焉。若可改也，大國亦可叛也。」

知武子謂獻子曰：「我實不德，而要人以盟，豈禮也哉？非禮，何以主盟？姑盟而退，修德息師而來，終必獲鄭，何必今日？我之不德，民將棄我，豈唯鄭？若能休和，遠人將至，何恃於鄭？」乃盟而還。

When the covenant was about to be sworn, the six ministers of Zheng— Zisi[a], Ziguo[a], Zikong[a], Zi'er[a], Zijiao[a], Gongsun Shezhi—as well as Zheng high officers and the heirs of ministerial lineages, all followed the Liege of Zheng. Shi Ruo[a] of Jin composed the covenant document, which said: "From this day on, after the swearing of the covenant, if Zheng does not abide only by Jin's commands but harbors some other intent, let this covenant bear witness against us!"

Zisi[a] hastened forward, saying, "Heaven brought disaster upon the domain of Zheng and has situated it in a place wedged between two great domains.[210] Your great domain has not bestowed on us virtuous words and has instead used disorder to bind us to this covenant, so that our ghosts and spirits do not get to savor their cleansed sacrifices, our people do not get to enjoy the advantages of the land, and husbands and wives toil to exhaustion with nowhere to turn to for redress of grievances. From this day on, after the swearing of the covenant, if the domain of Zheng does not submit only to the one that has the ritual propriety and the power to protect its people and if it dares to have perfidious intentions, let this covenant bear witness against us!"[211]

Zhonghang Yan[a] said, "Change that convenant document!"

Gongsun Shezhi said, "We have made ourselves clear to the great spirits with binding words. If the covenant can be changed, then one can also revolt against the great domain."

Zhi Ying[a] said to Zhonghang Yan[c]: "It is we who are without virtue, and yet we tried to bind others against their will with a covenant. How could this be in accordance with ritual propriety? Not being in accordance with ritual propriety, how can we preside over the covenant? We should for now swear the covenant and withdraw our forces. If we come after cultivating virtue and letting the army rest, we will in the end gain control over Zheng. Why must it be today? If we have no virtue, the people will cast us off: how could it be only Zheng that would do so? If we can achieve peace and repose, even those from afar will come to us. Why need we rely on Zheng?" Jin thus swore the covenant and turned back.

---

210 That is, Zheng lies between Jin and Chu.

211 Zisi thereby makes Zheng's submission to Jin conditional on the latter's policies and also proleptically justifies Zheng's shift of allegiance to Chu.

9.6 晉人不得志於鄭，以諸侯復伐之。十二月癸亥，門其三門。閏月戊寅，濟
于陰阪，侵鄭。次於陰口而還。子孔曰：「晉師可擊也，師老而勞，且有
歸志，必大克之。」子展曰：「不可。」

9.7 公送晉侯，晉侯以公宴于河上，問公年。季武子對曰：「會于沙隨之歲，
寡君以生。」
　　　　晉侯曰：「十二年矣，是謂一終，一星終也。國君十五而生子，冠而
生子，禮也。君可以冠矣。大夫盍為冠具？」
　　　　武子對曰：「君冠，必以祼享之禮行之，以金石之樂節之，以先君
之祧處之。今寡君在行，未可具也，請及兄弟之國而假備焉。」
　　　　晉侯曰：「諾。」公還，及衛，冠于成公之廟，假鍾磬焉，禮也。

9.8(6) 楚子伐鄭。子駟將及楚平，子孔、子蟜曰：「與大國盟，口血未乾而背
之，可乎？」

212　The three gates are Zhuan (east) Gate, Shizhiliang (west) Gate, and North Gate. Jin
and its allies do not attack the South Gate, probably because they want to wait to
confront (or avoid) Chu forces that might be coming from the south.

213　The received text has *runyue wuyin* 閏月戊寅. There was no *wuyin* day in the intercalary month, and the Jin invasion should take place in the twelfth month. According to Du Yu's (ZZ 30.528) emendation, *runyue* may be a corruption of *men wuri* 門
五日, "they stormed the gates for five days."

214　Yinban 陰阪 was located in Zheng west of present-day Xinzheng County 新鄭縣,
Henan.

215　Jin and its allies met at Shasui (575 BCE; Cheng 16.6) to plan an attack against Zheng.

216　He is referring to the Year-Planet (Jupiter), whose cycle (11.86 years) is thought to
span twelve years (Yang, 3:970). Many predictions are tied to Jupiter's cycle (see, e.g.,
Xiang 28.1, 28.8, 30.10, Zhao 7.14, 8.6, 9.4, 10.1, 11.2, 32.2).

217　What little we know of the capping ceremony in pre-Han times is based on *Yili*-
Zheng 1.2, *Yili*-Jia 1.2.

218　Lord Cheng of Wei (r. 634–600) was the great-grandfather of the reigning Lord Xian
of Wei.

Jin attacks Zheng again but appears vulnerable to Zheng leaders.

Because the men of Jin had not fulfilled their aims in Zheng, they led the princes to attack it again. In the twelfth month, on the *guihai* day (5), Jin and its allies stormed Zheng's three gates.[212] On the *wuyin* day (20),[213] they crossed the Wei River at Yinban and invaded Zheng.[214] They set up camp at Yinkou and then turned back. Zikong said, "We can strike the Jin troops! Their troops are worn out and exhausted and moreover have the desire to turn back. We are sure to crush them completely." Gongsun Shezhi[a] said, "This will not do."

9.6

Following the suggestion of Lord Dao of Jin, Lord Xiang of Lu undergoes the capping ceremony on his way back from the allies' expedition against Zheng.

Our lord escorted the Prince of Jin on his way. The Prince of Jin held a feast for our lord on the banks of the Yellow River. He asked our lord's age. Ji Wuzi replied, "Our unworthy ruler was born the year when there was a meeting at Shasui."[215]

9.7

The Prince of Jin said, "That was twelve years ago. This is called one completed cycle, for one planet completes its cycle in twelve years.[216] That the ruler of a domain begets sons at fifteen, or that he begets sons after the capping ceremony,[217] is in accordance with ritual propriety. Your ruler can now have the capping ceremony. Why do your high officers not prepare all the things necessary for it?"

Ji Wuzi[c] replied, "Our ruler's capping ceremony must begin with the ritual of libation of fragrant wine. It must be regulated with the music of bells and chime-stones. It must take place in the temple of his former rulers. Now our unworthy ruler is on the road, and these things cannot be furnished. I beg leave to reach a brother domain and borrow what is needed for preparation there."

The Prince of Jin said, "I agree." Our lord turned homeward. When he reached Wei, he had his capping ceremony at Lord Cheng's temple.[218] They borrowed the bells and the chime-stones. This was in accordance with ritual propriety.

Zheng, torn between Jin and Chu, now veers toward Chu after Jin fails to protect it from Chu retaliation. Zheng ministers argue that covenants based on coercion are not binding.

The Master of Chu attacked Zheng. Zisi planned to seek a peace agreement with Chu. Zikong and Zijiao said, "To have sworn a covenant with a great domain and then to turn against it before the blood has even dried on the mouth—is that acceptable?"

9.8(6)

子駟、子展曰：「吾盟固云『唯彊是從』，今楚師至，晉不我救，則楚彊矣。盟誓之言，豈敢背之？且要盟無質，神弗臨也。所臨唯信，信者，言之瑞也，善之主也，是故臨之。明神不蠲要盟，背之，可也。」

乃及楚平。公子罷戎入盟，同盟于中分。

楚莊夫人卒，王未能定鄭而歸。

9.9　晉侯歸，謀所以息民。魏絳請施舍，輸積聚以貸。自公以下，苟有積者，盡出之。國無滯積，亦無困人；公無禁利，亦無貪民。祈以幣更，賓以特牲，器用不作，車服從給。行之期年，國乃有節。三駕而楚不能與爭。

219　Zisi and Gongsun Shezhi are protesting that they have not violated the covenant as defined by the Zheng participants.

220　Fu Qian glosses *zhi* 質 as *cheng* 誠, "sincerity," extending the meaning of "substance" as "inner truth" and also anticipating the references to "good faith" later in the argument (Hong Liangji, *Chunqiu Zuozhuan gu*, 515).

221　Good faith is what gives speech the power of a tally. Zheng Xuan glosses *rui* 瑞 as *fuxin* 符信, the tally for conveying commands (*Zhouli*-Zheng 20.312). See also Ai 14.4.

222　The text gives no subject for "swore a covenant together" (*tongmeng* 同盟). Taking Xi 28.3h as an example, we assume that the rulers swear a covenant after the more powerful partner of the covenant is represented by its dignitary in a preliminary settlement. Zhongfen 中分 was the name of a road in the Zheng capital.

223　She was the mother of King Gong of Chu.

Zisi and Gongsun Shezhi[a] said, "Our covenant already stated: 'We will submit only to the domain that has the power.' Now the Chu army has arrived, and Jin is not coming to our aid. Chu then is the powerful one. How would we dare to turn against the words of a covenant vow?[219] Moreover, covenants based on coercion have no substance.[220] The spirits do not oversee them. What they do oversee are only covenants sworn in good faith. For good faith is the tally[221] of speech and the mainstay of excellence. That is why the spirits oversee it. The bright spirits do not purify a covenant made binding by force. To turn against it is acceptable."

Zheng thus reached a peace agreement with Chu. Gongzi Pirong entered the Zheng capital to swear the covenant. The rulers of Zheng and Chu swore a covenant together at Zhongfen.[222]

The wife of King Zhuang of Chu died.[223] The king turned back before he could settle the disorder in Zheng.

The Jin high officer Wei Jiang is credited with realizing an idealized vision of society based on due moderation, frugality, and a more equitable distribution of wealth. Despite evidence of Jin weakness during these years, it is said to prevail over Chu. The formulaic language here echoes similar summaries in Min 2.10, Xi 27.4c, Wen 6.1, and Cheng 18.3.

When the Prince of Jin returned home, he deliberated over how to let the people rest. Wei Jiang asked permission to grant them exemptions from conscript labor[224] and to transport the accumulated wealth of the domain in order to lend it to the people. From the lord downward, whosoever had any accumulation of goods brought them all forward. There were no accumulations of goods held back in the domain, nor were there destitute people. There were no prohibitions on opportunities for profit,[225] nor were there covetous people. Supplications to the spirits were made with silk and fur instead of sacrificial victims. Guests were honored with a single head of cattle. No new vessels were cast. Carriages and robes were no more than sufficient. After these practices were carried out for a year, the domain then had proper order. Three times were the chariots mounted,[226] and Chu was not able to contend with Jin.

9.9

---

224 We read *shi* 施 as *chi* 弛 ("exemptions"), following Zheng Xuan's gloss of the term in *Zhouli*-Zheng 11.168, and as distinct from the term *shishe* 施舍 in Xuan 12.2b, Zhao 13.2, and Zhao 25.3, which refers to gifts and giving.

225 That is, the domain does not monopolize resources and the people are allowed to profit from access to forests, mountains, marshes, or rivers.

226 This statement is referring to the campaigns at Niushou (Xiang 10.8), the eastern gate of the Zheng capital, and Xiang (both in Xiang 11.3).

春秋

10.1(1)　十年，春，公會晉侯、宋公、衛侯、曹伯、莒子、邾子、滕子、薛伯、杞伯、小邾子、齊世子光會吳于柤。

10.2(2)　夏，五月甲午，遂滅偪陽。

10.3　公至自會。

10.4(3)　楚公子貞、鄭公孫輒帥師伐宋。

10.5(4)　晉師伐秦。

10.6(7)　秋，莒人伐我東鄙。

10.7(8)　公會晉侯、宋公、衛侯、曹伯、莒子、邾子、齊世子光、滕子、薛伯、杞伯、小邾子伐鄭。

10.8(9)　冬，盜殺鄭公子騑、公子發、公孫輒。

10.9(10)　戍鄭虎牢。

10.10(11)　楚公子貞帥師救鄭。

10.11　公至自伐鄭。

左傳

10.1(1)　十年，春，會于柤，會吳子壽夢也。
　　　三月癸丑，齊高厚相大子光，以先會諸侯于鍾離，不敬。士莊子曰：「高子相大子以會諸侯，將社稷是衛，而皆不敬，棄社稷也，其將不免乎！」

227　Zha 柤 was located to the northwest of Pi County 邳縣 in present-day Jiangsu.

228　Biyang 偪陽, to the northwest of Zha, was at the border of present-day Shangdong and Jiangsu, about 135 kilometers southeast of the Lu capital and just south of present-day Yi County 嶧縣, Shandong.

ANNALS

In the tenth year, in spring, our lord met with the Prince of Jin, the Duke of Song, the Prince of Wei, the Liege of Cao, the Master of Ju, the Master of Zhu, the Master of Teng, the Liege of Xue, the Liege of Qi, the Master of Lesser Zhu, and the Qi heir apparent Guang and then met with Wu at Zha.[227]   10.1(1)

In summer, in the fifth month, on the *jiawu* day (8), they then extinguished Biyang.[228]   10.2(2)

Our lord arrived from the meeting.   10.3

Gongzi Zhen (Zinang) of Chu and Gongsun Zhe (Zi'er) of Zheng led out troops and attacked Song.   10.4(3)

Jin troops attacked Qin.   10.5(4)

In autumn, Ju leaders attacked our eastern marches.   10.6(7)

Our lord met with the Prince of Jin, the Duke of Song, the Prince of Wei, the Liege of Cao, the Master of Ju, the Master of Zhu, the Qi heir apparent Guang, the Master of Teng, the Liege of Xue, the Liege of Qi, and the Master of Lesser Zhu and attacked Zheng.   10.7(8)

In winter, brigands killed Gongzi Fei (Zisi), Gongzi Fa (Ziguo), and Gongsun Zhe (Zi'er).   10.8(9)

We garrisoned Hulao in Zheng.   10.9(10)

Gongzi Zhen (Zinang) of Chu led out troops and went to the aid of Zheng.   10.10(11)

Our lord arrived from the attack on Zheng.   10.11

ZUO

The Jin minister Shi Ruo, who showed his prescience earlier (Xiang 9.1), predicts disaster for the Qi heir apparent and the Qi minister Gao Hou because of their irreverence at a meeting.

In the tenth year, in spring, the princes met at Zha: this was to meet with   10.1(1)
Shoumeng, the Master of Wu.

In the third month, on the *guichou* day (26), Gao Hou of Qi acted as assistant to the Qi heir apparent Guang so as to have a prior meeting with the princes at Zhongli. Both behaved irreverently. Shi Ruo[a] said, "Gao Hou[a] acted as assistant to the heir apparent so as to meet with the princes. They were to guard the altars of the domain, and yet both behaved irreverently. Having cast off the altars of the domain, they will probably not escape disaster!"

夏，四月戊午，會于柤。

10.2a(2) 晉荀偃、士匄請伐偪陽，而封宋向戌焉。荀罃曰：「城小而固，勝之不武，弗勝為笑。」固請。丙寅，圍之，弗克。孟氏之臣秦菫父輦重如役。偪陽人啟門，諸侯之士門焉。縣門發，郰人紇抉之。以出門者，狄虒彌建大車之輪，而蒙之以甲，以為櫓。左執之，右拔戟，以成一隊。孟獻子曰：「《詩》所謂『有力如虎』者也。」主人縣布，菫父登之，及堞而絕之。隊，則又縣之。蘇而復上者三，主人辭焉，乃退。帶其斷以徇於軍三日。

10.2b 諸侯之師久於偪陽，荀偃、士匄請於荀罃曰：「水潦將降，懼不能歸，請班師。」

In summer, in the fourth month, on the *wuwu* day (1), the princes met at Zha.

Jin and its allies extinguish the small domain of Biyang. The campaign is marked by the extraordinary feats of Lu men, including Qin Jinfu, Di Simi, and Shuliang He, Confucius' father (for Confucius' ancestry, see Zhao 7.12).

10.2a(2)

Zhonghang Yan[a] and Fan Gai[a] of Jin requested to attack Biyang and to put Xiang Xu of Song in power there. Zhi Ying[b] said, "The city is small yet well defended. To win it would be no great martial achievement, yet to fail to win it would make us a laughingstock." They persisted in their request. On the *bingyin* day (9), they laid siege to it and failed to overcome it. A retainer of the Meng lineage, Qin Jinfu, pulled a heavy supply wagon to the site of the campaign. The men of Biyang opened the gate, and the officers of the princes stormed it. The portcullis of the inner gate was released,[229] but a man of Zou named He[230] held it up to allow the officers storming the gate to go in. Di Simi stood up the wheel of a big carriage, covered it with hides, and used it as a big shield. Holding it with his left hand and pulling out a lance with his right hand, he led a platoon.[231] Meng Xianzi said, "This is what the *Odes* calls one who 'has strength like a tiger.'"[232] Those guarding Biyang[233] hung a strip of cloth over the wall, by which Qin Jinfu[a] climbed up. When he reached the parapets, they cut it. He fell, and they hung it again. Three times he revived and climbed it again. Those guarding Biyang acknowledged his feats and desisted, and Qin Jinfu[a] then withdrew.[234] For three days he made his circuits among the troops showing the cut cloth, which he wrapped around himself as a belt.

The Jin commander Zhi Ying overcomes the irresolution and flagging will of the other leaders, and Jin achieves victory. Trying to consolidate Song's allegiance, Jin gives Biyang to the Song ruler after the Song minister Xiang Xu declines to be put in power there.

10.2b

The armies of the princes were long detained at Biyang. Zhonghang Yan[a] and Fan Gai[a] requested of Zhi Ying[b]: "Heavy rain is about to fall. We fear we will not be able to turn back, and ask permission to withdraw our troops now."

---

229 For the portcullis (*xuanmen* 縣門), see also Zhuang 28.3.

230 He (or Shuliang He), the father of Confucius, was from Zou 耶, a city near the Lu capital, Qufu. Zou has also been identified as the birthplace of Confucius.

231 The number of soldiers in one *dui* 隊 (translated here as "platoon") has been given as one hundred or as fifty by various commentators.

232 *Maoshi* 38, "Jian xi" 簡兮, 2C.100.

233 The text has *zhuren* 主人, which usually means "host" or "master."

234 The point may be that Qin Jinfu's persistent bravery is finally acknowledged and he can therefore withdraw with dignity.

知伯怒，投之以机，出於其間，曰：「女成二事，而後告余。余恐亂命，以不女違。女既勤君而興諸侯，牽帥老夫以至于此，既無武守，而又欲易余罪，曰：『是實班師。不然，克矣。』余羸老也，可重任乎？七日不克，必爾乎取之！」

五月庚寅，荀偃、士匄帥卒攻偪陽，親受矢石，甲午，滅之。

書曰「遂滅偪陽」，言自會也。

以與向戌。向戌辭曰：「君若猶辱鎮撫宋國，而以偪陽光啟寡君，群臣安矣，其何貺如之！若專賜臣，是臣興諸侯以自封也，其何罪大焉！敢以死請。」乃予宋公。

---

235   Zhi Ying was commander of the central army.

236   The text has *ji* 机 (armrest). Zhang Binglin suggests that *ji* 机 is a loanword for *ji* 機, the trigger on a big crossbow (*Zuozhuan du*, cited in Yang, 3:976). *Sunzi* 5.116 compares an army's momentum to the release of a crossbow trigger. Wu Jing'an (*Chunqiu Zuoshi zhuan jiuzhu shuzheng xu*, 87) suggests that Zhi Ying hurls the trigger to emphasize how retreat is not an option.

237   "The two things" refer to the invasion of Biyang and putting Xiang Xu in power there.

238   Conflicting views among the commanders will lead to confusion.

239   Following Karlgren, gl. 502. Du Yu (*ZZ* 31.538): "Lacking the martial achievement to hold on to." Yang (3:976) glosses the term *wushou* 武守: "to firmly defend and to attack in a martial manner."

Enraged, Zhi Ying[c235] hurled the crossbow trigger at them,[236] which flew between the two of them, and then said, "You had already made up your minds about these two things, and only then did you notify me.[237] I was afraid commands from us would get confused,[238] and for that reason did not oppose you. Now you have made the ruler labor, roused the princes, and dragged this old man here. Lacking the martial prowess to hold on,[239] you yet want to lay the blame on me by saying, 'It was that man who withdrew the troops. Otherwise, we would have overcome Biyang.' I am already old and feeble. Can I bear the heavy responsibility for defeat?[240] If you do not overcome the city in seven days, I will certainly take it out of your hide!"[241]

In the fifth month, on the *gengyin* day (4), Zhonghang Yan[a] and Fan Gai[a] led soldiers to attack Biyang, and they personally bore the shower of arrows and stones. On the *jiawu* day (8), they extinguished it.

The text says, "They then extinguished Biyang": this is to indicate that they did so coming from the meeting at Zha.[242]

The Jin ruler gave Biyang to Xiang Xu, but he declined, saying: "If you, my lord, still condescend to bring stability and solace to the domain of Song and use Biyang to expand the realm of our unworthy ruler, all his subjects will be content.[243] What generous gift could compare to this? If you bestow it on me alone, then I would have roused the princes just to have myself put in power in a place. What offense could be greater than that? I presume to brave death with my request." The Jin ruler thus gave Biyang to the Duke of Song.

---

240 We follow Kong Yingda (*ZZ-Kong* 31.539), who reads 重 as *zhong* ("heavy"). Yang (3:976) reads 重 as *chong* ("again"): "Can I again bear the responsibility for defeat?" Zhi Ying was taken captive during the Bi campaign (Xuan 12.2h).

241 We follow Takezoe (15.5) and read *er hu* 爾乎 as *yu er* 於爾, literally, "take it from you." Zhi Ying is saying that Zhonghang Yan and Fan Gai will certainly have to bear the blame.

242 The goal of the meeting at Zha was the campaign against Biyang; cf. the similar grammar and context in Xi 4.1. Jin's allies, gathered at Zha, have been forced to join this campaign.

243 Xiang Xu is implying that if he is given Biyang, there will be discontent, jealousy, and slander among the other Song leaders (Takezoe, 15.5).

10.2c　宋公享晉侯于楚丘，請以桑林。荀罃辭。荀偃、士匄曰：「諸侯宋、魯，
　　於是觀禮。魯有禘樂，賓祭用之。宋以桑林享君，不亦可乎？」舞，師題
　　以旌夏。晉侯懼而退入于房。去旌，卒享而還。及著雍，疾。卜，桑林見。
　　荀偃、士匄欲奔請禱焉，荀罃不可，曰：「我辭禮矣，彼則以之。猶有鬼
　　神，於彼加之。」

　　　　晉侯有間，以偪陽子歸，獻于武宮，謂之夷俘。偪陽，妘姓也。使
　　周內史選其族嗣納諸霍人，禮也。

　　　　師歸，孟獻子以秦堇父為右。生秦丕茲，事仲尼。

10.3(4)　六月，楚子囊、鄭子耳伐宋，師于訾毋。庚午，圍宋，門于桐門。

244　On Chuqiu, see *Annals*, Yin 7.6, n. 111.

245　On the meanings of the *di* 禘 sacrifice, see also Min 2.2, n.17. According to *Liji* 31.577,
the *di* sacrifice is offered in the sixth month to the Zhou duke at the Ancestral
Temple, and the music used includes the music of Zhou, Xia, the Eastern Yi, and the
Man. The music for the *di* sacrifice would be inappropriately momentous for entertaining guests, even as Zhi Ying judges the music of Mulberry Woods to be excessive
for the occasion of entertaining Lord Dao of Jin. In *Liji* 21.420, Confucius said, "The
sacrifice in the outskirts and *di* sacrifice of Lu violate ritual propriety. The line of the
Zhou duke has declined!"

246　Du Yu (*ZZ* 31.539) identifies the music of Mulberry Woods (Sanglin) as the music of
the Shang kings. Mulberry Woods was supposedly where Tang, the ancestor of
Shang, prayed for rain, and it came to be identified as the place for Shang ancestral
sacrifices. On the connection between Song and Shang, see Xi 22.8, n. 271. In
Zhuangzi 3.117, Cook Ding's art of cutting up the ox is said to accord with "the dance
of Mulberry Woods." See also *Lüshi chunqiu* 9.479, 12.634, 14.844.

247　The *jingxia* banner is decorated at the head of the pole with pheasant feathers dyed
in five colors (Yang, 3:977). Karlgren (gl. 505) reads *jing* 旌 as a verb ("to signal with
banners") and *ti* 題 as a loanword for *ti* 提: "The musicians began (*ti* 題) to signal
with banners (*jing* 旌) the grand Xia music."

248　They are already in Jin. Zhonghang Yan and Fan Gai want to rush back to Song to
pray to the spirit of Mulberry Woods.

An inappropriately grand musical entertainment offered by Song is linked to Lord Dao of Jin's sickness. On matching music with ritual propriety, see also Zhuang 20.1, Cheng 12.4, Xiang 4.3, and Zhao 1.12.

The Duke of Song offered the Prince of Jin ceremonial toasts at Chuqiu.[244] He requested to use the music of Mulberry Woods. Zhi Ying[b] declined. Zhonghang Yan[a] and Fan Gai[a] said, "Among the princes, it is only in Song and Lu that we can observe the proper rituals. Lu has the music of the *di* sacrifice and uses it with important guests and at major sacrifices.[245] Would it not be acceptable for Song to use Mulberry Woods to offer ceremonial toasts to our ruler?"[246] They danced, and the musicians led the way with banners decorated with colorful feathers.[247] The Prince of Jin was fearful and retreated into one of the side chambers. They removed the banners, and he then attended the ceremonial toasts before he turned homeward. When he reached Zhuyong, he fell ill. They conducted divination and the spirit of Mulberry Woods manifested itself. Zhonghang Yan[a] and Fan Gai[a] wanted to rush back to Song and offer supplicatory prayers.[248] Zhi Ying[b] did not permit this, saying, "We had already declined the ritual, but they used it nonetheless. If there are indeed ghosts and spirits, they will inflict the consequences on Song."

As soon as there was a break in the Prince of Jin's illness, he took the Master of Biyang back with him and presented him at the Wu palace, calling him "the captive of Yi tribe." The house of Biyang has the clan name of "Yun." The Jin ruler made the court scribe of Zhou choose a descendant from that lineage and install him in power in Huoren.[249] This was in accordance with ritual propriety.[250]

When the Lu army returned, Meng Xianzi made Qin Jinfu his spearman on the right. He fathered Qin Pizi, who served Confucius[c].[251]

10.2c

Chu and Zheng attack Song, now Jin's confirmed ally.

In the sixth month, Zinang of Chu and Zi'er of Zheng attacked Song, stationing their armies at Ziwu.[252] On the *gengwu* day (14), they laid siege to Song, storming its Paulownia Gate.[253]

10.3(4)

---

249 Huoren 霍人 was located in the domain of Jin east of present-day Fanzhi County 繁峙縣, Shanxi.

250 A descendant of the Yun line, presumably not too closely related to the ruler of Biyang, is to continue sacrifices to the Yun ancestors at Huoren, a city in Jin. A Zhou scribe is asked to make this choice to indicate that Jin is acting with deference to the royal house.

251 Pizi 丕茲, also written as Buci 不慈, is the courtesy name of Qin Shang 秦商, one of Confucius' disciples. See *Shiji* 67.2223; *Kongzi jiayu* 9.89.

252 Ziwu 訾毋 was in the domain of Song south of present-day Luyi County 鹿邑縣, Henan.

253 This gate was the northern gate of the Song capital.

10.4(5)　晉荀罃伐秦，報其侵也。

10.5　衛侯救宋，師于襄牛。鄭子展曰：「必伐衛。不然，是不與楚也。得罪於晉，又得罪於楚，國將若之何？」

子駟曰：「國病矣。」

子展曰：「得罪於二大國，必亡。病，不猶愈於亡乎？」諸大夫皆以為然。故鄭皇耳帥師侵衛，楚令也。

孫文子卜追之，獻兆於定姜。姜氏問繇。曰：

> 兆如山陵，
> 有夫出征，
> 而喪其雄。

姜氏曰：「征者喪雄，禦寇之利也。大夫圖之！」衛人追之，孫蒯獲鄭皇耳于犬丘。

10.6　秋，七月，楚子囊、鄭子耳侵我西鄙。還，圍蕭。八月丙寅，克之。九月，子耳侵宋北鄙。

孟獻子曰：「鄭其有災乎！師競已甚。周猶不堪競，況鄭乎！有災，其執政之三士乎！」

254　Xiangniu was in the domain of Wei (see Xi 28.1, n. 406).

255　Ding Jiang, wife of Lord Ding of Wei and the official mother of Lord Xian, again shows her perspicacity. In plastromancy and scapulimancy, exposure of the shell or bone to heat produces a crack that is interpreted as an omen.

256　The armies of Chu and Zheng seem to have invaded Lu only as an afterthought; Lu's proximity to Song meant that it could have been attacked "on the way." It is curious that this incident is not mentioned in the *Annals*.

257　On Xiao, see Zhuang 12.1, n. 68.

258　These three officers are Zisi, Ziguo, and Zi'er.

Zhi Ying[b] of Jin attacked Qin: this was in retaliation for Qin's invasion of Jin.   10.4(5)

Wei comes to Song's aid as Jin's ally, and Zheng, now siding with Chu, invades Wei. Ding Jiang, one of Zuozhuan's prescient women (Cheng 14.1, 14.5), interprets divination results in a way that boosts Wei morale.

The Prince of Wei came to Song's aid and stationed his army at Xiang-   10.5
niu.[254] Gongsun Shezhi[a] of Zheng said, "We must attack Wei. Otherwise, it would amount to a failure on our part to side with Chu. We have offended Jin. If we also offend Chu, then what is our domain to do?"
   Zisi said, "Our domain is already afflicted."
   Gongsun Shezhi[a] said, "If we offend two great domains, we are sure to perish. Is it not still better to be afflicted than to perish?" The high officers all agreed. That was why Huang Er of Zheng led out troops to invade Wei; this was Chu's command.
   Sun Linfu[a] of Wei divined about pursuing the enemy and presented the omen crack to Ding Jiang.[255] Lady Jiang asked about the omen verse. It said,

> The crack is like a mound.
> There are men who leave for battle
> And lose their leader.

Lady Jiang said, "For the invaders to lose their leader is an advantage for those resisting the enemy. You, high officers, should consider this!" The men of Wei pursued the Zheng forces. Sun Kuai, Sun Linfu's son, took Huang Er of Zheng captive at Quanqiu.

The Zheng leaders' perception that Zheng is an "afflicted" victim is belied by continued aggression against Lu and Song. The Lu minister Meng Xianzi's prediction of doom for Zheng leaders is fulfilled three months later.

In autumn, in the seventh month, Zinang of Chu and Zi'er of Zheng   10.6
invaded our western marches.[256] On the way back, they laid siege to Xiao.[257] In the eighth month, on the *bingyin* day (11), they overcame it. In the ninth month, Zi'er invaded the northern marches of Song.
   Meng Xianzi said, "Disaster will surely strike Zheng! Its army has been combative in the extreme. Even the Zhou house cannot bear too much combativeness, let alone Zheng! If there is disaster, it will surely strike the three officers in charge of government!"[258]

10.7(6)　莒人間諸侯之有事也，故伐我東鄙。

10.8(7)　諸侯伐鄭，齊崔杼使大子光先至于師，故長於滕。己酉，師于牛首。

10.9a(8)　初，子駟與尉止有爭，將禦諸侯之師，而黜其車。尉止獲，又與之爭。子駟抑尉止曰：「爾車非禮也。」遂弗使獻。

初，子駟為田洫，司氏、堵氏、侯氏、子師氏皆喪田焉。故五族聚群不逞之人因公子之徒以作亂。

於是子駟當國，子國為司馬，子耳為司空，子孔為司徒。冬十月戊辰，尉止、司臣、侯晉、堵女父、子師僕帥賊以入，晨攻執政于西宮之朝，殺子駟、子國、子耳，劫鄭伯以如北宮。子孔知之，故不死。書曰「盜」，言無大夫焉。

10.9b　子西聞盜，不儆而出，尸而追盜。盜入於北宮，乃歸，授甲，臣妾多逃，器用多喪。

<hr>

259　Leaders of other domains should have precedence over Guang, the Qi heir apparent. Jin leaders may be showing him special regard because Qi support is vital to Jin's struggle with Chu.

260　Niushou in Zheng was located in present-day Henan; see also Huan 14.4, n. 119.

261　Zisi is denying Wei Zhi credit for his achievement.

262　The text is referring here to the four lineages just mentioned as well as Wei Zhi.

263　This refers to the noble sons whom Zisi put to death in Xiang 8.2.

264　Wei Zhi, Si Chen, Hou Jin, Du Rufu, and Zishi Pu are all officers (*shi* 士), not high officers.

265　See, for example, the Song scholar Chao Buzhi's 晁補之 judgment, cited in Cheng Gongshuo, *Chunqiu fenji*, *j.* 69.

266　This could also include the other corpses, but the limited time suggests that he may be recovering only his father's corpse.

Ju leaders seized the opportunity of the princes' involvement in affairs of war, and that was why they attacked our eastern marches. 10.7(6)

The princes attacked Zheng. Cui Zhu of Qi had the Qi heir apparent Guang arrive first among the troops, and that was why he took precedence over Teng.[259] On the *jiyou* day (25), the troops were stationed at Niushou.[260] 10.8(7)

During internecine conflicts in Zheng, disaffected Zheng officers lead brigands to murder Zheng ministers in charge of government. The chief minister Zisi, who plotted the death of Lord Xi of Zheng (Xiang 7.9) and suppressed his rivals (Xiang 8.2), falls victim to his enemies.

Earlier, Zisi and Wei Zhi had clashed with one another. Just when Zheng was about to defend itself against the troops of the princes, Zisi decreased the number of Wei Zhi's chariots. Wei Zhi took some captives, and Zisi again clashed with him. Zisi suppressed Wei Zhi's claims, saying, "Your chariots are not in accordance with ritual propriety."[261] He thereupon did not let Wei Zhi present his captives at court. 10.9a(8)

Earlier, Zisi had laid out ditches between fields. The Si, Du, Hou, and Zishi lineages had all lost lands. That was why the five houses[262] gathered various disaffected persons and, relying on the support of the noble sons'[263] followers, raised a rebellion.

At that time Zisi was in charge of the domain. Ziguo was supervisor of the military, Zi'er was supervisor of works, and Zikong was supervisor of conscripts. In winter, in the tenth month, on the *wuchen* day (14), Wei Zhi, Si Chen, Hou Jin, Du Rufu, and Zishi Pu entered the palace with a gang of brigands. In the morning, they attacked those in charge of government in the court of the Western Palace and killed Zisi, Ziguo, and Zi'er. They abducted the Liege of Zheng and took him to the Northern Palace. Zikong knew about this plot, and for this reason he did not die. The text has "brigands" to indicate that there were no high officers involved.[264]

The different reactions of Zixi and Zichan to the rebellion show the latter's superior judgment.[265] For later moralists who regard filial piety as a more absolute moral imperative, however, Zixi's impulsive reaction is more praiseworthy than Zichan's careful defense of his property. The rebels are killed or driven into exile.

When Zisi's son Zixi heard about the brigands, he left the house without taking any precautions, recovered his father's corpse,[266] and then pursued the brigands. After the brigands had entered the Northern Palace, he went back home and distributed arms to his followers. Many of his servants and concubines had run away, and many vessels were missing. 10.9b

子產聞盜，為門者，庀群司，閉府庫，慎閉藏，完守備，成列而後
出，兵車十七乘。尸而攻盜於北宮，子蟜帥國人助之，殺尉止、子師僕，
盜眾盡死。侯晉奔晉，堵女父、司臣、尉翩、司齊奔宋。

10.9c　子孔當國，為載書，以位序、聽政辟。大夫、諸司、門子弗順，將誅之。
子產止之，請為之焚書。子孔不可，曰：「為書以定國，眾怒而焚之，是
眾為政也，國不亦難乎？」

子產曰：「眾怒難犯，專欲難成，合二難以安國，危之道也。不如
焚書以安眾，子得所欲，眾亦得安，不亦可乎？專欲無成，犯眾興禍，子
必從之！」

乃焚書於倉門之外，眾而後定。

10.10(9)　諸侯之師城虎牢而戍之，晉師城梧及制，士魴、魏絳戍之。書曰「戍鄭
虎牢」，非鄭地也，言將歸焉。鄭及晉平。

267　We follow Karlgren, gl. 506. Reinforced hierarchy in the government may also mean
that Zikong is effectively accruing power to himself and barring officials from inter-
fering with his own decisions. Recall that he knew about the plot against the other
Zheng ministers but did not intervene, which suggests that he was exploiting the
unrest to gain more power. Zichan understands his ambition but, instead of directly
confronting him, chooses a mediatory role. Zikong will control Zheng government
for nine years. For his downfall and murder, see Xiang 19.9.
268　Zikong would have control of the government.
269　For Hulao, see Xiang 2.5, n. 30, Yin 5.4, n. 95.

When Ziguo's son Zichan heard about the brigands, he established a gatekeeper, had the various supervisors in full readiness, closed the arsenal, carefully secured the respositories, completed the preparations for defense, formed ranks, and only then came out, with seventeen war chariots. He recovered his father's corpse and then attacked the brigands at the Northern Palace. Zijiao led the inhabitants of the capital to assist him, killing Wei Zhi and Zishi Pu. Every last man in the gang of brigands died. Hou Jin fled to Jin. Du Rufu, Si Chen, Wei Pian, and Si Qi fled to Song.

In the aftermath of the rebellion, Zikong's attempt to dominate the government provokes further unrest. Note that Zikong is not mentioned when Zixi, Zichan, and Zijiao are dealing with the rebellion. Zichan urges compromise because one has to reckon with "the anger of the multitude." On this idea, see also Zhao 13.2, 25.6, 26.4, and Ai 25.1.

Zikong took charge of the domain. He made a covenant document with the provision that required each according to his position to heed the commands of his immediate superior.[267] The high officers, various supervisors, and the heirs of ministerial lineages refused to follow these injunctions, and Zikong planned to execute them. Zichan stopped him and requested permission to burn the document on their account. Zikong refused, saying, "We made the document to stabilize the domain. If we burn it because of the anger of the multitude, then that would mean the multitude is in charge of government. Will it not be difficult to govern the domain?"

Zichan said, "It is difficult to contravene the anger of the multitude; it is difficult to achieve success with a desire for sole control. To combine both in an effort to calm the domain is the road to danger. It would be better to burn the document to reassure the multitude. You will get what you desire,[268] and the multitude will also be reassured. Would that not be acceptable? A desire for sole control will achieve nothing, and contravening the multitude will provoke disaster. You must follow my advice!"

They therefore burned the document outside the Cang Gate. Only then was the multitude more settled.

The armies of the princes fortified Hulao and garrisoned it.[269] The Jin army fortified Wu and Zhi,[270] with Shi Fang and Wei Jiang garrisoning them. The text says, "We garrisoned Hulao in Zheng": this is to indicate that though this was no longer Zheng territory, it was about to be returned to Zheng. Zheng and Jin reached a peace agreement.

10.9c

10.10(9)

---

270 Zhi 制 was another name for Hulao. Wu 梧 was probably close to Hulao. Jin's military presence in Hulao over the last eight years seems to have failed to consolidate Jin control over Zheng.

楚子囊救鄭。十一月，諸侯之師還鄭而南，至於陽陵。楚師不退。知武子欲退，曰：「今我逃楚，楚必驕，驕則可與戰矣。」

欒黶曰：「逃楚，晉之恥也。合諸侯以益恥，不如死。我將獨進。」師遂進。己亥，與楚師夾潁而軍。

子蟜曰：「諸侯既有成行，必不戰矣。從之將退，不從亦退。退，楚必圍我。猶將退也，不如從楚，亦以退之。」宵涉潁，與楚人盟。

欒黶欲伐鄭師，荀罃不可，曰：「我實不能禦楚，又不能庇鄭，鄭何罪？不如致怨焉而還。今伐其師，楚必救之。戰而不克，為諸侯笑。克不可命，不如還也。」

丁未，諸侯之師還，侵鄭北鄙而歸。楚人亦還。

The Jin commander Zhi Ying again shows his caution (see Xiang 9.5, 10.2), and Jin and its allies desist from attacking Zheng with full force and directly confronting Chu.

Zinang of Chu went to the aid of Zheng. In the eleventh month, the armies of the princes made a detour circuit around Zheng and headed southward, advancing as far as Yangling.[271] The Chu army did not retreat. Zhi Ying[a] wanted to retreat, saying: "If we now flee from Chu, Chu will certainly become complacent. Once it is complacent, we can then engage it in battle."[272]

Luan Yan said, "To flee from Chu would be Jin's disgrace. To have assembled the princes with the result of adding to our own disgrace would be worse than death. I will advance alone."[273] The Jin army thus advanced. On the *jihai* day (16), the Jin and Chu armies stationed their troops on opposite banks of the Ying River.

Zijiao said, "Since the princes already have formed ranks,[274] they will certainly not engage in battle. If we submit to Jin, they will retreat; if we do not submit to Jin, they will also retreat. If they retreat, Chu will certainly lay siege to us. Since they will retreat anyway, it would be better to submit to Chu, so as to make their army retreat also." Crossing the Ying River by night, he swore a covenant with the leaders of Chu.[275]

Luan Yan wanted to attack the Zheng army, but Zhi Ying[b] would not permit it. He said, "We are the ones who can neither stop Chu nor protect Zheng. What offense is Zheng guilty of? It would be better to turn back, leaving Chu as the target of resentment.[276] If we now attack Zheng's army, Chu will certainly come to its aid. If we engage in battle and do not overcome them, we will be the laughingstock of the princes. When victory cannot be decreed,[277] it is better to turn back."

On the *dingwei* day (24), the armies of the princes turned back, invaded Zheng's northern marches, and returned. The men of Chu likewise turned back.

---

271 Yangling 陽陵 was located in the domain of Zheng northwest of present-day Xuchang County 許昌縣, Henan.

272 Zhi Ying is arguing that Chu will be lulled into a state of careless arrogance and will therefore be vulnerable.

273 Cf. similar arguments in Xuan 12.2c.

274 That is, they are prepared to march and, by implication, to withdraw their troops.

275 Zheng and the armies of the princes are both north of the Ying River, while Chu forces are south of the river.

276 Upon Zheng's submission, Chu will make excessive demands on Zheng and arouse Zheng's resentment (Yang, 3:982). Karlgren (gl. 508) has a different reading: "It is better to make public our resentment (and admonish Zheng)."

277 Alternatively, "victory cannot be fated" (Takezoe, 15.14). Both readings imply that victory cannot be certain or be taken for granted.

王叔陳生與伯輿爭政，王右伯輿。王叔陳生怒而出奔。及河，王復之，殺史狡以說焉。不入，遂處之。晉侯使士匄平王室，王叔與伯輿訟焉。王叔之宰與伯輿之大夫瑕禽坐獄於王庭，士匄聽之。王叔之宰曰：「篳門閨竇之人而皆陵其上，其難為上矣。」

瑕禽曰：「昔平王東遷，吾七姓從王，牲用備具，王賴之，而賜之騂旄之盟，曰：『世世無失職。』若篳門閨竇，其能來東厎乎？且王何賴焉？今自王叔之相也，政以賄成，而刑放於寵。官之師旅，不勝其富，吾能無篳門閨竇乎？唯大國圖之！下而無直，則何謂正矣？」

范宣子曰：「天子所右，寡君亦右之；所左，亦左之。」使王叔氏與伯輿合要，王叔氏不能舉其契。王叔奔晉。

不書，不告也。單靖公為卿士以相王室。

---

278   Both Wangshu Chensheng and Boyu were royal ministers (*qingshi*). Boyu was involved in a similar power struggle with the Zhou Duke Chu in 580 BCE (Cheng 11.5). Upon his defeat, Chu fled to Jin, as did Chensheng in this episode.

279   We may surmise that the scribe Jiao was one of Chensheng's enemies at the Zhou court. It is possible to read *yue* 說 as *shuo* 說, "to make a case" (Takezoe, 15.15).

280   What we translate as "reside" (*chu* 處) can also mean "judge": "the king thus had the case judged by the Yellow River." See Wu Jing'an, *Chunqiu Zuoshi zhuan jiuzhu shuzheng xu*, 103.

281   The term here is *zuoyu* 坐獄 (literally, "sit in a court case"); elsewhere we also have simply *zuo* 坐 ("sit"). Jin was often the arbitrator in arguments within or between domains (including Zhou); see Xi 28.8, Zhao 23.2. Du Yu (ZZ 31.542) suggests that persons holding high offices were not supposed to personally argue their cases, hence the presence of their representatives here.

282   Following Takezoe (15.16) and Karlgren (gl. 512), we read *fang* 放 as "let go" or "set aside." Alternatively, Du Yu (ZZ 31.549) has "punishments have been only in the hands of favorites."

A Jin minister arbitrates the claims of two Zhou ministers contending for dominance in the Zhou court (see also Wen 14.9). The minister of lower rank is presented as having a more justified case.

Wangshu [which means "royal uncle"] Chensheng vied with Boyu for control of the government.[278] The king sided with Boyu. Enraged, Wangshu Chensheng left the Zhou capital and fled. When he reached the Yellow River, the king restored his position and put to death the scribe Jiao in order to please him.[279] He did not reenter the capital but from that time resided by the Yellow River.[280] The Prince of Jin sent Fan Gai[a] to make peace in the royal house. Wangshu Chensheng[a] and Boyu brought charges against one another before Fan Gai. The royal uncle's steward and Boyu's high officer, Xia Qin, disputed their claims at the royal court.[281] Fan Gai[a] heard their cases. The royal uncle's steward said, "When even all those living in hovels with brushwood gates and narrow doorways lord it over their superiors, it is difficult to be in superior ranks."

10.12

Xia Qin said, "Formerly, when King Ping resettled in the east, we were among the seven clans that followed the king, and we provided the full complement of sacrificial victims and equipment. The king relied on us and bestowed on us a covenant, offering a red bull as sacrifice. The covenant said, 'For generations to come, do not fail your office.' If we had truly come from hovels with brushwood gates and narrow doorways, could we have come east and stayed? Moreover, what would the king have relied on? Now since the royal uncle became chief minister, policies have been decided through bribes, while punishments have not been applied to favorites.[282] When officials of the various ranks have become so intolerably rich, how can the likes of us not live in hovels with brushwood gates and narrow doorways? Let the great domain consider this! If for those in inferior ranks there is no justice, how can this be called fair?"

Fan Gai[c] said, "Let the one the Son of Heaven favors be the one our unworthy ruler also favors. Let the one the Son of Heaven disfavors be the one our unworthy ruler also disfavors." He made the royal uncle and Boyu give their respective accusations and statements, which were to be reviewed together. The royal uncle could not give the evidence supporting his case, and he fled to Jin.

This was not recorded because we in Lu were not notified. The Shan Duke Jing became the minister serving the royal house.

春秋

11.1(1)　十有一年，春，王正月，作三軍。

11.2　夏，四月，四卜郊，不從，乃不郊。

11.3(2)　鄭公孫舍之帥師侵宋。

11.4(3)　公會晉侯、宋公、衛侯、曹伯、齊世子光、莒子、邾子、滕子、薛伯、杞伯、小邾子伐鄭。

11.5(3)　秋，七月己未，同盟于亳城北。

11.6　公至自伐鄭。

11.7(4)　楚子、鄭伯伐宋。

11.8(5)　公會晉侯、宋公、衛侯、曹伯、齊世子光、莒子、邾子、滕子、薛伯、杞伯、小邾子伐鄭，會于蕭魚。

11.9　公至自會。

11.10(5)　楚人執鄭行人良霄。

11.11(6)　冬，秦人伐晉。

ANNALS

In the eleventh year, in spring, in the royal first month, the three armies were created. — 11.1(1)

In summer, in the fourth month, we divined four times about performing the sacrifice in the outskirts. The results were not favorable, so we did not perform the sacrifice in the outskirts.[283] — 11.2

Gongsun Shezhi of Zheng led out troops and invaded Song. — 11.3(2)

Our lord met with the Prince of Jin, the Duke of Song, the Prince of Wei, the Liege of Cao, the Qi heir apparent Guang, the Master of Ju, the Master of Zhu, the Master of Teng, the Liege of Xue, the Liege of Qǐ, and the Master of Lesser Zhu and attacked Zheng. — 11.4(3)

In autumn, in the seventh month, on the *jiwei* day (10), they swore a covenant together north of Bocheng.[284] — 11.5(3)

Our lord arrived from the attack on Zheng. — 11.6

The Master of Chu and the Liege of Zheng attacked Song. — 11.7(4)

Our lord met with the Prince of Jin, the Duke of Song, the Prince of Wei, the Liege of Cao, the Qi heir apparent Guang, the Master of Ju, the Master of Zhu, the Master of Teng, the Liege of Xue, the Liege of Qǐ, and the Master of Lesser Zhu and attacked Zheng. They met at Xiaoyu.[285] — 11.8(5)

Our lord arrived from the meeting. — 11.9

Chu leaders arrested the Zheng envoy Liang Xiao. — 11.10(5)

In winter, Qin leaders attacked Jin. — 11.11(6)

---

283 For similar incidents, see Xi 31.3, Xiang 7.2.
284 Bocheng 亳城 was located in the domain of Zheng near present-day Zhengzhou 鄭州, Henan.
285 Xiaoyu 蕭魚 was located in present-day Xuchang City 許昌市, Henan.

11.1(1) 十一年，春，季武子將作三軍，告叔孫穆子曰：「請為三軍，各征其軍。」穆子曰：「政將及子，子必不能。」武子固請之。穆子曰：「然則盟諸？」乃盟諸僖閎，詛諸五父之衢。

正月，作三軍，三分公室而各有其一。三子各毀其乘。季氏使其乘之人，以其役邑入者無征，不入者倍征。孟氏使半為臣，若子若弟。叔孫氏使盡為臣，不然不舍。

286　According to *Zhouli*, each army (*jun* 軍) consisted of 12,500 soldiers (Yang, 3:986). Kong Yingda (ZZ-Kong 31.544) consistently applies this rule, although it is doubtful whether the formulations in *Zhouli* have any direct relevance for *Zuozhuan*. The word *zuo* 作 ("create") here probably means reorganization of, and additions to, existing military resources.

287　Yang (3:986) suggests that the word *zheng* 征 means "to have possession of." That Lord Xiang, who was about thirteen or fourteen at this point, should be bypassed in such important deliberations testifies to the weakness of the Lu ruling house. Ji Wuzi, who succeeded Ji Wenzi in Xiang 5, might still be young at this point, and Shusun Bao is consulted because of both his seniority and his position as supervisor of the military.

288　That is, "unable to do this equitably and bring about unity" (Takezoe, 15.19; Yang, 3:986). Alternatively, Ji Wuzi is "unable to accept the division of power" once he assumes charge of the government. Du Yu (ZZ 31.544) reads *zheng* 政 as "the overlord's (Jin) commands": "The overlord's commands will come upon you, and you will certainly be unable to deal with them." Du Yu might have taken his cue from *Guoyu*, "Lu yu 2," 5.186, where Shusun Bao admonishes Ji Wuzi against the creation of the three armies on the ground that it is transgressive and would anger the great domains.

289　The Crossroad of the Five Fathers (*wufu zhi qu* 五父之衢), also mentioned in Ding 6.7, 8.10, was just outside present-day Qufu and appears to have been an important landmark in Lu. The location implies that the imprecation is deliberately made known to the inhabitants of the capital. Cf. Zhao 5.1, n. 258. According to *Liji* 6.113, the crossroad is where Confucius buries his mother.

290　Du Yu (ZZ 31.544) interprets the phrase *sanfen gongshi* 三分公室 ("divided the lord's house into three") as a tripartite division of the people. Takezoe (15.20) surmises that the division concerned financial resources and tax revenue. Here we follow Yang's (3:986) reading of *gongshi* as "military resources (or forces) of the lord's house."

Lu reorganizes its military: the forces of the lord's house are expanded and divided into three armies (Lu had two before), and troops of the powerful lineages are assimilated into the new armies in different ways. This in effect transfers control of the military from the Lu ruling house to the Ji, Meng, and Shusun lineages. Since the households sending in conscripts also paid taxes, military reorganization is linked to changes in taxation (Xuan 15.8, Cheng 1.2, Ai 12.1), and control of the armies meant political and economic power. Fearful of the dissension that this may cause, Shusun Bao demands a covenant and a public oath. The Lu house is further diminished in the reorganization of the armies in Zhao 5.1a.

In the eleventh year, in spring, Ji Wuzi planned to create the three armies.[286] He told Shusun Bao[b]: "We request to organize three armies. Each of us will tax resources to support his own army."[287] Shusun Bao[c] said, "Control of the government will come to be in your hands. You are sure to be unable to do this well."[288] Ji Wuzi[c] persisted with his request. Shusun Bao[c] said, "Should we then swear a covenant about it?" They thus swore a covenant at the gate of Lord Xi's temple. The oath of imprecation was made at the Crossroad of the Five Fathers.[289]

11.1(1)

In the first month, the three armies were created. The three lineages divided the forces of our lord's house into three, each taking possession of one part.[290] Each of the three lineage heads disbanded his own contingent of chariots.[291] As for the chariot soldiers, the Ji lineage head absolved from levies those who enlisted from his conscript-supplying settlements but doubled the levies for those who did not do so.[292] The Meng lineage head made half of his lineage troops into conscripts; they were either sons or younger brothers of those who did not join the army.[293] The Shusun lineage head made all his lineage troops into conscripts; otherwise, he would not have given them up for inclusion in the new armies.[294]

---

291   With the expectation of controlling one-third of the military resources of the lord's house, there is no need for the three lineages to keep their own private chariots. There is the further implication that the disbanded chariots would enter a common "pool," enhancing the total number of chariots that are to be divided among the three lineages.

292   This follows Yang's (3:986–87) reading. Yang further surmises that the bondsmen in Ji's settlements were in effect freed, and they then had the choice of either paying levies or becoming conscripts.

293   The narrative implies that the older males—the fathers and older brothers—remained free men, while the younger males were conscripted into the army.

294   Whereas Shusun Bao opposes the creation of the three armies in *Guoyu*, "Lu yu 2," 5.186 (as consistent with his image of judiciousness and ritual propriety), he is party to the whole process in *Zuozhuan*. Here he appears as the most conservative of the leaders of the three lineages in the way he reorganizes the army under his control.

11.2(3)　鄭人患晉、楚之故，諸大夫曰：「不從晉，國幾亡。楚弱於晉，晉不吾疾也。晉疾，楚將辟之。何為而使晉師致死於我？楚弗敢敵，而後可固與也。」

子展曰：「與宋為惡，諸侯必至，吾從之盟。楚師至，吾又從之，則晉怒甚矣。晉能驟來，楚將不能，吾乃固與晉。」

大夫說之，使疆場之司惡於宋。宋向戌侵鄭，大獲。子展曰：「師而伐宋可矣。若我伐宋，諸侯之伐我必疾，吾乃聽命焉，且告於楚。楚師至，吾乃與之盟，而重賂晉師，乃免矣。」夏，鄭子展侵宋。

11.3(4, 5)　四月，諸侯伐鄭。己亥，齊大子光、宋向戌先至于鄭，門于東門。其莫，晉荀罃至于西郊，東侵舊許。衛孫林父侵其北鄙。六月，諸侯會于北林，師于向。右還，次于瑣。圍鄭，觀兵于南門，西濟于濟隧。鄭人懼，乃行成。

295　The word *ji* 疾 can also be read as "hate" or "resent": "Jin does not hate us."

296　Qi was situated to the northeast of Zheng, and Song was to the east, so their forces gathered at the Zheng capital's east gate.

297　The former Xǔ has been identified as the "lands of Xǔ" that Lu ceded to Zheng in exchange for the district of Beng near Mount Tai (Yin 8.2) or, alternatively, as the former domain of Xǔ, against which Zheng made repeated incursions, starting in 712 BCE (Yin 11.3). Yang (3:989) points out that the two areas were in any case quite close to each other. Fearing Zheng aggression, Xǔ resettled in She in 576 BCE (Cheng 15.7), which suggests that the territories formerly claimed by Xǔ had been annexed by Zheng.

298　Jin was situated to the west of Zheng, and Wei to its north.

299　On Beilin, see Xuan 1.8, n. 14. Xiang 向 was located in Zheng near present-day Weishi County 尉氏縣, Henan.

300　*Youhuan* 右還 means, literally, "returned to the right." The translation follows Du Yu's (ZZ 31.545) interpretation of the troop movement. Suo 瑣 was north of present-day Xinzheng County 新鄭縣, Henan.

301　Jisui 濟隧 River was a tributary of the Yellow River when the latter's course was different from its present one. It was probably located just north of present-day Yuanyang County 原陽縣, Henan.

Zheng leaders maneuver to achieve an alliance with Jin by attacking Song. The complicated calculations show Zheng making the most of its weakness and timely capitulation. The reasoning is circuitous—only when Jin jealously guards its influence over Zheng will Zheng be safe from Chu aggression, and Zheng plans to provoke Jin and invite Jin invasion by attacking Song, a Jin ally.

As a consequence of the Zheng leaders' being troubled over Jin and Chu, various high officers of Zheng said, "We did not follow Jin, and our domain almost perished. Chu is weaker than Jin, and Jin is not anxious to gain our allegiance.[295] If Jin does become anxious about us, Chu will avoid confrontation with it. What can we do to make the Jin army brave death to attack us? For only then, when Chu dares not oppose it, can we firmly adhere to Jin."

    Gongsun Shezhi[a] said, "If we create hostility with Song, the princes are sure to arrive, and we can submit and swear a covenant with them. When the Chu army arrives, and we submit to them as well, then Jin will be very angry indeed! If Jin can come at us again and again, Chu will not be able to oppose it. Then we can adhere firmly to Jin."

    The high officers were pleased with this plan and sent supervisors of the borders to provoke hostilities with Song. Xiang Xu of Song invaded Zheng and seized men and goods on a grand scale. Gongsun Shezhi[a] said, "Now we can mobilize and attack Song. If we attack Song, the princes are sure to furiously descend on us. We can then abide by their command and also notify Chu. When the Chu army arrives, we will then swear a covenant with it and give heavy bribes to the Jin army. We shall thus escape disaster." In summer, Gongsun Shezhi[a] of Zheng invaded Song.

The princes attack Zheng, and Gongsun Shezhi's plan materializes. The resulting covenant document outlines principles of common interest and mutual assistance. Zheng leaders will violate this oath immediately after swearing it.

In the fourth month, the princes attacked Zheng. On the *jihai* day (19), the Qi heir apparent Guang and Xiang Xu of Song, arriving at Zheng in advance of the others, stormed the eastern gate of the Zheng capital.[296] That evening, Zhi Ying[b] of Jin arrived in the western outskirts of the Zheng capital and moved eastward to invade the former Xǔ.[297] Sun Linfu of Wei invaded Zheng's northern marches.[298] In the sixth month, the princes had a meeting at Beilin and stationed their armies at Xiang.[299] Then they moved toward the northwest and set up camp at Suo.[300] They laid siege to the Zheng capital, displayed their military might at its southern gate, and crossed westward over the Jisui River.[301] Frightened, the men of Zheng sought a peace accord with the princes.

11.2(3)

11.3(4, 5)

秋，七月，同盟于亳。范宣子曰：「不慎，必失諸侯。諸侯道敝而無成，能無貳乎？」

乃盟。載書曰：「凡我同盟，毋蘊年，毋壅利，毋保姦，毋留慝，救災患，恤禍亂，同好惡，獎王室。或間茲命，司慎、司盟，名山、名川，群神、群祀，先王、先公，七姓、十二國之祖，明神殛之，俾失其民，隊命亡氏，踣其國家。」

11.4(7) 楚子囊乞旅于秦。秦右大夫詹帥師從楚子，將以伐鄭。鄭伯逆之。丙子，伐宋。

11.5a(8, 10) 九月，諸侯悉師以復伐鄭，鄭人使良霄、大宰石㚟如楚，告將服于晉，曰：「孤以社稷之故，不能懷君。君若能以玉帛綏晉，不然，則武震以攝威之，孤之願也。」楚人執之。書曰「行人」，言使人也。

諸侯之師觀兵于鄭東門。鄭人使王子伯駢行成。甲戌，晉趙武入盟鄭伯。冬，十月丁亥，鄭子展出盟晉侯。十二月戊寅，會于蕭魚。庚辰，赦鄭囚，皆禮而歸之；納斥候；禁侵掠。晉侯使叔肸告于諸侯。

---

302 This applies especially when another domain is afflicted by famines.

303 According to Du Yu (ZZ 31.546), "ancestral kings" refers to first ancestors, and "ancestral lords" refers to those first granted a domain.

304 Jin, Lu, Wei, Cao, and Teng shared the clan name Ji 姬; the clan name of both Zhu and Lesser Zhu was Cao 曹; that of Song, Zi 子; Qi, Jiang 姜; Ju, Ji 己; Qǐ, Si 姒; Xue, Ren 任.

305 Alternatively, we could translate this as "bring down his life" (Yang, 3:990).

In autumn, in the seventh month, they swore a covenant together at Bo. Fan Gai[c] said, "If we are not careful, we are sure to lose the allegiance of the princes. When the princes grow weary on the road to battle but achieve nothing, how can they not shift their allegiance?"

They thus swore a covenant. The covenant document said: "All of us who swear this covenant together will not hoard ripened grain,[302] will not monopolize resources, will not offer refuge to miscreants from other domains, and will not harbor malefactors. Each will relieve calamities and troubles, offer succor against disasters and rebellions, share what is loved and hated, and support the royal house. He who contravenes this command, may the spirit overseeing reverence and the spirit overseeing covenants, the spirits of great mountains and great rivers, the many spirits and recipients of sacrifices, the ancestral kings and ancestral lords,[303] the ancestors of the seven clans and the twelve domains,[304] and the bright spirits smite him, make him lose his people, cast down his mandate,[305] destroy his lineage, and devastate his domain and patrimony."

A Qin-Chu coalition attacks Zheng, and Zheng strikes Song as planned.

Zinang of Chu pleaded for troops at Qin. The high officer of the right in Qin, Zhan, led an army to follow the Master of Chu, intending to use it to attack Zheng. The Liege of Zheng met the invading troops. On the *bingzi* day (27), Zheng attacked Song.

11.4(7)

Zheng envoys seeking Chu military assistance are seized, paving the way for an accord with Jin, as Zheng leaders anticipated (Xiang 11.2).

In the ninth month, the princes all mobilized their armies in order to attack Zheng again. The leaders of Zheng sent Liang Xiao and the grand steward Shi Chuo to Chu to notify the latter of their intention to submit to Jin, declaring in the Zheng ruler's name: "I, the lone one, on account of the altars of the domain, cannot hold fast to you, my lord. What I wish for is that you, my lord, might use jade and silk to placate Jin or, failing that, use devastating martial power to overawe it. That is my very wish." The men of Chu arrested them. The text says, "envoy": this is to indicate that Liang Xiao had been sent.

11.5a(8, 10)

The armies of the princes reviewed their troops at the eastern gate of the Zheng capital. The men of Zheng sent Wangzi Bopian on a mission to seek an accord. On the *jiaxu* day (26), Zhao Wu of Jin entered and swore a covenant with the Liege of Zheng. In winter, in the tenth month, on the *dinghai* day (9), Gongsun Shezhi[a] of Zheng came out and swore a covenant with the Prince of Jin. In the twelfth month, on the *wuyin* day (1), they met at Xiaoyu. On the *gengchen* day (3), Jin leaders pardoned the Zheng prisoners, treated them all with ritual propriety, and sent them home. They called in scouting patrols and forbade raids and pillaging. The Prince of Jin sent Shuxiang[b] to notify the princes.

公使臧孫紇對曰：「凡我同盟，小國有罪，大國致討，苟有以藉
手，鮮不赦宥，寡君聞命矣。」

11.5b　鄭人賂晉侯以師悝、師觸、師蠲；廣車、軘車淳十五乘，甲兵備，凡兵車
百乘；歌鐘二肆，及其鎛、磬；女樂二八。

晉侯以樂之半賜魏絳，曰：「子教寡人和諸戎狄以正諸華，八年之
中，九合諸侯，如樂之和，無所不諧，請與子樂之。」

辭曰：「夫和戎狄，國之福也；八年之中，九合諸侯，諸侯無慝，君
之靈也，二三子之勞也，臣何力之有焉？抑臣願君安其樂而思其終也。
《詩》曰：

> 樂只君子，
> 殿天子之邦。
> 樂只君子，

306　The term *jishou* 藉手 means literally "service rendered" or "gift given by hand."

307　Kong Yingda cites Zheng Xuan, who glosses *guangche* 廣車 as "chariots arrayed
in a horizontal formation" (*hengchen zhi che* 橫陳之車) (ZZ-Kong 31.574). These
chariots were probably of the same type used in the "right sector" (*youguang* 右廣)
and "left sector" (*zuoguang* 左廣) when Chu confronted Jin in the battle of Bi (Xuan
12.2). Fu Qian glosses *tunche* 軘車 as chariots for defending and guarding the army
base (ZZ-Kong 31.547). We no longer know the details of how these two types of
chariots were equipped differently.

308　These other chariots were probably not equipped with armor and weapons.

309　In 1997 Zheng bells were unearthed in sacrificial pits at the remnants of the Zheng
capital. For this remarkable find, see von Falkenhausen, *Chinese Society in the Age
of Confucius*, 359–60. The most impressive set of bronze bells unearthed to date is
from the tomb of Prince Yi of Zeng. Discovered in 1978, this set of sixty-four bells
arranged in three tiers includes musical inscriptions that label strike points with the
names of the notes. The notations lead Yang (3:992) to surmise that only bells with
certain notes and pitches may qualify as a "set" (*si* 肆), identified by some commentators as meaning "a set of thirty-two bells." For more on the bells from the tomb of
Prince Yi of Zeng, see Bagley, "Percussion"; von Falkenhausen, "The Zeng Hou Yi
Finds in the History of Chinese Music."

310　For Wei Jiang's remonstrance with Lord Dao of Jin on the importance of achieving
peace with the Rong and Di tribes, see Xiang 4.7.

311　Lord Dao is referring to the meetings at Qi and Chengdi (Xiang 5.8, 5.9), Wei (Xiang
7.8), Xingqiu (Xiang 8.4), Xi (Xiang 9.5), Zha and Hulao (Xiang 10.1, 10.10), Bo and
Xiaoyu (Xiang 11.3, 11.5).

312　Here, as in the rest of the exchange, there are references to the double meanings of
the character *le* 樂 or *yue* 樂 as "music" and "joy."

Our lord sent Zang Wuzhong[e] to give this reply, "For all who are our covenant partners: when a small domain commits an offense, the great domain visits chastisement upon it; but so long as the small domain has ways to render service,[306] rarely does the great domain not extend forgiveness. Our unworthy ruler has heeded your command!"

The word he 和 *can mean "musical harmony" and "peaceful accord," and the Jin minister Wei Jiang is associated with both in Zuozhuan. Lord Dao bestows half of the gifts of musicians and musical instruments submitted by Zheng on Wei Jiang, in recognition of his role in achieving peace with the Rong and the Di (Xiang 4.7), an accord that has in turn facilitated the submission of Zheng. These two developments are considered the centerpiece of Lord Dao's reassertion of Jin's status as overlord (fuba). Some scholars consider the gift incommensurate with Wei Jiang's relatively low rank and interpret this episode as deliberate glorification of the Wei line. The gift confirms Wei's importance, while his initial refusal underlines his ritual propriety. Wei Jiang also uses the opportunity to remonstrate about the dangers of excess and indulgence. "The gift of musicians and musical instruments" sometimes signals danger and corrupting influence and can be used to undermine another domain (e.g., Zuozhuan, Xiang 15.4; Analects 18.4; Han Feizi 10.186–87).*

As gifts, Zheng leaders gave the Prince of Jin the music masters Kui, Zhu, and Juan; fifteen pairs of combat chariots and defense chariots complete with armor and weapons;[307] a hundred chariots of other kinds;[308] two sets of musical bells, with their small bells and chime-stones;[309] and sixteen female singers and dancers.

The Prince of Jin bestowed on Wei Jiang half of the musicians, singers, dancers, and musical instruments, saying, "You taught me, the unworthy one, to make peace with the various Rong and Di tribes in order to rectify our leadership of the various central domains.[310] In eight years, I assembled the princes nine times.[311] As with musical harmony, there is nothing not in accord. I ask permission to share with you the music and the joy."[312]

Wei Jiang declined the gifts: "Making peace with the Rong and Di tribes meant good fortune for the domain. Assembling the princes nine times in eight years, with the princes committing no transgression, was the result of my lord's numinous power and of the exertion of these fine men. What part did my efforts play in these things? And yet I hope that you, my lord, will enjoy the music and think about its proper ends. As it says in the *Odes*,

> Joyous is the noble man,
> Securing the realm of the Son of Heaven.
> Joyous is the noble man,

福祿攸同。
便蕃左右，
亦是帥從。

夫樂以安德，義以處之，禮以行之，信以守之，仁以厲之，而後可以殿邦國、同福祿、來遠人，所謂樂也。書曰：

居安思危。

思則有備，有備無患。敢以此規。」
　　公曰：「子之教，敢不承命？抑微子，寡人無以待戎，不能濟河。夫賞，國之典也，藏在盟府，不可廢也。子其受之！」魏絳於是乎始有金石之樂，禮也。

11.6(11)　秦庶長鮑、庶長武帥師伐晉以救鄭。鮑先入晉地，士魴禦之，少秦師而弗設備。壬午，武濟自輔氏，與鮑交伐晉師。己丑，秦、晉戰于櫟，晉師敗績，易秦故也。

313　*Maoshi* 222, "Caishu" 采菽, 15A.502. The received text has "myriad good fortunes" (*wanfu* 萬福) instead of "good fortune and position" (*fulu* 福祿); "in good order" (*pingping* 平平) instead of "well governed" (*bianfan* 便蕃).

314　This line is not found in the received text of the *Documents*. There is a comparable formulation in *Yi Zhou shu* 12.1936 : "In calmness, think of dangers; at the beginning, think of the end." In *Zhanguo ce* ("Chu ce 4," 17.582), Yu Qing cites, "In calmness, think of dangers, and in dangers, deliberate calmness" as a line from *Chunqiu* (i.e., its exegetical tradition). The same line appears in *Lüshi chunqiu* 15.843.

315　This line is incorporated in "Yue ming zhong" 說命中 (*Shangshu* 13.141) in the Ancient Script version of the *Documents*.

316　That is, he would not have been able to bring about Zheng's submission. Some commentators have noted how the eulogy of Lord Dao exceeds his recorded accomplishment (e.g., Wu Kaisheng, *Zuozhuan wei*, 483), while others note how he maximizes Jin power and stability given the circumstantial constraints (e.g., Gu Donggao, "Jin Dao gong lun" 晉悼公論, in *Chunqiu dashi biao*, 2:2025–26).

317　Du Yu (*ZZ* 31.547) claims that such archives contained writings on principles of rewards (*shanggong zhi zhi* 賞功之制), but it is more likely that the writings refer to proclamations of merit, as mentioned in Xi 5.8 and Xi 26.3.

In whom blessings and position are brought together.
Well governed are the small domains on left and right.
They too follow his leadership.[313]

Now, music is for calming virtue; dutifulness is for situating it; ritual propriety is for realizing it; good faith is for guarding it; and nobility of spirit is for encouraging it. Only with these can one lay the foundation for the realm, bring together good fortune and position, and draw close those from afar: this is called joy. As the *Documents* says,

> While living in calmness, think of dangers.[314]

To dwell on this is to be prepared; to be prepared is to have no cause for anxiety.[315] I have presumed to offer these words of correction, my lord.”

The lord said, “Should I presume not to receive your teachings as a command? However, if it had not been for you, I, the unworthy one, would have had neither the means to deal with the Rong nor the ability to cross the Yellow River.[316] Now rewards become part of the permanent heritage of the domain, and they are stored up in the covenant archives, where they cannot be discarded.[317] You, sir, should accept the reward!” It was from this time, then, that Wei Jiang first had the ceremonial music of bells and chime-stones.[318] This was in accordance with ritual propriety.

Two Qin colonels,[319] Bao and Wu, led out troops and attacked Jin in order to go to Zheng’s aid. Bao was the first to enter Jin territories. Shi Fang resisted them but underestimated the Qin army and did not make adequate defensive preparations. On the *renwu* day (5), Wu crossed the river from Fushi and with Bao attacked the Jin troops from both sides.[320] On the *jichou* day (12), Qin and Jin did battle at Li.[321] That the Jin army was completely defeated was because it had made light of Qin.

11.6(11)

---

318 At this point Wei Jiang, as assistant commander of the new army, ranked eighth among Jin leaders. That he should be singled out for a reward for Jin’s victory over Zheng seems somewhat incongruous. By the same token, Wei Jiang’s general importance during these years, including his speech on peace with the Rong, is not explained by his position. Like the prediction of the greatness of Bi Wan’s progeny (Min 1.6) or the praise of Wei music (Xiang 29.13), these may be derived from Wei sources aggrandizing that lineage. These Wei materials thus represent one stratum of *Zuozhuan*.

319 The term *shuzhang* 庶長 (translated here as “colonels”), also used in Xiang 12.4, designates an official title peculiar to Qin. On the use of this and another Qin rank, *bugeng*, to date the text, see Cheng 13.3, n. 287.

320 Fushi 輔氏 was located just east of present-day Dali County 大荔縣, Shaanxi.

321 This place named Li 櫟, likely in Jin, should be distinguished from the places with the same name in Zheng and Chu, see Huan 15.9, n. 125 and Zhao 1.13, n. 106.

12.1(1) 十有二年，春，王二月，莒人伐我東鄙，圍台。

12.2(1) 季孫宿帥師救台，遂入鄆。

12.3(2) 夏，晉侯使士魴來聘。

12.4(3) 秋，九月，吳子乘卒。

12.5(4) 冬，楚公子貞帥師侵宋。

12.6(6) 公如晉。

左傳

12.1(1, 2) 十二年，春，莒人伐我東鄙，圍台。季武子救台，遂入鄆，取其鐘以為
公盤。

12.2(3) 夏，晉士魴來聘，且拜師。

12.3(4) 秋，吳子壽夢卒，臨於周廟，禮也。凡諸侯之喪，異姓臨於外，同姓於宗
廟，同宗於祖廟，同族於禰廟。是故魯為諸姬，臨於周廟；為邢、凡、蔣、
茅、胙、祭，臨於周公之廟。

12.4(5) 冬，楚子囊、秦庶長無地伐宋，師于楊梁，以報晉之取鄭也。

---

322 Tai 台 was located in the domain of Lu southeast of Fei County 費縣, Shandong.

323 Fu Qian claims that "Shoumeng" is the phonetically drawn out version of "Sheng" 乘 (ZZ-Kong 31.537). He seems to be suggesting that the "barbarian" Wu language tends towards a poly-syllabic structure.

324 Yun was under Lu control (Wen 12.7). The basin (*pan* 盤) could be used for holding food or water.

325 According to Du Yu (ZZ 31.548), the Zhou Temple was the temple of King Wen of Zhou. The Wu ancestor was Taibo, older brother of King Wen; and the Lu ancestor was the Zhou Duke, younger brother of King Wu and son of King Wen. The kinship ties made the temple of King Wen an appropriate place to bewail Shoumeng. On lamentation in mourning rituals and the word *lin* 臨, see also Xuan 12.1, n. 180.

326 Du Yu (ZZ 31.548) reads: "Outside the city wall and facing the domain of the deceased."

327 The six enumerated houses here were descended from the Zhou Duke.

328 Yangliang 楊梁 was located in the domain of Song southeast of Shangqiu County 商丘縣, Henan.

ANNALS

In the twelfth year, in spring, in the royal second month, Ju leaders attacked our eastern marches and laid siege to Tai.[322]

Jisun Su (Ji Wuzi) led out troops and went to the aid of Tai. He then entered Yun.

In summer, the Prince of Jin sent Shi Fang to come on an official visit.

In autumn, in the ninth month, Sheng (Shoumeng),[323] the Master of Wu, died.

In winter, Gongzi Zhen (Zinang) of Chu led out troops and invaded Song.

Our lord went to Jin.

12.1(1)

12.2(1)

12.3(2)

12.4(3)

12.5(4)

12.6(6)

ZUO

In the twelfth year, in spring, Ju leaders attacked our eastern marches and lay siege to Tai. Ji Wuzi went to the aid of Tai. He then entered Yun. He took their bronze bells and made them into a basin for our lord.[324]

A Jin leader thanks Lu for its participation in the Jin-led campaign against Zheng (Xiang 11.5).

In summer, Shi Fang of Jin came to us on an official visit and moreover bowed in thanks for our troops.

Wu was castigated as barbarian twenty-three years earlier (Cheng 7.1) but is here recognized for its special ties with the Zhou house.

In autumn, Shoumeng, the Master of Wu, died. Our lord lamented his passing at the Zhou Temple:[325] this was in accordance with ritual propriety. In all cases concerning the funeral of a prince, if he was of a different clan, the lord would lament his passing outside the city wall;[326] if he was of the same clan, the lord would lament his passing at the Ancestral Temple; if he was of the same line, the lord would lament his passing at the founding ruler's temple; if he was of the same house, the lord would lament his passing at his father's temple. That was why a Lu lord lamented the passing of lords of the same clan name Ji at the Zhou Temple and lamented the passing of lords with the clan names of Xing, Fan, Jiang, Mao, Zuo, and Zhai at the Zhou Duke's temple.[327]

In winter, Zinang of Chu and Colonel Wudi of Qin attacked Song, stationing their troops at Yangliang.[328] This was in retaliation for Jin's act of taking control of Zheng.

12.1(1, 2)

12.2(3)

12.3(4)

12.4(5)

12.5 靈王求后于齊，齊侯問對於晏桓子。桓子對曰：「先王之禮辭有之。天子求后於諸侯，諸侯對曰：『夫婦所生若而人，妾婦之子若而人。』無女而有姊妹及姑姊妹，則曰：『先守某公之遺女若而人。』」齊侯許婚。王使陰里結之。

12.6(6) 公如晉朝，且拜士魴之辱，禮也。

12.7 秦嬴歸于楚。楚司馬子庚聘于秦，為夫人寧，禮也。

春秋

13.1(1) 十有三年，春，公至自晉。

13.2(2) 夏，取邿。

13.3(4) 秋，九月庚辰，楚子審卒。

13.4(6) 冬，城防。

---

329   Yan Ruo, father of Yan Ying, is first mentioned in Xuan 14.4.
330   We follow Gu Yanwu in reading *ruo er ren* 若而人 as hypothetical names (*Rizhi lu jishi*, 32.752–53; Karlgren, gl. 521). The prince would refer to his paternal aunts as daughters of his grandfather.
331   The word *jie* 結 refers to "binding words" 結言, words that seal an agreement.
332   See Xiang 12.2.

The proposed marriage between the Zhou king and a lady of the Qi house, formalized three years later (Xiang 15.2), may indicate closer Zhou-Qi ties (Xiang 14.8). For an earlier Zhou-Qi marriage alliance, see Xuan 6.4.

King Ling sought a queen from Qi. The Prince of Qi asked Yan Ruo[a] how he should reply.[329] Yan Ruo[c] replied, "The ritual language of the former kings had the proper formulations. When the Son of Heaven seeks a queen from a prince, the prince replies, 'Of daughters by husband and wife, there are so-and-so; of daughters by my concubines, there are so-and-so.' If the prince has no daughters but has sisters and paternal aunts, then he says, 'The former ruler, Lord so-and-so, left behind daughters so-and-so.'[330] The Prince of Qi agreed to the marriage. The king sent Yin Li to make the agreement.[331]

12.5

Our lord went to visit the court of Jin and moreover bowed for the condescension of Shi Fang's visit.[332] This was in accordance with ritual propriety.

12.6(6)

Qin and Chu form closer ties as they unite against Jin (Xiang 9.4).

Qin Ying returned to Chu.[333] The Chu supervisor of the military, Zigeng,[334] went on an official visit to Qin because of the visit of the ruler's wife to her natal state. This was in accordance with ritual propriety.

12.7

LORD XIANG 13 (560 BCE)
ANNALS

In the thirteenth year, in spring, our lord arrived from Jin.

13.1(1)

In summer, we took Shi.[335]

13.2(2)

In autumn, in the ninth month, on the *gengchen* day (14), Shen, the Master of Chu, died.

13.3(4)

In winter, we fortified Fang.

13.4(6)

333　According to Du Yu (ZZ 31.549), Qin Ying was the younger sister of Lord Jing of Qin and consort of King Gong of Chu. She had visited her mother in Qin and was at this point returning to Chu.

334　Zigeng's tomb was discovered in the Xiasi cemetery. See Zhang Jian and Zhang Shigang, "Henan sheng Xichuan xian Xiasi Chunqiu Chu mu."

335　Shi 邿 was a small domain located south of present-day Jining City 濟寧市, Shandong.

左傳

13.1(1) 十三年，春，公至自晉，孟獻子書勞于廟，禮也。

13.2(2) 夏，邶亂，分為三。師救邶，遂取之。凡書取，言易也；用大師焉曰滅；弗地曰入。

13.3a 荀罃、士魴卒，晉侯蒐于綿上以治兵。使士匄將中軍，辭曰：「伯游長。昔臣習於知伯，是以佐之，非能賢也。請從伯游。」荀偃將中軍，士匄佐之。

使韓起將上軍，辭以趙武。又使欒黶，辭曰：「臣不如韓起，韓起願上趙武，君其聽之。」使趙武將上軍，韓起佐之；欒黶將下軍，魏絳佐之。新軍無帥，晉侯難其人，使其什吏率其卒乘官屬，以從於下軍，禮也。晉國之民是以大和，諸侯遂睦。

---

336 We are told earlier that upon a lord's return from his journey, whether it be to visit the Zhou court, to meet other princes, or to undertake a military expedition, he had to report on his mission at the Ancestral Temple, offer ceremonial toasts to his officials, and have his services written down (Huan 2.7). The ritual of "recording merits on bamboo slips" (*cexun* 策勳) in Huan 2.7 is probably the same as "writing of his exertion" (*shulao* 書勞) here.

In the thirteenth year, in spring, our lord arrived from Jin. Meng Xianzi 13.1(1)
wrote of his exertion at the temple. This was in accordance with ritual
propriety.[336]

In summer, Shi fell into disorder and was partitioned into three sec- 13.2(2)
tions. Our troops went to Shi's aid and went on to take it. In all cases
when the text has "took," it is to say that it was easy; when a great army
was employed, it says "extinguished"; when territories were not retained,
it says "entered."

*Jin commanders show exemplary disinterestedness in vying to yield power
to the most worthy. We have seen similar rhetoric in Cheng 2.3, 2.7, 4.4,
6.11, 8.2. This narrative on the virtues of modesty and yielding also serves
to explain how Zhao Wu and Wei Jiang bypass the normal order of ranks
and rise to new prominence.*

Zhi Ying[b] and Shi Fang died. The Prince of Jin mustered troops at Mian- 13.3a
shang, where he drilled them. He appointed Fan Gai[a] commander of the
central army, but he declined: "Zhonghang Yan[d] is my senior. Formerly,
I had rapport with Zhi Ying[c]. On the basis of that connection, I assisted
him; it was not because I was capable and worthy. I beg to follow Zhonghang Yan[d]." Zhonghang Yan[a] commanded the central army, and Fan
Gai[a] assisted him.

The Jin ruler appointed Han Qi commander of the upper army, but
he declined in favor of Zhao Wu. He then appointed Luan Yan, who
declined: "I do not compare to Han Qi, and even Han Qi wishes to have
Zhao Wu above him. You, my lord, should heed him." He appointed
Zhao Wu commander of the upper army, and Han Qi assisted him. Luan
Yan commanded the lower army, and Wei Jiang assisted him.[337] The new
army did not have any commanders. The Prince of Jin, finding it difficult
to choose the proper men, made its ten senior officers lead their infantry
soldiers, chariot soldiers, and officers to follow the lower army. This was
in accordance with ritual propriety. On this basis a great harmony pre-
vailed among the people of Jin, and the princes were thus in concord
with Jin.

---

337 Du Yu (ZZ 32.555) notes that Zhao Wu, in taking over Zhonghang Yan's former
post as commander of the upper army, was promoted four ranks. As commander of
the new army, Zhao Wu had ranked seventh among the eight ministers, but now he
ranked third. Wei Jiang was also promoted, from the eighth rank (as assistant commander of the new army) to the sixth (as assistant commander of the lower army).

君子曰：「讓，禮之主也。范宣子讓，其下皆讓，欒黶為汰，弗敢違也。晉國以平，數世賴之，刑善也夫！一人刑善，百姓休和，可不務乎！《書》曰：

> 一人有慶，
> 兆民賴之，
> 其寧惟永。

其是之謂乎！周之興也，其《詩》曰：

> 儀刑文王，
> 萬邦作孚。

言刑善也。及其衰也，其《詩》曰：

> 大夫不均，
> 我從事獨賢。

言不讓也。世之治也，君子尚能而讓其下，小人農力以事其上，是以上下有禮，而讒慝黜遠，由不爭也，謂之懿德。及其亂也，君子稱其功以加小人，小人伐其技以馮君子，是以上下無禮，亂虐並生，由爭善也，謂之昏德。國家之敝，恆必由之。」

---

338 See Xiang 14.3.

339 The term *baixing* 百姓 ("a hundred clan names"), which means "common people" in modern Chinese, here refers to the clans of officials.

340 *Shangshu*, "Lü xing" 呂刑, 19.300. In the original context of the quotation, "one person" refers to the "Son of Heaven." Here it simply refers to a person of high station.

341 *Maoshi* 235, "Wen wang" 文王, 16A.537.

342 *Maoshi* 205, "Beishan" 北山, 13A.444. The poem is written in the plaintive voice of a high officer toiling in faraway places; he sings of bearing an unfair share of the burden of services. See Wang Fuzhi's gloss of the word *xian* 賢 as "many" in *Shijing baishu* 詩經稗疏, cited in Cheng Junying and Jiang Jianyuan, *Shijing zhuxi*, 2:643: "The high officers are unequal, / I alone toil in many missions." Here the quotation "breaks off the section and appropriates the meaning" (*duanzhang quyi* 斷章取義) and presents the voice of boastful self-assertion.

343 Following Hong Liangji (*Chunqiu Zuozhuan gu*, 527) and Wang Yinzhi (*Jingyi shuwen*, 705), who both cite *Guangya*, we read *nong* 農 as *mian* 勉 ("utmost effort"). Takezoe (15.37) suggests that the word *nong* 農 connotes strength and density; thus, *nong* 醲, with the wine radical added, means "strong wine."

344 The argument here concerns contention about merit or superiority.

345 See, for example, Xi Zhi's self-congratulation, criticized in Cheng 16.12.

The noble man's comments elaborate the meanings and effects of the virtue of yielding. The speech is reminiscent of Zinang's earlier praise of Jin leaders (Xiang 9.4) and stands in stark contrast to the accounts of ruthless struggles among rival Jin lineages that unfold elsewhere in Zuozhuan.

The noble man said, "Yielding is the mainstay of ritual propriety. Fan Gai[b] yielded, and those below him all yielded. Even Luan Yan, who was guilty of excesses,[338] did not presume to go against it. On the basis of yielding, the domain of Jin achieved stability, relying on it for several successive generations. Is this not the effect of taking the good as model? One person took the good as model, and there was calm and harmony among the hundred clans.[339] Can one do anything other than strive for it? As it says in the *Documents*,

> One person has the goodness.
> The myriad people rely on it.
> The peace it brings will be lasting.[340]

Surely this refers to such a case! At the time of the rise of Zhou, its *Odes* says,

> Take as model King Wen,
> And the ten thousand realms have trust.[341]

They were speaking of taking the good as model. By the time of Zhou's decline, its *Odes* says,

> The high officers are unequal.
> I serve, I alone am worthy.[342]

They were speaking of refusing to yield. In an era of good government, noble men honor the capable and yield to those below them, while the common men labor to the utmost[343] to serve those above them. That is why, above and below, there is ritual propriety, and the slanderous and iniquitous ones are banished afar. This comes about because they do not come into conflict,[344] and this is called 'beautiful virtue.' When the polity falls into disorder, noble men call attention to their achievements in order to lord it over the common men,[345] and the common men boast of their special skills in order to impose on noble men. That is why, above and below, there is no ritual propriety, and disorder and violence arise together. This comes about because they contend over their respective merits, and this is called 'obscured virtue.' The ruin of the domain and patrimony must always derive from this."

13.4(3) 楚子疾，告大夫曰：「不穀不德，少主社稷。生十年而喪先君，未及習師保之教訓而應受多福，是以不德，而亡師于鄢；以辱社稷，為大夫憂，其弘多矣。若以大夫之靈，獲保首領以歿於地，唯是春秋窀穸之事、所以從先君於禰廟者，請為『靈』若『厲』。大夫擇焉。」莫對。及五命，乃許。

　　秋，楚共王卒。子囊謀諡。大夫曰：「君有命矣。」子囊曰：「君命以共，若之何毀之？赫赫楚國，而君臨之，撫有蠻夷，奄征南海，以屬諸夏，而知其過，可不謂共乎？請諡之『共』。」大夫從之。

13.5 吳侵楚，養由基奔命，子庚以師繼之。養叔曰：「吳乘我喪，謂我不能師也，必易我而不戒。子為三覆以待我，我請誘之。」子庚從之。戰于庸浦，大敗吳師，獲公子黨。

　　君子以吳為不弔，《詩》曰：

346　The term "high officers" can include ministers.

347　King Gong's father, King Zhuang, died in 589 BCE (Cheng 2.8).

348　"The position of many blessings" or "the greatly blessed position" (*duofu* 多福) refers to kingship. For the phrase *yingshou* 應受, we read *ying* 應 as *ying* 膺, which has the same meaning as *shou* 受, "to receive" or "to have something come upon oneself"; see Wang Yinzhi, *Jingyi shuwen*, 698. In *Guoyu*, "Chu yu 1," 17.627–31, King Zhuang appoints Shi Wei and Shen Shushi as teachers of the heir apparent (later King Gong), and Shen Sushi gives an account of an exemplary princely education.

349　Yan stands for Yanling; for Chu defeat at the battle of Yanling, see Cheng 16.5.

350　For this expression, see also Yin 3.5, Zhao 25.8.

351　The practice of giving a posthumous honorific, which presumably summed up the achievements or failures of the deceased, seems to have arisen in the middle of Western Zhou; see Wang Shoukuan, *Shifa yanjiu*. The choice of honorifics was sometimes discussed when a person was about to die, as in this instance. "Ling" and "Li" both convey negative judgments. According to Du Yu (*ZZ* 32.556), "Disorder without damage is called 'Ling'; slaughter of the innocent is called 'Li.'" This episode is told more briefly in *Guoyu*, "Chu yu 1," 17.531–32. On "Ling" as a negative posthumous honorific, see our introductory remarks to Lord Xuan. Cf. Wen 1.7.

352　*Lin* 臨, "to look down from above," is also associated with the compassionate gaze of the spirits (Karlgren, gl. 525).

353　Although Chu is sometimes presented as being "not of the same kith and kin" (*fei wo zulei* 非我族類) by the central domains in *Zuozhuan* (e.g., Cheng 4.4), here Zinang's rhetoric indicates that Chu sees itself as mediating relations between the "barbarians" beyond the pale and the central domains. If anything, Chu adopts the voice of the central domains in dealing with the "barbarians."

354　This echoes Qu Wuchen's curse on Chu commanders (Cheng 7.5).

355　Yongpu 庸浦 was located in the domain of Chu south of present-day Wuwei County 無為縣, Anhui.

The Chu king dies and Zinang urges the use of "Gong" (Reverent) as post-humous honorific, in part because the Chu king is said to have turned Chu into the mediator between the central domains and the barbarians. Taking responsibility for the Chu defeat at Yanling fifteen years ago (Cheng 16.5), the king has asked to be given a posthumous honorific that conveys a negative judgment. Zinang argues that such a gesture indicates the king's reverence (gong), and the proper honorific would thus be "Gong." Whereas the other Chu ministers adhere to the letter of the Chu king's final charge, Zinang claims to distill the spirit in which the command was given.

When the Master of Chu was seriously ill, he addressed his high officers:[346] "I, the deficient one, lack virtue. I have presided over the altars of the domain since my early years. At the age of ten, I lost the former ruler,[347] and before I could master the instructions of teachers and guardians, the greatly blessed position came upon me.[348] That was how, lacking virtue, I lost troops at Yan,[349] brought disgrace to the altars of the domain, and made the high officers grieve. All these failings were grave indeed. If, thanks to my officers' numinous power, I manage to die a natural death with my head still upon my shoulders,[350] then on this matter, for the purposes of spring and autumn sacrifices and funeral ritual, whereby I will follow the former lord at my father's temple, I request to be given the posthumous honorific 'Ling' (Disordered) or 'Li' (Murderous).[351] You, high officers, shall choose between them." None replied. After he had given the command five times, they assented.

In autumn, King Gong of Chu died. Zinang held discussions about the posthumous honorific. The high officers said, "The ruler already gave his command." Zinang said, "His command was given in reverence. How can we betray it? He came to oversee the great and glorious domain of Chu,[352] he soothed and gained sway over the Man and Yi barbarians, canvassing far and wide in his expeditions to the Southern Sea and bringing them to submit to the central domains.[353] And yet he recognized his errors. Can he not be called 'reverent'? I request to honor him posthumously as 'Gong.'" The high officers followed his suggestion.

Wu invades Chu, continuing earlier hostilities (Xiang 3.1), but succumbs to Chu ambushes.

Wu invaded Chu. Yang Youji rushed about to fulfill commands,[354] and Zigeng followed with the army. Yang Youji[a] said: "Wu is taking advantage of our mourning period because they think we cannot field an army. They are sure to make light of us and not take any precautions. If you will prepare three ambushes and await my arrival, I ask permission to bait them." Zigeng followed his plan. Chu and Wu did battle at Yongpu.[355] Chu roundly defeated the Wu army and took Gongzi Dang captive.

The noble man considered Wu ruthless. As it says in the *Odes*,

13.4(3)

13.5

不弔昊天，
亂靡有定。

13.6(4)　冬，城防。書事，時也。於是將早城，臧武仲請俟畢農事，禮也。

13.7　鄭良霄、大宰石㒟猶在楚。石㒟言於子囊曰：「先王卜征五年，而歲習其
祥，祥習則行。不習，則增修德而改卜。今楚實不競，行人何罪？止鄭一
卿，以除其偪，使睦而疾楚，以固於晉，焉用之？使歸而廢其使，怨其君
以疾其大夫，而相牽引也，不猶愈乎？」楚人歸之。

356　*Maoshi* 191, "Jie nanshan" 節南山, 12A.396. Here we follow Jia Kui's reading of
budiao 不弔 as "failing to condole" (Hong Liangji, *Chunqiu Zuozhuan gu*, 528).
Heaven considers Wu ruthless for "failing to condole with Chu for its loss." Du Yu
(*ZZ* 32.556) reads *diao* 弔 as *xu* 恤 ("to show compassion for"): "High Heaven has no
compassion, / And there is no end to disorder." (This is the reading we chose for the
earlier quotation of these lines in Cheng 7.1.) In other words, "high Heaven" is
retributory: because Wu shows no compassion for Chu, attacking it while it is in
mourning, Heaven shows no compassion for Wu.

357　Cf. Huan 16.4.

358　Legge (458) surmises that it was about this time that the city of Fang was granted to
the Zangsun (Zang) lineage.

359　There is no reference to such practices in the Zhou court in other early texts. Shen
Tong suggests that "former kings" here may refer to early Chu kings (Yang, 3:1003).

360　According to Lu Deming, the line reads 不習則增，修德而改卜: "If it is not repeated,
they would add time (i.e., postpone their plans), cultivate their virtue, and divine
again" (Karlgren, gl. 528).

> High Heaven deems him ruthless,
> And there is no end to disorder.[356]

In winter, we fortified Fang. This event was recorded to show its timeli- 13.6(4)
ness.[357] There had been plans to fortify the city earlier, but Zang Wuzhong
asked to wait till agricultural labor was completed.[358] This was in accordance with ritual propriety.

A detained Zheng envoy (Xiang 11.5) convinces Chu leaders that by send-
ing himself and a fellow detainee back, they can create greater dissension
and weakness in Zheng. Chu follows his advice, and one of the repatriated
Zheng officers, Liang Xiao, will wreak havoc in Zheng (Xiang 30.2, 30.10).

Liang Xiao and the grand steward Shi Chuo of Zheng were still in Chu. 13.7
Shi Chuo said to Zinang, "The former kings divined for five successive
years when it came to military expeditions.[359] Year after year they repeated the question of whether it would be auspicious, and only with repeated auspicious results would they set forth. If they were not repeated,
then they would even more assiduously cultivate their virtue and divine
anew.[360] Now it is Chu that is lacking in strength: what offense are we
envoys guilty of? You detain one minister from Zheng in order to fend
off their importunate demands,[361] but you end up resolving conflicts for
Zheng and uniting Zheng leaders in hatred for Chu, and on those grounds
they hold fast to Jin. What use is that? If you let the envoy return after
having failed in his mission,[362] he will resent his ruler and hate the other
high officers, and they will be entangled in disagreements and mutual
recriminations. Would that not be better?"[363] The leaders of Chu repatriated them.

---

361 Shi Chuo is referring to Zheng demands for Chu to attack or make peace with Jin
(Karlgren, gl. 529). According to Kong Yingda (ZZ 32.556), the line pertains to Liang
Xiao: "You detain one minister from Zheng and, in doing so, remove the cause for
strife and oppression in Zheng."

362 Liang Xiao would be blamed for having failed in his mission upon his return to
Zheng.

363 Liang Xiao does bring about disorder in Zheng later (Xiang 30.10). In this sense, Shi
Chuo allows self-interest—his desire to return to Zheng—to override the interests
of the domain.

春秋

14.1(1) 十有四年，春，王正月，季孫宿、叔老會晉士匄、齊人、宋人、衛人、鄭公孫蠆、曹人、莒人、邾人、滕人、薛人、杞人、小邾人會吳于向。

14.2 二月乙未朔，日有食之。

14.3(3) 夏，四月，叔孫豹會晉荀偃、齊人、宋人、衛北宮括、鄭公孫蠆、曹人、莒人、邾人、滕人、薛人、杞人、小邾人伐秦。

14.4(4) 己未，衛侯出奔齊。

14.5 莒人侵我東鄙。

14.6(7) 秋，楚公子貞帥師伐吳。

14.7(9) 冬，季孫宿會晉士匄、宋華閱、衛孫林父、鄭公孫蠆、莒人、邾人于戚。

左傳

14.1a(1) 十四年，春，吳告敗于晉。會于向，為吳謀楚故也。范宣子數吳之不德也，以退吳人。

　　　　執莒公子務婁，以其通楚使也。

364　Du Yu (ZZ 32.557) held that Xiang 向 was a place in Zheng. Jiang Yong maintained that Xiang was in Wu (Yang, 3:1004), as did Takezoe (15.41). If this latter theory is correct, it probably would have been located west of present-day Huaiyuan County 懷遠縣, Anhui.

365　In *Zuozhuan*, Xiang 20.7, Ning Zhi enjoins his son Ning Xi to restore the Wei ruler so that the fact that "Sun Linfu and Ning Zhi drove their ruler into exile" can be "covered up" in the records of the lords. Is the present entry a result of that "covering up" or a reflection of how the victorious Wei ministers notify the other domains about Lord Xian's exile?

366　Qi, in present-day Henan, was Sun Linfu's settlement.

ANNALS

In the fourteenth year, in spring, in the royal first month, Jisun Su (Ji Wuzi) and Shu Lao met with Shi Gai (Fan Gai) of Jin, a Qi leader, a Song leader, a Wei leader, Gongsun Chai (Zijiao) of Zheng, a Cao leader, a Ju leader, a Zhu leader, a Teng leader, a Xue leader, a Qǐ leader, and a Lesser Zhu leader and then met with Wu at Xiang.[364]   14.1(1)

In the second month, on the *yiwei* day, the first day of the month, there was an eclipse of the sun.   14.2

In summer, in the fourth month, Shusun Bao met with Xun Yan (Zhonghang Yan) of Jin, a Qi leader, a Song leader, Beigong Kuo of Wei, Gongsun Chai (Zijiao) of Zheng, a Cao leader, a Ju leader, a Zhu leader, a Teng leader, a Xue leader, a Qǐ leader, and a Lesser Zhu leader and attacked Qin.   14.3(3)

On the *jiwei* day (26), the Prince of Wei departed and fled to Qi.[365]   14.4(4)

Ju leaders invaded our eastern marches.   14.5

In autumn, Gongzi Zhen (Zinang) of Chu led out troops and attacked Wu.   14.6(7)

In winter, Jisun Su (Ji Wuzi) met with Shi Gai of Jin, Hua Yue of Song, Sun Linfu of Wei, Gongsun Chai (Zijiao) of Zheng, a Ju leader, and a Zhu leader at Qǐ.[366]   14.7(9)

ZUO

Jin refuses to support Wu against Chu but continues to try to isolate the latter.

In the fourteenth year, in spring, Wu notified Jin of its defeat. The princes met at Xiang: this was for the purpose of conferring about an attack against Chu on Wu's behalf. Fan Gai[c] reprimanded Wu for its lapses from virtue and dismissed the Wu leader.[367]   14.1a(1)

　　Jin arrested Gongzi Wulou of Ju on the grounds that Ju had been in contact with emissaries from Chu.

367　Wu and Jin had sworn a covenant. Wu notified Jin of its defeat, presumably expecting Jin to attack Chu on its behalf. Jin summons the meeting at Xiang ostensibly to address Wu's concerns but actually to assert its own authority. Jin might have decided to take this course because the other princes refuse to attack Chu and hold that Wu was in the wrong. Takezoe (15.42–43) opines that Jin is less dependent on Wu's support because it had secured Zheng's allegiance, which in turn came about because Chu was busy fending off the threat posed by Wu. Moreover, at this point Jin is geared for a confrontation with Qin and cannot manage another front against Chu. It is also possible that Wu's invasion of Chu while Chu was mourning King Gong was such a violation of ritual norms that Jin had to distance itself from Wu.

將執戎子駒支，范宣子親數諸朝，曰：「來！姜戎氏！昔秦人迫逐乃祖吾
離于瓜州，乃祖吾離被苫蓋、蒙荊棘來歸我先君，我先君惠公有不腆之
田，與女剖分而食之。今諸侯之事我寡君不如昔者，蓋言語漏洩，則職
女之由。詰朝之事，爾無與焉。與，將執女。」

　　對曰：「昔秦人負恃其眾，貪于土地，逐我諸戎。惠公蠲其大德，
謂我諸戎，是四嶽之裔胄也，毋是翦棄。賜我南鄙之田，狐狸所居，豺
狼所嗥。我諸戎除翦其荊棘，驅其狐狸豺狼，以為先君不侵不叛之臣，
至于今不貳。昔文公與秦伐鄭，秦人竊與鄭盟，而舍戍焉，於是乎有殽
之師。晉禦其上，戎亢其下，秦師不復，我諸戎實然。譬如捕鹿，晉人角
之，諸戎掎之，與晉踣之。戎何以不免？自是以來，晉之百役，與我諸戎

368　The Rong of Guazhou consisted of the Jiang and Yun lineages, which Du Yu (ZZ
32.557) misidentifies as variant names of the same group. The Yun lineage of Luhun
(a place in Guazhou) was moved by Qin and Jin to Yichuan or the Yi River area (Xi
22.4, Zhao 9.3). At one point it submitted to Jin (Cheng 6.4) but eventually sided with
Chu and was eliminated by Jin in 525 BCE (Zhao 17.4). The Jiang Rong lineage, on
the other hand, was closer to Jin and consistently acknowledged Jin leadership. See
notes by Quan Zuwang and Qian Daxin, cited in Takezoe, 15.43. Guazhou 瓜州 is
traditionally identified as a place in Gansu, but Gu Jiegang claims that it refers to
the northern and southern slopes of the Qinling Mountains (Yang, 3:1005). According to Gu Jiegang, the Jiang Rong, the Rong of Luhun (also called Yin Rong or the
Rong of Jiuzhou), the Rong of the Yi and Luo Rivers, and the Man lineage all settled
around Yichuan (cited in Wu Jing'an, *Chunqiu Zuoshi zhuan jiuzhu shuzheng xu*,
171–72).

369　The uncouth garb suggests backwardness. Cf. the early Chu king Xiongyi's "tattered
hemp" mentioned in Zhao 12.11a.

370　We read *zhi* 職 as *zhi* 只, "only" (Karlgren, gl. 531). Jiang Rong is said to have leaked
Jin's secrets or passed on rumors that undermine the princes' allegiance to Jin.

371　The term "Four Peaks" (*si yue* 四嶽、四岳) or "Grand Peaks" (*da yue* 大嶽) is mentioned in Yin 11.3b, Zhuang 22.1, Zhao 4.1b. *Si yue* also appears in *Guoyu*, "Zhou yu
2," 3.104, and *Shangshu* 2.26, 2.28, 3.35, 3.43–44, 3.46, 18.269, 18.271. Cf. Yin n. 150.

372　Juzhi is both proclaiming Rong allegiance to Jin and also staking out its indepen-
dence from Jin. He qualifies Rong's indebtedness to Jin, claiming that the land Jin
ceded to Rong was inhospitable wilderness tamed only through Rong efforts. The
Rong should thus be considered civilizing agents rather than barbarians. In return,
Rong's ties with Jin are to be defined through negation, as the absence of aggression
and rebellion.

373　See Xi 30.3.

374　See Xi 33.1, 33.3.

375　The meaning of "above" and "below" is not clear: it may mean that while Jin engages
Qin in open confrontation, the Rong undermine Qin in surprise attacks.

Jin was about to arrest Juzhi, Master of the Rong. Fan Gai[c] personally   14.1b
reprimanded him at court, saying, "Come! You Master of the Jiang
Rong lineage! Formerly, the men of Qin pressed your ancestor Wuli
hard and drove him from Guazhou.[368] Your ancestor Wuli, draped in a
white rush cape and wearing a headdress made from brambles,[369] came
to our former ruler for protection. Though our former ruler, Lord Hui,
had but meager lands, he divided them with you to provide you with
sustenance. Now the reason that the princes no longer serve our unworthy ruler in the same way as before is because word of our negotiations
leaked out, and this could have happened only on account of you.[370] You
are not to take part in the event of the next morning. If you do, we shall
have you arrested."

He replied, "Formerly, the men of Qin, relying on their numbers and
covetous of territory, expelled us, the various Rong tribes. Lord Hui,
making manifest his great virtue, said that we, the various Rong tribes,
were the descendants of the chiefs of the Four Peaks, and that we were
not to be cut off and abandoned.[371] He bestowed on us the lands of Jin's
southern marches, where foxes and wild cats made their lairs, and where
jackals and wolves howled. We, the various Rong, removed and cut down
their brambles and drove away their foxes and wild cats, jackals and
wolves, and became subjects of the former lord. Neither aggressive nor
rebellious, we have been unwavering in our allegiance until now.[372] Formerly, Lord Wen of Jin, together with Qin, attacked Zheng. Qin secretly
swore a covenant with Zheng and set up garrisons there.[373] That was why
armies were mobilized at Yao.[374] Jin resisted Qin from above, and the
Rong withstood it from below.[375] That the Qin army did not come back
is due to none other than us, the various Rong. Just as in the pursuit of a
deer, the men of Jin seized its antlers, and the various Rong tribes caught
its legs, and with Jin brought it to the ground. How have the Rong failed
to absolve themselves from your charges of betrayal? From that time
until the present, in the hundred campaigns of Jin, we, the various Rong

相繼于時，以從執政，猶殽志也，豈敢離逷？今官之師旅無乃實有所
關，以攜諸侯，而罪我諸戎！我諸戎飲食衣服不與華同，贄幣不通，言
語不達，何惡之能為？不與於會，亦無瞢焉。」賦〈青蠅〉而退。宣子辭
焉，使即事於會，成愷悌也。

於是子叔齊子為季武子介以會，自是晉人輕魯幣而益敬其使。

14.2　吳子諸樊既除喪，將立季札。季札辭曰：「曹宣公之卒也，諸侯與曹人不
義曹君，將立子臧。子臧去之，遂弗為也，以成曹君。君子曰『能守節』。
君，義嗣也，誰敢奸君，有國，非吾節也。札雖不才，願附於子臧，以無
失節。」固立之，棄其室而耕，乃舍之。

376　This is one of the few references in *Zuozhuan* to language differences. See also
remarks about the Chu language (Xuan 4.3b) and the Wu language as "the barbaric
way of speaking" (*yiyan* 夷言, Ai 12.4b). It is ironic, of course, that having dis-
claimed interactions with the central domains and dwelling on obstacles to communication, Juzhi should show himself to have mastered a common cultural
heritage embodied by the *Odes*. *Maoshi* 219, "Qing ying" 青蠅, 14C.489, laments the
dangers of slander: "Joyous and civil is the noble man; / He does not believe in words
of slander." The burden of otherness is thus displaced from the barbarian to the
slanderer. The quotation apparently clinches the case for Fan Gai, who in acknowledging his error proves himself to be the "joyous and civil noble man."

377　Shu Lao is the son of Zishu Shengbo (see Cheng 6.7, 6.8, 8.3, 11.3, 16.8, 16.11, 17.8). It
was customary to send one high officer to assist a minister on a diplomatic mission.
Here Lu is sending two ministers to show its respect, and Jin reciprocates by lightening the burden of contributions from Lu. Fan Gai might have been prompted to scale
back demands because of Juzhi's speech.

378　Zhufan's father, Shoumeng, died in the ninth month of 561 BCE (Xiang 12.3). Zhufan
acceded to his position in the first month of 560 BCE. The mourning period of three
years (or twenty-five months) might have already been in place during this period
(see also Zhao 15.7). (Here Zhufan completed his mourning in slightly over two
years.) According to *Gongyang*, Xiang 29 (21.266), Zhufan did not yield the throne
to Jizha but instead proposed that the throne be passed from the older to the
younger brother. Zhufan, as the eldest, would pass it on to Yuzhai, Yuzhai to Yimei,
and Yimei to Jizha, the youngest. *Shiji* 31 follows the account from *Zuozhuan*.

tribes, have taken part unremittingly. Following those in charge of Jin government, our intent has ever been the same as at Yao. How would we dare to distance ourselves from you or go against you? Now is it not your officials of various ranks who themselves are remiss, and who have in this way alienated the princes, while you lay the blame on us, the various Rong tribes? Our drink, our food, our clothing, and our regalia are all different from those of the central domains. We do not exchange gifts with them, and our language and theirs do not allow communication. How can we possibly harm you? Not to participate in the meeting will be no cause for grief." He chanted "Blue Fly" and withdrew.[376] Fan Gai[b] acknowledged his error and allowed Juzhi to take part in affairs at the meeting, thus realizing the attributes of being "joyous and civil."

At this time Shu Lao[b] served as Ji Wuzi's assistant to attend the meeting.[377] From then on, the leaders of Jin reduced the obligatory contributions of Lu and treated its envoys with even greater respect.

The Wu heir Zhufan wants to yield the throne to his worthy younger brother Jizha, who adamantly refuses. Jizha is one of the most idealized figures in Zuozhuan *and* Gongyang. *Here he cites the noble man's approbation of Gongzi Xinshi of Zheng, which may indicate how the noble man's comment circulates as "public opinion," or it may suggest that Jizha-related materials represent a later stratum of the text.*

The Master of Wu, Zhufan, having put aside his mourning garb,   14.2
intended to establish Jizha as ruler.[378] Jizha declined, saying, "When Lord Xuan of Cao died, the princes and the men of Cao considered the new Cao ruler undutiful and planned to establish Gongzi Xinshi[a] as ruler. Gongzi Xinshi[a] left Cao, so they did not carry out the plan, and in this way he secured the position for the Cao ruler.[379] The noble man said of him that he 'was able to keep his principles.'[380] You, my lord, are the rightful heir. Who would dare to oppose you? To possess the domain is not my idea of principles. Although I lack talent, I wish to follow the example of Gongzi Xinshi[a], so as not to lose my principles." When Zhufan persisted about establishing him as ruler, he abandoned his property and took to farming, at which point his brother left him alone.

---

379   When Lord Xuan of Cao died, Fuchu (later Lord Cheng) murdered the heir apparent and established himself as ruler. Outraged, the leaders of Cao wanted to support Gongzi Xinshi as ruler, but he declined (Cheng 13.5).

380   Gongzi Xinshi was the one who spoke of "keeping one's principles" (*shoujie* 守節); see Cheng 15.1.

夏，諸侯之大夫從晉侯伐秦，以報櫟之役也。晉侯待于竟，使六卿帥諸侯之師以進。及涇，不濟。叔向見叔孫穆子，穆子賦〈匏有苦葉〉，叔向退而具舟。魯人、莒人先濟。

鄭子蟜見衛北宮懿子曰：「與人而不固，取惡莫甚焉，若社稷何？」懿子說。二子見諸侯之師而勸之濟。濟涇而次。秦人毒涇上流，師人多死。鄭司馬子蟜帥鄭師以進，師皆從之，至于棫林，不獲成焉。

荀偃令曰：「雞鳴而駕，塞井夷竈，唯余馬首是瞻。」

欒黶曰：「晉國之命，未是有也。余馬首欲東。」乃歸。下軍從之。

左史謂魏莊子曰：「不待中行伯乎？」

莊子曰：「夫子命從帥，欒伯，吾帥也，吾將從之。從帥，所以待夫子也。」

伯游曰：「吾令實過，悔之何及！多遺秦禽。」

乃命大還。晉人謂之「遷延之役。」

欒鍼曰：「此役也，報櫟之敗也。役又無功，晉之恥也。吾有二位於戎路，敢不恥乎？」與士鞅馳秦師，死焉。士鞅反。

---

381   *Maoshi* 34, "Pao you kuye" 匏有苦葉, 2B.87–89. Now commonly interpreted as a song of courtship, it contains images of crossing the river: "The gourd has bitter leaves; / The crossing is deep for wading. / Where it is deep, wade as you are dressed; / Where it is shallow, wade as you raise your skirt." Shuxiang infers from these lines that Shusun Bao is intent on crossing the river. In *Guoyu*, "Lu yu 3," 5.190, Shusun Bao does not actually sing the song but alludes to it as his "enterprise," and Shuxiang further dwells on the association between the gourd and crossing. "Shuxiang withdrew and summoned the boatmen and officers of war, saying, 'For the bitter gourd is for humans useless; it is only good as an aid for crossing. Shusun of Lu cited "The Bitter Gourd Has Leaves": he is sure to cross the river.'"

382   The Zheng leader is urging the Wei leader to continue to support Jin. Jin's resentment would have dire consequences for Wei and Zheng.

383   Yulin 棫林 was located northeast of present-day Ye County 葉縣, Henan.

384   For a similar strategy, see Cheng 16.5. Zhonghang Yan wants to prepare for swift troop movements and to demonstrate Jin's determination to press on. "Look to follow where the horses' heads are pointing" (*mashou shi zhan* 馬首是瞻) becomes an idiom for the disciplined execution of directions.

385   Qin lay to the west of Jin. Luan Yan is saying that he wants to return to Jin.

386   Luan Yan, as commander of the lower army, was the direct superior of Wei Jiang, the assistant commander.

387   The same word *dai* 待 is translated here differently as "to wait" and "to heed" or "to await the command of" (*daiming* 待命). Yang (3:1009) suggests that the second *dai* also has the meaning of "treat" or "regard" (*duidai* 對待): "the way to heed (or treat) the master."

388   Karlgren (gl. 535) believes that the "extension" (*yan* 延) refers to the troop movements involved in long-distance mobilizations. Here we translate *yan* as "procrastinations."

389   Luan Qian was next in rank to the driver of the commander's chariot (*rong lu* 戎路). In an alternative reading, Du Yu (ZZ 32.559) reads this as a comment that includes his brother: "There are two of us in the commander's chariot."

In summer, the princes' high officers followed the Prince of Jin and attacked Qin: this was in retaliation for the campaign of Li. The Jin ruler waited at the border and had the six ministers lead the princes' armies to advance. They reached the Jing River but did not cross it. Shuxiang had an audience with Shusun Bao[b], and Shusun Bao[c] sang "The Gourd Has Bitter Leaves." Shuxiang withdrew to prepare the boats.[381] The men of Lu and Ju were the first to cross the river.

Zijiao of Zheng had an audience with Beigong Kuo[a] of Wei and said to him, "There is nothing that provokes greater antipathy than to support someone and yet not persevere in it. What, then, about the altars of the domain?"[382] Beigong Kuo[b] was pleased. The two men presented themselves to the armies of the princes and convinced them to cross the river. Having crossed the Jing River, they set up camp. The men of Qin poisoned the upper reaches of the Jing River, and many among the troops died. The Zheng supervisor of the military, Zijiao, led the Zheng army to press on, and all the troops followed him, advancing as far as Yulin,[383] but they did not achieve success.

Zhonghang Yan[a] ordered, "When the roosters crow, yoke your chariots, fill in the wells, and level the stoves.[384] Look only to follow where my horses' heads are pointing."

Luan Yan said, "The domain of Jin has never had an order like this. My horses' heads wish to point east."[385] He thus turned back, and the lower army followed him.

The scribe of the left said to Wei Jiang[a]: "Should we not wait for Zhonghang Yan[e]?"

Wei Jiang[b] said, "Our master Zhonghang Yan ordered that we should follow our commanders. Luan Yan[a] is my commander.[386] I intend to follow him. To follow our commander, Luan Yan, is the way to heed Zhonghang Yan."[387]

Zhonghang Yan[d] said, "It was my command that was in error. Of what avail is regret now? We are only leaving captives in the hands of Qin."

He therefore ordered a large-scale retreat. The men of Jin called this the "Campaign of Changes and Procrastinations."[388]

Luan Qian said, "This campaign was supposedly in retaliation for our defeat at Li. Yet the campaign achieved nothing, much to Jin's shame. As I have the second place in the commander's chariot,[389] do I dare not to acknowledge the shame?" Together with Fan Yang[a] he galloped into the ranks of the Qin army and died there. Fan Yang[a] made it back.

樂黶謂士匄曰：「余弟不欲往，而子召之。余弟死，而子來，是而子
殺余之弟也。弗逐，余亦將殺之。」士鞅奔秦。

14.3b 於是齊崔杼、宋華閱、仲江會伐秦。不書，惰也。向之會亦如之。衛北宮
括不書於向，書於伐秦，攝也。

秦伯問於士鞅曰：「晉大夫其誰先亡？」
對曰：「其欒氏乎！」
秦伯曰：「以其汰乎？」
對曰：「然。欒黶汰虐已甚，猶可以免，其在盈乎！」
秦伯曰：「何故？」
對曰：「武子之德在民，如周人之思召公焉，愛其甘棠，況其子
乎？欒黶死，盈之善未能及人，武子所施沒矣，而黶之怨實章，將於是
乎在。」秦伯以為知言，為之請於晉而復之。

Luan Yan said to Fan Gai[a], "My younger brother did not want to go, and your son beckoned him. My younger brother died, and your son came back. This means your son killed my younger brother. If you do not expel him, I will likewise kill him." Fan Yang[a] fled to Qin.

The Jin high officer Fan Yang, in exile in Qin because of his brother-in-law Luan Yan's enmity,[390] predicts doom for the Luan lineage. According to Fan Yang, the merits of Luan Shu (Luan Yan's father) and the potential goodness of Luan Ying (Luan Yan's son) cannot outweigh the baleful effects of Luan Yan's excesses. Fan Yang, together with his father, Fan Gai, will eliminate the Luan lineage seven year later (Xiang 21.5). The Qin ruler intercedes for Fan Yang's reinstatement in Jin.

At that time Cui Zhu of Qi and Hua Yue and Zhong Jiang of Song joined forces to attack Qin. That the text does not record their names was because they were remiss. It was the same with the meeting at Xiang.[391] That the text does not record the name of Beigong Kuo of Wei for Xiang but does record it for the attack on Qin is because he helped in the latter case.

14.3b

The Liege of Qin asked Fan Yang[a], "Who among the Jin high officers will be the first to perish?"

He replied, "It will surely be the Luan lineage!"

The Liege of Qin said, "Is it because of their excesses?"

He replied, "Just so. Luan Yan's excesses and violence are already extreme. But he can still escape disaster, which will probably befall his son Luan Ying[a]!"

The Liege of Qin said, "Why is that?"

He replied, "Luan Shu[c]'s virtue has lived on among the people. Compare this to the men of Zhou, who, longing for the Shao Duke, love his sweet pear tree.[392] How much more would the Jin people love Luan Shu's son? By the time Luan Yan dies, Luan Ying[a]'s goodness will still not have reached the people, while what Luan Shu[c] had bestowed will already have faded, and it will be the resentment Luan Yan[b] provoked that will become manifest. Disaster will strike at that time." The Liege of Qin deemed his words astute and interceded on his behalf with Jin to have his position there restored.

---

390 Luan Yan married Fan Gai's daughter (Xiang 21.5).

391 At that meeting the *Annals* also records only "a Qi leader" and "a Song leader."

392 *Maoshi* 16, "Gantang" 甘棠, 1D.54–55. The people of Zhou, for love of the Shao Duke, will not cut down the pear tree which he loved and under which he found repose. Recall that Luan Shu was one of the ministers responsible for Lord Li's assassination, yet here he is praised for his virtue. Shuxiang also praises Luan Shu's virtue in *Guoyu*, "Jin yu 6," 14.480. In the Shanghai Museum Manscript, Luan Shu is the chief instigator of the Xi lineage's destruction and Lord Li's murder. Note that Zhao Dun is also remembered for his loyalty despite his probable role in Lord Ling's assassination (Cheng 8.6).

衛獻公戒孫文子、甯惠子食，皆服而朝，日旰不召，而射鴻於囿。二子從之，不釋皮冠而與之言。二子怒。孫文子如戚，孫蒯入使。公飲之酒，使大師歌〈巧言〉之卒章。大師辭。師曹請為之。

初，公有嬖妾，使師曹誨之琴，師曹鞭之。公怒，鞭師曹三百。故師曹欲歌之，以怒孫子，以報公。公使歌之，遂誦之。蒯懼，告文子。文子曰：「君忌我矣，弗先，必死。」

并帑於戚而入，見蘧伯玉，曰：「君之暴虐，子所知也。大懼社稷之傾覆，將若之何？」

對曰：「君制其國，臣敢奸之？雖奸之，庸知愈乎？」遂行，從近關出。

---

393   Court robes consisted of a black cap, a black top garment, and a white silk lower garment with folds.

394   Leather caps made from the hide of white deer were worn during hunting. A ruler receiving officials dressed in court robes should take off his cap, as in Zhao 12.11. Lord Xian is deliberately humiliating Sun Linfu and Ning Zhi. *Lüshi chunqiu* 25.1681 tells the anecdote as an example of a ruler's careless act that has disastrous consequences.

395   *Maoshi* 198, "Qiaoyan" 巧言, 12C.425. The last stanza of "Clever Words" denounces the slanderer who brings about disorder: "Who is that man? / He lives by the banks of the river. / Lacking strength and courage, / He is indeed the ladder leading to disorder." Lord Xian obviously implies a parallel between Sun Linfu and the man castigated in "Clever Words." He may also want to suggest that Sun Linfu is plotting rebellion (*ZZ* 32.560).

396   He refuses presumably because he realizes that the ode would goad Sun Linfu to rebellion.

397   Alternatively, "the lord had him sing it and then recite and explain it." *Song* 誦 means "to recite" and "to explain" (Karlgren, gl. 538). Musical accompaniment might have made the words less comprehensible, hence the recitation. The initiative to drive home the provocation can be Lord Xian's or Cao's, although Cao's desire for vengeance against Lord Xian suggests that the initiative to recite comes from Cao.

398   Sun Linfu's family and followers had been in two places: his settlement Qi and the Wei capital, Diqiu. As preparation for his insurrection, he consolidated the group in Qi and then attacked the capital.

Lord Xian of Wei, whose reign began inauspiciously because he showed no grief at his father's funeral eighteen years ago (Cheng 14.5), wantonly antagonizes his ministers Sun Linfu and Ning Zhi. Sun Linfu, who has his own long history of ritual impropriety (Xiang 7.7) and of conflicts with Wei rulers (Cheng 7.6, 14.1), attacks Wei from his power base in Qī with implicit Jin support.

Lord Xian of Wei invited Sun Linfu[a] and Ning Zhi[a] to a meal. They both dressed in formal robes for attending court.[393] Even when the sun was setting, the lord still did not summon them but was instead shooting wild geese at the park. When the two men followed him there, he spoke to them without taking off his leather cap.[394] The two men were furious. Sun Linfu[a] went to Qī, and his son Sun Kuai entered the court to offer his service. The lord entertained Sun Kuai with wine and told the grand music master to sing the last stanza of "Clever Words."[395] The grand music master refused,[396] and the music master Cao asked to perform it.

14.4a(4)

Earlier, the lord had had a favored concubine. He had sent the music master Cao to teach her how to play the horizontal lute, and the music master Cao had whipped her. Enraged, the lord had had the music master Cao whipped three hundred blows. That was why the music master Cao wished to sing "Clever Words." He did so to enrage Sun Kuai, so as to exact revenge against the lord. The lord had him sing it, and he then recited it.[397] Sun Kuai was fearful and told Sun Linfu[c]. Sun Linfu[c] said, "The ruler distrusts us. If we do not act first, we are sure to die."

Sun Linfu assembled his family and followers at Qī and then entered the Wei capital.[398] He saw Qu Boyu and said,[399] "You know full well the oppressive violence of the ruler. I live in great fear that the altars of the domain will be overturned. What is to be done?"

Qu Boyu replied, "The ruler controls his domain. How would a subject dare to challenge him? Even if we challenge him, how do we know that things will be better?" He then went on his way, leaving the domain by way of a nearby pass.[400]

---

399 The absence of a line break between *ru* 入 and *jian* 見 would yield a different reading: "and then he entered the Wei capital to have an audience with Qu Boyu." Yang (3:1015) suggests an accidental encounter. He argues that Qu Boyu, who served in the court of Lord Ling, the grandson of Lord Xian, must have been very young at this point and would not be in any important position in government. There would have been no reason for Sun Linfu to seek him out.

400 The boundaries between domains were marked by passes (*guan* 關). Qu Boyu, eager to escape the disorder that he expects to ensue, leaves by the closest pass. Twelve years later, he again leaves by a nearby pass (Xiang 26.2) to distance himself from the plot to restore the exiled Lord Xian. (The two passages may be variants of the same anecdote.) Confucius praises Qu Boyu as one who chooses perspicacious withdrawal in an age of disorder (*Analects* 15.7). He embodies Daoist transformations in *Zhuangzi* and *Huainanzi* (*Zhuangzi jishi* 4.165, 25.905; *Huainanzi* 1:25).

14.4b 公使子蟜、子伯、子皮與孫子盟于丘宮，孫子皆殺之。四月己未，子展奔齊，公如鄄。使子行請於孫子，孫子又殺之。公出奔齊，孫氏追之，敗公徒于河澤，鄄人執之。

初，尹公佗學射於庾公差，庾公差學射於公孫丁。二子追公，公孫丁御公。子魚曰：「射為背師，不射為戮，射為禮乎？」射兩軥而還。尹公佗曰：「子為師，我則遠矣。」乃反之。公孫丁授公轡而射之，貫臂。

14.4c 子鮮從公。及竟，公使祝宗告亡，且告無罪。定姜曰：「無神，何告？若有，不可誣也。有罪，若何告無？舍大臣而與小臣謀，一罪也。先君有冢卿以為師保，而蔑之，二罪也。余以巾櫛事先君，而暴妾使余，三罪也。告亡而已，無告無罪！」

---

401 Qiu Palace should be in the Wei capital, Diqiu. Sun's forces were probably already pressing close to the lord's palace, and Lord Xian had no choice but to seek a peace agreement.

402 He was presumably preparing for Lord Xian to take refuge in Qi.

403 Juan 鄄 was located in present-day Shandong, northwest of Juancheng County 鄄城縣; see *Annals*, Zhuang 14.4, n. 79.

404 He Marsh (Heze 河澤) was located northeast of present-day Yanggu County 陽穀縣, Shandong.

405 These were yokes over the two middle horses in the team of four horses drawing the chariot. By shooting at the yokes Cha seeks to both fulfill his charge and not betray his teacher.

406 In an anecdote with significant parallels and divergences in *Mencius* 4B.24, Yugong Zhisi of Wei, sent to pursue Zizuo Ruzi of Zheng's invading army, shoots at the latter only after removing the arrowhead because Zizuo Ruzi had taught archery to Yingong Zhituo, Yugong Zhisi's own teacher. For Yugong Zhisi, loyalty to his teacher's teacher outweighs a political command, which he fulfills only symbolically. Kong Yingda (ZZ-Kong 32.561) takes for granted that the *Zuozhuan* account is historical while the story in *Mencius* is elaborated to embellish an argument, but there is no reason to believe that the *Zuozhuan* account has greater historical veracity.

407 This is the first explicit expression of doubts regarding the existence of spirits in the text.

408 Ding Jiang is referring to Sun Linfu and Ning Zhi, whom Lord Xian humiliated repeatedly.

409 Wang Yinzhi (*Jingyi shuwen*, 706) claims that the word sequence here might have been corrupted. Instead of "he treated me with a scorn more fitting for a concubine" 蔑之，暴妾使余, he suggests "he treated me with scorn, as if I were a concubine" 暴蔑之，妾使余. Both *bao* 暴 and *mie* 蔑 mean dismissive scorn; see *Han Feizi* 47.977: "For a ruler to treat his subjects scornfully is called *bao*" 人主輕下曰暴. Karlgren (gl. 542) reads *bao* (with its usual meaning of violence) as an adjective modifying "concubine": "he treated me like an abused concubine."

410 Ding Jiang was not Lord Xian's birth mother, but she should have been honored as his mother and is cited as an exemplary mother in *Lienü zhuan* 1.9–11. *Maoshi* 28, "Yan yan" 燕燕, 2A.77–78, said to have been composed by Zhuang Jiang of Wei for a departing concubine in the Mao tradition, is read as Ding Jiang's admonition to Lord Xian in *Liji*-Zheng 11.866. The interpretation of "Yan yan" as an admonition to Lord Xian belongs to the Lu tradition; see Ma Zonglian, *Zuozhuan buzhu* (cited in Yang, 3:1013). According to *Lienü zhuan* 1.9, Ding Jiang composes the ode for her departing daughter-in-law.

The lord sent Zijiao, Zibo, and Zipi, noble sons of Wei, to swear a cove-nant with Sun Linfu[b] at Qiu Palace.[401] Sun Linfu[b] killed all of them. In the fourth month, on the *jiwei* day (26), the lord's younger brother Zizhan fled to Qi.[402] The lord went to Juan[403] and sent Zihang, another Wei noble son, to negotiate with Sun Linfu[b]. Sun Linfu[b] killed him too. The lord left the domain and fled to Qi. Sun Linfu[d] pursued him and defeated his followers at He Marsh.[404] The men of Juan arrested the rem-nants of the lord's followers.

Earlier, the Yin Lord Tuo had studied archery with the Yu Lord Cha, and the Yu Lord Cha had studied archery with Gongsun Ding. The two men pursued the lord, and Gongsun Ding was driving the lord's chariot. The Yu Lord Cha[a] said, "If I shoot, I will be turning against my teacher. If I don't shoot, I will be punished. Will shooting perhaps accord with ritual propriety?" He shot twice at the two yokes over the horses' necks and turned back.[405] The Yin Lord Tuo said, "You did that for your teacher, but for me he is farther removed." He thus reversed his course and resumed the pursuit. Gongsun Ding gave the reins to the lord and shot the Yin Lord Tuo, piercing his arm.[406]

Zhuan[a], the lord's younger full brother, followed the lord. When they reached the border, the lord sent the invocator and the ancestral atten-dant to announce his flight and also to announce that he had committed no offense. Ding Jiang said, "If there are no spirits, why bother to announce it?[407] If there are spirits, they cannot be deceived. Since he has committed offenses, how can he announce that he has not? He set the great officials aside and conferred instead with the minor officials. That was his first offense. The former ruler had eminent ministers to serve as his teachers and guardians, but he treated them with contempt. That was his second offense.[408] I served the former ruler with towel and comb, but he treated me with a scorn more fitting for a concubine.[409] That was his third offense. He should announce his flight and make an end of it. He is not to announce that he has committed no offense!"[410]

公使厚成叔弔于衛，曰：「寡君使瘠，聞君不撫社稷，而越在他竟，若之何不弔？以同盟之故，使瘠敢私於執事，曰：『有君不弔，有臣不敏；君不赦宥，臣亦不帥職，增淫發洩，其若之何？』」

衛人使大叔儀對，曰：「群臣不佞，得罪於寡君。寡君不以即刑，而悼棄之，以為君憂。君不忘先君之好，辱弔群臣，又重恤之。敢拜君命之辱，重拜大貺。」

厚孫歸，復命，語臧武仲曰：「衛君其必歸乎！有大叔儀以守，有母弟鱄以出。或撫其內，或營其外，能無歸乎！」

14.4d　齊人以郲寄衛侯。及其復也，以郲糧歸。

右宰穀從而逃歸，衛人將殺之。辭曰：「余不說初矣。余狐裘而羔袖。」乃赦之。

411　On the two readings of *budiao*, see Cheng 13.3, n. 263, Xiang 13.5, n. 356.

412　"Accumulated excesses" refers to the long-standing tensions between Sun Linfu and Wei rulers (Yang, 3:1014). The phrase may also refer to Lord Xian's transgresssions. The subject of "burst forth" may be the resentment of Wei officers and ministers (Lin Yaosou, cited in Karlgren, gl. 545), or it may describe how the mutual ill will has become widely known and can invite intervention (Takezoe, 15.54). Note the demarcation of a "private exchange" in a formal diplomatic mission (see also Wen 4.7, Xuan 16.4, Cheng 2.9, 8.1, Xiang 26.7, Zhao 3.3).

413　Here, as elsewhere, the use of the term "unworthy" is conventional self-deprecation (on behalf of one's own ruler). It does not imply criticism of the exiled Wei ruler.

414　The word *ji* 寄, translated here as "make a refuge for," comes up in relation to displaced or ousted princes. *Jigong* 寄公 or *yugong* 寓公 refers to displaced lords seeking temporary refuge in another domain.

415　According to Yang (3:1112), the title *youzai* ("steward of the right") had become the lineage name.

416　The translation follows Takezoe's reading (15.54). Cf. Du Yu's (ZZ 32.562) reading: "Earlier I did not follow the lord gladly; I did so because I could not help it."

Our lord sent Hou Chengshu to offer condolence in Wei. He said, "Our unworthy ruler has sent me. We have heard that your ruler no longer oversees the altars of the domain and has been exiled to another realm. How can he not offer his condolences?[411] On account of our ties as covenant partners, he has sent me to presume to speak privately to your functionaries: 'You have a ruler who is ruthless, and you have subjects who lack understanding. The ruler is unforgiving, and the subjects also do not fulfill their duties. Accumulated excesses have burst forth. What is to be done?'"[412]

The leaders of Wei sent Taishu Yi to reply. He said, "We, the subjects, are lacking in talent and have offended our unworthy ruler.[413] Our unworthy ruler did not apply punishment and instead has now mournfully cast us off, bringing grief to your ruler. Your ruler has not forgotten the good relations of our former rulers but has deigned to offer condolences to us and has moreover time and again expressed his sympathetic concern. We presume to bow in thanks for the condescension of your ruler's command and to bow a second time for the great gift of your consideration."

Hou Chengshu[a] returned and reported discharge of his mission. He said to Zang Wuzhong: "The Wei ruler is certain to return! There is Taishu Yi to guard the domain and there is his younger full brother Zhuan, who left with him. One settles what is within the domain, while the other manages what is outside the domain. How can he fail to return!"

Lord Xian of Wei is granted refuge in Lai, a small domain annexed by Qi eight years earlier (Xiang 6.7). That he eventually returns to Wei twelve years later (Xiang 26.2) with Lai grains shows his avarice. Lord Xian's defecting follower quotidianizes political choices with a sartorial metaphor.

The men of Qi made Lai into a temporary refuge for the Prince of Wei.[414]   14.4d
When it came to the time of his restoration, he returned to Wei with grain from Lai.

Youzai Gu had followed Lord Xian but escaped and returned to Wei.[415] The leaders of Wei were about to kill him. He offered this defense: "I am no longer happy with my earlier decision.[416] I am like a fox-fur coat with sleeves of lambskin."[417] They therefore pardoned him.

---

417   According to Du Yu (*ZZ* 32.562), the more precious fox fur refers to the greater good, and the common lambskin refers to a minor blemish—Youzai Gu is thus comparing his initial decision to follow the lord as the minor flaw that should not negate his general goodness. Tao Hongqing suggests that the difference between fox fur and lambskin is a metaphor for the divergence between appearance and reality, intention and execution—Youzai is saying that although he followed the lord, he was not loyal to him (Yang, 3:1015).

14.4e 衛人立公孫剽，孫林父、甯殖相之，以聽命於諸侯。

衛侯在郲，臧紇如齊唁衛侯。衛侯與之言，虐。退而告其人曰：「衛侯其不得入矣。其言糞土也。亡而不變，何以復國？」

子展、子鮮聞之，見臧紇，與之言，道。臧孫說，謂其人曰：「衛君必入。夫二子者，或輓之，或推之，欲無入，得乎？」

14.5 師歸自伐秦。晉侯舍新軍，禮也。成國不過半天子之軍。周為六軍，諸侯之大者，三軍可也。

於是知朔生盈而死，盈生六年而武子卒，彘裘亦幼，皆未可立也。新軍無帥，故舍之。

14.6 師曠侍於晉侯。晉侯曰：「衛人出其君，不亦甚乎？」

---

418 Gongsun Piao was the grandson of Lord Mu of Wei, the son of Zishu Heibei (Cheng 10.2), and Lord Xian's cousin.

419 They awaited commands for meetings and covenants, which would mark the princes' recognition of Gongsun Piao as the Wei ruler.

420 According to *Shuowen jiezi* 2A.5b, the word *yan* 唁 means "to condole with the living" (*diao sheng ye* 弔生也). Du Yu (ZZ 32.562) claims that *yan* in this case refers specifically to condolences offered to one who has lost his kingdom (*diao shiguo ye* 弔失國也).

421 These final words echo Hou Chengshu's. Both emphasize the instrumental role of Lord Xian's supporters (Zizhan, Zhuan, Taishu Yi) in cementing goodwill inside and outside Wei. Both Zizhan and Zhuan were Lord Xian's younger brothers.

422 Jin military organization underwent many changes in the period covered by *Zuozhuan*. The Jin army seems to have been largest in the aftermath of the battle of An, when Lord Jing created six armies (Cheng 3.8). The new army broken up in 560 BCE (Xiang 13.3) is mentioned in Cheng 13.3, 16.5, 16.6, and Xiang 3.7. It hardly seems possible that Zhou had a larger military force than Jin, so the ritual prescription may pertain only to the number of armies, which may vary in size.

   Zuo Tradition

The leaders of Wei established Gongsun Piao as ruler.[418] Sun Linfu and Ning Zhi assisted him so as to await the commands of the princes.[419]   14.4e

While the Prince of Wei was in Lai, Zang Wuzhong[a] went to Qi to pay him a visit of condolence.[420] The Prince of Wei spoke viciously to him. Zang Wuzhong withdrew and said to his men, "The Prince of Wei is unlikely to succeed in reentering Wei! His words were like dung and dirt. Even in exile, he still has not changed his ways. How can he regain his domain?"

Zizhan and Zhuan[a] heard of this and had an audience with Zang Wuzhong[a]. They spoke to him in the proper way. Zang Wuzhong[c] was pleased and said to his men: "The Wei ruler is sure to reenter Wei. With two such fine men, one pulling him and one pushing him, even if he did not wish to reenter Wei, how would it be possible not to do so?"[421]

The new army in Jin is abolished: a ritual justification (proper relations between the Zhou king and the princes) is juxtaposed with a political explanation (the heirs of the Fan [Shi] and Zhi lineages, which controlled the new army, are too young).

When the armies of the princes returned from attacking Qin, the Prince   14.5
of Jin abolished the new army. This was in accordance with ritual propriety. The armies of a full-size domain should not exceed half the number of the armies of the Son of Heaven. Zhou had six armies. For the great ones among princes, three armies were sufficient.[422]

At that time, Zhi Shuo fathered Zhi Daozi[e] and then died. When Zhi Daozi[e] was six, his grandfather Zhi Ying[d] died. Shi Fang's son Zhi Qiu was also young. Neither of them could be established as commanders as yet. The new army thus had no commanders, and that was why it was abolished.

The music master Kuang, known elsewhere in Zuozhuan for his good judgment, divinatory skills, and musical knowledge, justifies the expulsion of Lord Xian of Wei. He articulates a political vision wherein a ruler's power has inherent limits. Authority is based on just rule and reciprocity, and opinions from various levels of society are supposed to constrain the ruler's choices. On how the expulsion of a ruler may be justified, see also Zhao 32.4. That the justification of rulership lies in the people's welfare is a recurrent theme in Zuozhuan and is echoed in various early texts, including Mencius 7B.14, Xunzi 18.389, 27.622, and Shuoyuan 1.39.

The music master Kuang was attending the Prince of Jin. The Prince of   14.6
Jin said, "The leaders of Wei have expelled their ruler. Is that not going too far?"

對曰：「或者其君實甚。良君將賞善而刑淫，養民如子，蓋之如天，容之如地；民奉其君，愛之如父母，仰之如日月，敬之如神明，畏之如雷霆，其可出乎？夫君，神之主而民之望也。若困民之主，匱神乏祀，百姓絕望，社稷無主，將安用之？弗去何為？天生民而立之君，使司牧之，勿使失性。有君而為之貳，使師保之，勿使過度。是故天子有公，諸侯有卿，卿置側室，大夫有貳宗，士有朋友，庶人、工、商、皁、隸、牧、圉皆有親暱，以相輔佐也。善則賞之，過則匡之，患則救之，失則革之。自王以下各有父兄子弟以補察其政。史為書，瞽為詩，工誦箴諫，大夫規誨，士傳言，庶人謗，商旅于市，百工獻藝。故《夏書》曰：

遒人以木鐸徇于路，官師相規，工執藝事以諫。

正月孟春，於是乎有之，諫失常也。天之愛民甚，豈其使一人肆於民上，以從其淫，而棄天地之性？必不然矣。」

423　The received text has *kun min zhi zhu* 困民之主 ("a master that straitens the people" [Lin Yaosou, cited in Karlgren, gl. 550]), but Liu Xiang quotes the passage as *kun min zhi xing* 困民之性 in *Xinxu* 1.16, which can mean "he straitens (i.e., oppresses) the proper nature of the people" (Karlgren, gl. 550). Since the characters *xing* 性 and *sheng* 生 are often used interchangeably in ancient texts, we emend the text to *kun min zhi sheng* 困民之生 ("ruins the livelihood of the people") (see the readings of Hong Liangji, *Chunqiu Zuozhuan gu*, 535; and Takezoe, 15.56).

424　We follow the reading of *xing* 性 as *sheng* 生: "Not letting them lose their livelihood"; or if we combine *sheng* and *xing*: "not letting them lose the natural basis of livelihood." On the reading of *xing* as *sheng*, see also Fu Sinian, "Xing Ming guxun bianzheng"; *Fayan yishu* 3.86; *Baihu tong shuzheng*, "Xingqing," 381: "Nature is what one is born with [or what one lives by]" 性者, 生也. Cf. a similar usage in Zhao 8.1: "no one can protect his livelihood" 莫保其性.

425　"Helpers" (*er* 貳) may also be translated as "(lesser) doubles." In this vision of polity, the ruler is not unique and indispensable. His function is supported and duplicated by his officers and ministers, who also serve to keep him within proper bounds. Cf. Huan 2.8.

426　Cf. Huan 2.8: *shi you li zi di* 士有隸子弟, "the officers have sons and younger brothers who are subordinate to them." Of course, *pengyou* 朋友, here "subordinate younger kinsmen or like-minded colleagues," has a different meaning ("friends") in modern Chinese.

427　We follow Wang Yinzhi (*Jingyi shuwen*, 707) and read *lü* 旅 as *lu* 臚, meaning "to set forth words" (*chenyan* 陳言) or "to transmit words" (*chuanyan* 傳言). Du Yu (ZZ 32.563) takes this to mean "to set forth (goods)": "merchants set forth their goods in the marketplace." A similar formulation of how subjects articulate their critiques of the ruler's errors is found in *Guoyu*, "Zhou yu 1," 1.9–10.

428　Our translation of *guanshi* 官師 as "low-ranking officers" is based on Wang Yinzhi, *Jingyi shuwen*, 708–9. This passage is incorporated into "Yin zheng" 胤征 (*Shangshu* 4.102) in the Ancient Script version of the *Documents*.

429　Alternatively, we might translate this line as "remonstrance has lost its regular constancy," possibly because for minor officials and artisans it can be done only once in a year.

430　A shorter version of this exchange is found in *Xinxu* 1.16. This passage enunciates a vision of polity with inherent limits on power. Hence, it is often cited by scholars

He replied, "Perhaps it was their ruler who went too far. A good ruler will reward excellence and punish excesses. He will nurture the people like his own children, covering them like the sky and holding them like the earth. The people will hold up their ruler, love him like a parent, look up to him as the sun and the moon, revere him as the bright spirits, and hold him in awe as they do thunderbolts. How can he be expelled? Now the ruler is the master of the spirits and the hope of the people. If he ruins the livelihood[423] of the people and deprives the spirits of sacrifices, so that all the clans lose hope and the altars of the domain have no master, of what use is he? What is to be done but have him expelled? Heaven gives birth to the people and establishes rulers to oversee them and take care of them, not letting them lose their livelihood.[424] There being rulers, Heaven establishes helpers for them to act as their teachers and guardians, not letting them exceed limits.[425] That is why the Son of Heaven has his lords, and princes have their ministers; ministers establish their collateral lineages; high officers have their secondary lines; officers have their subordinate younger kinsmen or like-minded colleagues;[426] commoners, artisans, merchants, minions, lackeys, shepherds, and grooms all have their kin and close associates—so that they can assist and support each other. When there is excellence, the helpers praise them; when there are wrongs, they rectify them; when there are troubles, they come to their aid; when there are errors, they change them. From the king down, everyone has fathers, older brothers, sons, and younger brothers to observe and amend the flaws of their governing decisions. Scribes make their writings, blind music masters make their odes, musicians recite admonitions and remonstrances, high officers rectify and instruct, officers transmit opinions, commoners complain, merchants and travelers argue in the marketplace,[427] and all kinds of artisans present their views through their skills. Therefore, it says in the *Xia Documents*,

> The itinerant officers, waving their metal bells with wooden
> tongues, made their circuits on the roads. Various low-ranking
> officers admonished one another.[428] Artisans used their skills and
> crafts to offer remonstrances.

That is why in the first month, at the beginning of spring, this practice was followed. This was for the sake of remonstrating against any loss of constancy and regularity.[429] Great indeed is Heaven's love for the people! Why would it let one person exert his will over the people and indulge his excesses while abandoning the nature of heaven and earth? This would certainly not be allowed."[430]

---

eager to see "progressive" elements in early political thought; see, e.g., Liang Qichao, *Xian Qin zhengzhi sixiang shi*, 35–44; Xu Fuguan, *Zhongguo renxing lun shi*, 51–61; Xiao Gongquan, *Zhongguo zhengzhi sixiang shi*, 1:91.

14.7(6) 秋，楚子為庸浦之役故，子囊師于棠，以伐吳。吳人不出而還。子囊殿，以吳為不能而弗儆。吳人自皋舟之隘要而擊之。楚人不能相救，吳人敗之，獲楚公子宜穀。

14.8 王使劉定公賜齊侯命，曰：「昔伯舅大公右我先王，股肱周室，師保萬民。世胙大師，以表東海。王室之不壞，繄伯舅是賴。今余命女環，茲率舅氏之典，纂乃祖考，無忝乃舊。敬之哉！無廢朕命！」

14.9(7) 晉侯問衛故於中行獻子。對曰：「不如因而定之。衛有君矣，伐之，未可以得志，而勤諸侯。史佚有言曰：『因重而撫之。』仲虺有言曰：『亡者侮之，亂者取之。推亡、固存，國之道也。』君其定衛以待時乎！」
　　　冬，會于戚，謀定衛也。

431　Tang 棠 was located in the domain of Wei slightly northwest of present-day Liuhe County 六合縣, Jiangsu.

432　The precise location of Gaozhou 皋舟 is unknown.

433　Karlgren (gl. 554) reads "eastern seas" as the direct object of the verb *biao* 表 ("glorify"): "who glorified the eastern seas."

434　Lord Dao is asking whether Jin should punish those who drove out Lord Xian of Wei.

435　More literally, "accede to what is weighty [i.e., what cannot be changed easily] and calm the situation." The scribe Yi is also quoted in Xi 15.4, Wen 15.4, Xuan 12.3, Cheng 4.4, Zhao 1.13.

436　For Zhonghui, see Xuan 12.2, n. 197. He is also quoted in Xiang 30.10a.

437　The fact that the princes are meeting at the power base of Sun Linfu implies acceptance of the Wei ruler's expulsion.

In a continuation of last year's skirmishing (Xiang 13.5), Chu underestimates Wu and is defeated.

In autumn, the Master of Chu, on account of the campaign of Yongpu, had Zinang station his troops at Tang in order to attack Wu.[431] The men of Wu did not come forth, so the Chu army turned back. Zinang brought up the rear and, thinking that Wu was unable to fight, took no precautions. The men of Wu came out through the narrow pass at Gaozhou,[432] cut the Chu forces in the middle, and struck them. The men of Chu could not come to each other's aid. The men of Wu defeated them and captured Gongzi Yigu of Chu.

14.7(6)

King Ling of Zhou charges Lord Ling of Qi, in the archaic and elevated diction characteristic of royal commands, to continue the work of his ancestors in supporting the royal house. Elsewhere in Zuozhuan, Lord Ling (r. 581–554) is generally depicted as incompetent.

The king sent the Liu Duke Ding to bestow the following charge on the Prince of Qi: "In the past the senior uncle, the Grand Lord, assisted our former king. He was like the arms and the legs of the Zhou house, and he was teacher and guardian to the myriad people. For successive generations, there was recompense for the grand tutor, who was the glorious exemplar for the eastern seas.[433] That the royal house was not destroyed was due to its reliance on the senior uncle. Now I charge you, Huan, to assiduously follow the statutes of the uncle. Continue the work of your ancestors and do not shame your forebears. Be reverent! Do not neglect my command!"

14.8

The Jin minister Zhonghang Yan gives a practical assessment of the power struggle in Wei: Jin is to support the victor and bide its time before intervening.

The Prince of Jin asked Zhonghang Yan[b] about affairs in Wei.[434] He replied, "It is better to go along with the status quo and stabilize it accordingly. Wei already has a ruler. If we attack it, we may not fulfill our aims, and we will have taxed the efforts of the princes. The scribe Yi had these words: 'Go along with what is established and settle it.'[435] Zhonghui had these words: 'For the failing domain, shame it. For the domain in turmoil, take it. To overthrow what is failing and to preserve what is surviving is the way of dealing with domains.'[436] You, my lord, should stabilize Wei and wait for the right time."

14.9(7)

In winter, the meeting at Qī was designed to confer about stabilizing Wei.[437]

14.10　范宣子假羽毛於齊而弗歸，齊人始貳。

14.11　楚子囊還自伐吳，卒。將死，遺言謂子庚：「必城郢！」
　　　君子謂子囊忠。「君薨，不忘增其名；將死，不忘衛社稷，可不謂
忠乎？忠，民之望也。《詩》曰：

行歸于周，
萬民所望。

忠也。」

春秋

15.1(1)　十有五年，春，宋公使向戌來聘。二月己亥，及向戌盟于劉。

15.2(2)　劉夏逆王后于齊。

15.3(5)　夏，齊侯伐我北鄙，圍成。公救成，至遇。

438　Both bird feathers and oxtail hair were used in ritual dances. They often formed part of the decorations on flags and banners.

439　Zigeng was to succeed to the position of chief minister after Zinang died.

440　*Maoshi* 225, "Duren shi" 都人士, 15B.510. The ode is often taken to be an epithalamium, with the first line as the words of the bride or the groom: "He/She returns to Zhou." *Maoshi*-Zheng, 15B.210, reads *zhou* as "loyalty and good faith": "In his actions he turns to loyalty and good faith." For Zinang's role in deciding on King Gong's honorific, see Xiang 13.2.

A Jin leader's act of bad faith leads to Qi disaffection. A similar incident will occur more than fifty years later, with the same detrimental consequences (Ding 4.1b).

Fan Gai^c borrowed feathers and oxtail hair[438] from Qi and did not return them. From then on Qi began to shift their allegiance.

14.10

The Chu chief minister, Zinang, dies. He is commended for loyalty because of his final wish to fortify Ying, although the same plan by Nang Wa, another Chu minister, will be criticized (Zhao 23.9). In the ten years he was in power, Zinang led military expeditions against Chen, Zheng, Jin, Song, and Lu without, however, decisive successes.

Zinang of Chu returned from the attack on Wu and died. When he was about to die, his last words were addressed to Zigeng:[439] "You must fortify Ying!"

14.11

The noble man considered Zinang loyal: "When the ruler expired, he did not forget to enhance his good name. When he himself was about to die, he did not forget to defend the altars of the domain. Is he not a byword for loyalty? The loyal one is the hope of the people. As it says in the *Odes*,

> In his actions he turns to Zhou,
> Being the hope that myriad people look to.[440]

This refers to loyalty."

LORD XIANG 15 (558 BCE)
ANNALS

In the fifteenth year, in spring, the Duke of Song sent Xiang Xu to come on an official visit. In the second month, on the *jihai* day (11), we swore a covenant with Xiang Xu at Liu.[441]

15.1(1)

Liu Xia (the Liu Duke Ding) met the queen and escorted her home from Qi.

15.2(2)

In summer, the Prince of Qi attacked our northern marches and laid siege to Cheng. Our lord went to the aid of Cheng, advancing as far as Yu.[442]

15.3(5)

---

441 According to Kong Yingda, Liu 劉 was a place in the outskirts of the Lu capital, Qufu (Yang, 3:1020).

442 The text implies that Qi abandoned the siege of Cheng by the time the Lu army reached Yu.

15.4(5) 季孫宿、叔孫豹帥師城成郛。

15.5 秋，八月丁巳，日有食之。

15.6(6) 邾人伐我南鄙。

15.7(6) 冬，十有一月癸亥，晉侯周卒。

左傳

15.1(1) 十五年，春，宋向戌來聘，且尋盟。見孟獻子，尤其室，曰：「子有令聞而美其室，非所望也。」對曰：「我在晉，吾兄為之。毀之重勞，且不敢間。」

15.2(2) 官師從單靖公逆王后于齊。卿不行，非禮也。

15.3 楚公子午為令尹，公子罷戎為右尹，蒍子馮為大司馬，公子橐師為右司馬，公子成為左司馬，屈到為莫敖，公子追舒為箴尹，屈蕩為連尹，養由基為宮廏尹，以靖國人。

---

443 Cheng 成 was located to the northwest of Ningyang County in present-day Shandong (see *Annals*, Huan 6.2, n. 45).

444 Du Yu (*ZZ* 32.565) notes rightly that there was no *dingsi* day in the eighth month. *Dingsi* was the first day of the seventh month.

445 Lord Dao, who acceded to his position in 573 BCE (Cheng 18.3) at fourteen, was only thirty years old when he died in 558.

446 According to Du Yu (*ZZ* 32.565), the account shows Meng Xianzi's honesty and fraternal loyalty. One can, however, also read this as an attempt to justify extravagance. Meng Xianzi has the opposite image in various early texts. In *Liji* 6.119 Meng Xianzi is praised for an abstemious adherence to ritual that places him above his peers. In *Liji* 60.988, his opinion on how the ruling classes should not compete for profit with the people is quoted with approbation. An anecdote in *Han Feizi* 33.699–700 debates the meaning and appropriateness of Meng Xianzi's frugality. *Xinxu* 6.210 contrasts his abstemiousness with Fan Gai's extravagance.

447 For the term *guanshi* 官師, see Xiang 14.6, n. 428, above.

448 This implies that the Shan Duke Jing did not go all the way to Qi. Among the "low-ranking officers" was Liu Xia. Though posthumously honored as Liu Duke Ding, he was not a minister at this point. The ritual propriety of a Zhou minister escorting the bride for the king, mentioned only here and in *Annals*, Huan 8.6, and *Zuozhuan*, Huan 8.4, may not amount to a "rule" as some traditional commentators suggest.

Jisun Su (Ji Wuzi) and Shusun Bao led out troops and fortified the outer city walls of Cheng.[443]   15.4(5)

In autumn, in the eighth month, on the *dingsi* day,[444] there was an eclipse of the sun.   15.5

Zhu leaders attacked our southern marches.   15.6(6)

In winter, in the eleventh month, on the *guihai* day (9), Zhou, the Prince of Jin, died.[445]   15.7(6)

ZUO

While on a diplomatic mission in Lu to repay a Lu visit (Xiang 2.6) and to renew the Covenant of Bo (Xiang 11.3), Xiang Xu of Song criticizes the extravagance of the Lu chief minister's home. This is a recurrent concern in Zuozhuan *and other texts from the period. The Qi minister Yan Ying, for example, refuses to aggrandize his home (Zhao 3.3). In* Guoyu, *"Chu yu 1," 17.541–46, Wu Ju remonstrates with King Ling of Chu, warning that the grandeur of the Terrace of Zhanghua bodes ill for Chu. See also* Yanzi chunqiu 2.115, 6.415–16, *and* Xinshu 7.145.

In the fifteenth year, in spring, Xiang Xu of Song came to us on an official visit, and also to renew the Covenant of Bo. He had an audience with Meng Xianzi and found fault with his abode: "You, sir, have a fine reputation and yet you have aggrandized your abode. This is not what we had hoped for." Meng Xianzi replied, "When I was in Jin, my older brother did it. To take it down would be to redouble the labor. Moreover, I do not dare criticize him."[446]   15.1(1)

Various low-ranking officers came along as the Shan Duke Jing met the queen and escorted her home from Qi.[447] That a minister did not go violated ritual propriety.[448]   15.2(2)

New appointments are made following the death of the Chu chief minister, Zinang (Xiang 14.11). Choosing the right men for offices is a recurrent concern in Zuozhuan.

Zigeng[a] of Chu became the chief minister; Gongzi Pirong, the deputy of the right; Wei Ziping, the grand supervisor of the military; Gongzi Tuoshi, the supervisor of the right army; Gongzi Cheng, the supervisor of the left army; Qu Dao, the maréchal; Zinan[a], the deputy for remonstrance; Qu Dang, the court deputy; Yang Youji, the deputy for palace stables. These appointments were made to pacify the inhabitants of the capital.   15.3

　　君子謂「楚於是乎能官人。官人，國之急也。能官人，則民無覦心。《詩》云：

> 嗟我懷人，
> 寘彼周行。

能官人也。王及公、侯、伯、子、男，甸、采、衛大夫，各居其列，所謂周行也。」

15.4　鄭尉氏、司氏之亂，其餘盜在宋。鄭人以子西、伯有、子產之故，納賂于宋，以馬四十乘，與師茷、師慧。三月，公孫黑為質焉。司城子罕以堵女父、尉翩、司齊與之，良司臣而逸之，託諸季武子，武子寘諸卞。鄭人醢之三人也。

　　師慧過宋朝，將私焉。其相曰：「朝也。」
　　慧曰：「無人焉。」
　　相曰：「朝也，何故無人？」
　　慧曰：「必無人焉。若猶有人，豈其以千乘之相易淫樂之矇？必無人焉故也。」
　　子罕聞之，固請而歸之。

15.5(3, 4)　夏，齊侯圍成，貳於晉故也。於是乎城成郕。

449　*Maoshi* 3, "Juan'er" 卷耳, 1B.33. In the first stanza, a woman longs for an absent lover or husband and in her distraction and sadness cannot fill a basket as she picks *juan'er* (curly grass). In the context of the ode, the quoted lines should read: "Sighing, I long for the man, / And leave the basket by the great road." "The great road" (*zhouhang* 周行) in the original is understood here as "the ranks of Zhou." The Mao commentary and the Zheng Xuan commentary also identify noble men who could properly fill offices as objects of longing (*Maoshi*-Zheng 1B.33).

450　*Dian* 甸, *cai* 采, and *wei* 衛 are three of the five administrative districts (*houfu* 侯服, *dianfu* 甸服, *nanfu* 男服, *caifu* 采服, *weifu* 衛服), each of 500 *li* (according to *Guliang*, Xuan 15, 12.222, one *li* is the equivalent of 300 steps or about 0.15 mile), supposedly arranged in concentric squares from the *qi* 圻, the royal domain, covering 1,000 *li*. See *Zhouli*, "Zhi fang shi" 職方氏, 33.501; *Shangshu*, "Yu gong" 禹貢, 6.91.

451　Zixi's father (Zisi), Liang Xiao's father (Zi'er), and Zichan's father (Ziguo) were all killed by the Wei and Si lines, see Xiang 10.9.

452　One *sheng* 乘 consists of a carriage or chariot drawn by a team of four horses; *sheng* here thus indicates foursome teams.

453　Music masters, who were often blind, had special assistants.

454　That is, Song responds to the bribe of horses and Zheng music masters rather than the request of its ministers. Confucius claims that Zheng music should be cast aside because it is licentious (*Analects* 15.11). Zheng musicians and musical instruments were also offered as a bribe to Jin in Xiang 11.5.

The noble man said, "Chu was at this time capable of putting the right men in offices. To put the right men in offices is the urgent matter for the domain. If one can put the right men in offices, then the people will have no overreaching desires. It says in the *Odes*,

> Sighing, I long for the men,
> And would place them in all the ranks.[449]

This is about being capable of putting the right men in offices. The king and the dukes, the princes, the lieges, the chiefs, the heads, and the high officers of the second, the fourth, and the fifth outer rims, all occupy their proper places.[450] This is what is meant by 'all the ranks.'"

A blind musician exposes the misjudgment of Song leaders, who would not agree to the demands of Zheng ministers to repatriate miscreants and would comply only after receiving gifts of horses and musicians.

After the turmoil caused by the Wei and Si lineages in Zheng, the brigands who escaped justice were in Song. The leaders of Zheng, on account of Zixi, Liang Xiao[a], and Zichan,[451] sent to Song gifts of forty teams of horses,[452] as well as the music master Pei and the music master Hui. In the third month, Gongsun Hei of Zheng became hostage there. Yue Xi[b], the supervisor of fortifications in Song, handed over Du Rufu, Wei Pian, and Si Qi to Zheng. Thinking Si Chen a fine man, Yue Xi let him escape, entrusting him to Ji Wuzi's protection. Ji Wuzi placed him in Bian. The leaders of Zheng minced and pickled the flesh of the other three persons.

The music master Hui passed by the Song court and was about to relieve himself there. His assistant[453] said, "This is the court."

Hui said, "There is no one here."

The assistant said, "This is the court. How can there be no one here?"

Hui said, "For sure, there is no one. If there are still any proper men, why should ministers of a domain with a thousand chariots be exchanged for blind men playing licentious music?[454] Surely this was done because there is no one here."

Yue Xi[a] heard about this and insistently urged the Song ruler to return the music masters to Zheng.

Qi, Lu, and Jin were covenant partners. Having turned away from Jin because of the feathers incident (Xiang 14.10), Qi now feels no compunctions about attacking Lu, and Lu prepares accordingly.

In summer, the Prince of Qi laid siege to Cheng because Lu had shifted their allegiance from Jin. That was why Lu fortified the outer city walls of Cheng.

15.6(6, 7)　秋，邾人伐我南鄙，使告于晉。晉將為會以討邾、莒，晉侯有疾，乃止。冬，晉悼公卒，遂不克會。

15.7　鄭公孫夏如晉奔喪，子蟜送葬。

15.8　宋人或得玉，獻諸子罕。子罕弗受。獻玉者曰：「以示玉人，玉人以為寶也，故敢獻之。」

　　　子罕曰：「我以不貪為寶，爾以玉為寶。若以與我，皆喪寶也，不若人有其寶。」

　　　稽首而告曰：「小人懷璧，不可以越鄉，納此以請死也。」

Lord Dao of Jin's premature death at thirty forestalls Jin's timely protection of its covenant partners.

In autumn, Zhu leaders attacked our southern marches. We sent word to Jin. Jin was about to summon a meeting to chastise Zhu and Ju, but the Prince of Jin fell ill, and they thus desisted. In winter, Lord Dao of Jin died, and they therefore could not hold the meeting.[455]

15.6(6, 7)

Two Zheng ministers attend the funeral and burial of Lord Dao of Jin. This arrangement exceeds not only the ancient ritual prescription for a high officer and an officer to attend (Zhao 30.2) but also the rule for a high officer and a minister to attend when Lords Wen and Xiang of Jin were overlords (Zhao 3.1).

Zixi[a] of Zheng went to Jin to mourn at the funeral. Zijiao escorted the funeral cortege.

15.7

The hidden jade is a metaphor for unrecognized worth in Han Feizi *13.238. Here the offer of a jade becomes the occasion for considering the meaning of value. The Song minister Yue Xi demonstrates his integrity and sagacity by refusing a gift of jade and by making sure that its value is revealed and that it should benefit its rightful owner. Versions of this anecdote appear in* Han Feizi *21.404,* Lüshi chunqiu *10.552,* Huainanzi *7.236, and* Xinxu *7.233. In* Han Feizi, *the story is used to illustrate the idea of "desiring the absence of desire" in* Laozi. *Analogous reasoning is found in* Xinxu *6.210, where Meng Xianzi is praised for valuing wise men rather than wealth.* Mozi *46.392–93 pursues the same logic in a passage comparing the worth of gems to that of good government. A jade ring also provokes a deliberation over rightful ownership and the proper relationship between a minister and a commoner in Zhao 16.3b.*

There was a man of Song who obtained a piece of jade and presented it to Yue Xi[a]. Yue Xi[a] refused to accept it. The presenter of the jade said, "I showed this to the jade smith, and the jade smith thought it a treasure. That is why I presume to present it."

15.8

Yue Xi[a] said, "I consider not being covetous a treasure, while you consider the jade a treasure. If you give it to me, then we both lose what we treasure most. It is better for each of us to keep his own treasure."

The man bowed with his forehead touching the ground and told his story: "A commoner cherishing a precious jade disk cannot go through a village without meeting harm.[456] I am submitting this so as to avoid death."

---

455 The Jin ruler's death at a young age accounts for the honorific "Dao," which means "mourned."

456 Cf. the Zhou proverb quoted in Huan 10.4: "A common man may be without crime until cherishing a valuable jade becomes his crime."

子罕寘諸其里，使玉人為之攻之，富而後使復其所。

15.9　十二月，鄭人奪堵狗之妻，而歸諸范氏。

春秋

16.1(1)　十有六年，春，王正月，葬晉悼公。

16.2(1)　三月，公會晉侯、宋公、衛侯、鄭伯、曹伯、莒子、邾子、薛伯、杞伯、小邾子于湨梁。戊寅，大夫盟。

16.3(1)　晉人執莒子、邾子以歸。

16.4　齊侯伐我北鄙。

16.5　夏，公至自會。

16.6　五月甲子，地震。

16.7(2)　叔老會鄭伯、晉荀偃、衛甯殖、宋人伐許。

16.8(4)　秋，齊侯伐我北鄙，圍成。

16.9　大雩。

16.10(5)　冬，叔孫豹如晉。

Yue Xi[a] placed him in the lane where he himself lived and had a jade-smith work on the jade and refine it. After the man became rich, he sent him back to his place.

In the twelfth month, the men of Zheng seized Du Gou's wife and returned her to the Fan lineage.[457]   15.9

LORD XIANG 16 (557 BCE)
ANNALS

In the sixteenth year, in spring, in the royal first month, Lord Dao of Jin was buried.   16.1(1)

In the third month, our lord met with the Prince of Jin, the Duke of Song, the Prince of Wei, the Liege of Zheng, the Liege of Cao, the Master of Ju, the Master of Zhu, the Liege of Xue, the Liege of Qi, and the Master of Lesser Zhu at the Ju Dam.[458] On the *wuyin* day (26), the high officers swore a covenant.   16.2(1)

Jin leaders arrested the Master of Ju and the Master of Zhu and took them home with them.   16.3(1)

The Prince of Qi attacked our northern marches.   16.4

In summer, our lord arrived from the meeting.   16.5

In the fifth month, on the *jiazi* day (13), there was an earthquake.   16.6

Shu Lao met with the Liege of Zheng, Xun Yan of Jin, Ning Zhi of Wei, and a Song leader and attacked Xǔ.   16.7(2)

In autumn, the Prince of Qin attacked our northern marches and laid siege to Cheng.   16.8(4)

There was a great rain sacrifice.   16.9

In winter, Shusun Bao went to Jin.   16.10(5)

---

457 Du Gou was of the same lineage as Du Rufu. Having put the latter to death, the men of Zheng were concerned that Du Gou might be able to incite the Fan lineage of Jin to help in some scheme of revenge, and thus they took away his wife so that the link between Du Gou and the Fan lineage would be severed. Cross-domain marriage alliances seem to have been common.

458 The Ju Dam 湨梁 was located in Jin west of present-day Jiyuan County 濟源縣, Henan.

16.1(1) 十六年，春，葬晉悼公。平公即位，羊舌肸為傅，張君臣為中軍司馬，祁
奚、韓襄、欒盈、士鞅為公族大夫，虞丘書為乘馬御。改服、修官，烝于
曲沃。警守而下，會于溴梁。命歸侵田。以我故，執邾宣公、莒犁比公，
且曰「通齊、楚之使」。

晉侯與諸侯宴于溫，使諸大夫舞，曰：「歌詩必類。」齊高厚之詩
不類。荀偃怒，且曰：「諸侯有異志矣。」使諸大夫盟高厚，高厚逃歸。
於是叔孫豹、晉荀偃、宋向戌、衛甯殖、鄭公孫蠆、小邾之大夫盟，曰：
「同討不庭。」

16.2(7) 許男請遷于晉。諸侯遂遷許，許大夫不可，晉人歸諸侯。

鄭子蟜聞將伐許，遂相鄭伯以從諸侯之師。穆叔從公。齊子帥師
會晉荀偃。書曰「會鄭伯」，為夷故也。

夏，六月，次于棫林。庚寅，伐許，次于函氏。

---

459 Shi Wozhuo was made grand guardian in 573 BCE (Cheng 18.3). Shuxiang appears
to be taking over his position. In *Guoyu*, "Jin yu 7," 13.445, Shuxiang is appointed as
tutor for the heir apparent Biao (the future Lord Ping) because of his knowledge of
historical annals.

460 Zhang Junchen is the son of Zhang Lao, the leader of scouts (Cheng 18.3).

461 Han Xiang is the son of Han Wuji, who took charge of the high officers of ruling
lineages (Xiang 7.6).

462 The dance is accompanied by the singing of odes. "Odes for dancing" (*wushi* 舞詩)
are mentioned in *Mozi* (*Mozi xiangu* 48.418). The "right order" (or "proper category,"
lei 類) refers to the correspondence between the music and the dance or to the connection between the performance and the proper intent (ZZ 33.573). The "right
order" may also include political hierarchy and ritual propriety. *Lei* has also been
glossed as "good" (*Erya*).

463 On the term *buting* 不庭 ("those who turn against us"), see Cheng 12.2, n. 243.

464 Jin leaders intend to use only the Jin army to attack Xǔ.

465 This passage is a flashback on how the various armies were initially mobilized. The
old enmity between Zheng and Xǔ might explain why the Zheng ruler wants to
personally take part in the campaign. When Zheng decided to join the campaign,
Jin had not yet sent the princes' armies back.

466 The literal meaning of *yi* 夷 is "level." The sequencing of names in the *Annals* is
explained: Shu Lao is mentioned with the Zheng ruler (i.e., treated as being "of the
same level") because he is a Lu minister (ZZ 33.573), and the Zheng ruler is mentioned ahead of the Jin commander leading the campaign because of his higher
station as a prince.

467 Yulin 棫林 was located in the domain of Xǔ northeast of present-day Ye County
葉縣, Henan.

468 Hanshi 函氏 was located very close to Yulin.

Upon Lord Ping of Jin's accession, new leaders are appointed in Jin. Asserting his role as overlord, Lord Ping arrests the rulers of Ju and Zhu for their aggression against Lu and their ties with Qi. At a meeting in Wen, Jin leaders use odes and dance to judge the level of the princes' allegiance, and the Qi delegate betrays his disaffection.

In the sixteenth year, in spring, Lord Dao of Jin was buried. Lord Ping acceded to his position. Shuxiang[a] became grand guardian;[459] Zhang Junchen[460] became the supervisor of the military for the central army; Qi Xi, Han Xiang,[461] Luan Ying, and Fan Yang[a] became high officers of the ruling lineages; Yuqiu Shu became the chariot driver with foursome teams of horses. Lord Ping put aside his mourning clothes, chose able men for office, and offered the winter sacrifice at Quwo. Having made preparations for guarding the capital, he came down along the Yellow River and gathered the princes for a meeting at the Ju Dam. He commanded the princes to return to one another the territories they had invaded. On our account, Jin arrested Lord Xuan of Zhu and Lord Libi of Ju and in addition accused them: "You colluded with envoys from Qi and Chu."

The Prince of Jin and the princes feasted at Wen. He made the high officers dance, saying, "The ode sung has to match the right order."[462] The ode by Gao Hou of Qi did not match the right order. Enraged, Zhonghang Yan[a] said, "The princes are not of one mind with us." He had the high officers swear a covenant with Gao Hou, but the latter escaped and returned to Qi. As a consequence, Shusun Bao, Zhonghang Yan[a] of Jin, Xiang Xu of Song, Ning Zhi of Wei, Zijiao[a] of Zheng, and the high officers of Lesser Zhu swore a covenant that said, "Together we shall chastise those who turn against us."[463]

Xǔ became a de facto Chu protectorate when it moved its capital to She in 576 BCE (Cheng 15.7). Here the Xǔ ruler wants to shift allegiance to Jin by moving its capital again, but his high officers do not support him. Jin thus attacks Xǔ.

The Head of Xǔ asked permission from Jin to move its capital. The princes then agreed to move the Xǔ capital, but the Xǔ high officers would not allow it. The leaders of Jin sent the princes back to their domains.[464]

When Zijiao of Zheng heard that the allies intended to attack Xǔ, he assisted the Liege of Zheng in following the armies of the princes.[465] Shusun Bao[a] followed our lord, while Shu Lao[a] led an army to join with Zhonghang Yan[a] of Jin. That the text says, "met with the Liege of Zheng," is for the sake of proper leveling.[466]

In summer, in the sixth month, they set up camp at Yulin.[467] On the *gengyin* day (9), they attacked Xǔ and set up camp at Hanshi.[468]

16.1(1)

16.2(7)

16.3 　晉荀偃、欒黶帥師伐楚，以報宋楊梁之役。楚公子格帥師，及晉師戰于湛阪。楚師敗績。晉師遂侵方城之外，復伐許而還。

16.4 　秋，齊侯圍成，孟孺子速徼之。齊侯曰：「是好勇，去之以為之名。」速遂塞海陘而還。

16.5 　冬，穆叔如晉聘，且言齊故。晉人曰：「以寡君之未禘祀，與民之未息，不然，不敢忘。」

　　　穆叔曰：「以齊人之朝夕釋憾於敝邑之地，是以大請。敝邑之急，朝不及夕，引領西望曰：『庶幾乎！』比執事之間，恐無及也。」

　　　見中行獻子，賦〈圻父〉。獻子曰：「偃知罪矣，敢不從執事以同恤社稷，而使魯及此？」

　　　見范宣子，賦〈鴻雁〉之卒章。宣子曰：「匄在此，敢使魯無鳩乎？」

---

469 Zhanban 湛阪 was located in Chu north of Pingdingshan City 平頂山市, Henan.

470 For Fangcheng, a big buffer zone to the north of Chu that stretched for several hundred miles between the Huai River and the Jiang and Han Rivers, see Xi 4.1 (Yang 1:292–93), n. 42.

471 We follow Takezoe (16.5) in reading *jiao* 徼 as *yao* 要.

472 Cheng in northern Lu was close to Qi. Haijing might have been a narrow pass running from Lu to Qi. The word *hai* 海 indicates that there might have been waterways in this area, not necessarily that the pass was by the sea.

473 Shusun Bao wants to speak about Qi's aggression against Lu and to get help from Jin.

474 The *di* sacrifice was offered when the spirit tablet of the recently deceased former ruler was placed in the Ancestral Temple after the mourning period was over (*ZZ* 33.573). *Liji* 31.577 gives a different explanation of the sacrifice. The *di* sacrifice is also mentioned in Min 2.2, Xi 8.3, Xi 33.1, Xiang 10.2, Zhao 15.1, Zhao 25.6, and Ding 8.10.

475 The phrase *shuji* 庶幾 indicates hope and uncertainty.

476 *Maoshi* 185, "Qi Fu" 圻父, 11A.377–78. In this ode, Qi Fu is blamed for failing his duty as the king's minister. As a result, Zhou is defeated by the Qiang and Rong tribes and the people suffer instability and deprivations. Here Shusun Bao is comparing Zhonghang Yan to Qi Fu.

477 *Maoshi* 181, "Hong yan" 鴻雁, 11A.373–74. The ode compares the sorrows of displaced persons to a wild goose in flight. The last stanza reads: "The wild goose in flight: / Doleful are its sad cries. / These wise men / say we toil. / Those foolish men / Say we parade our arrogance." Shusun Bao is comparing the plight of Lu to the wild goose in flight and implicitly beseeching Fan Gai to be as discerning as "these wise men." This ode is also cited in Wen 13.5.

478 We follow Wei Zhao's annotation in *Guoyu*, "Jin yu 9," 15.491–92, reading *jiu* 鳩 as *an* 安; cf. Karlgren, gl. 561.

Jin's punitive expedition against Xŭ becomes a broader campaign against Chu, in retaliation for Chu's earlier aggression (Xiang 12.4). Chu's defeat allows Jin to move to the area just beyond the Fangcheng mountain range, a natural barrier said to be of great defensive value (Xi 4.1).

Zhonghang Yan[a] and Luan Yan, both of Jin, led an army to attack Chu in retaliation for the campaign of Yangliang in Song. Gongzi Ge of Chu led out troops and did battle with the Jin army at Zhanban.[469] Chu troops were completely defeated. Jin troops thus invaded the area beyond Fangcheng[470] and then returned after attacking Xŭ again.

16.3

The Qi ruler, said to lack courage (Xiang 18.3), here avows appreciation of a young Lu nobleman's valor and thus gives up the siege of the Lu city Cheng.

In autumn, the Prince of Qi laid siege to Cheng. Meng Zhuangzi[a] cut the Qi force in the middle.[471] The Prince of Qi said, "This is a brave man. Let us leave this place and so make his name famous." Meng Zhuangzi thereupon blocked Haijing Pass and returned.[472]

16.4

The Lu envoy Shusun Bao shows his mastery of ritual propriety by appealing to Jin leaders for help against Qi aggression with apposite recitations from the Odes.

In winter, Shusun Bao[a] went to Jin on an official visit and also to speak about Qi affairs.[473] The leaders of Jin said, "It is just that our unworthy ruler has not yet offered the *di* sacrifice[474] and that the people have not yet had rest. Otherwise, we would not have presumed to forget your troubles."

16.5

Shusun Bao[a] said, "We press our request because the men of Qi have been day and night venting their discontent in the territories of our humble settlement. The urgency for our humble settlement is such that from the morning we may not last to the evening. We anxiously crane our necks, looking westward and say, 'Perhaps help is close!'[475] By the time your functionaries have time for us, I fear it may be too late!"

He had an audience with Zhonghang Yan[b] and recited "Qi Fu."[476] Zhonghang Yan[c] said, "I know my offense. How could I presume not to follow our men in charge and together with them care for the altars of your domain, and consequently let Lu be reduced to this state!"

He had an audience with Fan Gai[c] and recited the last stanza of "The Wild Goose."[477] Fan Gai[b] said, "I am here. How could I presume to let Lu have no peace!"[478]

春秋

17.1　十有七年，春，王二月，庚午，邾子牼卒。

17.2(1)　宋人伐陳。

17.3(2)　夏，衛石買帥師伐曹。

17.4(3)　秋，齊侯伐我北鄙，圍桃。高厚帥師伐我北鄙，圍防。

17.5　九月，大雩。

17.6(5)　宋華臣出奔陳。

17.7(4)　冬，邾人伐我南鄙。

左傳

17.1(2)　十七年，春，宋莊朝伐陳，獲司徒卬，卑宋也。

17.2(3)　衛孫蒯田于曹隧，飲馬于重丘，毀其瓶。重丘人閉門而詢之，曰：「親逐
而君，爾父為厲。是之不憂，而何以田為？」
　　夏，衛石買、孫蒯伐曹，取重丘。曹人愬于晉。

ANNALS

In the seventeenth year, in spring, in the royal second month, on the *gengwu* day (23), Jing, the Master of Zhu, died.[479]

17.1

A Song leader attacked Chen.

17.2(1)

In summer, Shi Mai of Wei led out troops and attacked Cao.

17.3(2)

In autumn, the Prince of Qi attacked our northern marches and laid siege to Tao.[480] Gao Hou led out troops, attacked our northern marches, and laid siege to Fang.

17.4(3)

In the ninth month, there was a great rain sacrifice.

17.5

Hua Chen of Song departed and fled to Chen.

17.6(5)

In winter, Zhu leaders attacked our southern marches.

17.7(4)

ZUO

In the seventeenth year, in spring, Zhuang Zhao of Song attacked Chen and seized Ang, the supervisor of conscripts. This happened because Chen looked down on Song.

17.1(2)

The Wei campaign against Cao is explained as the consequence of a personal grudge. The leaders of Cao berate Sun Kuai, Sun Linfu's son, for his father's crimes and also blame him for the exile of Lord Xian of Wei (Xiang 14.4). Sun Kuai leads an attack against Cao in retaliation.

Sun Kuai of Wei was hunting at Sui in Cao when he let his horses drink at Chongqiu and broke the pitcher for drawing water.[481] The men of Chongqiu closed the gate and reviled him with these words: "You personally drove away your ruler. Your father is as vicious as a vengeful ghost.[482] How is it that you do not worry about these things and instead indulge in hunting?"

17.2(3)

In summer, Shi Mai and Sun Kuai of Wei attacked Cao and took Chongqiu. The men of Cao complained to Jin.

---

479   Lord Xuan of Zhu was taken as captive to Jin the year before (Xiang 16.1). He seems to have returned to Zhu before he died.

480   Tao 桃 belonged to the domain of Lu and was located northeast of Wenshang County 汶上縣, Shandong.

481   Chongqiu 重丘 was in the domain of Cao southwest of present-day Chiping County 茌平縣, Shandong.

482   Cf. Karlgren, gl. 562: "Your father will become a vicious ghost." Hong Liangji (*Chunqiu Zuozhuan gu*, 540), following *Maoshi* and *Guangya*, reads *li* 厲 as *e* 惡, "the evil one." In *Zhuangzi*, *li* is "the ugly one" or "the evil one" (*Zhuangzi jishi* 2.70, 12.450).

17.3(4) 　齊人以其未得志于我故，秋，齊侯伐我北鄙，圍桃。高厚圍臧紇于防。師自陽關逆臧孫，至于旅松。郰叔紇、臧疇、臧賈帥甲三百，宵犯齊師，送之而復。齊師去之。

　　　　齊人獲臧堅，齊侯使夙沙衛唁之，且曰「無死」。堅稽首曰：「拜命之辱。抑君賜不終，姑又使其刑臣禮於士。」以杙抉其傷而死。

17.4(7) 　冬，邾人伐我南鄙，為齊故也。

17.5(6) 　宋華閱卒，華臣弱皋比之室，使賊殺其宰華吳，賊六人以鈹殺諸盧門合左師之後。左師懼，曰：「老夫無罪。」賊曰：「皋比私有討於吳。」遂幽其妻，曰：「畀余而大璧。」

　　　　宋公聞之，曰：「臣也不唯其宗室是暴，大亂宋國之政，必逐之。」

483　The precise location of Lüsong is unknown, but it was obviously close to Fang 防 near present-day Fei County 費縣, Shanxi.

484　Zang Jian believes that the message of mercy is compromised by the messenger's status as a mere eunuch. Our translation follows the interpretation of Du Yu (*ZZ* 33.574) and Takezoe (16.8), reading *gu* 姑 as *gouqie* 苟且, "for mere expediency" (Xiang 17.8). Yang (3:1031) reads *gu* 姑 as *gu* 故 (*guyi* 故意): "The ruler has bestowed the gift of reprieve, yet he has deliberately sent a mutilated subject to express courtesy to an officer." The shame of castration is repeatedly emphasized in Sima Qian's letter to Ren An (*Hanshu* 62.2727).

485　Hua Gaobi is Hua Yue's son.

Qi attacks Lu again in the aftermath of its failed campaign against Lu (Xiang 16.4). Lu commanders show their valor by breaking the siege. Zang Jian, taken captive by Qi, commits suicide to vindicate his honor.

On account of the fact that the leaders of Qi had not yet achieved their goals with regard to us, in autumn, the Prince of Qi attacked our northern marches and laid siege to Tao. Gao Hou laid siege to Zang Wuzhong[a] at Fang. The Lu army came from Yangguan to meet up with Zang Wuzhong[c] and advanced as far as Lüsong.[483] Shuliang He[a] of Zou, Zang Chou, and Zang Jia led three hundred armored soldiers to raid the Qi army during the night. They escorted Zang Wuzhong to Lüsong and then returned to Fang. The Qi army withdrew.

The men of Qi captured Zang Jian. The Prince of Qi sent Susha Wei to console him and also to tell him, "You don't have to die." Zang Jian bowed with his forehead touching the ground and said, "I bow to the condescension of your command. Yet the gift the lord bestowed is not final, for he has, for mere expediency, sent a mutilated subject to show courtesy to an officer."[484] He drove a stake into his wound and died.

While the Zhu incursion into Lu is placed close to the end of the entries in the Annals *because of chronology, it is here juxtaposed with Qi aggression against Lu to emphasize the collusion of Qi with Zhu.*

In winter, that Zhu leaders attacked our southern marches was on account of Qi.

The Song minister Hua Chen instigates the murder of his nephew's steward and demands bribes from the steward's widow. The chief minister, Xiang Xu, urges compromise (for comparable examples, see Xiang 6.2, 10.9c, Zhao 1.7). Hua Chen is finally driven out not through orders from Duke Ping of Song or Xiang Xu but by a group of outraged inhabitants of the capital.

Hua Yue of Song died. His younger brother Hua Chen, deeming the house of his nephew Hua Gaobi[a485] vulnerable, sent brigands to murder Hua Gaobi's steward Hua Wu. These six brigands used daggers to kill him at the Lu Gate, behind the abode of Xiang Xu[a], the minister of the left whose settlement was He. Xiang Xu[b] was fearful and said, "I am not guilty." The brigands said, "Hua Gaobi[a] is chastising Hua Wu[a] because of private grudges." Hua Chen thereupon imprisoned Hua Wu's wife and said, "Give me your great jade disk."

The Duke of Song heard about these events and said, "Not only did Hua Chen use violence against none other than his own ancestral line, but he has also wrought great havoc on the government of the domain of Song. We must drive him out."

左師曰：「臣也，亦卿也。大臣不順，國之恥也。不如蓋之。」乃舍之。左師為己短策，苟過華臣之門，必騁。

十一月甲午，國人逐瘈狗。瘈狗入於華臣氏，國人從之。華臣懼，遂奔陳。

17.6　宋皇國父為大宰，為平公築臺，妨於農收。子罕請俟農功之畢，公弗許。築者謳曰：

> 澤門之晳，
> 實興我役。
> 邑中之黔，
> 實慰我心。

子罕聞之，親執扑，以行築者，而抶其不勉者，曰：「吾儕小人皆有闔廬以辟燥濕寒暑。今君為一臺，而不速成，何以為役？」謳者乃止。

或問其故。子罕曰：「宋國區區，而有詛有祝，禍之本也。」

486　Xiang Xu might have urged this perversion of justice out of fear for his own life, having seen how Hua Chen had brigands and assassins at his disposal. Kong Yingda (ZZ-Kong 33.5750) suggests that Xiang Xu used the short whip to help the driver make the horses gallop because he deeply abhors Hua Chen. (The whip has to be short so others cannot see that he is aiding the driver.) It would seem that Xiang Xu is motivated by the desire for self-protection rather than righteous indignation.

487　Huang Guofu is the fair-skinned man who lived at the Marsh Gate (Zemen), which might have been the same as the Gate of Dieze (Mound and Marsh) mentioned in *Mencius* 7A.36, the south gate of the eastern city wall (Yang, 3:1032). The dark-skinned man inside the city refers to Yue Xi.

Xiang Xu[b] said, "Hua Chen[a], too, is a minister. Insubordination among the great ministers is a disgrace to the domain. It is better to cover this up." The Song ruler thus dropped the case. Xiang Xu[b] made for himself a short whip. Whenever he passed by Hua Chen's gate, he never failed to make the horses gallop.[486]

In the eleventh month, on the *jiawu* day (22), the inhabitants of the capital were chasing a rabid dog. The rabid dog ran into Hua Chen's residence, and the inhabitants of the capital followed it in. Hua Chen was fearful and thus fled to Chen.

Humble men express their criticism of nobles through songs (as in Xuan 2.1, Xiang 4.8). Yue Xi, despite their commendation of his stance, suppresses such expressions as the source of political instability. For the opposite position on this issue, see Zichan's refusal to demolish village meeting places (Xiang 31.11). Yan Ying is substituted for Yue Xi in a similar story in Yanzi chunqiu *2.111. In* Han Feizi *2.111, 35.763,* Huainanzi *12.391–92,* Hanshi waizhuan *7.291–92, and* Shuoyuan *1.43, Yue Xi's refusal to accept praise from the people is coupled with his eagerness to take blame. Such gestures paradoxically magnify his authority, and he eventually drives the Song ruler into exile. (In* Zuozhuan, *Yue Xi is praised throughout as a worthy minister.)*

Huang Guofu of Song, as grand steward, was building a terrace for Duke Ping. Its construction interfered with the harvest. Yue Xi[a] requested that their work wait until the completion of agricultural labor, but the lord did not grant it. The builders sang:

17.6

> The fair one at Marsh Gate,
> He it is who brings about our toil.
> The dark one inside the city,
> He it is who gladdens our hearts.[487]

When Yue Xi heard this, he personally clutched a bamboo whip and made circuits among the builders, flogging those who were not diligent and saying, "Humble men like us[488] all have abodes to protect us from dryness and dampness, heat and cold. Now the ruler is building one terrace, and yet you will not complete it quickly. How can you call this toil?" The singers thus stopped.

Someone asked why he acted thus. Yue Xi[a] said, "Tiny as the domain of Song is, whenever there are imprecations and acclamations, these become the taproot of disaster."[489]

488　Perhaps to ameliorate the severity of his rebuke, Yue Xi emphasizes his sympathy or solidarity with the builders despite obvious "class difference." Yue Xi may also be making a point about his humble dwelling. In *Lüshi chunqiu* 20.1361, Yue Xi's meager abode signifies his frugality and compassion for the people.

489　Both *zu* 詛 (imprecation) and *zhu* 祝 (acclamation) invoke gods and spirits.

17.7 齊晏桓子卒，晏嬰麤縗斬，苴絰、帶、杖，菅屨，食鬻，居倚廬，寢苫、枕草。其老曰：「非大夫之禮也。」曰：「唯卿為大夫。」

春秋

18.1(1) 十有八年，春，白狄來。

18.2(2) 夏，晉人執衛行人石買。

18.3(3) 秋，齊師伐我北鄙。

18.4(3) 冬，十月，公會晉侯、宋公、衛侯、鄭伯、曹伯、莒子、邾子、滕子、薛伯、杞伯、小邾子同圍齊。

18.5 曹伯負芻卒于師。

18.6(4) 楚公子午帥師伐鄭。

左傳

18.1(1) 十八年，春，白狄始來。

18.2(2) 夏，晉人執衛行人石買于長子，執孫蒯于純留，為曹故也。

---

490 A similar anecdote is found in *Yanzi chunqiu* 5.367. The broader meaning of the term "high officer" (*dafu* 大夫) does include ministers, but it is often used more restrictively to refer to those with ranks lower than ministers. Yan Ying may be modestly claiming that he is inadequate for the rank of high officer, or he may be implying that while ministers could mourn like high officers, high officers should mourn like lower-ranking officers (*shi* 士). Takezoe (16.11–12) paints a picture—whose historical accuracy cannot be ascertained—whereby the higher one's station, the less demanding the rites of mourning. Shen Qinhan suggests that warfare and diplomacy might have become the contemporary excuse for diminishing mourning ritual (Wu Jing'an, *Chunqiu Zuoshi zhuan jiuzhu shuzheng xu*, 247–48).

The Qi minister Yan Ying chooses to mourn his father's death with more stringent rituals than is common among high officers. Probably intended as a critique of declining mores, this anecdote presents Yan Ying as adhering to a more ancient and honorable code of conduct. It may also imply that ancient morality survives more stubbornly among the lower ranks of nobility.

When Yan Ruo[a] of Qi died, his son Yan Ying wore a vest of coarse hemp and unhemmed mourning robes, hempen headdress and girdle, carried a bamboo staff, and put on grass shoes. He ate gruel, lived in an austere mourning hut, and slept on a straw mat and a grass pillow. His elder steward said, "This is not the ritual for a high officer." Yan Ying said, "Only ministers can be considered high officers."[490]

17.7

LORD XIANG 18 (555 BCE)
ANNALS

In the eighteenth year, in spring, the White Di came.[491]

18.1(1)

In summer, Jin leaders arrested the Wei envoy Shi Mai.

18.2(2)

In autumn, Qi troops attacked our northern marches.

18.3(3)

In winter, in the tenth month, our lord met with the Prince of Jin, the Duke of Song, the Prince of Wei, the Liege of Zheng, the Liege of Cao, the Master of Ju, the Master of Zhu, the Master of Teng, the Liege of Xue, the Liege of Qǐ, and the Master of Lesser Zhu and laid siege to Qi.

18.4(3)

Fuchu, the Liege of Cao, died among the troops.

18.5

Gongzi Wu (Zigeng) of Chu led out troops and attacked Zheng.

18.6(4)

ZUO

In the eighteenth year, in spring, the White Di came for the first time.

18.1(1)

In summer, Jin leaders arrested the Wei envoy Shi Mai at Changzi and arrested Sun Kuai at Chunliu.[492] This was on account of Cao.[493]

---

491 According to Du Yu (ZZ 33.576), borrowing from *Gongyang*, Xiang 18 (30.255), the customary expression *laichao* 來朝 ("come to our court") is not used because the White Di did not know how to perform the proper ritual for attending a lord's court.

492 Both Changzi 長子 and Chunliu 純留 were in the domain of Jin. The former was west of present-day Changzi County 長子縣, Shanxi, while the latter was south of Tunliu County 屯留縣, Shanxi.

493 See Xiang 17.2.

秋，齊侯伐我北鄙。中行獻子將伐齊，夢與厲公訟，弗勝。公以戈擊之，首隊於前，跪而戴之，奉之以走，見梗陽之巫皋。他日，見諸道，與之言，同。巫曰：「今茲主必死。若有事於東方，則可以逞。」獻子許諾。

晉侯伐齊，將濟河，獻子以朱絲繫玉二穀，而禱曰：「齊環怙恃其險，負其眾庶，棄好背盟，陵虐神主。曾臣彪將率諸侯以討焉，其官臣偃實先後之。苟捷有功，無作神羞，官臣偃無敢復濟。唯爾有神裁之。」沈玉而濟。

---

494   That is, the military expedition against Qi.

495   Huan is the given name of Lord Ling of Qi.

496   "The masters of the spirits" here refers to the people (Huan 6.2, Xi 19.3), although it can also mean the ruler (Xiang 14.6).

497   Biao is the given name of Lord Ping of Jin. The term "servant of servant" or "subject of subject" (*cengchen* 曾臣 or *peichen* 陪臣) refers to a twice-removed relationship with the source of authority. In this case Biao, Lord Ping of Jin, is the servant of the Zhou king, who is the servant of the gods. Analogously, the term also applies to the ministers and officers of great princes, who are subjects of the Zhou king. Gu Yanwu (*Rizhi lu jishi*, 23.546), citing *Huainanzi* 13.444, notes that a subject can call a ruler by name in prayers. Gu also enumerates instances in *Zuozhuan* when a son calls his father or grandfather by name when addressing the ruler; see Cheng, n. 120.

*Jin comes to Lu's assistance and attacks Qi. The Jin commander Zhong-
hang Yan dreams of disputing a court case with Lord Li and being decapitated by the latter. Eighteen years ago, Zhonghang Yan murdered Lord Li
(Cheng 18.1), whose favorites had conspired to kill Zhonghang Yan. Zhonghang Yan's dream is said to portend his death and Jin's victory. Most imperial commentators claim that the anecdote condemns Zhonghang Yan for
the murder, but he is in fact presented in a positive light as one who accepts
his fate and holds the interests of the realm paramount.*

In autumn, the Prince of Qi attacked our northern marches. Zhonghang   18.3a(3, 4)
Yan[b] was planning to attack Qi when he dreamed of disputing a legal
case with Lord Li. He did not win. The lord struck him with a dagger-
axe, and his head fell down in front of him. He knelt down and put it
back on. While running and holding on to his head, he saw Shaman Gao
of Gengyang. A few days after this dream, he did see Shaman Gao on the
road. He spoke to Gao, and it turned out they had had the same dream.
The shaman said, "This year you, master, will certainly die. Should you
have affairs in the east,[494] your ambition will be fulfilled." Zhonghang
Yan[c] assented.

The Prince of Jin attacked Qi and was about to cross the Yellow River
when Zhonghang Yan[c] tied two pairs of jade pieces up with red silk
threads and prayed: "Huan[495] of Qi, relying on the strategic advantages
of his lands and trusting in his multitudes, has cast aside good relations,
turned against the covenant, and treated cruelly the masters of the spirits.[496] The servant of your servant, Biao,[497] intends to lead the princes to
chastise him, and it is I, Yan, his royally apppointed subject, who will go
before or behind him to offer assistance.[498] If we are victorious and
achieve merit and bring no disgrace to you gods, then I, Yan, the royally
appointed subject, will not dare to presume to cross the Yellow River
again.[499] Only you gods will decide in this case." He let the jade pieces
sink into the Yellow River and then crossed.

---

498 According to *Zhouli*-Zheng 18.279, the term *guanchen* 官臣 refers to officials who
     received charges from the king to appoint their own stewards to administer their
     settlements (Yang, 3:1036).
499 Zhonghang Yan believes Shaman Gao's interpretation of his dream and does not
     presume to pray for his own deliverance. Instead, he prays only for Jin victory.

18.3b　冬，十月，會于魯濟，尋溴梁之言，同伐齊。齊侯禦諸平陰，塹防門而守之，廣里。夙沙衛曰：「不能戰，莫如守險。」弗聽。諸侯之士門焉，齊人多死。范宣子告析文子，曰：「吾知子，敢匿情乎？魯人、莒人皆請以車千乘自其鄉入，既許之矣。若入，君必失國。子盍圖之！」

　　　　子家以告公。公恐。晏嬰聞之，曰：「君固無勇，而又聞是，弗能久矣。」

18.3c　齊侯登巫山以望晉師。晉人使司馬斥山澤之險，雖所不至，必旆而疏陳之。使乘車者左實右偽，以旆先，輿曳柴而從之。齊侯見之，畏其眾也，乃脫歸。丙寅晦，齊師夜遁。師曠告晉侯曰；「鳥烏之聲樂，齊師其遁。」邢伯告中行伯曰：「有班馬之聲，齊師其遁。」叔向告晉侯曰：「城上有烏，齊師其遁。」

500　Participants of the Covenant of the Ju Dam agreed to respect each other's territorial integrity and to recognize Jin as overlord. Qi, however, has repeatedly attacked Lu and turned away from Jin.

501　Susha Wei is implying that Qi should abandon that moat, which would not serve the same defensive function as Qi's geographical advantage—the high ridges and narrow passes of Mount Tai.

502　According to Du Yu (ZZ 33.577), this means that Lord Ling cannot persist in his resistance too much longer. But Yan Ying might simply imply that Lord Ling does not have long to live. He will die the following year (Xiang 19.5).

503　The Jin army used the same tactic in the battle of Chengpu (Xi 28.3).

504　*Sunzi* 9.166–67: "Crows gather where troops are absent" (cited in Takezoe, 16.17; Yang, 3:1038). In Zhuang 28.3, crows are also observed in predictions regarding the enemy troops.

505　We follow Du Yu's reading (ZZ 33.577) of *ban* 班 as *bie* 別 ("separated"): this is the sound of horses running around loose because they have been abandoned by the fleeing troops. Other readings of *ban* suggest circular movements (Shen Qinhan) or retreat (Hui Dong): the sounds of horses departing (Yang, 3:1038).

Jin and its allies renew the Covenant of the Ju Dam (Xiang 16.1) and attack Qi. Lord Ling of Qi is shown to lack both judgment and courage.

In winter, in the tenth month, the princes met at the Ji River in Lu to renew the words of the Covenant of the Ju Dam.[500] Together they attacked Qi. The Prince of Qi resisted the incursion at Pingyin, where he dug a one-*li*-wide moat outside the Gate of Defense to guard it. Susha Wei said, "If we cannot fight, it would be better to guard our strategic advantage."[501] Lord Ling of Qi did not heed him. The officers of the princes stormed the gate. Many died among the men of Qi. Fan Gai[c] told the Qi high officer Xi Guifu[b], "I know you. Would I presume to hide the truth of the matter from you? The men of Lu and Ju have both requested to take a thousand chariots and come into Qi from the directions of their domains. We have already agreed to their plans. If they enter, your ruler will be sure to lose the domain. Why don't you plan accordingly!"

Xi Guifu[a] told the lord about this. The lord was terrified. Yan Ying heard about it and said, "The ruler had no courage to begin with. Now that he has heard this, he cannot last for long."[502]

The Jin army maneuvers to give the impression of being numerous and formidable. Lord Ling of Qi, intimidated, turns back. Unlike the Qi ruler, Jin leaders accurately assess the movement of the enemy. The retreating Qi army suffers further setbacks.

The Prince of Qi climbed Mount Wu in order to survey the Jin army. Jin leaders had sent their supervisor of the military to forge a way through strategic points in the mountains and the marshes. Even at the places that the army would not reach, they had unfailingly set up military formations with banners, albeit only sparsely. They had sent chariots, with real soldiers on the left and fake ones on the right, to move ahead with banners, with carts dragging branches following them.[503] The Prince of Qi saw this and feared that enemy troops were numerous; he thus absconded and turned back. On the *bingyin* day (29), the last day of the month, the Qi army fled during the night. The music master Kuang told the Prince of Jin: "The cawing of the crows is joyful. The Qi army has probably fled."[504] Xing Bo told Zhonghang Yan[e], "There are sounds of horses breaking loose:[505] the Qi army has probably fled." Shuxiang told the Jin ruler, "There are crows on the city wall: the Qi army has probably fled."[506]

---

506 Takezoe (16.17) notes the timing of these observations: "When the crows caw joyfully, it is the next morning. The sounds of returning horses are traced to the evening. The crows on the city walls are sighted at the moment of speaking."

十一月丁卯朔，入平陰，遂從齊師。夙沙衛連大車以塞隧而殿。殖綽、郭最曰：「子殿國師，齊之辱也。子姑先乎！」乃代之殿。衛殺馬於隘以塞道。晉州綽及之，射殖綽，中肩，兩矢夾脰，曰：「止，將為三軍獲；不止，將取其衷。」

顧曰：「為私誓。」州綽曰：「有如日！」乃弛弓而自後縛之。其右具丙亦舍兵而縛郭最，皆衿甲面縛，坐于中軍之鼓下。

18.3d 晉人欲逐歸者，魯、衛請攻險。己卯，荀偃、士匄以中軍克京茲。乙酉，魏絳、欒盈以下軍克邿；趙武、韓起以上軍圍盧，弗克。十二月戊戌，及秦周，伐雍門之萩。范鞅門于雍門，其御追喜以戈殺犬于門中；孟莊子斬其橑以為公琴。己亥，焚雍門及西郭、南郭。劉難、士弱率諸侯之師焚申池之竹木。王寅，焚東郭、北郭，范鞅門于揚門。州綽門于東閭，左驂迫，還于東門中，以枚數闔。

---

507 Pingyin 平陰 was located in Qi northeast of present-day Pingyin County 平陰縣, Shandong.

508 We read *lian* 連 as *nian* 輦 (Yang, 3:1038); cf. Karlgren, gls. 556, 572.

509 To have a eunuch bring up the rear is presumably the cause for shame.

510 Zhi Chuo describes the oath he demands as "private" (*si* 私) because it is made between individuals.

511 The ruler of Xu also had his hands bound behind him when he surrendered (Xi 6.4). In his discussion of that passage, Takezoe (5.38) suggests that *mianfu* 面縛 means "to have one's hands bound in front." The context of this passage, however, suggests that their hands were tied behind them.

512 Jingzi 京茲, Shi 邿, and Lú 盧 were all places along the range of Mount Tai. Jingzi and Shi were both near present-day Pingyin County 平陰縣, Shandong. On Lú, see Yin 3.6.

513 Qinzhou 秦周 was close to Yong Gate, the west gate of the Qi capital, present-day Linzi City 臨淄城. Catalpa is a fine-grained wood that can be used for vessels and coffins; see Xiang 2.3, 4.4.

514 The trees near Yong Gate (Yongmen) must have yielded superior wood for lutes. In *Shuoyuan* 11.367–68, Zizhou from Yongmen plays the lute for Meng Changjun and moves him to tears. "The lute of Yongmen" (*Yongmen zhi qin* 雍門之琴) becomes a common allusion to the affective power of music.

515 Chariots were drawn by teams of four horses. The two flanking horses were called *can* 驂. Here the flanking horse on the left could not move forward, probably because the passage was narrow or there were many other chariots making their way. When the left flanking horse stops and the other horses continue to move forward, the chariot turns around.

516 It takes Zhou Chuo quite a while to realign his horses and redirect his chariot, but instead of losing his composure, he demonstrates his self-possession and reassures the soldiers who follow him.

In the eleventh month, on the *dingmao* day, the first day of the month, the Jin army entered Pingyin and then pursued the Qi army.[507] Susha Wei pulled up[508] a great chariot to block the mountain paths since he was to bring up the rear. Zhi Chuo and Guo Zui said, "For you to bring up the rear for the army of the domain would be a disgrace to Qi.[509] You would do better to just move ahead!" They thus took his place in the rear. Susha Wei[a] killed some horses at a narrow pass to block passage. Zhou Chuo of Jin caught up with the Qi forces, shot Zhi Chuo in the shoulders so that two arrows flanked his neck, and said, "If you stop, you will be taken captive by the three armies; if you do not stop, I will take aim at your midsection."

Zhi Chuo looked back and said, "Make a private oath."[510] Zhou Chuo said, "Let the sun be my pledge!" He then untied his bow and bound Zhi Chuo's hands from behind. His spearman on the right, Ju Bing, also put down his weapon to bind Guo Zui. Wearing armor but with their hands bound behind them,[511] they were seated underneath the drums of the central army.

Jin and its allies attack various strategic points in Qi. Their plundering seems methodical, and one commander, Zhou Chuo, demonstrates his extraordinary self-possession. The Qi ruler, anxious to turn back, is prevented from doing so by the adamant intervention of his son Guang, the Qi heir apparent.

The leaders of Jin wished to pursue the Qi forces that fled, but Lu and Wei requested to attack the strategic points in Qi. On the *jimao* day (13), Zhonghang Yan[a] and Fan Gai[a] overcame Jingzi with the central army. On the *yiyou* day (19), Wei Jiang and Luan Ying overcame Shi with the lower army; Zhao Wu and Han Qi laid siege to Lú with the upper army but failed to overcome it.[512] In the twelfth month, on the *wuxu* day (2), the princes' forces advanced as far as Qinzhou and cut down catalpa trees at the Yong Gate.[513] Fan Yang stormed the Yong Gate, and his chariot driver Zhui Xi used his dagger-axe to kill the dog at the gate. Meng Zhuangzi cut down the wild varnish trees there to make lutes for Lord Xiang of Lu.[514] On the *jihai* day (3), the princes' forces burned down the Yong Gate as well as the western and southern outskirts of the Qi capital. Liu Nan and Shi Ruo, both of Jin, led the princes' troops to burn the bamboos and trees at Shen Pond. On the *renyin* day (6), they burned the eastern and northern outer walls. Fan Yang stormed the Yang Gate. Zhou Chuo was storming the East Gate when his flanking horse on the left, having been pressed to a halt, caused the chariot to turn around in the middle of the gate.[515] He used the interval to count the bosses that decorated the gate.[516]

18.3d

齊侯駕，將走郵棠。大子與郭榮扣馬，曰：「師速而疾，略也。將退矣，君何懼焉？且社稷之主不可以輕，輕則失眾。君必待之！」將犯之。大子抽劍斷鞅，乃止。甲辰，東侵及濰，南及沂。

18.4a(6) 鄭子孔欲去諸大夫，將叛晉而起楚師以去之。使告子庚，子庚弗許。楚子聞之，使楊豚尹宜告子庚曰：「國人謂不穀主社稷而不出師，死不從禮。不穀即位，於今五年，師徒不出，人其以不穀為自逸而忘先君之業矣。大夫圖之，其若之何？」

子庚歎曰：「君王其謂午懷安乎！吾以利社稷也。」見使者，稽首而對曰：「諸侯方睦於晉，臣請嘗之。若可，君而繼之。不可，收師而退，可以無害，君亦無辱。」

子庚帥師治兵於汾。於是子蟜、伯有、子張從鄭伯伐齊，子孔、子展、子西守。二子知子孔之謀，完守入保。子孔不敢會楚師。

---

517 Also known simply as Tang 棠, Youtang 郵棠 was located southeast of present-day Pingdu County 平度縣, Shandong.

518 Cf. Du Yu (*ZZ* 33.578): "this is to pass quickly through the land, with no plan for an extended attack."

519 The martingale attaches the middle two horses to the horizontal beam of the chariot. Lord Ling can no longer control his chariot properly once this connection is cut.

520 The meaning of the official title, *tunyin* 豚尹, is hard to fathom. *Tun* 豚 means "piglet," but this is clearly not an official in charge of animals. The *tunyin* mentioned in *Shuoyuan* 12.396 is an emissary. Wu Jing'an (*Chunqiu Zuoshi zhuan jiuzhu shuzheng xu*, 261) suggests that since the earliest meaning of "Yi" 宜 is "meat" (or, more precisely, the placement of two pieces of meat on the sacrificial table), "Tunyin" may be Yang Yi's courtesy name. (Given names and courtesy names are often semantically related.)

521 "It" refers to assertion of Chu's challenge to Jin.

  Zuo Tradition

The Prince of Qi had his horses harnessed to his chariot and was about to flee to Youtang.[517] The heir apparent and Guo Rong pulled up the horses and said, "Their armies are moving hastily and ferociously. This means they are intent on plunder.[518] They are about to withdraw. Why should you, my lord, be fearful? Moreover, the master of the altars of the domain cannot undertake his movements lightly, lest he lose the allegiance of the multitude. You, my lord, must wait!" Lord Ling was about to dash at them. The heir apparent pulled out his sword and cut through the martingale of the lord's chariot,[519] and only then did the lord stop. On the *jiachen* day (8), the princes' armies made incursions eastward, advancing as far as Wei, and they also moved southward, advancing as far as the Yi River.

Zikong of Zheng conspires to eliminate his rivals by securing Chu assistance in return for Zheng allegiance. King Kang of Chu is tempted by the offer, but Zigeng, chief minister of Chu, insists on caution. Zikong's plot to collude with Chu does not materialize.

Zikong of Zheng wanted to remove various high officers. He planned to turn against Jin and rouse the Chu army to remove them. He sent word to Zigeng, but Zigeng would not permit it. The Master of Chu heard about this and sent the deputy for diplomacy,[520] Yang Yi, to tell Zigeng: "The inhabitants of the capital say that I, the deficient one, preside over the altars of the domain and yet I refuse to dispatch the army, and that if I die, I cannot be honored with the proper rituals. It has been five years since I acceded to my position, and our troops have not been dispatched. People are going to regard me as being concerned with my own comfort and oblivious to the legacy of the former rulers. You, high officer, should consider this. What is to be done?"

18.4a(6)

Zigeng said, sighing, "Does the king think that I long for ease? I acted as I did to benefit the altars of the domain." He received the emissary, bowed with his forehead touching the ground and replied, "The princes have just reached accord with Jin, and I beg to test the situation. If it is feasible,[521] then the ruler can follow. If it is not, we can collect our troops and withdraw. We can then avoid harm, and the ruler will also suffer no disgrace."

Zigeng led out the troops and drilled the soldiers at the Fen River. At this time Zijiao, Liang Xiao[a], and Gongsun Heigong[a] were accompanying the Liege of Zheng as he attacked Qi, while Zikong, Gongsun Shezhi[a], and Zixi guarded the domain. The other two, knowing of Zikong's plot, completed the fortifications and entered the city to protect it. Zikong did not dare meet up with the Chu army.

18.4b　楚師伐鄭，次於魚陵。右師城上棘，遂涉潁。次于旃然。蒍子馮、公子格率銳師侵費滑、胥靡、獻于、雍梁，右回梅山，侵鄭東北，至于蟲牢而反。子庚門于純門，信于城下而還，涉於魚齒之下。甚雨及之。楚師多凍，役徒幾盡。

　　　晉人聞有楚師，師曠曰：「不害。吾驟歌北風，又歌南風，南風不競，多死聲。楚必無功。」董叔曰：「天道多在西北。南師不時，必無功。」叔向曰：「在其君之德也。」

春秋

19.1(1)　十有九年，春，王正月，諸侯盟于祝柯。晉人執邾子。

19.2　公至自伐齊。

19.3(1)　取邾田，自漷水。

19.4(3)　季孫宿如晉。

19.5　葬曹成公。

522　Plum Mountain (Meishan 梅山) was northwest of the Zheng capital, with Shangji 上棘 and Yongliang 雍梁 to the southwest. The Chu troops appear to have marched northward, turned eastward at Plum Mountain, and attacked the capital from the northeast. On the location of the Zheng capital, known as Xinzheng 新鄭, see map 3.

523　The Chun Gate was on the outer city wall of the Zheng capital.

524　Musical notes are tied to military movements, and one form of divination involves listening to the reverberations of musical notes to predict the fate of military endeavors. See *Zhouli*, "Tai shi" 大師, 23.357; *Guoyu*, "Zhou yu 2," 3.132–33; *Shiji* 25.139.

*The Chu army attacks Zheng, which has acknowledged Jin leadership
since the meeting at Xiaoyu (Xiang 11.5), but initial gains for Chu give way
to grave setbacks because of heavy rain. Musical notes and the movements
of stars are used for military predictions.*

The Chu army attacked Zheng and set up camp at Yuling. The army of
the right fortified Shangji. It then crossed the Ying River and set up
camp at the Zhanran River. Wei Ziping and Gongzi Ge led crack troops
to make incursions into Bihua, Xumi, Xianyu, and Yongliang, returning
on the right by way of Plum Mountain.[522] They invaded Zheng from the
northeast, advancing as far as Chonglao before they turned back. Zigeng
stormed the Chun Gate,[523] passed two nights underneath the city wall,
and returned, crossing the river at the foot of Mount Yuchi. Torrential
rains overtook them. Many in the Chu army suffered from the cold, and
the conscripts almost all perished.

    The men of Jin heard about the Chu army attacking Zheng. The music
master Kuang said, "No harm will be done. I have sung music to northern airs and also to southern airs several times. The southern airs cannot
prevail, for they are filled with the sounds of death.[524] Chu will certainly
accomplish nothing." Dong Shu said, "The Way of Heaven is mostly in
the northwest.[525] Unless troops from the south come at the right season,
they are certain to accomplish nothing." Shuxiang said, "All depends on
the virtue of the ruler."

LORD XIANG 19 (554 BCE)
ANNALS

In the nineteenth year, in spring, in the royal first month, the princes
swore a covenant at Zhuke.[526] Jin leaders arrested the Master of Zhu.   19.1(1)

Our lord arrived from the attack on Qi.   19.2

We took the lands of Zhu, starting from the Guo River.[527]   19.3(1)

Jisun Su (Ji Wuzi) went to Jin.   19.4(3)

Lord Cheng of Cao was buried.   19.5

---

525   Dong Shu is referring to the movement of the Year-Planet. See Takezoe, 19.23. For other
       references to planetary movements as "the Way of Heaven," see Xiang 9.1, Zhao 9.4,
       and 11.2.
526   Zhuke 祝柯 was located in Qi northeast of present-day Changqing County 長清縣,
       Shandong.
527   That is, lands west of the Guo River, reaching as far as Lu, were turned over to Lu.

19.6(2)　夏，衛孫林父帥師伐齊。

19.7(5)　秋，七月辛卯，齊侯環卒。

19.8(6)　晉士匄帥師侵齊，至穀，聞齊侯卒，乃還。

19.9　八月丙辰，仲孫蔑卒。

19.10(8)　齊殺其大夫高厚。

19.11(9)　鄭殺其大夫公子嘉。

19.12　冬，葬齊靈公。

19.13(11)　城西郛。

19.14(12)　叔孫豹會晉士匄于柯。

19.15(12)　城武城。

左傳

19.1a(1, 3)　十九年，春，諸侯還自沂上，盟于督揚，曰：「大毋侵小。」

執邾悼公，以其伐我故。遂次于泗上，疆我田，取邾田，自漷水歸之于我。

晉侯先歸。公享晉六卿于蒲圃，賜之三命之服；軍尉、司馬、司空、輿尉、候奄皆受一命之服；賄荀偃束錦、加璧、乘馬，先吳壽夢之鼎。

528　For Gu, see map 2.

529　Ke 柯 was in Jin northeast of present-day Neihuang County 內黃縣, Henan.

530　This Wucheng 武城, to be distinguished from the city in Chu of the same name, was located in Lu near present-day Jiaxiang County 嘉祥縣, Shandong.

531　See Xiang 17.4. Lord Dao's father, Lord Zhuang, was arrested by Jin in 557 BCE for the same reason (Xiang 16.1).

532　The word *gui* 歸 seems to suggest that the Zhu lands had once belonged to Lu, although it is also possible to read *gui* as "give," which would imply that these had always been Zhu territories. Here Jin defines the boundary between Lu and Zhu along the Guo River, with the lands west of the river belonging to Lu.

533　See Cheng 2.3, n. 76.

534　One bundle (*shu* 束) consisted of ten rolls (*duan* 端), and two rolls made up one bolt (*pi* 匹).

535　The word *xian* 先 ("precede") indicates that the objects enumerated before were deemed less valuable than the cauldron. Karlgren (gl. 576) reads *xian* as referring to the cauldron: "the cauldron formerly given to Lu by King Shoumeng of Wu."

In summer, Sun Linfu of Wei led out troops and attacked Qi.   19.6(2)

In autumn, in the seventh month, on the *xinmao* day (28), Huan, the   19.7(5)
Prince of Qi, died.

Shi Gai (Fan Gai) of Jin led out troops and invaded Qi. When he had   19.8(6)
advanced as far as Gu,[528] he heard that the Prince of Qi had died, and he
then began his return journey.

In the eighth month, on the *bingchen* day (23), Zhongsun Mie (Meng   19.9
Xianzi) died.

Qi put to death its high officer Gao Hou.   19.10(8)

Zheng put to death its high officer Gongzi Jia (Zikong).   19.11(9)

In winter, Lord Ling of Qi was buried.   19.12

We fortified the western outer city walls.   19.13(11)

Shusun Bao met with Shi Gai (Fan Gai) of Jin at Ke.[529]   19.14(12)

We fortified Wucheng.[530]   19.15(12)

ZUO

After victories over Qi and Chu, Jin defends its allies' interests and trans-
fers Zhu territories to Lu. Lord Xiang of Lu offers generous gifts and cere-
monial toasts to Jin ministers.

In the nineteenth year, in spring, the princes returned from the banks of   19.1a(1, 3)
the Yi River and swore a covenant at Duyang (Zhuke), which said: "The
great domains are not to invade the small ones."

The Jin leaders arrested Lord Dao of Zhu because he had attacked
us.[531] The Jin army thereupon set up camp on the Si River and defined the
boundaries for our lands. The lands of Zhu, starting from the Guo River,
were returned to us.[532]

The Prince of Jin returned to Jin first. Our lord offered ceremonial
toasts to the six Jin ministers at the Pu Gardens and bestowed on them
regalia appropriate to dignitaries of three commands.[533] The army commandant, the supervisor of the military, the supervisor of works, the
senior officer of military administration, and the leader of scouts all
received the regalia appropriate to dignitaries of one command. He conferred on Zhonghang Yan[a] five bolts of brocade,[534] adding to them a jade
disk and a team of four horses, and these preceded the cauldron that had
been given to Lu by King Shoumeng of Wu.[535]

荀偃癉疽，生瘍於頭。濟河，及著雍，病，目出。大夫先歸者皆反。士匄請見，弗內。請後，曰：「鄭甥可。」二月甲寅，卒，而視，不可含。宣子盥而撫之，曰：「事吳敢不如事主！」猶視。欒懷子曰：「其為未卒事於齊故也乎？」乃復撫之曰：「主苟終，所不嗣事于齊者，有如河！」乃瞑，受含。宣子出，曰：「吾淺之為丈夫也。」

19.2(6)　晉欒魴帥師從衛孫文子伐齊。

19.3(4)　季武子如晉拜師，晉侯享之。范宣子為政，賦〈黍苗〉。季武子興，再拜稽首，曰：「小國之仰大國也，如百穀之仰膏雨焉。若常膏之，其天下輯睦，豈唯敝邑？」賦〈六月〉。

536　Zhonghang Yan is referring to Zhonghang Wu (Xun Wu), whose mother was from Zheng.

537　It was customary to put pearls, jade, shells, grains, or rice in the mouth of the deceased. The ritual was called *han* (含、唅), "to hold in the mouth." On unclosed eyes as a sign of being aggrieved in death, see also Wen 1.7.

538　Huan Tan (cited in *ZZ-Kong* 34.585) and Wang Chong (*Lunheng* 21.63.892–93) try to give a natural explanation of what happened—Zhonghang Yan has protruding eyes and clenched teeth in the final stage of his illness, but some time after he dies the tension relaxes, his eyes shut, and his mouth opens. The narrative here, however, obviously intends to show Zhonghang Yan's spirit responding to Luan Ying's promise.

539　Fan Gai regrets that he tried to appeal to Zhonghang Yan's self-interest, thereby underestimating him and showing his own limited understanding. Cf. Takezoe 16.26: "I am but a lesser man of shallow understanding"; and Karlgren, gl. 577: "I took him as shallow, but he was a real man."

540　We may surmise that Luan Ying sends Luan Fang on this expedition to fulfill the promise he made Zhonghang Yan. Sun Linfu has a special interest in attacking Qi because his foes, the exiled Lord Xian of Wei and his followers, are in Qi.

541　Ji Wuzi is thanking Jin for attacking Qi but probably also for defining the boundary between Lu and Zhu to Lu's advantage.

542　*Maoshi* 227, "Shumiao" 黍苗, 15B.513–15. The ode celebrates the Zhou Duke Shao's successful expedition against Xie and also praises him for honoring the exertion of his troops (or other lords who participated in the campaign). Fan Gai is using the ode to celebrate Jin's successful campaign and to honor the exertion of its allies.

The meaning of Zhonghang Yan's dream (Xiang 18.3) is fulfilled in his death. His sense of duty is such, however, that the rituals of death cannot be completed unless his spirit is assured that his expedition against Qi will continue. Despite Zhonghang Yan's role in the murder of Lord Li of Jin (Cheng 18.1), he is commended for his loyalty and determination.

Zhonghang Yan[a] was suffering from a tumor, which grew and ulcerated on his head. By the time he crossed the Yellow River and reached Zhuyong, he had become seriously ill and his eyes were protruding. The high officers who had returned to Jin earlier all came back. Fan Gai[a] requested to have an audience with him, but Zhonghang Yan refused to admit him. Fan Gai sent someone to ask who should succeed him, and he said, "My son born of the one from Zheng."[536] In the second month, on the *jiayin* day (19), he died, but his eyes were still open and staring, and his mouth could not be made to hold anything.[537] Fan Gai[b] went through the ablutions and then stroked his corpse, saying, "Dare I serve your son, Wu, in any way less than I serve you, master!" But he was still staring and they were unable to close his eyes. Luan Ying said, "Is it because he had not completed his undertaking against Qi?" He thus again stroked his corpse and said, "If, after the master dies, I do not continue your undertaking against Qi, let the Yellow River bear witness against me!" Zhonghang Yan's eyes thus closed and he received the jade to be put in his mouth.[538] Fan Gai[a] came out and said, "I with my shallow understanding took him to be a lesser man."[539]

19.1b

Luan Fang of Jin led out an army and followed Sun Linfu[a] of Wei as he attacked Qi.[540]

19.2(6)

Jin and Lu dignitaries use quotations from the Odes *to cement their ties. The celebration of military success is conjoined with images of amity, protection, and sustenance.*

Ji Wuzi went to Jin to bow in thanks for Jin's military assistance.[541] The Prince of Jin offered him ceremonial toasts. Fan Gai[b], who was in charge of government, recited "Millet Shoots."[542] Ji Wuzi rose, bowed twice with his forehead touching the ground, and said, "A small domain looks up to a great domain just as the hundred grains look up to nourishing rain. If they are constantly nourished, then there will be peace and harmony for all-under-heaven. How can it be merely our humble settlement that will benefit?" He recited "The Sixth Month."[543]

19.3(4)

---

543 Ji Wuzi's response alludes to the first two lines of "Millet Shoots": "Luxuriant are the millet shoots. / The cool rain has nourished them." *Maoshi* 177, "Liuyue" 六月, 10B.357–60, celebrates Yin Jifu's campaign against the Xianyun tribe. Ji Wuzi is comparing the Jin ruler or Jin commanders to Yin Jifu. Both "Millet Shoots" and "The Sixth Month" are set during the reign of King Xuan of Zhou (r. 827–782). Lord Mu of Qin recited "The Sixth Month" in Xi 23.6f.

19.4　季武子以所得於齊之兵作林鐘而銘魯功焉。臧武仲謂季孫曰：「非禮也。夫銘，天子令德，諸侯言時計功，大夫稱伐。今稱伐，則下等也；計功，則借人也；言時，則妨民多矣，何以為銘？且夫大伐小，取其所得，以作彝器，銘其功烈，以示子孫，昭明德而懲無禮也。今將借人之力以救其死，若之何銘之？小國幸於大國，而昭所獲焉以怒之，亡之道也。」

19.5(7)　齊侯娶于魯，曰顏懿姬，無子。其姪鬷聲姬，生光，以為大子。諸子仲子、戎子，戎子嬖。仲子生牙，屬諸戎子。戎子請以為大子，許之。仲子曰：「不可。廢常，不祥；間諸侯，難。光之立也，列於諸侯矣。今無故而廢之，是專黜諸侯，而以難犯不祥也。君必悔之。」公曰：「在我而已。」遂東大子光。使高厚傅牙，以為大子，夙沙衛為少傅。

544　Following Du Yu (*ZZ* 34.585), we read *ling* 令 as a verb, meaning "to inscribe" or "to manifest," to better sustain the symmetry with the following two clauses. But it is also possible to take the phrase *lingde* 令德 in its customary meaning of "exemplary virtue."

545　In *Wenxin diaolong* 11.387–425, Liu Xie uses the distinctions between virtue, achievements, and military campaigns to classify categories of inscriptions.

546　This can mean either that Lu's efforts under Jin's command are not commendable enough for it to "name campaigns" or that to "name campaigns" is already the least worthy motive for creating inscriptions.

547　Zi was their clan name, which meant they were daughters of Song.

548　Guang represented Qi in various covenants and expeditions; see, e.g., *Annals*, Xiang 3.5, 5.7, 5.11, 9.5, 10.1, 10.7, 11.4, and 11.8.

549　Since Guang has been widely recognized as heir apparent by the other princes, to displace him for no reason would be to treat the other princes with contempt. Zhong Zi's remonstrance earns her a place in the chapter on "Benevolent Sagacity" (Renzhi) in *Lienü zhuan* (3.58–59).

Inscribing Lu's martial achievement on a bronze bell, Ji Wuzi shows heedless arrogance, in contrast to his humble protestations in Jin (Xiang 19.3). The incident echoes his father Ji Wenzi's similarly presumptuous exploit when he built the Martial Palace to commemorate Lu's victory over Qi (Cheng 6.2). Zang Wuzhong remonstrates with Ji Wuzi. On the dangers of martial success for a small domain, see also Xiang 8.3.

Jin Wuzi used the metal from the weapons he obtained in Qi to cast a bell, tuned to the note of *lin*, and inscribed on it Lu's achievements. Zang Wuzhong said to Ji Wuzi[d], "This is not in accordance with ritual propriety. When it comes to inscriptions, the Son of Heaven manifests virtue;[544] the princes speak of good timing and tabulate achievements; and the high officers name their campaigns.[545] Now, we are of the lower echelons when it comes to naming campaigns;[546] we have relied on another's power to justify tabulating achievements; we have interfered with agricultural labor in too many ways to speak of good timing. What was there to inscribe? Moreover, when a great domain attacks a small one and takes its spoils to cast ritual vessels, it inscribes glorious achievements and shows its descendants how it manifested bright virtue and punished those who violated ritual propriety. Now when we have relied on another's power to save ourselves from death, why would we inscribe it? For a small domain that has, through sheer good fortune, overcome a great domain to then display its spoils in order to anger the latter is the way to destruction."

19.4

A crisis of succession arises in Qi: Lord Ling deposed his heir apparent, Guang, and instated Ya, the son of a favorite. Guang regains his position with the support of the Qi minister Cui Zhu and eliminates his opponents.

The Prince of Qi had taken a wife in Lu. She was called Yan Yi Ji, and she bore him no son. Her niece Zong Sheng Ji gave birth to Guang, who became the heir apparent. Among his concubines were Zhong Zi and Rong Zi,[547] and the latter was his favorite. Zhong Zi bore Ya and entrusted him to Rong Zi. Rong Zi requested that Ya should become the heir apparent. The Qi ruler assented. Zhong Zi said, "This will not do. To abandon the regular rule is inauspicious. To offend the princes will bring difficulties. Having been established as heir apparent, Guang is ranked among the princes.[548] Now to cast him aside for no reason is to arbitrarily defy the princes.[549] By trying something difficult to accomplish, you will also be committing an inauspicious transgression. You, my lord, will certainly regret it." The lord said, "It is all up to me." He thus moved heir apparent Guang to the eastern border. He sent Gao Hou to tutor Gongzi Ya[a], who became the heir apparent. Susha Wei became his junior preceptor.

19.5(7)

齊侯疾，崔杼微逆光，疾病而立之。光殺戎子，尸諸朝，非禮也。
婦人無刑。雖有刑，不在朝市。

　　夏，五月壬辰晦，齊靈公卒。莊公即位。執公子牙於句瀆之丘。以
夙沙衛易己，衛奔高唐以叛。

19.6(8)　晉士匄侵齊，及穀，聞喪而還，禮也。

19.7　於四月丁未，鄭公孫蠆卒，赴於晉大夫。范宣子言於晉侯，以其善於伐
秦也。六月，晉侯請於王，王追賜之大路，使以行，禮也。

19.8(10)　秋，八月，齊崔杼殺高厚於灑藍，而兼其室。書曰「齊殺其大夫，」從君
於昏也。

550　Qi used the Xia calendar and Lu the Zhou calendar, hence the discrepancy of two
months.

551　Gaotang 高唐 was located southeast of Gaotang County 高唐縣 in present-day
Shandong.

552　On this ritual, see also Xiang 4.21, Ai 10.3 and 15.2.

When the Prince of Qi fell ill, Cui Zhu secretly went to meet Guang and escorted him back. When the ruler's illness became critical, Cui Zhu established Guang as heir apparent. Guang had Rong Zi killed and exposed her corpse at court. This was not in accordance with ritual propriety. Women are not to be subjected to mutilating punishments. Even if one enforces such punishments, they would not be carried out in court or in the marketplace.

In summer, in the fifth month, on the *renchen* day (29), the last day of the month, Lord Ling of Qi died.[550] Lord Zhuang acceded to his position. He arrested Gongzi Ya at Goudou Knoll. He thought that Susha Wei was the one who had had him replaced by Gongzi Ya. Susha Wei[a] fled to Gaotang[551] and led it in revolt.

Fan Gai[a] of Jin invaded Qi. When he had advanced as far as Gu, he heard that the Qi ruler had died and thus began his return journey. This was in accordance with ritual propriety.[552]

19.6(8)

The Zheng nobleman Zijiao receives posthumous honors in recognition of his sound advice that the allies should cross the Jing River (Xiang 14.3) during the campaign against Qin.

In the fourth month, on the *dingwei* day (13), Zijiao[a] of Zheng died, and notice of his death was sent to the high officers of Jin. Fan Gai[a] spoke to the Prince of Jin about him, because he had acquitted himself well while attacking Qin. In the sixth month, the Prince of Jin made a request to the king. The king bestowed on him posthumously a great carriage,[553] which was used in the funeral procession. This was in accordance with ritual propriety.

19.7

The Qi high officer Gao Hou is put to death for having supported Gongzi Ya, Lord Zhuang's former rival. Gao Hou was criticized nine years earlier for irreverence (Xiang 10.1) and three years ago for inappropriate recitations from the Odes *(Xiang 16.1).*

In autumn, in the eighth month, Cui Zhu of Qi killed Gao Hou at Salan and appropriated his land and property.[554] That the text says, "Qi put to death its high officer," is because he followed the ruler blindly.

19.8(10)

---

553   According to *Maoshi*-Zheng 9C.333 (cited in *ZZ*-Kong 34.586), *dalu* 大路 refers to carriages used by those holding the rank of minister or above. Du Yu (*ZZ* 5.91) asserts that all carriages bestowed by the Zhou king could be called *dalu*; see Huan 2.2.

554   Salan 灑藍 was located just outside the Qi capital of Linzi 臨淄, Shandong.

19.9(11) 鄭子孔之為政也專，國人患之，乃討西宮之難與純門之師。子孔當罪，
以其甲及子革、子良氏之甲守。甲辰，子展、子西率國人伐之，殺子孔而
分其室。書曰「鄭殺其大夫」，專也。

　　子然、子孔，宋子之子也；士子孔，圭媯之子也。圭媯之班亞宋
子，而相親也；二子孔亦相親也。僖之四年，子然卒；簡之元年，士子孔
卒。司徒孔實相子革、子良之室，三室如一，故及於難。子革、子良出奔
楚。子革為右尹。鄭人使子展當國，子西聽政，立子產為卿。

19.10 齊慶封圍高唐，弗克。冬，十一月，齊侯圍之。見衛在城上，號之，乃下。
問守備焉，以無備告。揖之，乃登。聞師將傅，食高唐人。殖綽、工僂會
夜縋納師，醢衛于軍。

19.11(13) 城西郛，懼齊也。

---

555 See Xiang 10.8 and 18.4.

556 Both Song Zi and Gui Gui were concubines of Lord Mu of Zheng.

557 The fourth year of the rule of Lord Xi of Zheng was 567 BCE.

558 The first year of the rule of Lord Jian was 565 BCE.

559 Susha Wei and Lord Zhuang of Qi are probably separated by a moat surrounding the city during this exchange. Du Yu (ZZ 34.587), following Jia Kui, believes that Lord Zhuang bows to Susha Wei to thank him for his frankness, and possibly to convey the wish to spare him. Takezoe (16.31) claims that Lord Zhuang is bowing to bid Susha Wei farewell.

560 Zhi Chuo was captured by Jin (Xiang 18.3) but has been repatriated to Qi. This scheme succeeds probably because the men of Gaotang are away at Susha Wei's feast.

Further conflicts occur between rival lineages in Zheng: Zikong, guilty of complicity in an earlier rebellion (Xiang 10.9) and collusion with Chu (Xiang 18.4), is killed for trying to monopolize power. Zichan, who demonstrated his sagacity earlier (Xiang 8.3, 10.9, 15.4), becomes a minister.

Zikong of Zheng monopolized power in the way he ran the government. Troubled by this, the inhabitants of the capital chastised him for the disaster at the Western Palace and the military action at the Chun Gate,[555] for which Zikong bore the guilt. He used his own armored soldiers and armored soldiers from Ran Dan[a]'s and Ziliang's lineages as guards. On the *jiachen* day (11), Gongsun Shezhi[a] and Zixi led the inhabitants of the capital to attack him. They put Zikong to death and divided his lands and property. That the text says, "Zheng put to death its high officer," is because he had monopolized power.

    Ziran and Zikong were the sons of Song Zi. Shi Zikong was the son of Gui Gui.[556] Gui Gui's rank was lower than Song Zi's, but the two were attached to each other, as were the half brothers, the two Zikongs. In the fourth year of Lord Xi,[557] Ziran died. In the first year of Lord Jian,[558] Shi Zikong died. It was none other than the supervisor of conscripts, Zikong[b], who assisted with the management of the lands and property of both Ran Dan[a] (son of Ziran) and Ziliang (son of Shi Zikong). The three houses were as one, and that was why they were embroiled in the disaster. Ran Dan[a] and Ziliang left the domain and fled to Chu, and Ran Dan[a] became deputy of the right in Chu. The men of Zheng had Gongsun Shezhi[a] take charge of the domain. They had Zixi attend to administration and established Zichan as minister.

Lord Zhuang of Qi completes the purge of Gongzi Ya's supporters. The eunuch Susha Wei seems ingenuous and self-assured as he meets his doom.

Qing Feng of Qi laid siege to Gaotang but failed to overcome it. In winter, in the eleventh month, the Prince of Qi laid siege to it. He saw Susha Wei[a] on the city wall and called out to him, so the latter came down. When the Qi ruler asked him about his preparations for defense, he told him there was no preparation. The Qi ruler bowed to Susha Wei, who then ascended the wall.[559] When Susha Wei[a] heard that the Qi army was planning to press close to the city walls, he feasted the men of Gaotang. Zhi Chuo and Gonglü Hui let down ropes to bring up Qi troops during the night.[560] They minced and pickled Susha Wei[a] amid the army.

We fortified the western outer city walls because we feared Qi.

19.9(11)

19.10

19.11(13)

19.12(14,15)　齊及晉平，盟于大隧。故穆叔會范宣子于柯。穆叔見叔向，賦〈載馳〉之
四章。叔向曰：「肸敢不承命！」穆叔歸，曰：「齊猶未也，不可以不懼。」
乃城武城。

19.13　衛石共子卒，悼子不哀。孔成子曰：「是謂蹶其本，必不有其宗。」

春秋

20.1(1)　二十年，春，王正月辛亥，仲孫速會莒人盟于向。

20.2(2)　夏，六月庚申，公會晉侯、齊侯、宋公、衛侯、鄭伯、曹伯、莒子、邾子、
滕子、薛伯、杞伯、小邾子盟于澶淵。

20.3　秋，公至自會。

20.4(3)　仲孫速帥師伐邾。

20.5(4)　蔡殺其大夫公子燮。蔡公子履出奔楚。

20.6(4)　陳侯之弟黃出奔楚。

20.7(5)　叔老如齊。

20.8　冬，十月丙辰朔，日有食之。

20.9(6)　季孫宿如宋。

561　Dasui 大隧 was located in Gaotang County 高唐縣, Shandong.

562　*Maoshi* 54, "Zai chi" 載馳, 3B.124–26. Shusun Bao cites the fourth stanza to convey
his plaint and appeal to Jin for protection: "I go forth in the wilderness. / Luxuriant
grows the caltrop. / I appeal to the great domain. / To whom could I go, on whom
rely? / High officers and noble men, / Do not hold me guilty. / All your many plans
/ Are not equal to what I propose." "Gallop" is said to have been composed by Lady
Mu of Xǔ (Min 2.5b) as she planned to seek Qi help to revive the fortunes of her natal
Wei. Gongzi Guisheng of Zheng also recited the last stanza of "Gallop" in Wen 13.5.

563　Shuxiang pledges to assist Lu to counter Qi aggression.

Qi and Jin reached an accord and swore a covenant at Dasui.[561] That was why Shusun Bao[a] met with Fan Gai[c] at Ke. Shusun Bao[a] had an audience with Shuxiang and recited the fourth stanza of "Gallop."[562] Shuxiang said, "Would I presume not to receive your command?"[563] When Shusun Bao[a] came back, he said, "Qi has not yet stopped its aggressive ambitions. We cannot but be fearful." We therefore fortified Wucheng.

19.12(14,15)

The Wei minister Kong Chengzi predicts doom for a Wei nobleman who shows no grief at his father's funeral. The nobleman is exiled nine years later (Xiang 28.3). For comparable prophecies, see Cheng 14.5 and Xiang 31.5.

Shi Mai[a] of Wei died, and his son Shi E[a] showed no grief. Kong Chengzi said, "This is called tearing out the roots. He will surely not keep his ancestral line."

19.13

LORD XIANG 20 (553 BCE)
ANNALS

In the twentieth year, in spring, in the royal first month, on the *xinhai* day (21), Zhongsun Su (Meng Zhuangzi) met with a Ju leader and swore a covenant at Xiang.

20.1(1)

In summer, in the sixth month, on the *gengshen* day (3), our lord met with the Prince of Jin, the Prince of Qi, the Duke of Song, the Prince of Wei, the Liege of Zheng, the Liege of Cao, the Master of Ju, the Master of Zhu, the Master of Teng, the Liege of Xue, the Liege of Qi, and the Master of Lesser Zhu and swore a covenant at Chanyuan.[564]

20.2(2)

In autumn, our lord arrived from the meeting.

20.3

Zhongsun Su (Meng Zhuangzi) led out troops and attacked Zhu.

20.4(3)

Cai put to death its high officer Gongzi Xie. Gongzi Lü of Cai departed and fled to Chu.

20.5(4)

The younger brother of the Prince of Chen, Huang, departed and fled to Chu.

20.6(4)

Shu Lao went to Qi.

20.7(5)

In winter, in the tenth month, on the *bingchen* day, the first day of the month, there was an eclipse of the sun.

20.8

Jisun Su (Ji Wuzi) went to Song.

20.9(6)

---

564 According to Yao Nai, Chanyuan 澶淵, formerly in Wei, is at this point in Jin (Yang, 3:1052). It was located northwest of present-day Puyang County 濮陽縣, Henan.

左傳

20.1(1)　二十年，春，及莒平。孟莊子會莒人盟于向，督揚之盟故也。

20.2(2)　夏，盟于澶淵，齊成故也。

20.3(4)　邾人驟至，以諸侯之事弗能報也。秋，孟莊子伐邾以報之。

20.4(5, 6)　蔡公子燮欲以蔡之晉，蔡人殺之。公子履，其母弟也，故出奔楚。
　　　　陳慶虎、慶寅畏公子黃之偪，愬諸楚曰：「與蔡司馬同謀。」楚人以為討，公子黃出奔楚。
　　　　初，蔡文侯欲事晉，曰：「先君與於踐土之盟，晉不可棄，且兄弟也。」畏楚，不能行而卒。楚人使蔡無常，公子燮求從先君以利蔡，不能而死。書曰「蔡殺其大夫公子燮」，言不與民同欲也；「陳侯之弟黃出奔楚」，言非其罪也。公子黃將出奔，呼於國曰：「慶氏無道，求專陳國，暴蔑其君，而去其親，五年不滅，是無天也。」

565　Lord Wen of Cai died in 592 BCE (*Annals*, Xuan 17.4). For the Covenant of Jiantu, see Xi 28.3i.

566　Chu might have made ever more severe and unpredictable demands, but Cai has been closer to Chu than to Jin, and Cai leaders probably fear reprisals from Chu.

567　The implied "rule" in the *Annals* is that the designation of Huang as the Chen ruler's younger brother indicates that he is not guilty—hence Kong Yingda's subcommentary (ZZ-Kong 34.588): "When an elder brother harms a younger brother, the latter is called 'younger brother' to make manifest the older brother's guilt."

568　For the death of Qing Hu and Qing Yin three years later, see Xiang 23.2.

The Covenant of Duyang (Xiang 19.1) paves the way for an accord between Lu and Ju, which lasts until 538 BCE (Zhao 4.5).

In the twentieth year, in spring, we reached an accord with Ju. Meng Zhuangzi met with a Ju leader and swore a covenant at Xiang: this was on account of the Covenant of Duyang.

The peace agreement between Qi and Jin now extends to other domains.

In summer, the princes swore a covenant at Chanyuan: this was on account of the peace agreement with Qi.

Hostilities between Lu and Zhu break out despite the Covenant of Chanyuan.

The men of Zhu repeatedly attacked us. We could not retaliate on account of our involvement in the affairs of the princes. In autumn, Meng Zhuangzi attacked Zhu in retaliation.

The relationship with Chu determines the fate of nobles in smaller domains: Gongzi Xie of Cai is put to death for trying to make Cai shift allegiance from Chu to Jin, and Gongzi Huang of Chen, accused of being Gongzi Xie's accomplice, flees to Chu to clear his name.

Gongzi Xie of Cai wanted to bring Cai over to Jin, and for that the leaders of Cai put him to death. It was for this reason that Gongzi Lü, who was Xie's younger full brother, departed and fled to Chu.

Qing Hu and Qing Yin of Chen feared the encroachment of Gongzi Huang and slandered him to Chu leaders: "He was in league with the Cai supervisor of the military Gongzi Xie." The men of Chu intended to chastise him for it, but Gongzi Huang departed and fled to Chu.

Earlier, Lord Wen of Cai had wanted to serve Jin. He said, "The former ruler participated in the Covenant of Jiantu. Jin cannot be cast off. Moreover, we are brother domains." But he was afraid of Chu, and he died before he could make the trip to Jin.[565] The leaders of Chu made demands on Cai without any regard for regular procedure. Gongzi Xie sought to follow the wishes of the former lord in order to benefit Cai, but he failed and died for it. The text says, "Cai put to death its high officer Gongzi Xie": this is to indicate that he did not share the same wishes with the people.[566] "The younger brother of the Prince of Chen, Huang, left the domain and fled to Chu": this is to indicate that the fault was not his.[567] When Gongzi Huang was about to depart and flee, he proclaimed in the capital: "These Qings lack the Way and seek to monopolize power in Chen. They defy and scorn their ruler and remove his kin. If they are not destroyed in five years, then there is no Heaven."[568]

20.5(7)　齊子初聘于齊，禮也。

20.6(9)　冬，季武子如宋，報向戌之聘也。褚師段逆之以受享，賦〈常棣〉之七章以卒。宋人重賄之。歸，復命，公享之，賦〈魚麗〉之卒章。公賦〈南山有臺〉。武子去所，曰：「臣不堪也。」

20.7　衛甯惠子疾，召悼子曰：「吾得罪於君，悔而無及也。名藏在諸侯之策，曰『孫林父、甯殖出其君』。君入，則掩之。若能掩之，則吾子也。若不能，猶有鬼神，吾有餒而已，不來食矣。」悼子許諾，惠子遂卒。

<hr>

569　Xiang Xu went on an official visit to Lu five years earlier (Xiang 15.1).

570　*Maoshi* 164, "Chang di" 常棣, 9B.320–23 also cited in Xi 24.2b, Zhao 1.4, 7.11. The ode celebrates the concord of brothers. The context might well have been a clan feast. The last two stanzas further emphasize fraternal harmony in joyous households.

571　*Maoshi* 170, "Yu li" 魚麗, 9D.341–42. The final stanza affirms how the feast is fine and bountiful because of timely action. Ji Wuzi is praising the Song mission as a timely charge.

Shu Lao[a] went on an official visit to Qi for the first time in Lord Zhuang's reign. This was in accordance with ritual propriety.

20.5(7)

As envoy in Song, Ji Wuzi emphasizes Lu-Song amity through an ode on fraternal harmony. The success of the mission is underlined in an exchange of Odes *citations between Lord Xiang of Lu and Ji Wuzi upon the latter's return. Despite the exchange of compliments, the rift between the Lu ruling house and the powerful Ji lineage is deepening.*

In winter, Ji Wuzi went to Song in answer to Xiang Xu's official visit.[569] The market overseer Duan met him and led him to receive the ceremonial toasts. Ji Wuzi recited the seventh and final stanzas of "Cherry Trees."[570] The leaders of Song gave him handsome gifts. He returned and reported the discharge of his mission. The lord offered him ceremonial toasts, and he recited the final stanza of "Fish Netted."[571] The lord recited "On the Southern Hills Grows Nut Grass." Ji Wuzi[c] left his place at the feast and said, "I am not worthy of that."[572]

20.6(9)

The Wei minister Ning Zhi drove Lord Xian into exile six years earlier (Xiang 14.4) but is compelled on his deathbed by the fear of leaving a bad name in historical records to enjoin his son Ning Xi to bring back the exiled ruler. The entry in Annals, Xiang 14.4, may reflect the "covering up" that Ning Zhi refers to.[573] Ning Xi eventually restores Lord Xian (Xiang 26.2). On how anticipation of how one's actions will be recorded influences choices, see also Zhuang 23.1 and Wen 15.2.

When Ning Zhi[a] of Wei was very ill, he summoned his son Ning Xi[a] and said to him, "I am guilty of a crime against the ruler. I regret it, but it is too late to do anything about it. My name has been stored up in the bamboo slips of the princes, which say, 'Sun Linfu and Ning Zhi drove out their ruler.' If the ruler reenters the domain, then that can be covered up. If you can cover that up, then you are truly my son. If you cannot, then I will not come to imbibe your offerings even if there are ghosts and spirits and I am one of them: I would rather suffer hunger."[574] Ning Xi[a] assented and promised to do so, and Ning Zhi[b] then died.

20.7

---

572 *Maoshi* 172, "Nan shan you tai" 南山有臺, 10A.347. The ode praises the noble man as "the foundation of the realm and home" and "the light of the realm and home." Ji Wuzi protests that the praise is excessive.

573 See n. 365 above.

574 Ning Zhi is saying that he will disavow Ning Xi as his son. On hungry ghosts, see also Xuan 4.2.

春秋

21.1(1)　二十有一年，春，王正月，公如晉。

21.2(2)　邾庶其以漆、閭丘來奔。

21.3　夏，公至自晉。

21.4(5)　秋，晉欒盈出奔楚。

21.5　九月庚戌朔，日有食之。

21.6　冬，十月庚辰朔，日有食之。

21.7(6)　曹伯來朝。

21.8(7)　公會晉侯、齊侯、宋公、衛侯、鄭伯、曹伯、莒子、邾子于商任。

左傳

21.1(2)　二十一年，春，公如晉，拜師及取邾田也。

21.2a(2)　邾庶其以漆、閭丘來奔，季武子以公姑姊妻之，皆有賜於其從者。於是魯多盜。季孫謂臧武仲曰：「子盍詰盜？」
　　　　武仲曰：「不可詰也。紇又不能。」

575　It is not possible to have solar eclipses in two successive months, although partial eclipses may be observed in two different places over that period of time This is a mistake either with observation or with recording (Yang, 3:1056; Huang Zongxi, cited in Takezoe, 16.20).

576　Shangren 商任 was located in present-day Anyang County 安陽縣, Henan.

577　In *Maoshi* 255, "Dang" 蕩, 18A.641–44, "giving entry to brigands and criminals" (*kou rang shi nei* 寇攘式內) is also one of the charges King Wen of Zhou levels against Shang.

578　Lord Xiang's aunt should be Lord Cheng's sister and Lord Xuan's daughter. Lord Xuan died thirty-nine years ago, and this aunt must therefore be around forty or older. She might have been a widow. Shen Qinhan (cited in Karlgren, gl. 579) maintains that *guzi* 姑姊 refers to a daughter of Lord Xiang's aunt.

579　Alternatively, there may be an implied connection: "as a result, there were many brigands in Lu."

In the twenty-first year, in spring, in the royal first month, our lord went to Jin.

21.1(1)

Shuqi of Zhu, bringing Qi and Lüqiu with him, came in flight.

21.2(2)

In summer, our lord arrived from Jin.

21.3

In autumn, Luan Ying of Jin departed and fled to Chu.

21.4(5)

In the ninth month, on the *gengxu* day, the first day of the month, there was an eclipse of the sun.

21.5

In winter, in the tenth month, on the *gengchen* day, the first day of the month, there was an eclipse of the sun.[575]

21.6

The Liege of Cao came to visit our court.

21.7(6)

Our lord met with the Prince of Jin, the Prince of Qi, the Duke of Song, the Prince of Wei, the Liege of Zheng, the Liege of Cao, the Master of Ju, and the Master of Zhu at Shangren.[576]

21.8(7)

ZUO

Lord Xiang repeats Ji Wuzi's mission, thanking Jin (Xiang 19.3) for using its army against Qi (Xiang 18.3) and for giving Zhu territories to Lu (Xiang 19.1).

In the twenty-first year, in spring, our lord went to Jin to bow in thanks for its military assistance and for taking the fields of Zhu.

21.1(2)

Shuqi of Zhu is generously rewarded for offering Zhu settlements to Lu leaders. We may surmise that Shuqi tried unsuccessfully to rebel against the Zhu ruler and is seeking refuge in Lu by offering the Zhu settlements of Qi and Lüqiu as a bribe. Zang Wuzhong argues that harboring Shuqi amounts to a miscarriage of justice that causes brigandry to flourish in Lu. For similar arguments equating acceptance of miscreants with complicity, see Wen 18.7, Xiang 26.2, Zhao 7.2, Ai 14.2.[577] On how a ruler's example can change mores, see Yin 5.1, Huan 2.2, and Zhuang 23.1, 24.1, 24.2.

Shuqi of Zhu, bringing Qi and Lüqiu with him, came in flight. Ji Wuzi gave our lord's aunt to him as wife[578] and bestowed gifts on all his followers. At that time there were many brigands in Lu.[579] Ji Wuzi[d] said to Zang Wuzhong, "Why have you not stopped the brigands?"

21.2a(2)

Zang Wuzhong[a] said, "They cannot be stopped. And in any case, I would be incapable of doing it."

季孫曰：「我有四封，而詰其盜，何故不可？子為司寇，將盜是務去，若之何不能？」

武仲曰：「子召外盜而大禮焉，何以止吾盜？子為正卿，而來外盜；使紇去之，將何以能？庶其竊邑於邾以來，子以姬氏妻之，而與之邑。其從者皆有賜焉。若大盜禮焉以君之姑姊與其大邑，其次皁牧輿馬，其小者衣裳劍帶，是賞盜也。賞而去之，其或難焉。紇也聞之：在上位者洒濯其心，壹以待人；軌度其信，可明徵也，而後可以治人。夫上之所為，民之歸也。上所不為，而民或為之，是以加刑罰焉，而莫敢不懲。若上之所為，而民亦為之，乃其所也，又可禁乎？《夏書》曰：

> 念茲在茲，
> 釋茲在茲，
> 名言茲在茲，
> 允出茲在茲，
> 惟帝念功。

將謂由己壹也。信由己壹，而後功可念也。」

21.2b　庶其非卿也，以地來，雖賤，必書，重地也。

580　Du Yu claims that the settlements in question refer to Qi and Lüqiu, but these are probably Lu settlements; otherwise, they would not count as a gift (Takezoe, 16.38).

581　The word translated here and later in the passage as "integrity" is *yi* 壹, which means, literally, "oneness"—the complete coincidence of appearance and reality, word and deed.

582　Cf. *Mencius* 3A.2: "If those in positions above desire something, those below are sure to do so in an even more extreme way."

583　This fragment becomes part of "Da Yu mo" in *Shangshu* 4.52–59. For "Da Yu mo," see n. 106.

Ji Wuzi said, "We have borders on all four sides. Why should it be impossible to stop the brigands? You are the supervisor of corrections, and removing brigands is precisely what you should strive to do. How can you be incapable of it?"

Zang Wuzhong said, "You, sir, have summoned brigands from abroad and have honored them with a great show of courtesy. How can we curb our own brigands? You, sir, are the chief minister, and yet brigands from abroad have been brought in because of you. You would have me eliminate our brigands, but on what basis can I do so? When Shuqi stole settlements from Zhu and used them to seek refuge with us, you married Lady Ji to him and also offered him settlements.[580] His followers all have gifts bestowed on them. If a prominent brigand is treated with a show of courtesy by being given the ruler's aunt and her major settlement, and if for the lesser ones there are lackeys, herdsmen, carriages, and horses, and if even for the least among them there are clothes, swords, and belts, then this amounts to rewarding brigands. Will it not perhaps be difficult to eliminate them by giving them rewards? I have heard, those in positions above can govern others only when they cleanse their hearts of deviance, treat others with integrity,[581] and set their good faith within proper bounds to which one can clearly appeal. For what those above do is that to which the people turn.[582] What those above do not do, some among the people may yet do. Consequently, punishment is meted out to them, and none would dare not to accept chastisement. If the people also do what those above do, then the situation we have is inevitable. Indeed, how could it be prevented? It says in the *Xia Documents*,

> That which you think of depends on this,
> That which you forgive depends on this.
> That which you speak of in your command depends on this,
> That which you truly reject depends on this.
> Only the god on high is to think of these achievements.[583]

Perhaps this refers to how results must come from one's own integrity. When good faith comes from one's own integrity, then achievements can be recorded."

The following exegetical comment claims that the Annals *places special importance on territorial gains, an attitude that, however, has just been decried as immoral.*

Shuqi was not a minister but he came bringing land. Although his position was lowly, this had to be recorded because of the importance placed on land.

21.2b

21.3(2) 齊侯使慶佐為大夫，復討公子牙之黨，執公子買于句瀆之丘。公子鉏來奔。叔孫還奔燕。

21.4 夏，楚子庚卒。楚子使蔿子馮為令尹，訪於申叔豫。叔豫曰：「國多寵而王弱，國不可為也。」遂以疾辭。方暑，闕地，下冰而牀焉。重繭，衣裘，鮮食而寢。楚子使醫視之。復曰：「瘠則甚矣，而血氣未動。」乃使子南為令尹。

21.5a(4) 欒桓子娶於范宣子，生懷子。范鞅以其亡也，怨欒氏，故與欒盈為公族大夫而不相能。桓子卒，欒祁與其老州賓通，幾亡室矣。懷子患之。

---

584 Since Wei Ziping seems too sick to be apointed, King Kang settles on his uncle
     Zinan as the next choice. Zinan was King Gong's younger brother.

585 See Li Long-shien, "Xian Qin xushi wenxian."

586 Fan Yang was forced to flee to Qin because Luan Yan accused him of bringing about
     the death of his younger brother Luan Qian and threatened to kill him. Fan Yang
     had predicted the Luan lineage's downfall in an exchange with the Qin ruler seven
     years earlier (Xiang 14.3).

587 This may refer to mismanagement or Zhou Bin's appropriation of the Luan lineage's
     property. Cf. Qian Zhongshu's alternative reading of *wangshi* 亡室 (*wushi* 無室)
     as "effacing division between inner quarters (*shi* 室) and the outside world"; i.e., the
     liaison was flagrant and became public knowledge (*Guanzhui bian*, 1:213–14). See
     Zhao 25.6 for another story of a widow's disastrous liaison with an inferior.

The Qing lineage rises in Qi, and Lord Zhuang of Qi continues to persecute the party of Gongzi Ya, his rival for the Qi throne.

The Prince of Qi appointed Qing Zuo high officer. He further chastised the party of Gongzi Ya, arresting Gongzi Mai at Goudou Knoll. Gongzi Chu came in flight. Shusun Xuan fled to Yan.   21.3(2)

Wei Ziping of Chu avoids being appointed chief minister by feigning illness. Shen Shuyu, who implicitly counsels him to refuse the appointment, turns out to be right. Zinan, the new chief minister, comes to grief the following year (Xiang 22.4).

In summer, Zigeng of Chu died. The Master of Chu appointed Wei Ziping chief minister, and the latter consulted with Shen Shuyu. Shen Shuyu[a] said, "There are many who enjoy special favor in the domain, and the king is young. The domain cannot be governed properly." Wei Ziping thus declined on the grounds of illness. Just then the weather was hot. He dug a hole in the ground, filled it with ice, and set up his bed over it. He wore two padded silk robes and a fur coat, ate little, and lay on the bed. The Chu ruler sent a physician to examine him. The physician reported, "He was emaciated in the extreme, but his blood and breath are not yet unsettled." The king thus appointed Zinan[584] chief minister.   21.4

The old enmity between the Luan and Fan lineages (Xiang 14.3) flares up again because Luan Qi, daughter of Fan Gai and wife of Luan Yan, is involved in an adulterous and ruinous liaison and plots against her own son Luan Ying in order to forestall the latter's punishment of her lover. Fan Gai eliminates supporters of the Luan lineage. While Zuozhuan focuses on the power struggle between the Luan and Fan lineages, Guoyu ("Jin yu 8," 14.447–51) presents the Jin ruler Lord Ping and his adviser Yang Bi as the ones who destroy the Luan lineage in the interest of centralizing power. Xinian (bamboo strips 91–95) and Shiji (39.1683–84) subsume Luan's rebellion into a narrative about Qi-Jin relations.[585]

Luan Yan[c] married a daughter of Fan Gai[c]. She bore Luan Ying[c]. Fan Gai's son Fan Yang resented the Luan lineage because of his exile.[586] That was why, though he and Luan Yan both served as high officers of ruling lineages, they could not abide each other. After Luan Yan[d] died, his wife Luan Qi had a liaison with the senior steward of the Luan lineage, Zhou Bin, who liquidated almost all the land and property of the Luan lineage.[587] Luan Ying[b] was outraged by this.   21.5a(4)

祁懼其討也，愬諸宣子曰：「盈將為亂，以范氏為死桓主而專
政矣，曰：『吾父逐鞅也，不怒而以寵報之，又與吾同官而專之。吾父死
而益富。死吾父而專於國，有死而已，吾蔑從之矣。』其謀如是，懼害於
主，吾不敢不言。」范鞅為之徵。

懷子好施，士多歸之。宣子畏其多士也，信之。懷子為下卿，宣子
使城著而遂逐之。秋，欒盈出奔楚。宣子殺箕遺、黃淵、嘉父、司空靖、
邴豫、董叔、邴師、申書、羊舌虎、叔羆，囚伯華、叔向、籍偃。

21.5b　人謂叔向曰：「子離於罪，其為不知乎？」叔向曰：「與其死亡若何？
《詩》曰：

優哉游哉，
聊以卒歲。

知也。」

588　Fan Yang should not have been allowed to return but instead was appointed, along
with Luan Yan, as a high officer of a ruling lineage (Xiang 16.1).
589　As Wei Xi (cited in Takezoe, 16.42) points out, Luan Ying seems to have been the
precursor of the Warring States nobleman supporting a group of talented men who
are in turn fanatically devoted to him.
590　He was the assistant commander of the lower army, ranking sixth among the
ministers.
591　Fan Gai thus plucks Luan Ying from a military milieu where he had direct control
over his troops. He sends Luan Ying to Zhu presumably because of its distance from
the Jin capital. This Zhu 著, a place in Jin, should not be confused with the small
domain of Zhu 邾 near Lu.
592　These ten are of the same party as Luan Ying.
593　All three seem to have been subsequently released.

His mother, Luan Qi[a], feared he would punish Zhou Bin and slandered Luan Ying to her father, Fan Gai[b]: "Luan Ying[a] is about to start a revolt. He thinks the Fan lineage brought about Luan Yan's death in order to monopolize power in the government. He says, 'My father drove Fan Yang[d] away. Upon his return, Fan Gai, instead of being angry, requited him with special favor.[588] Moreover, Fan Yang's rank is the same as mine, yet he monopolizes power. My father died and the Fan lineage became even richer. Since he brought about my father's death and has monopolized power in the domain, I would rather die: I am not going to go along with him!' Such is his plot, and I fear that he may harm you, Father. I did not dare not to speak up." Fan Yang confirmed what she said by his own testimony.

Luan Ying[b] was generous and liberal with gifts, and many officers became loyal to him.[589] Fan Gai[b], apprehensive that Luan Ying had the support of so many officers, believed the accusation. Luan Ying[b] was the lower minister.[590] Fan Gai[b] appointed him to fortify Zhu and then drove him away.[591] In autumn, Luan Ying departed and fled to Chu. Fan Gai[b] put to death Ji Yi, Huang Yuan, Jia Fu, Supervisor of Works Jing, Bing Yu, Dong Shu, Bing Shi, Shen Shu, Yangshe Hu, and Shu Pi[592] and imprisoned Yangshe Chi[a], Shuxiang (Yangshe Xi), and Ji Yan.[593]

Through his half brother Yangshe Hu, the Jin minister Shuxiang is implicated in the purge of the Luan lineage, but he maintains his equanimity. He ignores an offer for help from the Jin ruler's favorite, Yue Wangfu, and places his hopes in Qi Xi, who showed his impartiality earlier (Xiang 3.4). Qi Xi is also the prescient judge of Shuxiang's character in Shuoyuan *11.372 and in* Kongzi jiayu *3.29. Shuxiang's judgment of Qi Xi's fair-mindedness summarizes the message of the anecdote and harks back to Xiang 3.4.*

Someone asked Shuxiang, "You have been implicated in a crime. Is that not because you are unwise?" Shuxiang said, "How does that compare to death or exile? It says in the *Odes*,   21.5b

> Freely, easily,
> Just let the year come to an end like this.[594]

This is wisdom."

---

594 These lines are from an ode no longer extant. The first quoted line appears in the final stanza of *Maoshi* 222, "Cai shu" 采菽, 15A.503, which praises the noble man for fulfilling the king's commands. Whereas Shuxiang emphasizes composed detachment, that ode glorifies engagement with duties. Shuxiang is chided for failing to confirm his alliance with the Fan lineage, and he responds by citing lines lauding the wisdom of being uninvolved.

樂王鮒見叔向，曰：「吾為子請。」叔向弗應。出，不拜。其人皆咎叔向。叔向曰：「必祁大夫。」室老聞之，曰：「樂王鮒言於君，無不行，求赦君子，吾子不許。祁大夫所不能也，而曰必由之，何也？」

叔向曰：「樂王鮒，從君者也，何能行？祁大夫外舉不棄讎，內舉不失親，其獨遺我乎？《詩》曰：

> 有覺德行，
> 四國順之。

夫子覺者也。」

21.5c　晉侯問叔向之罪於樂王鮒。對曰：「不棄其親，其有焉。」

於是祁奚老矣，聞之，乘馹而見宣子，曰：「《詩》曰：

> 惠我無疆，
> 子孫保之。

書曰：

> 聖有謨勳，
> 明徵定保。

Yue Wangfu had a meeting with Shuxiang and said, "I will intercede on your behalf." Shuxiang did not respond. When he went out, Shuxiang did not bow. His followers all rebuked Shuxiang. Shuxiang said, "It has to be the high officer Qi Xi." His senior steward heard about this and said, "Nothing that Yue Wangfu tells the ruler fails to be done! He sought to have you pardoned, and you, sir, refused. A pardon is something the high officer Qi Xi will not be able to accomplish, and yet you say it has to be done through him. How can it be?"

Shuxiang said, "Yue Wangfu is one who follows the ruler. How can he accomplish this? The high officer Qi Xi, in recommending those outside his lineage, did not cast out his enemy; and in recommending those inside his lineage, he did not neglect his kin.[595] How could I alone be passed over by him? As it says in the *Odes*,

> To the power of upright virtue
> Domains on four sides will submit.[596]

That fine man is an upright man."

Shuxiang's predictions are fulfilled. Yue Wangfu implies Shuxiang's guilt, while Qi Xi eloquently praises his indispensable talents and argues against guilt by association.

The Prince of Jin asked Yue Wangfu about Shuxiang's guilt. He replied, "He would not have abandoned his kin and probably played a role."

At that time Qi Xi was already old and had retired.[597] He heard about this and rode in a courier-carriage to have an audience with Fan Gai[b].[598] He said, "It says in the *Odes*,

> Their beneficence for us is boundless;
> May sons and grandsons forever guard it.[599]

It says in the *Documents*,

> The sages have their plans and instructions, for which there is
> clear evidence and steady protection.[600]

21.5c

---

598 The carriage Qi Xi rides, *ri* 馹, is probably the same as the courier-carriage (*chuan-che*) mentioned in Cheng 5.4. His choice of the *ri* carriage emphasizes the urgency of his mission. Gu Yanwu (*Rizhi lu jishi*, 29.671) identifies the *ri* 馹 as *yi* 驛.

599 *Maoshi* 269, "Lie wen" 烈文, 18A.710–12. Qi Xi is using a hymn glorifying Zhou dynastic destiny to remind Fan Gai that a virtuous and talented man like Shuxiang is crucial for the continuation of just and glorious rule.

600 These lines are included in "Yin zheng" (*Shangshu* 7.102). For "Yin zheng," see n. 428.

夫謀而鮮過、惠訓不倦者，叔向有焉，社稷之固也，猶將十世宥之，以勸
能者。今壹不免其身，以棄社稷，不亦惑乎？鯀殛而禹興；伊尹放大甲
而相之，卒無怨色；管、蔡為戮，周公右王。若之何其以虎也棄社稷？子
為善，誰敢不勉？多殺何為？」

　　宣子說，與之乘，以言諸公而免之。不見叔向而歸，叔向亦不告免
焉而朝。

21.5d　初，叔向之母妒叔虎之母美而不使，其子皆諫其母。其母曰：「深山大
澤，實生龍蛇。彼美，余懼其生龍蛇以禍女。女，羝族也。國多大寵，不
仁人間之，不亦難乎？余何愛焉？」使往視寢，生叔虎，美而有勇力，欒
懷子嬖之，故羊舌氏之族及於難。

601　The "single misstep" or "one thing" refers to Shuxiang's being the half brother of
　　　Yangshe Hu, who was favored by Luan Ying.

602　Gun, the father of the legendary sage-king Yu, did not fulfill his charge of stopping
　　　the floods and was put to death by Shun. Yu succeeded where his father failed.

603　Yi Yin, the chief minister of Tang, the first Shang king, exiled Tang's grandson,
　　　Taijia, to the Tong Palace for three years when he deemed Taijia unfit for kingship.
　　　Taijia showed no resentment after he was restored as king.

604　Guan Shu, Cai Shu, and the Zhou Duke were all sons of King Wen, brothers of King
　　　Wu, and uncles of King Cheng. The Zhou Duke quelled the rebellion of Guan Shu
　　　and Cai Shu and supported King Cheng.

605　In the first case, the son was not blamed for the father's failure. In the second case,
　　　ruler and minister rose above rancor. In the third case, a minister is not blamed for
　　　his brothers' rebellion. Qi Xi thus questions guilt by association and criticizes exces-
　　　sive resentment.

606　Qi Xi cannot go to court with the courier-carriage; hence, Fan Gai offers his
　　　carriage.

607　This story also appears in *Lüshi chunqiu* 21.1427, where it serves a broader argument
　　　about judicious rewards and punishment. The injustice of excessive punishment is
　　　said to be far worse than that of excessive rewards, a point also made in Xiang
　　　26.10a.

Shuxiang is one who rarely errs in making plans and who tirelessly benefits us with instruction. He is the firm basis of the altars of our domain, and even his descendants ten generations hence should be pardoned so as to encourage men of talent. Is it not deluded if now you fail to spare his life because of a single misstep and, in doing so, abandon the altars of the domain?[601] Gun was put to death but Yu was raised to office.[602] Yi Yin exiled Taijia but later Yi Yin continued as Taijia's minister, and to the end Taijia showed no resentment.[603] Guan Shu and Cai Shu[604] were executed, but their brother the Zhou Duke was the king's chief helper.[605] How can you, on account of Yangshe Hu[b], abandon the altars of the domain? If you do good, who will dare not to try their best? What is the point of putting so many to death?"

Fan Gai[b] was pleased. Riding with Qi Xi in the same carriage, he spoke to the lord about the matter and had Shuxiang pardoned.[606] Qi Xi returned without seeing Shuxiang, and Shuxiang, for his part, had not told him of his acquittal before he attended court.[607]

Yangshe Hu and Shuxiang are implicated through no apparent flaw in their characters or judgment. The beauty of Yangshe Hu's mother is retrospectively presented as the cause of troubles for the Yangshe lineage. The femme fatale Xia Ji's daughter, who marries Shuxiang, features in a similar argument thirty-eight years later (Zhao 28.2) in the account of the fall of the Yangshe lineage. Both prescient judgments come from Shuxiang's mother, who might have been motivated by jealousy. References to possible jealousy are removed in her story in the chapter entitled "Benevolent Sagacity" (Renzhi 仁智) in Lienü zhuan 3.61–64.

Earlier, Shuxiang's mother was jealous of Yangshe Hu's mother, who was beautiful but was not sent to wait on their husband. Her sons all remonstrated with their mother. Their mother said, "It is great mountains and deep marshes that produce dragons and snakes. She is beautiful, and I fear she will give birth to dragons and snakes to bring disaster upon you.[608] Yours is a declining house, and the domain has many that enjoy great favor. Will it not be ruinous when ignoble persons set them against you? Why else would I begrudge her our husband?" Shuxiang's mother thus sent her to wait on their husband in the bedchamber. She bore Yangshe Hu, who was handsome, valiant, and strong. Luan Ying[c] was enamored of him. That was why the Yangshe house came to grief.

21.5d

---

608 Shuxiang's mother argues in Zhao 28.2b that great beauty is pernicious. Cf. *Guoyu,* "Jin yu 1," 7.255–63, where the scribe Su lists the beautiful femme fatales in history and concludes that great beauty comes with a heart of evil; cf. *Xunzi* 12.278; *Lunheng jiaoshi* 66.958.

21.5e 欒盈過於周，周西鄙掠之。辭於行人曰：「天子陪臣盈得罪於王之守臣，將逃罪。罪重於郊甸，無所伏竄，敢布其死：昔陪臣書能輸力於王室，王施惠焉。其子黶不能保任其父之勞。大君若不棄書之力，亡臣猶有所逃。若棄書之力，而思黶之罪，臣，戮餘也，將歸死於尉氏，不敢還矣。敢布四體，唯大君命焉。」

　　王曰：「尤而效之，其又甚焉。」使司徒禁掠欒氏者，歸所取焉，使候出諸轘轅。

21.6(7) 冬，曹武公來朝，始見也。

21.7(8) 會於商任，錮欒氏也。

　　齊侯、衛侯不敬。叔向曰：「二君者必不免。會朝，禮之經也；禮，政之輿也；政，身之守也。怠禮，失政；失政，不立，是以亂也。」

609　That is, Luan Ying has offended Lord Ping of Jin. Fan Gai banished Luan Ying in the name of the Jin ruler. Du Yu (*ZZ* 34.592) thinks that "the subject guarding the king" (*wang zhi shouchen* 王之守臣) refers to Fan Gai, but it is hard to imagine that Luan Ying would be so complimentary toward his enemy.

610　According to Du Yu (*ZZ* 34.592), "distant outskirts" (*dian* 甸) is the area beyond "outskirts" (*jiao* 郊). In addressing his plaint to the king, Luan Ying has to politely efface the boundary between victim and offender. He thus describes his plight in terms of his own presumed guilt.

611　Literally, "to set forth four limbs." Here we follow Du Yu's reading (*ZZ* 34.593). Takezoe (16.46) suggests that the phrase means "to be ready for any punishments." Both interpretations are plausible.

612　King Ling of Zhou is saying that Jin wronged the Luan lineage by persecuting it, and further mistreatment of Luan Ying would make the injustice even greater. Takezoe (16.46) suggests that the "wrong" refers to some unspecified crime of Luan Yan's (Xiang 21.46).

613　For the term *hou* or *houren* ("attending officer"), see Xuan 12.2f.

614　Huanyuan 轘轅 Mountain was located northwest of Dengfeng County 登封縣 in present-day Henan.

615　Fan Gai is trying to bar Luan Ying from seeking refuge in other domains. Both *Gongyang*, Xiang 21 (20.257), and *Guliang*, Xiang 21 (16.157), record the birth of Confucius in an entry following the Shangren meeting, the last entry for this year: "In the eleventh month, on the *gengzi* day, Confucius was born" (*Gongyang*); "On the *gengzi* day, Confucius was born" (*Guliang*).

Luan Ying, fleeing persecution in Jin, is robbed in Zhou. He states his case with humility and dignity to the royal envoy, arguing that his grandfather's merit outweighs his father's possible culpability.

When Luan Ying was passing through Zhou, a group on its western marches robbed him. He set forth his case to the king's envoy: "I, Ying, the subject of one serving the Son of Heaven, have offended against the king's subject, the guardian of his land.[609] I had intended to escape the consequences of my guilt, but I am again found guilty at the distant outkirts of the king's domain.[610] With nowhere to hide or escape, I presume to set forth what may cost me death: formerly, the subject of your subject, Luan Shu[e], was able to fully exert himself on behalf of the royal house, and the king bestowed favors on him. His son, Luan Yan[b], could not guard the fruits of his father's toil. If the great ruler does not cast off the efforts of Luan Shu[e], then there is still a place to which this exiled subject can escape. If the great ruler casts off Luan Shu[e]'s efforts and instead thinks of Luan Yan[b]'s guilt, then this subject, who barely escaped punishment, intends to face death under your sentencing officer. I dare not go back. I have presumed to hide nothing[611] and will abide by nothing but the command of the great ruler."

21.5e

The king said, "To imitate a wrong makes for an even greater wrong."[612] He sent the supervisor of conscripts to stop those who had been robbing Luan Ying and to make them return what they had taken. He sent the attending officer[613] to lead him out by way of Huanyuan Mountain.[614]

In winter, Lord Wu of Cao came to visit our court. This was the first time he had an audience with us.

21.6(7)

At the meeting at Shangren, Shuxiang predicts disaster for the rulers of Qi and Wei, which comes to pass in Xiang 25.2 and 26.2.

The princes met at Shangren: this was to bar Luan Ying from refuge in other domains.[615]

21.7(8)

The Prince of Qi and the Prince of Wei were not respectful. Shuxiang said, "The two rulers will certainly not escape disaster. Meetings and court visits are the warp threads of ritual propriety; ritual propriety is the vehicle for government; government is the means for guarding one's person. To debase ritual propriety is to lose control of government; to lose control of government is to fail to establish oneself as a person. On this account disorder will ensue."

21.8 知起、中行喜、州綽、邢蒯出奔齊，皆欒氏之黨也。樂王鮒謂范宣子曰：
「盍反州綽、邢蒯？勇士也。」宣子曰：「彼欒氏之勇也，余何獲焉？」王
鮒曰：「子為彼欒氏，乃亦子之勇也。」

　　齊莊公朝，指殖綽、郭最曰：「是寡人之雄也。」州綽曰：「君以為
雄，誰敢不雄？然臣不敏，平陰之役，先二子鳴。」莊公為勇爵，殖綽、
郭最欲與焉。州綽曰：「東閭之役，臣左驂迫，還於門中，識其枚數，其
可以與於此乎？」公曰：「子為晉君也。」對曰：「臣為隸新，然二子者，譬
於禽獸，臣食其肉而寢處其皮矣。」

春秋

22.1 二十有二年，春，王正月，公至自會。

22.2 夏，四月。

616　This is already very close to the ethos of "keeping retainers" (*yangshi* 養士) during
the Warring States period. It transpires that Fan Gai does not act on Yue Wangfu's
advice.

617　I.e., they are his "superb warriors." The word *xiong* 雄 means literally "male birds,"
and the bird metaphor continues with Zhou Chuo's remark on "crowing" (in the lore
of cockfights, the victor is supposed to be the first to crow). Lord Zhuang may be specifically comparing the brave men at his court to fighting cocks.

618　See Xiang 18.3.

Brave men who belong to Luan Ying's party flee to Qi. The question arises as to whether and how talent can be dissociated from loyalty. Fan Gai refuses to employ his enemy's adherents, but these men protest their worth to their new master, the Qi ruler, also a former enemy. One of them, Zhou Chuo, boasts of his valor and composure during the Qi-Jin conflict at Pingyin. On the issue of valuing talent, see also Gongsun Guisheng's famous speech in Xiang 26.10.

Zhi Qi, Zhonghang Xi, Zhou Chuo, and Xing Kuai departed and fled to Qi. They were all partisans of the Luan lineage. Yue Wangfu said to Fan Gai^c, "Why not have Zhou Chuo and Xing Kuai come back? These are valiant men." Fan Gai^b said, "Their valor is for the Luan lineage. What do I have to gain by it?" Wangfu said, "If you were to be their Luan Ying, they would then be your valiant men."[616]

    Lord Zhuang of Qi was holding court and pointed to Zhi Chuo and Guo Zui: "These are my fighting cocks."[617] Zhou Chuo said, "If you, my lord, consider them fighting cocks, who would dare to consider them otherwise? However, this subject, for all his lack of talent, crowed before these two at the Pingyin campaign."[618] Lord Zhuang created a special official rank to honor valiant men.[619] Zhi Chuo and Guo Zui wanted to belong to it. Zhou Chuo said, "During the East Gate campaign, my flanking horse on the left, having been pressed to a halt, caused the chariot to turn around in the middle of the gate. I came to know the number of bosses upon the gate.[620] Can I, because of that, share in this rank?" The lord said, "You were doing that for the Jin ruler." He replied, "I am new as your servant. But as for these two men, if I may compare them to beasts—I wish I could eat their flesh and sleep on their pelts already!"[621]

LORD XIANG 22 (551 BCE)
ANNALS

In the twenty-second year, in spring, in the royal first month, our lord arrived from the meeting.

Summer, the fourth month.

21.8

22.1

22.2

---

619   This follows Du Yu's (*ZZ* 34.593) reading. Takezoe (16.48) reads *jue* 爵 as "wine cups."

620   See Xiang 18.3.

621   Literally, "I would have already eaten their flesh and slept on their pelts!" Zhou Chuo despises them because he shot Zhi Chuo and took both Zhi Chuo and Guo Zui prisoners in Xiang 18.3c. Similar (but more laconic) expressions conveying contempt come up in Xiang 28.9 and Zhao 3.10.

22.3 秋，七月辛酉，叔老卒。

22.4(5) 冬，公會晉侯、齊侯、宋公、衛侯、鄭伯、曹伯、莒子、邾子、薛伯、杞伯、
小邾子于沙隨。

22.5 公至自會。

22.6(6) 楚殺其大夫公子追舒。

左傳

22.1 二十二年，春，臧武仲如晉。雨，過御叔。御叔在其邑，將飲酒，曰：「焉
用聖人？我將飲酒，而己雨行，何以聖為？」穆叔聞之，曰：「不可使也，
而傲使人，國之蠹也。」令倍其賦。

22.2 夏，晉人徵朝于鄭。鄭人使少正公孫僑對，曰：

In autumn, in the seventh month, on the *xinyou* day (16), Shu Lao died.　　22.3

In winter, our lord met with the Prince of Jin, the Prince of Qi, the Duke　　22.4(5)
of Song, the Prince of Wei, the Liege of Zheng, the Liege of Cao, the
Master of Ju, the Master of Zhu, the Liege of Xue, the Liege of Qǐ, and the
Master of Lesser Zhu at Shasui.

Our lord arrived from the meeting.　　22.5

Chu put to death its high officer Gongzi Zhuishu (Zinan).　　22.6(6)

ZUO

The Lu high officer Yu Shu is punished for mocking Zang Wuzhong's assi-
duity. Yu Shu contrasts his pleasures (symbolized by drinking) with Zang's
reputation of wisdom that leads only to hard work.

In the twenty-second year, in spring, Zang Wuzhong went to Jin. It was　　22.1
raining, and he passed by Yu Shu's abode. Yu Shu, who happened to be
in his settlement, was about to drink wine and said, "What use is there
for a sage? I am about to drink, while he is traveling in the rain. What
good does it do to be a sage?" Shusun Bao[a] heard this and said, "He cannot be employed, and yet he disdains the person sent as envoy.[622] He is
the vermin in the domain." He ordered to have his levy doubled.

The Zheng minister Zichan blames Zheng's vacillations (Xiang 8.7) on Jin's
ritual impropriety and implies that Zheng may claim the moral high
ground precisely because of its victimization by Jin and Chu. Reminding
Jin of Zheng's earlier defiance at Xi (Xiang 9.5) and its submission at
Xiaoyu (Xiang 11.5), Zichan combines resistance to Jin's demands with the
professed intent of loyalty. This is the first of Zichan's rhetorical defenses
of Zheng's rights vis-à-vis Jin (see also Xiang 24.2a, 25.10, 28.8, 31.6, Zhao
16.3).

In summer, the leaders of Jin summoned Zheng to attend court. The　　22.2
leaders of Zheng sent its junior director,[623] Zichan[a], to reply as follows:

622　Du Yu (ZZ 35.598) links both *shi* 使 to the diplomatic mission: "He cannot be sent
　　as envoy, and yet he disdains the person sent as envoy." Our reading of the first *shi* as
　　"use" or "employ" (*shiyong* 使用) follows Lu Deming (cited in Karlgren, gl. 589;
　　Takezoe, 16.49).
623　Zichan ranked third among ministers in Zheng; see Xiang 19.9.

在晉先君悼公九年，我寡君於是即位。即位八月，而我先大
夫子駟從寡君以朝于執事，執事不禮於寡君，寡君懼。因
是行也，我二年六月朝于楚，晉是以有戲之役。楚人猶竟，
而申禮於敝邑。敝邑欲從執事，而懼為大尤，曰：「晉其謂
我不共有禮。」是以不敢攜貳於楚。我四年三月，先大夫子
蟜又從寡君以觀釁於楚，晉於是乎有蕭魚之役。謂我敝邑，
邇在晉國，譬諸草木，吾臭味也，而何敢差池？

　　楚亦不競，寡君盡其土實，重之以宗器，以受齊盟。遂
帥群臣隨于執事，以會歲終。貳於楚者，子侯、石盂，歸而
討之。湨梁之明年，子蟜老矣，公孫夏從寡君以朝于君，見
於嘗酎，與執燔焉。間二年，聞君將靖東夏，四月，又朝以
聽事期。不朝之間，無歲不聘，無役不從。以大國政令之無
常，國家罷病，不虞荐至，無日不惕，豈敢忘職？

---

624   The first year of Lord Jian of Zheng was the ninth year of Lord Dao of Jin and the eighth year of Lord Xiang of Lu (565 BCE).

625   Zisi must have accompanied Lord Jian to Jin after the meeting at Xingqiu (Xiang 8.4).

626   Jin and Zheng disputed the terms of the covenant at Xi, and Jin was unable to make Zheng submit (Xiang 9.5).

627   Note the deliberate contrast between Jin treating the Zheng ruler "without ritual propriety" (*buli* 不禮) and Chu "extending ritually proper treatment" (*shenli* 申禮) to Zheng.

628   Zichan designates Jin as "the domain that abides by ritual propriety" as a reminder that Jin should be held to high moral standards.

629   It is part of Zichan's diplomatic rhetoric that Zheng's trip to Chu to attend court should be presented as an attempt to distance itself from Chu or perhaps even to observe Chu's vulnerability and seek the possible opening for military action.

630   Ji Wuzi employs the same analogy in referring to the relationship between Jin and Lu (Xiang 8.8, n. 174).

631   For the Covenant of the Ju Dam (557 BCE), see Xiang 16.1.

632   Zichan is referring to Jin's expedition against Qi, situated to the east of Jin. In 555 BCE, Zheng joined the princes to lay siege to Qi (Xiang 18.2), and two years later Zheng participated in the Covenant of Chanyuan (Xiang 20.2).

633   Zheng thus visited the Jin court two months prior to the meeting at Chanyuan.

It was in the ninth year of the reign of Lord Dao, former ruler of Jin, when our unworthy ruler acceded to his position.[624] Eight months later, our former high officer Zisi accompanied our unworthy ruler to visit the court of those charged with government in Jin.[625] They failed to treat our unworthy ruler with ritual propriety, and our unworthy ruler was fearful. It was because of this trip that, in the sixth month of the second year of our lord's reign, we visited the Chu court. That was the reason that Jin undertook the Xi campaign.[626] Chu was still strong, and extended ritually proper treatment to our humble settlement.[627] We wished to follow those charged with government in Jin, but were afraid of incurring great blame. We said, "Jin will think that we were disrespectful toward the domain that abides by ritual propriety."[628] We thus did not dare waver in our allegiance by turning to Chu. In the third month of the fourth year of our lord's reign, our former high officer Zijiao again accompanied our unworthy ruler to Chu to look for an opening for maneuvers.[629] That was why Jin undertook the Xiaoyu campaign. We considered our humble settlement so close to Jin that, to take an analogy from plants, we are to Jin what fragrance is to flowers and fruits.[630] How should we dare to diverge from them?

Also, Chu was no longer strong. In order to take part in a Jin-led covenant solemnized by fasting and purification, our unworthy ruler exhausted the produce of his land and in addition offered ancestral vessels. He thus led some of his subjects to follow those charged with government in Jin and attended the meeting at the year's end in the Jin court. Upon our return we chastised Zihou and Shi Yu, who had shifted allegiance to Chu. The year following the Covenant of the Ju Dam, Zijiao retired on account of old age, and Zixi[a] accompanied our unworthy ruler to visit the court of your ruler.[631] He was received at the summer sacrifice that involved offerings of thrice-distilled spirits and took his share of the sacrificial meat. Two years passed, and we heard that your ruler was planning to pacify the Eastern Xia.[632] In the fourth month, we again visited the court of Jin to await your command regarding the time of the meeting.[633] In the intervals when there was no court visit, there has been no year in which we did not make an official visit to Jin, no campaign in which we did not follow Jin. As the policies and commands of your great domain are inconstant, our domain and patrimony are weakened and diminished. With unexpected troubles frequently coming upon us, there have been no days when we could let down our guard. How would we dare to forget our duties toward Jin?

大國若安定之，其朝夕在庭，何辱命焉？若不恤其患，
而以為口實，其無乃不堪任命，而翦為仇讎？敝邑是懼，其
敢忘君命？委諸執事，執事實重圖之。

22.3　秋，欒盈自楚適齊。晏平仲言於齊侯曰：「商任之會，受命於晉。今納欒
氏，將安用之？小所以事大，信也。失信，不立。君其圖之。」弗聽。退告
陳文子曰：「君人執信，臣人執共。忠、信、篤、敬，上下同之，天之道也。
君自棄也，弗能久矣。」

22.4　九月，鄭公孫黑肱有疾，歸邑于公，召室老、宗人立段，而使黜官、薄
祭。祭以特羊，殷以少牢，足以共祀，盡歸其餘邑，曰：「吾聞之：生於亂
世，貴而能貧，民無求焉，可以後亡。敬共事君與二三子。生在敬戒，不
在富也。」

<hr>

634　Karlgren (gl. 529) relates "empty words" to Zheng's distress: "But if you have no
compassion for our distress, and instead regard it as empty complaints . . ."
635　Xiang 21.7.
636　The same line appears in Xiang 8.7a and Ai 7.4a.
637　Lord Zhuang of Qi is murdered three years later (Xiang 25.2).

If your great domain will grant us peace and stability, we will attend your court day and night. Why would you need to condescend to command us? But if you have no compassion for our distress, and instead fob us off with empty words,[634] will that not make us unfit to bear your commands? Will you not be discarding us and turning us into enemies? This is what our humble domain fears. How would we dare to forget your ruler's commands? We entrust this case to those charged with government in Jin, in the hope that they will give it serious consideration.

The Jin noble Luan Ying, persecuted by the Fan lineage (Xiang 21.5), flees to Qi, following his supporters who had already found refuge there (Xiang 21.8). Yan Ying urges their removal for fear of offending Jin, but the Qi ruler does not heed him.

In autumn, Luan Ying went from Chu to Qi. Yan Ying[a] said to the Prince of Qi, "At the meeting at Shangren,[635] we received the command from Jin. Now if we take Luan Ying in, how do we plan to use him? That by which the small domain serves the great one is good faith.[636] If one loses good faith, one will not stand. You, my lord, should consider it." The lord did not heed him. Yan Ying withdrew and told Chen Xuwu[a], "Those who would rule over men well hold on to good faith; those who would serve men well hold on to reverence. When those in high and low positions share loyalty, good faith, steadfastness, and reverence, it is the Way of Heaven. The ruler has abandoned what he owes himself. He cannot last for long."[637]

The Zheng noble Gongsun Heigong (son of Ziyin and grandson of Lord Mu of Zheng), on his deathbed, seeks to protect his Yin lineage by making it less wealthy and powerful. Heigong's ideas anticipate a similar argument by the Qi minister Yan Ying (Xiang 28.11a, 29.13e, Zhao 10.2c).

In the ninth month, Gongsun Heigong of Zheng was ill. He returned his settlement to the lord. Having summoned his senior steward and ancestral attendant to establish Yin Duan as his successor, he made them reduce the number of his retainers and diminish the elaborateness of sacrifices. One single sheep was to be used for a regular sacrifice; a lesser set of animals, comprising only a sheep and a pig, was to be used for a grand sacrifice. He kept enough land to provide for the sacrifices and had the rest of the settlement all returned to the lord, saying, "I have heard that if high-placed men, being born in an age of disorder, can make themselves poor, so that the people make no demands of them, they will be able to perish later than others. Reverently serve the ruler and his various fine men. Survival depends on reverence and vigilance, not on wealth."

己巳，伯張卒。君子曰：「善戒。《詩》曰：

> 慎爾侯度，
> 用戒不虞。

鄭子張其有焉。」

22.5(4) 冬，會于沙隨，復錮欒氏也。
欒盈猶在齊。晏子曰：「禍將作矣。齊將伐晉，不可以不懼。」

22.6a(5) 楚觀起有寵於令尹子南，未益祿而有馬數十乘。楚人患之，王將討焉。
子南之子棄疾為王御士，王每見之，必泣。棄疾曰：「君三泣臣矣，敢問誰之罪也？」
王曰：「令尹之不能，爾所知也。國將討焉，爾其居乎？」
對曰：「父戮子居，君焉用之？洩命重刑，臣亦不為。」
王遂殺子南於朝，轘觀起於四竟。

---

638 *Maoshi* 256, "Yi" 抑, 18A.644–49.

639 That Guan Qi received emoluments rather than titles and ranks suggests that Guan Qi was a commoner. His possession of these horses thus went well beyond his station.

640 Qiji was King Kang's cousin.

On the *jisi* day (25), Gongsun Heigong[b] died. The noble man said, "He excelled at urging vigilance. As it says in the *Odes*,

> Pay heed to your manner and measure as prince,
> And in this way use vigilance against the unforeseen.[638]

Gongsun Heigong[a] of Zheng probably had such qualities!"

The Qi minister Yan Ying repeats his earlier warning (Xiang 22.3) about impending Jin hostilities prompted by Luan Ying's presence in Qi. A year later, Luan Ying returns to Jin with Qi help, and Qi attacks Jin in retaliation for the Pingyin campaign (Xiang 18.3). Yan Ying foresees the disastrous consequences of Qi aggression.

In winter, the princes met at Shasui to try again to bar Luan Ying from refuge in other domains.   22.5(4)

Luan Ying was still in Qi. Yan Ying[b] said, "Disaster is about to rear its head. Qi is about to attack Jin. We cannot but be fearful."

The Chu chief minister, Zinan, favors a commoner who flaunts his consequence. For this and other unspecified crimes, King Kang of Chu executes him but wants to spare his son Qiji. Torn between filial duty and loyalty, Qiji kills himself. Chu rulers prune overreaching ministers, in contrast to Jin rulers, who have been sidelined by powerful lineages in Jin.

Guan Qi of Chu found favor with the chief minister, Zinan. His official emoluments had not yet been increased; nonetheless, he had scores of teams of horses.[639] The men of Chu were troubled by it, and the king planned to chastise Zinan and Guan Qi. Zinan's son Qiji was in the king's royal guard.[640] The king always wept whenever he saw Qiji. Qiji said, "Three times now you have wept before me, my lord. Dare I ask whose crime it is?"   22.6a(5)

The king said, "The chief minister's malfeasance is well known to you. The domain plans to chastise him. Will you still stay if that happens?"

He replied, "If the father is executed and the son stays, what can you, my lord, use the son for? But I will never reveal your command, lest I incur even greater punishment."[641]

The king thus put Zinan to death at court and had chariots tear Guan Qi limb from limb at the place where roads from four directions converged.[642]

---

641 Qiji would have been guilty of betraying the king's confidence had he disclosed his command. Had he communicated the king's plan to Zinan, the latter might also have started an insurrection and incurred even greater punishment.

642 Following Karlgren, gl. 595. Cf. Du Yu's (ZZ 35.600) different reading: "torn by chariots and circulated" (*che lie yi xun* 車裂以徇), which implies that the torn limbs were circulated among "territories in four directions" (*sijing* 四竟).

子南之臣謂棄疾：「請徙子尸於朝。」曰：「君臣有禮，唯二三子。」三日，棄疾請尸。王許之。既葬，其徒曰：「行乎？」曰：「吾與殺吾父，行將焉入？」曰：「然則臣王乎？」曰：「棄父事讎，吾弗忍也。」遂縊而死。

22.6b 復使薳子馮為令尹，公子齮為司馬，屈建為莫敖。有寵於薳子者八人，皆無祿而多馬。他日朝，與申叔豫言，弗應而退。從之，入於人中。又從之，遂歸。退朝，見之，曰：「子三困我於朝，吾懼，不敢不見。吾過，子姑告我，何疾我也？」

對曰：「吾不免是懼，何敢告子？」

曰：「何故？」

對曰：「昔觀起有寵於子南，子南得罪，觀起車裂，何故不懼？」

自御而歸，不能當道。至，謂八人者曰：「吾見申叔，夫子所謂生死而肉骨也。知我者如夫子則可；不然，請止。」辭八人者，而後王安之。

---

643 Zinan's retainers are proposing to steal Zinan's corpse so that it can be buried with the proper rites. Qiji, however, does not wish to move Zinan's corpse without the king's permission.

644 Had King Kang not felt a personal attachment to Qiji and divulged his plans to him, Qiji could have sought refuge in another domain because he would not have been party to his father's death.

Zinan's retainers said to Qiji: "We beg to move the master's corpse from the court." Qiji said, "There is ritual propriety that obtains between ruler and subject. It will be up to the various ministers to decide."[643] Three days later, Qiji begged to have his father's corpse, and the king gave his permission. After Zinan had been buried, his followers said, "Are you leaving?" Qiji said, "I was party to the killing of my father; if I leave, where can I go?" They said, "In that case, will you then be the king's subject?" He said, "I cannot bear to abandon my father and serve the enemy." He thereupon hanged himself.[644]

The new Chu chief minister, Wei Ziping, makes the same mistake as his predecessor and gathers favorites who parade their privileges. Shen Shuyu, who earlier advised Wei against accepting the appointment (Xiang 21.4), dramatizes his censure.

The king again appointed Wei Ziping chief minister. Gongzi Yi became supervisor of the military, and Qu Jian became maréchal. Those who found favor with Wei Ziping were eight in number, and without exception they had no emolument but many horses. Some days later at court, Wei Ziping tried to talk to Shen Shuyu, but the latter withdrew without responding. Wei Ziping followed him, but he disappeared into the crowd. He again followed him, whereupon the latter returned home. After Wei Ziping had retired from court, he went to see Shen Shuyu and said, "Three times you have shunned me at court. I am fearful and do not dare not to see you. If I am at fault, you should just tell me. Why do you abhor me so?"

He replied, "What I fear is that I will not escape disaster. How would I presume to tell you anything?"

Wei Ziping said, "What is this all about?"

He replied, "Formerly, Guan Qi gained favor with Zinan. Zinan was found guilty, and Guan Qi was torn apart with carriages. Why should I not be fearful?"

Wei Ziping then drove the carriage himself and returned home, but he could not keep his chariot on the road properly.[645] When he arrived, he said to the eight persons, "I had an audience with Shen Shuyu[b]. It may be said of the master that he breathes life into the dead and puts flesh on bleached bones. Those among you who know me as the master does can stay. Otherwise, please go." Only after he had dismissed these eight men did the king feel at peace with him.

22.6b

---

645 Wei drives home himself presumably because he is eager to disband his favorites, but he is so preoccupied with Shen Shuyu's warning that he cannot drive his carriage properly.

十二月，鄭游販將歸晉，未出竟，遭逆妻者，奪之，以館于邑。丁巳，其夫攻子明，殺之，以其妻行。

子展廢良而立大叔，曰：「國卿，君之貳也，民之主也，不可以苟。請舍子明之類。」求亡妻者，使復其所。使游氏勿怨。曰：「無昭惡也。」

春秋

23.1　二十有三年，春，王二月癸酉朔，日有食之。

23.2(1)　三月己巳，杞伯匄卒。

23.3　夏，邾畀我來奔。

23.4　葬杞孝公。

23.5(2)　陳殺其大夫慶虎及慶寅。

23.6　陳侯之弟黃自楚歸于陳。

23.7(3)　晉欒盈復入于晉，入于曲沃。

23.8(4)　秋，齊侯伐衛，遂伐晉。

23.9(4)　八月，叔孫豹帥師救晉，次于雍榆。

23.10(5)　己卯，仲孫速卒。

23.11(5)　冬，十月乙亥，臧孫紇出奔邾。

646　*Dingsi* was the fourteenth day of the eleventh month. The "twelfth month" above might be a mistake for "eleventh month."

647　We may surmise that Liang is also suspected of being ruthless like his father.

The Zheng noble You Fan abuses his power by taking away the wife of a presumably lower-ranking man, who kills him. The Zheng chief minister, Gongsun Shezhi, pardons the killer and establishes You Fan's younger brother You Ji as head of the You lineage.

In the twelfth month, You Fan of Zheng was about to return to Jin. Before he passed beyond the border of the domain, he encountered someone escorting home his new bride. He seized the bride and lodged her in his settlement. On the *dingsi* day,[646] the bride's husband attacked You Fan[a], killed him, and, taking back his wife, went away.

Gongsun Shezhi[a] deposed You Fan's son Liang and instead established You Ji[a], the oldest of You Fan's younger brothers, as his successor. He said, "A minister of the domain is the ruler's second and the master of the people. One cannot be careless about his appointment. Let us cast aside You Fan's[a] kind."[647] He sought the man who had lost his wife and had him return home.[648] He made sure the You lineage did not resent him, saying, "Do not make a wrongdoing even more flagrant."

LORD XIANG 23 (550 BCE)
ANNALS

In the twenty-third year, in spring, in the royal second month, on the *guiyou* day, the first day of the month, there was an eclipse of the sun.   23.1

In the third month, on the *jisi* day (28), Gai, the Liege of Qi, died.   23.2(1)

In summer, Biwo of Zhu came in flight.   23.3

Lord Xiao of Qi was buried.   23.4

Chen put to death its high officers Qing Hu and Qing Yin.   23.5(2)

Huang, the younger brother of the Prince of Chen, went home from Chu to Chen.   23.6

Luan Ying of Jin again entered Jin. He entered Quwo.   23.7(3)

In autumn, the Prince of Qi attacked Wei. He then attacked Jin.   23.8(4)

In the eighth month, Shusun Bao led out troops, went to the aid of Jin, and set up camp at Yongyu.[649]   23.9(4)

On the *jimao* day (10), Zhongsun Su (Meng Zhuangzi) died.   23.10(5)

In winter, in the tenth month, on the *yihai* day (7), Zangsun He (Zhang Wuzhong) departed and fled to Zhu.   23.11(5)

---

648 Having killed You Fan, that man presumably fled Zheng.
649 Yongyu 雍榆 was located in Jin southwest of present-day Jun County 浚縣, Henan.

23.12(6)　晉人殺欒盈。

23.13(7)　齊侯襲莒。

左傳

23.1(2)　二十三年，春，杞孝公卒，晉悼夫人喪之。平公不徹樂，非禮也。禮，為
鄰國闕。

23.2(5)　陳侯如楚，公子黃愬二慶於楚，楚人召之。使慶樂往，殺之。慶氏以陳
叛。夏，屈建從陳侯圍陳。陳人城，板隊而殺人。役人相命，各殺其長，
遂殺慶虎、慶寅。楚人納公子黃。君子謂慶氏不義，不可肆也。故《書》
曰：「惟命不于常。」

23.3a(7)　晉將嫁女于吳，齊侯使析歸父媵之，以藩載欒盈及其士，納諸曲沃。欒
盈夜見胥午而告之。對曰：「不可。天之所廢，誰能興之？子必不免。吾
非愛死也，知不集也。」

650　Lord Ping's mother, the widow of Lord Dao, was the younger sister of Lord Xiao of
　　　Qí. Her marriage to Lord Dao was arranged in 573 BCE (Cheng 18.7).

651　Wooden frames holding pounded earth between them were used in the construc-
　　　tion of city walls.

652　The translation follows Du Yu's reading (ZZ 35.602). Takezoe (17.3) suggests that the
　　　plank fell down and killed someone. But it is less obvious why that accident should
　　　lead to the workmen's insurrection.

653　*Shangshu*, "Kang gao," 14.206. Fan Xie quotes the same line during the battle of
　　　Yanling (Cheng 16.5k). Cf. *Maoshi* 235, "Wen wang" 文王, 16A.536: "Heaven's Man-
　　　date is not constant."

654　Takezoe (5.35, 12.64–65) suggests that *ying* 媵 can sometimes mean just "escort" and
　　　can apply to either a man or a woman: "the Prince of Qi sent Xi Guifu to escort her
　　　(the Jin lady)."

655　Luan Ying sought refuge in Qi the year before, much to Yan Ying's chagrin (Xiang
　　　22.3). Here Qi smuggles Luan Ying into Jin to foment disorder there. Du Yu (ZZ
　　　35.602) claims that Quwo was Luan Ying's settlement, but as Jin's former capital,
　　　Quwo should not have become a minister's settlement. It is possible that Quwo
　　　covered a large area and had subdivisions, one of which became Luan's settlement.
　　　There could also have been two places named Quwo, one in Shanxi and one in
　　　Henan, as Zhang Qi suggests in his study of geography in *Zhanguo ce* (Yang, 3:1073;
　　　Takezoe, 17.3).

Jin leaders put Luan Ying to death.   23.12(6)

The Prince of Qi made a surprise attack on Ju.   23.13(7)

ZUO

Lord Ping of Jin is criticized for failing to observe mourning for the ruler of a neighboring domain who was also his maternal uncle. On the occasions that call for the cessation of musical performances, see also Cheng 5.4, Xiang 26.10, and Zhao 9.5.

In the twenty-third year, in spring, Lord Xiao of Qi died. The widow of   23.1(2)
Lord Dao of Jin went into mourning for him. Lord Ping did not stop the usual musical performances. This was not in accordance with ritual propriety. According to ritual, music should be suspended on the occasion of the death of a ruler of a neighboring domain.[650]

Gongzi Huang of Chen, slandered by the Qing lineage (Xiang 20.4), brings about the latter's defeat with Chu's help. An insurrection of workmen abused by the Qing lineage contributes to their downfall.

The Prince of Chen went to Chu. Gongzi Huang complained about Qing   23.2(5)
Hu and Qing Yin at the Chu court, and the leaders of Chu summoned them. They had Qing Yue go to Chu, and he was put to death. The Qing lineage used Chen as a base for revolt. In summer, Qu Jian went with the Prince of Chen and laid siege to Chen. The men of Chen fortified their city. The frame collapsed,[651] and leaders of the Qing lineage put some workmen to death.[652] The workmen passed orders to one another, and each group of men killed their respective chief, and then they killed Qing Hu and Qing Yin. The leaders of Chu restored Gongzi Huang to his domain. The noble man said that the Qing lineage was undutiful: its excesses could not be left unchecked. That is why it says in the *Documents*, "It is the Mandate that does not remain constant."[653]

Luan Ying returns to Jin through Qi support. After confirming his retainers' loyalty, he emerges from hiding.

The Jin ruler was about to marry one of his daughters to the Wu ruler.   23.3a(7)
The Prince of Qi sent Xi Guifu to bring Qi ladies to serve as secondary wives[654] and used a screened carriage to convey Luan Ying and his retainers to Jin, installing them in Quwo.[655] Luan Ying met with Xu Wu by night and told him about his plans. Xu Wu replied, "This will not do. Who can raise up what Heaven has cast down? You, sir, will certainly not escape disaster. It is not that I begrudge death. I know this plan will not come to fruition."

盈曰：「雖然，因子而死，吾無悔矣。我實不天，子無咎焉。」許諾。伏之而觴曲沃人，樂作，午言曰：「今也得欒孺子何如？」對曰：「得主而為之死，猶不死也。」皆歎，有泣者。爵行，又言。皆曰：「得主，何貳之有！」盈出，遍拜之。

23.3b 四月，欒盈帥曲沃之甲，因魏獻子，以晝入絳。初，欒盈佐魏莊子於下軍，獻子私焉，故因之。趙氏以原、屏之難怨欒氏。韓、趙方睦。中行氏以伐秦之役怨欒氏，而固與范氏和親。知悼子少，而聽於中行氏。程鄭嬖於公。唯魏氏及七輿大夫與之。

欒王鮒侍坐於范宣子。或告曰：「欒氏至矣。」宣子懼。桓子曰：「奉君以走固宮，必無害也。且欒氏多怨，子為政，欒氏自外，子在位，其利多矣。既有利權，又執民柄，將何懼焉？欒氏所得，其唯魏氏乎，而可強取也。夫克亂在權，子無懈矣！」

---

656   Luan Ying is referred to as Luan Ruzi 欒孺子. The term *ruzi* usually means "youth," but in some cases it also means "successor," without implying youth. Luan Ying was already assistant commander of the lower army in 555 BCE (Xiang 18.3), so he could not have been that young. We may surmise that these retainers in Quwo served Luan Yan before and thus regarded Luan Ying as the "successor" or "the junior master."

657   Wei Xi (Takezoe, 17.4) notes Luan Ying's perfect timing. Xu Wu's questions, twice posed, have stirred up strong emotions, which may ebb if Luan Ying waits longer.

658   When Zhao Tong and Zhao Kuo were accused of staging a rebellion in 583 BCE, the Luan and Xi lineages confirmed the charges against them. The Zhao lineage was almost completely destroyed (Cheng 8.6).

659   In 583 BCE, Han Jue saved the Zhao house by convincing Lord Jing of Jin that Zhao Wu should continue the Zhao lineage (Cheng 8.6). He acknowledged nine years later, in the context of another argument, that he had been brought up by the Zhao lineage (Cheng 17.10). When Lord Dao appointed Han Qi (Han Jue's son) commander of the upper army in 560 BCE, he declined in favor of Zhao Wu (Xiang 13.3).

660   In the conflict with Qin in 559 BCE ("Campaign of Changes and Procrastinations"), Zhonghang Yan, assisted by Fan Gai, tried to lead the army to advance, but Luan Yan, Luan Ying's father, was insubordinate and turned back with the lower army (Xiang 14.3).

661   Zhi Daozi, the grandson of Zhi Ying, was seventeen at the time. Recall that Zhi and Zhonghang were lineages of the Xun house.

662   Cheng Zheng belonged to a branch lineage of the Zhonghang line.

663   For the term "seven high officers of the chariots" (*qiyu dafu* 七輿大夫), see also Xi 10.3 (Yang, 1:336).

664   The name "Gu" 固 suggests that the palace was fortified and well guarded. Being with Lord Ping of Jin allows Fan Gai to present his side as the legitimate defender of the lord's house.

665   The "eight handles" (*babing* 八柄) in *Zhouli* 2.28 refer to enumerated rewards and punishments.

Luan Ying[a] said, "Nevertheless, so long as I can rely on you, even if I die, I will have no regrets. I am the one who lacks Heaven's favor. You will bear no blame." Xu Wu agreed to his request and, having concealed him, invited the men of Quwo to a feast. When the music struck up, Xu Wu said, "How would it be if we could have the junior Luan master[656] with us here today?" They replied, "If we had our master and could die for him, it would be as if we were undying even in death." They all sighed, and there were some who wept. As the cups circulated, Xu Wu spoke again. They all said, "If we had our master, how could we have another allegiance!" Luan Ying[a] came out and bowed to all of them.[657]

What follows is a brief survey of how the lines are drawn in the struggle between the powerful lineages in Jin. The Han, Zhao, and Zhonghang lineages all resent the Luan lineage because of earlier grudges (Cheng 8.6, Xiang 14.3). Wei Shu alone supports Luan Ying and helps him reenter Jiang, the Jin capital.

In the fourth month, relying on the help of Wei Shu[a], Luan Ying led his armored Quwo followers and entered Jiang in broad daylight. Earlier, Luan Ying had assisted Wei Jiang[a], Wei Shu's father, in the lower army. Wei Shu[b] had private ties with Luan Ying, and that was why the latter relied on him. The Zhao lineage bore a grudge against the Luan lineage on account of the disaster suffered by Zhao Tong[a] and Zhao Kuo[b].[658] This was just when the Han and Zhao lineages were on good terms.[659] The Zhonghang lineage bore a grudge against the Luan lineage because of the campaign against Qin but had always had peaceful and intimate relations with the Fan lineage.[660] Zhi Daozi was young and followed the leadership of the Zhonghang lineage.[661] Cheng Zheng was the lord's favorite.[662] Only the Wei lineage and the seven high officers of the chariots supported the Luan lineage.[663]

Yue Wangfu was sitting in attendance on Fan Gai[c]. Someone told him, "Luan Ying[d] has arrived." Fan Gai[b] was fearful. Yue Wangfu[a] said, "Take the ruler under your care and hurry to the Fortified Palace.[664] Then certainly no harm will come to you. Moreover, the Luan lineage has had many enemies, while you have been in charge of government. Luan Ying is coming from outside, while you are in the position of power inside. The advantages of this are many indeed! Since you have the advantage and the authority and moreover hold the handle of reward and punishment for the people,[665] why should you be fearful? As for the support that the Luan lineage has garnered, is it not limited to the Wei lineage alone? Even that we can wrest from them by force. Overcoming disorder depends entirely upon exercising authority. You are not to be negligent!"

23.3c　公有姻喪，王鮒使宣子墨縗、冒、絰，二婦人輦以如公，奉公以如固宮。范鞅逆魏舒，則成列既乘，將逆欒氏矣。趨進，曰：「欒氏帥賊以入，鞅之父與二三子在君所矣，使鞅逆吾子。鞅請驂乘。」持帶，遂超乘。右撫劍，左援帶，命驅之出。僕請，鞅曰：「之公。」宣子逆諸階，執其手，賂之以曲沃。

　　　　初，斐豹，隸也，著於丹書。欒氏之力臣曰督戎，國人懼之。斐豹謂宣子曰：「苟焚丹書，我殺督戎。」宣子喜，曰：「而殺之，所不請於君焚丹書者，有如日！」乃出豹而閉之。督戎從之。踰隱而待之，督戎踰入，豹自後擊而殺之。

23.3d　范氏之徒在臺後，欒氏乘公門。宣子謂鞅曰：「矢及君屋，死之！」鞅用劍以帥卒，欒氏退，攝車從之。遇欒樂，曰：「樂免之。死，將訟女於天。」樂射之，不中；又注，則乘槐本而覆。或以戟鉤之，斷肘而死。欒魴傷。欒盈奔曲沃。晉人圍之。

666　The term *yinsang* 姻喪 refers to mourning for relatives related to the lord's house by marriage. In this case, the lord is mourning for his uncle, the Lord of Qi (Xiang 23.1).

667　Fan Gai is disguised as one of the female attendants of Lord Dao's widow presumably because he fears that Luan Ying has supporters or informers inside the capital or even the palaces. Female disguise is also used in Cheng 17.6 and Ai 15.5.

668　The alternative reading, "two women pulled the carriage and went to the lord," seems implausible.

669　Du Yu (*ZZ* 35.603) punctuates the text differently: "I beg leave to take the third place in your chariot and to hold the strap" 鞅請驂乘持帶. Yu Yue (cited in Takezoe, 17.7) argues convincingly that it is by holding on to Wei Shu's belt—though *dai* 帶 probably refers to the chariot's strap—that Fan Yang sprang into the chariot.

670　Crimes that resulted in a person being branded as a slave were recorded in red ink on bamboo slips.

671　Fan Gai is saying that as Luan Ying and his men shoot from the gate at the lord's abode, Fan Yang should be prepared to die defending it.

672　Shen Qinhan (Yang, 3:1076) glosses *sheche* 攝車 as *chaosheng* 超乘, "to spring into a carriage or chariot."

673　Although Fan is the one pursuing the men of the Luan lineage, Luan Yue has put him in a disadvantageous position.

Following Yue Wangfu's counsel, Fan Gai, disguised as a woman in mourning, goes to the Jin ruler's palace. Combining coercion with enticement (the promise of Luan Ying's erstwhile settlement), Fan Gai brings Wei Shu over to his side. He also promises to erase all records of Fei Bao's crime and enslavement when Fei offers to kill the strongman among Luan's retainers.

The lord was in mourning for his maternal uncle.[666] Yue Wangfu[b] had Fan Gai[b] wear black hempen mourning clothes, a black scarf, and a black girdle.[667] He then rode in a hand-drawn carriage with two women and went to the lord[668] and, bringing the lord with him, made his way to the Fortified Palace. By the time Fan Yang went to meet Wei Shu, the latter's soldiers had formed ranks and were already seated in drawn-up chariots, all prepared to meet Luan Ying[d]. Fan Yang hastened forward and said, "Luan Ying has entered the capital at the head of a band of brigands. My father and various fine men are already with the ruler in his palace. He has sent me to meet you, sir. I beg leave to take the third place in your chariot." He had been holding the mounting strap, and with these words he sprang into the chariot.[669] Stroking his sword with his right hand and grasping the strap in his left, he commanded that they should leave the ranks at full gallop. The chariot driver asked where they were going, and Fan Yang[d] said, "To the lord." Fan Gai[b] met them at the steps, held Wei Shu's hands, and offered to give him Quwo.

Earlier, Fei Bao had been a slave, his crime recorded in a red writ.[670] Luan Ying had a strong retainer named Du Rong, whom the inhabitants of the capital feared. Fei Bao said to Fan Gai[a], "If you will just burn the red writ, I will kill Du Rong." Fan Gai[a] was pleased and said, "If you kill him, then should I fail to request that the ruler burn the red writ, may the sun bear witness against me!" He thus sent Fei Bao[a] forth and closed the palace gate. Du Rong went after him. Fei Bao[a] jumped over a low wall, hid there and waited for him. Then, when Du Rong jumped over, Fei Bao[a] struck him from behind and killed him.

Fan Yang shows his valor as he pushes back the Luan fighters. Luan Ying flees to Quwo.

The followers of the Fan lineage stayed behind the terrace as men of the Luan lineage climbed up the lord's gate. Fan Gai[a] said to Fan Yang[d], "If their arrows reach the ruler's chamber, go and fight to the death."[671] Fan Yang[d] wielded his sword as he led the soldiers. As the men of the Luan lineage were retreating, Fan Yang sprang into a chariot and pursued them.[672] Met by Luan Yue, he said, "Yue, have done! If I die, I will accuse you in heaven."[673] Luan Yue shot an arrow at him and missed. When he was putting another arrow on the bowstring, his chariot hit the roots of a locust tree and overturned. Someone caught him by the hook of his dagger-axe and cut off his arm, whereupon he died. Luan Fang was wounded. Luan Ying fled to Quwo, and the men of Jin laid siege to it.

23.3c

23.3d

23.4a(8, 9) 秋，齊侯伐衛。先驅，穀榮御王孫揮，召揚為右；申驅，成秩御莒恆，申鮮虞之傅摯為右。曹開御戎，晏父戎為右。貳廣，上之登御邢公，盧蒲癸為右；啟，牢成御襄罷師，狼蘧疏為右；胠，商子車御侯朝，桓跳為右；大殿，商子游御夏之御寇，崔如為右；燭庸之越駟乘。自衛將遂伐晉。

23.4b 晏平仲曰：「君恃勇力，以伐盟主。若不濟，國之福也。不德而有功，憂必及君。」

崔杼諫曰：「不可。臣聞之：『小國間大國之敗而毀焉，必受其咎。』君其圖之。」弗聽。

陳文子見崔武子，曰：「將如君何？」武子曰：「吾言於君，君弗聽也。以為盟主，而利其難。群臣若急，君於何有？子姑止之。」

文子退，告其人曰：「崔子將死乎！謂君甚而又過之，不得其死。過君以義，猶自抑也，況以惡乎？」

---

674 The text can be rendered literally as "Shen Xianyu's Fuzhi." For a similar usage, see Cheng 16.5.

675 Yang (3:1076) notes that the different sections of the army are named after body parts—thus, the left wing is called *qi* 啟 or 臀, meaning the intestines; the right wing is called *qu* 胠 or 胉, meaning the underarm area; the rear is called *dian* 殿 (or *tun* 臀 in modern Chinese), meaning buttocks. Both *qi* and *qu* also mean "open," for these are the left and right flanks of the army, which "open up" on the side.

676 In the parallel passage in *Yanzi chunqiu* 3.175, Yan Ying addresses this speech to Lord Zhuang, whose heedless rejection of Yan Ying's remonstrance leads directly to his assassination. For other examples of forebodings about the consequences of victory, see *Zuozhuan*, Cheng 16.5 and Xiang 8.3.

677 Chen Xuwu implies that Cui Zhu's subversive intent is already evident. Cui Zhu seems to suggest that Qi ministers might have to depose Lord Zhuang to appease Jin.

678 We follow Lin Yaosou (cited in Karlgren, gl. 604). Alternatively, we can read *guo* 過 as "to fault" (rather than "to exceed"): "Even if one faults the ruler by the standard of dutifulness, one should still restrain oneself. How much more so when one faults the ruler from base motives!"

Qi attacks Jin by way of Wei. Details on the structure of the command, not given to this extent for other Qi military operations, suggest the importance of this campaign.

In autumn, the Prince of Qi attacked Wei. In the vanguard, Gu Rong drove the chariot for Wangsun Hui, while Shao Yang was the spearman on his right. In the second line of attack, Cheng Zhi drove the chariot for Ju Heng, while Shen Xianyu's son Fuzhi was the spearman on his right.[674] Cao Kai drove the chariot for Lord Zhuang, while Yan Furong was the spearman on his right. In the lord's secondary chariot, Shang Zhideng was the driver of the Lord of Xing, while Lupu Gui was the spearman on his right. On the left wing, Lao Cheng drove the chariot for Xiang Pishi, while Lang Qushu was the spearman on his right. On the right wing, Shang Ziche drove the chariot for Hou Zhao, while Huan Tiao was the spearman on his right. In the rear, Shang Ziyou drove the chariot for Yukou of Xia, while Cui Ru was the spearman on his right and Yue of Zhuyong was the fourth person in the chariot. Qi thereupon planned to attack Jin from Wei.[675]

Exploiting unrest in Jin, Lord Zhuang of Qi turns against earlier covenants (Xiang 20.2, 21.7, 22.5) to attack Jin, in retaliation for Qi's defeat in the Pingyin campaign (Xiang 18.3). Yan Ying predicts disaster, and Cui Zhu's halfhearted remonstrance presages his assassination of Lord Zhuang two years later (Xiang 25.2).

Yan Ying[a] said, "The ruler is relying on valor and strength as he attacks the covenant chief. If he fails, it will be good fortune for the domain. If, lacking virtue, he nevertheless achieves success, grief will surely come to him."[676]

Cui Zhu remonstrated with the Qi ruler, "This will not do. I have heard, 'If a small domain exploits a great domain's troubles to wreak havoc there, it will certainly bring baleful consequences.' You, my lord, should consider this." The Qi ruler did not heed him.

Chen Xuwu[a] had an audience with Cui Zhu[a] and said, "What should we do with the ruler?" Cui Zhu[b] said, "I have already spoken to the ruler, but he would not listen to me. Having acknowledged Jin as covenant chief, he is yet taking advantage of its troubles. If all his subjects are caught up in the urgency of the matter, then what do they care about the ruler? You, sir, should simply desist."

Chen Xuwu[b] withdrew and told his followers, "Cui Zhu[e] will probably die! He called the ruler excessive, yet his fault exceeds the ruler's.[677] He will not die a natural death. Even if one exceeds the ruler in the sense of duty, one should still restrain oneself. How much more so when one exceeds the ruler in deviance!"[678]

23.4a(8, 9)

23.4b

齊侯遂伐晉，取朝歌。為二隊，入孟門，登大行。張武軍於熒庭，戍郫邵，封少水，以報平陰之役，乃還。趙勝帥東陽之師以追之，獲晏氂。八月，叔孫豹帥師救晉，次于雍榆，禮也。

23.5a　季武子無適子，公彌長，而愛悼子，欲立之。訪於申豐曰：「彌與紇，吾皆愛之，欲擇才焉而立之。」申豐趨退，歸，盡室將行。他日，又訪焉。對曰：「其然，將具敝車而行。」乃止。

　　訪於臧紇。臧紇曰：「飲我酒，吾為子立之。」季氏飲大夫酒，臧紇為客。既獻，臧孫命北面重席，新樽絜之。召悼子，降，逆之。大夫皆起。及旅，而召公鉏，使與之齒。季孫失色。

<hr>

679　Zhaoge 朝歌 was located in present-day Qi County 淇縣, Henan.

680　Xingting 熒庭, identified as the same as Xingting 陘庭 mentioned in Huan 2.8, was located in present-day Yicheng County 翼城縣, Shandong. The military monument at Xingting probably also involved some sort of mass grave for enemy soldiers, like the one mentioned in Xuan 12.2i.

681　Pishao 郫邵 is the same as Pi 郫, mentioned in Wen 6.5, see n. 100.

682　Today the Shao River 少水 is called the Qin River 沁水; it is a tributary of the Yellow River in Shanxi.

683　In *Guoyu*, "Lu yu 2," 5.198–200, the Lu minister Zifu Huibo (Meng Jiao) reminds Han Qi of this episode as an example of Lu's support of Jin.

684　"Mi" is Gongchu's given name, and "He" is Daozi's given name. Gongchu and Daozi (Ji Daozi), the names we are using for the translation, are posthumous honorifics. Gongchu became the name of a branch lineage of the Jisun lineage. Daozi was established as heir but died before he could be made minister.

685　Shen Feng was one of Ji Wuzi's retainers (*jiachen* 家臣). He did not want to be party to Ji Wuzi's plan, which he apparently regarded as unjustified and dangerous, and thus withdrew without giving an answer.

686　The number and direction of the mats were markers of a person's status. According to *Yili* 10.100–102, lords sit on three mats and officials on two. The north side, where the person sitting will face south, was the position of honor. Zang Wuzhong is treating Ji Daozi as if he were the successor of Ji Wuzi.

The Prince of Qi thereupon attacked Jin and took Zhaoge.[679] He divided his army into two branches, one entering the narrow road of Mengmen, the other ascending the Taihang Pass. In retaliation for the Jin campaign at Pingyin, he established a military monument at Xingting,[680] garrisoned Pishao,[681] and set up a giant grave mound at the Shao River.[682] He then returned to Qi. Zhao Sheng led the army of Dongyang to pursue him and took Yan Li (Yan Ying's son) captive. In the eighth month, Shusun Bao led out troops, went to the aid of Jin, and set up camp at Yongyu.[683] This was in accordance with ritual propriety.

Zang Wuzhong, known for his sagacity (Xiang 19.4, 21.2, 22.1, 23.8), here uses his cleverness for a dubious cause. He stages a dramatic legitimation of Ji Wuzi's establishment of his younger son as his heir. The inversion of the order of succession in the Ji lineage will result in similar breaches in the Meng and the Zang lineages.

Ji Wuzi had no son by his principal wife. Gongchu[a] was the eldest of his sons, but Ji Wuzi loved Daozi and wanted to establish him as heir. He conferred with Shen Feng: "I love both Mi and He[684] and wish to choose the more talented of the two to be established as my heir." Shen Feng hastily withdrew, returned home, and prepared to move away with his entire household.[685] A few days later, Ji Wuzi conferred with Shen Feng again. The latter replied, "If it is to be like this, I intend to prepare my humble carriage and be on my way." Ji Wuzi thus desisted.

Ji Wuzi conferred with Zang Wuzhong[a]. Zang Wuzhong[a] said, "Entertain me with wine, and I will establish him as heir for you, sir." Ji Wuzi[a] entertained the high officers with wine, and Zang Wuzhong[a] was the honored guest. After one round of wine offering, Zang Wuzhong[c] ordered that one mat be stacked upon another at the north end of the hall and that new cups be washed. He summoned Daozi and came down the steps to meet him. The high officers all rose.[686] Only when it came to the moment when host and guests were inviting one another to drink did he summon Gongchu, and he had him sit with the other guests according to the order of age. Ji Wuzi blanched.[687]

23.5a

---

687 After several rounds of polite exchanges when the host, the aide to the hosts, the master of ceremonies, and the guests took turns to express their felicity and invite the others to drink, the more humble guests would also be summoned. Then a more general invitation to drink and to sit according to age and rank (*lü* 旅, *lüchou* 旅酬, or *chou* 酬、醻) would ensue. Gongchu is thus treated like an officer of lower rank or like any other son born of a concubine. Du Yu (ZZ 35.605) suggests that Ji Wuzi blanches because he is afraid that Gongchu will not submit to his sudden displacement. But it is just as likely that Ji Wuzi is simply shocked by this sudden turn of events. Although Zang Wuzhong is supposedly fulfilling Ji Wuzi's own wish, the latter is reduced to being a helpless observer. This is also an uncomfortable reminder that a person's status in life is defined through other people's perception and recognition rather than birthright or intrinsic merit.

23.5b　季氏以公鉏為馬正，慍而不出。閔子馬見之，曰：「子無然。禍福無門，唯人所召。為人子者，患不孝，不患無所。敬共父命，何常之有？若能孝敬，富倍季氏可也。姦回不軌，禍倍下民可也。」公鉏然之，敬共朝夕，恪居官次。季孫喜，使飲己酒，而以具往，盡舍旃。故公鉏氏富，又出為公左宰。

23.5c(10)　孟孫惡臧孫，季孫愛之。孟氏之御騶豐點好羯也，曰：「從余言，必為孟孫。」再三云，羯從之。孟莊子疾，豐點謂公鉏：「苟立羯，請讎臧氏。」公鉏謂季孫曰：「孺子秩固其所也。若羯立，則季氏信有力於臧氏矣。」弗應。己卯，孟孫卒。公鉏奉羯立于戶側。季孫至，入，哭而出，曰：「秩焉在？」公鉏曰：「羯在此矣。」季孫曰：「孺子長。」公鉏曰：「何長之有？唯其才也。且夫子之命也。」遂立羯。秩奔邾。

688　On how misfortune and good fortune are changeable and mutually dependent, see also *Zhanguo ce*, "Chu 4," 17.551; *Xunzi* 27.608; *Huainanzi* 18.587; *Shiji* 128.3233.

689　Min Zima is urging Gongchu to hold on to the principle of reverence and filial piety, because other things are inconstant and unpredictable. Yu Yue (Karlgren, gl. 606) reads *fu* 富 ("wealth") as *fu* 福 ("good fortune"), which is also plausible.

690　Alternatively: "I will, with your permission, wreak vengeance against Zang Wuzhong" (Karlgren, gl. 608). Throughout this conversation, Meng Xiaobo is referred to by his given name "Jie." Meng Xiaobo, the name we have chosen for the translation, is his posthumous honorific.

691　On the use of the term *ruzi* ("junior") to refer to the successor, see n. 656 above.

692　According to Du Yu (*ZZ* 35.505), Gongchu is arguing that if Zang Wuzhong proved his power by following Ji Wuzi's wish and changing his successor, Ji Wuzi could go one step further by changing the order of succession in the Meng lineage without consulting Meng Zhuangzi. Alternatively, Gongchu may be arguing that if Ji Wuzi supports Meng Xiaobo, the latter will be beholden to him. In both cases, power is defined as arbitrary intervention. It is by going against the rules of lawful succession and ritual propriety that one can prove one's power.

693　According to the funeral rites of the times, the corpse was placed in the chamber while the successor stood beside the door, facing south, as he received the condolences of the guests. Gongchu has thus presented Meng Xiaobo as the successor. As with Gongchu's own displacement, the public setting and the tacit acknowledgment of the other high officers turn an arbitrary change into a fait accompli.

694　Of course, Meng Zhuangzi left no such command. Ji Gongchu is using the same argument that Ji Wuzi made to Shen Feng. By calling Meng Zhi "the junior Meng," Ji Wuzi shows that he still recognizes him as the Meng heir. He gives in, however, to his son Gongchu.

Ji Gongchu (Ji Wuzi's eldest son, who was cast aside) follows the wise counsel of Min Zima and accepts the new status quo with equanimity and seeks to establish himself in his new office through reverence and dutifulness.

Ji Wuzi[a] appointed Gongchu manager of horses. Angered, he did not take up the office. Min Zima had a meeting with him and said, "You, sir, should not behave this way. Disaster and good fortune have no special gate whereby they enter: they are precisely what people bring upon themselves.[688] As a son one should be troubled about being unfilial, not about having no proper place. Respect and honor your father's command. What constancy is there in gain and loss? If you can be filial and reverent, your wealth could well double that of the Ji lineage head.[689] If you are deviant and lawless, and if you flout the proper way, your ruin could well be twice as disastrous as that of lowly commoners." Gongchu assented. He respected and honored his father day and night and fulfilled the duties of his office carefully and assiduously. Ji Wuzi[d] was pleased. He had Gongchu entertain him with wine, then brought along his own vessels for feasting and left them all there. That was why Gongchu's lineage was rich. He also took office as our lord's steward of the left.

Succession struggles in the Meng lineage mirror those in the Ji lineage. Meng Zhuangzi's younger son, Meng Xiaobo, displaces the legitimate heir, Meng Zhi, through a retainer's machinations and Ji Gongchu's assistance. Gongchu's goal is to align forces against Zang Wuzhong, but to avenge the injustice he suffered he inflicts the same injustice on Meng Zhi.

Meng Zhuangzi[c] hated Zang Wuzhong[c], while Ji Wuzi[d] was partial to him. Meng Zhuangzi's chariot driver and groom, Feng Dian, was fond of Meng Zhuangzi's younger son Meng Xiaobo[a] and said to the latter, "If you follow my advice, you are sure to become your father's heir." He pressed the point again and again, and Meng Xiaobo[a] agreed to it. When Meng Zhuangzi was ill, Feng Dian said to Gongchu, "If you establish Jie as heir, I will, with your permission, make sure that he regards Zang Wuzhong[d] as an enemy."[690] Gongchu said to Ji Wuzi[d], "The junior Meng, Meng Zhi, is of course in his rightful place as the heir.[691] But if Meng Jie is established as heir, then the Ji lineage will indeed be more powerful than the Zang lineage."[692] Ji Wuzi did not respond. On the *jimao* day, Meng Zhuangzi[c] died. Gongchu, attending on Meng Xiaobo[a], had him stand by the door of the chamber.[693] Ji Wuzi[d] arrived, entered, wailed, came out, and said, "Where is Meng Zhi[a]?" Gongchu said, "Jie is already here." Ji Wuzi[d] said, "The junior Meng, Meng Zhi, is the elder." Gongchu said, "What does being the elder have to do with it? It is only a matter of talent. Moreover, this is the master's command."[694] So Meng Xiaobo[a] was established as heir. Meng Zhi[a] fled to Zhu.

23.5d(11)　臧孫入哭，甚哀，多涕。出，其御曰：「孟孫之惡子也，而哀如是。季孫若死，其若之何？」

臧孫曰：「季孫之愛我，疾疢也；孟孫之惡我，藥石也。美疢不如惡石。夫石猶生我，疢之美，其毒滋多。孟孫死，吾亡無日矣。」

孟氏閉門，告於季孫曰：「臧氏將為亂，不使我葬。」季孫不信。臧孫聞之，戒。冬，十月，孟氏將辟，藉除於臧氏。臧孫使正夫助之，除於東門，甲從己而視之。孟氏又告季孫。季孫怒，命攻臧氏。乙亥，臧紇斬鹿門之關以出，奔邾。

23.5e　初，臧宣叔娶于鑄，生賈及為而死。繼室以其姪，穆姜之姨子也，生紇，長於公宮。姜氏愛之，故立之。臧賈、臧為出在鑄。

695　More specifically, *yao* 藥 refers to herbal medicine, while *shi* 石 designates either mineral substances from various stones that could be used as medicine or the stones used for preparing acupuncture needles.

696　What we translate as "benign" can mean "beguiling" or "beautiful." Moral or spiritual sickness is often rooted in the pursuit of desires that promise to bring pleasure and gratification; on this theme, see also Zhao 1.12 The medicinal stone is used to prepare needles for acupuncture, which is painful.

697　Takezoe (17.14), following Lin Yaosou, suggests that Zang Wuzhong knows that disaster is brewing for him when he sees Gongchu supporting Meng Xiaobo as Meng Zhuangzi's heir—hence his grief. Zang's explanation dignifies power politics with self-knowledge and moral rhetoric.

698　Meng Xiaobo is trying to stir up resentment against Zang Wuzhong, as Feng Dian promised Gongchu. He is claiming that Zang Wuzhong tries to disrupt the burial, probably because Zang Wuzhong disputes Meng Xiaobo's claim to be Meng Zhuangzi's successor.

699　Zang Wuzhong comes with armored soldiers because he is afraid of being attacked, but their presence lends credence to Meng Xiaobo's slander.

700　Zhù 鑄, a domain of the Ren clan name, seems to have been annexed by Qi. It was situated south of present-day Feicheng County 肥城縣, Shandong. It is mentioned also in Zhao 25.6.

Zang Wuzhong's prediction of his own exile following Meng Zhuangzi's death is soon fulfilled. Though the immediate cause is Meng Xiaobo's slander, Zang looks to his relationship with the Meng and Ji lineage heads for explanation: Ji Wuzi's partiality to Zang is dangerous though beguiling, while Meng Zhuangzi's aversion to him is corrective though painful.

Zang Wuzhong[c] entered and wailed. He grieved bitterly, weeping copious tears. After he had come out, his chariot driver said, "Meng Zhuangzi[c] hated you, sir, and yet you are grieving like this. If Ji Wuzi[d] were to die, how would you bear it?"

Zang Wuzhong[c] said, "Ji Wuzi[d]'s partiality to me was a malady; Meng Zhuangzi[c]'s hatred for me was medicine.[695] A benign sickness is worse than the pain from a medicinal stone.[696] That stone may yet restore life to me, while the malady is all the more poisonous for being apparently benign. Now that Meng Zhuangzi[c] is dead, my exile is not far off."[697]

Meng Xiaobo[c] shut the gate and said to Ji Wuzi[d], "Zang Wuzhong[d] is planning to foment unrest. He is not letting me bury my father."[698] Ji Wuzi[d] did not believe him. Zang Wuzhong[c] heard about this and took precautions. In winter, in the tenth month, Meng Xiaobo[c] planned to build a ramp down into the grave and borrowed conscripted workers from the Zang household to do the clearing work. Zang Wuzhong sent the manager of workmen to help them. They were doing clearing work at the East Gate, as Zang Wuzhong, followed by armored soldiers, surveyed the procedure. Meng Xiaobo[c] again accused Zang Wuzhong to Ji Wuzi[d].[699] Furious, Ji Wuzi[d] gave orders to attack Zang Wuzhong[d]. On the *yihai* day (7), Zang Wuzhong[a] hacked through the crossbar of Deer Gate, left the domain, and fled to Zhu.

Comparable succession struggles occur in the Zang lineage. Zang Wuzhong, himself a younger son, became the head of the lineage through connections with Lord Xuan's wife Mu Jiang, thereby violating the order of succession. His eldest half brother, Zang Jia, to whom he entrusts the lineage, is tricked out of his patrimony by his younger brother Zang Wei. Since Zang's fate is tied up with the inversion of the order of succession in the Ji and Meng lineages, the explanation of Zang Wuzhong's exile would expose the Ji and Meng lineages' dubious maneuverings, whose skillful concealment in the covenant statement elicits Zang Wuzhong's admiration.

Earlier, Zang Xuanshu had taken a wife in Zhù,[700] who had died after giving birth to Zang Jia[a] and Zang Wei[a]. He then raised to her place her niece, the daughter of Mu Jiang's younger sister. She gave birth to Zang Wuzhong[e], who grew up in our lord's palace. Mu Jiang loved him, and that was why he was established as heir. Zang Jia and Zang Wei were sent out to Zhù.

23.5d(11)

23.5e

臧武仲自邾使告臧賈，且致大蔡焉，曰：「紇不侫，失守宗祧，敢告不弔。紇之罪不及不祀，子以大蔡納請，其可。」

賈曰：「是家之禍也，非子之過也。賈聞命矣。」再拜受龜，使為以納請，遂自為也。

臧孫如防，使來告曰：「紇非能害也，知不足也。非敢私請。苟守先祀，無廢二勳，敢不辟邑？」乃立臧為。

臧紇致防而奔齊。其人曰：「其盟我乎？」臧孫曰：「無辭。」將盟臧氏，季孫召外史掌惡臣而問盟首焉。

對曰：「盟東門氏也，曰『毋或如東門遂不聽公命，殺適立庶』。盟叔孫氏也，曰『毋或如叔孫僑如欲廢國常，蕩覆公室』。」

季孫曰：「臧孫之罪皆不及此。」

孟椒曰：「盍以其犯門斬關？」

季孫用之，乃盟臧氏，曰：「毋或如臧孫紇干國之紀，犯門斬關！」

臧孫聞之，曰：「國有人焉，誰居？其孟椒乎！」

701 Cf. Du Yu (*ZZ* 35.606): "I presume to tell how Heaven has no compassion for me." On the two readings of *budiao*, see Cheng 13.3, n. 263.

702 The turtle was valued because it was used in divination. The larger the turtle, the greater the spiritual power attributed to it.

703 Fang 防 was the settlement of the Zang lineage.

704 Zang Wuzhong's message conveys great humility, but there is a harsher interpretation of Zang Wuzhong's intention in *Analects* 14.14, where he is said to "threaten the ruler" (*yaojun* 要君)—that is, he implies that he would rebel, with Fang as his base, if Lu does not allow the Zang lineage to continue.

705 That is, there is no wording that would not draw unwelcome attention to the problematic succession in the Meng and Ji lineages.

706 Du Yu (*ZZ* 35.607) believes that this refers to "the first section of the covenant." The reading here follows Wang Yinzhi (*Jingyi shuwen*, 699), who reads *mengshou* 盟首 as *mengdao* 盟道, "the way of (phrasing) the covenant."

Zang Wuzhong sent word from Zhu to apprise Zang Jia of what had happened, and he also sent along a large turtle: "I lack ability and have thus failed to guard the Ancestral Temple. I presume to tell how I have failed.[701] My crime did not reach the point punishable by the abrogation of sacrifices. You should use the large turtle to submit your request to continue the Zang sacrifices. The request may well be granted."[702]

Zang Jia[a] said, "This is our family's misfortune, not any crime on your part, sir. I have heard your command!" He bowed twice and received the turtle, then sent Zang Wei[a] to use it to submit his request. Zang Wei[a] thereupon made the request on his own behalf.

Zang Wuzhong[c] went to Fang.[703] An envoy came from him with this message: "It was not in my power to do any harm. It was just that I lacked wisdom. I do not presume to make any request for myself. As long as we can guard our ancestral sacrifices, so that the glorious achievements of our forefathers, Zang Wenzhong and Zang Xuanshu, will not be cast aside, how would I presume not to leave this settlement!"[704] Zang Wei was thus established as heir.

Zang Wuzhong[a] gave Fang back to our lord and fled to Qi. His men said, "Will they swear a covenant against us?" Zang Wuzhong[c] said, "There is no proper wording for the case."[705] Planning to swear a covenant against Zang Wuzhong[a], Ji Wuzi[d] summoned the scribe of the outer court, whose task was to deal with deviant officials, and asked him about the wording of the covenant.[706]

He replied, "The covenant against the head of the Dongmen lineage said, 'Let no one be like Xiangzhong[d], who did not abide by our lord's command, who killed the rightful heir, and who established as heir the son of a secondary wife.'[707] The covenant against Shusun Qiaoru said, 'Let no one be like Shusun Qiaoru, who wanted to cast aside the constant order of the domain and overturn our lord's house.'"[708]

Ji Wuzi[d] said, "Zang Wuzhong[c]'s offense is not as heinous as either of these."

Zifu Huibo[a] said, "Why not accuse him of trespassing at the gate and hacking through its crossbar?"[709]

Ji Wuzi[d] adopted his suggestion and thus swore a covenant against Zang Wuzhong[d] that said, "Let no one be like Zang Wuzhong[e], who transgressed against the principles of the domain, trespassed at the gate, and hacked through its crossbar!"

Zang Wuzhong[c] heard this and said, "The domain has its man of talent. Who could it be then? Would it not be Zifu Huibo[d]?"

---

707 See Wen 18.5.
708 See Cheng 16.11.
709 Zifu Huibo (Meng Jiao) is the grandson of Meng Xianzi. Zifu became a branch of the Meng lineage.

23.6(11)　晉人克欒盈于曲沃，盡殺欒氏之族黨。欒魴出奔宋。書曰「晉人殺欒盈」，不言大夫，言自外也。

23.7(12)　齊侯還自晉，不入，遂襲莒。門于且于，傷股而退。明日，將復戰，期于壽舒。杞殖、華還載甲夜入且于之隧，宿於莒郊。明日，先遇莒子於蒲侯氏。莒子重賂之，使無死，曰：「請有盟。」華周對曰：「貪貨棄命，亦君所惡也。昏而受命，日未中而棄之，何以事君？」莒子親鼓之，從而伐之，獲杞梁。莒人行成。

　　　齊侯歸，遇杞梁之妻於郊，使弔之。辭曰：「殖之有罪，何辱命焉？若免於罪，猶有先人之敝廬在，下妾不得與郊弔。」齊侯弔諸其室。

710　Takezoe notes that this was the first time in early Chinese history that an offender's lineage members (*zu* 族) and followers (*dang* 黨) were summarily executed.

711　Juyu 且于 was located in present-day Ju County 莒縣, Shandong. Shoushu 壽舒, mentioned just below, was nearby.

712　Qi Liang's wife comes to be celebrated as an exemplar of female virtue and felicitous rhetoric in a number of early texts, including *Liji* 10.191, *Mencius* 6B.26, *Shuoyuan* 4.114–15, and *Lienü zhuan* 4.81–82. These accounts are more embellished and dramatic than the one in *Zuozhuan*. In *Mencius*, the widows of Qi Liang and Hua Zhou

The Fan lineage, with the support of other powerful lineages in Jin, kills Luan Ying and almost all his followers.

The men of Jin overcame Luan Ying at Quwo and killed all the members and partisans of the Luan house.[710] Luan Fang left the domain and fled to Song. The text says, "Jin leaders put Luan Ying to death." It does not say, "high officer," because he arrived from abroad.   23.6(12)

Lord Zhuang of Qi attacks Ju while on his way home from a successful campaign against Jin (Xiang 23.4b). After initial setbacks, Qi achieves an inconclusive victory. Qi Liang's widow, who meets Lord Zhuang upon his return, demonstrates her ritual propriety and rhetorical prowess. A Qi woman who meets returning troops also appears in Cheng 2.3.

The Prince of Qi was returning from Jin. He did not enter the domain but went on to make a surprise attack on Ju. He stormed the gate at Juyu,[711] withdrawing after suffering a wound in his thigh. The following day, he intended to resume battle and arranged to meet his troops at Shoushu. Qi Liang[a] and Hua Zhou[a] put armored soldiers in chariots, and during the night they entered the narrow pass in Juyu, staying overnight in the outskirts of Ju. The following day, they were the first to encounter the Master of Ju at the Puhou residence. The Master of Ju gave them lavish gifts and wanted them to agree to not fight to the death, saying, "I beg leave to have a covenant." Hua Zhou replied, "To be greedy for profit and to abandon commands is indeed something you, my lord, would abhor. If, having received the ruler's command in the evening, we abandon it before midday, how can we serve any ruler?" The Master of Ju personally beat the war drum against Qi. He pursued and attacked Qi troops and seized Qi Liang's corpse. The leaders of Ju went to seek an accord.   23.7(12)

As the Prince of Qi returned, he encountered Qi Liang's wife in the outskirts of the capital. He sent a messenger to offer his condolences. She declined, "If Qi Liang[b] had committed offenses, why condescend to give this command? If he had managed to avoid committing offenses, then the humble abode of our ancestor still exists, and this lowly concubine cannot accept condolences in the outskirts of the capital." The Prince of Qi offered condolences at her abode.[712]

---

are said to "transform the mores of their domain" through their lamentation. In *Shuoyuan* and *Lienü zhuan*, her wailing brought down the city wall, and this trope eventually merges with the legend of Meng Jiangnü 孟姜女, whose lament brought down the Great Wall; see Gu Yanwu, *Rizhi lu jishi*, 25.585–86 ("Qi Liang qi" 杞梁妻). She also appears often in classical poetry as a symbol of the mournful wife (e.g., "Nineteen Old Poems").

23.8 齊侯將為臧紇田。臧孫聞之，見齊侯。與之言伐晉，對曰：「多則多矣，抑君似鼠。夫鼠，晝伏夜動，不穴於寢廟，畏人故也。今君聞晉之亂而後作焉，寧將事之，非鼠如何？」乃弗與田。

仲尼曰：「知之難也。有臧武仲之知，而不容於魯國，抑有由也，作不順而施不恕也。《夏書》曰：『念茲在茲』，順事、恕施也。」

春秋

24.1(1) 二十有四年，春，叔孫豹如晉。

24.2(3) 仲孫羯帥師侵齊。

24.3(4) 夏，楚子伐吳。

24.4 秋，七月甲子朔，日有食之，既。

24.5(6) 齊崔杼帥師伐莒。

24.6 大水。

---

713   This is a final echo of the theme of Zang Wuzhong's reputed cleverness and its misuse. Although the word *zhi* 智 is usually translated as "wisdom," Zang Wuzhong's exploits in this section of *Zuozhuan* seem to lack the moral compass implied by the word "wisdom." His sagacity and moral judgment are evident elsewhere in *Zuozhuan*. Confucius may be trying to explain the inconsistency, or he may be using *zhi* to mean "cleverness."

*Lord Zhuang of Qi is about to grant land to Zang Wuzhong when the lat-
ter's deliberately offensive remark makes him revoke his gift. Perhaps Zang
foresees the disasters that will befall Qi and does not want to be too closely
associated with it, as Du Yu suggests. Such prescience was not evident in
his intervention in the affairs of the Ji lineage, which "Confucius" summarizes as contravention of right order and failure of reciprocity.*

The Prince of Qi intended to grant land to Zang Wuzhong[a]. Zang
Wuzhong[c] heard this and had an audience with the Prince of Qi, who
then spoke to him about attacking Jin. Zang Wuzhong replied, "Your
military achievements have indeed been considerable. But you, my lord,
are like a mouse. For a mouse lies low during the day and moves about
at night. It does not dig its hole in Ancestral Temples because it is afraid
of people. Now you, my lord, raised your troops only after you had heard
of the disorder in Jin. Had Jin been at peace, you would have served it.
What are you like if not a mouse?" The Qi ruler thus did not grant him
land.

23.8

Confucius[c] said, "It is indeed difficult to be wise. For someone with
Zang Wuzhong's wisdom to find no place in Lu, there should yet be a
reason.[713] What he did went against the right order, and in his dealings
with others he did not show empathy.[714] The *Xia Documents* says, 'That
which you think of depends on this.'[715] This refers to putting affairs in the
right order and showing empathy in dealing with others."

LORD XIANG 24 (549 BCE)
ANNALS

In the twenty-fourth year, in spring, Shusun Bao went to Jin.

24.1(1)

Zhongsun Jie (Meng Xiaobo) led out troops and invaded Qi.

24.2(3)

In summer, the Master of Chu attacked Wu.

24.3(4)

In autumn, in the seventh month, on the *jiazi* day, the first day of the
month, there was an eclipse of the sun. It was a total eclipse.

24.4

Cui Zhu of Qi led out troops and attacked Ju.

24.5(6)

There was a great flood.

24.6

---

714   See *Analects* 15.24: asked whether there is one principle that one can abide by for
one's whole life, Confucius replies, "It is probably empathy! What one does not
desire for oneself, do not apply it to another person." What we translate as "empathy" (*shu* 恕) is what dictates the imperative of reciprocity.

715   Also quoted in Xiang 21.2. See nn. 106 and 583.

24.7　八月癸巳朔，日有食之。

24.8(7)　公會晉侯、宋公、衛侯、鄭伯、曹伯、莒子、邾子、滕子、薛伯、杞伯、小邾子于夷儀。

24.9(8)　冬，楚子、蔡侯、陳侯、許男伐鄭。

24.10　公至自會。

24.11(10)　陳鍼宜咎出奔楚。

24.12(11)　叔孫豹如京師。

24.13　大饑。

左傳

24.1(1)　二十四年，春，穆叔如晉，范宣子逆之，問焉，曰：「古人有言曰：『死而不朽』，何謂也？」穆叔未對。宣子曰：「昔匄之祖，自虞以上為陶唐氏，在夏為御龍氏，在商為豕韋氏，在周為唐杜氏，晉主夏盟為范氏，其是之謂乎！」

　　穆叔曰：「以豹所聞，此之謂世祿，非不朽也。魯有先大夫曰臧文仲，既沒，其言立，其是之謂乎！豹聞之：『大上有立德，其次有立功，其次有立言。』雖久不廢，此之謂不朽。若夫保姓受氏，以守宗祊，世不絕祀，無國無之。祿之大者，不可謂不朽。」

716　If there was a complete solar eclipse the month before, there could not have been another eclipse now. Some commentators suggest that the entry refers to the solar eclipse on the *guisi* day, the last day of the month in Wen 11 (616 BCE), and that the confusion arose from misplaced bamboo slips.

717　The precise location of Yiyi 夷儀 is not known.

718　According to Shen Qinhan, in the ritual for official visits, when the envoy from another domain reached the outskirts of the capital, the ruler would send a minister in court robes to meet him, giving him a bolt of silk as a gift to honor his exertion (Yang, 3:1087).

719　On the Yulong (Dragon-Rearing) lineage, see also Zhao 29.4.

720　According to *Guoyu*, "Zheng yu," 16.511, Shiwei was descended from Zhurong and was one of the "Shang overlords" eventually destroyed by Shang kings. Cf. Cheng 2.3f, n. 68.

721　The theory that "Han is descended from Yao" (*Han wei Yao hou* 漢為堯後), championed by, among others, Liu Xiang (*Hanshu* 1.81), Ban Gu ("Dian yin" 典引, in *Wenxuan* 48.2159), and Jia Kui (*Hou Hanshu* 26.1237), is based on this account of the Fan lineage (see also Zhao 29.4) and the presumed link between the Fan lineage and the surname Liu (Wen 13.2). Cf. Zhao n. 1177. These passages have been used to "prove" that *Zuozhuan* contains Han interpolations, but the evidence is not convincing.

In the eighth month, on the *guisi* day, the first day of the month, there was an eclipse of the sun.[716]   24.7

Our lord met with the Prince of Jin, the Duke of Song, the Prince of Wei, the Liege of Zheng, the Liege of Cao, the Master of Ju, the Master of Zhu, the Master of Teng, the Liege of Xue, the Liege of Qǐ, and the Master of Lesser Zhu at Yiyi.[717]   24.8(7)

In winter, the Master of Chu, the Prince of Cai, the Prince of Chen, and the Head of Xǔ attacked Zheng.   24.9(8)

Our lord arrived from the meeting.   24.10

Qian Yijiu of Chen departed and fled to Chu.   24.11(10)

Shusun Bao went to the Zhou capital.   24.12(11)

There was a great famine.   24.13

ZUO

The Jin minister Fan Gai, after suppressing the revolt of his longtime rival Luan Ying (Xiang 23.3, 23.6), boasts of the ancient roots and enduring power of the Fan lineage to the Lu minister Shusun Bao. The latter, however, deflates his self-aggrandizement and famously defines the "three ways to never perish."

In the twenty-fourth year, in spring, Shusun Bao[a] went to Jin. Fan Gai[c] came out to escort him in[718] and asked, "The ancients have this saying, 'To die but not perish.' What does that mean?" Shusun Bao[a] had not yet answered when Fan Gai[b] continued, "Long ago, before the reign of King Shun, my ancestors became the Taotang lineage; under Xia, they became the Yulong lineage;[719] under Shang, the Shiwei lineage;[720] under Zhou, the Tangdu lineage; under Jin, which presides over the covenant of the central domains, the Fan lineage.[721] Surely this is what is meant!"   24.1(1)

Shusun Bao[a] said, "From what I have heard, this is called hereditary office and emolument; those do not signify 'never perishing.' Lu has a former high officer called Zang Wenzhong. He died, but his words have been established among us. Surely this is what is meant! According to what I have heard, 'the highest of all is to establish virtue; next to that is to establish achievements; next to that is to establish words.' Even with the passage of time these glories are not cast aside. This is called 'never perishing.' As for keeping one's clan name and receiving lineage status, so as to guard one's Ancestral Temple and to maintain sacrifices for generations, there is no domain without such things. Hereditary office and emolument, even at their greatest, cannot be called 'never perishing.'"

24.2a　范宣子為政，諸侯之幣重，鄭人病之。二月，鄭伯如晉，子產寓書於子西，以告宣子，曰：

子為晉國，四鄰諸侯不聞令德，而聞重幣，僑也惑之。僑聞君子長國家者，非無賄之患，而無令名之難。夫諸侯之賄聚於公室，則諸侯貳。若吾子賴之，則晉國貳。諸侯貳，則晉國壞；晉國貳，則子之家壞，何沒沒也？將焉用賄？

夫令名，德之輿也；德，國家之基也。有基無壞，無亦是務乎！有德則樂，樂則能久。《詩》云：

樂只君子，
邦家之基。

有令德也夫！

上帝臨女，
無貳爾心。

有令名也夫！恕思以明德，則令名載而行之，是以遠至邇安。毋寧使人謂子「子實生我」，而謂「子浚我以生」乎？象有齒以焚其身，賄也。

宣子說，乃輕幣。

722　*Maoshi* 172, "Nan shan you tai" 南山有臺, 10A.347.

723　*Maoshi* 236, "Da ming" 大明, 16B.544.

724　The word we translate as "use up" is *jun* 浚, which Du Yu (*ZZ* 35.610) glosses as "take" 取, and which also means "to hollow out," as in dredging a river (*Annals, Zhuang* 9.7) or digging a well (*Mencius* 4A.2). See Karlgren, gl. 613.

725　Fu Qian reads *fen* 焚 ("to burn") as *fen* 僨 ("to fall down," "to stiffen and die"); see Hong Liangji, *Chunqiu Zuozhuan gu*, 568.

Zichan resists Jin demands for offerings in an eloquent letter to Fan Gai.
He warns that the accumulation of material gain will cause alienation and
dissension and thereby endanger both the domain and the Fan lineage.
Zichan's remonstrance succeeds in lightening the burden of Jin demands
on subordinate domains.

When Fan Gai[c] was in charge of government, the offerings demanded of   24.2a
the princes were burdensome, and Zheng leaders were distressed by
them. In the second month, the Liege of Zheng went to Jin. Zichan sent
a letter with Zixi to tell Fan Gai[b] the following:

> With you, sir, in charge in Jin, your neighboring princes on all
> four sides have not heard of your exemplary virtue but only of
> burdensome offerings. I am perplexed by this. I have heard that
> noble men who lead domains and patrimonies are not troubled
> by the lack of gifts but are disturbed by the lack of a good name.
> When the princes' gifts are gathered in the lord's house, then the
> princes will have divided allegiance. If you, sir, rely so much on
> all these gifts, then the domain of Jin will have divided alle-
> giance. If the princes have divided allegiance, then the domain of
> Jin will be ruined, and if the domain of Jin has divided alle-
> giance, then your patrimony will be ruined. How can you be so
> misguided? Of what use can the gifts be?
>
> Now a good name is the vehicle of virtue, and virtue is the
> foundation of domain and patrimony. Should one not strive to
> have a foundation and not let it be ruined? With virtue one is joy-
> ful, and with joy one is able to endure. As it says in the *Odes*,
>
>> Joyful is the noble man—
>> He is the foundation of domain and patrimony.[722]
>
> Surely this is because he has exemplary virtue!
>
>> The god on high is watching over you.
>> Do not let your heart be divided.[723]
>
> Surely this is because he has a good name! Use the longing for
> reciprocity to illuminate virtue, which will then be carried forth
> by a good name, so that those afar will be drawn close and those
> nearby will be calmed. Would you rather have others say about
> you, sir, "It is you who sustain us," or "You use us up to sustain
> yourself"?[724] It is because elephants have tusks that their bodies
> are destroyed:[725] such is the danger of gifts.

Fan Gai[b] was pleased, and thus he lightened the burden of offerings.

24.2b　是行也，鄭伯朝晉，為重幣故，且請伐陳也。鄭伯稽首，宣子辭。子西相，曰：「以陳國之介恃大國，而陵虐於敝邑，寡君是以請請罪焉，敢不稽首？」

24.3(2)　孟孝伯侵齊，晉故也。

24.4(3)　夏，楚子為舟師以伐吳，不為軍政，無功而還。

24.5　齊侯既伐晉而懼，將欲見楚子。楚子使薳啟彊如齊聘，且請期。齊社，蒐軍實，使客觀之。陳文子曰：「齊將有寇。吾聞之：兵不戢，必取其族。」

24.6(5)　秋，齊侯聞將有晉師，使陳無宇從薳啟彊如楚，辭，且乞師。崔杼帥師送之，遂伐莒，侵介根。

24.7(6, 8)　會于夷儀，將以伐齊。水，不克。

726　Some texts have only one *qing* 請; see Yang, 3:1090.

727　Du Yu (*ZZ* 35.610) glosses *junzheng* 軍政 (literally, "military administration") as "the distinctions of reward and punishment"; and Kong Yingda (*ZZ*-Kong, 23.390) explains it as "instruction in the army." See also Xuan 12.2a.

728　Yang (3:1090) suggests that sacrifices are performed at the altar of earth that has been set up by the army (*junshe* 軍社).

729　Following Karlgren (gl. 617), who cites Xu Shen on the implied homology of *zu* 族 and *zu* 鏃 ("arrowhead"). Cf. Du Yu's (*ZZ* 35.610) reading of *zu* as "kin" or "clan": "A display of weapons will surely harm one's own."

730　The precise location of the Qi domain settlement Jiegen 介根 is unknown.

The Zheng ruler bows to the Jin chief minister with rituals reserved for the Zhou king in order to seek Jin's acquiescence to Zheng's plans to attack Chen, a Chu ally. Jin seems to have withheld its assent, because Zichan has to defend the Zheng campaign the following year (Xiang 25.10).

On this trip, the Liege of Zheng visited the court of Jin because of the heavy burden of offerings and also to beg leave to attack Chen. The Liege of Zheng bowed with his forehead touching the ground, and Fan Gai[b] declined to accept such reverence. Zixi, who was serving as the lord's assistant, said, "Chen, relying on the support of a great domain, unleashed its tyranny upon our humble settlement. That is why our unworthy ruler begs leave to hold Chen accountable for its offenses.[726] Would he dare not bow with his forehead touching the ground?"

Lu invades Qi in retaliation for the Qi campaign against Jin (Xiang 23.4).

Meng Xiaobo invaded Qi on account of Jin.

Chu engages in a fruitless campaign against Wu.

In summer, the Master of Chu attacked Wu with a flotilla. He did not enforce military discipline[727] and so returned without accomplishing anything.

Qi seeks an alliance with Chu but takes pains to display its strength, lest it appear subservient. The Qi minister Chen Xuwu's prediction of disaster for Qi is fulfilled the following year (Xiang 25.2).

Having attacked Jin, the Prince of Qi was fearful and wished to have an audience with the Master of Chu. The Master of Chu sent Wei Qiqiang to Qi on an official visit and also to request a date for the meeting. Qi leaders performed sacrifices at the altar of earth[728] and reviewed the troops and equipment, having invited the guests to observe the parade. Chen Xuwu[a] said, "Qi will suffer raiders. I have heard that a display of weapons will surely cause arrowheads to fly."[729]

Qi prepares for conflict with Jin.

In autumn, when the Prince of Qi heard that Jin troops were coming, he sent Chen Wuyu to follow Wei Qiqiang to Chu to decline the meeting and also to beg for troops. Cui Zhu led out troops to send him off. He thereupon attacked Ju and invaded Jiegen.[730]

The princes met at Yiyi: they were planning then to attack Qi. There were floods, and they did not succeed in mounting an attack.

24.8(9)　冬，楚子伐鄭以救齊，門于東門，次于棘澤。諸侯還救鄭。

晉侯使張骼、輔躒致楚師，求御于鄭。鄭人卜宛射犬，吉。子大叔戒之曰：「大國之人不可與也。」對曰：「無有眾寡，其上一也。」大叔曰：「不然。部婁無松柏。」

二子在幄，坐射犬于外；既食，而後食之。使御廣車而行，己皆乘乘車。將及楚師，而後從之乘，皆踞轉而鼓琴。近，不告而馳之。皆取胄於櫜而胄，入壘，皆下，搏人以投，收禽挾囚。弗待而出。皆超乘，抽弓而射。既免，復踞轉而鼓琴，曰：「公孫！同乘，兄弟也，胡再不謀？」對曰：「曩者志入而已，今則怵也。」皆笑，曰：「公孫之亟也！」

楚子自棘澤還，使薳啟彊帥師送陳無宇。

731　Brambles Marsh (Jize 棘澤) was located in the domain of Zheng south of present-day Xinzheng County 新鄭縣, Henan.

732　On the practice of using a single chariot to "challenge the enemy" by some extraordinary feat of bravery, see Xuan 12.2. Jin commanders want a Zheng chariot driver because he would be more familiar with the terrain.

733　Cf. Yang (3:1091): "It does not matter whether a domain has a great army or a small one; the chariot driver should have a higher position all the same." You Ji is trying to convince Yuan Shequan to defer to the two Jin officers, but Yuan Shequan counters that the usual hierarchy (regarding positions in a chariot) applies irrespective of the size and power of the domains involved. Takezoe (17.26) notes, however, that the person on the left side of the chariot should have a higher position than the chariot driver.

734　We follow Hu Yujin's reading of *zhuan* 轉 as *zhen* 軫 (Yang, 3:1092). Cf. Du Yu's (*ZZ* 35.611) reading of *zhuan* as "bundles of clothing," which Takezoe (17.26) supports and links to the related words *zhuan* 縳 and *tuan* 摶.

The following passage offers a memorable vignette from the battlefield. When the Jin-Zheng coalition confronts the Qi-Chu alliance, two Jin officers slight the Zheng nobleman who is driving their chariot. The latter argues that rank does not depend on the size and power of the domain (for an opposite argument, see Cheng 3.7) and tries to put the Jin officers in their place through his valor and ready wit. The Jin officers for their part seem unruffled as they display their courage and supercilious calmness.

In winter, the Master of Chu attacked Zheng to relieve Qi. Chu troops stormed the eastern gate of the Zheng capital and set up camp at Brambles Marsh.[731] The princes turned back to relieve Zheng.

The Prince of Jin sent Zhang Ge and Fu Li to challenge the Chu army, and they sought a chariot driver from Zheng.[732] The men of Zheng divined about sending Yuan Shequan, and the result was auspicious. You Ji[b] cautioned him, "You should not put yourself on a par with men from a great domain." He replied, "It does not matter whether a domain has multitudes or few people, those above are honored in the same way."[733] You Ji[a] said, "Not so. There are no pines and cypresses on puny knolls."

The two officers, Zhang Ge and Fu Li, were inside their tent, but they made Yuan Shequan[a] sit outside and gave him his meal only after they had eaten. They had him drive a combat chariot and proceed while they themselves rode in a regular chariot. Only when they were about to reach the Chu army did they join Yuan Shequan in his chariot. They both perched on the horizontal beam at the back of the chariot[734] and strummed their lutes. As the combat chariot approached the Chu camp, Yuan Shequan dashed in without notifying them. Zhang Ge and Fu Li took their helmets from the armory case and put them on. When they entered the ramparts, both got down from the chariot, seized enemy soldiers, and hurled them back, tying up some captives and clamping others under their arms. Without waiting for them, Yuan Shequan sped out of the ramparts. Zhang Ge and Fu Li both sprang onto the chariot, pulled out their bows, and shot at the enemy. Having escaped from the danger zone, they again perched on the horizontal beam at the back of the chariot and strummed their lutes. They said, "Noble grandson![735] Sharing a chariot makes us brothers. Why did you twice fail to confer with us?" He replied, "The first time I was intent only on entering the enemy camp. Just now I was worried."[736] They both laughed and said, "What a hasty temperament the noble grandson has!"

The Master of Chu returned from Brambles Marsh and had Wei Qiqiang lead out troops to send off Chen Wuyu.

---

735   Yuan Shequan is the grandson of a Zheng lord.

736   Yuan Shequan claims to be worried about the Jin-Zheng coalition army being outnumbered. With these blatantly unconvincing excuses, Yuan Shequan thus manages to show his displeasure without admitting that he is offended.

24.9 吳人為楚舟師之役故，召舒鳩人。舒鳩人叛楚。楚子師于荒浦，使沈尹壽與師祁犁讓之。舒鳩子敬逆二子，而告無之，且請受盟。二子復命。王欲伐之。薳子曰：「不可。彼告不叛，且請受盟，而又伐之，伐無罪也。姑歸息民，以待其卒。卒而不貳，吾又何求？若猶叛我，無辭，有庸。」乃還。

24.10(11) 陳人復討慶氏之黨，鍼宜咎出奔楚。

24.11(12) 齊人城郟。穆叔如周聘，且賀城。王嘉其有禮也，賜之大路。

The men of Wu, because of the campaign by Chu naval forces, summoned the men of Shujiu,[737] who then rebelled against Chu. The Master of Chu mobilized the army at Huangpu and sent Shou, governor of Shěn, and Shiqi Li to reprimand them. The Master of Shujiu respectfully met the two Chu high officers, told them that there was no such rebellion, and moreover asked to receive a covenant. The two men reported the discharge of their mission to the king. The king wanted to attack Shujiu. The chief minister, Wei Ziping[a], said, "This will not do. They submitted that they were not rebelling, and moreover, they asked to receive a covenant. If we attack them, we are attacking the guiltless. For now, we should just return, let the people rest, and await the outcome. If the outcome is that they do not shift allegiance, what more can we ask for? If they nevertheless rebel against us, then they will have no excuse, and we can act with success." The Chu army thus turned back.

24.9

The leaders of Chen continue to persecute the Qing lineage because of its earlier rebellion (Xiang 23.2).

The leaders of Chen again chastised partisans of the Qing lineage. Qian Yijiu departed and fled to Chu.

24.10(11)

Qi fortifies Jia for the Zhou king, possibly to gain support in the wake of its breach with Jin.

The men of Qi fortified Jia.[738] Shusun Bao[a] went to Zhou on an official visit and also to congratulate the king on the fortification. The king commended him for his ritual propriety and bestowed on him a great carriage.

24.11(12)

---

737   Shujiu 舒鳩 was located in present-day Shucheng County 舒城縣 in Anhui.
738   Jia is the same as Jiaru, the Zhou royal city mentioned in Xuan 3.3.

24.12 晉侯嬖程鄭，使佐下軍。鄭行人公孫揮如晉聘，程鄭問焉，曰：「敢問降階何由？」子羽不能對，歸以語然明。然明曰：「是將死矣。不然，將亡。貴而知懼，懼而思降，乃得其階。下人而已，又何問焉？且夫既登而求降階者，知人也，不在程鄭。其有亡釁乎！不然，其有惑疾，將死而憂也。」

春秋

25.1(1) 二十有五年，春，齊崔杼帥師伐我北鄙。

25.2(2) 夏，五月乙亥，齊崔杼弒其君光。

25.3(3) 公會晉侯、宋公、衛侯、鄭伯、曹伯、莒子、邾子、滕子、薛伯、杞伯、小邾子于夷儀。

25.4(5) 六月壬子，鄭公孫舍之帥師入陳。

25.5(6) 秋，八月己巳，諸侯同盟于重丘。

739　See Xiang 23.3b.

740　The implied question is "Dare I ask how one may attain a lower rank?"

741　Cheng Zheng came to be assistant commander of the lower army because he was a favorite of Lord Ping of Jin. The assumption is that he could not have been genuinely interested in self-abnegation. For similar formulations on the importance of restraint

The Prince of Jin was enamored of Cheng Zheng[739] and made him the assistant commander of the lower army. When the Zheng envoy, Gongsun Hui, went to Jin on an official visit, Cheng Zheng asked him, "May I presume to ask how one can descend the steps?"[740] Gongsun Hui[a] could not reply and upon his return spoke about this to Ran Ming. Ran Ming said, "He must be about to die—or else, he will go into exile. To be in an exalted position and know fear, to be fearful and think of stepping down: such are the ways one can obtain the proper rank. The key is to place oneself beneath others and nothing more. What is there to ask about? Moreover, those who seek to step down after rising high are the wise ones, not the likes of Cheng Zheng.[741] This is probably a sign that he will be exiled! Otherwise, he has perhaps become sick with confusion. He is about to die and is worried about it."   24.12

LORD XIANG 25 (548 BCE)
ANNALS

In the twenty-fifth year, in spring, Cui Zhu of Qi led out troops and attacked our northern marches.   25.1(1)

In summer, in the fifth month, on the *yihai* day (17), Cui Zhu of Qi assassinated his ruler, Guang.   25.2(2)

Our lord met with the Prince of Jin, the Duke of Song, the Prince of Wei, the Liege of Zheng, the Liege of Cao, the Master of Ju, the Master of Zhu, the Master of Teng, the Liege of Xue, the Liege of Qi, and the Master of Lesser Zhu at Yiyi.   25.3(3)

In the sixth month, on the *renzi* day (24), Gongsun Shezhi of Zheng led out troops and entered Chen.   25.4(5)

In autumn, in the eighth month, on the *jisi* day, the princes swore a covenant together at Chongqiu.[742]   25.5(6)

---

and vigilance, see Xi 22.7, Xuan 16.1, and Xiang 11.5. Cf. *Zhouyi* 9.188: "to ascend without stopping will certainly result in an impasse."

742 Du Yu (ZZ 36.617) notes that *jisi* was the twelfth day of the seventh month. There was no *jisi* day in the eighth month. The precise location of the Qi settlement of Chongqiu 重丘 is unknown. This should not be confused with Chongqiu in Cao (n. 481).

25.6 公至自會。

25.7(9) 衛侯入于夷儀。

25.8(8) 楚屈建帥師滅舒鳩。

25.9 冬，鄭公孫夏帥師伐陳。

25.10(12) 十有二月，吳子遏伐楚，門于巢，卒。

左傳

25.1(1) 二十五年，春，齊崔杼帥師伐我北鄙，以報孝伯之師也。公患之，使告于晉。孟公綽曰：「崔子將有大志，不在病我，必速歸，何患焉？其來也不寇，使民不嚴，異於他日。」齊師徒歸。

25.2a(2) 齊棠公之妻，東郭偃之姊也。東郭偃臣崔武子。棠公死，偃御武子以弔焉。見棠姜而美之，使偃取之。偃曰：「男女辨姓，今君出自丁，臣出自桓，不可。」

Our lord arrived from the meeting.   25.6

The Prince of Wei entered Yiyi.   25.7(9)

Qu Jian of Chu led out troops and extinguished Shujiu.   25.8(8)

In winter, Gongsun Xia (Zixi) of Zheng led out troops and attacked   25.9
Chen.

In the twelfth month, E (Zhufan), the Master of Wu, attacked Chu and 25.10(12)
stormed its gate at Chao. He died.

ZUO

Qi invades Lu, but the Qi commander Cui Zhu is too intent on his ambi-
tions at home to truly challenge Lu. If this is the same person as the Cui
Zhu exiled in 599 BCE (Xuan 10.2), he must be at least seventy at this point.

In the twenty-fifth year, in spring, Cui Zhu of Qi led out troops and   25.1(1)
attacked our northern marches in retaliation for Meng Xiaobo's incursion.[743] Our lord was troubled by this and sent word to Jin. Meng Gong-
chuo said, "Cui Zhu[c] will have grand ambitions, and he is not bent on
hurting us. He is sure to return soon. Why be troubled? Since he has
come, there have been no raids, and he has not treated our people with
severity. This is different from before." The Qi army returned without
gaining anything.

Cui Zhu, in defiance of inauspicious divination results, takes Dongguo
Jiang, the widow of the Lord of Tang, as his wife (who comes to be known
as Lady Jiang). Lord Zhuang, whom Cui Zhu had helped to establish as
ruler six years earlier (Xiang 19.5), flaunts his adulterous relations with
Lady Jiang. Cui Zhu plots his assassination.

The wife of the Lord of Tang in Qi, Dongguo Jiang, was an older sister   25.2a(2)
of Dongguo Yan, who served Cui Zhu[a] as a retainer. When the Lord of
Tang died, Dongguo Yan[a] drove Cui Zhu to offer condolences. Upon
seeing Dongguo Jiang[a], Cui Zhu was struck with her beauty and sent
Dongguo Yan[a], acting as intermediary, to take her as his wife. Dongguo
Yan[a] said, "Man and wife should be of different clan names. Now you,
my lord, come from the line of Lord Ding, while I, your servant, come
from the line of Lord Huan. This will not do."[744]

---

743 For Meng Xiaobo's invasion of Qi, see Xiang 24.3.
744 Lord Ding was the son of the Grand Lord, the ancestor of the Qi house. Lord Huan
     was the famous overlord. Thus, both Cui Zhu and Dongguo Yan had the clan name
     Jiang. On the taboo against marrying someone with the same clan name, see Xi
     23.6d, Zhao 1.12, *Guoyu*, "Jin yu 4," 10.349.

武子筮之，遇困䷮之大過䷛。史皆曰「吉」。示陳文子，文子曰：「夫
從風，風隕妻，不可娶也。且其繇曰：『困于石，據于蒺梨，入于其宮，不
見其妻，凶。』困于石，往不濟也；據于蒺梨，所恃傷也；入于其宮，不見
其妻，凶，無所歸也。」崔子曰：「嫠也，何害？先夫當之矣。」遂取之。

莊公通焉，驟如崔氏，以崔子之冠賜人。侍者曰：「不可。」公曰：
「不為崔子，其無冠乎？」崔子因是，又以其間伐晉也，曰：「晉必將
報。」欲弒公以說于晉，而不獲間。公鞭侍人賈舉，而又近之，乃為崔子
間公。

25.2b　夏，五月，莒為且于之役故，莒子朝于齊。甲戌，饗諸北郭，崔子稱疾，不
視事。乙亥，公問崔子，遂從姜氏。姜入于室，與崔子自側戶出。公拊楹
而歌。侍人賈舉止眾從者而入，閉門。

745　"Impasse" ䷮ (Kun 困) is hexagram 47 and "Great Surpassing" ䷛ (Daguo 大過) is
　　hexagram 28 in the received version of *Zhouyi*. When the broken, or yin, line, third
　　from the bottom in the hexagram "Impasse," is transformed into an unbroken, or
　　yang, line, the result is the hexagram "Great Surpassing."

746　The scribes are presumably trying to please Cui Zhu. Hexagram 47 is made up of the
　　trigrams "Sinkhole" ☵ (Kan 坎) below and "Joy" ☱ (Dui 兌) above. In terms of
　　family relationships "Sinkhole" and "Joy" denote middle son and young daughter,
　　respectively. On that basis one can claim that hexagram 47 symbolizes the well-
　　matched union of "middle son" and "young daughter."

747　Hexagram 28 is made up of the trigrams "Compliance" ☴ (Sun 巽) below and "Joy"
　　☱ (Dui) above. The image of "Compliance" is wind. Thus, when hexagram 47 is
　　transformed into hexagram 28, "Sinkhole" becomes "Compliance," which may be
　　interpreted as the middle son or husband being overcome by the wind. The wind
　　can also undermine the "Joy" above—hence the image of the wind blowing down
　　the young daughter or wife.

748　This is the omen verse for the third line of hexagram 47.

749　The trigram "Sinkhole," the lower component of hexagram 47, has the attribute of
　　"dangerous" and the image of water, which may account for Chen Xuwu's
　　explanation.

750　We follow Du Yu's reading (ZZ 36.618). Cf. Yu Yue's reading (cited in Karlgren, gl.
　　621): "But no! Isn't he Cui Zhu? How can he lack hats?"

Cui Zhu[b] divined by milfoil about this and came upon the hexagram "Impasse" ䷮ and the line whereby it becomes the hexagram "Great Surpassing" ䷛."[745] The scribes all pronounced the result auspicious.[746] But when Cui Zhu showed it to Chen Xuwu[a], the latter said, "The husband follows the wind, and the wind blows down the wife.[747] You must not take her as wife. Also, the omen verse says, 'Caught among rocks, he leans on thorns and thistles. He enters his chamber and does not see his wife. Inauspicious.'[748] 'Caught among rocks' means that going forward with your plan will bring no success.[749] 'He leans on thorns and thistles' means being harmed by what one depends on. 'He enters his chamber and does not see his wife. Inauspicious' means that there is no place to return to." Cui Zhu[e] said, "She is a widow. What harm is there? Her former husband already suffered the consequences of the ill omen." He then took her as wife.

Lord Zhuang had a liaison with Lady Jiang. As he went often to Cui Zhu's residence, he took Cui Zhu[e]'s hats and bestowed them on others. His attendant said, "This will not do." The lord said, "Can it be that one must have no hat if one does not happen to be Cui Zhu?"[750] Prompted by these acts and also because of the way the lord had used Jin's troubles as the opportunity to attack it, Cui Zhu[e] said, "Jin will certainly retaliate." He wanted to assassinate the lord to curry favor with Jin but had not found the opportunity. The lord had whipped an attendant, Jia Ju, and yet had continued to keep him close at hand. Jia Ju thus looked for an opportunity for Cui Zhu.

Cui Zhu's followers murder Lord Zhuang when the latter comes to Cui's residence for an assignation with Cui Zhu's wife. Pretending to be ignorant of his identity, they kill Lord Zhuang in the name of defending the lord's palace. Despite Lord Zhuang's depravity, many of his followers remain loyal to him and die with him.

In summer, in the fifth month, the Master of Ju visited the court of Qi on account of the Juyu campaign.[751] On the *jiaxu* day (16), the lord offered him ceremonial toasts at the northern outer wall of the capital. Cui Zhu[e] pleaded illness and did not oversee the event. On the *yihai* day (17), the lord went to inquire after Cui Zhu, and he then followed Lady Jiang, who entered the chamber and left with Cui Zhu[e] from the side door. The lord tapped a pillar and sang.[752] The eunuch Jia Ju stopped all the lord's entourage, entered himself, and shut the gate.

25.2b

---

751   For the Juyu campaign, see Xiang 23.7.

752   According to Fu Qian, the lord may be trying to get Lady Jiang's attention because he thinks she does not know that he is waiting outside; or he may already be aware that he is trapped and is singing to express his regret (Hong Liangji, *Chunqiu Zuozhuan gu*, 572).

甲興，公登臺而請，弗許；請盟，弗許；請自刃於廟，弗許。皆曰：
「君之臣杼疾病，不能聽命。近於公宮，陪臣干擏有淫者，不知二命。」
　　公踰牆，又射之，中股，反隊，遂弒之。賈舉、州綽、邴師、公孫敖、
封具、鐸父、襄伊、僂堙皆死。祝佗父祭於高唐，至，復命，不說弁而死
於崔氏。申蒯，侍漁者，退，謂其宰曰：「爾以帑免，我將死。」其宰曰：
「免，是反子之義也。」與之皆死。崔氏殺鬷蔑于平陰。

25.2c　晏子立於崔氏之門外，其人曰：「死乎？」
　　　　曰：「獨吾君也乎哉，吾死也？」
　　　　曰：「行乎？」
　　　　曰：「吾罪也乎哉，吾亡也？」
　　　　曰：「歸乎？」
　　　　曰：「君死，安歸？君民者，豈以陵民？社稷是主。臣君者，豈為其
口實，社稷是養。故君為社稷死，則死之；為社稷亡，則亡之。若為己
死，而為己亡，非其私暱，誰敢任之？且人有君而弒之，吾焉得死之？而
焉得亡之？將庸何歸？」

753　The received text has *you* 又 ("again"), which will make sense only if Lord Zhuang
　　　had already been shot. Yu Yue (Yang, 3:1097) suggests that the graph should be read
　　　as *you* 有, meaning "there was someone."

754　This is a different Jia Ju, not to be confused with the attendant of the same name who
　　　plotted with Cui Zhu against Lord Zhuang.

755　On Zhou Chuo's valor, see Xiang 18.3c, 18.3d, 21.8.

756　Pingyin was a strategic area in the outskirts of the Qi capital, Linzi, see n. 477 above.
　　　Zong Mie was probably related to Zong Sheng Ji, mother of Lord Zhuang.

757　According to Du Yu (ZZ 36.619), the eight men who die defending Lord Zhuang are all
　　　his personal favorites. Ma Su points out that Lord Zhuang's followers (Lupu Kui, Wang
　　　He) later avenge his murder by wiping out the Qing lineage, but the fact that it is his
　　　favorites rather than Qi ministers who remain loyal to him underlines his failings as
　　　a ruler (Wu Jing'an, *Chunqiu Zuoshi zhuan jiuzhu shuzheng xu*, 413–14).

Cui Zhu's armed men rose up from their ambush. The lord climbed up a terrace and begged to be spared. They would not grant it. He begged to swear a covenant. They would not grant it. He begged to put himself to the sword at the Ancestral Temple. They would not grant it. They all said, "The ruler's subject, Cui Zhu[c], is very ill. He cannot personally attend to the lord's commands. Being close to the lord's palace, we, the subjects of the lord's subject, are to make our night circuit and round up the depraved. We know of no other command."

The lord was trying to jump over the wall when someone[753] shot him and hit him in the thigh. He fell back, and they then assassinated him. His followers—Jia Ju,[754] Zhou Chuo,[755] Bing Shi, Gongsun Ao, Feng Ju, Duofu, Xiang Yi, and Lü Yin—all died. Invocator Tuofu had been offering sacrifices at Gaotang. He arrived, reported discharge of his mission, and died at Cui Zhu's residence without taking off his ceremonial cap. Shen Kuai, the superintendent of the fishery, withdrew and said to his steward, "Spare yourself and take care of my family. I am prepared to die." His steward said, "If I spare myself, I will be going against your principle of abiding by duty." He died with Shen Kuai. Cui Zhu killed Zong Mie at Pingyin.[756]

The sagacious Yan Ying mourns Lord Zhuang in a ritually appropriate fashion but refuses to die or go into exile for him. His judgment exemplifies the choices and dilemmas of a noble man in an age of disorder (see also Zhao 10.2).

Yan Ying[b] stood outside the gate of Cui Zhu's residence. His followers said, "Will you die?"

He said, "Was he my ruler only? Why should I die?"

"Will you leave?"

"Is it my crime? Why should I leave?"

"Will you return home?"

"With the ruler dead, where is the home to return to? He who rules over the people, how can he use his position to lord it over the people? It is the altars of the domain that he should take as master. He who serves the ruler, how can he do it for the sake of material recompense? It is the altars of the domain that he should nurture. Thus, if a ruler dies for the altars of the domain, then the subject dies for him. If the ruler is exiled for the altars of the domain, then the subject goes into exile for him. If a ruler dies for himself or is exiled because of his deeds, who, except for his personal favorites, would presume to bear the responsibility?[757] Besides, it was that person, Cui Zhu, who had made him ruler and assassinated him, so how could I die for him? And how could I go into exile for him? Where then is the home to return to?"

門啟而入，枕尸股而哭，興，三踊而出。人謂崔子：「必殺之」。崔子曰：「民之望也，舍之，得民。」

25.2d 盧蒲癸奔晉，王何奔莒。

叔孫宣伯之在齊也，叔孫還納其女於靈公，嬖，生景公。丁丑，崔杼立而相之，慶封為左相，盟國人於大宮，曰：「所不與崔、慶者——」晏子仰天歎曰：「嬰所不唯忠於君、利社稷者是與，有如上帝！」乃歃。辛巳，公與大夫及莒子盟。

大史書曰：「崔杼弒其君。」崔子殺之。其弟嗣書，而死者二人。其弟又書，乃舍之。南史氏聞大史盡死，執簡以往。聞既書矣，乃還。

---

758 The Chinese original, *zhen shi gu* 枕尸股, can also be read as "putting his head on the corpse's thighs." Our translation follows Du Yu's (*ZZ* 36.619) reading, which is based on the phrase *zhen zhi gu* 枕之股 in analogous accounts of mourning ritual (Xi 28.5, Xiang 27.3, 30.10). See Xi 28.5, n. 444. Both *Yanzi chunqiu* 5.296 and *Shiji* 32.1501 present Yan Ying putting his head on the corpse. On the three leaps as mourning ritual, see also *Liji* 20.726.

759 The parallel passage from *Yanzi chunqiu* 5.295–96 more clearly delineates moral choices. In *Yanzi chunqiu*, Yan Ying wisely withdraws from government because of Lord Zhuang's mistrust and incivility. He sighs and smiles as he returns lands and titles to the Qi ruler. He explains to his servant, "I sigh, grieving that my lord will not escape from calamity. I smile, being glad of what I have gained. I will be spared death." Defying Cui Zhu, who reproaches him for not committing suicide, he implies ultimate goals of "preserving the (rightful) ruler" (*cunjun* 存君) and "establishing merit" (*ligong* 立功).

When the gates were opened, Yan Ying entered, pillowed the corpse's head on his thigh[758] and wailed, rose, leaped thrice, and left Cui Zhu's residence. Someone said to Cui Zhu[e], "He must be killed!" Cui Zhu[e] said, "He is the one to whom the people feel allegiance. Let him be, so that we can gain the people's support."[759]

Yan Ying manages to uphold his integrity and protect himself when forced to swear a covenant with Cui Zhu and Qing Feng. The scribes of Qi defend truthful historical records with their lives. The political power of the usurper is shown to be ultimately no match for the moral authority of historical judgment. These Qi scribes, along with Dong Hu (Xuan 2.3c), become the emblem of the historian's integrity in the tradition. This is one of the most famous passages in the text.

Lupu Gui fled to Jin. Wang He fled to Ju.[760]   25.2d

When Shusun Qiaoru[b] was in Qi, Shusun Xuan had Shusun Qiaoru's daughter taken into Lord Ling's harem. He was enamored of her, and she gave birth to Lord Jing.[761] On the *dingchou* day (19), Cui Zhu established the latter as ruler and made himself the chief minister. Qing Feng became the minister of the left. They swore a covenant with the inhabitants of the capital at the Ancestral Temple, and as they said, "Should we not support Cui and Qing . . . ," Yan Ying[b] raised his head heavenward and sighed, "Should I fail to support those who are loyal to the ruler and who benefit the altars of the domain, let the god on high bear witness against me!"[762] Then he smeared his mouth with the blood. On the *xinsi* day (23), the lord and the high officers swore a covenant with the Master of Ju.

The grand scribe wrote, "Cui Zhu assassinated his ruler." Cui Zhu[e] put him to death. The scribe's younger brothers succeeded him and wrote the same thing, and so two more persons were killed. Another younger brother again wrote it, whereupon Cui Zhu desisted. The scribe of the south, having heard that the grand scribes had all died, clutched the bamboo strips and set out. When he heard that the record had already been made, he turned back.[763]

---

760   Both men were of the party of Lord Zhuang.

761   The Lu minister Shusun Qiaoru fled to Qi in 575 BCE (Cheng 16.11). Lord Jing was thus the half brother of the murdered Lord Zhuang. Lord Jing's mother, Mu Meng Ji, is mentioned in Zhao 10.2c, n. 487.

762   In the analogous passage in *Yanzi chunqiu* 5.298–99, Yan Ying denounces Cui Zhu and Qing Feng in a more direct and forceful manner. On interrupted speech, see n. 73 above.

763   The version of this story in *Xinxu* 7.231 concludes with a noble man's commendation: "These are the fine scribes of ancient times" (*gu zhi liangshi* 古之良史).

25.2e　閻丘嬰以帷縛其妻而載之，與申鮮虞乘而出，鮮虞推而下之，曰：「君昏不能匡，危不能救，死不能死，而知匿其暱，其誰納之？」行及弇中，將舍。嬰曰：「崔、慶其追我。」鮮虞曰：「一與一，誰能懼我？」遂舍，枕轡而寢，食馬而食，駕而行。出弇中，謂嬰曰：「速驅之！崔、慶之眾，不可當也。」遂來奔。

　　　　崔氏側莊公于北郭。丁亥，葬諸士孫之里。四翣，不蹕，下車七乘，不以兵甲。

25.3(3)　晉侯濟自泮，會于夷儀，伐齊，以報朝歌之役。齊人以莊公說，使隰鉏請成，慶封如師。男女以班。賂晉侯以宗器、樂器。自六正、五吏、三十帥、三軍之大夫、百官之正長、師旅及處守者皆有賂。晉侯許之。使叔向告於諸侯。公使子服惠伯對曰：「君舍有罪，以靖小國，君之惠也。寡君聞命矣。」

764　Yanzhong 弇中 was located southwest of the Qi capital Linzi 臨淄.

765　The pass is so narrow that they will be fighting their pursuers one chariot at a time.

766　We follow Hong Liangji's (*Chunqiu Zuozhuan gu*, 574) reading of *ce* 側 as *ze* 仄, "not proper." Yu Yue (Yang, 3:1100) reads *ce* as *ji* 堲, "to burn earth and make it into mud bricks" (i.e., Cui Zhu surrounded Lord Zhuang's coffin with mud bricks).

767　The Lane of Shisun must have been located at the northern outer wall. Criminals are banished from family burial grounds (Ai 2.3a). A lord of the domain should have been interred at the ancestral cemetery. The interval between death and burial should have been five months (instead of thirteen days). Here the roads are not cleared as they should have been for the funeral; there are four instead of the customary six fans, seven inferior carriages instead of nine fine carriages; and armed soldiers that should have been employed are absent.

Two supporters of Lord Zhuang escape. Their different reactions to exigencies will result in divergent fates (Xiang 27.9, 31.2). Lord Zhuang is buried in a manner beneath his station.

Lüqiu Ying wrapped his wife in carriage drapes and took her in a carriage. As he rode out with Shen Xianyu, the latter pushed the woman down from the carriage and said to Lüqiu Ying, "When the ruler was benighted, you failed to correct him. When he was in danger, you failed to save him. When he died, you failed to die with him. And yet you know how to conceal your loved one. Who will take us in?" They journeyed forth and reached the narrow pass at Yanzhong,[764] preparing to rest there for the night. Lüqiu Ying[a] said, "Cui Zhu[d] and Qing Feng[a] are pursuing us." Shen Xianyu[a] said, "It will be one against one. Who can make us afraid?"[765] They thus rested for the night and slept using their reins as pillows. After feeding their horses, they ate, yoked the horses, and drove on. Once they came out of Yanzhong, Shen Xianyu said to Lüqiu Ying[a], "Spur on the horses at top speed! We are no match for the multitudes of Cui Zhu[d] and Qing Feng[a]!" And so they came in flight.

Cui Zhu buried Lord Zhuang improperly at the northern outer wall of the capital.[766] On the *dinghai* day (29), Lord Zhuang was interred at the Lane of Shisun. There were four plume-fans flanking the carriage carrying the coffin, the roads were not cleared, seven inferior carriages formed the funeral procession, and no soldiers with weapons and armor were employed.[767]

Jin plans to attack Qi in retaliation for the Zhaoge campaign (Xiang 23.4) but agrees to an accord when Qi leaders offer abundant gifts. Jin may also have been placated by the removal of Lord Zhuang, who was largely responsible for the deterioration of Qi-Jin relations. Note that Cui Zhu cited Jin enmity as one of the reasons why Lord Zhuang should be deposed (Xiang 25.2a).

The Prince of Jin crossed the Pan River. He gathered the princes for a meeting at Yiyi with a view to attacking Qi in retaliation for the Zhaoge campaign. The leaders of Qi made Lord Zhuang their excuse for past troubles and sent Xi Chu to request an accord. Qing Feng went to the Jin army with rows of men and women, signifying submission. He offered the Prince of Jin gifts of sacrificial vessels and musical instruments. All received gifts—from the six directors on down through the ranks of the five senior officers, the thirty subcommanders, the high officers of the three armies, the superintendents of the hundred offices and their subordinates, to those who remained to guard the domain. The Prince of Jin granted his assent to the accord and had Shuxiang notify the princes. Lord Xiang of Lu sent Zifu Huibo to reply: "You, my lord, have let the guilty off in order to bring peace to a small domain. This is your beneficence. Our unworthy ruler has heeded your command!"

25.2e

25.3(3)

25.4 晉侯使魏舒、宛沒逆衛侯，將使衛與之夷儀。崔子止其帑，以求五鹿。

25.5(4) 初，陳侯會楚子伐鄭，當陳隧者，井堙，木刊，鄭人怨之。六月，鄭子展、子產帥車七百乘伐陳，宵突陳城，遂入之。

陳侯扶其大子偃師奔墓，遇司馬桓子，曰：「載余！」曰：「將巡城。」遇賈獲，載其母妻，下之，而授公車。公曰：「舍而母。」辭曰：「不祥。」與其妻扶其母以奔墓，亦免。

子展命師無入公宮，與子產親御諸門。陳侯使司馬桓子賂以宗器。陳侯免，擁社，使其眾男女別而纍，以待於朝。子展執縶而見，再拜稽首承，飲而進獻。子美入，數俘而出。祝祓社，司徒致民，司馬致節，司空致地，乃還。

---

768 For a man and a woman who are unrelated to each other to ride together violates propriety and is therefore inauspicious. Recall how a Jin officer makes his sons dismount his chariot (and sacrifice their lives) and yield their place to a minister of higher rank in the battle of Bi (Xuan 12.2h).

769 *Yu* 御 can also be read as *yu* 禦, "to defend": "and together with Zichan he personally defended the palace at the gates."

770 Cf. Han Jue's manner toward Lord Qing of Qi following Jin's victory in the An campaign (Cheng 2.2).

771 In other words, Zichan just ascertains the extent of Zheng victory without taking Chen captives back to Zheng as prisoners of war.

772 According to Yang (3:1103), these are Zheng officers who restored the people, the tallies, and the land to their Chen counterparts.

Lord Xian of Wei, who had fled to Qi eleven years earlier (Xiang 14.4), will gain a power base in Yiyi with Jin's help, even as Cui Zhu tries to use Lord Xian's family as hostages to bargain for Wei territories.

The Prince of Jin sent Wei Shu and Yuan Mo to meet the Prince of Wei [the exiled Lord Xian]. He planned to have Wei give Yiyi to the exiled Wei ruler. Cui Zhu[e] detained the family of the exiled Wei ruler in order to demand Wulu from Wei.

25.4

Zheng attacks Chen in retaliation for the Chen-Chu incursion of the previous winter (Annals, Xiang 24.9; Zuozhuan, Xiang 24.8). Chen's defeat is dignified by the ritually proper behavior of its high officer Jia Huo. Zheng victors enforce military discipline and restore order in Chen. The account glorifies Zheng leaders as benevolent victors.

Earlier, the Prince of Chen had joined with the Master of Chu to attack Zheng. Along the route taken by the Chen army, wells were filled up and trees cut down. The men of Zheng resented this. In the sixth month, Gongsun Shezhi[a] and Zichan of Zheng, leading seven hundred chariots, attacked Chen, broke through the walls of its capital at night, and then entered it.

25.5(4)

The Prince of Chen, helping along his heir apparent, Yanshi, fled to the graveyard. They encountered the supervisor of the military, Huanzi, and said, "Let us ride in your chariot!" Huanzi replied, "I am preparing to make a circuit of the city walls." They then encountered Jia Huo, who was riding with his mother and wife. Jia Huo made them come down and gave the chariot to the lord. The lord said, "Leave your mother." He declined, saying, "That would be inauspicious."[768] Along with his wife, Jia Huo helped his mother along and fled to the graveyard. They were also spared.

Gongsun Shezhi[a] ordered the army not to enter the lord's palace, and together with Zichan he personally took charge at the palace gates.[769] The Prince of Chen sent the supervisor of the military, Huanzi, to offer them gifts of sacrificial vessels. The Prince of Chen, in mourning clothes and embracing the tablets of the altars, had numerous men and women in bondage arranged in separate rows, and with them he awaited Zheng commands at court. Gongsun Shezhi[a], holding on to a bridle, had an audience with the Chen ruler. He bowed twice with his forehead touching the ground, held up a wine cup, and came forward to offer it ceremoniously.[770] Zichan[b] entered, counted the number of captives, and then left.[771] They had the invocator cleanse all baleful influences at the altar of earth. The supervisor of conscripts restored their people to them, the supervisor of the military restored their tallies of command to them, and the supervisor of works restored their land to them, and they then returned to Zheng.[772]

25.6(5) 秋，七月己巳，同盟于重丘，齊成故也。

25.7 趙文子為政，令薄諸侯之幣，而重其禮。穆叔見之，謂穆叔曰：「自今以往，兵其少弭矣。齊崔、慶新得政，將求善於諸侯。武也知楚令尹。若敬行其禮，道之以文辭，以靖諸侯，兵可以弭。」

25.8(8) 楚蒍子馮卒，屈建為令尹，屈蕩為莫敖。舒鳩人卒叛，楚令尹子木伐之，及離城，吳人救之。子木遽以右師先，子彊、息桓、子捷、子駢、子盂帥左師以退。吳人居其間七日。子彊曰：「久將墊隘，隘乃禽也，不如速戰。請以其私卒誘之，簡師，陳以待我。我克則進，奔則亦視之，乃可以免。不然，必為吳禽。」從之。五人以其私卒先擊吳師，吳師奔；登山以望，見楚師不繼，復逐之，傅諸其軍，簡師會之。吳師大敗。遂圍舒鳩，舒鳩潰。八月，楚滅舒鳩。

---

773 "Finely patterned arguments," also translated as "ornamented words and phases" below (Xiang 25.10b), refer specifically to efficacious diplomatic language.

774 Licheng 離城 was probably very close to Shujiu 舒鳩 just west of present-day Shucheng County 舒城縣, Anhui.

In autumn, in the seventh month, on the *jisi* day (12), the princes swore   25.6(5)
a covenant together at Chongqiu: this was on account of good relations
with Qi.

*Zhao Wu succeeds Fan Gai as chief minister in Jin and lessens demands
on the princes. His goal to end conflicts with Chu results in the Covenant
of Song two years later (Xiang 27.4), although the quest for peace ultimately proves futile.*

Zhao Wu[a] was in charge of government. He issued orders to lighten the   25.7
burden of offerings from the princes and to redouble ritual honors for
them. When Shusun Bao[a] had an audience with him, he said to Shusun
Bao[a], "Henceforth, military conflicts will likely abate somewhat. In Qi,
Cui Zhu[d] and Qing Feng[a] have newly obtained control of the government
and are planning to secure the goodwill of the princes. I also know the
chief minister of Chu. If we respectfully fulfill ritual propriety and open
the way with finely patterned arguments,[773] thereby calming the princes,
then military conflicts can be made to abate."

*Shujiu revolts with Wu aid after its earlier halfhearted submission to Chu
(Xiang 24.9). Chu strategic ploys lead to its elimination, a culmination of
Chu aggression against various Shu domains, including Shuliao (Wen 12.3,
14.10, Xuan 8.3) and Shuyong (Cheng 17.11).*

Wei Ziping of Chu died, and Qu Jian became chief minister. Qu Dang   25.8(8)
became maréchal. The leaders of Shujiu finally revolted, and the Chu
chief minister Qu Jian[a] attacked it. When the Chu forces reached
Licheng,[774] the men of Wu came to the aid of Shujiu. Qu Jian[a] swiftly
deployed the right army to move ahead and had Ziqiang, Xi Huan, Zijie,
Zipian, and Ziyu lead the left army in retreat. The men of Wu were positioned between the right and left armies of Chu for seven days. Ziqiang
said, "A prolonged stalemate will weaken us, and in that weakened state
we will be captured. It is better to fight soon. I request to use our private
soldiers to lead the enemy on, while you select our crack troops and wait
for me with ready battle formations. If we overcome the enemy, then
you advance. Even if we flee, you can still observe the situation and act
accordingly, and we can then be spared. Otherwise, we will certainly be
captured by Wu." They followed his plan. The five men used their clan
troops to first strike the Wu army. The Wu army fled, climbed the mountain to survey the scene, saw that the Chu soldiers were not backed up,
and pursued them again. Once they had drawn the Wu troops close to
the Chu army, the select crack troops closed in on them. The Wu army
was roundly defeated. Chu then laid siege to Shujiu, which collapsed. In
the eighth month, Chu extinguished Shujiu.

　衛獻公入于夷儀。

25.10a　鄭子產獻捷于晉，戎服將事。晉人問陳之罪。對曰：

> 昔虞閼父為周陶正，以服事我先王。我先王賴其利器用也，與其神明之後也，庸以元女大姬配胡公，而封諸陳，以備三恪。則我周之自出，至于今是賴。桓公之亂，蔡人欲立其出，我先君莊公奉五父而立之，蔡人殺之，我又與蔡人奉戴厲公。至於莊、宣，皆我之自立。夏氏之亂，成公播蕩，又我之自入，君所知也。
>
> 今陳忘周之大德，蔑我大惠，棄我姻親，介恃楚眾，以憑陵我敝邑，不可億逞，我是以有往年之告。未獲成命，則有我東門之役。當陳隧者，井堙、木刊。敝邑大懼不競而恥大姬，天誘其衷，啟敝邑之心。陳知其罪授手于我。用敢獻功。

> 晉人曰：「何故侵小？」

775　The ensuing exchange shows that the speaker is Shi Ruo.

776　The former king referred to is King Wu of Zhou.

777　According to *Liji* 39.696, after the Zhou conquest of Shang, King Wu put the descendants of the Yellow Emperor, Yao, and Shun in power in Ji, Zhu, and Chen, respectively. The "three respected lines" thus refer to the descendants of the Yellow Emperor, Yao, and Shun (Yang, 3:1104). Du Yu (*ZZ* 36.622) claims that the term refers to the ruling houses before Zhou, that is, Yu, Xia, and Shang.

778　The Chen heir born of a Cai lady is the future Lord Li (r. 706–700). Lord Zhuang of Zheng at first supported Wufu, Lord Huan's (r. 744–707) younger brother, but eventually recognized Lord Li (Lord Huan's son) after Wufu was killed by the leaders of Cai; see Huan 5.1, Zhuang 22.1; *Annals*, Huan 6.4.

779　Lords Zhuang (r. 699–693) and Xuan (r. 692–648) are sons of Lord Li. There is no mention of Zheng's role in establishing these two Chen rulers in *Zuozhuan*.

780　Chu played a major role intervening in Chen affairs at this point. Zichan ignores that and instead focuses on how Lord Cheng, in exile in Jin, came back to Chen through Zheng's help, which is not mentioned in the account in Xuan 11.5.

781　See Xiang 24.2.

782　Chu invaded Zheng on the request of Chen, see Xiang 24.8.

783　Zichan is implying that since Zhou, Jin, and Zheng all share the clan name Ji, Zheng's weakness will bring shame on the Zhou princess Tai Ji, "Grand Lady Ji," the ancestress of Chen.

Lord Xian of Wei entered Yiyi.   25.9(7)

Zheng requested Jin permission to attack Chen last year (Xiang 24.2b) but did not seem to have obtained it. Here Zichan defends the Zheng invasion of Chen by mixing moral and pragmatic arguments. He appeals to Zhou-Zheng ties, Jin-Zheng ties, and historical examples of beneficial Zheng intercession in Chen, but he also frankly avows the logic of power politics (see also Zhao 1.2b).

Zichan of Zheng presented the spoils of victory to Jin and wore his mili-   25.10a
tary garb while attending to affairs. A Jin leader[775] asked about Chen's offenses. Zichan replied,

> Long ago, Yu Efu became the Zhou director of pottery produc-
> tion so as to serve our former king.[776] Commending the beneficial
> utility of his vessels and his descent from the sage-king Shun, our
> former king gave his eldest daughter, Grand Lady Ji, in marriage
> to Yu Efu's son, the Hu Lord, and put him in power in Chen to
> complete the honors due the "three respected lines."[777] Thus,
> Chen came from our Zhou house and to this day relies on its
> beneficence. With the unrest following the death of Lord Huan
> of Chen, the leaders of Cai wanted to establish as ruler the Chen
> heir born of a Cai lady. Our former ruler, Lord Zhuang, sup-
> ported Wufu and established him as ruler. The leaders of Cai
> killed him, and we worked with them to support and maintain
> Lord Li.[778] Coming to Lords Zhuang and Xuan, each was estab-
> lished as ruler by us.[779] During the rebellion of Xia Zhengshu,
> Lord Cheng wandered as an exile and was also brought back into
> Chen through our effort. That is something you, my lord, knew
> about.[780]
>
> Now Chen has forgotten the great virtue and beneficence of
> Zhou, rejected our ties by marriage, and relied on Chu forces to
> threaten the demolition of our humble settlement. It could not
> be satisfied. That was why we had last year's request.[781] Before we
> received your complete approval, there was the East Gate cam-
> paign.[782] Along the route taken by the Chen army, wells were
> stopped up and trees cut down. Our humble settlement was greatly
> fearful that, failing to assert ourselves, we would bring great shame
> on Grand Lady Ji.[783] Heaven's sentiments were swayed and
> opened our minds to the idea of attacking Chen. Chen realized
> its guilt and accepted punishment from us. That is why we pre-
> sume to offer the spoils of our victorious achievement.

The Jin leader said, "For what reason did you invade a small domain?"

對曰；「先王之命，唯罪所在，各致其辟。且昔天子之地一圻，列國一同，自是以衰。今大國多數圻矣，若無侵小，何以至焉？」

晉人曰：「何故戎服？」

對曰：「我先君武、莊為平、桓卿士。城濮之役，文公布命，曰：『各復舊職。』命我文公戎服輔王，以授楚捷——不敢廢王命故也。」

士莊伯不能詰，復於趙文子。文子曰：「其辭順。犯順，不祥。」乃受之。

25.10b　冬，十月，子展相鄭伯如晉，拜陳之功。子西復伐陳，陳及鄭平。

仲尼曰：「《志》有之：『言以足志，文以足言。』不言，誰知其志？言之無文，行而不遠。晉為伯，鄭入陳，非文辭不為功。慎辭也。」

Zichan replied, "By the command of the former kings, the only thing that matters is where the guilt lies. To each and every offender punishment is meted out. Moreover, long ago the territories of the Son of Heaven amounted to one thousand square *li*; that of the various domains, one hundred square *li*; and with the lower ranks, the territories were smaller still. Now most of the great domains span several thousand square *li*. If they had not invaded small domains, how could they have reached that?"

The Jin leader said, "Why are you wearing military garb?"

He replied, "Our former rulers Lords Wu and Zhuang were the ministers in attendance on Kings Ping and Huan.[784] After the Chengpu campaign, Lord Wen of Jin proclaimed the command, saying, 'All should resume their former duties.' He commanded our Lord Wen to don military attire and assist the king as Jin presented its Chu spoils.[785] We would not presume to cast aside the king's command."

Shi Ruo[b] could not press further and reported discharge of his mission to Zhao Wu[a]. Zhao Wu[b] said, "His words follow propriety and good sense. It is inauspicious to go against propriety and good sense." He then accepted the Zheng spoils.

Confucius commends the power of masterful diplomatic rhetoric. His comment is often cited in writings on literary thought that address the relationship between intent and expression, meaning and rhetoric.[786] In the context here, however, the emphasis is on efficacious language that justifies political gains.

In winter, in the tenth month, Gongsun Shezhi[a] assisted the Liege of Zheng as they went to Jin to bow in thanks for Jin's acceptance of Zheng's achievements in Chen. Zixi again attacked Chen. Chen and Zheng reached a peace agreement.

Confucius[c] said, "As the *Records* has it: 'Use words that are adequate to the intent; use ornamentation that is adequate to the words.' Without words, who can know the intent? Words without ornamentation cannot go far. For Jin to become overlord, and Zheng to enter Chen, there would have been no merit had it not been for ornamented words and phrases. Words and phrases must be used with care!"

25.10b

---

784 See Yin 3.3.

785 This is a reminder of Zheng's role in Jin's moment of glory; see Xi 28.3.

786 E.g., *Wenxin diaolong* 31.1144–75. In the annotation to Lu Ji's "Wen fu" 文賦, these lines are cited differently: "the words are adequate for conveying intent, and the ornamentation is adequate for facilitating words" 言足以志，文足以言 (Wu Jing'an, *Chunqiu Zuoshi zhuan jiuzhu shuzheng xu*, 441). Cf. *Xunzi* 5.85 and 5.89 on the relationship between words, intent, and action.

25.11 楚蒍掩為司馬，子木使庀賦，數甲兵。甲午，蒍掩書土田，度山林，鳩藪澤，辨京陵，表淳鹵，數疆潦，規偃豬，町原防，牧隰皋，井衍沃，量入修賦，賦車、籍馬，賦車兵、徒兵、甲楯之數。既成，以授子木，禮也。

25.12(10) 十二月，吳子諸樊伐楚，以報舟師之役。門于巢。巢牛臣曰：「吳王勇而輕，若啟之，將親門。我獲射之，必殪。是君也死，疆其少安。」從之。吳子門焉，牛臣隱於短牆以射之，卒。

25.13 楚子以滅舒鳩賞子木。辭曰：「先大夫蒍子之功也。」以與蒍掩。

25.14 晉程鄭卒，子產始知然明，問為政焉。對曰：「視民如子。見不仁者，誅之，如鷹鸇之逐鳥雀也。」子產喜，以語子大叔，且曰：「他日，吾見蔑之面而已，今吾見其心矣。」

---

787 This *jiawu* day is the eighth day of the tenth month.

788 An alternative reading is "defined the boundaries of districts liable to flooding."

Chu leaders systematically review the conditions and resources of the domain.

Wei Yan of Chu became supervisor of the military. Qu Jian[a] had him regulate revenues and review weapons and armor. On the *jiawu* day,[787] Wei Yan recorded the conditions of resources and lands: he measured the timber of mountain forests, examined wetlands and marshes, made distinctions between high altitudes and lesser mounds, marked out saline fields with trees, defined districts with dense soil liable to flooding,[788] drew boundaries for reservoirs, divided lands up into small parcels for cultivation, used wetlands for pastures, established subdivisions for flat, fertile lands, calculated the domain's revenues and regularized levies, and determined the contribution of chariots, of horses, and of the weapons for chariot drivers and for foot soldiers, as well as the number of armor suits and shields. Having completed this, he delivered the results to Qu Jian[a]. This was in accordance with ritual propriety.

Wu attacks Chu in retaliation for the latter's flotilla-borne attack (Xiang 24.4). The reckless Wu king dies in battle.

In the twelfth month, Zhufan, the Master of Wu, attacked Chu in retaliation for the campaign of the flotilla. Wu forces stormed the gate of Chao. Niuchen of Chao said, "The Wu king is valiant and reckless. If we open the gate, he will personally break through it. I will get the chance to shoot him, and he will be sure to die. If that ruler dies, our borders will enjoy peace for a little while." The men of Chao followed his suggestion. The Master of Wu stormed the gate, and Niuchen, hiding behind a low wall, shot him, and he died.

The Master of Chu rewarded Qu Jian[a] for extinguishing Shujiu. The latter declined, "This was the achievement of the former high officer Wei Ziping[a]." The reward was thus given to Wei Ziping's son Wei Yan.

Cheng Zheng's death reminds Zichan of Ran Ming's negative judgment of Cheng Zheng (Xiang 24.12). Ran Ming's ugliness (Zhao 28.3c) means that Zichan is slow to appreciate his foresight. Ran Ming had seen through Cheng Zheng's apparent humility, and now Zichan can get past Ran Ming's appearance. Ran Ming and Zichan offer similar views on discipline and assiduity in government.

Cheng Zheng of Jin died, and only then did Zichan recognize Ran Ming's prescience. Zichan asked the latter about the way of government. Ran Ming replied, "Regard the people as your children. If you see an ignoble person, put him to death the way hawks pounce on sparrows." Zichan was glad and told You Ji[b] about this, adding, "In the old days I saw only Ran Ming[a]'s face, but now I have seen his heart."

子大叔問政於子產。子產曰：「政如農功，日夜思之，思其始而成其終，朝夕而行之。行無越思，如農之有畔，其過鮮矣。」

25.15　衛獻公自夷儀使與甯喜言，甯喜許之。大叔文子聞之，曰：「烏呼！《詩》所謂

> 我躬不說，
> 皇恤我後

者，甯子可謂不恤其後矣。將可乎哉？殆必不可。君子之行，思其終也，思其復也。書曰：

> 慎始而敬終，終以不困。

《詩》曰：

> 夙夜匪解，
> 以事一人。

今甯子視君不如弈棋，其何以免乎？弈者舉棋不定，不勝其耦；而況置君而弗定乎？必不免矣。九世之卿族，一舉而滅之，可哀也哉！」

789　For a similar comparison, see Yin 6.4, Zhao 1.1b.

790　These lines appear in both *Maoshi* 35, "Gufeng" 谷風, 2B.90, and *Maoshi* 197, "Xiao pan" 小弁, 12C.423.

791　These lines are not found in the received version of *Shangshu*. They appear in a slightly altered version in *Yi Zhou shu* 1.3.1929a and in Xu Gan, *Zhong lun* 2.11. In *Liji* 54.918, being "cautious at the beginning and reverential at the end" is said to be "the way to serve rulers."

You Ji[b] asked Zichan about the way of government. Zichan said, "Governing is like farming,[789] in that one thinks about it day and night, in that one thinks about its beginnings so as to achieve its ends, in that one acts on these thoughts from morning till evening. Do not act on what you have not thought through; do this in the same way that fields follow dividing boundaries. In this way there will be few errors."

The Wei minister Ning Xi, whose father drove out Lord Xian of Wei (Xiang 14.4), promises to restore the latter, fulfilling his father's dying wish (Xiang 20.7). The Wei minister Taishu Yi's prediction of Ning Xi's doom will be fulfilled two years later (Xi 27.3a).

From Yiyi Lord Xian of Wei sent someone to talk to Ning Xi about his restoration. Ning Xi gave his assent. Taishu Yi[a] heard about this and said, "Alas! There are those of whom the *Odes* says,

> Even for my person there is no place,
> Whence the means to worry about what comes after me?[790]

Ning Xi[c] can be said not to worry about what comes after him! Can what is planned be done? Surely it cannot be done. When it comes to a noble man's action, he thinks about its consequences and its continuance. As the *Documents* says,

> Be cautious at the beginning and reverential at the end, and you
> will finish with no difficulty.[791]

It says in the *Odes*,

> Day and night, unflaggingly,
> He serves the One Man.[792]

Now that Ning Xi[c] regards dealing with the ruler as a lesser game than chess, how can he escape disaster? If a chess player holds a piece and cannot decide, he will not overcome his opponent. How much more is it so with one who is about to put a ruler in his place and cannot decide? He will certainly not escape disaster. A house that has held ministerial positions for nine generations will be destroyed with one stroke. It is lamentable indeed!"

---

792   *Maoshi* 260, "Zhengmin" 蒸民, 18C.675. Yin Jifu, a Zhou nobleman, is praising another Zhou nobleman, Zhong Shanfu, for his service to the royal house. "One Man" refers to King Xuan of Zhou (r. 827–781). These lines are also cited in Wen 3.4.

25.16　　會于夷儀之歲，齊人城郟。其五月，秦、晉為成，晉韓起如秦涖盟，秦伯車如晉涖盟。成而不結。

春秋

26.1(2)　二十有六年，春，王二月辛卯，衛甯喜弒其君剽。

26.2(2)　衛孫林父入于戚以叛。

26.3(2)　甲午，衛侯衎復歸于衛。

26.4(5)　夏，晉侯使荀吳來聘。

26.5(7)　公會晉人、鄭良霄、宋人、曹人于澶淵。

26.6(8)　秋，宋公殺其世子痤。

26.7(7)　晉人執衛甯喜。

26.8(11)　八月壬午，許男甯卒于楚。

26.9(11)　冬，楚子、蔡侯、陳侯伐鄭。

26.10(11)　葬許靈公。

Qin and Jin made a peace agreement in the previous year, but the realization of the covenant in the coming year, to which this entry properly belongs, is fraught with difficulties.

The year when the meeting at Yiyi took place, the leaders of Qi fortified Jia. In the fifth month of that year, Qin and Jin reached a peace agreement. Han Qi of Jin went to Qin to oversee the covenant. Qian[b] of Qin went to Jin to oversee the covenant. The peace agreement was made but did not last.[793]

25.16

LORD XIANG 26 (547 BCE)
ANNALS

In the twenty-sixth year, in spring, in the royal second month, on the *xinmao* day (7), Ning Xi of Wei assassinated his ruler Piao.

26.1(2)

Sun Linfu of Wei entered Qī and led it in revolt.

26.2(2)

On the *jiawu* day (10), the Prince of Wei, Kan, went home again to Wei.

26.3(2)

In summer, the Prince of Jin sent Xun Wu (Zhonghang Wu) to us on an official visit.

26.4(5)

Our lord met with a Jin leader, Liang Xiao of Zheng, a Song leader, and a Cao leader at Chanyuan.[794]

26.5(7)

In autumn, the Duke of Song put to death his heir apparent Cuo.

26.6(8)

Jin leaders arrested Ning Xi of Wei.

26.7(7)

In the eighth month, on the *renwu* day (1), Ning, the Head of Xǔ, died in Chu.

26.8(11)

In winter, the Master of Chu, the Prince of Cai, and the Prince of Chen attacked Zheng.

26.9(11)

Lord Ling of Xǔ was buried.

26.10(11)

---

793   This narrative is separated from its continuation in Xiang 26.1 by *Annals* entries.

794   Chanyuan 澶淵 was in the domain of Wei northwest of Puyang County 濮陽縣, Henan.

26.1 二十六年，春，秦伯之弟鍼如晉修成，叔向命召行人子員。行人子朱曰：
「朱也當御。」三云，叔向不應。子朱怒，曰：「班爵同，何以黜朱於朝？」
撫劍從之。叔向曰：「秦、晉不和久矣。今日之事，幸而集，晉國賴之。不
集，三軍暴骨。子員道二國之言無私，子常易之。姦以事君者，吾所能御
也。」拂衣從之。人救之。

平公曰：「晉其庶乎！吾臣之所爭者大。」師曠曰：「公室懼卑。臣
不心競而力爭，不務德而爭善，私欲已侈，能無卑乎？」

26.2a 衛獻公使子鮮為復，辭。敬姒強命之。對曰：「君無信，臣懼不免。」敬姒
曰：「雖然，以吾故也。」許諾。

初，獻公使與甯喜言，甯喜曰：「必子鮮在。不然，必敗。」故公使
子鮮。子鮮不獲命於敬姒，以公命與甯喜言，曰：「苟反，政由甯氏，祭
則寡人。」

甯喜告蘧伯玉。伯玉曰：「瑗不得聞君之出，敢聞其入？」遂行，從
近關出。

795　See Xiang 4.3 and 8.7b.
796　*Guoyu*, "Jin yu 8," 14.463, has an almost identical passage.
797　Cf. Xiang 14.4, n. 400.

Two Jin envoys fight over the right to serve during Qin-Jin negotiations. Shuxiang, elsewhere commended for his wisdom, here seems more partisan. The music master Kuang sees the signs of Jin decline.

In the twenty-sixth year, in spring, Qian, the younger brother of the Liege of Qin, went to Jin to cultivate good relations. Shuxiang gave orders to summon the envoy Ziyun. The envoy Zizhu said, "But I am the one who should go up." Thrice he said this, and Shuxiang did not respond. Enraged, Zizhu said, "Ziyun and I have the same rank. Why are you dismissing me from court?" Holding his sword, he went after Shuxiang. Shuxiang said, "Qin and Jin have not been at peace for a long time. If fortunately today's affair comes to fruition, the domain of Jin will depend on it. If it does not come to fruition, our three armies will be slaughtered and will have their bones exposed on the battlefield. Ziyun conveys the words of the two domains without interposing his private views,[795] whereas you often alter them. I will fight any who serve the ruler with treachery!" He shook his robes and went after Zizhu. The others stopped them.

26.1

Lord Ping said, "Jin seems to be improving its good government! What my subjects fight over are important matters." The music master Kuang said, "I fear the lord's house will be brought low. The subjects are not competing with their minds but fighting with their strength. They do not strive for virtue but fight for approval. Their private desires are already excessive. How can the lord's house not be brought low?"[796]

Ning Xi carries out his father's deathbed wish (Xiang 20.7) and prepares to restore the exiled Lord Xian, although various prescient characters predict disaster.

Lord Xian of Wei assigned his younger brother Zhuan[a] the task of preparing for his restoration. Zhuan declined. Their mother, Jing Si, forced him by command to do so. He replied, "The ruler is faithless. I fear we will not escape disaster." Jing Si said, "Even so, do this for my sake." Zhuan[a] agreed to comply.

26.2a

Earlier, Lord Xian had sent someone to talk to Ning Xi. Ning Xi said, "Zhuan[a] has to be there. Otherwise, we will fail for sure." That was why the lord sent Zhuan[a]. Not having been instructed on the details of his mission by Jing Si, he conveyed the lord's command to Ning Xi: "If I return, the government will be in the hands of the Ning lineage, but I, the unworthy one, will be in charge of sacrifices."

Ning Xi told Qu Boyu. Boyu said, "I did not get to hear about the lord's exile. How dare I hear about his reentry?" He then went on his way, leaving the domain by way of a nearby pass.[797]

告右宰穀。右宰穀曰：「不可。獲罪於兩君，天下誰畜之？」悼子曰：「吾受命於先人，不可以貳。」穀曰：「我請使焉而觀之。」遂見公於夷儀。反，曰：「君淹恤在外十二年矣，而無憂色，亦無寬言，猶夫人也。若不已，死無日矣。」悼子曰：「子鮮在。」右宰穀曰：「子鮮在，何益？多而能亡，於我何為？」悼子曰：「雖然，不可以已。」

26.2b(1, 2)　孫文子在戚，孫嘉聘於齊，孫襄居守。二月庚寅，甯喜、右宰穀伐孫氏，不克，伯國傷。甯子出舍於郊。伯國死，孫氏夜哭。國人召甯子，甯子復攻孫氏，克之。辛卯，殺子叔及大子角。

　　書曰「甯喜弒其君剽」，言罪之在甯氏也。孫林父以戚如晉。書曰「入于戚以叛」，罪孫氏也。臣之祿，君實有之。義則進，否則奉身而退。專祿以周旋，戮也。

Ning Xi told Youzai Gu. The latter said, "This will not do. When your lineage will have committed crimes against two rulers,[798] who in the world will take you in?" Ning Xi[a] said, "I received the command from my late father. I cannot swerve onto another course." Youzai Gu[a] said, "I beg leave to be sent as emissary so that I can observe the situation." He thus had an audience with the lord at Yiyi. Upon his return, he said, "The ruler has been mired in troubles and sorrows abroad for twelve years. Yet he did not appear worried, nor did he have any generous words. He still remains that same person. If you do not desist, our death is not far off." Ning Xi[a] said, "Zhuan[a] is there." Youzai Gu said, "Even if Zhuan[a] is there, what good will it do? At the most he will go into exile. What can he do for us?" Ning Xi[a] said, "Even so, we cannot stop now."

Ning Xi kills Piao, who ruled in Wei during Lord Xian's exile. He also attacks the lineage of Sun Linfu, his father's accomplice in driving out Lord Xian. Although Sun Linfu is criticized for turning Qī into a semiautonomous Jin protectorate (in a manner comparable to Yu Shi's position in Pengcheng [Cheng 18.5]), it is obvious that Lord Xian deserves no loyalty.

Sun Linfu[a] was in Qī. His son Sun Jia was on an official visit in Qi, while another son, Sun Xiang, remained in the Wei capital. In the second month, on the *gengyin* day (6), Ning Xi and Youzai Gu attacked the Sun lineage. They did not overcome them, but Sun Xiang[a] was wounded. Ning Xi[c] came out of the capital and lodged in the outskirts. Sun Xiang[a] died, and members of the Sun lineage wailed at night. The inhabitants of the capital summoned Ning Xi[c], who again attacked the Sun lineage and overcame them. On the *xinmao* day (7), Ning Xi killed the Wei ruler Piao[a] and the heir apparent Jiao.

26.2b(1, 2)

The text says, "Ning Xi assassinated his ruler Piao": this is to indicate that the guilt lay with Ning Xi[b]. Sun Linfu, taking Qī, went over to Jin. The text says that he "entered Qī and led it in revolt": this is to hold Sun Linfu guilty. It is the ruler who possesses the emolument of the subject. When dutiful action is viable, then one advances to serve; if not, one withdraws, preserving one's honor. To lay sole claim to one's emolument and use it to maneuver for advantages is a crime that deserves public execution.[799]

---

798 Sun Linfu and Ning Zhi (Ning Xi's father) drove out Lord Xian of Wei in 559 BCE (Xiang 14.4), and Ning Xi is now planning to murder the current Wei ruler, Piao. In *Chunqiu shiyu*, Youzai Gu predicts that Lord Xian will not honor his promises because he is gaining reentry through bribery.

799 Fu Qian defines *zhuanlu* 專祿 ("lay sole claim to one's emolument") as "regarding one's settlement as a small domain." Li Yide links *zhouxuan* 周旋 ("maneuver for advantages") to the way Sun deals with Wei and Jin (Wu Jing'an, *Chunqiu Zuoshi zhuan jiuzhu shuzheng xu*, 465).

26.2c 甲午，衛侯入。書曰「復歸」，國納之也。

大夫逆於竟者，執其手而與之言；道逆者，自車揖之；逆於門者，頷之而已。公至，使讓大叔文子曰：「寡人淹恤在外，二三子皆使寡人朝夕聞衛國之言，吾子獨不在寡人。古人有言曰：『非所怨，勿怨。』寡人怨矣。」對曰：「臣知罪矣。臣不佞，不能負羈絏以從扞牧圉，臣之罪一也。有出者，有居者，臣不能貳，通外內之言以事君，臣之罪二也。有二罪，敢忘其死？」乃行，從近關出。公使止之。

26.3 衛人侵戚東鄙，孫氏愬于晉，晉戍茅氏。殖綽伐茅氏，殺晉戍三百人。孫蒯追之，弗敢擊。文子曰：「厲之不如。」遂從衛師，敗之圉。雍鉏獲殖綽。復愬于晉。

---

800   This could be the gate of the capital or of the palace.

801   Taishu Yi is referring to Lord Xian's exile and Piao's instatement as the Wei ruler. He implies that they are equally legitimate and he cannot betray Piao. Taishu Yi's argument echoes the covenant Ning Wuzi swore with Wei leaders (Xi 28.5). In *Chunqiu shiyu* from the Mawangdui manuscripts, Lord Xian eventually makes Taishu Yi minister because of his "undivided allegiance" (*bu'er* 不貳); see also Xiang 27.3.

802   Qī was about 80 *li* to the northeast of the Wei capital, Diqiu. According to Du Yu (ZZ 37.631), Maoshi 茅氏 was on the eastern side of Qī.

803   Zhi Chuo, the Qi officer whose exploits are told in Xiang 18.3, 19.11 and 21.8, might have fled to Wei following the murder of Lord Zhuang of Qi.

On the *jiawu* day (10), the Prince of Wei entered the capital. The text
says that he "went home again" because the domain took him in.   26.2c

As for the high officers who met him at the border, he held their
hands and spoke with them. As for those who met him on the road, he
bowed to them from his carriage. As for those who met him at the
gate,[800] he merely nodded to them. When the lord arrived, he sent
someone to reprimand Taishu Yi[a]: "I, the unworthy one, was mired in
troubles and sorrows abroad. Various fine men have all, day and night,
let me hear of news from Wei. You alone, sir, have shown no concern
for me. The ancients had this saying, 'Do not resent what should not be
resented.' I do feel resentment." Taishu Yi replied, "Your subject knows
his offenses. I lack talent and was not able to carry bridles and reins to
follow you and defend your property as herdsman and groom. That was
my first offense. There was the one who left the domain, and there was
the one who stayed.[801] I was not able to shift allegiance and serve the
ruler by becoming a conduit for talk inside and outside the domain.
That was my second offense. Being guilty of these two offenses, how
could I presume to forget that I deserve to die?" He thus went on his
way, leaving the domain by way of a nearby pass. The lord sent someone
to stop him.

*Lord Xian pursues another foe, the exiled Wei minister Sun Linfu. The
latter, who has relied on Jin for almost four decades to oppose errant Wei
rulers (e.g., Cheng 7.6, 14.1), complains about Wei to Jin.*

The men of Wei invaded the eastern marches of Qí. Sun Linfu[d] accused   26.3
Wei to Jin. Jin garrisoned Maoshi.[802] Zhi Chuo attacked Maoshi and
killed three hundred Jin soldiers garrisoned there.[803] Sun Kuai, one of
Sun Linfu's sons, pursued Zhi Chuo but did not dare to strike. Sun Linfu[c]
said, "You are not even the equal of vengeful ghosts."[804] Sun Kuai then
pursued the Wei troops and defeated them at Yu.[805] Yong Chu took Zhi
Chuo captive. Sun Linfu again accused Wei to Jin.

---

804   The three hundred Jin soldiers, having been killed by Zhi Chuo, would presumably
      turn into vengeful ghosts. In Xiang 17.2, the men of Cao reviled Sun Kuai by calling
      his father, Sun Linfu, "a vengeful ghost."
805   Yu 圉 was in the domain of Wei in the east of Puyang County 濮陽縣, Henan.

26.4　鄭伯賞入陳之功，三月甲寅朔，享子展，賜之先路三命之服，先八邑；賜子產次路再命之服，先六邑。子產辭邑，曰：「自上以下，降殺以兩，禮也。臣之位在四，且子展之功也，臣不敢及賞禮，請辭邑。」公固予之，乃受三邑。公孫揮曰：「子產其將知政矣。讓不失禮。」

26.5(4)　晉人為孫氏故，召諸侯，將以討衛也。夏，中行穆子來聘，召公也。

26.6a　楚子、秦人侵吳，及雩婁，聞吳有備而還。遂侵鄭。五月，至于城麇。鄭皇頡戍之，出，與楚師戰，敗。穿封戌囚皇頡，公子圍與之爭之，正於伯州犁。伯州犁曰：「請問於囚。」乃立囚。伯州犁曰：「所爭，君子也，其何

806　See Cheng 2.3h, n. 76. In the ritual of gift giving, the most important gifts are given last; hence, other gifts precede the gift of land here.

807　According to Xiang 27.5, Zichan is ranked after Gongsun Shezhi, Liang Xiao, and Zixi.

808　Yulou 雩婁 was in the domain of Chu east of Shangcheng County 商城縣 and north of Jinzhai County 金寨縣, Anhui.

809　The precise location of Chengjun 城麇 is not known.

Lord Jian of Zheng rewards his ministers for victory in Chen. Zichan tries to decline the honors bestowed on him and thereby demonstrates his suitability for even greater responsibility.

The Liege of Zheng rewarded his ministers for their achievement in entering the Chen capital. In the third month, on the *jiayin* day, the first day of the month, he offered Gongsun Shezhi[a] ceremonial toasts and bestowed on him superior carriages and regalia appropriate to dignitaries of three commands,[806] and these gifts were followed by eight settlements. He bestowed on Zichan second-tier carriages and regalia appropriate to dignitaries of two commands, and these gifts were followed by six settlements. Zichan declined the settlements: "Going from above to below, for each lower rank the number of gifts and honors is diminished by two. That is in accordance with ritual propriety. Your subject ranks fourth among the ministers.[807] What is more, the achievement was Gongsun Shezhi[a]'s. I do not dare to be included in the ritual of rewards. I beg to decline the settlements." The lord insisted on giving them to him, so he accepted three settlements. Gongsun Hui said, "Zichan will probably assume responsibility for government. In yielding he did not go against ritual propriety."

26.4

Jin rallies its allies to attack Wei because of Sun Linfu's machinations.

The leaders of Jin, on account of Sun Linfu[d], summoned the princes so as to prepare to chastise Wei. In summer, Zhonghang Wu[a] came to us on an official visit: this was to summon our lord.

26.5(4)

A Qin-Chu coalition attacks Zheng. Chuanfeng Xu, a district governor, and Gongzi Wei both claim credit for taking a Zheng officer captive. The adjudicating Chu minister Bo Zhouli, who had fled to Chu from Jin and showed good judgment earlier (Cheng 15.5, 16.5), here twists the truth to pander to Gongzi Wei. When Gongzi Wei becomes king six years later, he will punish Bo Zhouli (Zhao 1.13) and will reward Chuanfeng Xu (Zhao 8.6).

The Master of Chu and the men of Qin invaded Wu, advancing as far as Yulou.[808] Having heard that Wu was well prepared, they turned back and then invaded Zheng. In the fifth month, they reached Chengjun.[809] Huang Jie of Zheng, who was garrisoned there, came out and did battle with Chu troops, and he suffered defeat. Chuanfeng Xu took Huang Jie prisoner. Gongzi Wei fought with him over the credit for taking a Zheng nobleman prisoner, and so they had Bo Zhouli determine who was in the right. Bo Zhouli said, "I submit that we ask the prisoner." They thus had the prisoner stand before them. Bo Zhouli said, "They are fighting over you, and

26.6a

不知？」上其手，曰：「夫子為王子圍，寡君之貴介弟也。」下其手，曰：
「此子為穿封戌，方城外之縣尹也。誰獲子？」囚曰：「頡遇王子，弱焉。」
戌怒，抽戈逐王子圍，弗及。楚人以皇頡歸。

26.6b 印堇父與皇頡戍城麇，楚人囚之，以獻於秦。鄭人取貨於印氏以請之，
子大叔為令正，以為請。子產曰：「不獲。受楚之功，而取貨於鄭，不可
謂國，秦不其然。若曰『拜君之勤鄭國。微君之惠，楚師其猶在敝邑之
城下』，其可。」弗從，遂行。秦人不予。更幣，從子產，而後獲之。

26.7a(5, 7) 六月，公會晉趙武、宋向戌、鄭良霄、曹人于澶淵，以討衛，疆戚田。取衛
西鄙懿氏六十以與孫氏。
　　　趙武不書，尊公也。向戌不書，後也。鄭先宋，不失所也。
　　　於是衛侯會之。晉人執甯喜、北宮遺，使女齊以先歸。衛侯如晉，
晉人執而囚之於士弱氏。

810　This story gives rise to a common idiom, "to raise and lower one's hand" (*shangxia
qi shou* 上下其手), which means interference that perverts justice or correct
judgment.

811　Instead of the reality of the Qin-Chu coalition invading Zheng (Xiang 26.6a), Zichan
presents Qin as the force restraining Chu aggression.

812　The implication is that these are ritually proper gifts, which Qin can accept without
suspicion of receiving a bribe from the Yin lineage.

you are a nobleman. How can you fail to understand?" He raised his hand and said, "This fine man is Gongzi Wei[a], our humble ruler's exalted younger brother." He lowered his hand and said, "This man is Chuanfeng Xu, the governor of the district outside Fangcheng. Now who took you captive?" The prisoner said, "I encountered the king's son, who showed I was the weaker man." Infuriated, Chuanfeng Xu pulled out his dagger-axe and pursued Gongzi Wei[a] but could not overtake him. The leaders of Chu took Huang Jie with them and turned back.[810]

Zichan's skillful diplomatic rhetoric conceals the reality of a transaction, enlists a former foe as ally, and secures the return of a Zheng officer held in Qin.

Yin Jinfu was garrisoned with Huang Jie at Chengjun. The men of Chu took Yin Jinfu prisoner and offered him to Qin. The leaders of Zheng took goods from the Yin lineage to request Yin Jinfu's ransom. You Ji[b], who was serving as director of decrees, was to submit the request. Zichan said, "You will not get him back. Receiving the fruit of Chu's victory and then using it to obtain goods from Zheng is hardly what we call the behavior of a proper domain. Qin will not do that. But it will work if you say, 'I bow to acknowledge my lord's exertions on behalf of Zheng. If it were not for your beneficence, Chu troops would still be beneath the city wall of our humble domain.'"[811] You Ji did not follow his advice. He then set out for Qin. The leaders of Qin did not give him Yin Jinfu. They sent another envoy bringing another set of gifts, following Zichan's advice, and only then did they get Yin Jinfu back.[812]

Jin leaders summon a meeting to strengthen Sun Linfu's lineage and to punish the Wei ruler and his supporters.

In the sixth month, our lord met with Zhao Wu of Jin, Xiang Xu of Song, Liang Xiao of Zheng, and a Cao leader at Chanyuan to chastise Wei and also to set up boundaries for the territories of Qí. They took sixty settlements of the Yi lineage on the western marches of Wei and gave them to the Sun lineage.

That Zhao Wu is not recorded is to honor our lord. That Xiang Xu is not recorded is because he came late. That Zheng is recorded before Song is because the Zheng delegates arrived on time and did not lose their place.

At that time the Prince of Wei met with them. The leaders of Jin arrested Ning Xi and Beigong Yi and had Ru Qi first take them back to Jin. The Prince of Wei went to Jin. The leaders of Jin arrested him and imprisoned him at Shi Ruo's residence.

秋，七月，齊侯、鄭伯為衛侯故如晉，晉侯兼享之。晉侯賦〈嘉樂〉。國
景子相齊侯，賦〈蓼蕭〉。子展相鄭伯，賦〈緇衣〉。叔向命晉侯拜二
君，曰：「寡君敢拜齊君之安我先君之宗祧也，敢拜鄭君之不貳也。」

　　國子使晏平仲私於叔向，曰：「晉君宣其明德於諸侯，恤其患而
補其闕，正其違而治其煩，所以為盟主也。今為臣執君，若之何？」叔
向告趙文子，文子以告晉侯。晉侯言衛侯之罪，使叔向告二君。國子
賦〈轡之柔矣〉，子展賦〈將仲子兮〉，晉侯乃許歸衛侯。

　　叔向曰：「鄭七穆，罕氏其後亡者也，子展儉而壹。」

813　*Maoshi* 249, "Jia le" 假樂, 17C.615–16. Also cited or mentioned in Wen 3.7, Cheng 2.8, Zhao 21.2, and Ai 5.4, this ode praises the virtuous government of the noble man that is rewarded by Heaven and brings good to all. Lord Ping of Jin is probably using the ode to praise the Qi and Zheng rulers. Cf. The uses of "Chang di" in Xi 24.b, Xiang 20.7, and Zhao 7.11.

814　*Maoshi* 173, "Luxiao" 蓼蕭, 10A.348–50. This is a feast poem celebrating the fraternal harmony between the Zhou king and the princes. The great joy of "having seen my lord" (*ji jian junzi* 既見君子) lies in the certainty that he is "good for the elder brother and the younger brother" (*yi xiong yi di* 宜兄宜弟). Guo Ruo is implicitly appealing to Jin to release the Wei ruler in the interest of harmonious relations among "brother domains." This ode also features in Jin-Wei negotiations in Zhao 7.11. Lu ministers recite this ode for the Song envoy Hua Ding in Zhao 12.3, but Hua Ding fails to respond properly.

815　*Maoshi* 75, "Ziyi" 緇衣, 4B.159–61. Zheng is protesting its loyalty to Jin as Zheng implicitly intercedes on behalf of the Wei ruler, comparing itself to the lady who mends the black robe for the lord in the poem. Gongsun Shezhi emphasizes how the Zheng ruler's journey underlines Jin-Zheng amity: "We have come to your lodgings" (*shi zi zhi guan xi* 適子之館兮). The image of the mended robe may also refer to reconciliation between the Jin and Wei rulers.

816　Shuxiang understands the appeals of Qi and Zheng on behalf of the Wei ruler but is deliberately deflecting the issue. Since "Luxuriant Artemisia" praises the lord's "good name and rightful place" (*yu chu* 譽處), Shuxiang thanks Qi for augmenting Jin rule, possibly also harking back to the assistance that Lord Huan of Qi rendered Chong'er, later Lord Wen of Jin (Xi 23.6b). Shuxiang also acknowledges Zheng loyalty as expressed in "Black Robe," without, however, accepting Zheng mediation.

Jin, with a history of supporting Wei ministers accusing their rulers (Xi 28.8, Cheng 14.1), again sides with Sun Linfu against Lord Xian of Wei. At the meeting at Chanyuan, diplomatic negotiations conducted through the recitation of odes eventually convince the Jin ruler to release the Wei ruler.

In autumn, in the seventh month, the Prince of Qi and the Liege of Zheng went to Jin on behalf of the Prince of Wei. The Prince of Jin offered them ceremonial toasts together. The Prince of Jin recited "Great Happiness."[813] Guo Ruo[a] acted as assistant to the Prince of Qi and recited "Luxuriant Artemisia."[814] Gongsun Shezhi[a] acted as assistant to the Liege of Zheng and recited "Black Robe."[815] Shuxiang told the Prince of Jin to bow to the two rulers and said, "Our unworthy ruler presumes to bow to the Qi ruler for securing the Ancestral Temples of our former rulers. He presumes to bow to the Zheng ruler for his unwavering allegiance."[816]

Guo Ruo[b] sent Yan Ying[a] to speak privately to Shuxiang: "The Jin ruler manifests his bright virtue among the princes, allays their troubles and supplements their deficiencies, corrects their errors and brings order to their turmoil. That is how he can be the covenant chief. Now Jin has seized the ruler on behalf of the subject. What is to be done?" Shuxiang told Zhao Wu[a], and Zhao Wu[b] told the Prince of Jin. The Prince of Jin spoke of the crimes of the Prince of Wei and sent Shuxiang to report them to the two rulers. Guo Ruo recited "The Reins Are Soft."[817] Gongsun Shezhi[a] recited "Please, Zhongzi."[818] The Prince of Jin thus agreed to let the Prince of Wei return to his domain.

Shuxiang said, "Of the seven lineages descended from Lord Mu of Zheng, the Han lineage will probably be the last to perish. Gongsun Shezhi[a] is temperate and constant."[819]

---

817 This is an "uncollected ode" not found in the received text of the *Odes*. It may be associated with a citation from an ode in *Yi Zhou shu* (64.1982) that summons the image of "soft reins." Guo Ruo is urging the Jin ruler to use leniency to bring peace to the lords, just as soft reins may be employed to control recalcitrant horses.

818 *Maoshi* 76, "Qiang Zhongzi" 將仲子, 4B.161–62. In this song, a woman admonishes her overly ardent lover to desist, "fearing the many things people would say" (*wei ren zhi duoyan* 畏人之多言). Gongsun Shezhi is suggesting that "public opinion" would turn against Jin if it sides with a subject against his ruler.

819 Gongsun Shezhi (Zizhan) belongs to the Han lineage. On the seven Mu lineages, see Xuan 3.6b. Nothing is known of the fate of the Han lineage in Zheng, and this is one of the unverifiable predictions in *Zuozhuan*.

26.8(6) 　初，宋芮司徒生女子，赤而毛，棄諸堤下，共姬之妾取以入，名之曰棄。
長而美。平公入夕，共姬與之食。公見棄也，而視之，尤。姬納諸御，嬖，
生佐，惡而婉。大子痤美而很，合左師畏而惡之。寺人惠牆伊戾為大子
內師而無寵。

　　秋，楚客聘於晉，過宋。大子知之，請野享之，公使往。伊戾請從
之。公曰：「夫不惡女乎？」對曰：「小人之事君子也，惡之不敢遠，好之
不敢近，敬以待命，敢有貳心乎？縱有共其外，莫共其內，臣請往也。」
遣之。

　　至，則欿，用牲，加書，徵之，而騁告公，曰：「大子將為亂，既與楚
客盟矣。」公曰：「為我子，又何求？」對曰：「欲速。」公使視之，則信有
焉。問諸夫人與左師，則皆曰：「固聞之。」公囚大子。大子曰：「唯佐也
能免我。」召而使請，曰：「日中不來，吾知死矣。」左師聞之，聒而與之
語。過期，乃縊而死。佐為大子。公徐聞其無罪也，乃亨伊戾。

820　Gong Ji is the wife of Lord Gong of Song and the daughter of Lord Xuan of Lu and
Mu Jiang. The name "Qi" 棄 means "abandoned."

821　Fu Qian reads *you* 尤 as "excessive" or "too long": "He found her pleasing and stared
at her for too long" (cited in Hong Liangji, *Chunqiu Zuozhuan gu*, 585). Qian
Zhongshu (*Guanzhui bian* 1:223) glosses *you* as *yishi* 異視 (regarded her in a special
way). We read *you* as *youwu* 尤物 (Zhao 28.2), which refers to a bewitching and
dangerous woman.

822　The text gives no example of Cuo's ruthlessness, and Zuo later turns out to be a
faithless ruler. Hui Dong thus suggests the reading that Zuo is "inwardly evil but
appears gentle," while Cuo is "inwardly good but appears ruthless" (Wu Jing'an,
Chunqiu Zuoshi zhuan jiuzhu shuzheng xu, 479).

The Song ruler's heir apparent, Cuo, falls victim to groundless allegations of treason. Similar stories in the text often feature victimized innocence (e.g., Huan 16.5, Xi 5.2), but Cuo is said to be ruthless, and Zuo, the half brother who profits by his demise, is supposedly kind. Zuo's mother, Qi, however, fits the stereotype of the bewitchingly beautiful but devious and dangerous woman. Xiang Xu, sometimes praised elsewhere, here seems conniving and manipulative. Although Zuo (later Lord Yuan of Song) is praised here, he will be judged negatively as a ruler (Zhao 20.3).

Earlier, the Song supervisor of conscripts Rui had sired a girl. As she was born red-skinned and hairy, he had had her abandoned at the bottom of an embankment. A concubine subordinate to Gong Ji took her in and named her "Qi."[820] She grew up and became beautiful. Once, when Lord Ping entered his mother Gong Ji's quarters to pay an evening visit, Gong Ji gave him a meal. Catching sight of Qi, the lord gazed at her, entranced by her bewitching loveliness.[821] Gong Ji[d] included her among the lord's concubines. She was favored and gave birth to Zuo, who was ugly but gentle. The heir apparent, Cuo, was handsome but ruthless.[822] Xiang Xu[b], the minister of the left, feared and hated Cuo. The eunuch Huiqiang Yili was the heir's court preceptor but did not enjoy any favor.

In autumn, a Chu visitor came on an official visit to Jin and passed through Song. The heir apparent knew him and requested that he be allowed to offer him ceremonial toasts in the countryside. The lord let him go. Huiqiang Yili[a] asked for permission to go with the heir apparent. The lord said, "Does he not hate you?" He replied, "If a petty man serving a noble man is hated, he would not presume to distance himself; if he is loved, he would not presume to draw close. Respectfully he awaits commands. How could he presume to shift allegiance? Even if there are those supplying the heir's needs in external affairs, there is none supplying his needs in internal affairs. Your servant begs leave to go." The lord sent him.

Upon his arrival, he dug a hole, sacrificed an animal, placed a written document there to serve as proof, and then galloped back and told the lord, "The heir apparent is about to raise a rebellion. He has already sworn a covenant with the visitor from Chu." The lord said, "He is my heir. What else can he ask for?" He replied, "He wants to become ruler sooner." The lord sent someone to examine the site, and there was indeed evidence. He asked his consort, Qi, and Xiang Xu[b] about this, and they both said, "We have actually heard about it." The lord imprisoned the heir apparent, who said, "Only Zuo can save me." He summoned Zuo and sent him to intercede on his behalf with the lord, saying, "If by midday he does not come, I know I will die." Xiang Xu[b] heard about this and kept up an endless conversation with Zuo. The appointed time passed, and Cuo thus hanged himself and died. Zuo became the heir apparent. The lord gradually came to hear that Cuo was guiltless, and he thus had Huiqiang Yili[a] boiled alive.

26.8(6)

左師見夫人之步馬者，問之。對曰：「君夫人氏也。」左師曰：「誰
為君夫人？余胡弗知？」圉人歸，以告夫人。夫人使饋之錦與馬，先之
以玉，曰：「君之妾棄使某獻」。左師改命曰「君夫人」，而後再拜稽首
受之。

26.9　　鄭伯歸自晉，使子西如晉聘，辭曰：「寡君來煩執事，懼不免於戾，使夏
謝不敏。」君子曰：「善事大國。」

26.10a　初，楚伍參與蔡大師子朝友，其子伍舉與聲子相善也。伍舉娶於王子
牟。王子牟為申公而亡，楚人曰：「伍舉實送之。」伍舉奔鄭，將遂奔晉。
聲子將如晉，遇之於鄭郊，班荊相與食，而言復故。聲子曰：「子行也，
吾必復子。」

　　　　及宋向戌將平晉、楚，聲子通使於晉，還如楚。令尹子木與之語，
問晉故焉，且曰：「晉大夫與楚孰賢？」

823　Xiang Xu thereby demonstrates his power over his erstwhile co-conspirator Qi as
well as the new heir apparent Zuo. Having established her son as heir, Qi flaunts
her more elevated status. "When a concubine's son becomes the ruler, his mother
could be regarded as the lord's wife" (ZZ-Kong 1.50). *Gongyang* 1, 1.11, maintains
that "the mother is elevated through the son" (*mu yi zi gui* 母以子貴) But Xiang
Xu here makes it clear that the de facto "promotion" of Qi from concubine to the
lord's wife depends on his support.

824　In the analogous passage in *Guoyu*, "Chu yu 1," 17.534–36, Gongsun Guisheng enumerates roughly the same examples (Wangsun Qi, Lord of Xi, Yongzi, Qu Wu), but
more briefly.

825　Cf. Hong Liangji, *Chunqiu shilun*, 7, "Chunqiu shi Chu guo renwen zui sheng lun"
春秋時楚國人文最盛論. In Zhao 26.9a, Wangzi Zhao took Zhou canonical documents and fled to Chu, and Hong takes this as one indication of Chu cultural
eminence.

826　See the Covenant of Song (Xiang 27.4).

Xiang Xu[b] saw the groom walking the horses for the lord's wife and asked whose horses they were. He replied, "The ruler's wife." Xiang Xu[b] said, "Who is the ruler's wife? How is it that I do not know?" The groom came back and told the lord's wife. The ruler's wife sent Xiang Xu gifts of brocade and horses, preceding these with jades, along with this message: "The lord's concubine, Qi, sent this emissary to present them." Xiang Xu[b] changed the wording to "the ruler's wife," and then he bowed twice with his forehead touching the ground and accepted the gifts.[823]

The following passage records Zheng's humble diplomatic rhetoric vis-à-vis Jin.

The Liege of Zheng returned from Jin and sent Zixi to Jin on an official visit with this statement: "Our unworthy ruler has brought troubles to your functionaries. He fears that he will not escape blame and has sent me to apologize for his lapses." The noble man said, "He was skillful in serving the great domain."

26.9

Gongsun Guisheng, a Cai noble serving in Chu, convinces the Chu chief minister, Qu Jian, that the exiled high officer Wu Ju should be allowed to return to Chu.[824] His brilliant rhetorical performance, which Zhu Xi characterized as proto–Warring States, gives rise to an idiom on losing talented people to the enemy: "Jin employs Chu talents" (Chu cai Jin yong 楚材晉用). His examples remind us of the political and cultural achievements of Chu.[825] He begins by arguing against excessively harsh punishments. It is true that throughout Zuozhuan, ministers and commanders fall victim to the suspicions and persecution of their rulers more frequently in Chu than in other domains.

Earlier, Wu Can of Chu and grand preceptor Zizhao of Cai, were friends. Wu Can's son, Wu Ju, was on good terms with Zizhao's son Gongsun Guisheng[b]. Wu Ju married a daughter of Wangzi Mou, who became the Lord of Shen before going into exile. The leaders of Chu said, "It was none other than Wu Ju who sent him off." Wu Ju fled to Zheng and then was planning to flee to Jin. Gongsun Guisheng[b], who was about to go to Jin, met him in the outskirts of Zheng. They spread hay on the ground as a kind of mat, ate together, and spoke about the way Wu Ju could be restored. Gongsun Guisheng[b] said, "You go on your way. I will certainly have you restored."

26.10a

By the time Xiang Xu was preparing for peace between Jin and Chu,[826] Gongsun Guisheng[b] was sent as envoy to Jin. On his return to Chu, the chief minister, Qu Jian[a], had a talk with him and asked about Jin affairs. Qu Jian further asked, "If we compare Jin high officers and Chu ones, who are more worthy?"

對曰：「晉卿不如楚，其大夫則賢，皆卿材也。如杞梓、皮革，自楚
往也。雖楚有材，晉實用之。」
子木曰：「夫獨無族、姻乎？」
對曰：

雖有，而用楚材實多。歸生聞之：善為國者，賞不僭而刑不
濫。賞僭，則懼及淫人；刑濫，則懼及善人。若不幸而過，寧
僭，無濫。與其失善，寧其利淫。無善人，則國從之。《詩》
曰：

人之云亡，
邦國殄瘁。

無善人之謂也。故夏書曰『與其殺不辜，寧失不經』，懼失
善也。商頌有之曰：

不僭不濫，
不敢怠皇。
命于下國，
封建厥福。

此湯所以獲天福也。

---

827 The graph *cai* 材 in the passage is variously translated as "timber," "materials," and
"talents."

828 As noted before (introduction to Xuan), there were far fewer members of the lord's
lineage employed in high positions in Jin than anywhere else during the Spring and
Autumn period.

829 The Mao commentary cites this line to explain the line "Not indiscriminate, not
excessive" 不僭不濫 in *Maoshi* 305, "Yin wu" 殷武, 20D.805, which Gongsun Guisheng also quotes below.

830 There are similar passages on rewards and punishments in *Xunzi* 14.309 and *Lüshi
chunqiu* 21.1427. *Huainanzi* 13.455 and *Shangjun shu* 18.147 speak more generally
about the importance of judicious rewards and punishments.

Gongsun Guisheng replied, "The Jin ministers are not the equal of the
Chu ministers. Its high officers, however, are worthy; they all have the
talent to be ministers. Just like the timber from medlar and catalpa trees
and fur and leather, they made their way there from Chu. Although Chu
has the talents,[827] it is Jin that makes use of them."

Qu Jian[a] said, "Does Jin alone not have worthy members of the ruling
house or relatives by marriage?"[828]

He replied,

> Although there are those, the fact remains that in many cases it
> is Chu talent that is employed. I have heard that those who are
> adept at governing a domain are neither indiscriminate with
> rewards nor excessive with punishments.[829] If rewards are indis-
> criminately handed out, then one fears that they will reach
> depraved men; if punishments are excessively meted out, then
> one fears that they will reach worthy men. If, unfortunately, one
> is to err, then one would rather be indiscriminate with rewards
> than be excessive with punishments. Instead of losing the worthy
> ones, one would rather benefit the depraved ones.[830] If there are
> no worthy men, then the domain follows the path of ruin. As it
> says in the *Odes*,
>
>> The good men have gone into exile.
>> The realm is sickly and wasting away.[831]
>
> That refers to not having superior men. That is why it says in the
> *Xia Documents*, "Rather than killing the innocent, it is better to
> miss out on punishing the deviant."[832] This is for fear of losing the
> superior ones. As the "Shang Hymns" has it,
>
>> Not indiscriminate, not excessive—
>> None dare to be lax or wallow in leisure.
>> The command is given to domains below
>> To grandly establish their blessings.[833]
>
> That was how the first Shang ruler, Tang, obtained the blessings
> of Heaven.

831 *Maoshi* 264, "Zhanyang" 瞻卬, 18E.696.

832 Du Yu (*ZZ* 37.635) identifies this as a passage not found in the *Documents* he knew.
These lines are incorporated into "Da Yu mo" (*Shangshu* 4.55). For "Da Yu mo," see
nn. 106 and 583. Two Han texts cite them as lines from the *Documents* (*Hanshu*
51.2369; *Shuoyuan* 5.139); they could be citing *Zuozhuan*.

833 *Maoshi* 305, "Yinwu" 殷武, 20D.805.

古之治民者，勸賞而畏刑，恤民不倦。賞以春夏，刑以秋冬。是
以將賞，為之加膳，加膳則飫賜，此以知其勸賞也。將
刑，為之不舉，不舉則徹樂，此以知其畏刑也。夙興夜
寐，朝夕臨政，此以知其恤民也。三者，禮之大節也。有
禮，無敗。

　今楚多淫刑，其大夫逃死於四方，而為之謀主，以害楚
國，不可救療，所謂不能也。子儀之亂，析公奔晉，晉人寘
諸戎車之殿，以為謀主。繞角之役，晉將遁矣，析公曰：「楚
師輕窕，易震蕩也。若多鼓鈞聲，以夜軍之，楚師必遁。」晉
人從之，楚師宵潰。晉遂侵蔡，襲沈，獲其君，敗申、息之師
於桑隧，獲申麗而還。鄭於是不敢南面。楚失華夏，則析公
之為也。

834　It is possible that Jin sources devote less attention to advisers from other domains.

835　See Zhuang 20.1.

836　We follow Du Yu's (ZZ 37.635) reading. Yang (3:1121) reads *buneng* 不能 as *bunai*
不耐, "being unable to bear with (minor infractions)." Talented men are lost to the
realm if they are too easily deemed guilty.

837　See Wen 14.10.

Gongsun Guisheng maintains that rewards should be emphasized over punishments. Two exiled Chu nobles, the Lord of Xi and Yongzi, are said to be instrumental in the erosion of Chu influence over the central and eastern domains by bringing about Chu's defeat by Jin at the campaigns of Raojiao (Cheng 6.11) and Mijiao (Xiang 5.7) respectively, although they are not mentioned in the Zuozhuan accounts of those battles.[834]

Those who governed the people well in ancient times encouraged rewards and dreaded punishments, and they cared for the people untiringly. Rewards were granted in spring and summer; punishments were meted out in autumn and winter. That was why, when preparing to dispense rewards, the lords added dishes to meals. Adding dishes to meals meant that what remained after satiation could be bestowed as gifts. That is how we know they encouraged rewards. When preparing to mete out punishments, the lords did not dine with full ceremony.[835] Not dining with full ceremony meant that they stopped the music. That is how we know they dreaded punishments. They rose early and went to sleep late, and from morning till evening they presided over government. That is how we know they cared for the people. These three things are the great tenets of ritual propriety. Where there is ritual propriety, there is no failure.

Now Chu has many unwarranted punishments. Its high officers flee death in domains of the four quarters, for which they have become chief strategists, inflicting on Chu harm that cannot be remedied or healed. This is what is called failure to employ one's own talented people.[836] In the aftermath of Dou Ke[a]'s insurrection,[837] the Lord of Xi fled to Jin. Jin leaders placed him at the back of the Jin ruler's battle chariot and made him their chief strategist. At the Raojiao campaign, as Jin was preparing to flee, the Lord of Xi said, "The Chu troops show levity and debility. They will be easily dazed and destroyed.[838] If we play the war drums many times, rivaling their sounds, and use the cover of night to attack them with full force, Chu troops will certainly flee." Jin leaders followed his plans, and the Chu army collapsed during the night. Jin then invaded Cai, attacked Shĕn by surprise and took its ruler captive, and defeated the army of Shen and Xi at Sangsui, took Shen Li[a] captive, and returned.[839] That was why Zheng did not dare to turn south and follow Chu. That Chu lost the allegiance of the central domains was the doing of the Lord of Xi.

26.10b

---

838   We follow Wei Zhao's gloss in *Guoyu*, "Zhou yu 3," 147, and read *dang* 蕩 as *huai* 壞, "destroy" (cited in Karlgren, gl. 638).

839   In the account of the battle in Cheng 8.2, Zhi Ying, Fan Xie, and Han Jue, not the Lord of Xi, are mentioned as the strategists responsible for Jin victories.

雍子之父兄譖雍子，君與大夫不善是也，雍子奔晉，晉
人與之鄐，以為謀主。彭城之役，晉、楚遇於靡角之谷。晉
將遁矣，雍子發命於軍曰：「歸老幼，反孤疾，二人役，歸一
人。簡兵蒐乘，秣馬蓐食，師陳焚次，明日將戰。」行歸者，
而逸楚囚。楚師宵潰，晉降彭城而歸諸宋，以魚石歸。楚失
東夷，子辛死之，則雍子之為也。

26.10c　子反與子靈爭夏姬，而雍害其事，子靈奔晉，晉人與之邢，以
為謀主，扞禦北狄，通吳於晉，教吳叛楚，教之乘車、射
御、驅侵，使其子狐庸為吳行人焉。吳於是伐巢、取駕、克
棘、入州來，楚罷於奔命，至今為患，則子靈之為也。

840　We follow Yang's (3:1121) reading of *shan* 善 as "resolve" or "mediate." Cf. Du Yu's
　　　(*ZZ* 37.636) implied reading of *shi* 是 as *shi* 諟 ("rectify") in the phrase *bu shan shi*
　　　不善是, "not skilled at judging right and wrong" (*bu shi qi quzhi* 不是其曲直).
841　The city of Chù 鄐 was located in the domain of Jin near Wen County 溫縣, Henan.
842　See Cheng 18.5 and 18.12.
843　Yongzi wants Chu to hear about Jin's preparations for battle.
844　See Xiang 1.1.

Yongzi's father and older brother slandered Yongzi. The ruler
and the high officers did not resolve their conflicts.[840] Yongzi fled
to Jin. The Jin leaders gave him the city of Chù and made him
their chief strategist.[841] At the Pengcheng campaign, the Jin and
Chu armies confronted each other at the Valley of Mijiao.[842] Jin
was about to flee when Yongzi issued a command to the soldiers:
"Let the old and the young return. Repatriate the orphans and
sickly ones. If two brothers are on military duty, let one of them
return. Choose the best foot soldiers, and review the chariots and
their troops. Feed the horses well, and give the soldiers a good
meal. Array the troops in battle formations, and burn the tents
for setting up camp. Be prepared for battle tomorrow." Those to
be returned were sent on their way, and he allowed Chu prisoners
to escape.[843] The Chu army collapsed during the night. Jin vanquished Pengcheng, returned it to Song, and took Yu Shi back to
Jin.[844] That Chu lost the allegiance of the Eastern Yi, a loss that
led to Zixin's death,[845] was the doing of Yongzi.

*Gongsun Guisheng elaborates two more examples: Qu Wuchen's defection
to Jin, which leads to the rise of Wu, Chu's nemesis (Cheng 2.6, Ding 4.3),
and Fen Huang's role in bringing about Jin's victory over Chu during the
Yanling campaign (Cheng 16.5). Qu Jian is persuaded to restore Wu Ju's
position.*

Zifan, who fought over Xia Ji with Qu Wuchen[c], obstructed and   26.10c
ruined the latter's plans.[846] Qu Wuchen[c] fled to Jin, and Jin leaders gave him Xing and made him their chief strategist. He
defended Jin against the Northern Di, established relations
between Wu and Jin, taught Wu to rebel against Chu, taught Wu
men how to ride chariots, shoot, drive, and charge into battle,
and he made his son Huyong an envoy in Wu.[847] Wu thus
attacked Chao, took Jia, overcame Ji, and entered Zhoulai. That
Chu commanders became exhausted as they rushed to fulfill
urgent commands and that Chu is in distress down to this day
are the doing of Qu Wuchen[c].

---

845   See Xiang 3.8 and 5.7. Chen and other domains to the east of Chu revolted against
      Chu because of Chu's failure to relieve Pengcheng. Chen leaders blamed their defec-
      tion on the avarice of the Chu minister Zixin (Gongzi Renfu).
846   See Cheng 2.6.
847   See Cheng 7.5.

若敖之亂，伯賁之子賁皇奔晉，晉人與之苗，以為謀
主。鄢陵之役，楚晨壓晉軍而陳。晉將遁矣，苗賁皇曰：「楚
師之良在其中軍王族而已，若塞井夷竈，成陳以當之，欒、
范易行以誘之，中行、二郤必克二穆，吾乃四萃於其王族，
必大敗之。」晉人從之，楚師大敗，王夷、師熸，子反死之。
鄭叛、吳興，楚失諸侯，則苗賁皇之為也。

子木曰：「是皆然矣。」
聲子曰：「今又有甚於此者。椒舉娶於申公子牟，子牟得戾而亡，
君大夫謂椒舉：『女實遣之。』懼而奔鄭，引領南望，曰：『庶幾赦余。』
亦弗圖也。今在晉矣。晉人將與之縣，以比叔向。彼若謀害楚國，豈不
為患？」
子木懼，言諸王，益其祿爵而復之。聲子使椒鳴逆之。

26.11(8–10) 　許靈公如楚，請伐鄭，曰：「師不興，孤不歸矣。」八月，卒于楚。楚子曰：
「不伐鄭，何以求諸侯？」

848　See Xuan 4.3.

849　For Fen Huang's role in the battle of Yanling, see Cheng 16.5b. The strategy of filling
　　up wells and leveling stoves comes from Fan Gai (Cheng 16.5a).

850　Wu Ju was also known as Jiao Ju, or Ju of Jiao; Jiao is the settlement assigned to him.
　　Jiao becomes his son's lineage name.

In the aftermath of the Ruo'ao lineage's insurrection,[848] Dou Jiao[e]'s son Fen Huang fled to Jin. Jin leaders gave him Miao and made him their chief strategist. During the Yanling campaign, when at dawn Chu pressed close to Jin forces and deployed battle formations, Jin was preparing to flee, but Fen Huang[a] said, "The finest fighters of Chu are only with the central army of the royal house. If we fill up our wells and level our stoves, deploy battle formations to confront them, and have Luan Shu[d] and Fan Xie advance out of line to lure the Chu troops, then Zhonghang Yan[f], Xi Qi, and Xi Zhi will certainly overcome the two Chu commanders descended from King Mu, Zichong and Zixin. We can then bring our four armies to bear on the troops of the royal house, and we will be sure to roundly defeat them."[849] Jin leaders followed his plan, and the Chu army was roundly defeated. The king was injured, the army was snuffed out like flames, and Zifan died as a result. That Zheng revolted against Chu, Wu rose to power, and Chu lost the allegiance of the princes were the doing of Fen Huang[a].

Qu Jian[a] said, "It is indeed as you said."

Gongsun Guisheng[b] said, "Now we have something even worse than these examples. Wu Ju[a] married a daughter of Wangzi Mou[a], the Lord of Shen. Wangzi Mou[a] was incriminated and went into exile. The ruler and the high officers said to Wu Ju: 'It was indeed you who sent him off.' Fearful, he fled to Zheng, but longing for home, he craned his neck to gaze southward and said, 'If only I could be pardoned.' Even then Chu paid no attention. Now he is in Jin. Jin leaders are about to give him a dependency, making him the equal of Shuxiang. If he strategizes to harm Chu, will he not pose a threat?"

Qu Jian[a] was fearful and spoke to the king, who added to Wu Ju's rank and emoluments and restored his position. Gongsun Guisheng[b] sent Wu Ju's son Jiao Ming to meet him and escort him back.[850]

Zheng and Xǔ, with a long history of hostilities reaching back to the beginning of the period covered by Zuozhuan *(Yin 11.3), last confronted each other ten years earlier (Xiang 16.2). Here Chu attacks Zheng on behalf of Xǔ, but Zheng manages to defend itself without full-fledged fighting.*

Lord Ling of Xǔ went to Chu and asked Chu to attack Zheng: "If the army is not mobilized, I will not go back." In the eighth month, he died in Chu. The Master of Chu said, "If we do not attack Zheng, how can we seek the allegiance of the princes?"

26.11(8–10)

冬，十月，楚子伐鄭，鄭人將禦之。子產曰：「晉、楚將平，諸侯將
和，楚王是故昧於一來。不如使逞而歸，乃易成也。夫小人之性，釁於
勇、嗇於禍、以足其性而求名焉者，非國家之利也，若何從之？」

子展說，不禦寇。十二月乙酉，入南里，墮其城。涉於樂氏，門于師
之梁。縣門發，獲九人焉。涉于氾而歸。而後葬許靈公。

26.12　衛人歸衛姬于晉，乃釋衛侯。君子是以知平公之失政也。

26.13　晉韓宣子聘于周，王使請事。對曰：「晉士起將歸時事於宰旅，無他事
矣。」王聞之，曰：「韓氏其昌阜於晉乎！辭不失舊。」

In winter, in the tenth month, the Master of Chu attacked Zheng. The leaders of Zheng were planning to resist Chu. Zichan said, "Jin and Chu are about to make peace, and the princes are about to reach an accord. That is why the Chu king is reckless to have come.[851] It is better to let Chu have its way and turn back, for then a peace agreement will be easily achieved. Now it is in the nature of petty men to be roused by their own daring and to hanker after calamity so that they can satisfy their urges and seek fame. That will not be to the advantage of the domain and patrimony. Why should we follow them?"

Gongsun Shezhi[a] was pleased and Zheng did not resist the enemy. In the twelfth month, on the *yiyou* day (5), Chu entered Nanli and demolished its city walls.[852] They crossed the river at Yueshi and stormed the Shizhiliang Gate. The portcullis of the inner gate was let down, and nine persons were taken captive. Only after the men of Chu had crossed the Fan River and returned to Chu did they bury Lord Ling of Xǔ.

Lord Ping of Jin releases Lord Xian of Wei, whom Jin had arrested earlier (Xiang 26.7a), after Wei leaders send a Wei lady (Wei Ji) as consort. Union with a lady of the same clan name (Ji) is a sign of the ruler's moral laxity (Zhao 1.12).

The leaders of Wei sent Wei Ji to Jin, and Jin then released the Prince of Wei. That is how the noble man knew that Lord Ping was remiss in government.

Han Qi, as Jin envoy in Zhou, shows proper self-abasement.

Han Qi[a] of Jin was on an official visit in Zhou. The king sent an officer to inquire about his mission. He replied, "The officer of Jin, Qi, is preparing to present the offerings of the season to the steward's subordinates.[853] I have no other mission." The king heard about this and said, "The Han lineage will surely flourish in Jin! His words have not lost the old decorum."

26.12

26.13

---

851   We read *mei* 眛 as "being blinded" or "lacking in judgment." Cf. Du Yu's (ZZ 37.637) reading of *mei* as *tanmao* 貪冒 "avaricious": "The Chu king came because of his avarice."

852   On Nanli, see Xuan 3.6.

853   Han Qi, a minister in Jin, describes himself with the lower rank of "officer" (*shi* 士) because the royal court is supposed to have more exalted standards than the Jin court. To show proper deference, Han Qi mentions the steward's subordinates rather than the king or his ministers.

26.14 齊人城郟之歲，其夏，齊烏餘以廩丘奔晉，襲衛羊角，取之；遂襲我高魚。有大雨，自其竇入，介于其庫，以登其城，克而取之。又取邑于宋。於是范宣子卒，諸侯弗能治也。及趙文子為政，乃卒治之。文子言於晉侯曰：「晉為盟主，諸侯或相侵也，則討而使歸其地。今烏餘之邑，皆討類也，而貪之，是無以為盟主也。請歸之。」公曰：「諾。孰可使也？」對曰：「胥梁帶能無用師。」晉侯使往。

春秋

27.1(2) 二十有七年，春，齊侯使慶封來聘。

27.2(4) 夏，叔孫豹會晉趙武、楚屈建、蔡公孫歸生、衛石惡、陳孔奐、鄭良霄、許人、曹人于宋。

27.3(3) 衛殺其大夫甯喜。

27.4(3) 衛侯之弟鱄出奔晉。

---

854 See Xiang 24.11.

855 Linqiu 廩丘 was located northeast of present-day Juancheng County 鄄城縣, Shandong.

856 Gaoyu 高魚 was located north of present-day Yuncheng County 鄆城縣, Shandong. Yangjiao 羊角 was located northwest of Yuncheng County.

Wu Yu of Qi gains refuge in Jin by bringing Qi land with him. He acquired territories through surprise attacks and sought Jin protection with bribes (Xiang 24). Zhao Wu, who succeeds Fan Gai as chief minister, urges Lord Ping to return Wu Yu's unlawfully gained settlements to their owners. For comparable remonstrances, see Wen 18.7 and Xiang 21.1.

In the summer of the year that the leaders of Qi fortified Jia,[854] Wu Yu of Qi, taking the settlement of Linqiu with him,[855] fled to Jin. He made a surprise attack on Yangjiao in Wei and took it, and then he made a surprise attack on our Gaoyu.[856] There was then heavy rain, and he entered the city from the opened drains, armed his men with weapons from the arsenal of Gaoyu, climbed up its city walls, overcame the city, and took control of it. He also took settlements from Song. It was at that time that Fan Gai[c] died,[857] and the princes could not deal with the situation. When Zhao Wu[a] came to be in charge of government, he finally dealt with it. Zhao Wu[b] said to the Prince of Jin, "When the princes invade each other's territories, Jin, as covenant chief, should chastise the invaders and make them return the lands they have taken. Now Wu Yu's settlements are all in the category that deserves chastisement. If we covet them, then we will not have the wherewithal to be covenant chief. I request to have the land returned." The lord said, "I agree. Whom can we send for this mission?" He replied, "Xu Liangdai will be able to accomplish this without using force."[858] The Prince of Jin sent him on the mission.

26.14

LORD XIANG 27 (546 BCE)
ANNALS

In the twenty-seventh year, in spring, the Prince of Qi sent Qing Feng to us on an official visit.

27.1(2)

In summer, Shusun Bao met with Zhao Wu of Jin, Qu Jian of Chu, Gong sun Guisheng of Cai, Shi E of Wei, Kong Huan of Chen, Liang Xiao of Zheng, a Xǔ leader, and a Cao leader at Song.

27.2(4)

Wei put to death its high officer Ning Xi.[859]

27.3(3)

Zhuan, the younger brother of the Prince of Wei, departed and fled to Jin.

27.4(3)

---

857   Fan Gai died the year before (Xiang 25).

858   The narrative continues in Xiang 27.1 and is broken off because of the chronological arrangement of the text.

859   The sequence of entries in *Zuozhuan* suggests that the covenant sworn at Song takes place after the death of Ning Xi.

27.5(4)　秋，七月辛巳，豹及諸侯之大夫盟于宋。

27.6(10)　冬，十有二月乙亥朔，日有食之。

左傳

27.1　二十七年，春，胥梁帶使諸喪邑者具車徒以受地，必周。使烏餘具車徒以受封。烏餘以其眾出，使諸侯偽效烏餘之封者，而遂執之，盡獲之。皆取其邑，而歸諸侯。諸侯是以睦於晉。

27.2(1)　齊慶封來聘，其車美。孟孫謂叔孫曰：「慶季之車，不亦美乎！」
　　叔孫曰：「豹聞之：

服美不稱，
必以惡終。

美車何為？」
　　叔孫與慶封食，不敬。為賦〈相鼠〉，亦不知也。

In autumn, in the seventh month, on the *xinsi* day (5), Bao (Shusun Bao)   27.5(4)
and the high officers of the princes swore a covenant at Song.

In winter, in the twelfth month, on the *yihai* day, the first day of the   27.6(10)
month, there was an eclipse of the sun.

ZUO

In a continuation of the last entry of Xiang 26, Zuozhuan *here reports how
Xu Liangdai maneuvers to have Wu Yu seized and the settlements he
appropriated given back to their owners.*

In the twenty-seventh year, in spring, Xu Liangdai made the various   27.1
parties that had lost settlements to Wu Yu come equipped with chariots
and soldiers, so that they might get back their lands, and they were to
maintain the utmost secrecy. He made Wu Yu come equipped with chariots and soldiers to receive entitlement to the lands he had taken. Wu Yu
came with the throng of his followers. Xu Liangdai made the princes
pretend to be the ones conferring entitlement on Wu Yu. They then
arrested him, seized all his followers, retrieved all the settlements he had
taken, and returned them to the princes. That was why the princes had
harmonious relations with Jin.[860]

*Qing Feng, whose career has been ascendant after Cui Zhu's murder of
Lord Zhuang (Xiang 25.2), comes to Lu as a Qi envoy. His ignorance of
ritual, evident in his failure to register the criticism implied in a recited
ode, belies the splendor of his equipage. He will show his ignorance of odes
again in Xiang 28.9.*

Qing Feng of Qi came to us on an official visit. His carriage was splen-   27.2(1)
did. Meng Xiaobo[d] said to Shusun Bao[d], "Isn't Qing Feng[c]'s carriage
splendid!" Shusun Bao[d] said, "I have heard,

> He whose splendid garments do not match him
> Will certainly come to a bad end.[861]

Of what use is a splendid carriage?"
   Shusun Bao[d] gave a feast for Qing Feng, and the latter was disrespectful. Shusun Bao recited "Rats" on his account, but Qing Feng also did not
understand.[862]

---

860 In thus reversing the policy of Fan Gai, Zhao Wu is the implied hero of this account.
861 This appears to be an ancient proverb. It is echoed in *Maoshi* 151, "Houren" 候人,
     7C.269–71 (cited in Xi 24.3) and in *Liji* 54.911.
862 *Maoshi* 52, "Xiang shu" 相鼠, 3B.122–23. The ode pointedly criticizes those ignorant
     of ritual propriety and is cited for that purpose in Zhao 3.4 and Ding 10.4.

27.3a(3)　衛甯喜專，公患之，公孫免餘請殺之。公曰：「微甯子，不及此。吾與之言矣。事未可知，祇成惡名，止也。」

對曰：「臣殺之，君勿與知。」乃與公孫無地、公孫臣謀，使攻甯氏，弗克，皆死。

公曰：「臣也無罪，父子死余矣！」夏，免餘復攻甯氏，殺甯喜及右宰穀，尸諸朝。石惡將會宋之盟，受命而出，衣其尸，枕之股而哭之。欲斂以亡，懼不免，且曰：「受命矣。」乃行。

27.3b(4)　子鮮曰：「逐我者出，納我者死。賞罰無章，何以沮勸？君失其信，而國無刑，不亦難乎！且鱄實使之。」遂出奔晉。公使止之，不可。及河，又使止之，止使者而盟於河。

863　By turning against Ning Xi, Lord Xian will gain notoriety for bad faith.

864　Du Yu (ZZ 38.643) notes that Gongsun Chen's father was killed in 559 BCE, when Lord Xian was driven out of Wei (Xiang 14.4).

865　Zhuan is referring to Sun Linfu.

Ning Xi, who brought Lord Xian of Wei back from exile (Xiang 26.2), is killed because Lord Xian cannot tolerate his dominance over Wei affairs. Lord Xian has no intention of honoring their earlier agreement that Ning Xi would control the government while Lord Xian would preside over sacrifices.

Ning Xi of Wei was monopolizing power, and the lord worried about it. 27.3a(3)
Gongsun Mianyu requested to have him killed. The lord said, "If it were not for Ning Xi, I could not have attained my position. I already had a prior agreement with him. We cannot know whether this plan has any chance of success, and it may end up only making a bad name for me.[863] Please desist."

Gongsun Mianyu replied, "Your subjects will kill him. You, my lord, do not have to know about it." He thus plotted with Gongsun Wudi and Gongsun Chen to attack the Ning lineage. The latter two failed to prevail and both died.

The lord said, "Gongsun Chen[a] was guiltless. Father and son both died for me!"[864] In summer, Mianyu again attacked the Ning residence, killed Ning Xi[c] and Youzai Gu, and exposed their corpses at court. Having been preparing to join the meeting for swearing the covenant at Song, Shi E received his command and was just setting out. He dressed Ning Xi's corpse, rested its head on his thigh, and wailed for Ning Xi. He wanted to encoffin it and then go into exile, but he feared that he would not escape disaster. Further, he said, "I have already received the command to go," and he thus set forth.

Zhuan, Lord Xian's younger brother and loyal supporter during his exile, laments the injustice of Ning Xi's death, flees to Jin, and refuses to serve in any government. Gongsun Mianyu declines the settlements and honors bestowed on him as reward for destroying Ning Xi and his supporters. For similar arguments on the dangers of excessive wealth and power, see Xiang 22.4, 22.6b, 28.11a, 29.13e, Zhao 10.2c.

Zhuan[a] said, "He who drove us out is in exile;[865] he who installed us was 27.3b(4)
killed. Rewards and punishments have no obvious justifications, so how can one deter wrongdoings and encourage good deeds? The ruler has lost all credibility, and the domain has no just penalties. Is it not difficult to govern? What's more, I was the one who brought this about." He thus departed and fled to Jin. The lord sent someone to stop him. He refused. When he reached the Yellow River, the lord again sent someone to stop him. He stopped the messenger and swore a covenant with him by the Yellow River.

託於木門，不鄉衛國而坐。木門大夫勸之仕，不可，曰：「仕而廢其事，罪也；從之，昭吾所以出也。將誰愬乎？吾不可以立於人之朝矣。」終身不仕。公喪之如稅服終身。

公與免餘邑六十，辭曰：「唯卿備百邑，臣六十矣。下有上祿，亂也。臣弗敢聞。且甯子唯多邑，故死，臣懼死之速及也。」公固與之，受其半。以為少師。公使為卿，辭曰：「大叔儀不貳，能贊大事，君其命之。」乃使文子為卿。

27.4a(2) 宋向戌善於趙文子，又善於令尹子木，欲弭諸侯之兵以為名。如晉，告趙孟。趙孟謀於諸大夫。韓宣子曰：「兵，民之殘也，財用之蠹，小國之大菑也。將或弭之，雖曰不可，必將許之。弗許，楚將許之，以召諸侯，則我失為盟主矣。」晉人許之。如楚，楚亦許之。如齊，齊人難之。陳文子曰：「晉、楚許之，我焉得已？且人曰『弭兵』，而我弗許，則固攜吾民矣，將焉用之？」齊人許之。告於秦，秦亦許之。皆告於小國，為會於宋。

<hr>

866 According to Du Yu (ZZ 38.643), Mumen 木門 was a settlement in Jin. Gu Donggao (Yang, 3:1128) situates it to the northwest of Hejian County 河間縣, Hebei.

867 In *Gongyang*, Xiang 27 (21.264), Zhuan makes a pledge with his wife to never set foot on Wei soil or eat Wei grains. In *Guliang*, Xiang 27 (16.160), Zhuan, "to the end of his life, never spoke of Wei again."

868 Zhuan is saying that if he serves competently and successfully in another court, his exile from Wei will be seen in the light of Lord Xian's failings.

869 The implication is that Lord Xian observes mourning rites beyond what are due a younger brother. Lord Xian dies two years after Zhuan went into self-imposed exile (*Annals* 29.3). Zhuan might have died only a few months before him. Lu Can glosses *shui* 稅 as "hearing of the death and wearing mourning clothes retroactively" (Wu Jing'an, *Chunqiu Zuoshi zhuan jiuzhu shuzheng xu*, 515).

He lodged in reclusion at Mumen,[866] and whenever he sat down, he would not face the direction of the domain of Wei.[867] The high officers of Mumen tried to convince him to serve in government, but he refused: "To serve and cast off one's duties is an offense; to follow through in my duties would be to draw attention to the cause of my exile.[868] To whom can I plead my case? I can no longer be allowed to stand in anybody's court." To the end of his life he did not serve. Lord Xian mourned Zhuan's death by keeping to hempen mourning clothes to the end of his life.[869]

The lord gave Gongsun Mianyu[a] sixty settlements. He declined: "Only ministers are provided with a hundred settlements. I already have sixty. For the one below to have the emoluments of the one above creates disorder. I would not presume to hear of it. Moreover, it is precisely because Ning Xi[c] had many settlements that he died. I fear that death will come to me soon if I accept." The lord insisted on giving them to him. He accepted half of them and was appointed junior tutor. The lord wanted to make him minister, but he declined: "Taishu Yi did not shift allegiance and can be instrumental in important affairs. You, my lord, should charge him with the office." The lord thus made Taishu Yi[b] minister.

The Song minister Xiang Xu tries to halt conflicts among the princes by convening a covenant meeting at Song, following earlier intimations of this possibility (Xiang 25.7, 26.11). This laudable goal is, however, marred by Xiang Xu's selfish desire for fame and the continued rivalry between Jin and Chu.

Xiang Xu of Song was on good terms with Zhao Wu[a] of Jin and also with chief minister Qu Jian[a] of Chu. He wanted to make military conflicts abate among the princes and in this way make a name for himself. He went to Jin and told Zhao Wu[c] about his plans. Zhao Wu[c] conferred with the various high officers. Han Qi[a] said, "Military conflicts are devastation for the people, parasites on wealth and resources, and a great bane for small domains. If there is a plan that may make conflicts abate, even though some may say it will not work, we will certainly grant it. If we do not do so, Chu will grant it. With that assent Chu will summon the princes, and we will lose our position as covenant chief." The leaders of Jin agreed. Xiang Xu went to Chu, and Chu also agreed. He went to Qi, and the leaders of Qi raised difficulties about it. Chen Xuwu[a] said, "Jin and Chu have agreed, so how can we not take part? What's more, if others say 'make conflicts abate' and we do not agree, then we will have already alienated our people. What is the use of doing that?" The leaders of Qi agreed. He told Qin about it, and Qin also agreed. He told all the small domains, and a meeting was held at Song.

五月甲辰，晉趙武至於宋。丙午，鄭良霄至。六月丁未朔，宋人享趙文子，叔向為介。司馬置折俎，禮也。仲尼使舉是禮也，以為多文辭。

戊申，叔孫豹、齊慶封、陳須無、衛石惡至。甲寅，晉荀盈從趙武至。丙辰，邾悼公至。壬戌，楚公子黑肱先至，成言於晉。丁卯，宋向戌如陳，從子木成言於楚。戊辰，滕成公至。

子木謂向戌，請晉、楚之從交相見也。庚午，向戌復於趙孟。趙孟曰：「晉、楚、齊、秦，匹也，晉之不能於齊，猶楚之不能於秦也。楚君若能使秦君辱於敝邑，寡君敢不固請於齊？」

壬申，左師復言於子木，子木使馹謁諸王。王曰：「釋齊、秦，他國請相見也。」秋七月戊寅，左師至。是夜也，趙孟及子晳盟，以齊言。庚辰，子木至自陳。陳孔奐、蔡公孫歸生至。曹、許之大夫皆至。以藩為軍。

---

870 According to the dating of the *Gongyang* and *Guliang* traditions, as well as in *Shiji* 47, Confucius is about six or seven at this juncture. If the author of this *Zuozhuan* entry abides by the same chronology, then he is claiming that some years later Confucius draws attention to the record of this rhetorical display, presumably because it is praiseworthy, although there are commentators who suggest that Confucius is emphasizing the discrepancy between fine words and suspicious calculations. Fang Bao (*Zuozhuan yifa juyao*, 1.66–67) notes, for example, that the meeting highlights Jin weakness despite splendid rhetorical display.

871 Qu Jian is suggesting that the allies of Jin should attend court in Chu, and the allies of Chu should attend court in Jin.

Complex maneuvering and negotiations precede the Covenant of Song. Confucius notes the wealth of elaborate phrases in the diplomatic ritual, whose narrative context is the mutual suspicion of Jin and Chu. Commentators differ as to whether Confucius is expressing praise or criticism.

In the fifth month, on the *jiachen* day (27), Zhao Wu of Jin arrived at Song. On the *bingwu* day (29), Liang Xiao of Zheng arrived. In the sixth month, on the *dingwei* day, the first day of the month, the leaders of Song offered ceremonial toasts to Zhao Wu[a], and Shuxiang was his aide. The supervisors of the military put in place the meat, cutting it up and arranging it on stands. This was in accordance with ritual propriety. Confucius[c] had these rituals set forth and recorded, considering them replete with finely patterned arguments.[870]

On the *wushen* day (2), Shusun Bao of Lu, Qing Feng and Chen Xuwu of Qi, and Shi E of Wei arrived. On the *jiayin* day (8), Zhi Daozi[b] of Jin, following Zhao Wu, arrived. On the *bingchen* day (10), Lord Dao of Zhu arrived. On the *renxu* day (16), Gongzi Heigong of Chu arrived in advance and settled on the wording of the covenant with Jin. On the *dingmao* day (21), Xiang Xu of Song went to Chen and, deferring to Qu Jian[a], settled on the wording of the covenant with Chu. On the *wuchen* day (22), Lord Cheng of Teng arrived.

Qu Jian[a] spoke to Xiang Xu and requested that the allies of Jin and Chu each have an audience with their leader's rival.[871] On the *gengwu* day (24), Xiang Xu reported back to Zhao Wu[c]. Zhao Wu[c] said, "Jin, Chu, Qi, and Qin are peers. Jin cannot control Qi, just as Chu cannot control Qin. If the Chu ruler can make the Qin ruler deign to visit our humble settlement, will our unworthy ruler presume not to insist on requesting that the Qi ruler should do likewise with Chu?"

On the *renshen* day (26), the minister of the left, Xiang Xu, reported on his mission to Qu Jian[a]. Qu Jian[a] sent a courier-carriage to seek an audience with the Chu king. The king said, "Leave out Qi and Qin, and request that the other domains each have an audience with their leader's rival."[872] In autumn, in the seventh month, on the *wuyin* day (2), Xiang Xu[b] arrived. That night, Zhao Wu and Gongzi Heigong[a] worked on the covenant so that the parties could agree on the wording. On the *gengchen* day (4), Qu Jian[a] arrived from Chen. Kong Huan of Chen and Gongsun Guisheng of Cai arrived. The high officers of Cao and Xǔ all arrived. The delegates used bamboo fences to separate their respective troops.[873]

27.4b(5)

872　Note that Zhao Wu can act according to his own judgment, while Qu Jian has to seek approval from the Chu king.

873　The bamboo fences take the place of the customary ramparts.

晉、楚各處其偏。伯夙謂趙孟曰：「楚氛其惡，懼難。」趙孟曰：「吾左還，入於宋，若我何？」辛巳，將盟於宋西門之外。楚人衷甲。伯州犁曰：「合諸侯之師，以為不信，無乃不可乎？夫諸侯望信於楚，是以來服。若不信，是棄其所以服諸侯也。」固請釋甲。

子木曰：「晉、楚無信久矣，事利而已。苟得志焉，焉用有信？」

大宰退，告人曰：「令尹將死矣，不及三年。求逞志而棄信，志將逞乎？志以發言，言以出信，信以立志。參以定之。信亡，何以及三？」

趙孟患楚衷甲，以告叔向。叔向曰：「何害也？匹夫一為不信，猶不可，單斃其死。若合諸侯之卿，以為不信，必不捷矣。食言者不病，非子之患也。夫以信召人，而以僭濟之，必莫之與也，安能害我？且吾因宋以守病，則夫能致死。與宋致死，雖倍楚可也，子何懼焉？又不及是。曰弭兵以召諸侯，而稱兵以害我，吾庸多矣；非所患也。」

---

874 According to Du Yu (*ZZ* 38.645), Jin stayed on the north side and Chu on the south side.

875 We follow Du Yu (*ZZ* 38.645), who asserts that Bosu 伯夙 (the name written here) is another name for Zhi Daozi, but Fu Qian simply identifies Bosu as a high officer in Jin.

876 In a corresponding entry in *Guoyu*, "Jin yu 8," 14.464, Qu Jian plans to launch a surprise attack on the Jin delegation.

877 The graph *can* or *san* 參 means both "three" and "intertwine" or "interact."

878 If the Song capital becomes the battlefield, the men of Song will be fighting for the survival of their own domain.

Jin and Chu each stayed on its side.[874] Zhi Daozi[d875] said to Zhao Wu[c], "The atmosphere on the Chu side is very hostile. I fear disaster."[876] Zhao Wu[c] said, "If we veer left, we will enter Song. What can they do to us?" On the *xinsi* day (5), the delegates were about to swear a covenant outside the west gate of Song. The men of Chu wore armor under their clothes. Bo Zhouli said, "Is it not unacceptable to gather the armies of the princes for a meeting so as to act in bad faith? Now the princes look to Chu for good faith, and that is why they have come in submission. If we act in bad faith, we will be abandoning the very thing that has brought the princes to submission." He persisted in requesting the removal of the armor.

Qu Jian[a] said, "Jin and Chu have been faithless with each other for a long time, caring only to do whatever is advantageous. So long as we fulfill our ambition, what use do we have for good faith?"

The grand steward Bo Zhouli withdrew and told others, "The chief minister will die soon. He will not last even three years. He seeks to fulfill his ambition, yet he abandons good faith. Can his ambition be fulfilled? Ambition is to be expressed through words, words are for bringing forth good faith, and good faith is for establishing ambition. These three things are intertwined, sustaining and stabilizing each other.[877] If good faith is lost, how can he last three years?"

Zhao Wu[c], troubled by the fact that Chu men were wearing armor under their clothes, told Shuxiang about it. Shuxiang said, "What harm is there? One act of bad faith is unacceptable even for commoners. Without exception they fall to their death. If one gathers the ministers of the princes for a meeting so as to act in bad faith, one will certainly have no success. He who eats his words has no power to endanger others. This is not what should trouble you. For if one summons others in the name of good faith, and yet uses duplicity to achieve one's goal, the others will certainly not give their support or acquiescence. How can they harm us? Moreover, since we can use Song to guard against attempts to harm us, all of our men will fight to the death, and with Song men who will also fight to the death, we could resist Chu, even if its army were double its size.[878] What is there for you to fear? In addition, the course of events will not come to this point. If Chu claims to use abatement of military conflicts to summon the princes, and yet initiates military action against us, we can use the situation to our advantage in many ways. This is not something we have to worry about."

27.4d 季武子使謂叔孫以公命曰：「視邾、滕。」既而齊人請邾，宋人請滕，皆不與盟。叔孫曰：「邾、滕，人之私也；我，列國也，何故視之？宋、衛，吾匹也。」乃盟。故不書其族，言違命也。

晉、楚爭先。晉人曰：「晉固為諸侯盟主，未有先晉者也。」楚人曰：「子言晉、楚匹也，若晉常先，是楚弱也。且晉、楚狎主諸侯之盟也久矣，豈專在晉？」叔向謂趙孟曰：「諸侯歸晉之德只，非歸其尸盟也。子務德，無爭先。且諸侯盟，小國固必有尸盟者，楚為晉細，不亦可乎？」乃先楚人。書先晉，晉有信也。

27.4e 壬午，宋公兼享晉、楚之大夫，趙孟為客，子木與之言，弗能對；使叔向侍言焉，子木亦不能對也。

879 According to Du Yu (ZZ 38.646), Ji Wuzi wants Lu to be regarded as a small domain to forestall excessive demands from Jin and Chu for offerings. Qu Jian's proposal that Jin's allies should pay their respects to Chu, and Chu's allies should do likewise to Jin, may mean that the smaller domains will face demands from both Chu and Jin. Teng and Zhu, as subordinate allies, do not participate in the covenant and are not bound by its demands.

880 *Annals*, Xiang 27.5, refers to Shusun Bao as "Bao."

Exegetical explanations of why Shusun Bao's name is omitted (he violates a command) and Jin is recorded first (its leaders have good faith) are belied by implicit debates on what constitutes a reasonable command and good faith, as well as complex considerations of motives and circumstantial exigencies. Shusun Bao's political acumen justifies insubordination, and Jin's good faith may be the rhetorical cover for weakness.

Ji Wuzi sent word to Shusun Bao[d], conveying it as our lord's command: "Look to Zhu and Teng as equals."[879] Shortly thereafter the leaders of Qi requested to have Zhu as its subordinate ally, while the leaders of Song requested to have Teng as its subordinate ally, and as a result neither Zhu nor Teng participated in the covenant. Shusun Bao[d] said, "Zhu and Teng are like the private possessions of other domains, while we are arrayed with other domains. Why should we look to them as equals? Song and Wei are on a par with us." He thus swore the covenant. Hence, the name of his house is not recorded.[880] This is to say that he acted against the command.

27.4d

Jin and Chu fought over precedence. The leaders of Jin said, "Jin has always been the covenant chief among the princes. There has not been any instance of another domain taking precedence over Jin." The leaders of Chu said, "You, sir, said that Jin and Chu are on a par. If Jin always has precedence, then Chu is the weaker party. Moreover, Jin and Chu have alternated as covenant chiefs among the princes for a long time. How can Jin have exclusive claim to leadership?" Shuxiang said to Zhao Wu[c], "The princes turn to Jin for its virtue; they do not turn to Jin because it presides over the swearing of the covenant. You, sir, should just strive for virtue instead of fighting over precedence. Moreover, when the princes swear covenants, there have always been cases when small domains preside over the ceremony.[881] Is it not acceptable for Chu to be Jin's lesser partner?" Thus, precedence was given to the leaders of Chu. That Jin is recorded first is because Jin had good faith.

Memory of the Jin minister Fan Hui's virtue, as well as Shuxiang's eloquence and ritual knowledge, augments Jin's prestige with respect to the rivalry between Jin and Chu.

On the *renwu* day (6), the Duke of Song offered ceremonial toasts to the high officers of both Jin and Chu. Zhao Wu[c] was the honored guest. When Qu Jian[a] spoke with him, Zhao Wu could not reply. Zhao Wu sent Shuxiang to assist him in the exchange, and Qu Jian[a] also could not reply.

27.4e

---

881   The leader of the covenant would be the first to smear his mouth with blood and swear the oath, while high officers of other domains would preside over the ceremony by holding the bull's ears and officiating in other ways; see Ding 8.7, Ai 17.6. In other words, Shuxiang is trying to justify yielding precedence to Chu by redefining what it means to "preside over the covenant."

1199

乙酉，宋公及諸侯之大夫盟于蒙門之外。子木問於趙孟曰：「范武子之德何如？」對曰：「夫子之家事治，言於晉國無隱情，其祝史陳信於鬼神無愧辭。」

子木歸以語王。王曰：「尚矣哉！能歆神、人，宜其光輔五君以為盟主也。」子木又語王曰：「宜晉之伯也，有叔向以佐其卿，楚無以當之，不可與爭。」

晉荀盈遂如楚涖盟。

27.5a 鄭伯享趙孟于垂隴，子展、伯有、子西、子產、子大叔、二子石從。趙孟曰：「七子從君，以寵武也。請皆賦，以卒君貺，武亦以觀七子之志。」

子展賦〈草蟲〉，趙孟曰：「牀哉，民之主也！抑武也，不足以當之。」

伯有賦〈鶉之賁賁〉，趙孟曰：「床笫之言不踰閾，況在野乎？非使人之所得聞也。」

子西賦〈黍苗〉之四章，趙孟曰：「寡君在，武何能焉！」

子產賦〈隰桑〉，趙孟曰：「武請受其卒章。」

子大叔賦〈野有蔓草〉，趙孟曰：「吾子之惠也。」

印段賦〈蟋蟀〉，趙孟曰：「善哉，保家之主也！吾有望矣。」

---

882 Fan Hui was the spearman on the right under Lord Wen, the high officer of Lords Ling and Xiang, one of Lord Cheng's ministers, and grand tutor of Lord Jing.

883 Zhao Wu is returning to Jin from Song via Zheng. Chuilong 垂隴 is located to the northeast of present-day Xingyang County 滎陽縣 in Henan.

884 The text has "the two Zishis": both Yin Duan and the Gongsun Duan have the cognomen "Zishi" 子石.

885 *Maoshi* 14, "Cao cong" 草蟲, 1D.51–52. Gongsun Shezhi is using this ode, which articulates a woman's longing for "the noble man" before their meeting and her expectation of joy when they meet, to convey his hopes for the Zheng-Jin relationship. Zhao Wu declares that "the noble man" in the ode is "the master of the people" but considers himself unworthy of the comparison. As with Zichan and You Ji below, relationship between domains is compared to love and courtship.

886 *Maoshi* 49, "Chun zhi ben ben" 鶉之賁賁, 3A.114. The ode directly denounces the ruler and might have been associated with condemnation of licentiousness in the ruling house (as told in the Mao commentary), hence Zhao Wu's reference to "words spoken near the bedstead" and his later prediction of Liang Xiao's doom. It is also possible to interpret lines from this ode ("The man is no good, / But I treat him as older brother) as criticism of how Jin yielded precedence to Chu (Wu Jing'an, *Chunqiu Zuoshi zhuan jiuzhu shuzheng xu*, 531).

887 *Maoshi* 227, "Shu miao" 黍苗, 15B.513–15. The ode glorifies the exploits of the Shao Duke who built the settlement of Shen during the reign of King Xuan. Zixi implicitly compares Zhao Wu to the Shao Duke, hence Zhao Wu's disclaimer.

888 *Maoshi* 228, "Xi sang" 隰桑, 15B.515. Zichan is also using a woman's love for "the noble man" to convey Zheng's devotion to Jin. Zhao Wu's acceptance of the last stanza, which tells how love and devotion will always be remembered even if the emotions may not be expressed, implies that while he does not deserve to be compared to the fervently praised "noble man" in the earlier stanzas, he will not forget the ties between Zheng and Jin.

On the *yiyou* day (9), the Duke of Song and the high officers of the princes swore the covenant outside the Meng Gate. Qu Jian[a] asked Zhao Wu[c], "What was Fan Hui[i]'s virtue like?" He replied, "That fine man's domestic affairs were well governed, and when he spoke in the domain of Jin, he had nothing to hide. His invocator and scribe presented the truth to ghosts and spirits with no need for apologies."

Qu Jian[a], upon his return, told the Chu king. The king said, "Lofty indeed! He could delight spirits and men. It was fitting that he gloriously assisted five rulers who became covenant chiefs."[882] Qu Jian[a] also said to the king, "It is fitting that Jin should be the overlord. It has Shuxiang to assist its ministers. Chu has no one that can match up. We cannot contend with them."

Zhi Daozi[b] of Jin then went to Chu to oversee the covenant.

Seven Zheng nobles recite odes to convey their intent, which the Jin minister Zhao Wu successfully decodes. For a comparable episode, see Zhao 16.3d.

The Liege of Zheng offered ceremonial toasts to Zhao Wu[c] at Chuilong.[883] 27.5a
Gongsun Shezhi[a], Liang Xiao[a], Zixi, Zichan, You Ji[b], Yin Duan[b], and Gongsun Duan[b884] accompanied their ruler. Zhao Wu[c] said, "These seven fine men, in thus accompanying the ruler, show me favor. I request that they all recite odes to bring to completion the ruler's gift, and I will also thereby observe the intent of these seven fine men."

Gongsun Shezhi[a] recited "Crickets in the Grass." Zhao Wu[c] said, "Excellent indeed! This is the master of the people! However, I am inadequate to bear the comparison!"[885]

Liang Xiao[a] recited "Quails Forging Ahead." Zhao Wu[c] said, "Words spoken near the bedstead do not go beyond the threshold, let alone spread to the countryside! This is not something an envoy should get to hear."[886]

Zixi recited the fourth stanza of "Shoots of Millet." Zhao Wu[c] said, "Our unworthy ruler is there. What competence could I claim?"[887]

Zichan recited "Mulberry of the Marshes." Zhao Wu[c] said, "I beg leave to accept the last stanza."[888]

You Ji[b] recited "In the Wilds There Are Creepers." Zhao Wu[c] said, "This is your kindness, sir."[889]

Yin Duan recited "Crickets." Zhao Wu[c] said, "Excellent indeed! This is the master who guards the patrimony! I have hope indeed."[890]

---

889 *Maoshi* 94, "Ye you mancao" 野有蔓草, 4D.182. The ode celebrates the joyous encounter between a man and a woman, and You Ji is using it to express his gladness in meeting Zhao Wu for the first time.

890 *Maoshi* 114, "Xishuai" 蟋蟀, 6A.215–17. In this ode, a man with public responsibilities mourns the passage of time, cautions against excesses, and urges attention to duty.

公孫段賦〈桑扈〉，趙孟曰：「『匪交匪敖』，福將焉往？若保是言也，欲辭福祿，得乎？」

27.5b 卒享，文子告叔向曰：「伯有將為戮矣。詩以言志，志誣其上而公怨之，以為賓榮，其能久乎？幸而後亡。」叔向曰：「然，已侈，所謂不及五稔者，夫子之謂矣。」文子曰：「其餘皆數世之主也。子展其後亡者也，在上不忘降。印氏其次也，樂而不荒。樂以安民，不淫以使之，後亡，不亦可乎！」

27.6a 宋左師請賞，曰：「請免死之邑。」公與之邑六十，以示子罕。子罕曰：「凡諸侯小國，晉、楚所以兵威之，畏而後上下慈和，慈和而後能安靖其國家，以事大國，所以存也。無威則驕，驕則亂生，亂生必滅，所以亡也。天生五材，民並用之，廢一不可，誰能去兵？兵之設久矣，所以威不

891　*Maoshi* 215, "Sanghu" 桑扈, 14B.480–81. This is a feast song that celebrates the virtues and refinement of the king and his lords. Its last two lines—"Neither haughty nor arrogant: / Myriad blessings come and gather"—link moral attributes to blessings. The received text of the *Maoshi* has *bi jiao fei ao* 彼交匪傲, which is also how the line appears in Cheng 14.1.

892　Liang Xiao is killed three years later (Xiang 30.10).

893　"Crickets in the Grass" has the line "My heart is humbled" 我心則降. As superior minister in Zheng, Gongsun Shezhi nevertheless claims to be awed by the noble man (i.e., Zhao Wu). Gongsun Shezhi's Han lineage is also mentioned as long lasting in Xiang 26.7b, but little is known about it beyond sporadic references in *Zuozhuan*.

894　"Crickets in the Grass" has the line "To love joy without abandonment" 好樂無荒, hence Zhao Wu's comment.

895　Extant sources do not inform us about the fate of the Yin lineage in Zheng. Zichan, a prominent figure in *Zuozhuan*, is curiously not singled out for praise.

896　Had the negotiations for the cessation of conflict failed, Xiang Xu might have been punished by death. He thus presents his achievement as the feat whereby he escaped death (Takezoe, 18.40). Lü Zuqian suggests that Xiang Xu is asking for the privilege to "escape death" (*miansi* 免死) should he be accused of crimes (Wu Jing'an, *Chunqiu Zuoshi zhuan jiuzhu shuzheng xu*, 535).

897　The "Five Resources" (*wucai*) are also mentioned in Zhao 11.2. References to "five colors," "five tones," and "five tastes" (Zhao 25.3) are sometimes understood as a nascent version of the theory of "Five Phases." The term "five phases" (*wuxing* 五行) is used in Zhao 25.3, 29.4, and 32.3, but theories of "five phases" or "five agents" developed later (ca. 3rd to 2nd cent. BCE).

898　The meanings of the graph *bing* 兵 include "weapons," "warfare," and "military conflict." Weapons are made of at least one of the five elements (e.g., metal; Takezoe, 18.41), or their making can involve all five (metal, wood, water, fire, and earth; Yang, 3:1136). Yue Xi is arguing that the "naturalness" of weapons, as evinced by their derivation from the "Five Resources," means that military conflicts are inevitable. Similar arguments on the inevitability of conflict and warfare are found in *Zhuangzi jishi* 23.795; *Han Feizi* 49.1042; *Zhanguo ce*, "Zhao 3," 712–13; and *Lüshi chunqiu* 7.383–84. Ban Gu links warfare to punishment and cosmic order (*Hanshu* 32.1081–86). Cf. Qian Zhongshu, *Guanzhui bian*, 1:223–24.

Gongsun Duan recited "Mulberry Finch." Zhao Wu[c] said, "'Neither haughty nor arrogant.' Where else can good fortune go? If one can guard these words, even if one were to decline good fortune and emoluments, would it be possible?"[891]

The Jin ministers Zhao Wu and Shuxiang diagnose the recitations and link them to the destiny of the Zheng nobles.

When the ceremonial toasts were over, Zhao Wu[b] said to Shuxiang, "Liang Xiao[a] will be executed.[892] Odes are for articulating intent. His intent was to slander those above him and to publicly express his resentment against them, and he presents it as a way to honor the guest. Can he last for long? He would be lucky to end up in exile." Shuxiang said, "Indeed. He is excessively extravagant. The phrase 'not reaching five harvests' applies to that man." Zhao Wu[b] said, "The rest are all masters for several generations. Gongsun Shezhi[a]'s Han lineage will surely be among the last to perish. Being in a superior position, he yet does not forget to humble himself.[893] Next to Gongsun Shezhi is Yin Duan[a], who expresses joy without abandonment.[894] He uses joy to bring peace to the people and employs them with no excess. Is it not proper that his lineage should be among the last to perish?"[895]

The Song minister Yue Xi castigates Xiang Xu for trying to profit by his effort to halt military conflict. He further characterizes such attempts as fatuous and dangerous because warfare is said to play a positive role in creating order.

Xiang Xu[b], minister of the left in Song, requested a reward: "I request to be granted settlements for having escaped death."[896] The lord gave him sixty settlements, and Xiang Xu showed the document of the bestowal to Yue Xi[a]. Yue Xi[a] said, "In all cases concerning small domains of the princes, Jin and Chu use military might to establish authority over them. Only with awe are there compassion and harmony between those above and below. Only with compassion and harmony can they then bring peace and stability to their domains and patrimonies. In that way they serve the great domains, for such is their means of survival. Without authority there will be arrogance, and as a result of arrogance disorder will arise. When disorder arises, these small domains will be extinguished, for such is the road to destruction. Heaven gives rise to the Five Resources,[897] and the people use all of them. Discarding even one of them will not do. Who can remove weapons?[898] Weapons have been in use for a long time: such is the means for using authority to forestall

軌而昭文德也。聖人以興，亂人以廢。廢興、存亡、昏明之術，皆兵之由
也，而子求去之，不亦誣乎！以誣道蔽諸侯，罪莫大焉。縱無大討，而又
求賞，無厭之甚也。」削而投之。左師辭邑。

27.6b　　向氏欲攻司城。左師曰：「我將亡，夫子存我，德莫大焉。又可攻乎？」
　　　　君子曰：

　　　　「彼己之子，
　　　　　邦之司直。

樂喜之謂乎！

　　　　何以恤我，
　　　　我其收之。

向戌之謂乎！」

27.7a　齊崔杼生成及彊而寡，娶東郭姜，生明。東郭姜以孤入，曰棠無咎，與
東郭偃相崔氏。崔成有疾而廢之，而立明。成請老于崔，崔子許之，偃
與無咎弗予，曰：「崔，宗邑也，必在宗主。」

　　　成與彊怒，將殺之，告慶封曰：「夫子之身，亦子所知也，唯無咎
與偃是從，父兄莫得進矣。大恐害夫子，敢以告。」

899　　*Maoshi* 80, "Gao qiu" 羔裘, 4C.168.

900　　Du Yu (*ZZ* 38.649) claims that this ode is no longer extant, but the lines seem to be
　　　variants of "How will it be bestowed on me? / I will embrace it" 假以溢我，我其收之
　　　from *Maoshi* 267, "Wei tian zhi ming" 維天之命, 19A.708–9.

901　　See Xiang 25.2.

transgressions and for making manifest the virtue of culture. The sages rise by them, and those who foment disorder fall by them. The ways to determine rise and fall, preservation and destruction, darkness and illumination, all originate in weapons. Yet you seek to remove them. Is that not deceptive? There is no defense worse than using deceptive tactics to confound the princes! You are lucky to have escaped great chastisement. How can you be seeking rewards! This is the extreme of insatiable greed!" He cut out the words from the bamboo strips and threw them down. Xiang Xu[b] declined the settlements.

Xiang Xu accepts Yue Xi's judgment. A noble man praises both Song ministers with quotations from the Odes.

The Xiang lineage wanted to attack Yue Xi[b], the supervisor of fortifica- 27.6b
tions. Xiang Xu[b], the minister of the left, said, "I was about to perish, and that fine man let me live. No virtuous beneficence is greater than that! How can we attack him?"

The noble man said,

> "The fine man
> Is the supervisor of justice in the realm.[899]

Does that not refer to Yue Xi?

> How will you show concern for me?
> I will embrace it.[900]

Does that not refer to Xiang Xu?"

Dongguo Jiang brings strife into Cui Zhu's household. Her brother, Dongguo Yan, and her son from her first marriage, Tang Wujiu, plot against Cui Zhu's sons, who in turn seek revenge with the assistance of Qing Feng.

Cui Zhu of Qi had become a widower after the birth of Cheng and Qiang. 27.7a
He then took as wife Dongguo Jiang, who gave birth to Ming.[901] Dongguo Jiang took the child from her previous marriage into Cui Zhu's household. He was called Tang Wujiu, and together with Dongguo Yan he assisted Cui Zhu. Cui Cheng had a serious illness and Cui Zhu cast him aside, establishing Ming as his heir instead. Cui Cheng begged leave to retire in Cui. Cui Zhu granted it, but Dongguo Yan[a] and Tang Wujiu would not give it to him, saying, "Cui is the ancestral settlement. It must stay with the head of the lineage."

Enraged, Cui Cheng[a] and Cui Qiang[a] planned to kill them. They told Qing Feng, "You, sir, know well how our father conducts his affairs. He abides by none but Tang Wujiu[a] and Dongguo Yan[a], and the elders of the lineage can no longer put in a word. We are very anxious that they will harm our father, and we presume to tell you this."

慶封曰：「子姑退。吾圖之。」告盧蒲嫳。盧蒲嫳曰：「彼，君之讎也。天或者將棄彼矣。彼實家亂，子何病焉？崔之薄，慶之厚也。」他日又告。慶封曰：「苟利夫子，必去之。難，吾助女。」

27.7b 九月庚辰，崔成、崔彊殺東郭偃、棠無咎於崔氏之朝。崔子怒而出，其眾皆逃，求人使駕，不得。使圉人駕，寺人御而出，且曰：「崔氏有福，止余猶可。」遂見慶封。

慶封曰：「崔、慶一也。是何敢然？請為子討之。」使盧蒲嫳帥甲以攻崔氏。崔氏墉其宮而守之。弗克，使國人助之，遂滅崔氏，殺成與彊，而盡俘其家，其妻縊。嫳復命於崔子，且御而歸之。至，則無歸矣。乃縊。崔明夜辟諸大墓。辛巳，崔明來奔。慶封當國。

<hr>

902 Takezoe (18.45) comments on the word *qie* 且 ("but then"): "Cui Zhu actually did not want to go. He faced forward but his heart lagged behind."

903 Following Karlgren, gl. 645. Cui Zhu knows that a mission of vengeance is ultimately self-destructive. Cf. Du Yu (ZZ 38.649): "The Cui lineage will still be blessed if destruction stops with me"; Takezoe 18.45: "If the Cui lineage stops me from going, it can still be saved from destruction." Alternatively: "The Cui lineage is blessed. It will be acceptable even if only I am left alive."

Qing Feng said, "You retire for now. I will consider this." He told Lupu Pie about this. Lupu Pie said, "He is the former ruler's enemy. Perhaps Heaven is about to abandon him. Since he is the one whose house is in turmoil, why should you worry about it? Any diminution of the Cui lineage is an enhancement of the Qing lineage." Some days later, Cui Cheng and Cui Qiang again told Qing Feng about their concerns. Qing Feng said, "So long as it benefits that fine man your father, I will certainly get rid of them. In case of difficulties, I will assist you."

Cui Cheng and Cui Qiang kill Dongguo Yan and Tang Wujiu. Cui Zhu, with great foreboding, turns to Qing Feng for help to punish his sons. The inauspicious omen from two years earlier (Xiang 25.2) is fulfilled as Qing Feng uses the opportunity to annihilate Cui Zhu's lineage. Cui Zhu hangs himself, and Qing Feng takes over the government in Qi. This story is also told in Lüshi chunqiu *22.1482–83.*

In the ninth month, on the *gengchen* day (5), Cui Cheng and Cui Qiang killed Dongguo Yan and Tang Wujiu in Cui Zhu's court. Cui Zhu[e] left his residence in a fury. His followers had all run away, and he could not get anyone to harness the horses to his carriage. Having made a groom harness the horses to his carriage and a eunuch drive his carriage, he left. But then he said,[902] "The Cui lineage will be blessed if someone can stop me from going."[903]

27.7b

He thus went to see Qing Feng, who said, "The Cui and Qing lineages are one.[904] How did they dare do that? I beg to chastise them on your behalf." He sent Lupu Pie to lead armored soldiers to attack the Cui residence. Members of the Cui lineage fortified their palace walls and guarded it. Failing to overcome them, Qing Feng had the inhabitants of the capital assist him. They thus annihilated the Cui lineage, killed Cui Cheng[a] and Cui Qiang[a], and took all the members of the household as captives. Cui Zhu's wife hanged herself. Lupu Pie[a] reported the discharge of his mission to Cui Zhu[e] and also drove him home. When he arrived, there was no place to return to.[905] He thus hanged himself. Cui Ming escaped at night to his ancestral graveyard. On the *xinsi* day (6), Cui Ming came in flight. Qing Feng assumed charge of the government.

---

904 That is, they share the same interests and should behave as one close-knit unit.

905 Recall the omen verse of hexagram 47, "Impasse," cited in Xiang 25.2: "Caught among rocks, he leans on thorns and thistles. He enters his chamber and does not see his wife. Inauspicious."

27.8　楚薳罷如晉蒞盟，晉侯享之。將出，賦〈既醉〉。叔向曰：「薳氏之有後於楚國也，宜哉！承君命，不忘敏。子蕩將知政矣。敏以事君，必能養民，政其焉往？」

27.9　崔氏之亂，申鮮虞來奔，僕賃於野，以喪莊公。冬，楚人召之，遂如楚，為右尹。

27.10(6)　十一月乙亥朔，日有食之。辰在申，司歷過也，再失閏矣。

春秋

28.1(1)　二十有八年，春，無冰。

28.2(3)　夏，衛石惡出奔晉。

28.3(4)　邾子來朝。

28.4(5)　秋，八月，大雩。

Wei Pi, party to Gongzi Wei's usurpation (Xiang 30.1), will become chief minister when Gongzi Wei becomes King Ling of Chu (Zhao 1.14). However, all associations with transgression are suppressed here in Shuxiang's prediction of Wei Pi's great destiny, based on his apt recitation of an ode.

Wei Pi of Chu went to Jin to oversee the covenant, and the Prince of Jin offered him ceremonial toasts. When he was about to leave, he recited "Having Become Inebriated."[906] Shuxiang said, "That the Wei lineage should have descendants in Chu is fitting indeed! He received the ruler's command and is not remiss with a timely and astute response. Wei Pi[a] will be in charge of government. He who serves the ruler with astuteness will certainly be capable of nurturing the people. Where else can the charge of government go but to him?"

27.8

Shen Xianyu, who showed good judgment when he fled Qi (Xiang 25.2), mourns Lord Zhuang with proper ritual, augmenting the ranks of mourners by hiring servants to wear mourning clothes. He becomes a minister in Chu.

As a result of the havoc wreaked by Cui Zhu, Shen Xianyu came in flight. He hired servants in the countryside and had them wear mourning clothes for Lord Zhuang. In winter, the leaders of Chu summoned him. He thus went to Chu and became deputy of the right.

27.9

Calendrical miscalculations in the Annals are noted; see also Ai 12.5.

In the eleventh month, on the *yihai* day, the first day of the month, there was an eclipse of the sun. The Handle of the Ladle pointed to the Shen asterism. This was an error on the part of the supervisor of the calendar. Twice he had missed the intercalary months.[907]

27.10(6)

LORD XIANG 28 (545 BCE)
ANNALS

In the twenty-eighth year, in spring, there was no ice.

28.1(1)

In summer, Shi E of Wei departed and fled to Jin.

28.2(3)

The Master of Zhu came to visit our court.

28.3(4)

In autumn, in the eighth month, there was a great rain sacrifice.

28.4(5)

---

906 *Maoshi* 247, "Jizui" 既醉, 17B.603–7. The ode probably has a sacrificial context whereby the abundance of the feast is linked to satiation in virtue and the conferring of blessings. Wei Pi is comparing the Jin ruler to "the noble man" who receives blessings in the ode.

907 According to Yasui Kō 安井衡, the missed intercalary months should have been in 549 and 547 BCE (Takezoe, 18.46).

28.5(7)　　仲孫羯如晉。

28.6(9)　　冬，齊慶封來奔。

28.7(12)　　十有一月，公如楚。

28.8(10,14)　　十有二月甲寅，天王崩。

28.9(12)　　乙未，楚子昭卒。

左傳

28.1(1)　　二十八年，春，無冰。梓慎曰：「今茲宋、鄭其饑乎！歲在星紀，而淫於玄枵。以有時菑，陰不堪陽。蛇乘龍。龍，宋、鄭之星也。宋、鄭必饑。玄枵，虛中也。枵，秏名也。土虛而民秏，不饑何為？」

28.2　　夏，齊侯、陳侯、蔡侯、北燕伯、杞伯、胡子、沈子、白狄朝于晉，宋之盟故也。
　　　　齊侯將行，慶封曰：「我不與盟，何為於晉？」陳文子曰：「先事後賄，禮也。小事大，未獲事焉，從之如志，禮也。雖不與盟，敢叛晉乎？重丘之盟，未可忘也。子其勸行！」

908　There was no *yiwei* day in the twelfth month of this year.

909　The cycle of the Year-Planet (Jupiter), erroneously believed to last twelve years (it is actually 11.86 years), is matched with the twelve branches (*zhi*) and the twelve meeting points of the sun and the moon in one year. Asterial Order (Xingji 星紀) and Dark Hollow (Xuanxiao 玄枵) are names of asterisms at two of the twelve meeting points. Zi Shen unravels the figural equivalents and semantic associations of the names. Dark Hollow consists of three subconstellations: Woman (Nü 女), Empty (Xu 虛), and Danger (Wei 危). Xu and Wei are associated with the snake, and the Year-Planet is identified with the element wood and the blue dragon. An inversion of the order of nature is thus obtained when the Year-Planet moves too soon to Dark Hollow—the snake rides the dragon. Dark Hollow is "empty at the center" because the name of one of its subconstellations is Empty. Also, Dark Hollow contains the word *xiao* 枵, which means "hollow," "hunger," or "depletion." Dark Hollow is called Mound of Zhuanxu in Zhao 10.1.

910　Chen, Cai, Hu, and Shěn, formerly subordinate allies of Chu, now also acknowledge Jin leadership, as stipulated by the Covenant of Song.

911　Qi and Qin were left out of the Covenant of Song; see Xiang 27.4b.

912　Cf. Du Yu's (ZZ 38.652) reading: "In serving a great domain, one should follow its lead in administrative affairs and then offer gifts to confirm one's loyalty."

913　In other words, although Qi is not bound by the Covenant of Song, it should go out of its way to please its more powerful ally, Jin. For similar reasoning, see Zhao 30.2.

914　For the Covenant of Chongqiu, see Xiang 25.6.

Zhongsun Jie (Meng Xiaobo) went to Jin.   28.5(7)

In winter, Qing Feng of Qi came in flight.   28.6(9)

In the eleventh month, our lord went to Chu.   28.7(12)

In the twelfth month, on the *jiayin* day (16), the Heaven-appointed king   28.8(10,14)
succumbed.

On the *yiwei* day,[908] Zhao, the Master of Chu, died.   28.9(12)

The Lu high officer Zi Shen predicts famine in Song and Zheng when he traces the lack of ice to the irregular movement of the Year-Planet and to the Dark Hollow asterism. Famines occur in Song and Zheng the following year (Xiang 29.7).

In the twenty-eighth year, in spring, there was no ice. Zi Shen said, "Now   28.1(1)
Song and Zheng will probably have famines! The Year-Planet should be
at Asterial Order, but it has overreached and moved into Dark Hollow.
Because of that there is the calamity of climatic irregularities: yin is no
match for yang. The Snake rides the Dragon, and Dragon is the star
whose position corresponds to Song and Zheng. There will certainly be
famines in Song and Zheng. Dark Hollow is empty at the center, as "hollow" is a term for depletion. When the earth is empty and the people are
depleted, how can they avoid famine?"[909]

In the aftermath of the Covenant of Song, leaders of various domains prepare to attend the Jin court. Two Qi ministers, Qing Feng and Chen Xuwu, debate whether Qi should also acknowledge Jin leadership.

In summer, the Prince of Qi, the Prince of Chen, the Prince of Cai, the   28.2
Liege of Northern Yan, the Liege of Qĭ, the Master of Hu, the Master of
Shĕn, and the White Di visited the court of Jin. This was on account of
the Covenant of Song.[910]

The Prince of Qi was about to set forth, when Qing Feng said, "Since
we were not party to the covenant,[911] why should we attend the Jin court?"
Chen Xuwu[a] said, "Serve first and consider the cost of gifts later:[912] that
is in accordance with ritual propriety. When a small domain serves a
great one and fails to obtain the opportunity to serve, it should anticipate
the latter's wishes and comply accordingly: that is in accordance with
ritual propriety.[913] Even if we were not party to the covenant, do we dare
revolt against Jin? The Covenant of Chongqiu cannot yet be forgotten.[914]
You, sir, should encourage the ruler to set forth."

28.3(2) 衛人討甯氏之黨，故石惡出奔晉。衛人立其從子圃，以守石氏之祀，禮
也。

28.4(3) 邾悼公來朝，時事也。

28.5(4) 秋，八月，大雩，旱也。

28.6 蔡侯歸自晉，入于鄭。鄭伯享之，不敬。子產曰：「蔡侯其不免乎！日其過
此也，君使子展迋勞於東門之外，而傲。吾曰猶將更之。今還，受享而
惰，乃其心也。君小國，事大國，而惰傲以為己心，將得死乎？若不免，
必由其子。其為君也，淫而不父。僑聞之：如是者，恆有子禍。」

28.7(5) 孟孝伯如晉，告將為宋之盟故如楚也。

Shi E, after mourning Ning Xi's death (Xiang 27.3a), flees to Jin, fulfilling a prophecy from nine years earlier (Xiang 19.13). His lineage, however, is allowed to continue, perhaps because of the great merit of his ancestor (Yin 3.7, 4.5).

The leaders of Wei chastised the party of the Ning lineage, and that was why Shi E departed and fled to Jin. The leaders of Wei established his nephew Shi Pu[a] as his successor so that he could guard the sacrifices of the Shi lineage. This was in accordance with ritual propriety.

28.3(2)

Lord Dao of Zhu came to visit our court: that was a customary seasonal visit.

28.4(3)

In autumn, in the eighth month, there was a great rain sacrifice because of the drought.

28.5(4)

Lord Jing of Cai's negligent and arrogant manner leads the Zheng minister Zichan to predict disaster. Zichan's judgment is supposedly based on the Cai ruler's ritual infractions, but Zichan might also have been influenced by rumors of the Cai ruler's adulterous relations with his daughter-in-law. His son murders him two years later (Xiang 30.5).

When the Prince of Cai was returning from Jin, he entered Zheng. The Liege of Zheng offered him ceremonial toasts, and he was irreverent. Zichan said, "The Prince of Cai will not escape disaster, surely! The other day, when he passed through here on his way to Jin, the lord sent Gong-sun Shezhi[a] to go and honor his exertions outside the eastern gate, but he was arrogant. I said then that he might still change his ways. Now on his return, he received ceremonial toasts and yet was negligent. It is thus really a matter of his nature![915] As the ruler of a small domain serving a great one, he yet lets negligence and arrogance become his nature. How will he manage to die a natural death? If he cannot escape disaster, then it will certainly be because of his son. As a ruler, he is licentious, and he has not acted like a father.[916] I have heard that a man like this is always plagued by disasters instigated by his son."

28.6

Meng Xiaobo went to Jin to notify the Jin court that Lu, on account of the Covenant of Song, would go to Chu.

28.7(5)

---

915   The original has heart or mind (*xin* 心), which in this context means nature.
916   Zichan is referring to Lord Jing's adulterous relations with his daughter-in-law.

28.8a 蔡侯之如晉也，鄭伯使游吉如楚。及漢，楚人還之，曰：「宋之盟，君實親辱。今吾子來，寡君謂吾子姑還，吾將使馹奔問諸晉而以告。」
　　　子大叔曰：「宋之盟，君命將利小國，而亦使安定其社稷，鎮撫其民人，以禮承天之休，此君之憲令，而小國之望也。寡君是故使吉奉其皮幣，以歲之不易，聘於下執事。今執事有命曰：『女何與政令之有？必使而君棄而封守，跋涉山川，蒙犯霜露，以逞君心。』小國將君是望，敢不唯命是聽？無乃非盟載之言，以闕君德，而執事有不利焉，小國是懼。不然，其何勞之敢憚？」

28.8b 子大叔歸，復命。告子展曰：「楚子將死矣。不修其政德，而貪昧於諸侯，以逞其願，欲久，得乎？《周易》有之：在復☷之頤☶，曰『迷復，凶』，其

<hr>

917　Jin-Chu negotiations would determine the degree of submission each is exacting from the adherents of the other.

918　That is, the top (sixth) line of hexagram 24, "Return" ☷ (Fu 復). When this broken line is unbroken, we have hexagram 27, "Nourishment" ☶ (Yi 頤). For other examples of the rhetorical use the *Zhou Changes*, see Xuan 6.6, 12.2c.

Chu leaders indicate to the visiting Zheng envoy You Ji that they expect the Zheng ruler personally to attend court in Chu. You Ji eloquently criticizes such demands.

When the Prince of Cai was going to Jin, the Liege of Zheng sent You Ji to Chu. When he reached the Han River, the leaders of Chu sent him back, saying, "At the Covenant of Song, your ruler was the one who deigned to participate personally. Now that you have come, sir, our unworthy ruler is saying that you should turn back for now. We will send a courier-carriage posthaste to inquire about this of Jin and then notify you about it."[917]

You Ji[b] said, "At the Covenant of Song, your ruler commanded that there be plans to benefit the small domains, and also that you let them bring peace and stability to the altars of their domains, settle and comfort their people, and use ritual propriety to receive the munificence of Heaven. This was your ruler's binding command and the very hope of the small domains. That was why our unworthy ruler, considering the difficulties of the times, sent me to present the gifts of fur and silk on this official visit to those in charge of your government. Now those in charge have a command that says, 'How could you have anything to do with the orders of government in Zheng? We must have your ruler abandon the land which he was put in power to guard, climb mountains and wade through rivers, and expose himself to the hazards of frost and dew, so as to satisfy our ruler's desires.' Our small domain looks only to your ruler. Would we dare fail to abide by none but your command? Will it not undermine your ruler's virtue to make demands beyond those recorded in the original covenant? Will that not mean harm for those in charge of your government? This is what our small domains fears. Otherwise, what toils would we dare to shrink from?"

You Ji, on the basis of Chu's unreasonable demands, predicts the death of King Kang of Chu as well as Chu's failure to become covenant chief. The irregular movement of the Year-Planet, said to portend famines in Song and Zheng (Xiang 28.1), is here taken to be an omen of death for King Ling of Zhou and King Kang of Chu. Both die later this year.

You Ji[b] returned and reported discharge of his mission. He told Gongsun Shezhi[a], "The Master of Chu is going to die. He does not cultivate the virtues of his government and is instead driven by greed and blindness to satisfy his wishes when dealing with the princes. He may wish to last long, but will he succeed? As the *Zhou Changes* has it, with the line whereby the hexagram 'Return' ䷗ becomes the hexagram 'Nourishment' ䷚:[918] 'Lost, turn back. Inauspicious.' Does that not refer to the

楚子之謂乎！欲復其願，而棄其本，復歸無所，是謂迷復，能無凶乎？君
其往也，送葬而歸，以快楚心。楚不幾十年，未能恤諸侯也，吾乃休吾
民矣。」

　　裨竈曰：「今茲周王及楚子皆將死。歲棄其次，而旅於明年之次，
以害鳥帑，周、楚惡之。」

28.8c　　九月，鄭游吉如晉，告將朝于楚以從宋之盟。子產相鄭伯以如楚。舍不
為壇。外僕言曰：「昔先大夫相先君適四國，未嘗不為壇。自是至今亦
皆循之。今子草舍，無乃不可乎？」

　　子產曰：「大適小，則為壇；小適大，苟舍而已，焉用壇？僑聞之，
大適小有五美：宥其罪戾，赦其過失，救其菑患，賞其德刑，教其不及。
小國不困，懷服如歸，是故作壇以昭其功，宣告後人，無怠於德。

919　The graph *fu* 復 means both "to return" and "to fulfill a wish." Instead of "returning
to basic concerns," the Chu king seeks to "realize his wishes."

920　That is, he fails to adhere to the right path or cultivate virtue. This may also connect
to the image of "forgetting the right road" from the line statement cited above.

921　You Ji is predicting that the Chu ruler will die before or during the Zheng ruler's
visit. Despite You Ji's disparagement of Chu, he is basically capitulating to Chu's
demand that the Zheng ruler should personally attend the Chu court.

922　The statement of the top line of "Return": "To use this to send forth troops will end
in great defeat. For the ruler of the domain, this is inauspicious. Even in ten years
the expedition will not succeed."

923　The inauspicious consequences of the irregular movement of the Year-Planet affect
the Vermilion Bird (Zhuque 朱雀) constellation, which includes "Quail Fire"
(Chunhuo 鶉火) and "Quail's Tail Feathers" (Chunwei 鶉尾). According to the
theory of *fenye* 分野, or "field allocation astrology" (Pankenier's translation), the
latter two govern events in Zhou and Chu.

Master of Chu! He wants to realize[919] his wishes, yet he abandons the basic concerns.[920] To try to return but have no place to come back to is what is meant by 'lost, turn back.' How can this fail to be inauspicious? Our ruler should go there, send off the funeral procession, and come back, so as to gratify Chu's desires.[921] It will be close to ten years before Chu will be able to exert any sway over the Princes.[922] We can then let our people rest."

Pi Zao said, "This year the Zhou king and the Master of Chu will both die. The Year-Planet has abandoned its proper place and is moving to its position for next year, bringing harm to the 'Bird' and the 'Quail's Tail Feathers.' Zhou and Chu will suffer because of this."[923]

While complying with Chu demands, Zichan demonstrates Zheng's discontent by refusing to build the customary earthern platform. As with You Ji earlier (Xiang 28.8a), criticism of the stronger domain is the rhetorical compensation for submission.

In the ninth month, You Ji of Zheng went to Jin to notify Jin that Zheng would visit the court of Chu in accordance with the Covenant of Song. With Zichan acting as assistant to the Liege of Zheng, they went to Chu. Zichan set up a tent but did not build an earthen platform.[924] The external officer in charge of this ceremony said, "In the past, when the former high officers acted as the former rulers' assistants as they traveled to all the domains in the four quarters of the land, they never neglected to clear the ground and build an earthen platform. That is why to this day we still all follow this practice. Now you, sir, have set up a tent on the grass. Is that not unacceptable?"

Zichan said, "When those from a great domain travel to a small domain, they build an earthen platform. But when those from a small domain travel to a great domain, they merely make do with a tent. What need is there for an earthen platform? I have heard that there are five good things when those from a great domain travel to a small one: they forgive the latter's offenses, pardon its errors, relieve its troubles, reward it for its beneficence and punishments,[925] and instruct it about its lapses and inadequacies. Thus free from difficulties, the small domain cherishes submission to the great one, finding refuge as if it is returning home. That is why the great domain creates an earthen platform to make manifest its achievement and to proclaim to those who come after that they should not be remiss in cultivating virtue.

---

924 It was customary for the ruler of a domain, during an official visit to another domain, to build an earthen platform in the outskirts of the domain he was visiting to receive the host's gifts honoring the visiting ruler's exertions.

925 Takezoe (18.54): *de* 德 (virtue or beneficence) refers to rewards, *xing* 刑 refers to punishment. *De* and *xing* are often named together as complementary measures that are, respectively, ameliorative and punitive; see Xuan 12.2, n. 189

　　小適大有五惡：說其罪戾，請其不足，行其政事，共其職貢，從其
時命。不然，則重其幣帛，以賀其福而弔其凶，皆小國之禍也，焉用作壇
以昭其禍？所以告子孫，無昭禍焉可也。」

28.9a(7)　齊慶封好田而耆酒，與慶舍政，則以其內實遷于盧蒲嫳氏，易內而飲
酒。數日，國遷朝焉。使諸亡人得賊者，以告而反之，故反盧蒲癸。癸
臣子之，有寵，妻之。慶舍之士謂盧蒲癸曰：「男女辨姓，子不辟宗，何
也？」曰：「宗不余辟，余獨焉辟之？賦詩斷章，余取所求焉，惡識宗？」
癸言王何而反之，二人皆嬖，使執寢戈而先後之。

28.9b　公膳日雙雞，饔人竊更之以鶩。御者知之，則去其肉，而以其洎饋。子
雅、子尾怒。慶封告盧蒲嫳。盧蒲嫳曰：「譬之如禽獸，吾寢處之矣。」
使析歸父告晏平仲。

926　It is possible to have "the great domain" as the subject of the first two clauses: the
great domain "justifies its offenses with fine words, requests to be supplied with
what it lacks" (Yang, 3:1145). However, it makes more sense here to have the small
domain as the subject suffering all "five evils."

927　"Timely commands" (*shiming* 時命) are justified, as in Zhao 30.2. Here Zichan is
implying that the commands are supposedly seasonal but actually unpredictable.

928　Although Qing Feng has supposedly yielded control of the government to Qing She,
he is still acknowledged as the person in charge, and the ministers and high officers
must therefore attend court in Lupu Pie's residence.

929　The "exiled persons" are those exiled in the aftermath both of Lord Zhuang's assassination (Xiang 25.2) and of Cui Zhu's downfall (Xiang 27.7). The "malefactors" (*zei*
賊) are probably Lord Zhuang's supporters or the remnants of Cui Zhu's party.

930　Lupu Gui, formerly Lord Zhuang's supporter (Xiang 23.4a), had fled to Jin (Xiang
25.2d).

931　Both Lupu Gui and Qing Feng have the clan name Jiang. Note that Cui Zhu violated
the same taboo (Xiang 25.2a).

932　Self-interest that overrides taboos is compared to the practice of breaking off
stanzas to create meanings that fit the occasion during the recitation of odes (*duanzhang* 斷章). This indicates an awareness of the gap between performed and "originally intended" meanings in the quotation of odes. "Taking what one seeks" in the
recitation of odes is common practice in *Zuozhuan*.

933　The attendant understands the cook's intention of provoking Ziya and Ziwei into
opposing Qing Feng and makes the slight more offensive. For "food stories," see
Xuan 2.1a.

934　Ziya and Ziwei, Lord Hui's grandsons of the Luan and Gao lineages, respectively,
hold Qing Feng responsible for the diminution of their official meals.

935　Literally, "If I may compare them to beasts, I would readily sleep on their pelts."
Zhou Chuo makes the same remark about Zhi Chuo and Guo Zui in Xiang 21.8; see
n. 621. Cf. Zhao 3.10.

936　Since Qing Feng appeals to Yan Ying for help to get rid of Ziya and Ziwei, he must
have enlarged on stories of their disaffection and unruliness. Yan Ying's response
echoes his refusal to become embroiled in Qi internecine struggles in Xiang 25.2c
and Zhao 10.2b.

"There are five evils when those from a small domain travel to a great one: they have to explain the small domain's alleged offenses, request leniency for its deficiencies,[926] carry out the great domain's policies, supply it with obligatory offerings, and follow its supposedly timely commands.[927] If the small domain fails to do these things, the great domain will increase the burden of offerings, whether it be for congratulations on its good fortunes or for condolences over its misfortunes. All these are disasters for the small domain. What need is there to build an earthen platform to advertise its disasters? Tell our descendants this: do not advertise your disasters, and that will be all."

The seeds of doom for the Qing lineage are sown: having monopolized power in Qi (Xiang 27.7), Qing Feng indulges in licentious behavior. Probably through the intercession of Qing Feng's favorite Lupu Pie, Qing Feng's former enemies, including Lupu Gui and Wang He (Lord Zhuang's supporters who fled in Xiang 25.2d), are allowed to return to Qi.

Qing Feng of Qi, who loved hunting and drinking, handed government over to his son Qing She and moved with his women and valuables to Lupu Pie's residence, where the two men exchanged their women and drank. In a few days, the domain moved its court there.[928] Qing Feng allowed various exiled persons to return if they had reported any news about malefactors.[929] That was why he brought back Lupu Gui.[930] Lupu Gui[a] became a retainer serving Qing She[a], who favored Lupu Gui and gave his daughter to him as wife. Qing She's officers said to Lupu Gui, "Man and wife should have different clan names, yet you, sir, have not avoided marriage with someone who shares a common ancestor with you.[931] Why is this?" He said, "Since her father, who shares a common ancestor with me, has not avoided me, how can I for my part avoid him? Just as one breaks off stanzas when reciting odes, I take what I seek.[932] What do I know about common ancestors?" Lupu Gui[a] spoke to Qing She about Wang He and brought Wang He back. Qing She was enamored of both of them and had them guard him closely with dagger-axes, one in front and one behind him.

28.9a(7)

Qing Feng tries but fails to enlist the support of other factions to topple disaffected Qi nobles. The Chen lineage, which will eventually win out by the end of the period covered by Zuozhuan, predicts the downfall of the Qing lineage and seeks to profit by it.

For the official meals at court, there were two chickens every day. The cook secretly substituted ducks for them. The attendant bringing in the meal knew about this and took away the meat and served only the broth.[933] Ziya and Ziwei were furious.[934] Qing Feng told Lupu Pie, who said, "Those beasts—I wish I could sleep on their pelts already!"[935] Qing Feng sent Xi Guifu to tell Yan Ying[a].[936]

28.9b

　　平仲曰：「嬰之眾不足用也，知無能謀也。言弗敢出，有盟可也。」
子家曰：「子之言云，又焉用盟？」告北郭子車。子車曰：「人各有以事君，
非佐之所能也。」陳文子謂桓子曰：「禍將作矣，吾其何得？」對曰：「得
慶氏之木百車於莊。」文子曰：「可慎守也已。」

28.9c　　盧蒲癸、王何卜攻慶氏，示子之兆，曰：「或卜攻讎，敢獻其兆。」子之曰：
「克，見血。」

　　　　冬，十月，慶封田于萊，陳無宇從。丙辰，文子使召之，請曰：「無
宇之母疾病，請歸。」慶季卜之，示之兆，曰：「死。」奉龜而泣，乃使歸。
慶嗣聞之，曰：「禍將作矣。」謂子家：「速歸，禍作必於嘗，歸猶可及
也。」子家弗聽，亦無悛志。子息曰：「亡矣！幸而獲在吳、越。」陳無宇
濟水，而戕舟發梁。

Yan Ying[d] said, "My followers are not worth calling upon for this task. They lack the wits to devise any plan or strategy. I would not dare let the word out. Let us swear a covenant about this." Qing Feng[b] said, "You have already given your word. What need is there for a covenant?"[937] He told Beiguo Zuo[a]. Beiguo Zuo[b] said, "Each person has his way of serving the ruler. This is not something I can do." Chen Xuwu[a] said to his son Chen Wuyu[b], "Disaster is about to rear its head. What can we gain from it?" He replied, "We can gain a hundred cartloads of lumber from the Qing lineage on Broad Avenue."[938] Chen Xuwu[b] said, "You should be on your guard."

The plot against the Qing lineage thickens. Divination is tied to deception and hubris: Qing She and Qing Feng are repeatedly fooled by omens.

Lupu Gui and Wang He divined about attacking the Qing lineage and showed the omen cracks to Qing She[a]. They said, "Someone divined about attacking an enemy, and we presume to present to you the omen." Qing She[a] said, "Prevail. See blood."[939]

In winter, in the tenth month, Qing Feng was hunting at Lai, with Chen Wuyu in attendance. On the *bingchen* day (17), Chen Xuwu[b] had someone summon him and make this request: "Wuyu's mother is very ill. We ask your permission to let him return." Qing Feng[c] divined about this and showed the omen to Chen Wuyu, who said, "This portends death." He held the turtle shell and wept. Qing Feng thus let him return. When his kinsman Qing Si heard about this, he said, "Disaster is about to rear its head." He said to Qing Feng[b], "Go back quickly! Disaster is certain to rear its head at the time of autumnal sacrifice, but there is still time to go back." Qing Feng[b] did not heed him, nor did he show any signs of remorse or desire to change his ways. Qing Si[a] said, "He will surely be driven into exile! If he is lucky, he will manage to find refuge in Wu and Yue."[940] After Chen Wuyu crossed the river, he destroyed his boat and took down the bridge.

28.9c

---

937 Du Yu (ZZ 38.654) identifies Zijia, the speaker of this line, as Xi Guifu, which makes sense according to the logic of the sentence. However, Qing Feng is elsewhere referred to as Zijia (Xiang 28.9c), and if Xi Guifu has the same cognomen, the text would have marked it more explicitly.

938 Chen Xuwu is predicting ruin for the Qing lineage. His son replies likewise in code, asserting that they can hope to take over the resources of the Qing lineage and assume control of the Qi government.

939 This is Qing She's reading of the cracks on the turtle shell.

940 See Xiang 28.9e and Zhao 4.4.

28.9d　盧蒲姜謂癸曰：「有事而不告我，必不捷矣。」癸告之。姜曰：「夫子愎，莫之止，將不出。我請止之。」癸曰：「諾。」十一月乙亥，嘗于大公之廟，慶舍涖事。盧蒲姜告之，且止之，弗聽，曰：「誰敢者？」

　　　遂如公。麻嬰為尸，慶奊為上獻。盧蒲癸、王何執寢戈，慶氏以其甲環公宮。陳氏、鮑氏之圉人為優。慶氏之馬善驚，士皆釋甲束馬，而飲酒，且觀優，至於魚里。欒、高、陳、鮑之徒介慶氏之甲。子尾抽桷，擊扉三，盧蒲癸自後刺子之，王何以戈擊之，解其左肩。猶援廟桷，動於甍。以俎、壺投，殺人而後死。遂殺慶繩、麻嬰。公懼，鮑國曰：「群臣為君故也。」陳須無以公歸，稅服而如內宮。

Qing She's daughter, Lupu Jiang, sides with her husband, Lupu Gui, and goads her father to attend the autumnal sacrifice at the Qi Ancestral Temple, where Lupu Gui and his allies, emerging from ambush, murder Qing She and his supporters. Lupu Jiang's choice offers a striking contrast with women who side with their fathers against their husbands or sons in Zuozhuan (Huan 15.2, Xiang 21.5a). Paradoxically, Lupu Jiang ensnares her father in her husband's plot by revealing the truth and using it as a provocation.

Lupu Jiang, Qing She's daughter and Lupu Gui's wife, said to Lupu Gui[a], 28.9d "You will certainly not succeed if you are planning something and are not telling me!" Lupu Gui[a] told her about the plot to attack the Qing lineage during the autumnal sacrifice. Lupu Jiang[a] said, "My father is stubborn and contrary. If no one stops him, he will not go. I beg leave to stop him." Lupu Gui[a] said, "I agree." In the eleventh month, on the *yihai* day (7), the autumnal sacrifice was to take place at the temple of the Qi ancestor Grand Lord, and Qing She was to oversee the ceremony. Lupu Jiang told him about the plot and moreover tried to stop him from going. He did not heed her, saying, "Who would dare do such a thing?"

He thus went to the temple. Ma Ying was the personator receiving sacrifices. Qing Xie was the leading guest who would present the first offerings. Lupu Gui and Wang He were holding dagger-axes in close attendance, and Qing She used his armored men to surround the lord's palace. The grooms of the Chen and Bao lineages were the entertainers.[941] Since Qing She's horses were easily startled, the officers all took off their armor and tied up their horses. They then drank and also watched the entertainers, going off with them to Yuli. The followers of the Luan, Gao, Chen, and Bao lineages put on the armor left behind by the officers of the Qing lineage. Ziwei pulled out a beam and hit the door thrice.[942] Lupu Gui stabbed Qing She[a] from behind, while Wang He struck him with his dagger-axe, splitting open his left shoulder. Even then he still grabbed the square pillar of the temple and shook it till the roof tiles quivered. Hurling ritual vessels and a stand for sacrificial meat, he killed some men before he died. The attackers then killed Qing Xie[a] and Ma Ying. The lord was terrified, but Bao Guo said, "We, your subjects, are acting on behalf of the ruler." Chen Xuwu went back with the lord, who took off his sacrificial robes and went to the inner palace.

---

941 The temple was inside the palace. Possibly because of his daughter's duplicitous warning, Qing She is making provisions to defend the palace against attackers. The entertainers prepared by the Chen and Bao lineages might have been intended to distract Qing She's officers.

942 Ziwei (Gao lineage) is giving the signal for the attack to begin. The account of the attack indicates that the Luan, Gao, Chen, and Bao lineages are all plotting together with Lupu Gui and Wang He.

28.9e　慶封歸，遇告亂者。丁亥，伐西門，弗克。還伐北門，克之。入，伐內宮，弗克。反，陳于嶽，請戰，弗許，遂來奔。
　　　　獻車於季武子，美澤可以鑑。展莊叔見之，曰：「車甚澤，人必瘁，宜其亡也。」叔孫穆子食慶封，慶封氾祭。穆子不說，使工為之誦〈茅鴟〉，亦不知。既而齊人來讓，奔吳。吳句餘予之朱方，聚其族焉而居之，富於其舊。子服惠伯謂叔孫曰：「天殆富淫人，慶封又富矣。」穆子曰：「善人富謂之賞，淫人富謂之殃。天其殃之也，其將聚而殲旃。」

28.10(8)　癸巳，天王崩。未來赴，亦未書，禮也。

Qing Feng learns about the insurrection on his way back from hunting at Lai (Xiang 28.9c), and he flees to Lu after a series of skirmishes. Repeating motifs from his earlier visit (Xiang 27.2), his fine carriage, ritual impropriety, and ignorance of the Odes *invite negative judgments from Lu dignitaries. Defying such denunciations with new prosperity in Wu, Qing Feng will meet his end only seven years later (Zhao 4.4).*

When Qing Feng was on his way back from hunting, he met someone who told him about the turmoil. On the *dinghai* day (19), he attacked the western gate but did not prevail. Upon returning, he attacked the northern gate and did prevail. He entered the city and attacked the inner palace but did not prevail. He turned back and set forth his forces at Peaks Avenue. He requested engagement in battle, but his opponents did not agree. He thus came to Lu in flight.

28.9e

He presented to Ji Wuzi a carriage whose lustrous sheen was such that its surface could be used as a mirror. Zhan Zhuangshu saw this and said, "His carriage is so very splendid, there must be people who suffer for it.[943] It is fitting that he is in exile." Shusun Bao[b] invited Qing Feng to a meal, and Qing Feng first offered sacrifices to all the spirits.[944] Shusun Bao[c] was displeased and had the musicians chant for him "The Bird of Prey."[945] Yet again he did not understand. Not long afterward, the leaders of Qi came to reprimand Lu, and Qing Feng fled to Wu. Yimo[a], the ruler of Wu, gave him Zhufang.[946] He gathered his kinsmen and resided there, where he became even richer than before. Zifu Huibo said to Shusun Bao[d], "Heaven seems to enrich depraved people! Qing Feng is becoming rich again." Shusun Bao[c] said, "For a good man, riches are called 'just recompense.' For a depraved man, riches are called 'calamity.' Heaven is surely going to bring calamity on him. Perhaps it is gathering them all so that the lineage can be entirely destroyed."

On the *guisi* day, the twenty-fifth day of the eleventh month, the Heaven-appointed king succumbed.[947] Notice of his passing did not arrive, and it was also not recorded. This was in accordance with ritual propriety.

28.10(8)

943　That is, Qing Feng accumulates wealth at the expense of the people. Alternatively, *ren* 人 can refer to Qing Feng: "he must suffer for it" or "he must have wreaked destruction," reading *cui* 瘁 as either the state of illness and depletion or the act of inflicting pain and depletion.

944　Ritual requires the offering of sacrifices before a meal. However, making "sacrifices to all the spirits" (*fanji* 氾祭) is deemed ritually inappropriate, probably because it is too general or grandiose.

945　This ode is no longer extant. We may surmise that the ode criticizes transgression and the ignorance of ritual.

946　Zhufang 朱方 was located east of present-day Zhenjiang City 鎮江市, Jiangsu.

947　The *Annals* and *Zuozhuan* give different dates for the death of King Ling of Zhou. Cf. n. 961.

28.11a 崔氏之亂，喪群公子，故鉏在魯，叔孫還在燕，賈在句瀆之丘。及慶氏亡，皆召之，具其器用，而反其邑焉。與晏子邶殿其鄙六十，弗受。子尾曰：「富，人之所欲也。何獨弗欲？」

對曰：「慶氏之邑足欲，故亡。吾邑不足欲也，益之以邶殿，乃足欲。足欲，亡無日矣。在外，不得宰吾一邑。不受邶殿，非惡富也，恐失富也。且夫富，如布帛之有幅焉。為之制度，使無遷也。夫民，生厚而用利，於是乎正德以幅之，使無黜嫚，謂之幅利。利過則為敗。吾不敢貪多，所謂幅也。」與北郭佐邑六十，受之。與子雅邑，辭多受少。與子尾邑，受而稍致之。公以為忠，故有寵。釋盧蒲嫳于北竟。

---

948   Lord Zhuang drove them away because they had supported his rival Gongzi Ya. But Lord Zhuang was instated through Cui Zhu's help; hence, "the havoc wreaked by Cui Zhu" is presented as the cause for their exile; see Xiang 19.5, 21.3. Following Yang, 3:1150, we take it that Gongzi Mai 買 of Xiang 21.3 and the character here called Jia 賈, both associated with Goudou Knoll, are the same person. The graphs for the two names are very similar.

949   Beidian 邶殿 was located northwest of Changyi County 昌邑縣, Shandong.

950   It is also possible to read *zuyu* 足欲, translated here as "satisfy desires," as "worth desiring."

951   The word "measurements" here, *fu* 幅, is a homophone of the word for "wealth," *fu* 富.

952   Bolts of cloth and silk were supposed to be of fixed width.

953   In Wen 7.8, "correcting virtue, using things advantageously, and enriching livelihood" (*zhengde* 正德, *liyong* 利用, *housheng* 厚生) are named as the "three official affairs."

In the aftermath of the Qing lineage's downfall, the noble sons from Qi exiled seven years earlier (Xiang 21.3) are reinstated. In the dispensation of rewards that follows, Yan Ying declines settlements bestowed on him and discourses on the necessity of keeping wealth within "proper measure" (see also Xiang 27.3b).

As a consequence of the havoc wreaked by Cui Zhu, the noble sons had been dispersed. That was why Gongzi Chu[a] had been in Lu, Shusun Xuan had been in Yan, and Gongzi Mai[a] had been at Goudou Knoll.[948] By the time the Qing lineage head went into exile, they had all been summoned back. Vessels and household implements were provided for them, and their settlements were returned. Yan Ying[b] was granted sixty settlements on the border of Beidian,[949] but he declined to accept them. Ziwei said, "Riches are what men desire, so why do you alone not desire them?"

He replied, "The Qing lineage's settlements were enough to satisfy their desires, and that is why they are in exile. Admittedly, my settlements are not enough to satisfy my desires. But if Beidian were added to them, then they would satisfy my desires. Once they satisfied my desires, exile would not be far off.[950] If I were abroad, I could not be in charge of even one of my settlements. I refuse to accept Beidian, not because I abhor riches but because I fear losing them. What's more, riches are like bolts of cloth and silk that have proper measurements.[951] Dimensions are set up for them so that there will be no deviations.[952] Now the people all want their livelihood to prosper and their operations to be profitable. That is why correcting virtue is the way to keep them to proper measure,[953] so that there is neither want nor excess. This is called keeping profit within proper measure. Excessive profit makes for ruin. That I do not dare to covet excesses is what is called proper measure." The lord granted Beiguo Zuo sixty settlements, and he accepted them. He granted Ziya settlements, and he declined many but accepted a few. Ziwei accepted the settlements granted him, but he returned all of them to the lord.[954] The lord considered him loyal, and that was why he was favored. Lupu Pie was released at the northern territories.[955]

28.11a

---

954 Takezoe (18.62) notes that at this juncture the Qing lineage's property is divided among the high officers. Whatever Ziwei declines would have been further divided, but since he first accepts the settlements and only later returns them to Lord Jing, the latter is ensured gain and thus considers Ziwei loyal. Ziwei seems to be following the same reasoning as Yan Ying.

955 A parallel passage appears in *Yanzi chunqiu* 6.405.

28.11b　求崔杼之尸，將戮之，不得。叔孫穆子曰：「必得之。武王有亂臣十人，崔杼其有乎？不十人，不足以葬。」既，崔氏之臣曰：「與我其拱璧，吾獻其枢。」於是得之。十二月乙（己）亥朔，齊人遷莊公，殯于大寢，以其棺尸崔杼於市。國人猶知之，皆曰：「崔子也。」

28.12a(7)　為宋之盟故，公及宋公、陳侯、鄭伯、許男如楚。公過鄭，鄭伯不在，伯有迂勞於黃崖，不敬。穆叔曰：「伯有無戾於鄭，鄭必有大咎。敬，民之主也，而棄之，何以承守？鄭人不討，必受其辜。濟澤之阿，行潦之蘋藻，寘諸宗室，季蘭尸之，敬也。敬可棄乎？」

28.12b(9)　及漢，楚康王卒。公欲反。叔仲昭伯曰：「我楚國之為，豈為一人？行也！」子服惠伯曰：「君子有遠慮，小人從邇。飢寒之不恤，誰遑其後？不如姑歸也。」叔孫穆子曰：「叔仲子專之矣；子服子，始學者也。」榮成伯曰：「遠圖者，忠也。」公遂行。

<hr>

956　See *Analects* 8.20 and the "Great Oath" quoted in Zhao 24.1. For a short summary of the way a variant of 司 becomes confused with 亂, see Karlgren, *Grammata Serica Recensa*, 180a–b. Karlgren points to the solution also in his gl. 651.

957　Huangya 黃崖 was located in the domain of Zheng south of present-day Xinzheng County 新鄭縣, Henan.

958　See Xuan 2.3a: "he who does not forget reverence is the master of the people."

959　These lines appear to be a paraphrase or variant version of lines from *Maoshi* 15, "Cai pin" 采蘋, 1D.52–54, which is also quoted in Yin 3.3 to substantiate an argument about good faith. The idea is that even humble objects such as duckweed and algae can be proper sacrificial offerings so long as everything is done in a spirit of reverence. Some commentators suggest that Jilan should be read as a variant of *jiluan* 季巒, "the young and beautiful one" (Wu Jin'an, *Chunqiu Zuoshui zhuan jiuzhu shuzheng xu*, 577).

960　The somewhat abstract sense of duty here is concretized as an argument about Chu power in Shuzhong Zhaobo's much longer speech in *Guoyu*, "Lu yu 2," 5.191–93.

Cui Zhu's corpse is desecrated, and Lord Zhuang of Qi's improper burial (Xiang 25.2e) is rectified.

Qi leaders sought Cui Zhu's corpse, as they intended to publicly dese- 28.11b
crate it, but it was not found. Shusun Bao[b] said, "It is sure to be found. King Wu had ten ministers who brought order.[956] Did Cui Zhu have any? Without ten such men, there will not be the wherewithal for him to remain buried." Shortly thereafter, a retainer of Cui Zhu said, "Give me his great jade disk, and I will present his coffin." Thus, his corpse was found. In the twelfth month, on the *jihai* day, the first day of the month, the leaders of Qi reburied Lord Zhuang and had his coffin lie in state at the Grand Chamber in the Ancestral Temple. Cui Zhu's coffin was opened to have his corpse exposed in the marketplace. The inhabitants of the capital could still recognize him, and all said, "This is Cui Zhu[e]."

The Lu minister Shusun Bao predicts disaster for the Zheng noble Liang Xiao, who lacks reverence as he honors the exertions of Lu delegates on their way to Chu. Liang Xiao is killed two years later (Xiang 30.2, 30.10).

On account of the Covenant of Song, our lord, together with the Duke 28.12a(7)
of Song, the Prince of Chen, the Liege of Zheng, and the Head of Xǔ, went to Chu. Our lord passed through Zheng, and the Liege of Zheng was not there. Liang Xiao[a] went to honor our exertions at Huangya but was irreverent.[957] Shusun Bao[a] said, "If Liang Xiao[a] is not punished for his offense in Zheng, Zheng will certainly suffer great misfortune. Reverence sustains one as the master of the people.[958] If one abandons it, how can one uphold and guard one's patrimony? If the leaders of Zheng do not chastise him, they are sure to suffer from a calamity of his making. The thin soil by fords and marshes and the duckweed and algae in puddles by the wayside are placed as offerings in the Ancestral Temple, with Jilan acting as personator at the sacrifices.[959] This is what is meant by reverence. Can reverence be abandoned?"

King Kang of Chu dies as the rulers of various domains are on their way to attend court in Chu. Lu continues but Song turns back, and both choices seem justified.

By the time our lord reached the Han River, King Kang of Chu died. Our 28.12b(9)
lord wanted to turn back. Shuzhong Zhaobo said, "We have come for Chu, so how could one person matter? Let us go forth!"[960] Zifu Huibo said, "The noble man considers what lies far ahead, while the petty man acts by what is close at hand. But if we cannot allay hunger and cold, who has time to worry about what comes after? It would be better to return for now." Shusun Bao[b] said, "Shuzhong Zhaobo[c] has all the right on his side. Zifu Huibo[a] is one who is just beginning to learn." Rong Jia'e[a] said, "He who plans far ahead is loyal." Our lord thus continued on his way.

宋向戌曰：「我一人之為，非為楚也。飢寒之不恤，誰能恤楚？姑歸而息民，待其立君而為之備。」宋公遂反。

28.13　楚屈建卒，趙文子喪之如同盟，禮也。

28.14(8)　王人來告喪，問崩日，以甲寅告，故書之，以徵過也。

春秋

29.1(1)　二十有九年，春，王正月，公在楚。

29.2(4)　夏，五月，公至自楚。

29.3　庚午，衛侯衍卒。

29.4(6)　閽弒吳子餘祭。

29.5(8)　仲孫羯會晉荀盈、齊高止、宋華定、衛世叔儀、鄭公孫段、曹人、莒人、滕人、薛人、小邾人城杞。

29.6(10)　晉侯使士鞅來聘。

29.7(12)　杞子來盟。

29.8(13)　吳子使札來聘。

29.9　秋，九月，葬衛獻公。

29.10(14)　齊高止出奔北燕。

29.11(15)　冬，仲孫羯如晉。

961　The *Annals* entry is said to deliberately record the wrong date in order to censure those responsible for the error.

962　As noted by Wang Kekuan (cited in Yang, 1:115), starting from Zhuang 27.6, the *Annals* normally refers to the ruler of Qi as a liege (*bo* 伯). The only exceptions besides this one are in Xi 23.4 and Xi 27.1.

Xiang Xu of Song said, "We have come for one man, not for Chu. We cannot even allay hunger and cold, so who can allay the Chu threat? Let us return for now and bring rest to the people, wait for Chu to establish its ruler, and prepare for a possible attack." The Duke of Song thus turned back.

Qu Jian of Chu died. Zhao Wu[a] mourned him in the way appropriate for covenant partners. This was in accordance with ritual propriety.

28.13

Two dates are given for the death of King Ling of Zhou (Xiang 28.10, 28.14). The author of the following passage claims that the Annals *entry (28.8) is based on an erroneous Zhou report.*

The king's envoy came to notify us of the royal funeral. We asked about the date he succumbed and were told that it happened on the *jiayin* day (16). That was why the date was recorded, to chastise those responsible for the error.[961]

28.14(8)

LORD XIANG 29 (544 BCE)
ANNALS

In the twenty-ninth year, in spring, in the royal first month, our lord was in Chu.

29.1(1)

In summer, in the fifth month, our lord arrived from Chu.

29.2(4)

On the *gengwu* day, the sixth day of the fifth month, Kan, the Prince of Wei, died.

29.3

A gatekeeper assassinated Yuzhai, the Master of Wu.

29.4(6)

Zhongsun Jie (Meng Xiaobo) met with Xun Ying (Zhi Daozi) of Jin, Gao Zhi of Qi, Hua Ding of Song, Shishu Yi (Taishu Yi) of Wei, Gongsun Duan of Zheng, a Cao leader, a Ju leader, a Teng leader, a Xue leader, and a Lesser Zhu leader and fortified Qǐ.

29.5(8)

The Prince of Jin sent Shi Yang (Fan Yang) to us on an official visit.

29.6(10)

The Master of Qǐ came and swore a covenant.[962]

29.7(12)

The Master of Wu sent Zha (Jizha) to us on an official visit.

29.8(13)

In autumn, in the ninth month, Lord Xian of Wei was buried.

29.9

Gao Zhi of Qi departed and fled to Northern Yan.

29.10(14)

In winter, Zhongsun Jie (Meng Xiaobo) went to Jin.

29.11(15)

左傳

29.1(1) 二十九年，春，王正月，公在楚，釋不朝正于廟也。
楚人使公親禭，公患之。穆叔曰：「被殯而禭，則布幣也。」乃使巫以桃、茢先祓殯。楚人弗禁，既而悔之。

29.2 二月癸卯，齊人葬莊公於北郭。

29.3 夏，四月，葬楚康王，公及陳侯、鄭伯、許男送葬，至於西門之外，諸侯之大夫皆至于墓。楚郟敖即位，王子圍為令尹。鄭行人子羽曰：「是謂不宜，必代之昌。松柏之下，其草不殖。」

---

963 This story is also found in *Liji* 10.190–91.

964 The ruler attended court (*chao zheng* 朝正) following sacrifices at the Ancestral Temple on the first day of the month, this is called *gao shuo* 告朔, *shi shuo* 視朔, or *ting shuo* 聽朔. Rulers' attendance at such rituals seems to have been in decline since the mid-Chunqiu period. Cf. Xi 5.2, n. 60.

965 The ceremony of "dressing the dead" (*sui* 禭) is undertaken by envoys from other domains attending the funeral of a lord; see *Liji* 41.723. It may have involved actually putting a robe on the dead lord or symbolically placing it on the eastern side of the coffin. Since King Kang seems to have been encoffined by this point, we may surmise that the ceremony is symbolic.

Chu leaders try to humiliate Lord Xiang of Lu by asking him to dress the dead, a ritual usually performed by a subject for a ruler. Lu manages to return the insult by having Lord Xiang perform an exorcistic ritual reserved for a ruler when he attends funerals for his subjects, thus demoting the deceased Chu king to the status of subject.[963]

In the twenty-ninth year, in spring, in the royal first month, our lord was in Chu: this is to explain why he did not attend court following sacrifices at the Ancestral Temple that marked the beginning of the month.[964]   29.1(1)

The leaders of Chu had our lord personally dress the dead with burial garments.[965] Our lord was troubled by it. Shusun Bao[a] said, "If you exorcise the inauspiciousness of the funeral chamber and then dress the dead, it will be no different from setting forth gifts in court visits." Our lord thus had shamans use peach branches and reed brooms to first exorcise the inauspiciousness of the funeral chamber. The leaders of Chu did not prevent the ceremony, but shortly thereafter they regretted it.[966]

Lord Zhuang of Qi is reburied after the fall of the Cui and Qing lineages. Although Lord Zhuang lay in state at the Ancestral Temple, he was ultimately buried outside the city, possibly because his former enemies now regain their power (Xiang 28.11a).

In the second month, on the *guimao* day (6), the men of Qi buried Lord Zhuang at the northern outer wall of the city.   29.2

Jia'ao, the son of King Kang of Chu, accedes to his position, and his uncle Gongzi Wei becomes chief minister. The Zheng envoy Gongsun Hui warns of the danger of usurpation posed by an overly powerful minister, comparing the young king to grass and Gongzi Wei to imposing trees (for similar arguments, see Huan 18.3, Zhao 11.10). Gongzi Wei will murder Jia'ao three years hence (Zhao 1.13).

In summer, in the fourth month, King Kang of Chu was buried. Our lord, together with the Prince of Chen, the Liege of Zheng, and the Head of Xǔ, escorted the funeral cortege till they reached the area outside the west gate of the city. The high officers of the princes all went as far as the tomb. Jia'ao of Chu acceded to his position, and Gongzi Wei[a] became chief minister. The Zheng envoy Gongsun Hui[a] said, "This is what we call unfitting. Gongzi Wei will certainly flourish in place of the king. Under the pines and cypresses, the grass does not flourish."   29.3

---

966 Shusun Bao argues that by returning the insult, the Lu ruler can put the robe on the coffin without suffering humiliation—it will be like the customary practice of setting forth gifts during court visits. Chu leaders seem to grasp this only after the ceremony.

29.4a(2)　公還，及方城。季武子取卞，使公冶問，璽書追而與之，曰：「聞守卞者將叛，臣帥徒以討之，既得之矣。敢告。」公冶致使而退，及舍，而後聞取卞。公曰：「欲之而言叛，祇見疏也。」

公謂公冶曰：「吾可以入乎？」對曰：「君實有國，誰敢違君？」公與公冶冕服。固辭，強之而後受。公欲無入。榮成伯賦〈式微〉，乃歸。五月，公至自楚。

29.4b　公冶致其邑於季氏，而終不入焉。曰：「欺其君，何必使余？」季孫見之，則言季氏如他日；不見，則終不言季氏。及疾，聚其臣，曰：「我死，必無以冕服斂，非德賞也。且無使季氏葬我。」

29.5　葬靈王，鄭上卿有事。子展使印段往。伯有曰：「弱，不可。」子展曰：「與其莫往，弱，不猶愈乎？《詩》云：

---

967 Fangcheng seems to refer to an area south of the Huai River and north of the Han River. See n. 470; Xi 4.1, n. 42.

968 Gongye is called Jiye in *Guoyu*, "Lu yu 2," 5.194. According to Wei Zhao, Gongye belonged to a branch lineage of the Ji house.

969 Lord Xiang is saying, with bitter irony, that if Ji Wuzi wants the settlement, he only has to say so; there is no need to talk about a revolt and not take Lord Xiang into his confidence.

970 *Maoshi* 36, "Shi wei" 式微, 2B.92. Rong Jia'e is using the line "Why do we not return?" (*hu bu gui* 胡不歸) in the ode to urge Lord Xiang to go back.

Our lord began his homeward journey and reached Fangcheng.[967] Ji Wuzi, who had taken Bian and had sent Gongye[968] to inquire after our lord, dispatched someone to catch up with Gongye and gave him a letter stamped with a seal to be delivered to our lord. The letter said, "I heard that the person guarding Bian intended to revolt. I led my followers to chastise him and have gained sway over it. I presume to notify you, my lord." Gongye carried out his mission and then withdrew. Only when he reached his lodgings did he hear that Ji Wuzi had taken Bian. Our lord said, "To want the place and talk about a revolt only shows that he is keeping me at arm's length."[969]

Our lord said to Gongye, "Can I enter Lu?" He replied, "It is you, my lord, who have possession of the domain. Who will dare to oppose you?" Our lord granted Gongye ministerial cap and robes. He persisted in declining them and accepted only after our lord forced him. Our lord did not want to enter Lu. Rong Jia'e[a] sang "How Few of Us,"[970] and thus he returned. In the fifth month, our lord arrived from Chu.

Gongye gave his settlement back to the Ji lineage and to the end of his life did not enter Ji Wuzi's residence. He said, "When he deceived his ruler, why did he have to send me to do it?" If Ji Wuzi[d] went to see him, he would talk about affairs of the Ji lineage as before, but if Ji Wuzi did not go to see him, he never spoke about them. When Gongye was very ill, he gathered his retainers and said, "After I die, you must not bury me with ministerial cap and robes, for my virtue does not deserve such rewards. What's more, do not let Ji Wuzi[a] bury me."

At the time when King Ling of Zhou was to be buried, the high ministers of Zheng were occupied with affairs of state. Gongsun Shezhi[a] sent Yin Duan to go to Zhou. Liang Xiao[a] said, "He is too young. It will not do." Gongsun Shezhi[a] said, "Isn't it better to send someone young if the alternative is that no one would go? As it says in the Odes,

29.4a(2)

29.4b

29.5

> 王事靡盬，
> 不遑啟處。

東西南北，誰敢寧處？堅事晉、楚，以蕃王室也。王事無曠，何常之有？」
遂使印段如周。

29.6(4) 吳人伐越，獲俘焉，以為閽，使守舟。吳子餘祭觀舟，閽以刀弒之。

29.7 鄭子展卒，子皮即位。於是鄭饑，而未及麥，民病。子皮以子展之命餼國
人粟，戶一鍾，是以得鄭國之民，故罕氏常掌國政，以為上卿。

宋司城子罕聞之，曰：「鄰於善，民之望也。」宋亦饑，請於平公，
出公粟以貸；使大夫皆貸。司城氏貸而不書，為大夫之無者貸。宋無
飢人。

叔向聞之，曰：「鄭之罕，宋之樂，其後亡者也，二者其皆得國乎！
民之歸也。施而不德，樂氏加焉，其以宋升降乎！」

---

971 *Maoshi* 162, "Si mu" 四牡, 317–18.

972 Serving the king in an era dominated by great domains like Jin and Chu calls for
expedient measures: there is no invariable rule. On how circumstances justify devia-
tion from precedents, see also Xiang 23.5, Zhao 1.2b, 26.9.

973 One *zhong* equals approximately 1.3 *dan*, or 80 kilograms (Yang, 3:1157).

974 For other encomiums to the Han lineage, see Xiang 26.7b and 27.5.

The king's affairs admit of no carelessness;
I have no time to tarry or dwell.[971]

East and west, north and south, who would dare to dwell in complacent ease? We should steadily serve Jin and Chu so as to defend the royal house. The king's affairs are not to be neglected. But what is there about this principle that stipulates a constant way of acting?"[972] He thus sent Yin Duan to Zhou.

Yuzhai, the King of Wu, is assassinated.

The leaders of Wu attacked Yue and took captives, one of whom was made a gatekeeper. He was assigned to guard the boats. When Yuzhai, the Master of Wu, was inspecting the boats, the gatekeeper assassinated him with a knife.

29.6(4)

Han Hu of Zheng and Yue Xi of Song both deal with famines in their respective domains with remarkable compassion and efficiency. The Jin minister pronounces Yue Xi's generosity even more laudable.

Gongsun Shezhi[a] of Zheng died, and his son Han Hu[a] acceded to his position. At the time there was a famine in Zheng, and it was not yet time for the wheat harvest, so the people were suffering. Han Hu[a], acting on his late father's command, gave out rations of grain to the inhabitants of the capital, with one *zhong* for each household.[973] As a result he gained the support of the people of Zheng, and that was why the Han lineage was consistently in charge of government, with its leaders appointed as high ministers.[974]

29.7

Hearing about this, Yue Xi[b], the supervisor of fortifications in Song, said, "We are neighbor to excellence.[975] That is what the people look up to." There was also a famine in Song, and Yue Xi[a] requested of Lord Ping that grain from the lord's granary be given out as loans, and he made all the high officers lend their grain. Yue Xi[b] lent grain but kept no record of the transactions, and he also lent on behalf of the high officers who had no store of grain. As a result, there were no starving people in Song.

Shuxiang heard about it and said, "The Han lineage of Zheng and the Yue lineage of Song will be the last to perish.[976] Their descendants will surely remain in charge in their respective domains, for the people will turn to them. In giving and not considering it an act of virtue to be repaid, Yue Xi[b] is even better. His lineage will probably rise and fall with Song."

---

975 Cf. *Analects* 4.25: "The virtuous ones are not solitary, they will certainly have neighbors." Yue Xi is implying that Song and Zheng share virtues.

976 This is another unverifiable prediction.

29.8(5)　晉平公，杞出也，故治杞。六月，知悼子合諸侯之大夫以城杞，孟孝伯會之，鄭子大叔與伯石往。子大叔見大叔文子，與之語。文子曰：「甚乎其城杞也！」子大叔曰：「若之何哉！晉國不恤周宗之闕，而夏肄是屏，其棄諸姬，亦可知也已。諸姬是棄，其誰歸之？吉也聞之：棄同即異，是謂離德。《詩》曰：

　　　　　協比其鄰，
　　　　　婚姻孔云。

晉不鄰矣，其誰云之？」

29.9　齊高子容與宋司徒見知伯，女齊相禮。賓出，司馬侯言於知伯曰：「二子皆將不免。子容專，司徒侈，皆亡家之主也。」知伯曰：「何如？」對曰：「專則速及，侈將以其力斃，專則人實斃之，將及矣。」

Lord Ping of Jin demands that other domains contribute to the fortification of Qǐ, his mother's natal domain. Zheng and Wei ministers express their disaffection.

Lord Ping of Jin was born of a lady from Qǐ, so Jin managed its affairs. In the sixth month, Zhi Daozi assembled the high officers of the princes to fortify Qǐ. Meng Xiaobo attended the meeting, and You Ji[b] and Gong-sun Duan[a] of Zheng also went. You Ji[b] met with the Wei noble Taishu Yi[a] and spoke to him. Taishu Yi[b] said, "Excessive indeed is Jin's attempt to fortify Qǐ!" You Ji[b] said, "What is to be done? Jin does not care for the needs of the ancestral Zhou domains and instead protects the remnants of Xia.[977] That Jin thereby casts aside the various domains with the Ji clan name is indeed plain to see. Having cast aside those Ji domains, who will give their allegiance to it? I have heard: to cast aside those of the same name and to move close to those of different ones is called estranged virtue. As it says in the *Odes*,

> He is in accord with his neighbors
> And with kith and kin he is in harmony.[978]

Jin is not being neighborly. Who will be in harmony with it?"   29.8(5)

The Jin supervisor of the military Ru Qi predicts the downfall of Gao Zhi of Qi and Hua Ding of Song, which will come to pass later this year (Xiang 29.14) and twenty-four years hence (Zhao 20.3, 20.5), respectively.

Gao Zhi[a] of Qi and Hua Ding, the supervisor of conscripts in Song, had an audience with Zhi Daozi[c] of Jin, with Ru Qi, the supervisor of the military, assisting in the ceremony. After the guests had left, Ru Qi[b] said to Zhi Daozi[c]: "Neither of these two men will escape disaster. Gao Zhi[b] monopolizes power, and Hua Ding[a] indulges in excesses. Both are men who will bring ruin to their patrimonies." Zhi Daozi[c] said, "How so?" He replied, "He who monopolizes power will soon be overtaken by disaster. He who indulges in excesses will be destroyed by his own power, whereas he who monopolizes power will be destroyed by other people. Disaster will come upon them soon."   29.9

---

977   The ruling houses of Zheng, Wei, and Lu were all descended from Zhou and shared the clan name Ji. Qǐ was descended from Xia.

978   *Maoshi* 192, "Zheng yue" 正月, 12A.401. The received text of *Maoshi* has *qia* 洽 instead of *xie* 協. While in the ode the lines criticize the oblivious abandon of those in power, they are understood affirmatively in the quotation here. Du Yu (*ZZ* 39.667), following the "Mao Commentary" (*Maoshi* 12A.401), reads *yun* 云 as *xuan* 旋, implying concordant, circular movements. These lines are also quoted in Xi 22.6.

29.10(6) 范獻子來聘，拜城杞也。公享之，展莊叔執幣。射者三耦。公臣不足，取
於家臣。家臣展瑕、展王父為一耦；公臣公巫召伯、仲顏莊叔為一耦，
鄫鼓父、黨叔為一耦。

29.11 晉侯使司馬女叔侯來治杞田，弗盡歸也。晉悼夫人慍曰：「齊也取貨，
先君若有知也，不尚取之。」公告叔侯。叔侯曰：「虞、虢、焦、滑、霍、
楊、韓、魏，皆姬姓也，晉是以大。若非侵小，將何所取？武、獻以下，兼
國多矣，誰得治之？杞，夏餘也，而即東夷。魯，周公之後也，而睦於晉。
以杞封魯猶可，而何有焉？魯之於晉也，職貢不乏，玩好時至，公卿大
夫相繼於朝，史不絕書，府無虛月。如是可矣，何必癠魯以肥杞？且先君
而有知也，毋寧夫人，而焉用老臣？」

---

979   The archers displayed their skills as part of the entertainment at feasts. Commentators note that the feast of the Zhou king and the lords calls for six pairs of archers; that of the lords among themselves, four pairs; and that of the lords and ministers or high officers, three pairs.

980   We follow Fu Qian's equation of *bushang* 不尚 with *shang* 尚 (cited in *ZZ-Kong* 39.667): "He would have approved of taking Ru Qi and killing him." Cf. Du Yu's (*ZZ* 39.667) reading: "If the former lord could know of this, he would not approve of him taking bribes." Yang (3:1160) suggests that *huo* 貨 refers to Qi territories and reads *shang* 尚 as *you* 佑 (bless): "Thus did Ru Qi take back Qi territories. If the former lord could know of this, he would not bless such an undertaking."

981   These domains were annexed by Jin before and during the reign of Lord Xian (r. 676–651). Jin extinguished Geng (whose clan name was either Ji or Ying), Huo, and Wei in 661 BCE (Min 1.6), and it extinguished Yu and Guo in 655 BCE (Xi 5.8). According to the *Bamboo Annals*, Prince Wen of Jin (Jin Wen Hou) extinguished Han in 760 BCE. On Jin annexation of these and other domains, see Li Mengcun and Li Shangshi, *Jin guo shi*, 40–57.

982   Cf. Zichan's similar argument in Xiang 25.10a.

983   Cf. Takezoe's (19.9) alternative reading, based in part on Du Yu (*ZZ* 39.667): "Would he not blame his wife [for siding with her natal family against the interests of her husband's family]? Why would he use me to manage such an affair?"

Another indication of the decline of the Lu ruling house is reported in the following passage: when archers are lacking for entertainment at an official feast, retainers of ministers have to fill in. In a comparable incident twenty-seven years later, only two Wan dancers are available for a ceremony at Lord Xiang's temple (Zhao 25.6b). On ritual prescriptions regarding this dance, see Yin 5.7.

Fan Yang[b] came on an official mission to bow in thanks for Lu's contribution to the fortification of Qi. Our lord offered him ceremonial toasts, and Zhan Zhuangshu held the bolts of silk that were to be given as gifts. There were three pairs of archers.[979] Our lord's own officers had not sufficed, so archers were taken from the retainers of ministers. From the ministers' retainers, Zhan Xia and Zhan Zhuangshu formed one pair; from the lord's officers, Gongwu Shaobo and Zhongyan Zhuangshu formed one pair, and Zeng Gufu and Zhang Shu formed another pair. 29.10(6)

Under Jin pressure Lu returns some, but not all, of the lands it took from Qi. The case against Jin policy is argued in terms of historical affinities (Zhou versus Xia genealogies), power politics (the strong against the weak), and a woman's divided loyalties to her natal domain and her husband's domain (the ties of Lord Ping's mother with Qi and with Jin).

The Prince of Jin sent the supervisor of the military Ru Qi[d] to Lu to manage the return of Qi territories, but Lu did not return all of them. The wife of Lord Dao of Jin, Lord Ping's mother, said heatedly, "Ru Qi[c] has taken bribes. If the former lord had known of this, he would have taken Ru Qi and gotten rid of him."[980] The lord told Ru Qi[e] about this. Ru Qi[e] said, "Yu, Guo, Jiao, Hua, Huo, Yang, Han, and Wei were all domains ruled by lineages with the clan name Ji. Jin became great by annexing them.[981] How else can lands be taken, if not by invading small domains?[982] There have been so many cases, from Lord Wu and Lord Xian on, of Jin taking over other domains that no one can deal with them! Qi, a remnant of Xia, has gone over to the Eastern Yi. Lu is descended from the Zhou Duke and has harmonious relations with Jin. Even if Lu were to be put in power in Qi, it would still be acceptable. Why be concerned about this? Lu, when it comes to Jin, has not been remiss with dues and offerings. Fine things and precious objects have come regularly from Lu, and the lords, ministers, and high officers of Lu have come one after another to our court. The scribes have never ceased writing about these things, and not a month passes without our treasury receiving something from them. Such a state of affairs is acceptable enough. Why must we impoverish Lu to enrich Qi? What's more, if the former lord had known of this, wouldn't he have preferred to let his wife manage this? Why would he have had any use for this old servant?"[983] 29.11

29.12(7) 杞文公來盟，書曰「子」，賤之也。

29.13a(8) 吳公子札來聘，見叔孫穆子，說之。謂穆子曰：「子其不得死乎！好善而不能擇人。吾聞君子務在擇人。吾子為魯宗卿，而任其大政，不慎舉，何以堪之？禍必及子！」

29.13b 請觀於周樂。使工為之歌周南、召南，曰：「美哉！始基之矣，猶未也，然勤而不怨矣。」

　　為之歌邶、鄘、衛，曰：「美哉淵乎！憂而不困者也。吾聞衛康叔、武公之德如是，是其衛風乎！」

　　為之歌王，曰：「美哉！思而不懼，其周之東乎！」

　　為之歌鄭，曰：「美哉！其細已甚，民弗堪也。是其先亡乎！」

　　為之歌齊，曰：「美哉，泱泱乎！大風也哉！表東海者，其大公乎！國未可量也。」

984　On the concert for Jizha, see Schaberg, *Patterned Past*, 86–95; Wai-yee Li, *Readability of the Past*, 136–47.

985　The formulation here is echoed in the "Mao Preface," which describes the "Zhounan" and "Shaonan" as "the way of proper beginnings and the foundation of royal culture" (*zhengshi zhi dao wanghua zhi ji* 正始之道，王化之基). According to the "Mao Preface," *nan* 南 refers to how Zhou culture (here linked to the Zhou Duke and the Shao Duke) extends southward. Some scholars believe that *nan* designates a kind of music; see Gu Yanwu, *Rizhi lu jishi*, 3.49–50; Gu Jiegang, *Gushi bian*, 3:642–44. Chen Pan refutes the Mao tradition and claims that *nan* refers to how the poems in those sections were collected and put to music in the south; see his "Zhou Shao er nan yu Wenwang zhi hua" 周召二南與文王之化 in *Gushi bian* 3:424–39.

986　After the Zhou conquest of Shang, Shang territories were divided into Bei, Yong, and Wei. In the wake of a subsequent rebellion, the Zhou Duke amalgamated these territories and created the domains of Wei and put Kang Shu, King Wu's younger brother, in power there. See also Ding 4.1, for the identification of Wei as former Shang territory. Being anxious but not distressed may refer to how Kang Shu and Lord Wu endured rebellions and chaos or how errant Wei rulers in the period covered by *Zuozhuan* create "anxiety but no distress" because of their ancestors' virtue.

987　*Si* 思 can also mean "filled with longing" or "sorrowful" (as in *yousi* 憂思, *aisi* 哀思).

988　The Zhou court moved east in 770 BCE.

989　The "fine points" (*xi* 細) may refer to musical properties (high-pitched sounds or rapid rhythm) or personal, trivial feelings (as distinct from political concerns), or they may pertain to the proliferation of rules and regulations. Confucius is said to want to banish Zheng music because it is excessive or licentious (*yin* 淫) (*Analects* 15.11).

990　According to Jizha's reasoning, the "fine points" noted above thus imply moral laxity and pose a political danger. Zheng was destroyed in 376 BCE by Han, long after the de facto division of Jin by the Han, Zhao, and Wei houses in 453 BCE. This is either an inaccurate prophecy, or the comparison may be between Zheng and some other domains.

991　That is, it has a great destiny. Since by this point the Jiang ruling house of Qi is in decline (as Jizha points out in Xiang 29.13e), the "great destiny" may simply refer to

Lord Wen of Qi came to swear a covenant with us. The text says, "Master," to disparage him.

Before attending a concert, Jizha, noble son of Wu, warns the wise Lu minister Shusun Bao about the dangers of misjudging people. Six years hence Shusun Bao will die because of misplaced trust in his illegitimate son (Zhao 4.8). Jizha's appraisal of statesmen precedes and follows the concert held for him, suggesting the connection between "knowing music" (zhiyin 知音) and "knowing people" (zhiren 知人).

Jizha[a] of Wu came on an official mission. He met with Shusun Bao[b] and was pleased with him. He said to Shusun Bao[c], "You, sir, will likely not die a natural death! You may love goodness but you cannot choose the right men. I have heard that a noble man strives to choose the right men. You, sir, are the ancestral minister of Lu and bear the chief responsibility for government. If you are not cautious with your choice of persons for office, how can you bear the consequences? Disaster will certainly overtake you!"

A concert is held for Jizha in the Lu court. His aesthetic appreciation of music is tied to political and historical judgments. The order of the odes presented suggests broad parallels with the received text of the Odes. *This concert is often included in histories of Chinese aesthetics as a prime example illustrating the moral and political dimensions of musical understanding.*[984]

Since Jizha asked to hear Zhou music, the musicians were made to sing "Zhounan" and "Shaonan" for him. He said, "Beautiful indeed! The foundation is beginning to be laid down,[985] but the task is not yet accomplished. For all that, it shows industry but not rancor!"

The Airs of Bei, Yong, and Wei were sung for him, and he said, "Beautiful indeed! How profound! This is anxious but not distressed. I have heard that such was the virtue of Kang Shu of Wei and Lord Wu. These must be the Airs of Wei!"[986]

The Airs of the royal domain were sung for him, and he said, "Beautiful indeed! This is deliberate but not fearful.[987] This must have been composed when Zhou moved east!"[988]

The Airs of Zheng were sung for him, and he said, "Beautiful indeed! The fine points are extreme,[989] and the people will not be able to bear it. This must be the one that will perish first!"[990]

The Airs of Qi were sung for him, and he said, "Beautiful indeed! How expansive! Great airs indeed! As the exemplar of the eastern seas, this must be the Grand Lord! The domain cannot yet be fathomed!"[991]

29.12(7)

29.13a(8)

29.13b

---

the power and prosperity of the domain rather than of the ruling lineage. Up to this point the order of odes from various domains is the same as that in the received text of *Maoshi*.

　　為之歌豳，曰：「美哉，蕩乎！樂而不淫，其周公之東乎！」

　　為之歌秦，曰：「此之謂夏聲。夫能夏則大，大之至也，其周之舊乎！」

　　為之歌魏，曰：「美哉，渢渢乎！大而婉，險而易行，以德輔此，則明主也。」

　　為之歌唐，曰：「思深哉！其有陶唐氏之遺民乎！不然，何其憂之遠也？非令德之後，誰能若是？」

　　為之歌陳，曰：「國無主，其能久乎！」

　　自鄶以下無譏焉。

29.13c　為之歌小雅，曰：「美哉！思而不貳，怨而不言，其周德之衰乎？猶有先王之遺民焉。」

　　為之歌大雅，曰：「廣哉，熙熙乎！曲而有直體，其文王之德乎！」

992　Confucius (*Analects* 3.20) comments that "Guanju," the first poem in the Mao tradition, is "joyous but not licentious."

993　According to Du Yu (*ZZ* 39.669), this refers to the Zhou Duke's eastern expeditions after quelling the rebellion of Guan Shu and Cai Shu.

994　Areas formerly demarcated as Zhou territories are now under Qin rule. Du Yu (*ZZ* 39.669) links *xia* 夏 to "central domains" (as in the term *zhuxia* 諸夏), the implication being that Qin has embraced the civilization of the central domains although Qin is situated in the west. Takezoe (19.13) suggests that *xia* is identified with the west. Jizha is thus moving from *xia* as a geographical designation (west) to its semantic content ("greatness"). Yang (3:1163) cites *Fangyan*, according to which *xia* means "great" in the language spoken west of the Pass (i.e., in the Zhou homeland and in Qin).

995　Weì was a domain eliminated by Jin. The Jin minister Bi Wan was put in power there (Min 1.6).

996　Yao Nai ("*Zuoshi buzhu* xu" 左氏補注序, cited in Qian Mu, *Xian Qin zhuzi xinian*, 192–93) argues that glorification of the Wei lineage here and the anachronistic usage of the term "enlightened ruler" suggest an author (or editor) with special ties to Weì and Weì-based "additions" in the process of transmission. The term "enlightened ruler" (*mingzhu* 明主) appears as "covenant chief" (*mengzhu* 盟主) in *Shiji* 31.1452. See also Wai-yee Li, *Readability of the Past*, 54–56.

997　Yao 堯 was first enfeoffed at Tao 陶 and then at Tang 唐. The house of Tao and Tang thus refers to the ancient sage-king Yao. Shuyu 叔虞 (Tang Shuyu, Tang Shu), founder of Jin and younger brother of King Cheng of Zhou, was enfeoffed at Tang (see Zhao 1.12).

998　Chu extinguished Chen sixty-five years later (Ai 17.4).

999　Kuai was in present-day Zhengzhou in Henan. Kuai was extinguished by Lord Wu of Zheng (r. 770–744).

The Airs of Bin were sung for him, and he said, "Beautiful indeed! How grand! This is joyous but not licentious.[992] This must have been composed when the Zhou Duke moved east!"[993]

The Airs of Qin were sung for him, and he said, "These are called sounds of Xia. Now to be capable of being majestic (*xia*) is to be great. This is the epitome of greatness: this must have been composed in the former seat of Zhou!"[994]

The Airs of Wei[995] were sung for him, and he said, "Beautiful indeed! How fluid and flowing! This is forceful yet gentle, arduous yet easily realized. Use virtue to assist them, and they will be enlightened rulers."[996]

The Airs of Tang were sung for him, and he said, "Profound longing indeed! Do they not have the people remaining from those ruled by the Tao and Tang lineages![997] Otherwise, why would their concerns reach so far back? If they were not descendants of those of exemplary virtue, how could they be capable of this?"

The Airs of Chen were sung for him, and he said, "The domain has no master. How can it last long?"[998]

From the Airs of Kuai[999] on, Jizha did not make any comments.

Good government and ideal ritual relations between humans and spirits supposedly yield superior music, and Jizha becomes progressively more laudatory as the order of performance moves back in time. He reserves the highest praise for the "Hymns," an extended description of modulated emotional-mental states suggesting perfect balance and harmony. The implication of restraint and moderation echoes what Confucius (Analects 3.20) remarks about "Fish Hawk" ("Guanju") in the Odes: *"Joyous but not licentious, grieving yet not injurious" (le er buyin ai er bushang* 樂而不淫，哀而不傷*).*

29.13c

The Lesser Odes were sung for him, and he said, "Beautiful indeed! This is deliberate but not disloyal, expressing resentment, but not in so many words.[1000] Is this not Zhou virtue in its period of decline? There are still people remaining from those ruled by the former kings!"

The Greater Odes were sung for him, and he said, "Sweeping indeed! How resplendent![1001] Modulated yet forthright in nature, this must be explained by the virtue of King Wen!"

1000 It is said that the *Odes* "can be used to express resentment" (*keyi yuan* 可以怨) (*Analects* 17.9). In *Shiji* 84.2482, the Lesser Odes are described as "expressing resentment, but not to the extent of fomenting disorder" (*yuanfei er buluan* 怨誹而不亂). The formulation "expressing resentment, but without anger" (*yuan er bunu* 怨而不怒), often used to characterize the *Odes* in the tradition, suggests the restraint and modulation of emotions.

1001 We follow Karlgren, gl. 658. Cf. Takezoe's (19.15) reading of *xixi* 熙熙 as "all-encompassing" or "far-reaching."

為之歌頌，曰：「至矣哉！直而不倨，曲而不屈，邇而不偪，遠而不攜，遷而不淫，復而不厭，哀而不愁，樂而不荒，用而不匱，廣而不宣，施而不費，取而不貪，處而不底，行而不流。五聲和，八風平。節有度，守有序，盛德之所同也。」

29.13d　見舞〈象箾〉、〈南籥〉者，曰：「美哉！猶有憾。」

見舞〈大武〉者，曰：「美哉！周之盛也，其若此乎！」

見舞〈韶濩〉者，曰：「聖人之弘也，而猶有慚德，聖人之難也。」

見舞〈大夏〉者，曰：「美哉！勤而不德，非禹，其誰能修之？」

見舞〈韶箾〉者，曰：「德至矣哉，大矣！如天之無不幬也，如地之無不載也。雖甚盛德，其蔑以加於此矣，觀止矣。若有他樂，吾不敢請已。」

1002　Kong Yingda (ZZ-Kong, 39.671) interprets *qian* 遷 ("changing") as the dislocations suffered by the Zhou court.

1003　On the "eight winds" as a musical term, see Yin 5.7, Zhao 20.8, Zhao 25.3; *Lüshi chunqiu* 5.285, 22.1526; *Yanzi chunqiu* 7.443, "Fulu 2," 537; *Huainanzi* 1.15, 20.673; *Shiji* 14.1208–11; *Fayan* 2.54–56. Cf. Wang Yinzhi, *Jingyi shuwen*, 720–21.

　　　　　　　　　　　　　　　　　　　　Zuo Tradition

The "Hymns" were sung for him, and he said, "Supreme indeed! This is forthright yet not arrogant, modulated yet not bent, proximate yet not pressing, afar yet not alienating, changing yet not licentious,[1002] repetitive yet not tiresome, grieving yet not disconsolate, joyous yet not unbridled, put to use yet not used up, sweeping yet not revealing, giving yet not extravagant, taking yet not avaricious, staying yet not stagnant, going forth yet not wantonly flowing. The five sounds harmonize; the eight winds are balanced.[1003] The rhythm has proper measure, the gradations are in the right order: this is the common ground of great virtue."

The concert continues with the music and dance of even greater antiquity, and Jizha watches the dances identified with the first kings of Xia, Shang, Zhou, and the sage-kings Yao, Shun, and Yu. The highest virtue is revealed in the spectacle of greatest beauty.

He watched the dances of "Elephant Steps to Flute Music" and "Southern Tunes on the Pipes" and said, "Beautiful indeed! But there is still regret."[1004]

He watched "Great Martial Prowess"[1005] and said, "Beautiful indeed! The rise of Zhou to greatness must have been like this!"

He watched "Great Harmony"[1006] and said, "Even sages in their capacious understanding have causes for shame. It is difficult indeed to be a sage."[1007]

He watched "Great Xia"[1008] and said, "Beautiful indeed! He toiled without claiming merit. Who but Yu could have fashioned this?"

He watched "Harmony to Flute Music"[1009] and said, "Supreme virtue indeed! Great indeed! This is like heaven, which leaves nothing uncovered; like earth, which leaves nothing uncradled. This is the epitome of great virtue, to which nothing can be added. I should stop with this utmost spectacle. Even if there are other kinds of music, I would not dare to ask about them."

1004 Du Yu (*ZZ* 39.672) identifies these as "King Wen's music" and surmises that King Wen regrets how his virtue had not spread far before the Zhou conquest of Shang. It is perhaps fitting that the performance of the "Hymns" should culminate in dances. The "Mao Preface" characterizes the "Hymns" as "glorifying the spectacle of great virtue."

1005 Du Yu (*ZZ* 39.672) identifies this as "King Wu's music."

1006 Du Yu (*ZZ* 39.672) identifies this as "the music of Tang, the founder of Shang."

1007 The "shame" may refer to the violence of the Shang conquest of Xia (Du Yu, *ZZ* 39.672), but it is odd that the same is not said of the Zhou conquest of Shang in relation to the dance praising King Wu of Zhou.

1008 Du Yu (*ZZ* 39.672) identifies this as "[The Xia founder] Yu's music."

1009 Du Yu (*ZZ* 39.672) identifies this as "Shun's music."

29.13e 其出聘也，通嗣君也。故遂聘于齊，說晏平仲，謂之曰：「子速納邑與政。無邑無政，乃免於難。齊國之政將有所歸，未獲所歸，難未歇也。」故晏子因陳桓子以納政與邑，是以免於欒、高之難。

29.13f 聘於鄭，見子產，如舊相識。與之縞帶，子產獻紵衣焉。謂子產曰：「鄭之執政侈，難將至矣，政必及子。子為政，慎之以禮。不然，鄭國將敗。」
適衛，說蘧瑗、史狗、史鰌、公子荊、公叔發、公子朝，曰：「衛多君子，未有患也。」

29.13g 自衛如晉，將宿於戚，聞鐘聲焉，曰：「異哉！吾聞之也：辯而不德，必加於戮。夫子獲罪於君以在此，懼猶不足，而又何樂？夫子之在此也，猶燕之巢於幕上。君又在殯，而可以樂乎？」遂去之。文子聞之，終身不聽琴瑟。

1010 The "new ruler" 嗣 refers to Yimo (Fu Qian, Jia Kui). Du Yu (ZZ 39.673) identifies him as Yuzhai (r. 547–544) and implies that Yuzhai is assassinated after Jizha leaves Wu. Du might have wished to defend Jizha against the charge of attending a concert while in mourning.

1011 For the power struggle in Qi, with the Chen and Bao lineages on one side and the Luan and Gao lineages on the other, see Zhao 10.2. Yan Ying will refuse to get involved in the conflict.

1012 According to Xiang 26.2a (possibly from another source), Qu Boyu left Wei.

1013 Du Yu (ZZ 39.673) identifies Qiu as the upright Scribe Yu 史魚, who is also mentioned in *Analects* 15.7.

1014 Du Yu (ZZ 39.673) identifies Gongshu Fa as the sincere and generous Gongshu Wenzi 公叔文子, who is mentioned in *Analects* 14.13, 14.18; and *Liji* 8.146, 10.186.

1015 This man should not be confused with the Gongzi Zhao who is involved in a rebellion in Wei in Zhao 20.4.

1016 Du Yu (ZZ 39.673) reads *bian* 辯 as "contention" (*zheng* 爭). Liang Lüsheng reads *bian* as *bian* 變: "having been involved in a rebellion (*bianluan* 變亂), he yet [even now] has no virtue" (cited in Yang, 3:1166–67). Takezoe (19.21) reads *bian* 辨／辯 as "powers of judgment" and infers a broader meaning of *bian er bude* 辯而不德 as "talent without virtue."

1017 A tent can be dismantled at any moment, and therefore, the swallow is under constant threat without realizing it.

1018 Lord Xian of Wei, whom Sun Linfu ousted (Xiang 14.4) and whose restoration caused Sun to go into exile (Xiang 26.2), died earlier this year (*Annals*, Xiang 29.3).

That Jizha left the domain on official visits was to establish relations between his new ruler and other domains.[1010] That was why he then went on an official visit to Qi. He was pleased with Yan Ying[a] and said to him, "You, sir, should quickly turn in your settlements and your control of the government. You will be spared disaster if you have neither settlements nor control over the government. Government in Qi will then go where it should. But before it gets to go where it should, disaster will not abate." That was why Yan Ying, through Chen Wuyu[a], relinquished his control of the government and his settlements and as a result was spared the disaster that befell the Luan and Gao lineages.[1011]

29.13e

Jizha predicts unrest in Zheng (see Xiang 29.17, 30.10) and urges Zichan to rely on caution and ritual propriety. Despite recent turmoil in the wake of Lord Xian's restoration in Wei, Jizha sees the ameliorative effect of noble men.

When Jizha went on an official visit to Zheng, he met with Zichan, and it was as if the two had known each other for a long time. He gave Zichan a broad white-silk sash, and Zichan offered him a robe made from fine hemp. Jizha said to Zichan, "Those controlling government in Zheng are extravagant. Disaster will come soon, and government is sure to fall to you. When you take charge of government, conduct it cautiously by the rules of ritual propriety. Otherwise, the domain of Zheng will go to ruin."

29.13f

He went to Wei and was pleased with Qu Boyu[a],[1012] the scribe Gou, the scribe Qiu,[1013] Gongzi Jing, Gongshu Fa,[1014] and Gongzi Zhao.[1015] He said, "Wei has many noble men. It will not yet have troubles."

Jizha castigates Sun Linfu, in exile from Wei, for indulging in music. While in Jin, he approves of the rise of the Han, Wei, and Zhao lineages but translates their ascendancy into danger for Shuxiang, whose Yangshe lineage will be destroyed thirty years hence, some years after Shuxiang's own death (Zhao 28.2).

From Wei he went to Jin and was preparing to spend the night at Qī, where he heard the sound of bells and said, "Strange indeed! I have heard: he who is skillful with words and yet has no virtue will certainly be executed.[1016] This fine man is here because he offended his ruler. Even had he lived in fearful vigiliance, it might still have not been enough for keeping disaster at bay. How dare he indulge in music and pleasure? This fine man here is like a swallow that has built its nest atop a tent.[1017] What's worse, his ruler is still lying in state in the Ancestral Temple.[1018] Now is it acceptable to take pleasure in music?" He thus left. When Sun Linfu[c] heard about this, he did not, to the end of his life, listen to any lute or zither.

29.13g

適晉，說趙文子、韓宣子、魏獻子，曰：「晉國其萃於三族乎！」說叔向。將行，謂叔向曰：「吾子勉之！君侈而多良，大夫皆富，政將在家。吾子好直，必思自免於難。」

29.14(10) 秋，九月，齊公孫蠆、公孫竃放其大夫高止於北燕。乙未，出。書曰「出奔」，罪高止也。高止好以事自為功，且專，故難及之。

29.15(11) 冬，孟孝伯如晉，報范叔也。

29.16 為高氏之難故，高豎以盧叛。十月庚寅，閭丘嬰帥師圍盧。高豎曰：「苟使高氏有後，請致邑。」齊人立敬仲之曾孫酀，良敬仲也。十一月乙卯，高豎致盧而出奔晉，晉人城縣而寘旃。

29.17 鄭伯有使公孫黑如楚，辭曰：「楚、鄭方惡，而使余往，是殺余也。」伯有曰：「世行也。」子皙曰：「可則往，難則已，何世之有？」伯有將強使之。子皙怒，將伐伯有氏，大夫和之。十二月己巳，鄭大夫盟於伯有氏。

1019　These three houses partitioned Jin in 453 BCE.
1020　See Xiang 29.10.
1021　Mian 縣 is the same place as Mianshang 縣上 (see Xi 24.1).
1022　In fact, Chu-Zheng relations seem cordial at this point: Lord Jian of Zheng attended court in Chu (Xiang 28.12) and probably attended King Kang's funeral in Chu.

Jizha went to Jin and was pleased with Zhao Wu[a], Han Qi[a], and Wei Shu[a]. He said, "The government of Jin will likely be concentrated in the hands of these three houses!"[1019] He was pleased with Shuxiang. When he was about to leave, he said to Shuxiang, "You, sir, should exert yourself! Your ruler is extravagant but has many good ministers. The high officers are all wealthy. Government is going to fall into the hands of the great houses. You, sir, love justice and forthrightness. You must consider how to spare yourself disaster."

The exile of the Qi high officer Gao Zhi fulfills an earlier prophecy (Xiang 29.9).

In autumn, in the ninth month, Ziwei[a] and Ziya[a] of Qi exiled their high officer Gao Zhi to Northern Yan. On the *yiwei* day (2), he departed. That the text says, "departed and fled," is to blame Gao Zhi for his offense. Gao Zhi liked to claim merit for anything accomplished and, moreover, monopolized power. That was why disaster overtook him.

29.14(10)

In winter, Meng Xiaobo went to Jin: this was in answer to Fan Yang[e]'s visit to Lu.[1020]

29.15(11)

Gao Zhi's exile leads to his son's revolt in Qi.

On account of the disaster that overtook the Gao lineage, Gao Zhi's son Gao Shu used Lú as a base to rebel. In the tenth month, on the *gengyin* day (27), Lüqiu Ying led out troops and laid siege to Lú. Gao Shu said, "If the Gao lineage can be allowed to continue, I beg to return my settlements to the ruler." The leaders of Qi established Gao Xi[a]'s great-grandson Gao Yan as his successor out of high regard for Gao Xi[a]. In the eleventh month, on the *yimao* day (23), Gao Shu gave Lú back, departed, and fled to Jin. The leaders of Jin fortified Mian and put him there.[1021]

29.16

Contention in Zheng between Liang Xiao and Gongsun Hei, of the Liang and Si lineages, respectively, ends in temporary reconciliation. Zichan is pronounced the best hope for Zheng.

Liang Xiao[a] of Zheng appointed Gongsun Hei to go to Chu. He declined, saying, "As relations between Chu and Zheng are so hostile just now,[1022] to send me there is to have me killed." Liang Xiao[a] said, "For generations those of your lineage have gone." Gongsun Hei[a] said, "We go when it is feasible but desist when it is dangerous. What do generations have to do with it?" Liang Xiao[a] planned to force the issue. Furious, Gongsun Hei[a] was preparing to attack Liang Xiao[a]'s lineage when the high officers had them make peace. In the twelfth month, on the *jisi* day (7), the high officers of Zheng swore a covenant at Liang Xiao[a]'s residence.

29.17

裨諶曰：「是盟也，其與幾何？《詩》曰：

> 君子屢盟，
> 亂是用長。

今是長亂之道也，禍未歇也，必三年而後能紓。」然明曰：「政將焉往？」裨諶曰：「善之代不善，天命也，其焉辟子產？舉不踰等，則位班也。擇善而舉，則世隆也。天又除之，奪伯有魄，子西即世，將焉辟之？天禍鄭久矣，其必使子產息之，乃猶可以戾。不然，將亡矣。」

春秋

30.1(1) 三十年，春，王正月，楚子使薳罷來聘。

30.2(5) 夏，四月，蔡世子般弒其君固。

30.3(7) 五月甲午，宋災，宋伯姬卒。

30.4(6) 天王殺其弟佞夫。

30.5(6) 王子瑕奔晉。

30.6(9) 秋，七月，叔弓如宋，葬宋共姬。

30.7(10) 鄭良霄出奔許，自許入于鄭，鄭人殺良霄。

30.8 冬，十月，葬蔡景公。

30.9(12) 晉人・齊人・宋人・衛人・鄭人・曹人・莒人・邾人・滕人・薛人・杞人・小邾人，會于澶淵，宋災故。

1023 According to Takezoe (19.24), Pi Chen and Pi Zao are the same person. Du Yu (*ZZ* 39.674) seems to consider them different persons.

1024 *Maoshi* 198, "Qiao yan" 巧言, 12C.424. These lines are also cited in Huan 12.2.

1025 Zixi (Gongsun Xia) of the Si lineage was last mentioned in Xiang 27.5. He must have died in the interval. Zixi is supposed to be next in line to hold power in Zheng after Liang Xiao.

Pi Chen[1023] said, "How much can this covenant control? As it says in the *Odes*,

> Noble men repeatedly swear covenants,
> But disorder is thereby only prolonged.[1024]

What is happening now is the way to prolong disorder. Calamity will not yet come to an end. Three years will have to pass before it eases." Ran Ming said, "To whom will the charge of government go?" Pi Chen said, "To have worthy men replace unworthy ones is the command of Heaven. How can the charge of government elude Zichan? If the right order for raising men to office is not flouted, it should be Zichan's turn. If it is a matter of choosing worthy men to raise to office, then our generation esteems him. What's more, Heaven has cleared the way for him by undoing Liang Xiao[a]'s spirit. Zixi, next in line to Liang Xiao, has passed away.[1025] How can the charge of government elude Zichan? Heaven has inflicted calamities on Zheng for too long. It will surely send Zichan to pacify disorder, and only then can there be stability. If not, Zheng will be destroyed!"

LORD XIANG 30 (543 BCE)
ANNALS

In the thirtieth year, in spring, in the royal first month, the Master of Chu sent Wei Pi to us on an official visit. — 30.1(1)

In summer, in the fourth month, the Cai heir apparent Ban assassinated his ruler, Gu. — 30.2(5)

In the fifth month, on the *jiawu* day (5), there was a disastrous fire in Song. Bo Ji of Song died. — 30.3(7)

The Heaven-appointed king put to death his younger brother Ningfu (Wangzi Ningfu). — 30.4(6)

Wangzi Xia fled to Jin. — 30.5(6)

In autumn, in the seventh month, Shu Gong went to Song for the burial of Gong Ji of Song. — 30.6(9)

Liang Xiao of Zheng departed and fled to Xǔ, and from Xǔ he reentered Zheng. Zheng leaders put Liang Xiao to death. — 30.7(10)

In winter, in the tenth month, Lord Jing of Cai was buried. — 30.8

A Jin leader, a Qi leader, a Song leader, a Wei leader, a Zheng leader, a Cao leader, a Ju leader, a Zhu leader, a Teng leader, a Xue leader, a Qǐ leader, and a Lesser Zhu leader met at Chanyuan on account of the disastrous fire in Song. — 30.9(12)

30.1(1) 　三十年，春，王正月，楚子使薳罷來聘，通嗣君也。穆叔問王子圍之為政何如。對曰：「吾儕小人食而聽事，猶懼不給命，而不免於戾，焉與知政？」固問焉，不告。穆叔告大夫曰：「楚令尹將有大事，子蕩將與焉助之，匿其情矣。」

30.2 　子產相鄭伯以如晉，叔向問鄭國之政焉。對曰：「吾得見與否，在此歲也。駟、良方爭，未知所成。若有所成，吾得見，乃可知也。」叔向曰：「不既和矣乎？」對曰：「伯有侈而愎，子晳好在人上，莫能相下也。雖其和也，猶相積惡也，惡至無日矣。」

30.3a 　二月癸未，晉悼夫人食輿人之城杞者，絳縣人或年長矣，無子而往，與於食，有與疑年，使之年。曰：「臣，小人也，不知紀年。臣生之歲，正月甲子朔，四百有四十五甲子矣，其季於今三之一也。」更走問諸朝。

1026　Literally, "eat and heed commands concerning affairs."
1027　The assassination of a ruler is also referred to as "a great matter" 大事 in Wen 1.7.
1028　Gongsun Hei is of the Si lineage, and Liang Xiao is of the Liang lineage.

An evasive Chu envoy convinces Shusun Bao that the Chu chief minister, Gongzi Wei, will usurp the throne (see Zhao 1.13).

In the thirtieth year, in spring, in the royal first month, the Master of Chu sent Wei Pi to us on an official visit: this was to establish relations between the new ruler and Lu. Shusun Bao[a] asked how Gongzi Wei[a] was conducting government. He replied, "Petty men like us merely earn our keep and do as we are told.[1026] Even then, we fear that we are not adequate to the task of fulfilling our charges and thus will not be able to escape offenses. On what basis can we know about government?" Shusun Bao persisted in asking, but Wei Pi did not tell him anything. Shusun Bao[a] told the high officers, "The chief minister of Chu will take up a great matter.[1027] Wei Pi[a] will help him and be party to it. He is dissembling and hiding the truth."

30.1(1)

Zichan predicts that the reconciliation between Liang Xiao and Gongsun Hei (Xiang 29.17) will not last, and violence indeed erupts later because of their mutual ill will (Xiang 30.10).

Zichan, assisting the Liege of Zheng, went to Jin. Shuxiang asked him about government in the domain of Zheng. He replied, "This year will determine whether I get to see how the government turns out. The Si and Liang lineages[1028] are just now at loggerheads with each other, and we do not yet know how their conflict will be resolved. If there is a resolution and I get to see it, then I will be able to know." Shuxiang said, "Have they not already made peace?" He replied, "Liang Xiao[a] is extravagant and willful, and Gongsun Hei[a] loves to place himself above others. Neither will give way to the other. Although they have made peace, they are still accumulating mutual ill will, which will come to a head before too long."

30.2

An old man drafted to work on the fortification of Qi calculates the passage of time with uncommon precision and is rewarded for it. For other examples of characters of low social status showing sagacity, see Cheng 5.4 and Xiang 15.4.

In the second month, on the *guiwei* day (22), the wife of Lord Dao of Jin feasted the workmen who had been fortifying Qi. An aged man from the Jiang dependency went to work there because he had no sons. He partook of the feast. There were those who wondered about his age and had him talk about it. He said, "Your servant is but a petty man. I do not know about keeping a record of the years. Since the year I was born on a *jiazi* day, the first day of the first month, the *jiazi* day in the sexagenary cycle has come around four hundred and forty-five times, and we have gone through, by today, one-third of the last cycle." The officers ran to ask about this at court.

30.3a

　　師曠曰：「魯叔仲惠伯會郤成子于承匡之歲也。是歲也，狄伐魯，叔孫莊叔於是乎敗狄于鹹，獲長狄僑如及虺也、豹也，而皆以名其子。七十三年矣。」

　　史趙曰：「亥有二首六身，下二如身，是其日數也。」

　　士文伯曰：「然則二萬六千六百有六旬也。」

　　趙孟問其縣大夫，則其屬也。召之而謝過焉，曰：「武不才，任君之大事，以晉國之多虞，不能由吾子，使吾子辱在泥塗久矣，武之罪也。敢謝不才。」遂仕之，使助為政。辭以老。與之田，使為君復陶，以為絳縣師，而廢其輿尉。

30.3b　於是魯使者在晉，歸以語諸大夫。季武子曰：「晉未可婾也。有趙孟以為大夫，有伯瑕以為佐，有史趙、師曠而咨度焉，有叔向、女齊以師保其君。其朝多君子，其庸可婾乎！勉事之而後可。」

30.4　夏，四月己亥，鄭伯及其大夫盟。君子是以知鄭難之不已也。

30.5(2)　蔡景侯為大子般娶于楚，通焉。大子弒景侯。

1029　See Wen 11.2.

1030　See Wen 11.5. Shusun Qiaoru and Shusun Bao are both well-known figures in *Zuozhuan*. Takezoe (19.28) identifies Hui as Shuzhong Zhaobo or Shuzhong Dai. On the naming of sons to commemorate victory, see also Ding 8.5.

1031　The old man of Jiang was born in 616 BCE (Wen 11), the first day of the third month according to the Zhou calendar or the first day of the first month according to the Xia calendar.

1032　We cannot know what the Warring States Jin version of the graph *hai* 亥 was. Taking our cue from the seal script version of the graph in *Shuowen jiezi*, we may surmise that it has the sign for "two" on top and three shapes that can each be read as "six" at the bottom, hence the numeric associations of 26,660. It is not clear why Scribe Zhao uses the graph *hai* for computation. On this basis Hui Dong (*Zuozhuan buzhu, j.* 4) suggests that "Hai" is the old man's given name and identifies him as Hai Tang 亥唐, the commoner whom Lord Ping of Jin treats with great deference in *Mencius* 5B.12.

1033　That is, four hundred forty-five sexagenary cycles minus forty days, since only one-third of the last cycle has passed.

1034　*Futao* 復陶 is the name of the fur or feather coat that King Ling of Chu wore in Zhao 12.11, hence Du Yu's (ZZ 40.680) inference that the old man was appointed "keeper of the lord's wardrobe." That office would involve residence in the palace, but the position might have been symbolic enough for the old man to simultaneously serve as preceptor in Jiang.

1035　The text has *dafu* 大夫, in this case used in the broad sense that includes both ministers and high officers.

1036　See also *Guoyu*, "Jin yu 7," 13.445, and "Jin yu 8," 14.462.

The music master Kuang said, "That was the year when Shuzhong Huibo of Lu met with Xi Que[a] of Jin at Chengkuang.[1029] In that same year, the Di attacked Lu, and Shusun Dechen[b] at the time defeated the Di at Xian, seizing the leaders of the Chang Di, Qiaoru, Hui, and Bao, after whom he named his sons.[1030] This was seventy-three years ago."[1031]

The scribe Zhao said, "The graph *hai* has 'two' as head and shapes of 'six' as its body. Move the 'two' down to the body of the graph, and that will be the number of days."[1032]

Shi Gai[a] said, "In that case, we have twenty-six thousand six hundred sixty days."[1033]

Zhao Wu[c] asked the old man who was the high officer in his dependency, and it turned out that he was Zhao Wu's subordinate. Zhao Wu summoned the old man and apologized, "I lack talent but bear responsibility for the ruler's great affairs. On account of the many problems in Jin, I have not been able to employ you properly. I am to blame for the fact that you, sir, have to be shamed by being mired in a lowly position for so long. Allow me to apologize for my lack of talent." He then gave the old man an appointment and had him assist in government. He declined on account of old age. Zhao Wu then gave him land and made him keeper of the lord's wardrobe, serving as preceptor in the Jiang dependency.[1034] The senior officer of military administration in charge of the old man was relieved of his position.

The eagerness of Jin ministers to reward the old man of Jiang convinces Lu of their competence and good judgment.

At that time the Lu envoy was in Jin. Upon his return he told the various high officers about this incident. Ji Wuzi said, "Jin cannot yet be discounted, as it has Zhao Wu[c] as minister,[1035] Shi Gai[b] as his assistant, the scribe Zhao and the music master Kuang to provide consultation, and Shuxiang and Ru Qi to serve as the teacher and the guardian of the ruler.[1036] The Jin court has many noble men. How can it be discounted! The only acceptable course is to strive to serve them."

Repeated covenants in Zheng betray unresolved conflicts among its leaders.

In the fourth month, on the *jihai* day, the Liege of Zheng swore a covenant with his high officers. Thus did the noble man know that the troubles in Zheng had not yet come to an end.

Lord Jing of Cai commits adultery with his son's wife and is murdered by his son, as Zichan predicted (Xiang 28.6).

Prince Jing of Cai had taken a wife for his heir apparent, Ban, in Chu. The Cai ruler had a liaison with her. The heir apparent assassinated Prince Jing.

初，王儋季卒，其子括將見王，而歎。單公子愆期為靈王御士，過諸廷，聞其歎，而言曰：「烏乎！必有此夫！」入以告王，且曰：「必殺之！不慼而願大，視躁而足高，心在他矣。不殺，必害。」王曰：「童子何知！」

及靈王崩，儋括欲立王子佞夫。佞夫弗知。戊子，儋括圍蒍，逐成愆。成愆奔平畤。五月癸巳，尹言多、劉毅、單蔑、甘過、鞏成殺佞夫。括、瑕、廖奔晉。書曰「天王殺其弟佞夫」，罪在王也。

或叫于宋太廟曰：「譆譆，出出。」鳥鳴于亳社，如曰「譆譆」。甲午，宋大災。宋伯姬卒，待姆也。君子謂宋共姬女而不婦。女待人，婦義事也。

1037 Dan Kuo's father had just died. Dan Kuo's overweening ambition and lack of filial devotion are indicated by his having an audience with the king, coveting royal power, and showing no grief. Failure to mourn properly also leads to dire predictions in Cheng 14.5 and in Xiang 19.13 and 31.4.

1038 For another instance of subversive intent revealed through "high steps," see how Dou Bobi rightly predicts Qu Xia's defeat because "he lifts his feet high; his intentions are not firm" (Huan 13.1).

1039 Du Yu (*ZZ* 40.681) identifies Chengqian as a high officer in Wei 蒍. Some commentators suggest that Chengqian may be another name for Qianqi. Wei (not to be confused with the domain of Wei) was first mentioned in Yin 11.5.

1040 Pingzhi 平畤 was part of the royal domain of Zhou and was located near Luoyang City 洛陽市, Henan.

1041 *Gongyang*, Xiang 30 (21.268–69), even suggests that the purpose of the meeting (to relieve Song) is stated to honor Bo Ji (also known as Gong Ji, the name we chose for our translation). It also asserts that the lords are moved to aid Song because of Bo Ji, although according to *Zuozhuan* (Xiang 30.11) no aid is given. The account of Bo Ji in *Lienü zhuan* (4.74–75) follows *Gongyang*. By Han times, it is common to use Bo Ji as an example of self-sacrifice that inspires political rectitude; see, for

The newly installed King Jing of Zhou eliminates his presumed rival Wangzi Ningfu. Dan Kuo, a cousin of King Jing of Zhou, plots to put Wangzi Ningfu, King Jing's younger brother, on the throne. The root of the unrest is traced to Dan Kuo's earlier overreaching demeanor, which another minister correctly decodes. The result is a miscarriage of justice for Ningfu. King Jing is blamed for killing his younger brother, a mere pawn in the intrigues of his ministers.

Earlier, when King Ling's younger brother, Dan Ji, died, his son Dan Kuo was about to see the king and sighed. Qianqi, a son of the Shan Duke who was serving in King Ling's royal guard, passed him at court. Qianqi overheard him sighing and saying, "Alas, I must make all of this mine!" Qianqi entered and told the king, adding, "You must put him to death! Kuo is not grieving and his ambitions are great;[1037] his gaze is impatient and his steps are high.[1038] His heart is elsewhere. If he is not killed, there is sure to be harm." The king said, "What would a mere child like you know!"

 When it came to the time of King Ling's death, Dan Kuo wanted to establish Wangzi Ningfu, King Ling's younger son, as ruler. Ningfu did not know about it. On the *wuzi* day (28), Dan Kuo laid siege to Wei and drove away Chengqian,[1039] who fled to Pingzhi.[1040] In the fifth month, on the *guisi* day (5), Yin Yanduo, Liu Yi, Shan Mie, the Gan Duke Dao[a], and Gong Cheng killed Ningfu. Dan Kuo, Wangzi Xia, and Liao fled to Jin. The text says, "The Heaven-appointed king put to death his younger brother Ningfu": this is to indicate that the blame lay with the king.

Gong Ji, whose attitude toward ritual prescriptions could not be more different from that of her mother, Mu Jiang, dies in a fire in Song because she refused to leave the palace unaccompanied. Whereas Gongyang, Guliang, Lienü zhuan, and Huainanzi all praise her exemplary modesty and decorum,[1041] Zuozhuan implies criticism of such rigid adherence to ritual propriety.

Someone cried at the Song Ancestral Temple, making the sounds "Xi-xi! Out! Out!" Birds sang at the altar of earth at Bo, as if saying, "Xi-xi!" On the *jiawu* day, the fifth day of the fifth month, there was a catastrophic fire in Song. Gong Ji[c] died because she had been waiting for her chaperone. The noble man said of Gong Ji[c] that she acted like a young girl, not like a married woman. A young girl should wait for others, but a married woman should attend to her duties judiciously.[1042]

30.6(4, 5)

30.7(3)

---

example, Dongfang Shuo's remonstrancein *Hanshu* 65.2856: "In former times, Bo Ji burned herself, and the princes became fearful."

1042 Gong Ji married Duke Gong of Song in 582 BCE (Cheng 9.5). She was widowed six years later (Cheng 15.2) and must have been around sixty at the time of this fire.

30.8　六月，鄭子產如陳涖盟，歸，復命。告大夫曰：「陳，亡國也，不可與也。聚禾粟，繕城郭，恃此二者，而不撫其民。其君弱植，公子侈，大子卑，大夫敖，政多門，以介於大國，能無亡乎？不過十年矣。」

30.9(6)　秋，七月，叔弓如宋，葬共姬也。

30.10a(7)　鄭伯有耆酒，為窟室，而夜飲酒，擊鐘焉。朝至，未已。朝者曰：「公焉在？」其人曰：「吾公在壑谷。」皆自朝布路而罷。

　　既而朝，則又將使子晳如楚，歸而飲酒。庚子，子晳以駟氏之甲伐而焚之。伯有奔雍梁，醒而後知之。遂奔許。

　　大夫聚謀。子皮曰：「《仲虺之志》云：『亂者取之，亡者侮之。推亡固存，國之利也。』罕、駟、豐同生，伯有汰侈，故不免。」

1043　As the minister in charge of government, Liang Xiao meets the other ministers and the high officers in his own court of audience.

1044　"Hollow ravine" refers to the underground chamber. The retainer's rejoinder may convey a hint of criticism or even derision.

1045　Liang Xiao's attempt to send Gongsun Hei to Chu the year before caused tension between the Si and Liang lineages (Xiang 29.17).

1046　For Zhonghui, see Ding 1.1. He is also quoted in Xuan 12.2 and Xiang 14.9. The wording of this quotation is slightly different in Xiang 14.9.

1047　Han Hu, Gongsun Hei, and Gongsun Duan belong to the Han, Si, and Feng lineages, respectively. According to this, the ancestors of these three lineages were born of the same consort of Lord Mu of Zheng.

1048　That is, Liang Xiao's flaws as well as the natural ties among the three lineages opposing him make for his defeat.

Zheng's recent victory over Chen (Xiang 25.10) might have emboldened Zichan to enumerate its weaknesses and predict its doom. Chu will overrun Chen nine years hence (Zhao 8.6) and will extinguish Chen sixty-five years later (Ai 17.4).

In the sixth month, Zichan of Zheng went to Chen to oversee the covenant. Upon his return, he reported the discharge of his mission, telling the high officers, "Chen is a domain doomed to perish. We should not form ties with them. Their leaders have accumulated grain and repaired city walls. Relying on these two things, they do not care for the people. Their ruler is feebly implanted in his position, the noble sons are extravagant, the heir apparent is put in a lowly position, the high officers are arrogant, and the government is controlled by many rival houses. When it is thus afflicted while being situated among great domains, how can it not perish? It will not last more than ten years."

30.8

In autumn, in the seventh month, Shu Gong went to Song: this was for the burial of Gong Ji.

30.9(6)

Zheng is roiled by internal strife: Gongsun Hei leads the forces of the Si lineage to attack the Liang lineage. Liang Xiao, a drunkard, flees while drunk. Zichan tries to maintain impartiality in this conflict. Gongsun Hei will foment disorder in Zheng and will be put to death three years hence (Zhao 2.4).

Liang Xiao[a] of Zheng was a drunkard. He built an underground chamber and once drank there through the night as chime-bells played, and he had not stopped drinking by the time the high officers arrived at his court of audience.[1043] Those who came to his court said, "Where is your lord?" Liang Xiao's retainer said, "My lord is in the hollow ravine,"[1044] at which they gave up the wait and left by different roads.

30.10a(7)

Later, when Liang Xiao attended the Zheng ruler's court, he again wanted to send Gongsun Hei[a] to Chu.[1045] Upon his return from court, he fell to drinking. On the *gengzi* day (11), Gongsun Hei[a] used the armored men of the Si lineage to attack Liang Xiao's residence and burn it. Liang Xiao[a] fled to Yongliang, but only after he sobered up did he realize what was happening. He then fled to Xǔ.

The high officers gathered to confer about the situation. Han Hu[a] said, "It says in the *Records of Zhonghui*, 'Take the domain in turmoil. Shame the failing domain. It will benefit the domain to overthrow whatever is failing and to stabilize whatever can be preserved.'[1046] Our Han, Si, and Feng lineages[1047] were born of the same mother. Liang Xiao[a] is extravagant and arrogant, and that is why he could not escape disaster."[1048]

人謂子產就直助彊。子產曰：「豈為我徒？國之禍難，誰知所敝？或主彊直，難乃不生。姑成吾所。」辛丑，子產斂伯有氏之死者而殯之，不及謀而遂行。印段從之。子皮止之。眾曰：「人不我順，何止焉？」子皮曰：「夫子禮於死者，況生者乎？」遂自止之。

王寅，子產入。癸卯，子石入。皆受盟于子晳氏。乙巳，鄭伯及其大夫盟于大宮，盟國人于師之梁之外。

30.10b(7)　伯有聞鄭人之盟己也，怒，聞子皮之甲不與攻己也，喜，曰：「子皮與我矣。」癸丑晨，自墓門之瀆入，因馬師頡介于襄庫，以伐舊北門。駟帶率國人以伐之。皆召子產。子產曰：「兄弟而及此，吾從天所與。」伯有死於羊肆。子產襚之，枕之股而哭之，斂而殯諸伯有之臣在市側者，既而葬諸斗城。子駟氏欲攻子產。子皮怒之，曰：「禮，國之幹也。殺有禮，禍莫大焉。」乃止。

1049　In this case, justice is aligned with power. According to Du Yu (*ZZ* 40.682), Gongsun Hei is supposed to have justice on his side, and the Han, Si, and Feng lineages are powerful.

1050　Alternatively: "Even if I were to abide by the just and powerful ones, would disasters then not arise?" (Yang, 3:1176); "Had the three lineages been truly capable of justice and power, disasters would not have arisen" (Du Yu, *ZZ* 40.682; Takezoe, 19.33). Zichan is implicitly disagreeing with Han Hu and suggesting that the feud between the Si and Liang lineages cannot be cast in black-and-white terms.

1051　That is, Zichan will keep his place by exercising impartiality and neutrality. Readings of *suo* 所 as *wei* 為 ("action") (Takezoe, 19.33) and *yi* 意 ("intent") (Yang, 3:1176) would imply that Zichan is insisting on his principles: "For now, I will simply follow through with my action [or my intent]." Zichan's attitude is comparable to Yan Ying's in Xiang 25.2, 28.9, and Zhao 10.2.

1052　Both Si Dai and Liang Xiao were great-grandsons of Lord Mu. Zichan, Gongsun Hei, and Gongsun Duan were grandsons of Lord Mu.

1053　On the meaning of this gesture, see also Xi 28.6, Xiang 25.2c, and Xiang 27.3.

People said that Zichan should side with the just one and help the powerful ones.[1049] Zichan said, "How can they be of my ilk? Who among them knows how to put a stop to the troubles and disasters suffered by the domain? Perhaps if we abide by the truly just and powerful, disasters will then not arise.[1050] For now, I will simply keep my place."[1051] On the *xinchou* day (12), Zichan had the dead of Liang Xiao[a]'s lineage dressed in burial clothes and placed in coffins to lie in state. He then left the domain without waiting to confer with the other ministers and high officers. Yin Duan followed suit. Han Hu[a] tried to stop them. The others said, "If the two of them are not going along with us, why should we stop them?" Han Hu[a] said, "If that fine man is treating even the dead with ritual propriety, how much more would he do well by the living?" He thus personally tried to stop Zichan.

On the *renyin* day (13), Zichan reentered Zheng. On the *guimao* day (14), Yin Duan[b] did the same. They both accepted a covenant at Gongsun Hei[a]'s house. On the *yisi* day (16), the Liege of Zheng and his high officers swore a covenant at the Grand Ancestral Temple, and they swore a covenant with the inhabitants of the capital outside the Shizhiliang Gate.

The violent power struggle between the Si and Liang lineages continues, and Liang Xiao dies. His ghost will haunt Zheng eight years hence (Zhao 7.9a). Zichan tries to maintain neutrality. His Guo lineage and the You lineage, like the Yin lineage above, reach a truce with the Si lineage.

When Liang Xiao[a] heard that the leaders of Zheng had sworn a covenant against him, he was furious, but he brightened up when he heard that Han Hu[a]'s men in armor were not party to the attack against him, saying, "Han Hu[a] is on my side." On the morning of the *guichou* day (24), he entered the Zheng capital from the drains on the Tomb Gate. Relying on the help of Yu Jie[a], the trainer of horses, Liang Xiao armed his followers at the arsenal set up by Lord Xiang and led them to attack the old North Gate. Si Dai, the head of the Si lineage, led out the inhabitants of the capital to fight them. Both sides summoned Zichan, who said, "To be brothers and yet to have come to this! I can only follow the one favored by Heaven."[1052] Liang Xiao[a] died among the vendors of mutton at the marketplace. Zichan dressed the corpse, pillowed its head on his thigh, and wailed for him.[1053] He put the corpse in a coffin and had it lie in state in the house of one of Liang Xiao[a]'s retainers who lived beside the marketplace. Later, he buried him at Doucheng. The Si lineage wanted to attack Zichan. Furious at this, Han Hu[a] said, "Ritual propriety is the pillar of the domain. There is no greater disaster than to kill the one who has ritual propriety." The Si lineage thus desisted.

30.10b(7)

於是游吉如晉還，聞難，不入。復命于介。八月甲子，奔晉。駟帶追之，及酸棗。與子上盟，用兩珪質于河。使公孫鉏入盟大夫。己巳，復歸。

書曰「鄭人殺良霄」，不稱大夫，言自外入也。

30.10c 於子蟜之卒也，將葬，公孫揮與裨竈晨會事焉。過伯有氏，其門上生莠。子羽曰：「其莠猶在乎？」於是歲在降婁，降婁中而旦。裨竈指之，曰：「猶可以終歲，歲不及此次也已。」及其亡也，歲在娵訾之口，其明年乃及降婁。

僕展從伯有，與之皆死。羽頡出奔晉，為任大夫。

雞澤之會，鄭樂成奔楚，遂適晉。羽頡因之，與之比而事趙文子，言伐鄭之說焉。以宋之盟故，不可。子皮以公孫鉏為馬師。

At that time You Ji was on his way back from his mission in Jin. Having heard of the disaster, he did not enter the capital and sent his aide to report the discharge of his mission. In the eighth month, on the *jiazi* day (6), he fled to Jin. Si Dai pursued him, catching up with him at Suanzao. You Ji swore a covenant with Si Dai[a], sinking two jade tablets to call upon the Yellow River to bear witness. He then sent Gongsun Xi to enter the capital and swear a covenant with the high officers. On the *jisi* day (11), he came home again.

The text says, "the leaders of Zheng put Liang Xiao to death," and does not call him "high officer": this is to indicate that he came in from outside the domain.

Recapitulation of how eleven years earlier Pi Zao predicted Liang Xiao's demise by referring to planetary movements.

After Zijiao had died, when he was about to be buried,[1054] Gongsun Hui and Pi Zao met in the morning to confer about his funeral. They passed by Liang Xiao[a]'s residence, and foxtail weeds were growing on his gate. Gongsun Hui[a] said, "Are the foxtail weeds still there?"[1055] At that time the Year-Planet was at the Bound Bovine asterism, which was in the middle of the sky as dawn was breaking. Pi Zao pointed to it and said, "It seems he can still last through another cycle of the Year-Planet, only by then the Year-Planet will not have reached this asterism again." By the time Liang Xiao died, the Year-Planet was at the mouth of the Consort asterism,[1056] and only in the following year did it reach Bound Bovine.

30.10c

Pu Zhan followed Liang Xiao[a] and died with him. Yu Jie left the domain and fled to Jin, where he became a high officer in Ren.

At the meeting at Ji Marsh,[1057] Yue Cheng of Zheng fled to Chu and then went to Jin. Relying on Yue Cheng, Yu Jie became his partner in the service of Zhao Wu[a], and he made arguments in favor of an attack on Zheng. On account of the Covenant of Song, this was considered unacceptable. To replace Yu Jie, Han Hu[a] appointed Gongsun Chu as trainer of horses.[1058]

1054 See Xiang 19.7.

1055 Gongsun Hui is implicitly comparing Liang Xiao to the foxtail weeds.

1056 We derive our translation of Jianglou 降婁 (the equivalent of Aries) as "Bound Bovine" from *Gongyang*, Zhao 25 (24.302): "A bound bovine is called *lou*." *Shuowen jiezi* 12B.4a glosses *lou* as "being empty." We translate Juzi 娵訾 (the equivalent of Pisces) as "Consort" because Juzi is the name of Di Ku's consort in Han texts, although it is not clear that the association existed at the time of *Zuozhuan*'s compilation.

1057 See Xiang 3.5.

1058 Gongsun Chu was Zihan's son, Gongsun Shezhi's brother, and Han Hu's uncle.

30.11　楚公子圍殺大司馬蔿掩而取其室。申無宇曰：「王子必不免。善人，國之主也。王子相楚國，將善是封殖，而虐之，是禍國也。且司馬，令尹之偏，而王之四體也。絕民之主，去身之偏，艾王之體，以禍其國，無不祥大焉，何以得免？」

30.12(9)　為宋災故，諸侯之大夫會，以謀歸宋財。冬，十月，叔孫豹會晉趙武、齊公孫蠆、宋向戌、衛北宮佗、鄭罕虎及小邾之大夫會于澶淵。既而無歸於宋，故不書其人。

　　　　君子曰：「信其不可不慎乎！澶淵之會，卿不書，不信也。夫諸侯之上卿，會而不信，寵名皆棄，不信之不可也如是。《詩》曰：

文王陟降，
在帝左右。

信之謂也。又曰：

淑慎爾止，
無載爾偽。

1059　*Maoshi* 235, "Wen wang" 文王, 16A.533.

1060　Du Yu (ZZ 40.683) classifies this as an ode that is no longer extant, but the first line of the quotation appears in *Maoshi* 256, "Yi" 抑, 18A.648, which is also quoted in Zhao 1.1b to support an argument about good faith. "Yi" is also quoted in Xi 9.6, Xiang 31.13, Zhao 5.1b.

A Chu noble predicts doom for Gongzi Wei when the latter wantonly destroys Wei Yan, the Chu supervisor of the military, who was praised earlier for his achievements (Xiang 25.11). Body and limbs are elsewhere also used as a metaphor for loyalty and the cohesion of the polity (e.g., Xi 9.4, 26.3, Wen 7.3, Cheng 12.4, Xiang 14.8, Zhao 9.5, 13.2, Ai 6.4).

Gongzi Wei of Chu put to death Wei Yan, the grand supervisor of the military, and seized his possessions. Shen Wuyu said, "The royal son [Gongzi Wei] will certainly not escape disaster. Worthy men are masters of the domain. The royal son, serving as chief minister in Chu, should establish and nurture worthy men, but instead, he destroyed them, which amounts to bringing disaster to the domain. What's more, the supervisor of the military is like one side of the chief minister's body and the king's four limbs. Nothing can be more inauspicious than to destroy the master of the people, remove one side of the chief minister's own body, hack off limbs from the king's person, and consequently visit calamity on the domain. How can he escape disaster?"

Ministers from various domains meet to confer about disaster relief for Song, but in the end no aid is given. Such a breach of good faith is turned into an exegetical comment on why names and titles are omitted in the Annals. Zuozhuan *also tries to reconcile the absence of Shusun Bao in the* Annals *with its own record of his role at Chanyuan.*

On account of the disastrous fire in Song, the high officers of the princes met to confer about providing resources to Song. In winter, in the tenth month, Shusun Bao joined Zhao Wu of Jin, Ziwei of Qi, Xiang Xu of Song, Beigong Tuo of Wei, Han Hu of Zheng, and the high officers of Lesser Zhu in a meeting at Chanyuan. But thereafter no aid was offered to Song. That was why the names of the delegates are not recorded.

The noble man said, "One must not fail to be cautious about good faith! For the meeting at Chanyuan, the names of the ministers are not recorded, because they lacked good faith. Now when it is the high ministers of the princes who meet, and yet they lack good faith, both rank and name are cast aside. That is how unacceptable a failure of good faith is. As it says in the *Odes,*

> King Wen, be he in ascent or descent,
> Is always by the side of the god on high.[1059]

This refers to good faith. It also says,

> Use caution well in your conduct;
> Do not harbor any deceit.[1060]

不信之謂也。」書曰「某人某人會于澶淵，宋災故」，尤之也。不書魯大
夫，諱之也。

30.13a　鄭子皮授子產政。辭曰：「國小而偪，族大寵多，不可為也。」子皮曰：「虎
帥以聽，誰敢犯子？子善相之。國無小，小能事大，國乃寬。」

子產為政，有事伯石，賂與之邑。子大叔曰：「國皆其國也，奚獨
賂焉？」

子產曰：「無欲實難。皆得其欲，以從其事，而要其成。非我有成，
其在人乎？何愛於邑，邑將焉往？」

子大叔曰：「若四國何？」

子產曰：「非相違也，而相從也，四國何尤焉？《鄭書》有之曰：

安定國家，
必大焉先。

姑先安大，以待其所歸。」

既伯石懼而歸邑，卒與之。伯有既死，使大史命伯石為卿，辭。大
史退，則請命焉。復命之，又辭。如是三，乃受策入拜。子產是以惡其為
人也，使次己位。

1061　That is, he is not mentioned in order to conceal his participation in a covenant that
betrays good faith.

1062　Alternatively, Zichan may be claiming that so long as a task is accomplished, he can
claim credit as chief minister: "Wouldn't I be the one who achieves success? Or
would it be the others who achieve success?"

That refers to the lack of good faith." The text says, "So-and-so and so-and-so met at Chanyuan on account of the disastrous fire in Song": this is to blame them. That the high officer from Lu is not mentioned is for the sake of concealment.[1061]

Braving great difficulties, Zichan takes charge of policy decisions in Zheng. His pragmatism is evident in the ways he promotes the devious and hypocritical Gongsun Duan, the head of the Feng lineage.

Han Hu[a] wanted to give to Zichan the charge of government. Zichan declined: "Our domain is small and hard-pressed. The houses are powerful and favorites are numerous. It will be impossible to govern well." Han Hu[a] said, "With me leading them in abiding by your commands, who will dare to go against you, sir? You should do your best to assist in good government. The smallness of a domain does not matter. When a small domain can serve the great domains well, it will find relief."

Zichan took charge of the government. He wanted to enlist Gongsun Duan[a] for a certain task and gave him settlements as gifts. You Ji[a] said, "The domain is a domain for all. Why give gifts only to him?"

Zichan said, "It is indeed difficult to entirely ignore personal desires. Let them all obtain what they desire, so that they attend to their tasks and strive to accomplish them. It is not I alone who can accomplish all these tasks; does it not depend on others?[1062] Why begrudge settlements? Where can settlements go?"

You Ji[a] said, "What about our neighboring domains on four sides?"

Zichan said, "In granting these settlements we are not opposing but rather complying with each other. How can our neighboring domains on four sides blame us? As the *Zheng Documents* has it,

> To bring peace and stability to the domain and patrimony,
> It is necessary to give priority to the great lineages.

Let us for now give the great lineages a sense of security, and wait to see which way they go."

Shortly thereafter, Gongsun Duan[a] returned the settlements out of fear, but in the end they were given to him. Liang Xiao[a] had already died, so Zichan sent the grand scribe to appoint Gongsun Duan[a] minister. Gongsun Duan[a] declined. But when the grand scribe withdrew, he requested that the appointment be repeated. When Gongsun Duan[a] was appointed again, he again declined. Only after repeating this exchange three times did he accept the bamboo document of appointment and enter the court to bow in gratitude. Because of this, Zichan abhorred his character, but he made his position next to his own.

子產使都鄙有章，上下有服；田有封洫，廬井有伍。大人之忠儉者，從而
與之；泰侈者，因而斃之。

　　　豐卷將祭，請田焉。弗許，曰：「唯君用鮮，眾給而已。」子張怒，退
而徵役。子產奔晉，子皮止之，而逐豐卷。豐卷奔晉。子產請其田、里，
三年而復之，反其田、里及其入焉。

　　　從政一年，輿人誦之，曰：

取我衣冠而褚之，
取我田疇而伍之。
孰殺子產，
吾其與之！

及三年，又誦之，曰：

我有子弟，
子產誨之；
我有田疇，
子產殖之。
子產而死，
誰其嗣之？

春秋

三十有一年，春王正月。

1063　We follow Takezoe's (19.40) identification of *fu* 服 with the graph *fu* 𝄰 in *Shuowen
jiezi* 3B.4b, which Xu Shen glosses as *zhi* 治 ("manage"), with *jie* 卩 being "the regu-
lation of affairs" 事之節. Alternatively, we can follow the literal meaning of the line:
"Those above and those below had their distinctive regalia."

Zichan judiciously reins in powerful lineages and establishes rules and regulations that initially provoke the people's resentment but eventually win their allegiance. As in Zhao 4.6, Zichan tolerates but is ultimately not swayed by popular criticism. For political criticism expressed through songs, see also Xuan 2.1b, Xiang 4.8, 17.6.

Zichan brought it about that the cities and the country had distinctions, those above and those below had their respective duties,[1063] fields had their boundaries and irrigation ditches, and houses and wells had their levies regulated.[1064] He listened to and supported the loyal and frugal among the high officers, and he demoted the arrogant and extravagant among them accordingly.

Feng Juan was preparing for sacrifices and asked permission to go on a hunt. Zichan refused to grant it and said, "The ruler alone uses animals fresh from the hunt. The rest of us only make do."[1065] Furious, Feng Juan[a] withdrew and began enlisting troops. Zichan fled to Jin. Han Hu[a] stopped him and drove away Feng Juan.[1066] Feng Juan fled to Jin. Zichan requested to have his land and residence. Three years later, he let Feng Juan return and restored to him his land and residence, as well as the income that had accrued.

After Zichan had been in charge of government for one year, the common workers chanted about him:

> He takes our clothes and caps and imposes taxes on them.
> He takes our lands and fields and measures them for levies.
> Whoever wants to kill Zichan,
> We will join him.

After three years, they again chanted about him:

> We have sons and younger brothers;
> Zichan instructs them.
> We have lands and fields;
> Zichan makes them yield more.
> If Zichan were to die,
> Who would succeed him?

LORD XIANG 31 (542 BCE)
ANNALS

The thirty-first year, spring, the royal first month.

31.1(1)

1064 A number of households would gather around wells, which thus serve as a way to measure land use.

1065 All but the ruler make do with domestic animals or preserved meat of animals captured in earlier hunts.

1066 Feng Juan belongs to the Feng lineage mentioned above (Xiang 30.10a). He was probably Zifeng's son and Gongsun Duan's brother.

31.2(3)　夏，六月辛巳，公薨于楚宮。

31.3(3)　秋，九月癸巳，子野卒。

31.4(4)　己亥，仲孫羯卒。

31.5(5)　冬，十月，滕子來會葬。

31.6(6)　癸酉，葬我君襄公。

31.7(8)　十有一月，莒人弒其君密州。

左傳

31.1(1)　三十一年，春，王正月，穆叔至自會。見孟孝伯，語之曰：「趙孟將死矣。其語偷，不似民主。且年未盈五十，而諄諄焉如八、九十者，弗能久矣。若趙孟死，為政者其韓子乎！吾子盍與季孫言之，可以樹善，君子也。晉君將失政矣，若不樹焉，使早備魯，既而政在大夫，韓子懦弱，大夫多貪，求欲無厭，齊、楚未足與也，魯其懼哉！」

　　孝伯曰：「人生幾何，誰能無偷？朝不及夕，將安用樹？」

　　穆叔出，而告人曰：「孟孫將死矣。吾語諸趙孟之偷也，而又甚焉。」又與季孫語晉故，季孫不從。及趙文子卒，晉公室卑，政在侈家。韓宣子為政，不能圖諸侯。魯不堪晉求，讒慝弘多，是以有平丘之會。

1067　For a similar judgment, see Wen 17.7.

1068　Shusun Bao has been in disagreement with Ji Wuzi on several occasions (e.g., Xiang 11.1, 27.4d), and this may be why he asks Meng Xiaobo to convey his opinion.

1069　Jin leaders arrested Ji Wuzi at the meeting at Pingqiu (Zhao 13.3). Pingqiu 平丘 was in the domain of Wei east of present-day Fengqiu County 封丘縣, Henan.

In summer, in the sixth month, on the *xinsi* day (28), our lord expired at the Chu Palace. 31.2(3)

In autumn, in the ninth month, on the *guisi* day (11), Ziye died. 31.3(3)

On the *jihai* day (17), Zhongsun Jie (Meng Xiaobo) died. 31.4(4)

In winter, in the tenth month, the Master of Teng came and met with us for the burial. 31.5(5)

On the *guiyou* day (21), we buried our ruler Lord Xiang. 31.6(6)

In the eleventh month, Ju leaders assassinated their ruler, Mizhou. 31.7(8)

ZUO

Torpid words spell doom for Zhao Wu and Meng Xiaobo. The prescient Shusun Bao predicts Jin decline and urges Lu leaders to secure an alliance with Han Qi, but he is not heeded. Jin-Lu relations will deteriorate, and Jin will gather its allies for an expedition against Lu at the meeting at Pingqiu thirteen years later (Zhao 13.3).

In the thirty-first year, in spring, in the royal first month, Shusun Bao[a] arrived from the meeting. He met with Meng Xiaobo and said to him, "Zhao Wu[c] is about to die. His words are torpid and do not fit a master of the people.[1067] What's more, he is not yet fifty, but he is babbling like an eighty- or ninety-year-old. He cannot last much longer. If Zhao Wu[c] were to die, the one in charge of government would likely be Han Qi[c]. Why don't you, sir, speak to Ji Wuzi[d] about it?[1068] We should establish good relations with Han Qi, who is a noble man, since the Jin ruler is about to lose control of the government. If we fail to establish good relations with Han Qi and early on make him ready to act on Lu's behalf, then later, when the Jin government falls to the high officers, Han Qi will be timid and weak, the high officers will be greedy and insatiable in their demands, and with Qi and Chu being untrustworthy allies, Lu will indeed have much to fear!" 31.1(1)

Meng Xiaobo said, "How long is the span of human life? Who can avoid being torpid? From the morning we may not last till the evening. Of what use is it to establish good relations?"

Shusun Bao[a] came out and told his followers, "Meng Xiaobo[d] will soon die. I told him about Zhao Wu[c] being torpid, yet he is even more so." He also spoke to Ji Wuzi[d] about affairs in Jin, but Ji Wuzi[d] did not follow his advice. By the time Zhao Wu[a] died, the lord's house in Jin was brought low, and overreaching nobles controlled the government. Han Qi[a] was in charge of the government, but he could not enlist the allegiance of the princes. Lu could not bear Jin's many demands, and the slanderous charges against it multiplied. That was why the meeting at Pingqiu took place.[1069]

31.2　齊子尾害閭丘嬰，欲殺之，使帥師以伐陽州。我問師故。夏，五月，子尾殺閭丘嬰，以說于我師。工僂灑、渻竈、孔虺、賈寅出奔莒。出群公子。

31.3(2, 3)　公作楚宮。穆叔曰：「〈大誓〉云：

民之所欲，
天必從之。

君欲楚也夫，故作其宮。若不復適楚，必死是宮也。」六月辛巳，公薨于楚宮。

叔仲帶竊其拱璧，以與御人，納諸其懷，而從取之，由是得罪。
立胡女敬歸之子子野，次于季氏。秋九月癸巳，卒，毀也。

31.4(4)　己亥，孟孝伯卒。

1070 Ziwei belongs to the Gao lineage, whom Lüqiu Ying attacked two years earlier (Xiang 29.16). Yangzhou 陽州 was a Lu settlement on the border with Qi. It was located in the area of present-day Dongping County 東平縣, Shandong.

1071 The "Great Oath" that Du Yu (ZZ 40.685) and the various Han scholars before him saw did not contain these lines, which are incorporated into the "Great Oath" (*Shangshu* 11.154), one of the Ancient Script chapters in the *Documents*.

1072 Shuzhong Dai, earlier commended for his judgment, is here disgraced. His grandson, Shuzhong Zhi, "did not fulfill his ambitions in Lu" (Ding 8.10).

Ziwei of Qi feared the worst from Lüqiu Ying and wanted to kill him, so he had Lüqiu Ying lead out troops to attack Yangzhou.[1070] We demanded to know the reason for this military action. In summer, in the fifth month, Ziwei put Lüqiu Ying to death to placate our army. Gonglü Sa, Xing Zao, Kong Hui, and Jia Yin, all of Lüqiu Ying's party, left the domain and fled to Ju. The noble sons were exiled.

31.2

Lord Xiang's infatuation with Chu architecture seems vaguely inauspicious, and he dies in the Chu-style palace he built in Lu. For another ruler who takes to "barbarian" mores, see the Ousted Lord of Wei, who imitates "the barbaric way of speaking" and is thus destined to "die among the barbarians" (Ai 12.4, 26.1).

Our lord built the Chu Palace. Shusun Bao[a] said, "It says in the 'Great Oath,'

31.3(2, 3)

> What the people desire
> Heaven is sure to grant.[1071]

Perchance our lord desires Chu, and so built his palace. If he does not go again to Chu, he will certainly die in that palace." In the sixth month, on the *xinsi* day (28), our lord expired at the Chu Palace.

Shuzhong Dai stole Lord Xiang's big jade disk and gave it to his carriage driver. He inserted it into his clothing and afterward took it from him. As a result, Shuzhong Dai was deemed guilty.[1072]

Ziye, our lord's son born of Jing Gui, a Hu woman, was established as ruler. He dwelt temporarily in the Ji residence. That he died in autumn, on the *guisi* day (11), was because of excessive grief.[1073]

Meng Xiaobo dies, as Shusun Bao predicted (Xiang 31.1). Gongzi Chou, the future Lord Zhao, is instated as the Lu ruler against Shusun Bao's recommendation. His lack of grief and negligence (symbolized by his soiled lapels) at his father's funeral are said to portend his exile twenty-five years hence (Zhao 25.6).

On the *jihai* day (17), Meng Xiaobo died.

31.4(4)

1073 Ziye's mysterious death leads some commentators (e.g., Fang Bao, Gu Donggao, cited in Takezoe, 19.45–46) to suspect foul play, especially because earlier assassinations of Lu rulers also took place when those rulers "temporarily dwelt" in a minister's residence (Yin 11.8, Zhuang 32.5).

立敬歸之娣齊歸之子公子裯。穆叔不欲，曰：「大子死，有母弟，
則立之，無，則立長。年鈞擇賢，義鈞則卜，古之道也。非適嗣，何必娣
之子？且是人也，居喪而不哀，在慼而有嘉容，是謂不度。不度之人，鮮
不為患。若果立之，必為季氏憂。」

武子不聽，卒立之。比及葬，三易衰，衰絰如故衰。於是昭公十九
年矣，猶有童心，君子是以知其不能終也。

31.5(5)　冬，十月，滕成公來會葬，惰而多涕。子服惠伯曰：「滕君將死矣。怠於
其位，而哀已甚，兆於死所矣，能無從乎？」

31.6a(6)　癸酉，葬襄公。

Gongzi Chou, born of Jing Gui's younger sister Qi Gui, was established as ruler. Shusun Bao[a] opposed this, saying, "When the heir apparent dies, if he has a full younger brother, he should be established as heir. If not, then the oldest among the lord's sons should be established. If the sons are of the same age, the worthy one is chosen.[1074] If they are equally dutiful, then divination is used. This was the way of the ancients. Ziye was not the heir born of the principal consort, so why must we establish the son of a concubine's younger sister as ruler? Moreover, this person is in mourning and yet does not grieve; he is bereaved and yet has the countenance of gladness. This is called violation of rules and standards.[1075] Rarely does the person who violates rules and standards not make trouble. If he is indeed established as ruler, he is sure to cause distress for the Ji lineage."

Ji Wuzi[c] did not heed him and in the end established Gongzi Chou as ruler. By the time of the burial, he had changed his hempen mourning clothes three times, but the hempen lapels still looked soiled. At that time Lord Zhao was nineteen years old, yet he still had the mind of a child. By this, the noble man could know that he would not be able to come to a good end.

The Teng ruler's demeanor at Lord Xiang's funeral portends his own death three years later (Zhao 3.2).

In winter, in the tenth month, Lord Cheng of Teng came and met with us for the burial of our lord. He was negligent and shed many tears. Zifu Huibo said, "The Teng ruler is going to die. He was negligent in his place of mourning, and his grief was excessive. The omen pertains to how death will come to him. Can he but follow the dead?"

31.5(5)

Zichan and Lord Jian of Zheng go to Jin for an official visit and are treated dismissively. Zichan takes down the walls of the guest lodgings and eloquently defends the rights of Zheng as the subordinate ally.

On the *guiyou* day, the twenty-first day of the tenth month, we buried Lord Xiang.

31.6a(6)

1074 Cf. Zhao 26.9b.

1075 Yang (3:1185), on the basis of a *Xiaojing* quotation cited in *Liji*-Kong 49.830, argues that the phrase *budu* 不度 refers specifically to the unfilial conduct of lords. For other examples of improper mourning that portends doom, see Cheng 14.5, Xiang 30.6, Zhao 14.4.

公薨之月，子產相鄭伯以如晉，晉侯以我喪故，未之見也。子產使
盡壞其館之垣而納車馬焉。士文伯讓之，曰：「敝邑以政刑之不修，寇
盜充斥，無若諸侯之屬辱在寡君者何，是以令吏人完客所館，高其閈
閎，厚其牆垣，以無憂客使。今吾子壞之，雖從者能戒，其若異客何？以
敝邑之為盟主，繕完葺牆，以待賓客。若皆毀之，其何以共命？寡君使
匄請命。」
　　對曰：

> 以敝邑褊小，介於大國，誅求無時，是以不敢寧居，悉索敝
> 賦，以來會時事。逢執事之不閒，而未得見；又不獲聞命，未
> 知見時。不敢輸幣，亦不敢暴露。其輸之，則君之府實也，非
> 薦陳之，不敢輸也。其暴露之，則恐燥濕之不時而朽蠹，以
> 重敝邑之罪。
>
> 　僑聞文公之為盟主也，宮室卑庳，無觀臺榭，以崇大諸
> 侯之館，館如公寢；庫廄繕修，司空以時平易道路，圬人以
> 時塓館宮室；諸侯賓至，甸設庭燎，僕人巡宮；車馬有所，

1076　The Zheng delegation has been kept waiting for four months.

The month that Lord Xiang expired, Zichan acted as assistant to the Liege of Zheng as they went to Jin. The Prince of Jin, on account of our lord's death, had not yet received them.[1076] Zichan had the walls of their lodgings all taken down so he could bring in the carriages and horses. Shi Gai[a] reprimanded him: "Our humble domain, for want of attention to administration and punishment, is filled with bandits and brigands. Yet what is to be done when the princes and their retinues deign to visit our unworthy ruler? That is why we have ordered the officers to make the guests' lodgings perfect, making their doors and gates high and their walls and barriers thick, so as to free the guest envoys from worries. Now you, sir, have taken down the walls. Although your followers will be able to keep guard, what are we to do about guests from other domains? As covenant chief, our humble domain should refurbish the courtyards and repair the walls so as to treat our guests properly. If the walls are all demolished, how are we to meet the demands of our guests? Our unworthy ruler has sent me to inquire about your command."

Zichan replied,

> Our humble domain is small and situated among great domains that demand gifts on no set schedule. That is why we do not dare to dwell at ease and have mustered all our meager resources to come to meetings and court visits. It so happens that your functionaries here do not have time to spare, and we have not yet obtained an audience. Not having heard your commands, we do not yet know when we will be received in audience. We do not dare to submit our gifts, nor do we dare to leave them in the open air. As for submitting them, since these are to be the content of your treasuries, we would not dare to submit them without formally displaying and offering them. As for leaving them in the open air, we fear that they will rot from untimely heat and humidity, thereby doubling the offense ascribed to our humble settlement.

> I have heard, when Lord Wen was covenant chief, his palaces were small and low, devoid of terraces and towers that afford fine prospects. Such moderation meant that the lodgings of the princes could be made lofty and spacious. The lodgings then were like your lord's main chambers now. The storehouses and stables were refurbished and in good repair. The supervisor of works regularly leveled the roads. Plasterers regularly smoothed the walls of the chambers. When the princes arrived as guests, the managers of firewood prepared the torches in the courtyards, watchmen made their circuits around the quarters, carriages and horses had appropriate places to go, the guests' retinues had

賓從有代，巾車脂轄，隸人、牧、圉各瞻其事；百官之屬各展
其物；公不留賓，而亦無廢事；憂樂同之，事則巡之；教其
不知，而恤其不足。賓至如歸，無寧菑患；不畏寇盜，而亦
不患燥濕。

　　今銅鞮之宮數里，而諸侯舍於隸人，門不容車，而不可
踰越；盜賊公行，而天厲不戒。賓見無時，命不可知。若又
勿壞，是無所藏幣以重罪也。敢請執事：將何所命之？雖君
之有魯喪，亦敝邑之憂也。若獲薦幣，修垣而行，君之惠
也，敢憚勤勞！

文伯復命。趙文子曰：「信。我實不德，而以隸人之垣以贏諸侯，是吾罪
也。」使士文伯謝不敏焉。

31.6b　晉侯見鄭伯，有加禮，厚其宴、好而歸之。乃築諸侯之館。叔向曰：「辭
之不可以已也如是夫！子產有辭，諸侯賴之，若之何其釋辭也？《詩》
曰：

1077　Zichan is justifying why he had to take down the walls.

1078　Only by taking down the walls could Zichan enter the compound for visiting princes
　　　and envoys, and the gifts are to be stored inside that compound.

1079　Zheng, Lu, and Jin are all domains with the clan name Ji. The Jin ruler may use the
　　　Lu funeral as an excuse for negligence, but Zheng, with the same cause for distress,
　　　has not been deterred from making the trip to Jin.

1080　Alternatively, Du Yu (ZZ 40.687) has "he treated him with added courtesy."

replacements to take over their duties, the managers of carriages
oiled wheels and axles, menials, herdsmen, and grooms all
attended to their respective affairs, and the retinues of various
officials all set forth their supplies for the guests. The lord did not
detain the guests, yet there was no business neglected. Host and
guests shared their sorrows and joys. When something came up,
the lord attended to it. He instructed the guests in what they were
ignorant about and took care of what they lacked. The guests
arrived as if they were returning home. How could there be troubles or calamities? They did not fear bandits and brigands, nor
did they worry about heat and humidity.

Now the Palace of Tongti extends for several *li*, while the
princes are lodged in abodes fit for servants. The gates are not
wide enough to admit carriages, which of course cannot scale
the walls.[1077] Bandits and brigands move about openly, and there
is no guard against the pestilence of heaven. There is no set time
for the guests to be received, and the lord's command cannot be
known. If, facing such difficulties, we are also not to take down
the walls, then we will have no place to store our gifts and will
thereby double our offense.[1078] We presume to inquire of the
functionaries: how would you command us? Although your
ruler is occupied with the Lu funeral, that is also a cause of distress shared by our humble settlement.[1079] If we can manage to
offer the gifts, repair the walls, and leave, it will be due to your
ruler's beneficence. How would we dare to evade the toil and
the responsibility!

Shi Gai[c] returned to tell of his mission. Zhao Wu[a] said, "It is truly so. It
is we who are lacking in virtue and have used walls fit for servants quarters to receive the princes. This was my offense." He sent Shi Gai[a] to
apologize for his lapses.

*Lord Ping of Jin treats the Zheng ruler and other princes with new respect.
Zichan's diplomatic success prompts Shuxiang to laud the importance of
rhetorical prowess. Recall that Confucius praises Zichan's diplomatic
rhetoric in Xiang 25.10.*

The Prince of Jin received the Liege of Zheng in an audience, and he
treated him with additional ritual.[1080] He lavished feasts and gifts on him
before sending him home. He then rebuilt the lodgings for the princes.
Shuxiang said, "How indispensable eloquent words are! Zichan masters
eloquent words, and the princes benefited accordingly. How can we dis-
card eloquent words? As it says in the *Odes*,

31.6b

辭之輯矣，
民之協矣；
辭之繹矣，
民之莫矣。

其知之矣。」

31.7 鄭子皮使印段如楚，以適晉告，禮也。

31.8(7) 莒犁比公生去疾及展輿。既立展輿，又廢之。犁比公虐，國人患之。十一月，展輿因國人以攻莒子，弒之，乃立。去疾奔齊，齊出也。展輿，吳出也。書曰「莒人弒其君買朱鉏」，言罪之在也。

31.9 吳子使屈狐庸聘于晉，通路也。趙文子問焉，曰：「延州來季子其果立乎？巢隕諸樊，閽戕戴吳，天似啟之，何如？」
　　對曰：「不立。是二王之命也，非啟季子也。若天所啟，其在今嗣君乎！甚德而度。德不失民，度不失事。民親而事有序，其天所啟也。有吳國者，必此君之子孫實終之。季子，守節者也，雖有國，不立。」

1081　*Maoshi* 254, "Ban" 板, 17D.633. The received text has *yi* 懌 ("in accord," "glad") instead of *yi* 繹 ("continuous," "patterned," "reasonable"). Some scholars have argued that *ci* 辭 is a loanword for 辝, which means "I" or "we" in bronze inscriptions (Cheng Junying and Jiang Jianyuan, *Shijing zhuxi*, 2:843). According to this reading, the lines describe how those in positions of power set examples for the people without resorting to the power of words.

1082　The difference between "Mizhou" in the *Annals* and "Maizhuchu" in *Zuozhuan* may testify to variants in oral transmission.

1083　Qu Huyong is the son of Qu Wuchen, the Chu noble who went to Wu in Cheng 7.5.

1084　Jizha was first given the settlement of Yanling 延陵 (present-day Changzhou 常州, Jiangsu) and then Zhoulai (present-day Fengtai County, Anhui; see Cheng 7.5).

1085　According to *Shiji* 31.1460–65, this prediction is not fulfilled. Yimo's son Liao was assassinated by order of Zhufan's son Guang, whose son Fucha was the last Wu ruler. However, Fu Qian (cited in Kong Yingda's subcommentary) claims that Liao was Yimo's half brother and Guang was his son. As in the case of Gongzi Xinshi (Xiang 15.1), "to keep one's principles" is associated with rejecting the lure of power.

The words follow the right order;
The people are harmonious.
The words follow reason;
The people take them as example.[1081]

He already understood this."

Zheng notifies Chu of its leaders' visit to Jin, in accordance with the Covenant of Song (Xiang 27.4).

Han Hu[a] of Zheng sent Yin Duan to Chu to notify Chu that Zheng had gone to Jin. This was in accordance with ritual propriety.   31.7

The Ju ruler is assassinated by his son, but the victim is blamed for his own death.

Lord Libi of Ju sired Quji and Zhanyu. Having established Zhanyu as   31.8(7)
heir apparent, he then deposed him. Lord Libi was tyrannical, and the inhabitants of the capital were distressed by him. In the eleventh month, Zhanyu, relying on the support of the inhabitants of the capital, attacked the Master of Ju and assassinated him, after which Zhanyu was thus established as ruler. Quji fled to Qi because he was born of a lady of Qi. Zhanyu was born of a lady of Wu. The text says, "Ju leaders assassinated their ruler, Maizhuchu":[1082] this is to indicate that the guilt lies with Mai Zhuchu, Lord Libi.

The Wu envoy praises the Wu king Yimo, defending him against the perception that Jizha might have been the worthier ruler.

The Master of Wu sent Qu Huyong[1083] on an official visit to Jin, so as to   31.9
keep open the possibility of relations between the two domains. Zhao Wu[a] asked him, "Will Jizha[b] of Yanling and Zhoulai eventually be established as ruler?[1084] At Chao, Zhufan fell, and a gatekeeper slew Yuzhai[a]. Heaven seems to be opening a way for him. What of it then?"

He replied, "He will not be established as ruler. That was the fate of the two kings; it was not a matter of opening the way for Jizha[b]. As for the person for whom Heaven is opening the way, it is likely our succeeding ruler. He has great virtue and abides by rules and standards. Being virtuous, he will not lose the support of the people; abiding by rules and standards, he will not be remiss in the affairs of the domain. The people adhere to him and affairs are in proper order. He is the one for whom Heaven is opening the way. It will certainly be this ruler's descendants who will have possession of the domain of Wu to the very end.[1085] Jizha[b] is one who keeps to his principles. Although he could have possession of the domain, he will not be established as ruler."

十二月，北宮文子相衛襄公以如楚，宋之盟故也。過鄭，印段迋勞于
棐林，如聘禮而以勞辭。文子入聘。子羽為行人，馮簡子與子大叔逆客。
事畢而出，言於衛侯曰：「鄭有禮，其數世之福也，其無大國之討乎！
《詩》云：

> 誰能執熱，
> 逝不以濯？

禮之於政，如熱之有濯也。濯以救熱，何患之有？」

子產之從政也，擇能而使之：馮簡子能斷大事，子大叔美秀而文，公孫
揮能知四國之為，而辨於其大夫之族姓、班位、貴賤、能否，而又善為辭
令。裨諶能謀，謀於野則獲，謀於邑則否。鄭國將有諸侯之事，子產乃
問四國之為於子羽，且使多為辭令；與裨諶乘以適野，使謀可否；而告
馮簡子使斷之。事成，乃授子大叔使行之，以應對賓客，是以鮮有敗事。
北宮文子所謂有禮也。

1086 Lord Xiang was the son of the errant and ruthless Lord Xian, whose death and burial
are not recorded in *Zuozhuan*.

1087 Zheng troubles resumed around 460 BCE.

1088 *Maoshi* 257, "Sang rou" 桑柔, 18B.654.

1089 *Analects* 14.8 gives a structurallly similar but somewhat different account of the
different talents in Zheng. *Shuoyuan* 7.206 has a very similar passage.

In the twelfth month, Beigong Tuo[a] served as assistant to Lord Xiang of Wei as they went to Chu.[1086] The visit was on account of the Covenant of Song. They passed through Zheng, and Yin Duan went to meet them at Feilin to honor their exertions. The ceremony was like that for an official visit, but Yin Duan used the speech for honoring exertions. To reciprocate, Beigong Tuo[b] entered the Zheng capital on an official visit. Gongsun Hui[a] was the envoy, and Feng Jianzi and You Ji[a] went forth to meet the guest. When the visit was over, Beigong Tuo came out and said to the Prince of Wei, "Zheng abides by ritual propriety. This will bring blessings for several generations. It will likely be free from chastisement by the great domains.[1087] As it says in the *Odes*,

> Who can suffer the heat
> And not bathe or wash?[1088]

Ritual propriety is to government what taking a bath is to heat. When they save themselves from the heat with a bath, what do they have to worry about?"

The perfect ritual performance above is shown to be based on a judicious choice of talents and careful division of labor.

In taking charge of government, Zichan chose the able and employed them. Feng Jianzi was able to make decisions in important matters. You Ji[a] was handsome and gracious, refined and learned. Gongsun Hui was able to know the policies of domains in the four quarters and could make distinctions regarding their high officers' houses and clans, ranks and positions, nobility or lowliness, and competence or incompetence; in addition, he was adept with eloquent speeches. Pi Chen was able to plan strategically: when he made plans while he was in the countryside, he would get it right, but when he did so in the city, he would not. When the domain of Zheng was preparing for dealings with the princes, Zichan asked Gongsun Hui[a] about the policies of the domains in the four quarters and also made him prepare many eloquent speeches. He then rode with Pi Chen in a carriage to go to the countryside and made him plan about what was feasible and what was not. Then he told Feng Jianzi and had him make decisions. When these things were done, he gave the task to You Ji[a] and sent him as envoy to respond to guests and visitors.[1089] Consequently, there were rarely any failures. This was what Beigong Tuo[a] referred to as "abiding by ritual propriety."

31.11　鄭人游于鄉校，以論執政。然明謂子產曰：「毀鄉校何如？」

　　　子產曰：「何為？夫人朝夕退而游焉，以議執政之善否。其所善者，吾則行之；其所惡者，吾則改之，是吾師也。若之何毀之？我聞忠善以損怨，不聞作威以防怨。豈不遽止？然猶防川。大決所犯，傷人必多，吾不克救也。不如小決使道，不如吾聞而藥之也。」

　　　然明曰：「蔑也今而後知吾子之信可事也。小人實不才，若果行此，其鄭國實賴之，豈唯二三臣？」

　　　仲尼聞是語也，曰：「以是觀之，人謂子產不仁，吾不信也。」

31.12　子皮欲使尹何為邑。子產曰：「少，未知可否。」

　　　子皮曰：「愿，吾愛之，不吾叛也。使夫往而學焉，夫亦愈知治矣。」

Zichan regards the debates about Zheng policies in village meeting places as instructive rather than threatening and refuses to suppress potential dissent. Such compassionate tolerance wins the approval of "Confucius" and contrasts with anecdotes about Zichan's sterner side (e.g., Zhao 20.9). For an opposite view of "public opinion," see Xiang 17.6.

The men of Zheng gathered freely in the village meeting places and passed judgment on those in charge of government. Ran Ming said to Zichan, "What about dismantling the village meeting places?"

Zichan said, "Why should we do that? Having retired from their tasks, which last from morning till evening, people gather freely to debate whether those in charge of government have done well or not. I will then carry out whatever they deem to be good policies and emend whatever they regard as bad. They are my teachers. Why should we dismantle the village meeting places? I have heard of using loyalty and goodness to diminish resentment, but I have not heard of assuming the forceful pose of authority to block resentment. Wouldn't forceful authority swiftly put a stop to resentment? But that would be like blocking a river.[1090] The damage caused by a great break in the dyke would surely injure so many people that we would not have the means to save the situation! It is better to have a small break to lead the flow, and it is better that I hear criticism and let it be my medicine."

Ran Ming said, "Henceforth I know that you, sir, are truly one whom I should serve. I am indeed a petty man who lacks talent, but if this can actually be done, then it will be the domain of Zheng that benefits. How would the benefit be limited to a few ministers or officers?"[1091]

Confucius[c] heard this story and remarked, "Judging from this, when people say that Zichan was not humane, I do not believe it."[1092]

Zichan dissuades Han Hu from conferring power and authority on a novice. Han Hu trusts Zichan even more after the latter's criticism.[1093]

Han Hu[a] wanted to let Yin He take charge of his settlement. Zichan said, "He is young, and we cannot yet know whether this will be feasible."

Han Hu[a] said, "He is careful and well intentioned. I am fond of him, and he will not turn against me. If we send him to go and learn, he will eventually learn how to govern."

31.11

31.12

1090 "Public opinion" that cannot be repressed is compared to a river that cannot be blocked in *Guoyu*, "Zhou yu 1," 1.9.

1091 A similar passage is found in *Xinxu* 4.133 and *Kongzi jiayu* 9.41.98.

1092 Confucius was eleven at this point, so this was supposedly his comment when he later heard this story. The comment suggests that there were also critical assessments of Zichan.

1093 Note that Han Hu remains the leader even though Zichan seems to make the most important decisions.

　　子產曰：「不可。人之愛人，求利之也。今吾子愛人則以政，猶未能操刀而使割也，其傷實多。子之愛人，傷之而已，其誰敢求愛於子？子於鄭國，棟也。棟折榱崩，僑將厭焉，敢不盡言？子有美錦，不使人學製焉。大官、大邑，身之所庇也，而使學者製焉，其為美錦不亦多乎？僑聞學而後入政，未聞以政學者也。若果行此，必有所害。譬如田獵，射御貫，則能獲禽，若未嘗登車射御，則敗績厭覆是懼，何暇思獲？」

　　子皮曰：「善哉！虎不敏。吾聞君子務知大者、遠者，小人務知小者、近者。我，小人也。衣服附在吾身，我知而慎之；大官、大邑所以庇身也，我遠而慢之。微子之言，吾不知也。他日我曰：子為鄭國，我為吾家，以庇焉，其可也。今而後知不足。自今請，雖吾家，聽子而行。」

　　子產曰：「人心之不同如其面焉，吾豈敢謂子面如吾面乎？抑心所謂危，亦以告也。」

　　子皮以為忠，故委政焉，子產是以能為鄭國。

31.13　衛侯在楚，北宮文子見令尹圍之威儀，言於衛侯曰：「令尹似君矣，將有他志。雖獲其志，不能終也。《詩》云：

1094　Cf. *Analects* 11.25.

1095　On the relationship between mind (or "heart") and face, see also Xiang 25.14, Zhao 28.3c.

1096　The text has "majesty in his bearing" (*weiyi* 威儀). However, since Beigong Tuo goes on to argue that Wei lacks "majesty in his bearing," we have followed Wang Yinzhi's (*Jingyi shuwen*, 728) suggestion that the word *wei* is extraneous. As cited in *Hanshu* 27B1.1360, this line also has *yi* instead of *weiyi*.

1097　Some commentators suggest that *si* 似 is a mistake for *yi* 以, often used interchangeably with *yi* 已 in early texts.

Zichan said, "This will not do. When one is fond of someone, one seeks to benefit him. Now you, sir, just because you are fond of someone, would entrust him with the charge of government, which is like making someone cut something up before he can wield a knife properly. His injuries will be many, surely![1094] If your fondness for someone merely ends up injuring him, who will dare to seek your fond regard? You, sir, are the roof beam for the domain of Zheng. If the roof beam breaks and the rafters collapse, I will be crushed. Would I presume not to state the case to the fullest? If you have a piece of beautiful brocade, you would not let someone learn tailoring with it. Great government positions and great settlements are what protect one's person, and yet you would let a novice who is still learning 'tailor' them? Are they not much more important than a piece of beautiful brocade? I have heard that one learns first before entering government service; I have not heard that one uses the conduct of government to learn. If you do indeed proceed with this, you are sure to do harm. Take an example from hunting: if a man is schooled in shooting and driving, he will then be able to capture birds and animals. But if he has never climbed a carriage to shoot and drive, then the fear of being defeated in his purpose and of being crushed by his overturning carriage will overpower him. How can he spare any time or attention to think of capturing anything?"

Han Hu[a] said, "Well said! I lack discernment. I have heard that a noble man applies himself to understanding what is important and far-reaching, while a petty man applies himself to understanding what is minor and close at hand. I am but a petty man. I know how to take care of the clothes I put on my body, yet I treat lightly the great government offices and great settlements whereby I protect my person, keeping my distance from these issues. If it were not for your words, sir, I would not have understood. In the past I said that it would do if you took charge of the domain of Zheng, and I took charge of protecting my patrimony. Only now do I know that will not suffice. Henceforth, I request that even with my patrimony, I heed your commands and act accordingly."

Zichan said, "Men's minds are different, even as their faces are. How would I dare to say that your face is like mine?[1095] All the same, if my mind senses danger, I will tell you about it."

Han Hu[a] considered Zichan loyal and thus entrusted government to him. That is why Zichan was able to run the domain of Zheng.

The Wei envoy Beigong Tuo predicts Gongzi Wei's downfall because he has the demeanor of overreaching ambition but not majesty in his bearing.

The Prince of Wei was in Chu. When Beigong Tuo[a] saw the bearing[1096] of Chief Minister Wei, he remarked to the Prince of Wei, "The chief minister is already like a ruler.[1097] He will have another ambition. Even though he will fulfill his ambition, he will not be able to come to a good end. As it says in the *Odes*,

31.13

靡不有初，
鮮克有終。

終之實難，令尹其將不免。」
　　公曰：「子何以知之？」
　　對曰：「《詩》云：

敬慎威儀，
惟民之則。

令尹無威儀，民無則焉。民所不則，以在民上，不可以終。」
　　公曰：「善哉！何謂威儀？」
　　對曰：「有威而可畏謂之威，有儀而可象謂之儀。君有君之威儀，
其臣畏而愛之，則而象之，故能有其國家，令聞長世。臣有臣之威儀，其
下畏而愛之，故能守其官職，保族宜家。順是以下皆如是，是以上下能
相固也。衛詩曰：

威儀棣棣，
不可選也。

言君臣、上下、父子、兄弟、內外、大小皆有威儀也。周詩曰：

朋友攸攝，
攝以威儀。

言朋友之道必相教訓以威儀也。《周書》數文王之德，曰：

1098　*Maoshi* 255, "Dang" 蕩, 18A.641. Also cited in Xuan 2.3a.

1099　*Maoshi* 256, "Yi" 抑, 18A.645. Cf. n. 1060.

1100　On the importance of *weiyi* (majesty of bearing) in early Chinese thought, see Yang Rubin, *Rujia shenti guan*, 28–42.

1101　*Maoshi* 26, "Bozhou" 柏舟, 2A.74.

1102　*Maoshi* 247, "Ji zui" 既醉, 17B.605. Besides "Bozhou" and "Ji zui," the term *weiyi* also appears in *Maoshi* 253, "Min lao" 民勞; *Maoshi* 256, "Yi" 抑; *Maoshi* 260, "Zhengmin" 烝民; as well as in bronze inscriptions ("Wangsun yi zhu zhong" 王孫遺諸鐘; "Guoshu lüzhong" 虢叔旅鐘) and in the *Documents* ("Jiu gao" 酒誥; "Gu ming" 顧命).

There is none who does not have beginnings.
Few are those who fulfill them as endings.[1098]

It is indeed difficult to fulfill them as endings. The chief minister will likely not escape disaster."

The lord said, "How do you, sir, know it?"

He replied, "As it says in the *Odes*,

Be reverent and cautious about your majesty of bearing.
It will make you an example for the people.[1099]

As the chief minister has no majesty in his bearing, the people have no example to look up to. If he remains above the people without being held up by them as an example, he will not be able to come to a good end."

Beigong Tuo praises the majesty of bearing—the observable movements and gestures—that define moral exemplarity. These ideas are dominant in the Odes *and echo similar discussions in* Zuozhuan *(e.g., Huan 2.2, Zhao 5.4a).*[1100]

The lord said, "Well said! What is meant by the majesty of bearing?"

He replied, "To have majesty that can inspire awe is called 'majesty,' and to have bearing that can serve as a model is called 'bearing.' When a ruler has the ruler's majesty of bearing, his subjects hold him in awe and love him, take him as an example, and follow him as a model. That is how he can possess his domain and patrimony and how his good name can last through the generations. When a minister has the minister's majesty of bearing, those below him hold him in awe and love him. That is how he can guard his position and duties, protect his house, and bring harmony to his patrimony. If, following this order down the hierarchy, all behave like this, it will be the means for those above and those below to support each other. As its says in an ode from Wei,

The majesty of bearing is gentle and refined
In ways too many to be numbered.[1101]

This is saying that rulers and ministers, those above and those below, fathers and sons, older brothers and younger brothers, those inside and those outside, the big ones and the small ones, all have the majesty of bearing. As it says in an ode from Zhou,

Where your friends offer their assistance,
They assist you by their majesty of bearing.[1102]

This is saying that, with the way of friendship, friends must instruct each other in the majesty of bearing. The *Zhou Documents* enumerates King Wen's virtues:

大國畏其力，
小國懷其德。

言畏而愛之也。《詩》云：

不識不知，
順帝之則。

言則而象之也。紂囚文王七年，諸侯皆從之囚，紂於是乎懼而歸之，可
謂愛之。文王伐崇，再駕而降為臣，蠻夷帥服，可謂畏之。文王之功，天
下誦而歌舞之，可謂則之。文王之行，至今為法，可謂象之。有威儀也。
故君子在位可畏，施舍可愛，進退可度，周旋可則，容止可觀，作事可
法，德行可象，聲氣可樂；動作有文，言語有章，以臨其下，謂之有威儀
也。」

> The great domains are awed by his strength.
> The small domains cherish his virtues.[1103]

This is saying that they held him in awe yet loved him. It says in the *Odes*,

> Without being aware, without knowing how,
> He follows the example of the god on high.[1104]

This is saying that he followed the example and took it as a model. When the last king of Shang, Zhòu, imprisoned King Wen for seven years, the princes all followed him in his imprisonment. Zhòu thus became fearful and sent him home. It can be said that they loved King Wen. When King Wen attacked Chong, during his second expedition he made the ruler of Chong demote himself to become a subject.[1105] Tribes and border peoples led each other in submission. It can be said that they held him in awe. As for King Wen's achievements, all-under-heaven chanted them and sang and danced about them. It can be said that they took him as an example. King Wen's actions to this day serve as rules and standards. It can be said that the people follow him as a model. King Wen had the majesty of bearing. That is why the noble man in his position inspires awe, and in his acts of giving he inspires love. His steps forward and back can serve as a standard, his every turn can be imitated as an example, his demeanor is well worth observing, his conduct of affairs can be set up as rules, his virtues and actions can be realized as a a model, his voice and aura can bring joy, his gestures have refinement, and his speeches are elegant. With all these attributes he oversees those below him. This is called having the majesty of bearing."

1103 Similar lines are incorporated into "Wucheng" 武成 (*Shangshu* 11.161) in the Ancient Script version of the *Documents*.

1104 *Maoshi* 241, "Huang yi" 皇矣, 16D.573.

1105 This is also mentioned in Xi 19.5.